THE NEW YORK TIMES ENCYCLOPEDIA OF SPORTS **Volume 7**

BOXING

THE NEW YORK TIMES ENCYCLOPEDIA OF SPORTS

THE NEW YORK TIMES
ENCYCLOPEDIA OF SPORTS

VOLUME 7

BOXING

EDITED BY
GENE BROWN

INTRODUCTION BY
FRANK LITSKY

ARNO PRESS
A NEW YORK TIMES COMPANY
NEW YORK 1979

GROLIER EDUCATIONAL CORPORATION
SHERMAN TURNPIKE, DANBURY, CT. 06816

Library of Congress Cataloging in Publication Data

Main entry under title:

Boxing.

(The New York times encyclopedia of sports; v. 7) Collection of articles reprinted from the New York times.
Bibliography.
Includes index.
SUMMARY: Traces the history of boxing as presented in articles appearing in the "New York Times."
1. Boxing. [1. Boxing] I. Brown, Gene. II. New York times.
III. Series: New York times encyclopedia of sports; v. 7.
GV565.N48   vol. 7   [GV1133]   796s   [796.8'3]   79-19945
ISBN 0-405-12633-6

Manufactured in the United States of America

Appendix © 1979, *The Encyclopedia Americana.*

The editors express special thanks to The Associated Press, United Press International, and Reuters for permission to include a number of dispatches originally distributed by those news services.

The New York Times Encyclopedia of Sports

Founding Editors: Herbert J. Cohen and Richard W. Lawall
Project Editors: Arleen Keylin and Suri Boiangiu
Editorial Assistant: Jonathan Cohen

Photographs courtesy *UPI* on pages X, 3, 30, 33, 57, 79, 88, 98, 113, 136, 152, 156, 180, 197

CONTENTS

It has been called the Manly Art of Self-Defense. Romantics have referred to it as the sweet science. Law enforcement officials have cited it as the most corruption-ridden of all sports. Medical people say it can cause brain damage.

Whatever the view, the ancient sport of boxing has attained wide popularity throughout the world. Almost every country has amateur boxing, and the sport is prominent in the Olympic Games. Most nations, except for those in the Eastern bloc, also have professional boxers.

In the eras of such well-known fighters as Jack Dempsey, Joe Louis and Muhammad Ali, no sports event was bigger or commanded more media attention than a contest for the world heavyweight boxing title. No athlete in any era approached Ali's combined career earnings of more than $50 million or as much as $6 million for one fight.

No other sport in the United States has ridden such a television roller coaster. In the 1950's, when television and televised sports began to flower, boxing was often shown four or five nights a week. Such overexposure almost wiped out the sport in the United States, and only the public's dynamic fascination with Ali kept boxing on home or closed-circuit theater television. By the mid-1970's, television had become enamored with boxing again, and the weekend sports anthologies on the three national networks often featured boxing.

One result of this demand for boxing was a proliferation of champions. For most of the 20th century, professional boxing operated with eight weight divisions ranging from flyweight (112 pounds and less) to heavyweight (over 175 pounds). By 1980, there were thirteen weight divisions, almost all with two world champions.

Logically, there would be one champion per weight division. But the World Boxing Council and the world Boxing Association, rival organizations that governed professional boxing internationally, almost always recognized different champions. This provided promoters with more champions and more championship bouts, which pleased everyone concerned.

Underworld influence in boxing has been widespread. At times, the publically acknowledged manager of one fighter has been the undercover manager of his opponent. Fixed fights have been common. Primo Carnera, once a strongman in an Italian circus, became world heavyweight champion in 1934, supposedly after having won one fixed fight after another.

In 1977, the so-called United States Boxing Championships were suspended by ABC-TV, their television outlet and principal financier, because of scandal. There was talk of fixed fights, bribes to get fighters into the tournament and falsified records of fighters to make them more attractive. Despite that embarrassment, ABC and the other networks continued to expand boxing coverage.

One attraction for the television audience is the simplicity of boxing. Two men, wearing padded gloves, punch each other above the waist in a roped-off arena (known as a ring) 18 to 20 feet square. A professional bout is scheduled for four to fifteen rounds, each round consisting of three minutes of boxing and one minute of rest.

If a fighter is knocked to the floor and cannot regain his feet in ten seconds, he loses. If he is cut badly or is otherwise injured or unable to defend himself, the referee may end the bout and declare him the loser. Normally, if a fighter is knocked down three times in one round, the fight is ended and he loses.

If the fight does not end prematurely, the winner is decided by a vote of two judges and the referee, or by three judges alone. A fight may also end in a draw.

Amateur and professional boxing have a few differences. Amateur fights are scheduled for three rounds, each of two or three minutes of boxing time. The fighters may be required to wear headgear.

Amateur boxing in the United States is regulated by the Amateur Athletic Union, which conducts a national championship annually. The Golden Gloves national competition offers similar opportunities. The sport, once popular in colleges, was abandoned by the

National Collegiate Athletic Association in 1960 as too dangerous.

Boxing predated the ancient Greeks and Romans. About 900 B.C., the Greeks employed a form of boxing in which sitting opponents wore leather thongs and fought to the death. Later, to quicken the ending, the thongs were studded with metal spikes. One champion, Theagenes of Thasos, won more than 1,400 consecutive bouts, killing every opponent.

When Rome conquered Greece, it introduced to these bouts a more deadly weapon, the cestus, and the opponents stood rather than sat. Centuries later, a Roman king, deploring the waste of life, banned the cestus and allowed fights with fists only. Later, that was banned, too, and boxing disappeared until 17th-century England.

When it reappeared, it was more a free-for-all than pure boxing. Opponents could be punched, wrestled or thrown to the ground. In the early 18the century, only fists were allowed.

James Figg, the first champion of this era, was so good that he ran out of opponents, retired and in 1719 opened a boxing school. He fought again from 1720 to 1730, when he retired undefeated at age 34.

In 1743, Jack Broughton wrote rules for a fight he would referee. These were refined and became known as the London Prize Ring Rules. They governed boxing until the bare-knuckle era ended.

In 1865, the Marquis of Queensberry, a British sportsman, introduced twelve rules that he hoped would reduce barbarism. They included the use of gloves instead of bare knuckles, a 24-foot ring, no wrestling, three-minute rounds separated by a one-minute rest period, and ten seconds to get up after a knockdown. These rules were not used until an 1872 tournament in London, and bare-knuckle fights continued until 1889.

By this time, there was occasional boxing in the United States. Because fights were generally illegal, they were staged on barges and farms and anywhere else to escape law-enforcement officials. Many fighters were from England.

The first American heavyweight champion was Paddy Ryan. In 1880, he knocked out Joe Goss, the English champion, near Colliers Station, W. Va. The fight lasted 87 rounds and almost 1½ hours. In those days, a round ended when one man was knocked down or fell to the canvas floor, and a tired fighter would end a round and gain respite simply by going down without being hit.

In 1882, Ryan made his first title defense. In a brutal bare-knuckle fight in Mississippi County in Mississippi, John L. Sullivan of Boston knocked him out in nine rounds.

Sullivan had fought with gloves and felt that the future of boxing involved gloves. Later that year, he toured theaters and fought sparring partners, both adversaries wearing gloves.

Critics chided Sullivan, saying he had instructed his sparring partners not to hit him hard. An angered Sullivan offered $100 to anyone in the audience he could

not knock out within four rounds. Soon, the ante was raised to $500. Sullivan seldom had to pay.

In 1889, Sullivan defended against Jake Kilrain in Richburg, Miss., where the temperature was 104 degrees in the shade. Sullivan won in 75 rounds and 2 hours 16 minutes in the last heavyweight championship bout with bare knuckles.

Sullivan was a national hero. As Rex Lardner wrote years later, "He was a boozer and a bully and a braggart and as such was loved by every red-blooded American."

He was also careless, and when he defended against James J. Corbett in 1892 in New Orleans, he did not train seriously. Corbett knocked him out in 21 rounds, the only loss in Sullivan's career. That bout was fought under Marquis of Queensberry rules and with gloves.

New York State made certain boxing matches legal in 1896, and Nevada followed in 1897. But they and other states frequently banned boxing through the years.

Boxing has thrived on controversial fighters, and one of the most controversial was Jack Johnson. He won the world heavyweight championship in 1908 by knocking out Tommy Burns of Canada in 14 rounds in Sydney, Australia. In his first defense, he knocked Stanley Ketchel almost unconscious in 12 rounds in Solma, Calif., and broke all of Ketchel's front teeth at the gums.

Johnson was the first black heavyweight champion of modern times (the second was Joe Louis). He was flamboyant and arrogant, and in a day during which race relations in the United States were often strained, he twice married white women.

In 1915, at age 37 and past his prime, Johnson was knocked out by Jess Willard in 26 rounds in Havana and lost the title. There is a famous photograph of Johnson being counted out. He was lying on the canvas, face up, an arm apparently shading his eyes from the sun. That reinforced suspicions that Johnson had agreed to lose the fight and had allowed himself to be counted out.

The brutality of boxing was no more evident than in Willard's first title defense. It came in 1919 in Toledo, Ohio, against William Harrison (Jack) Dempsey, who had done most of his fighting in saloons for purses as low as $2. Dempsey knocked out Willard in three rounds. Historains disagree on exact figures, but Willard was knocked down six or seven times in the first round and suffered four or six broken teeth plus a broken jaw.

Dempsey made five successful title defenses. The fifth was in New York against Luis Angel Firpo of Argentina, who knocked him out of the ring and into the press row. Dempsey was pushed back into the ring and almost destroyed Firpo. He knocked down Firpo 10 times in 3 minutes 57 seconds before the fight ended in the second round.

In the ring, Dempsey was a mean, violent man. He hit below the belt, he hit after the bell and he hit an opponent still rising from the floor. "What do you want me to do, write him a letter that I'm going to hit him?" he asked. The public despised him for his savagery.

Outside the ring, Dempsey was a mild man, gentle and dignified. After retirement, he became immensely popular.

In 1926, he defended in Philadelphia against James J. (Gene) Tunney, the American light-heavyweight champion and a scientific fighter. Boxing people distrusted Tunney becuase he supposedly enjoyed reading Shakespeare, a rare activity in the rough-and-tumble world of boxing.

Tunney won the fight and the title. When Dempsey's wife asked what had happened, he told her simply, "Honey, I just forgot to duck." The next year, Tunney again won a decision from Dempsey in Chicago in a fight celebrated for the so-called "long count."

The fighters had been instructed before the bout that if one man was knocked down, the other had to go to the farthest neutral corner. When Dempsey knocked down Tunney, he stood over him until the referee persuaded him to go to the proper corner. The referee did not start to count over Tunney until Dempsey obeyed. As a result, Tunney was on the canvas at least 14 seconds. The extra seconds may have saved him.

The first Tunney-Dempsey fight attracted 120,757 spectators and a gross gate of $1,895,733. For the return fight, 104,943 paid $2,658,660. Tunney's purse for the second fight was $990,445.

In 1914, when Jack Johnson was heavyweight champion, Joe Louis Barrow was born in an Alabama sharecropper's shack that had no electricity and no indoor plumbing. In 1937, his name shortened to Joe Louis, he knocked out James J. Braddock in eight rounds and won the heavyweight title. He held it for 11 years 8 months, a record at the time. He earned $4.6 million in the ring and saved none of it.

The year before Louis became champion, Max Schmeling of Germany knocked him out in 12 rounds. Adolf Hitler made Schmeling a hero in Nazi Germany, and the 1938 return bout between Louis and Schmeling had racial overtones. Louis gave Schmeling a brutal beating and knocked him out in the first round.

From 1937 to 1942, Louis defended 21 times against opponents so outclassed that someone named them the Bum of the Month Club, Lous retired in 1950, but he fought again because he owed the federal government so much money for back taxes.

Louis was a beloved public figure, but his later life was marred by drugs, mental problems and poor health. As Dave Anderson wrote in The New York Times, "His life has been a tragedy, but somehow he is a tragedy to be revered."

In 1951, a promising young heavyweight named Rocky Marciano knocked out an aging Joe Louis, his idol, in eight rounds. In 1952, the stocky Marciano knocked out Jersey Joe Walcott in 13 rounds and became champion. After six defenses, Marciano retired in 1957, undefeated in 49 pro bouts.

In 1960, young Cassius Marcells Clay of Louisville, Ky. won the Olympic light-heavyweight championship and turned professional. By the time he retired in 1979,

when he was 37 years old and overweight, he had changed boxing history.

Charles (Sonny) Liston was the heavyweight champion in 1964 when he made his first defense against Clay in Miami Beach. The young braggart was a 7-1 underdog in the betting, but he won the title when Liston did not answer the bell for the seventh round, claiming a shoulder injury.

Many people resented Clay because he was so arrogant. There was more resentment after the fight from white America when Clay disclosed that he had joined the nation of Islam, the so-called Black Muslims, and had changed his name to Muhammad Ali.

In 1965, Ali knocked out Liston in one round in their return bout in Lewisston, Maine, on a right-hand punch that many people failed to see. In 1967, Ali refused induction into the United States Army, saying he was a Black Muslim unpaid minister and thus exempt from the draft.

Every boxing governing body stripped Ali of his title, and he did not fight for three years. Though sentenced to five years in prison for draft evasion, he remained free on appeal until the Supreme Court in 1971 overturned the conviction. Ali then fought Joe Frazier in New York for the title then held by Frazier, and suffered his first professional defeat.

George Foreman won the title in 1973 by stopping Frazier in Kingston, Jamaica, after six knockdowns in two rounds. In1974, in Kinshasa, Zaire, Ali knocked out the favored Foreman in eight rounds and regained the title. Each was paid $5 million for the fight.

In 1978, Ali fought Leon Spinks, the 1976 Olympic light-heavyweight champion, in Las Vegas for the title. It was only the eighth pro fight for Spinks, and Ali failed to take it seriously. Spinks won. Seven months later, Ali beat Spinks in New Orleans and became heavyweight champion for the third time.

That was the last fight for Ali. By this time, he was world famous. He was glib, charming and outrageous, loved and hated, always controversial, always the showman. Singlehandly, he had saved American boxing from oblivion.

The lighter weight division provided heroes through the years. In 1938, Henry Armstrong held the featherweight, lightweight and welterweight titles simultaneously, the only such triple. From 1948 to 1951, Sandy Saddler and Willie Pep staged four fierce fights for the featherweight title, with Saddler winning three, all by knockouts. In a career that ran from 1940 to 1965, Sugar Ray Robinson won the middleweight title five times and the welterweight title once and almost became light-heavyweight champion.

One of the brightest, fiercest and shortest careers belonged to Stanley Ketchel, who as middleweight champion in 1909 floored Jack Johnson, the heavyweight champion. A year later, he was dead. As John Lardner wrote, "Stanely Ketchel was 24 years old when he was shot and killed by the common-law husband of the lady who was cooking his breakfast."

—Frank Litsky

CHAPTER 1

THE RING AND RESPECTABILITY

Joe Louis buckles Joe Walcott with a hard right
in their 1947 fight. Louis is thought by many to
have been the greatest heavyweight ever. It is a
measure of the "Brown Bomber"'s greatness that
the skills of all good heavyweights since his reign
have been measured by how they might have
stood up to his.

CORBETT NOW IS CHAMPION

SULLIVAN MEETS HIS MATCH AT NEW-ORLEANS.

THE CALIFORNIAN KEPT AWAY FROM THE BIG FELLOW'S BLOWS, AND FINALLY FORCED THE FIGHTING—THE BOSTON PUGILIST KNOCKED OUT IN THE TWENTY-FIRST ROUND.

NEW-ORLEANS, La., Sept. 7.—John L. Sullivan, the heavyweight champion pugilist who has held the honor so long, was defeated to-night by James Corbett of California. The fight lasted for twenty-one rounds and took place before a crowd of over 10,000 persons in the arena of the Olympic Club.

Corbett came out of the fight fresh and without a mark. Sullivan was badly punished. It was a contest between science and strength. Corbett's expert boxing and his agility in dodging the big fellow's blows and eluding his rushes won him the fight. Corbett was given a great ovation at the close when he had given the Boston pugilist a knock-down and knock-out blow. Sullivan soon recovered and was able to make a short speech in which he said that he was glad the championship would remain in this country.

It was the old generation against the new. It was the gladiator against the boxer. Sullivan represented the first stage in the evolution of the American pugilist, and swept away old methods and old traditions. The old style was severe training and bloody battles, fights under difficulties in secluded spots, which the contestants performed for little money before the most objectionable classes. Although Sullivan has thrice defended the championship with bare knuckles, under London prize-ring rules, he was the virtual inventor of the modern glove contest.

He did better with the gloves than all his predecessors with naked fists, and did as much execution with padded hands in four rounds as the old-time fighters with ungloved battering rams. He Americanized the manly art, deprived it of much of its brutality, and made it possible to decide championships before athletic clubs under the best auspices before classes of people who formerly took little interest in the sport. Nature intended him for a gladiator, and although he abused nature to a considerable extent, not even the best trained rivals could defeat him. In England and America he defended the title of champion, and when anywhere near his true self there was no doubt as to the result. He stood out a central figure in the history of pugilism and attracted to him a following from every corner of the country.

Wherever Sullivan fought people flocked to see him, and no matter what his condition, no matter who his rival, no matter what the odds, the crowd was for Sullivan. It was so in to-night's battle. Whatever the attraction of the other two contests forming the triple event, the name of Sullivan contained the magic power.

The crowd which came before Monday night had the gladiator chiefly in mind. Those who did not arrive in time to see the other battles came with a rush before the hour for the heavyweights to meet. All day long Tuesday special trains arrived, and even yesterday hundreds of people from almost every State, from California to New-York, and from Minnesota to Texas, came pouring into the city. Canal Street and St. Charles Streets had a look of carnival season. Hotels, saloons, and all places of resort were crowded. Men of high and men of low degree mingled freely, and nearly all said Sullivan.

At night the streets were very animated. There was no rush to the other fights, but to the heavyweight contest the visitors and local admirers of the sport felt impressed with the necessity of starting early. Carriages, cabs, wagonettes, wagons turned into pleasure vehicles, and street cars began bearing spectators to the Olympic arena. And the rush kept up until nearly the hour for the call of time.

Everybody recognized the necessity of going early, for it was known that the arena would be packed to its utmost capacity, and those who had not secured reserved seats would have to struggle for a point of vantage.

The betting was not very heavy. The principal reason was the large majority which built its hopes upon Sullivan. The champion of champions was a strong favorite in the pool rooms. The morning odds were 1 to 4 Sullivan and 3 to 1 Corbett.

The night before, in banter between the backers of the men, Wakeley and Brady each deposited $50 to bind the bet of $2,000 to $1,000. This was at odds of 2 to 1, and the money was to have been put up at 1 o'clock P. M. yesterday. When Brady came down town and found 3 to 1 Corbett posted, he forfeited the $50 and turned over $1,000 to Harrison's turf exchange, getting $3,000 against it. There was another bet of $1,000 on Corbett, and D. B. Mitchell, New-York Commissioner, telegraphed $500 at the odds. Although $1,000 went in on Sullivan at 1 to 4, the Corbett bets forced a change in the odds, 3 to 10 being laid against Sullivan, 5 to 2 against Corbett. At those odds a large local cotton house placed $1,000 on Corbett, and a Californian sport made a similar bet. The Sullivan men, although Wakeley, Johnson, and the leading backers demurred at the odds, did not delay to back their favorite. Men formed in line and played from $100 to $500 each on the champion, and up to about 3 o'clock Harrison's room stood to pay out $26,000 on Corbett and $22,000 on Sullivan.

On combinations the room stood to pay out $14,000 if Sullivan won, and $9,000 if Corbett proved the victor. At the Crescent the betting on Sullivan was marked, $5,000 coming in within a short space of time, one bet being for $2,000. A rush of Corbett money in the morning also forced a drop in the odds from 3 to 1 to 5 to 6.

The Sullivan contingent was so confident of the champion's ability to win with ease that they made a number of bets on the duration of the affair. Hurd bet $500 that Sullivan would win inside of fifteen rounds, and Honest John Kelly laid a wager of $300 with "Alf" Kennedy, "Billy" Myer's backer, that Sullivan would win in thirteen rounds.

The great battle between Sullivan and Corbett for the pugilistic championship of the world was the culmination of interest and excitement to-night. All the streets leading from the busines portion of the city to the Olympic Club were brilliantly lighted and every one was crowded with enthusiasts, male and female, adult and infantile. Every car and carriage was greeted with huzzas and the atmosphere was infused with a suppressed excitement as if some stupendous event, some gigantic casualty was about to occur.

If there was excitement on the streets, there was something beyond that in the club itself. Every square inch of the stupendous structure was occupied. No seat was vacant, no box empty. In every direction there was a solid mass of men. Although the figures 10,000 is an immense number, it would be no overstatement to say that there were 1,500 more than that number who saw the great heavyweight battle to-night.

This huge assemblage comported itself faultlessly. There were enthusiastic and encouraging cheers for each man, but no disagreeable personalities. New-Orleans notables were well represented. Mayor John Fitzpatrick, who refereed the Sullivan-Kilrain contest at Richburg with eminent satisfaction, was an interested spectator. Chief of Police Dexter Gaster sat in a box in citizen's clothes. District Attorney Butler and Assistant Lowel Adams, both sporting enthusiasts, were awarded reserved seats, while the City Council and the Orleans Parish delegations to the State Senate and Hosue had each more than a quorum present.

The participants in the previous battles—McAuliffe, Myer, Dixon, Skelly—and the horde of famed pugilistic visitors to the city all had good points of vantage. The entrance of "Bob" Fitzsimmons, the middle-weight champion, and "Joe" Choyinski, Corbett's thrice-defeated heavy-weight opponent, gave the audience an opportunity to do some cheering during the wait for the appearance of the champions. A sensation was produced by a very innocent cause. At 8:30 in order to make the arena cool and comfortable. The tarpaulins which covered the place were pulled back from over all parts of the amphitheatre, save the ring itself. Therefore when a light shower fell there was a decided commotion in the assemblage. There were very few umbrellas in the crowd, but as the rain soon ceased and the tarpaulins were replaced over the roof, the disturbance subsided, and the spectators patiently awaited the approach of 9 o'clock and the entrance of the gladiators.

Ex-Mayor Guillotte entered the ring at 8:50 and made the address advising perfect quiet and fair treatment to each man without personal remarks. He was interrupted by the appearance of Sullivan, and a moment later by Corbett, both of whom were greeted with tremendous cheering. Sullivan was attired in green trunks with legs bare, his feet being covered with black socks and fighting shoes. Corbett wore the fancy mascot belt his wife knit for him, but detached it before the fight began and left it exposed to view only a gray pair of trunks; his legs were also bare. On behalf of the club, Capt. Barrett of the police force presented Prof. Duffy a handsome punch bowl of silver as a token of the appreciation by the club of his services as referee. Sullivan showed up in splendid shape, massive in proportions, and showing every sign of good training. Corbett, taller and slighter, looked equally well trained, but not as strong. He looked happy and confident, and chatted with friends outside of the ring while he waited for his gloves to be adjusted.

Sullivan, on the contrary, was cautious, and submitted to a little rubbing from McAuliffe without a word. When fighters and seconds were called up for final directions from the referee, he said hardly a word, while Corbett asked questions and gesticulated pleasantly. Agreeably to his promise, expressed early in the afternoon, Sullivan did not wear the plasters over his stomach to which Corbett had objected.

Sullivan experienced great difficulty in putting on the five-ounce gloves, and it took several powerful tugs and assistances from McAuliffe to put the giant's hands into the mittens. Corbett's shapely hands slipped into his pair with ease. Behind the gigantic form of the Boston man were "Charley" Johnson, "Jack" McAuliffe, "Joe" Lannon, and "Phil" Casey. Corbett's seconds were "Billy" Delaney, "Jim" Daley, and "Prof." John Donaldson. Prof. "Mike" Donovan, who had received instructions from the New-York Athletic Club not to go behind either man, could not resist the temptation to help. He lay outside Corbett's corner and fanned him industriously during each intermission. Sullivan's form was massive; his structure, so often described, was at its best. The big muscles behind his shoulders bulged out hard and heavy and his arms were embodiment of power. There was just a suggestion of heaviness about him. The flesh about his stomach was white, and that portion of his body was not at all as flat as prize fighters usually is. His weight just before entering the ring was 212 pounds.

Corbett was clotted with muscles. He was slight, but all the flesh on him was muscle. His stomach was covered with knots of sinew. His chest was hard but flexible. His back, while no ways as ponderous as Sullivan's, was hard, firm, and deep with muscle. His large arms were a mass of sinew molded into ideal athletic form. His weight, taken for record before he stepped into the ring, was 187 pounds.

Corbett from the beginning was confident, and he showed his ability to stop Sullivan and avoid his blows. He was happy and smiling. His tactics at first were purely defensive and he ducked, he sprang, he even ran out of Sullivan's reach; but it was by no means a walking-around match. Even at the beginning he faced his adversary, countered, stopped, and swung, and was away with lightning quickness before return could be administered. His early campaign was to tire and blow Sullivan. With this view he kept bothering the big man into following him, swinging heavily at him and not finding him there. Then, when he drew blood in the fifth, he made a target of Sullivan's nose and mouth, jabbed him alternately in the stomach and the nose, and battered his man badly.

About this time Sullivan began to appreciate the fact that it was the next thing to the impossible for him to reach the Californian. Nevertheless, he rushed at him and would only desist when his nose came up short against Corbett's left.

In the tenth Sullivan rushed the fighting in a vain attempt to finish the fight then. None of the big bets depended on a result in that round.

When the end came it was unexpected. John L. had been bleeding from the nose, and his lips were swollen and sore, but even Corbett men expected him to stay in the ring as many rounds more, but Corbett's finishing strokes were lightning in speed and force. Three times the left went into Sullivan's face. Four times the right smashed on the swollen nose and mouth. Then Sullivan collapsed. He went down hands first, then knees, then shoulders. He tried to push himself up, and did get his hands off the ground. The referee then began counting the ten seconds, but Sullivan had not really risen from the ground. The idol had fallen; the huzzas of the crowd greeted the new pugilist king.

The battle commenced at 9:10. Both men stepped lightly to the centre of the ring. Sullivan immediately became the aggressor. He made a left lead and was stopped. Corbett danced all about his opponent, eyeing him closely. Sullivan made a rush, but Jim backed away; he also attempted a left-hander, but Jim would not bite. Sullivan looked vicious as he played for an opening; he attempted a right-hand stomach punch, but the blow fell short. Sullivan tried to corner Jim, but the latter slipped away. The gong sounded and not a blow had been landed by either man.

Sullivan was still the aggressor in the second. He attempted a left for the head and missed it, Jim slipping neatly away from a left-hand swing. A moment later the men came to a clinch and Jim aimed a left-hander. Sullivan upper-cut Jim in a duck and touched him again with his left hand a little later. Jim eyed his man closely, and when Sullivan would rush the Californian would slip away. Sullivan landed a heavy right on the shoulder, but received a stomach punch in return.

Corbett ducked away in the third from a heavy lunge. Sullivan followed him about the ring, trying for stomach. Jim's head missed a heavy left-hander, and Sullivan looked vicious. Jim landed two heavy stomach punches, and duly missed a vicious right; both hit each other on the head. Corbett stepped out of harm's way. He came back quickly and landed his left on the stomach. He also planted heavy left on the champion's ear, sending his head back. Both men were fighting hard when the gong sounded. Sullivan was ringing wet from perspiration.

Sullivan missed his left again in the fourth, but he chased Jim around the ring. Sullivan landed a light left, Corbett stepped up close, attempting to punch the stomach, but John was guarding that member with his right hand. The champion followed his opponent all over the ring and received a heavy left-hand swing on the head for his pains. Corbett was standing well up in this round against the great gladiator with whom he was fighting. Jim landed both hands on Sullivan's head as the round ended, and the champion went to his corner with a sneering smile.

In the fifth round Sullivan stepped to the centre with a smile and Corbett touched his nose with a left. The champion tried to land a left on the stomach and the men clinched, Sullivan landing his first heavy right. Sullivan missed a fearful left hand, and staggered forward from the force of the blow. The men boxed cautiously for an opening and the champion seemed eager for hot work. He followed his antagonist all around the ring and first blood came from Sullivan's nose. The fight was fast and furious and Sullivan nearly fell on the ropes from left hand jabs on the head. As the round ended Corbett landed a heavy right on the champion's head.

Both men landed light lefts in the sixth, and Sullivan's nose was bleeding again. The champion was beginning to look tired, for he missed a heavy right aimed for the jaw. Corbett took plenty of time and used the entire ring to manœuvre in. He landed a light left on the stomach and punched the champion on the face. A little later there was heavy exchange of lefts on the head; Sullivan seemed to be angry, and slapped his opponent with his left hand. Corbett landed with blows on the head and ran away. The men were in the centre of the ring, and it began to look like some of the fight was out of Sullivan. Jim landed a heavy left on Sullivan's head, and the champion went to his corner looking tired.

Corbett in the seventh walked right up to Sullivan and barely avoided a left-hand punch. The champion was trying his hardest for the right on the jaw, but foxy Corbett was not there. The champion landed two light blows on the head and Corbett sent in a hot shot for the left on the nose. He jabbed Sullivan continually on the nose in this round and blood flowed freely. Jim was cheered to the echo for his skillful fighting. Sullivan's only hope was looked for from his heavy right. Sullivan was forced on the ropes by a heavy right on the jaw, and as the gong sounded he received a heavy left on the jaw.

On the eighth Sullivan landed light left on the stomach, and received the left on the mouth. Jim was now the aggressor, forcing the champion toward the post, and Sullivan, attempting a left-hand stomach punch, slipped away. Sullivan hit Corbett in a clinch and the audience yelled "foul;" both exchanged heavy lefts, but Jim's head missed the mighty right. Jim barely escaped the right and sent his left in the champion's stomach, forcing him to the ropes. Jim landed heavy left on the mouth, which brought blood and a smile from the champion. Sullivan looked very tired as the gong sent them to their corners.

The men got in the middle of the ring in the ninth and Jim's head barely missed two swings. Sullivan was puffing and both exchanged good lefts. Sullivan received a light one on the ear and got another on the nose, but evened up matters a little with his right. Jim landed a heavy left on the nose and both men hugged each other in the clinch. Sullivan was missing many blows now, though when he did land, it was twice as heavy as his antagonist's. Both men landed light lefts, but the Californian landed heavy on the stomach; as the gong sounded Jim had all the best of Sullivan and went to his corner looking like the victor.

Sullivan attempted to land his left in the tenth, but the blow was very short. He followed his opponent, however, and both exchanged lefts. Corbett's right found the champion's head and his left got there a moment later, but the champion landed on the head in return. This was a great fight so far, and Corbett apparently had the admiration of the crowd, as he was doing most of the hitting. When the round ended Corbett was lustily cheered.

Both landed good blows in the eleventh, and Sullivan got twisted around from the force of his left. Corbett showed great ability, even at clinching his more bulky opponent. Sullivan was extremely cautious, though he got a crushing blow on the nose. Jim tried to deliver a heavy right-hand blow, and the champion was forced to the ropes to avoid it. Sullivan received a punch in the stomach from the left and got it again a moment later.

In the twelfth Sullivan was last to respond, and when he did he got a left in the stomach. He got it again very heavily and a repetition a moment later. Sullivan landed a fairly good blow with his right, though he got the left in the stomach in return. Jim landed another left in the stomach and ran away smiling. The Californian landed a good left on the head, but the champion stopped the right with his shoulder. Sullivan made a vicious rush, and Corbett clipped him in the stomach with his left. The champion's head was forced back twice from two heavy left-handers, and the round wound up with both Corbett's hands in Sullivan's stomach.

Round thirteen found Jim first up again. Dodging the usual left lead from the champion, he slipped away from the left a moment later, and the men boxed scientifically for an opening. Sullivan could not draw his antagonist on with left-hand feints, but he

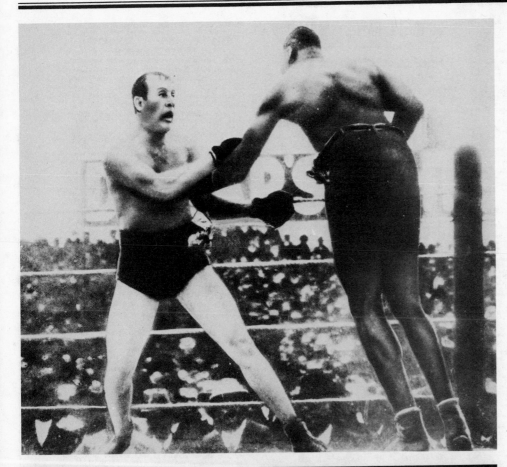

The legendary Jack Johnson fighting Tommy Burns in Australia, December 1908.

Benny Leonard (right) was a skillful, scientific boxer. He held the lightweight championship from 1917 to 1925.

barely touched his body with the left; the men's toes touched, they stood so close, and Sullivan never attempted to land the right, his left was short, Corbett stepping away. Sullivan was now forcing matters, but carefully. He got a left on the nose that sent his head far back, though the champion landed light on the head.

In the fourteenth the Californian's stock was sky-high, and he stepped to his opponent, though he got a left on the nose for his pains. Both men landed good blows. Corbett landed the left and Sullivan the right; both men got heavy blows on the head and Sullivan was pushed back with the left. Again both men got in good lefts, though the first blow was the heavier of the two. Jim landed a left on Sullivan's face and slipped away. Sullivan landed on the forehead, but in attempting to land his left fell into a corner, standing closely to his man. Honors were easy.

Corbett was first to the centre in the fifteenth. Sullivan made his famous rush and forced his man all over the ring, though he was nearly knocked down with a right. The men clinched and separated, Sullivan receiving a right on the ear. The latter landed his left on Jim's nose, but his stomach was uncoved and he received a heavy blow. Jim landed the usual left on the head, but he got the right on the body in return. Both men landed lefts, Sullivan missed his vicious right for the body. Both men received light lefts, though Jim recorded a heavy stomach punch as the round ended.

The sixteenth round commenced with a rally. Sullivan received the left on his dial; he attempted a left lead for the head, and Jim saved himself by pulling away.

The champion's head was pushed back once more. Sullivan landed heavily on the nose and stomach a moment later. Jim looked very fresh as he punched the champion in the head and stomach. Sullivan received two good punches, and Jim clinched. During the lock Sullivan hit his opponent and the audience yelled "foul," though Corbett refused to have the victory that way.

Jim was first up again, in the seventeenth round, looking none the worse for wear. Sullivan landed a good left, though his right for the body was short. Sullivan was breathing hard. Jim neatly avoided a left for the face, but sent his own fist home a moment later on Sullivan's head. Sullivan's face was very red, and he received a left-hand swing in the stomach for coming too close. Both exchanged light lefts and boxed for an opening for the right. No severe punishment was administered to either man in this round.

Jim Corbett was, as usual, first to respond in the eighteenth. A beautiful rally took place in the centre of the ring. Jim landed two stomach punches, but got two light punches on the head. A fearful left-hand jab on the nose was presented to John and he got a hot one on the head for being too familiar. Jim's left found the champion's stomach and face, and also the head; later, John L. landed a right punch on the ribs that sounded all over the house, though he got a left swing in the stomach a moment later. Sullivan was extremely cautious, although he got four heavy rights on the face. This was all Corbett's round.

In the nineteenth round both men were quick to respond. They boxed cautiously, Sullivan landing, and "Jim" retaliated on the stomach and then stepped away from a heavy right, and the champion looked tired. Sullivan's left was continually in motion, seemingly from the rattles. The Californian looked too clever for him and he laughed sarcastically at the champion as he leisurely boxed for an opening. Corbett landed two quick lefts in the stomach and Sullivan lost his temper from a staggering right, rushed at his opponent, but he looked like a beaten man.

Sullivan looked tired for the twentieth round, and his left was very short; he was blowing hard and seemed very cautious, but he was the same resolute, ferocious man of yore. Both exchanged rights, and Sullivan was beaten to the ropes with a right and left. The champion was nearly knocked down with the left on the stomach and right on the head. Corbett was dead game and unhurt so far. Sullivan tried a right, and received five clips on the head and stomach. The champion's knees were shaking, and he seemed unable to defend himself. Sullivan was fought to the ropes with heavy rights and lefts, and the gong seemed his only safety.

The twenty-first round was the last. Corbett was the first to respond to time. Sullivan's left lead was very weak, and he seemed anxious to wait. His opponent was with him, however, saw the championship bee in his bonnet, and the champion received a left on the nose. Sullivan was trying for the right, though he made little attempt to send it home. Sullivan was beaten down with heavy rights and lefts, falling to the ground. He attempted to rise and fight, but nature gave way and he fell and was counted out, and Corbett was proclaimed the champion of America by Referee Duffy.

The ovation that Corbett received was something tremendous, and he walked around the ring kissing and hugging his friends. Sullivan afterward made a speech in the centre of the ring, saying that he was glad America got the championship. He had fought once too often in the ring.

September 8, 1892

CORBETT FAIRLY WHIPPED

Fitzsimmons Wins the Fight at Carson City in the Fourteenth Round After a Hard Contest.

THE BLOW WHICH COUNTED.

Fitzsimmons Took Advantage of His Opportunity—Corbett Says He Is Anxious to Fight the Battle Over Again.

CARSON, Nev., March 17.—After two years of doubt and vexatious postponements the heavyweight championship of the world for pugilism was decided beyond cavil today when Robert Fitzsimmons sent James J. Corbett helpless to his knees with a left-hand blow under the heart after one minute and forty-five seconds in the fourteenth round.

The great contest was decided in the simplest manner and the "knockout" was the result of one unwary move on the part of Corbett. After the first minute of the fourteenth round had been spent in a few harmless clinches and counters Fitzsimmons made a "fake" lead with his right for the jaw. It was a simple ruse, but it caught the Californian napping. Instead of keeping his body inclined forward and throwing back his head just a trifle to allow the blow, which was of the very lightest kind, to slip by, Corbett contemptuously bent his head and chest backward and thus protruded his abdomen.

Fitzsimmons's small eyes flashed, and, like lightning he saw and availed himself of his advantage. Drawing back his left, he brought it up with terrible force, the forearm rigid and at right angles to the upper arm. With the full power of his wonderful driving muscles brought into play, the Australian fairly ripped the blow up the pit of Corbett's stomach at a point just under the heart. Corbett was lifted clean of his feet, and as he pitched forward Fitzsimmons shot his right up and around, catching Corbett on the jaw and accelerating his downward fall.

Corbett sank on his left knee, and with his outstretched right grasped the ropes for support. His left arm worked convulsively up and down, while his face was twitching with an expression of the greatest agony.

Referee Siler threw up his hands on the call of "ten" and left the ring. There were some cries of "Foul!" when the referee declared Corbett "out," but they were unheeded by anybody, as the battle was won fairly and squarely.

Corbett Takes His Defeat to Heart.

The defeat nearly drove Corbett wild. When he was able to feel his feet, after his seconds had helped him to his corner, he broke away from them and rushed at Fitzsimmons, who had not left the ring. A scene of dreadful confusion ensued. The ring was crowded with an excited mob, but Corbett burst through them and struck at Fitzsimmons. The Australian kept his arms by his sides, and with a great deal of generosity, made allowance for Corbett's half demented condition. Fitzsimmons merely ducked under the blow, and when Corbett clinched with him and struck him a feeble blow on the ear the champion only smiled. It was with great difficulty that "Billy" Brady and the seconds succeeded in quieting Corbett down and getting him back to the dressing room.

The fight was clean and speedy. It demonstrated two facts—that Corbett is the cleverest boxer of his weight in the world, and that Fitzsimmons is able to hit him. The California boy smothered the Cornishman with "left jabs" in the face and right and left body blows. Fitzsimmons's most effective attack was a semi-fake left swing, followed with a quick half-arm hook. The first time he tried it, which was in the third round, Corbett threw back his head from the fake, coming forward for a counter when he thought Fitzsimmons's glove was comfortably past his jaw. Quick as a flash, Fitzsimmons doubled back and barely missed Corbett's jaw with the hook. Corbett's smile died away for an instant, and he took no more chances on countering on that particular form of lead afterward.

On New Principles.

The battle was fought on purely scientific and almost new principles. Corbett made no attempt to bring around his right in breaking away, probably because Fitzsimmons held up his elbows too high. Corbett's only effort in the way of a parting shot was a full right upper cut, which he brought around very clumsily, and failed to land by at least a foot every time he tried. He did get in one good upper cut in the fourth round, splitting Fitzsimmons's under lip and starting the blood in a thick stream. Several times the men clinched and parted with both hands up. Frequently Fitzsimmons worked Corbett into his corner and reached for him right and left with blows that would win any championship battle if they had landed. Fitzsimmons himself admits that Corbett shuffled and side-stepped his way to safety in a manner which simply dazed him.

"I never saw such a clever man in my life," said Fitzsimmons to-night. "He got away from me time and again when I thought I had him dead to rights. I knew I could wear him out, and so I kept coming right along until my oportunity arrived. He was weak in the last round, and all his cleverness could not keep him out of that left punch under the heart. The only blow that really worried me was the one which split my lip. The others I never felt. He fought fair, and hereafter he may have my respect if he continues to merit it."

Corbett's View of His Defeat.

Corbett's version of his own Waterloo did not vary greatly from Fitzsimmons's. "I made a mistake in not keeping away," was the way he put it. "Fitzsimmons, I knew to be a terrible puncher, but I never calculated on his being able to reach me. If the sixth round had lasted ten seconds longer I would have landed him to a certainty. His nose was clogged with blood and his legs were wobbling. The gong sounded just as I was about to plug him with my right and end the battle. He recuperated wonderfully, and I stayed away from him until I thought he was about ripe for another drubbing at short range. My neglect in not standing off when he tapped me on the cheek in the fourteenth lost me the championship. That heart punch simply choked me up. I could not breathe or move for fifteen seconds, and it was several minutes before I realized that I had committed a breach of etiquette in trying to follow up my opponent after he put me out. I meant it when I said I would be his friend hereafter. He whipped me fair and square, but I don't think he is the best man yet, and we will have another go if money can bring him into the ring."

After the fight W. A. Brady, Corbett's manager, expressed a willingness to back Corbett for $20,000 for another fight.

March 18, 1897

JEFFRIES WINS FROM FITZSIMMONS

Youth and Muscle Overmatch Science and Pluck.

CONTEST ENDS IN 11TH ROUND

Boxers Get About $25,000 Cash and Contingent Profits.

The long-heralded prizefight, known by a pleasant fiction of New York law as a boxing contest, between Robert Fitzsimmons, who held the championship of the world, and James J. Jeffries, the aspiring boiler-maker from California, was fought last night in the building of the New Coney Island Sporting Club.

It resulted in an indisputable victory for

Jeffries in the eleventh round. Consequently the world has a new champion pugilist this morning, and Fitzsimmons, who knocked out Corbett, who knocked out Sullivan, has taken his place in the long procession of fistic heroes known in ring circles as "back numbers" or "has beens."

The work of changing champions occupied a little less than forty-four minutes. How much the two men gained in money nobody know . On a rough estimate it is said that Fitzsimmons, whose dignity demanded large pecuniary inducements to tempt him to display his prowess upon a comparatively unknown man, will receive about $25,000 of the gate receipts as his share, besides contingent profits from the vitascope, which took photographs of the fight and will reproduce them indefinitely.

Jeffries will do as well and is probably richer by a comfortable amount in side bets, to say nothing of gratuities from winners, who are naturally all his enthusiastic friends.

The room in which the battle was fought is 200 feet long by 100 wide, and is 40 feet high. Ceilings, walls, and rafters are stained a light brown. From the arena tiers of seats arise to within fifteen feet of the ceiling.

In the centre of the arena rises the square platform, with the three stout manila ropes inclosing the square in which the fighting was done. Over the ring, up among the rafters, four strong arc lamps were hung. Twenty other arc lamps, equidistant, hang alongside the arena. High above the ring hung a square, flying gallery, suspended from the rafters by iron rods.

At 9 o'clock all the arena seats were occupied, and the tiers of seats banked at each side and the ends presented masses of white faces and shirt fronts. There was a clamor of thousands of tongues and a cloud of tobacco smoke drifting up and gathering in a haze against the roof.

A WELL-DRESSED CROWD.

It was a well-dressed gathering. There was not a shabby man in sight anywhere, nor were there many whose dress indicated the sporting man. Immediately about the ring there were rows of middle-aged and elderly men, some of them with white hair and beards. These had a distinctively welled and well-groomed appearance, and diamonds flashed from their fingers and shirt fronts in the electric light. But for the diamonds and the formidable cigars at which many of them pulled, they might have been taken for vestrymen waiting for the opening of a religious service, so tranquil was their demeanor, so calm were their countenances and the peace of their attitudes.

There were old and young men who had traveled more than a thousand miles and spent hundreds of dollars to reach the ringside, and they were content to be there. Some of them had thousands and ten of thousands of dollars at stake, but it is against sporting ethics to display emotion and the prevalent face was impassive, even though it might sometimes pale or flush.

Only the newspaper men and the police seemed to be busy or interested. A casual observer, dropping in through the roof from some distant country, would have thought the crowd had gathered for an evening which it expected to be rather a bore.

The preliminary demonstration was all from the seats looking down upon the arena. The younger men there were more restless and eager and alert than the veterans below, and vented their feelings in cheers and handclapping on trivial provocations.

JEFFRIES LOOKED ANGRY.

There was a great cheer and a rattle of applause when Jeffries walked in a little after 9 o'clock, pushing his way through the men packed along the arena. He looked huge and rather angry than pleased, and, with his red sweater under a sack coat, and a flimsy cap on the back of his head resting on his thick black hair, was the most carelessly dressed and the roughest-looking man in the room. There was a fainter cheer as Fitzsimmons was announced, and after his disappearance there were symptoms of impatience and cries and hoots began to sound from around the house.

The rumor that there was a dispute over the rules had gone abroad, and it caused impatience and dissatisfaction. The uncertainty of Chief of Police Devery's intentions added to the uneasy feeling. The men there had not come to see whether Fitzsimmons or Jeffries was the better boxer. They wanted to see which was the "best man," which could hit hardest, endure the most pain and fatigue, keep his head, and use his skill the better when breath was coming hard and short and the body was sore and the muscles tired and resenting the fearful strain upon them.

At 10 o'clock there were yet vacant patches in the expanses of reserved seats opposite the ring on each side. The crowd amused itself watching workmen on the flying platform patch a broken railing and put the finishing touches on the rows of black vitascope machines, which looked like mortars trained on the ring below. Stamping in imitation of drum beats, whistles and cat calls, and ironical cheers relieved the monotony.

FLOWERS FOR FITZSIMMONS.

But the annoyance of waiting seemed to be forgotten when a cheer began at the eastern end of the great building, and the men there were seen to rise in their seats. The mass of humanity surged up like a great wave as a mound of roses appeared moving through the throng down on the floor. This was a gigantic horseshoe of pink, white, and crimson roses, with American flags above it, and bearing the inscription "Good Luck to the Champion."

Behind this aesthetic proclamation, which was carried by two men, Fitzsimmons stalked solemnly, like the chief figure in a classic spectacle. His bearing was solemn, like that of a man who felt that he was about to perform a rite with the eyes of an admiring world concentrated upon him. He wore a bath robe of pale blue, gathered at the waist, and his head was bare. His three attendants, in white flannel undershirts and long trousers, followed him, two of them bearing galvanized iron buckets and broad palm-leaf fans, one of them with a long bottle driven into his hip pocket.

Jefferies was more on the rough-and-ready order. He moved briskly and swung his shoulders and wore a red sweater, with suspenders over it, and the breeches of ordinary, commonplace humanity; but his three seconds carried the galvanized iron buckets and the bottles and fans and were also in their undershirts.

AN AESTHETIC FEATURE.

A stray wounded moth had been fluttering about the padded surface of the ring, and as the big floral piece was carried in many of the roses tumbled to pieces. Therefore, it was another aesthetic feature of the affair that the first actual preliminary was to clear the ring of moth and rose leaves, which was done with one of the big fans.

Fitzsimmons, sitting on his wooden stool in his corner, watched this operation with interest. Jeffries, from his stool in his corner, twisted his neckl and peered between the men, who surrounded him, trying to catch a view of his antagonist.

Then came the referee, George Siler, in blue and white striped undershirt collarless and bareheaded. He leaned negligently against the ropes in an unoccupied corner while the seconds inspected the gloves and other seconds fitted them on.

Fitzsimmons rubbed his hands together before he submitted to be gloved, his air being that of a man who rather expected to enjoy himself. Jeffries leaned over and rubbed his palms on the floor to get resin upon them. Billy Brady leaned against the ropes opposite the press stalls, and bit the top one idly. Nobody in or around the ring was excited or hurried. One of the seconds held a fan over Fitzsimmons's head as Eastern attendants hold umbrellas of state above potentates.

By this time the spectators had all arrived and it was seen that men of several classes were elbow to elbow and cheek by jowl. There were sporting men and business men, financiers and actors, society men and jockeys, and distributed among them all were the denizens of South Brooklyn, who always can afford to buy a front seat at a prize fight in or around New York.

MRS. FITZSIMMONS PRESENT.

Mrs. Fitzsimmons got into the clubhouse, and was in her husband's dressing room while he was preparing for the battle, but she decided not to attempt to witness the fight. She saw William A. Brady, the manager of Jeffries, shook hands with him, and remarked:

"We will beat your man again to-night, as we did the other at Carson City."

Brady smiled and replied that he hoped not, and Mrs. Fitzsimmons, after seeing that her husband was properly equipped for the fray, kissed him, and wishing him good luck, sent him out into the arena.

George E. Smith, ("Pittsburg Phil,") a man who never in his career on the turf, even when a decision of $100,000 depended on an inch of ground, was known to betray excitement, caused some surprise by becoming one of the most enthusiastic of the shouters. He was a Jeffries man, and his excitement was in marked contrast to the cool demeanor of some of the others.

About 10:17 Jeffries's seconds, with serious demeanor, began to withdraw his trousers, and a hundred pencils in the press stalls were instantly busy with the chronicle of this portentous fact.

Two journalists with split second watches had quite an energetic dispute as to whether the ceremony began at 10:17 or 10:17¼. There was also a solemn drawing of corks from the bottles and an unfolding and laying aside of large towels. About the same time Fitzsimmons untied and put away his pale-blue robe and revealed himself naked but for trunks and shoes with black stockings turned down nearly to his ankles. The trunks were ornamented with rosettes of red, white, and blue. Jeffries also wore trunks, shoes, and stockings. His trunks were plain white.

A PERFUNCTORY HANDSHAKE.

Then they gargled their throats from the bottles and met each other at the centre of the ring, where they shook hands coldly and perfunctorily.

There was silence throughout the house by this time. The contrast between the two was startling. Fitzsimmons looked little and white confronting his antagonist. Jeffries is a dark man. His eyes and hair are black and his skin almost a tan. Fitzsimmons is light-eyed and what hair he has is pale red. No woman has a skin whiter or smoother than his.

The word was given and the men rose from the stools to which they had returned. Neither looked cheerful. Jeffries swallowed hard; Fitzsimmons moistened his lips with his tongue, and as he faced his man and they slowly and cautiously circled about, feinting, advancing, and retreating, never within arm's length, their eyes intently fastened on each other, he began to work his lips nervously.

THEY FACE EACH OTHER.

If the crowd had been a crowd of dead men, the stillness could not have been deeper than it was. The two pugilists trod softly as cats. Nothing could be heard but the gentle thud, thud of their ever restless, shifting feet as they circled.

Then there was a sudden rush and the sharp slap of a glove landing, a gleaming of arms and twisting and violent motion of white bodies in the ring, a storm of cries, with applause and some roaring laughter from arena and encompassing seats.

Jeffries had led. He was not afraid to fight. That was one point settled.

Fitzsimmons's light blue eyes opened wide and blazed angrily. Jeffries crouched low, keeping his tremendous left arm well thrust out, his head down, looking from under his eyebrows.

In the second round the cheering and shouting began again. The crowd then felt that it would see what it had gathered to see—a fight with hard knocks. The two men in the ring smiled at each other as both missed and they came together in a clinch, but the big muscles in their thighs were already quivering and they did not relax their watchfulness the fraction of a second.

CROWD WITH JEFFRIES.

The crowd was evidently with Jeffries, and after Fitzsimmons had tumbled on his back, looking a much-surprised man, joy was unrestrained. It was evident then that the ideas of Chief of Police Devery on slugging were liberal, and that there would be no interference. The older sporting men around the ring, their last fear removed, settled down more placidly and calmly than ever and looked entirely and supremely happy.

After the sixth round a new change came into Fitzsimmons's face. He had looked furious at times and amused at times, as he felt that he had scored a point or that his antagonist had missed one.

FITZSIMMONS WORRIED.

Now he looked old and worn and anxious. Wrinkles seemed to come into his cheeks. He was aggressive, crafty, watchful, always moving, his rather cruel lips working and working as if he would like to bite; but he seemed like a man who is hunted. Once or twice thereafter his lips broke into a smile. When he and Jeffries broke out of a clinch and separated at the end of the eighth round, their mutual grins were almost affable. But as he sat on his stool and breathed fast and his seconds fanned him furiously with towels and fans and gave him from the bottle to gargle, he looked harassed.

When he came it seemed very quick and easy. The blow that really did the work was given with Jeffries's left glove. After it was delivered Fitzsimmons stood an instant, his hands hanging by his side, his knees bowed. The knock-out with the right came swiftly. It was given from the hip, much like a quick slap. It was not like one of the long, hard swings Jeffries had aimed at him several times, and which had gone over his head.

When it landed Fitzsimmons fell and turned on his right side. There was no need to count. His body was limp and doubled up. He passed the back of his hand wearily over his bald forehead and straightened out on his back, his lower lip hanging foolishly, his long upper lip scarlet.

Jeffries looked at him an instant and walked to his corner, breathing hard. A thousand men were storming and swirling about the ringside then.

Hats were waving and the big hall was ringing with yells and cheers and exultant laughter.

Fitzsimmons was dragged to his stool, his heels trailing helplessly on the floor. It was all over.

June 10, 1899

GANS KNOCKS OUT ERNE.

Negro Pugilist Wins the Fight at Fort Erie in Two Rounds.

FORT ERIE, Ont., May 12.—Joe Gans, the negro lightweight pugilist of Baltimore, defeated Frank Erne of Buffalo to-night in the second round of what was to have been a fight of twenty rounds. The sudden termination of the combat threw the sporting crowd into temporary consternation, for the men had hardly got warmed up to the fray before Erne was down and out. A large crowd of sporting men from New York, Boston, Buffalo, Baltimore, and different Canadian towns saw the fight. The limit weight was 136 pounds. Gans weighed in at 133¼ pounds and Erne at 132½ pounds.

The time of the fatal second round to Erne was one minute and forty seconds. Gans had the advantage in the first round. In the second Gans, while warily looking for an opening, caught Erne off his guard, giving the negro a chance to land his right on the ear. It was a deciding blow, although Gans hardly believed it at first. Erne at once started to spar somewhat wildly and in return Gans sent out his left hand, which broke down Erne's guard. A second later Gans followed up his advantage by a blow on the jaw. This was the culmination of the series of fierce blows which had been showered on him by Gans, and Erne fell to the floor in a heap. As the referee, Charley White, counted him out Erne rolled over on his stomach.

The consensus of opinion by the experts at the ring was that the fight was altogether too short to successfully determine the superiority of either man with the small gloves.

May 13, 1902

MARVIN HART IS CHAMPION.

Louisville Fighter Defeated "Jack" Root in Twelve Rounds.

RENO, Nev., July 3.—Marvin Hart of Louisville is champion heavyweight pugilist of the world. He won the title to-day by knocking out "Jack" Root of Chicago in twelve rounds, after one of the fiercest fights ever witnessed in the West. The blow which won for Hart the championship was a hard right to the left of Root's heart. The blow was delivered with terrific force, and it caught the Chicago man while he was coming up. Root reeled and fell in a heap. Referee James J. Jeffries counted the fateful seconds, but there was little necessity for this, as Root was beaten and still unconscious at the count of ten.

Root scaled 170 pounds, while Hart was twenty pounds heavier. The men fought for a five-thousand-dollar purse, 65 per cent. to the winner and 35 per cent. to the loser. Before the fight James J. Jeffries, who refereed the fight, stated that he had retired from the ring for good and that the winner would be entitled to the name of heavyweight champion of the world. Among those present were Attorney General Sweeney, Senator F. G. Newlands, Lieut. Gov. Allen and wife, Mayor O'Connor, Sheriff Ferrell, and District Attorney Craig of Nevada, and the entire constabulary and police force of Washoe County and the City of Reno.

Before the fight Root ruled favorite at odds of 3 to 1 and up to the knockout blow the Chicago man had an apparent lead over Hart. The two men were cautious during the first round, but Root soon gained confidence and went after his man in the most approved style. He gained a big lead in the first seven rounds. At the end of the seventh round Root knocked Hart down with a terrific right just as the gong sounded. A claim of foul was made for Hart, but Referee Jeffries disclaimed any foul and ordered the men to continue. Hart was in a bad way and the gong saved him.

Root continued to force the fighting in the eighth rolund, but Hart seemed to be growing stronger as the bout progressed. He secured a big lead over Root in the ninth round, and in the tenth he had his man going fast at the bell. From this on Hart continued to improve until the end came in the twelfth round. It was unexpected, as Root looked good for some time before receiving the blow which sent him to the floor helpless and gave the heavyweight championship to Marvin Hart.

The contest took place in a large open amphitheatre a mile east of Reno, and for nearly an hour the men fought before 5,000 persons under a blazing sun. There was a liberal sprinkling of women among the spctators.

The blow that knocked Root out was heard all over the arena. As the eighth second was called Root raised himself on his hands with his mouth open, dragged himself to a kneeling position, and then collapsed. His seconds carried him to his corner, where he remained three minutes.

July 4, 1905

STRAIGHT HITTING GETS BOXERS PLUMS

Champion Joe Gans Tells Why He Has Lasted So Long in the Prize Ring.

STYLES OF OTHER FIGHTERS

Jeffries Never Employed Fancy Boxing to Win His Battles—Men Who Fell by the Wayside.

Lightweight Champion Joe Gans was discussing his long and successful career with a number of friends the other night.

"I owe my present position in the ring," said the crack negro fighter, "to my ability to hit straight more than to anything else. This may sound rather strange, but it is the truth. Of course, careful living and correct methods have aided me to outlast all of my rivals in my class. Straight hitting is the foundation of most of my success, and I can prove it to you."

Then the champion illustrated how much useful energy and strength is spent in needless swinging blows and other so-called original punches.

"Wait for your opportunity," continued Gans, "and when it comes avail yourself of it. The idea of boring in and sending smashes helter skelter without reason doesn't amount to a row of pins. In the long run, save if you are a man of abnormal strength, nine times out of ten it will beat you. Every time you miss a swing it is worse than being hit. I could be the champion of the world until I was as old as Methusulah if I could have for opponents fellows who just rushed at me with swinging blows. All I would have to do would be to let them waste their energy and when they were weakened just land one blow, a straight one, to be sure, and it would be all over in a jiffy.

"Terry McGovern had the knack of hitting straight. Still he coupled his ability with occasional swings, and this helped to pave the way for his downfall. McGovern had great power behind his wallops, and when he connected with one of those swings his rival was certain to collide with the floor.

"I regard Bob Fitzsimmons as one of the greatest exponents of straight hitting that the prize ring has ever known," says Gans. "Fitz was a wonderful fighter, and all of his straight punches were very effective. Until age set in, and his hands went back on him, there were few fighters able to withstand that famous shift of his. When Fitz delivered this blow he carried the whole weight of his body with it. He executed it so deftly, too, that one marveled at its effectiveness. The truth is that Bob never tried the punch with the slightest loss of energy. When he landed it properly victory was his, as attested by his defeat of Gus Ruhlin, Jim Corbett, Tom Sharkey, and others.

"Young Corbett never cared to indulge in swings. He invariably frowned on this method of winning fights. He believed in the efficacy of straight hitting for success, and undoubtedly he would have been on top of the heap to-day had he stuck to the right path

"Some folks imagine that it is Jim Jeffries's bulk and huge strength that has enabled him to remain the undefeated champion of the world," continued Gans. "This is a most popular impression, but.

a wrong one. Jeffries, in my estimation, is one of the most accurate punchers in the business. I don't recall where Jeffries knocked out any one with swinging blows, but I do know that he has won the majority of his contests through straight hitting. Take, for instance, his 'mill' with Tom Sharkey at Coney Island. If you saw that scrap you will recall how Jeffries plied straight right drives to the sailor's ribs. All of Jeffries's strength was behind those stabs, and Sharkey seemingly never recovered after that encounter. One reason why Sharkey never became the champion heavyweight was because he was nothing more than a swinger. If Tom, when he started out upon his pugilistic career, had been taught to hit straight, I think he would have taken Jeffries's measure, and perhaps occupied the boilermaker's shoes to-day.

"'Kid' McCoy was not nominally a straight hitter, yet he has received the credit with winning all of his fights on these lines. The 'Kid' had a natural incentive to try something new—that is, he was invariably inventing some ruse or improving on old blows for his success. As most of these punches were swings, the effort taxed his strength, which was never great. McCoy's best blow was a short right hook and jab. But in the long run the jab was his best asset, because it is a straight blow.

"Peter Maher was a straight hitter, but lacked courage to amount to anything. I don't know of any heavyweight who could strike as hard a blow as Maher. Somehow those short, snappy, straight punches of his seemed to come from nowhere. The force of Maher's whole frame was behind the smashes, and very few of his rivals ever heard the count of the fatal ten seconds when Peter landed.

"Abe Attell, Young Ketcham, and Owen Moran of England are straight hitters. So is Tommy Murphy of Harlem. Jack Johnson, the negro heavyweight, is also in this class, and to my mind Johnson will soon be the superior of all the big men. He seldom swings. Young Griffo never swings. He was a straight hitter from the word 'go.' Had he possessed the punch and taken care of himself he would have been in harness to-day. As to the late George Dixon, he seldom resorted to swinging. All of his victories were the result of short-arm straight blows. He often used that famous double punch of his, a left drive to the wind and a smash on the jaw with the same glove. The drive to the wind was straight and the blow on the jaw slightly hooked. Still the straight punch was the one that invariably did the damage.

February 2, 1908

KETCHEL KNOCKS OUT PAPKE IN ELEVENTH

Michigan Boxer Regains Middleweight Title in Ring at San Francisco.

WINNER LEADS ALL THE WAY

Wrests Championship from Illinoisan with a Blow on the Jaw—Fighters Fall Off Platform.

SAN FRANCISCO, Nov. 26.—Stanley Ketchel of Grand Rapids, Mich., regained the middleweight championship of the world to-day and reversed his defeat of last September, when he sent Billy Papke, the Illinois "thunderbolt," crashing to the floor before a well-directed blow that caught his opponent flush upon the chin. The end came in the eleventh round, prior to which Ketchel showed clearly that he was master of his opponent at any kind of fighting. Round by round, Ketchel forced his opponent, and when opportunity offered, planted his right to head or body, generally escaping without a damaging return. Belying his appearance and forcing the fight throughout every minute, Ketchel was stronger up to the moment of the knockout blow than was his opponent. Once during an aggressive moment they fell in the ringside and toppled through the ropes, wrapped in a close embrace. It was a left to the stomach that sent Papke to the ropes at this juncture. In falling Papke seized his opponent, and the force of his rush carried him clear off the platform and over the heads of the spectators. Willing hands assisted them to the platform, and in a moment they were grappling in a clinch.

Ketchel was a victor throughout. His appearance during the early rounds did not tend to encourage those who had backed him at odds of 10 to 7 and 10 to 6, but his awkward delivery of blows fast seemed to lull Papke into a false sense of security. In the first round Ketchel drove Papke into a neutral corner, landing right and left almost at will, and thereafter the Illinois contender was always at a disadvantage. Stepping aside at critical junctures, Ketchel swung his right time and again flush upon his opponent's jaw, now and then alternating with left drives to the body. In the fifth round Ketchel drove a hard left to the stomach, and Papke had not put up his hands before he encountered a hard right to the jaw. Before this, in the fourth round, a light tap on the nose had brought blood from Papke that started the crowd yelling for the Michigander.

It was in the seventh that Ketchel used his right to the greatest advantage. Papke's only hope lay in his disposition to clinch, but he was hit twice, and both blows tended to lessen his recuperative powers.

From this time on the crowd awaited the knockout punch that Ketchel was apparently withholding. In the ninth Papke was sent tottering across the ring and nearly went to his knees by a powerful blow delivered in a clinch. He arose to meet Ketchel's right, which twice landed on the jaw. Papke went to his corner, bleeding freely from the nose. This was the beginning of the end. In the following round Papke twice turned his back on Ketchel's swift assaults and deliberately ran away.

In the eleventh and final round Ketchel was as fresh and strong as at any time during the fight. He tapped Papke lightly on the jaw and then rushed him half way across the ring, planting two hard rights to the stomach. A moment later, as they broke out of a clinch, Ketchel swung the left at three-quarters length, landing squarely on the point of the chin. Papke struck at full length, his head rapping the floor with terrible force. He had just enough strength to regain his feet, and while he crouched in an attitude half protected, Ketchel sent his right to the head four times in quick succession and almost pushed Papke over with a left hook. Papke fell forward on his knees, his hands supporting him and his head bowed as if in agony. Referee Jack Welsh counted eleven, as did also the timekeeper, and then, advancing toward Ketchel, threw the Michigan fighter's glove aloft. Papke, still dazed, seemed not to realize his defeat.

Papke said after the fight: "I am not satisfied with the outcome. I want a return. I did not hear the count. I heard the referee say 'Six,' and then he stopped. I would have been able to continue the fight, as I was not hurt and recovering fast. I want a return match."

Ketchel said: "I anticipated this result long before I entered the ring, and backed my opinion with my own money. Papke's victory in the South was an accident. Under proper conditions I am willing to fight him again."

The betting was seriously affected prior to the fight by rumors of Ketchel's failure to get into proper condition. The betting dropped from 10 to 7½, to 10 to 6, solely because of this.

November 27, 1908

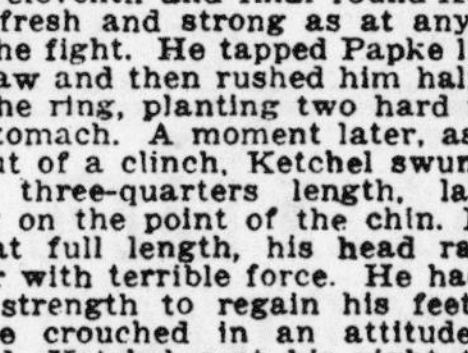

JACK JOHNSON WINS; POLICE STOP FIGHT

Negro's Punishment of Champion Burns Causes Authorities to End Bout.

MILL DECIDED ON POINTS

News of Saturday Morning's Battle in Australia Received Last Night in New York.

Heavyweight Championship Fight.

Principals—Jack Johnson, Galveston, Texas, and Tommy Burns, Canada.

Winner—Jack Johnson.

Number of rounds—Fourteen.

Place—Stadium, Sydney, N. S. W.

Purse—$35,000; $30,000 to Burns, $5,000 to Johnson.

Betting—Six to four in favor of Burns.

Referee—Hugh D. McIntosh.

Physical Comparison of Fighters.

Jack Johnson—Weight, 195 pounds; height, 6 feet 1¾ inches; reach, 72¾ inches; forearm, 13 inches; biceps, 14½ inches; neck, 17 inches; chest, 43¼ inches; waist, 33 inches; hip, 37 inches; thigh, 22½ inches; calf, 15½ inches; age, 30 years.

Tommy Burns—Weight, 180 pounds; height, 5 feet 7¼ inches; reach, 74½ inches; forearm, 12 inches; biceps, 13¼ inches; neck, 16 inches; chest, 40½ inches; waist, 32½ inches; hip, 38 inches; thigh, 23 inches; calf, 15½ inches; age, 27 years.

SYDNEY, Saturday noon, Dec. 26.—Jack Johnson, the big negro from Galveston, Texas is the world's champion, heavyweight pugilist. He won the title to-day in the big arena at Ruschutters Bay from Tommy Burns, the French-Canadian, who had held it since James J. Jeffries relinquished it, and after a chase of Burns that had led half way round the world.

The end came in the fourteenth round when the police, seeing Burns tottering and unable to defend himself from the savage blows of his opponent, mercifully stopped the fight. Previously it had been arranged that if the police interfered a decision should be rendered on points, and referee McIntosh without hesitation declared the big black man the winner, for all through the fight he had shown himself Burns's master in every style of fighting.

Burns in an interview after he had gone to his dressing room said:

"I did the best I could and fought hard. Johnson was too big and his reach was too great."

Johnson appeared fresh after the fight, while Burns's eyes were badly puffed and his mouth swollen to twice its normal size. The Canadian fought a game battle and showed indomitable pluck, but he was no match for the big black Texan.

The fight was for a purse of $35,000, of which Burns received $30,000 and Johnson $5,000. The ring was a 24-foot one, and was pitched in the centre of a big arena built especially for the purpose at Rushcutters Bay. The bout was to have been for twenty rounds.

The day dawned overcast and cool. Thousands of persons from all parts of the country were attracted to the scene of the encounter, and many reached there Christmas night and slept in the open. They came by street cars, automobiles, carriages, and on horseback, and at 10 o'clock this morning, one hour before the fight was scheduled to start, every seat was occupied. The prices of seats ranged from $25 to 2.50. The crowd was estimated at between 18,000 and 20,000 persons, and it kept perfect order throughout the fight.

Before the contestants entered the ring, "Bill" Squires, who thrice has been defeated by Burns, challenged the winner. Burns weighed in at 168 pounds and Johnson at 192. The betting was 7 to 4 on Burns at the start, but it veered after a few rounds to 2 to 1 on Johnson.

The spectators conceded that Johnson's victory was due to his physical advantages over burns, his superior knowledge of the fighting game, and his unruffled demeanor while being taunted by the champion. The stakes were paid the men while they were in the ring.

At 10:42 o'clock Johnson entered the Arena accompanied by his seconds, Sam Fitzpatrick, Mullins, Unholz, Lang, and Bryant. Wild cheering greeted him and the big black man turned and bowed to all four sides of the ring.

Just as Johnson took his seat Burns appeared. He was smiling and the plaudits of the spectators were even more enthusiastic than those accorded Johnson. Burns took up his position in the western corner of the ring surrounded by his seconds, Keating, O'Keefe, O'Donnell, Burke, and Russell. When the cheering had died down somewhat Johnson crossed over and shook Burns by the hand. The Canadian glanced at the big hands of the Texan and noticed that both were covered with bandages. Fearful that perhaps they might not be of the soft kind, he scrutinized them closely, but finding them to his satisfaction he made no objection.

The announcement was made that if during the contest the police should interfere and stop it the referee would immediately give a decision based on points scored.

When Burns stripped it was noticed that he wore elastic bandages about his elbows. Johnson shouted across the ring half angrily: "You must take those off." Then the men met in the centre of the ring, and for a few minutes argued the question. Then they retired again to their corners, but Burns did not remove the bandages.

From Johnson's seconds came the announcement that their man refused to fight unless Burns took off the wraps around his elbows, and it looked as though there was a possibility of the fight not taking place, for Burns was stubborn and Johnson insistent on his point. The referee, however, here took a hand in the controversy and said that the wearing of bandages was not against the rules. Johnson still demurred, nevertheless, and Burns, with a show of impatience, had his seconds unwind the tape. His action brought forth from the spectators a tremendous round of applause.

At 11:15 o'clock Johnson and Burns posed for a moving picture machine, and, having received final instructions from Referee McIntosh, retired to their corners. Then the battle began.

December 26, 1908

FIRST NEGRO CHAMPION.

Johnson Also Only Colored Man to Fight for Heavyweight Title.

Jack Johnson is the first negro who ever won the world's heavy-weight pugilistic championship—in fact, he is the only negro who ever was permitted to battle for the title. He was born in Galveston, Texas, in 1878, and began his ring career in 1901. He is 6 feet 1 1-3 inches in height and weighed at the ringside close to 190 pounds.

Burns was born in Hanover, Ontario, in 1881, and started fighting when he was 19 years old. He is 5 feet 7¼ inches in height and weighs, when trained for battle, about 175 pounds. Burns always was a rough-and-ready fighter, who delighted to sail in and mix things with his adversary. Favored with unusual length of arm (his reach measuring 74½ inches,) Burns has proved himself a dangerous man at close range. Despite the fact that Johnson overtopped him in height by 6½ inches, Burns had the better of the argument in reach by 1¾ inches.

A purse of $35,000 was hung up for the battle, which was scheduled to go twenty rounds. Of this amount Burns demanded and received $30,000, this sum to be paid him despite the outcome of the fight. Johnson had to be satisfied with $5,000 and return transportation for himself and his manager, Sam Fitzpatrick.

According to reports both Johnson and Burns bet heavily on themselves at the prevailing odds, which slightly favored Burns at the ringside. The men fought

before what probably was the largest crowd that ever witnessed a pugilistic contest. Burns did his training at Darling Point, while Johnson got in condition at Manley, a seaside suburb. Besides a retinue of skillful trainers, who gave the men daily practice at the game of hit, stop, and get away, both Burns and Johnson followed American training methods by doing hard road work. Each man picked up a lot of loose change by giving training exhibitions twice a week at the Stadium.

Since James J. Jeffries retired and Tommy Burns claimed the championship, Johnson has been trying to get the Canadian to meet him and he has trailed him throughought the United States and even to England in quest of a match. It was not until Mr. McIntosh, the promoter of this fight, and who also acted as referee, offered a purse of $35,000 for a battle at Rushcutter's Bay, a suburb of Sydney, that Burns consented to meet Johnson. Then he stipulated how the money should be split up, the size of the ring, and all the conditions surrounding the fight. Johnson immediately accepted and sailed from London for Australia to begin training.

Johnson, during his ring career has fought sixty-four battles, and twenty-two of his opponents have gone down to defeat by the knockout route. Prominent among those who have been put to sleep by the big negro are Jack Jeffries, a brother of the former heavyweight champion, who was knocked out by Johnson at Los Angeles in 1902 in five rounds, and Bob Fitzsimmons, who, in Philadelphia in 1907, was able to withstand Johnson's shifty work but two rounds. Fitzsimmons, however, had an injured arm when he engaged in this bout. Johnson has lost but two fights, one a twenty-round decision to Marvin Hart and the other on a foul to Joe Jeanette.

Not since the days of James J. Corbett has the prize ring seen so perfect a looking boxer as Johnson. Long and lithe and graceful, he is as true as an arrow in placing his blows. Especially deft is he with his left hand, and few boxers, unless they have great skill, are able to keep the big fighter from beating their faces to tatters.

In courage Burns was always a bulldog; Johnson, it was said by some, had a "yellow streak." In none of his many battles, however, has it been proved that Johnson would not take a good beating. Neither Burns nor Johnson, however, have been considered men of the stamp of Jeffries, Sullivan or Corbett in the fighting game.

December 26, 1908

JOHNSON DAZED AS KETCHEL GOES OUT

Black Champion Finishes White Fighter in Twelfth Round.

LAST SECONDS SENSATIONAL

Negro Rises from a Fall and Piles Into Ketchel with Crashing Blows— $40,000 Taken In.

SAN FRANCISCO, Oct. 16.—Jack Johnson to-day retained the heavyweight pugilistic championship by knocking out Stanley Ketchel in the twelfth round. The end came so suddenly that when Ketchel rolled to the floor and Referee Webb counted him out the 10,000 persons crowding the arena were absolutely quiet for a full minute. Even Johnson, who leaned against the ropes, half dazed by his own fall a moment before, did not seem to know what had happened.

The climax of the fight was crowded into thirty-four seconds. At the begin-

ning of what proved to be the last round there had been little in the preceding round on which to forecast the winner. The men in the centre of the ring clinched and wrestled to Johnson's corner. The negro broke away, and, poising himself, dashed at Ketchel, who sprang to meet him. Ketchel drove his right at the black's lowered head. Johnson ducked, and the blow landed behind his ear. He stumbled and fell, landing heavily.

Johnson Surprises Ketchel.

Ketchel backed toward the ropes with a faint smile on his battered, blood-streaked face. Johnson rose slowly as though dazed. As he straightened to his knees he looked at Ketchel and like a wild beast he leaped across the ten feet that separated them. His right fist shot to the white man's jaw. His left crashed to the stomach, and the right swung again with the speed of lightning, catching Ketchel's head as he reeled back from the onslaught.

Ketchel dropped in a heap, and Johnson, unable to stop his rush, sprawled across his beaten rival's legs and fell full length himself.

The negro sprang to his feet with a bound, but Ketchel was out. Once as the seconds were counted over him he feebly moved his arms and rolled his head. He gave no other sign of life and his seconds picked him up from the floor barely conscious.

Johnson was still dazed. He clung to the ropes and looked about him in a bewildered way.

The crowd broke into murmurings and seemed unable to realize that the first was over.

Ketchel won many friends by his show-, ing to-day. From the time he entered the ring until he was carried out, he was game to the core. Outweighted, overreached, and in every way the physical inferior to his gigantic opponent, he fought a cool, well-planned, gritty fight. His face was puffed and he was bleeding at the nose and mouth before three rounds had passed, but he kept following the negro about the ring undaunted.

Negro Fights Carefully.

Johnson appeared to be holding himself back all the time. Three times only did it look as though he went in to knock his man out; once when Ketchel landed a clean left hook on the jaw that broke the skin and raised a lump; once when a similar blow caught him from the other side, and the last time when he ended the fight.

Throughout the fight Johnson's "golden smile" flashed out at intervals over Ketchel's shoulder in the midst of their wrestling bouts. This happened whenever he picked the smaller man off the ground and set him down again in another place. He did it frequently, and apparently without effort.

Ketchel fought warily from the start. He kept at long range, avoiding many blows by clever ducking, but Johnson jabbed his left into Ketchel's face time after time. When they clinched Johnson towered inches above Ketchel.

Twice Ketchel was thrown to the floor by the rush of Johnson's attack. Neither time did a blow land. At other times Ketchel avoided the charges by skipping nimbly to right or left or backing swiftly away. They sparred for openings for long periods and there was little real fighting through the earlier rounds. For reasons known only to himself, Johnson preferred to keep away, and when he had felt the force of Ketchel's left hook he seemed more than ever ready to go slow about his work.

In his dressing room after the fight Johnson said:

"He is a good puncher and a strong man. I must say that he has given me a sorer chin than I ever had before," and he rubbed his swollen jaw reflectively.

"He can take some heavy blows," continued the negro. "See here," and he showed one of his gloves sodden with Ketchel's blood. "There were several cuts on the leather. That's where I uppercut him in the mouth," said Johnson.

Ketchel said after he recovered that a chance blow had finished him. "I am in better condition than Johnson now," he said. "Look at him; he is dazed. But for that one blow I would have beaten him."

The fight attracted the greatest crowd in years. More than 10,000 people were ranged around the walls and overflowed the seats. Fully 3,000 were turned away, Promoter Coffroth stated after the fight that $40,000 had been taken in.

October 17, 1909

TOPICS OF THE TIMES.

And May the Best Man Win!

There must be, we suppose, what is called "a note of sorrow" in our recognition of the fact that the matching of JEFFRIES and JOHNSON for a fist fight is an event of importance. Such it is, however, if only for the reason that in one way or another it keenly interests a large majority of the inhabitants of the United States, to say nothing of not a few million people in other countries.

But there are other reasons for ascribing moment to it, and among them this, that upon the outcome of the fight will depend in no small measure the lessening or the increasing of the friction that exists between the two races whose self-appointed representatives, ad hoc, these men will be. It is a really serious matter that, if the negro wins, thousands and thousands of other negroes will wonder whether, in claiming equality with the whites, they have not been too modest. In too many cases the wonder will be followed by belief, and the result will be an acerbation of relations already quite sufficiently bitter.

Not a few white pugilists, from an instinctive feeling of ethnic pride founded on a deeper wisdom than they had the intelligence to realize, have refused to meet negroes in the ring. It were desirable, we incline to think, that all of them should do so, for it is not well that the two races should meet in formally arranged and widely advertised competition when the conditions are such that victory and defeat are decided by the possession on one side or the other of a superiority so trivial as that given by weight, strength, and agility.

Of course, prize fighting is not a mere matter of brute prowess, but the demands it makes upon the intellect are narrowly limited, and, while the sort of efficiency which avails in pugilism is in itself a valuable asset for the members of a dominant race, it is perilous to risk even nominally the right of that race to exercise dominance in a conflict which brings so few of its higher superiorities into play. Therefore, as this fight cannot, or at least probably will not, be prevented, even those who have an absurdly exaggerated horror of prize fighting as a "brutal" sport should gently warm in their sensitive minds a little hope that tho white man may not lose, while the rest of us will wait in open anxiety the news that he has licked the—well, since it must be in print, let us say the negro, even though it is not the first word that comes to the tongue's tip.

November 1, 1909

JOHNSON WINS IN 15 ROUNDS; JEFFRIES WEAK

"I Couldn't Come Back," Says Former Champion, Helpless After Third Knockdown.

POOR FIGHT, SAYS SULLIVAN

White Man Outclassed by His Opponent from the First Tap of the Gong.

CROWD'S SYMPATHY AROUSED

Yells to Referee to Save Jeffries from a Knockout and His Seconds Jump Into the Ring.

JOHNSON'S SHARE, $70,600

While Jeffries Takes $50,400 from the Purse—The Moving-Picture Rights Bring Them More Thousands.

By JOHN L. SULLIVAN.
Special to The New York Times.

RENO, Nev., July 4.—The fight of the century is over and a black man is the undisputed champion of the world.

It was a poor fight as fights go, this less than fifteen-round affair between James J. Jeffries and Jack Johnson. Scarcely ever has there been a championship contest that was so one-sided.

All of Jeffries's much-vaunted condition and the prodigious preparations that he went through availed him nothing. He wasn't in it from the first bell tap to the last, and as he fell bleeding, bruised, and weakened in the twenty-seventh second of the third minute of the fifteenth round no sorrier sight has ever gone to make pugilistic history. He was practically knocked out twice in this round.

Johnson's deadly left beat upon his unprotected head and neck, and he went down for the count just before the second minute had gone in the fifteenth round. As Johnson felled him the first time he was conscious, but weakened. He tactfully waited for the timekeeper's call of nine before he rose. When he did Johnson caught him flush on the jaw again, and he fell almost in the same spot, but further out, and as he leaned against the lower rope his great bulk crashed through outside the ring.

His seconds and several newspaper men hauled him into the ring again, and he staggered weakly over to the other side. Johnson slowly followed him, measured his distance carefully, and as Jeff's head always hangs forward, struck him hard in the face, and again that terrible left hand caught him, sending him reeling around to a stooping posture.

Johnson pushed his right hand hard as Jeffries wheeled around, and quick as a flash whipped his left over again, and Jeff went down ror the last time. His seconds had given it up.

They didn't wait for the ten seconds to be counted, but jumped into the ring after their man. Billy Delaney, Johnson's chief second, always watchful for the technicalities, yelled his claim for the fight for his man on the breach of the rules by Jeff's handlers. Tex Rickard, in the meantime, was trying to make himself heard, and he was saying that the fight was Johnson's.

Result Left the Crowd Dazed.

By this time the crowd was realizing that Johnson had won out, but there was very little cheering. Jeff had been such a decided favorite they could hardly believe that he was beaten and that there wouldn't still be a chance for him to reclaim his lost laurels. The crowd was not even willing to leave the arena, and as poor old Jeff sat in his corner being sprayed with water and other resuscitating liquids he was pitied from all sides. The negro had few friends, but there was no real demonstration against him. They could not help but admire Johnson, because he is the type of prize fighter that is regarded highly by sportsmen. He played fairly at all times and fought fairly. He gave in wherever there was a contention and he demanded his rights only up to their limit, but never beyond them.

Had Picked Johnson to Win.

I have never witnessed a fight where I was in such a peculiar position. I all along refused to announce my choice as to the winner. I refused on Jeff's account, because he was sensitive and I wanted to be with him some time during his training. I refused on Johnson's account, because of my well-known antipathy to his race, and I didn't want him to think that I was favoring him from any other motive than a purely sporting one. He might have got this impression, although since I know him better, in the last few weeks, I am rather inclined to believe that he hasn't many of the petty meannesses of human character.

You will deduce from the foregoing that I really had picked Johnson as the winner. My personal friends all know it, and even Jeffries accused me of it one day, but I denied it in this way. I said:

"Jeff, I have picked the winner, but I haven't done it publicly. A few personal friends know who I think will win, and I am not going to tell you before the fight. I don't want you to get any wrong impression."

However, the fact remains that three weeks ago I picked Johnson to win. It seems almost too much to say, but I did say inside of fifteen rounds. It's all over now, and it does not matter who I picked to win to either Jeff or Johnson, but the main theory I based my decision on was the old one that put me out of the game. Jeff could not come back. Jeffries was a mere shell of his former self. All the months of weight reducing, involving great feats of exercise, had come to naught.

The experts who figured that a man must receive his reward for such long, conscientious, muscle-wearing and nerve-racking work, figured that he must get it even providentially.

It seemed only just to human nature that Jeffries must win, even in the face of all the features resting on the other side of the argument. For it is true, and probably would only be denied by Johnson himself, that the big colored, champion did not train conscientiously. As subsequent events proved he didn't have to train more than he did, but nevertheless

less he took a chance, and, by his manner and deportment, seemed perfectly willing to stand the consequences, whatever they were. The result was success for him in its fullest meaning.

Johnson got scarcely a hard knock during the whole encounter and was never bothered by Jeffries's actions one little bit. He came out of the fray without a mark, if one except the cut lip he got in the third round, which proved to be only the opening of the old cut that George Cotton gave him the other day when Gov. Dickerson was out at his training quarters.

Never before has there been a fight for the championship of the world with so many peculiar ends to it, because never before has a black man been a real contender for the championship. Johnson, of course, was the credited champion even before to-day's fight by virtue of his defeat of Tommy Burns, but just the same the rank and file of sporting people never gave him the full measure of his title. Jeffries has always been the bugaboo of Johnson's championship career, and it seemed to many that if only the big boilermaker would go back into the fighting game and get himself into condition he could obliterate this so-called blot on the pugilistic map.

Jeffries was persuaded against his will, and he went to work with a willingness and determination that brought about wonderful results, but that couldn't bring back outraged old nature.

Johnson Never in Doubt.

Probably never before was a championship so easily won as Johnson's victory to-day. He never showed the slightest concern during the fifteen rounds and from the fourth round on his confidence was the most glaring thing I ever saw in any fighter. He was the one person in the world at that moment who knew that Jeffries's best blow was packed away in his last fight and on the road and by the running brooks from which he lured the fish during his preliminary training for his fight.

He was a perfect picnic for the big negro, who seemed to be enjoying himself rather than fighting for 60 per cent. of a $101,000 purse. It could not have been all assumed, either, as his remarks during the contest to me, while I sat below and near him at the ringside, showed that he had honestly a good opinion of himself.

Once in the interval between the fifth and sixth rounds he leaned over and said: "John, I thought this fellow could hit."

I said: "I never said so, but I believe he could have six years ago."

Johnson continued with conversation when he should have been paying attention to the advice his seconds were giving him, and said: "Yes; five or six years ago ain't now, though."

By that time the bell had rung and he was up and at it again.

My, what a crafty, powerful, cunning left hand he has. He leads with it, of course, but he does most of his work in close, and some of his blows look as though he were trying to lead with his right while his left is traveling to its goal.

He is one of the craftiest, cunningest boxers that ever stepped into the ring, and poor old Jeffries could not get set or anywhere near him for an effective punch.

As a matter of fact, he didn't have any. They both fought closely all during the fifteen rounds. It was just the sort of a fight that Jeffries wanted. There was no running around and ducking like Corbett did with me in New Orleans.

Jeffries didn't miss so many blows, because he hardly started any. Johnson was on top of him all the time, and he scarcely attempted a blow that didn't land. There wasn't a full swing during the whole fifteen rounds, something unusual in this latter-day fighting.

The only thing that wasn't actual fighting to-day was the many clinches that occurred, and here, instead of Jeff getting in the fatal work, it was Johnson. None of the plans that all of the experts and critics have been talking about for the last six months materialized.

Jeffries's fearful rushes were not there. The awful wallops that he was going to land on Johnson's body, where were they? Johnson didn't receive a blow during the whole encounter that would have hurt a 12-year-old boy. From the time Jeff got his right eye closed in the sixth round it was all over as far as I was concerned. I felt then that if Jeffries had all this power behind that had been claimed for him, he would get mad and he would at least take a desperate chance. Probably he had some such idea in mind himself, for he did step in viciously in the next round, but a gloved fist always stopped his onward way.

When I saw Johnson throw Jeffries away from him in one of the many clinches in the eighth or ninth round I was still further convinced that the negro was the winner.

This had been one of his favorite stunts

during his training, and he was expected to at least attempt it here. He didn't get gay at all with Jeffries in the beginning, and it was always the white man who clinched, but Johnson was very careful, and he backed away and took no chances, and was good-natured with it all.

Probably the Last Big Fight Here.

There were those in the throng to-day who will probably say it was the greatest fight the world ever saw, but that is because it was the most peculiar fight crowd the world ever saw, for half of them never saw a fight before. It was the greatest fight this class ever saw, but, as a matter of fact, it was about the poorest fight that has ever been fought for the championship. It will probably be the last big fight in this country, notwithstanding the crowd's enthusiastic reception of Billy Muldoon's sentimental speech. "Let us give three cheers for the great, broad-minded State of Nevada and its great, broad-minded Governor," because it will be hard to work up the fervor that has existed all through the arrangements for this fight.

It will go down in history as the greatest fight that ever took place in some respects, and from a purely sporting point of view the very worst.

Nevertheless, the best man won, and I was one of the first to congratulate him, and also one of the first to extend my heartfelt sympathy to the beaten man.

JOHN L. SULLIVAN.

July 5, 1910

BAR FIGHT PICTURES TO AVOID RACE RIOTS

Washington, Atlanta, Baltimore, St. Louis, and Cincinnati Fear Effect on Negroes.

GAYNOR WON'T STOP THEM

Christian Endeavorers of Boston Agitating for Suppression in the United States, Europe, and Australia.

DEATHS FROM FIGHT RIOTS.

In these cities fatalities resulted from fights occasioned by the Johnson victory at Reno:

New York City	1
Uvaldia, Ga.	3
Little Rock, Ark.	2
Houston, Texas	1
Omaha, Neb.	1
Mounds, Ill.	1
Tyler, Texas	1
Total	10

Action was taken in several cities yesterday to prevent the exhibition there of moving pictures of the Johnson-Jeffries fight at Reno, Nev. In each instance the officials were stirred by the race fights, and in some cases actual riots, which followed the receipt of the news of Johnson's victory.

Washington, Atlanta, Baltimore, St. Louis, and Cincinnati are among the towns which already have decided not to permit the exhibition of the pictures. In Boston the United Society of Christian Endeavor is arranging to appeal to Mayor Fitzgerald for a ruling against the pictures, and at the same time is preparing to send appeals in aid of the movement to Mayors of cities all over the country, as

well as to President Taft, ministers, and societies for civil welfare.

Mayor Gaynor here, however, announced yesterday that he would make no effort to prevent the exhibition of the pictures. He said that the negro population in this city was not as great as in the cities in which action already had been taken or in which the officials were preparing to bar the fight pictures. He added that he had not the right to stop the pictures any more than he had to stop the publication of stories of the fight. Complaint might be made against any place showing the pictures, he suggested, and then the only recourse of the city would be to revoke the license of the place.

BOSTON, July 5.—Declaring that Independence Day had been dishonored and disgraced by a brutal prizefight; that the moral sense of the Nation had been outraged, but that this evil was as nothing compared to the harm which will be done by allowing children and women to view the production of the Jeffries-Johnson fight by moving pictures, William Shaw, General Secretary of the United Society of Christian Endeavor, in a formal statement to-night announced the beginning of a campaign against the exhibition of these pictures. The campaign will be taken up by three branches of the Christian Endeavor Society in Europe and Australia.

Telegrams calling special attention to the race riots which have followed in the wake of the fight were dispatched to-night to ex-President Roosevelt. Gov. Charles E. Hughes, and Mayor William J. Gaynor of New York, asking their co-operation in the start of the movement for the suppression of the pictures.

Mayor FitzGerald of Boston will be seen to-morrow, and asked to prevent the exhibition in Boston. In a day or two telegrams will be sent to Governors of all the States making a similar request.

Special to The New York Times.

WASHINGTON, July 5.—The disorders that have followed the victory of Johnson over Jeffries at Reno have had the result of starting a movement to prevent a possible repetition of trouble by barring from the local picture theatres reproductions of the fight. This movement has the indorsement of Chief of Police Sylvester and of many local ministers and private citizens.

Major Sylvester has announced that he will issue an order forbidding the theatres to show pictures of the fight on the ground that they tend to demoralization and disorder. He will also extend his order to include pictures of a lurid sort generally, such as train hold-ups and burglaries. Major Sylvester is not certain of the strict legality of his proposed action, but he wants to raise the point and let the theatres fight it out if they wish to.

"Anything that tends to increase race hatred or sectionalism has no place whatever in the affairs of the American people," said Major Sylvester to-day, "if we live up to the spirit of to-day."

Special to The New York Times.

ATLANTA, Ga., July 5.—There will be no revenue for the promoters of the Jeffries-Johnson fight films in Atlanta. This much will be definitely settled to-morrow afternoon, when the City Council meets to adopt a resolution prohibiting them from the city. This was made certain to-day by statements from Mayor Maddox and Carlos Mason, Chairman of the Police Board. Their decision was hastened as a result of the immense crowd which gathered in the centre of the city last night, beat up a negro, and threatened serious trouble, which only prompt and energetic action of the police nipped in the bud.

BALTIMORE, July —Backed by the authority of the Board of Police Commissioners, Marshal Farnan will request Mayor Mahool to prohibit the proposed exhibition in Baltimore of the moving pictures of the Jeffries-Johnson fight. The Mayor says that with a formal complaint before him he will stop the pictures.

Action by the Police Commissioners was taken this morning following the submission by Marshall Farnan of reports of the rioting all over the country, including Baltimore, last night, and the frequent clashes between whites and blacks.

Special to The New York Times.

ST. LOUIS, July 5.—St. Louisans are destined never to see the moving pictures of the Jeffries-Johnson prizefight. Chairman G. Reynolds of the Police Board declared to-night the matter will be brought before the board. to-morrow, and that he will recommend that the display of pictures be prohibited.

H. W. Becker. Secretary of the Patriotic Independence Day Association. said he would introduce a resolution calling upon the Mayor and Board of Police to prevent the display of the fight pictures.

Mrs. T. G. Comstock, President of the St. Louis Society for the Prevention of Cruelty to Children. says she is considering calling a meeting of her organization to protest against the police permitting the pictures of the fight to be displayed.

With such opposition, it is believed the Board of Police Commissioners, who, with the Mayor. have complete charge of the situation, will not permit the moving pictures to be shown.

Other St. Louisans are planning a Nation-wide movement against the pictures.

CINCINNATI, July 5.—Mayor Schwab said to-day that he would not allow the Johnson-Jeffries fight pictures to be shown in this city. The Mayor declared the pictures would promote race hatred, and for that reason he would bar them.

July 6, 1910

TIRED OF JOHNSON.

Pompous Ways of Black Champion Offend Mild-Tempered Britons.

Was it Jack Johnson's pompous ways in England and the flashiness the colored champion displayed with his white wife that caused such a reversal of feeling in the land of King George against the man who defeated Jim Jeffries?

Heretofore England has been a paradise for colored boxers, for in that country the black man has been given almost as much consideration as his white opponent; in fact, some of the blacks have been made a great deal of. Colored boxers always liked to visit England, because they were placed almost on an equality with the Briton. Jack Johnson has suddenly changed this order of things.

It is given out pretty straight that it was not the fact that Johnson was to box Bombardier Wells that caused the great outcry, although it had considerable to do with it, but simply the forward methods adopted by the champion and putting himself on too high a pedestal to suit even the mild-tempered Britons.

According to a letter just received from a close follower of the situation in London, Johnson is " in bad " with the sporting fraternity over there. Johnson's manners, which gained him so much animosity in America, a feeling that was never held toward such men as Peter Jackson, George Dixon, Joe Gans, and other colored boxers, have evidently caused a similar feeling in England. This is all the more remarkable in view of the fact that colored boxers have heretofore been treated with almost as much courtesy as white boxers. In spite of the strong feeling against negroes in many quarters, Johnson would never have been as unpopular in America as he is now if it were not for his actions outside of the ring since he won the championship. Johnson has drawn upon himself more animosity by his actions in public life than he did when he defeated a big favorite in the ring at Reno.

October 2, 1911

ABE ATTELL LOSES TO JOHN KILBANE

Cleveland Boy Wins Featherweight Boxing Title Before 10,000 Spectators.

HISS ATTELL'S FOUL TACTICS

Cuts Big Gash on Kilbane's Left Eye, Is Hissed by Crowd, and Warned by Referee—Outfought All the Way.

LOS ANGELES. Cal., Feb. 22.—A new pugilistic champion was made in the Vernon Arena to-day when John Kilbane of Cleveland, Ohio, decisively outfought, outgamed, and outpunched Abe Attell in a twenty-round contest, and at the close was awarded the featherweight title by Referee Charles Eyton.

Nearly 10,000 persons saw the fight. Fully 5,000 others were turned away at the gates. It was the greatest crowd that ever viewed a prize fight in Los Angeles. Receipts amounted to approximately $25,000. The men fought for a purse of $10,000, of which Attell was to receive $6,500, win, lose or draw, and Kilbane $3,500. Besides they agreed to divide evenly 50 per cent. of the moving picture privileges.

Attell was clearly outfought. His boasted speed and wonderful cleverness were not in evidence. Kilbane made him look like a novice in nearly every round. Only in one round, the seventh, did Attell have a lead, and that was not by any means as decisive as that of Kilbane in the remaining rounds.

Attell brought the wrath of the big crowd upon his head by foul tactics. Time and again he would hold Kilbane's arms in a clinch, and once in the eighth, he grabbed Kilbane's left arm with both hands and tried to bend it back. In the third he " heeled " the Cleveland boy while in a clinch and in nearly every succeeding round his work called forth hisses from the spectators. In the sixteenth round when, after rushing into a clinch to avoid Kilbane's tattoo on his face and body, Attell butted the Clevelander with his head, opening a big gash over Kilbane's left eye, from which blood spurted profusely.

At the beginning of the sixteenth round Referee Eyton stopped the fight, grabbed a towel, and thoroughly wiped off Attell's body. It was covered with some greasy substance. Attell protested, but the referee paid no attention to him. Kilbane's work was a revelation even to his friends. Entering the ring with the odds 10 to 4 against him, he never faltered for an instant. He fought fast and showed clever work with both hands and feet. A straight left jab to Attell's nose or sore left eye was his favorite blow. He would send this in, and then like a flash cross with his right to the other side of Attell's head and jump back out of harm's way. Attell seemed wild throughout the fight, but this was due as much to Kilbane's footwork as to any other cause. Time and again the bewildered Attell tried in vain to corner the Cleveland boy.

The decision of Referee Eyton was received with cheers, and Kilbane was carried from the building on the shoulders of his friends.

" I want to telephone to Mary," he said, meaning Mrs. Kilbane.

Attell. tired, his face drawn and bleeding, left the ring alone. As he reached the edge of the platform he said to a friend: " Well, I had to stand for it; I couldn't do any better."

CLEVELAND, Ohio, Feb. 22.—Two years ago Johnny Kilbane, the new featherweight champion was not known outside of Cleveland. He had been a contestant in minor bouts since 1905, but it was not until the fighting game opened in sev-

eral Northern Ohio towns in the Winter of 1909-10 that he really began to attract attention. Kilbane decisively defeated Joe Rivers, Patsy Kline, and Frankie Conley, his close rivals, thus earning the right to fight Attell in the battle for the championship.

Kilbane was born and reared in Cleveland. He will be 23 years old on April 8. He is married and has a baby daughter, Mary Coletta. His habits are of the best and he is devoted to his family. He is the support of his blind father.

February 23, 1912

WHITE MEN MAY NOT BOX NEGROES HERE

Athletic Commission Wipes Out Practice of Holding Mixed Bouts Within the State.

Boxing bouts between white men and negroes are no longer permissible in this State according to a ruling made yesterday by the State Athletic Commission at its regular weekly meeting. Such contests, which are termed " mixed bouts " have been under discussion at previous meetings of the Commission, but not until yesterday was any definite action taken. Although the exact vote on the question was not announced officially it is understood that all three members of the commission went on record as favoring the new rule. A similar resolution was introduced several days ago in the California Legislature.

February 6, 1913

PUGILIST KILLED BY BLOW IN RING

McCarty, the White Champion, Slowly Crumples Up After a Punch Near the Heart.

Special to The New York Times.

CALGARY, Alberta. May 24.—Luther McCarty, whose claim to the heavyweight white championship of the world has been generally recognized, was killed by a blow in the ring here to-day by his adversary. Arthur Pelkey, in what was scheduled as a ten-round bout.

The fatal blow was delivered in the first round, after one minute and forty-five seconds of fighting. Pelkey, with no idea of the fatal result of his blow, waited while McCarty was counted out. Then he hurried from the ring. Later he was arrested by a mounted policeman, and not until then did he know McCarty was dead. Pelkey subsequently was released on bail.

It was a short-arm blow below the heart in a clinch that killed the champion.

A physician who examined the body declared that the death of McCarty was due either to organic heart trouble or paralysis of the heart. The altitude of Calgary may have contributed to the weakness.

The fight was to have advertised

clean boxing in Calgary and was one of the incidents of Empire Day. Both fighters had been well trained and both were believed to be in fit condition. When they entered the ring at 1 o'clock the great arena was filled. McCarty laughed and joked with his seconds. He was the favorite in the betting.

May 25, 1913

NEGRO'S SUPREMACY IN RING NEAR END

Johnson, Langford, McVea, and Jeannette Are Deteriorating Rapidly as Boxers.

The supremacy of the negro in pugilism, which has not been disputed since Jack Johnson won the heavyweight title from Tommy Burns at Sydney five years ago, unless by those who took hope in Jeffries's return to the ring, seems to be at an end. Numerous elimination tournaments among the white heavyweights have failed to bring out any such leader as Jeffries, Fitzsimmons, Corbett, or Sullivan, and have shown little except the punching ability of Gunboat Smith, now regarded as the premier of the white heavyweights. The negro Big Four, made up of Jack Johnson, Sam Langford, Sam McVea, and Joe Jeannette, have not been unusually busy, but they have at last reached the stage where all four have ceased to inspire terror among the whites.

Johnson's miserable showing against his namesake, "Battling" Jim Johnson, at Paris a few night ago, verified the suspicions which many close followers of the game have had for some time. Jeffries could not come back, and the feeling was general that Johnson could not maintain his former strength and skill without real action in the ring—something that the dusky champion did not have. Only two fights in four years and two months was the extent of Jack Johnson's activity up to the time he climbed into the ring with "Battling" Jim Johnson at Paris, and the long rest exacted its toll. Johnson's mode of living did not work to his interests, either. Close students of boxing have said that the first good heavyweight to face Johnson in the ring would climb through the ropes with the title the negro has carried for five years. Jim Johnson does not come up to this class standard, but he nearly won the title last week when he had Jack Johnson groggy in his bout.

As for the new Johnson—new to fame through his bout with Jack Johnson, but not new to the boxing game—he is getting no consideration whatever as a possible champion. The result of the Paris bout is regarded more from the standpoint of Jack's weakness than for showing unusual strength in the other Johnson. Jim has been in the ring for several years, and never showed up beyond the mediocre stage. Certain it is that he has not developed into a champion with what little ring work he has done in the last few years. If he is better than Jack Johnson to-day Jack has retrograded beyond hope of recovery.

Langford completely eliminated Sam McVea before he left Australia, and Big Sam has not been heard of since that time. It is almost seven years since McVea last appeared in America, and he met with considerable success for a time in France, England, and Australia. He got one decision over Langford two years ago, but three bouts which followed showed McVea on the loser's end, the last bout resulting in a knockout in eleven rounds. This defeat put an end to McVea's pretensions as a heavyweight star.

Jeannette's showing against Langford at Paris the night after the two Johnsons got together just about ends Joe's claims. It was by the narrowest of margins that the Hoboken negro escaped being knocked out in the thirteenth round, in which he was floored three times, and the final bell found him very groggy and on the ropes. In his recent bout here with Langford Jeannette won on points, but gave unmistakable traces that he was going back as a boxer, a hitter and a mixer. Only Langford's lack of condition enabled the Hoboken negro to win, as Sam was clearly overweight. At that the Bostonian showed himself the better hitter.

Langford got his quietus from Gunboat Smith in a twelve-round bout at Boston recently. Langford realized that the tide was going against him, and tried hard, the only time he has been really extended by a white boxer in several years, but the old skill was lacking. He had trained hard, according to reports, yet he had been unable to get down to his old fighting weight. The success of the Gunner did much to drive away the trepidation which white heavyweights had felt in regard to Langford for some years. It was the general impression up to the time of the Smith bout that Langford was the class among all heavyweights, white or black, but Gunboat furnished a surprise.

Now the doubt about Jack Johnson has been removed, and Jeannette goes back among the also-rans within a few hours. Langford had already been tamed, and McVea got his quietus several months before. The black heavyweight dynasty is almost at an end, and with a big field of fairly good white heavyweights "coming along," it seems only a matter of a short time before the white race will furnish an undisputed heavyweight champion.

December 23, 1913

BOXING BARRED IN WEST.

California After Twenty Years Decides Against Pugilistic Contests.

Back in the early nineties, when James J. Corbett first stepped into ring prominence, California began to make pugilistic history, and ever since that time the "Golden State" has been looked upon as a great centre for the maintenance and encouragement of fistic sport. Many championship battles have been fought there, and followers of the fortunes of pugilists in every class, from heavies to bantams, evinced unusual interest when bouts were scheduled at San Francisco, Los Angeles, or any other of the many places where glove encounters were decided and titles passed. Two generations of fistic champions have enjoyed the privilege afforded by the State of California, and thousands of followers of the sport have been well satisfied with the results. But all this is to be changed, and the "knights of the glove and squared circle" will have to seek fresh fields outside of California.

At the recent State election the majority of California's voters decided that pugilism should not be accredited as legal sport, thus making it mandatory for the boxers to settle their differences as to relative merits elsewhere. At midnight of Tuesday, Dec. 15 "taps" will be sounded for other than amateur bouts of four rounds duration in the principal Pacific Coast State, and after a rather prosperous quarter of a century, pugilism will be taboo. In recent years the California promoters of this class of sport have given excellent inducements to the leading fighters of the world, and as a result the best men in every class have at one time or another appeared there and several championship titles have been lost and won.

Several notable heavyweight contests have taken place in San Francisco since the memorable sixty-one round draw between James J. Corbett and Peter Jackson was fought in 1891. This served to bring Corbett into the limelight and within eighteen months afterward, the then young bank clerk, had annexed the heavyweight honors by defeating John L. Sullivan somewhat unexpectedly at New Orleans in September, 1892. The young Californian was not considered seriously as a possible contender by Sullivan's legion of admirers and the Pacific Coast was elated when Corbett brought back the championship to his native State.

Among the many bouts between big men decided in San Francisco in the last twelve years the following may be mentioned: Jim Jeffries knocked out Bob Fitzsimmons in eight rounds. This was in 1902, just four years after Fitzsimmons had lost the championship to the big boilermaker at Coney Island in eleven rounds. Jack Munroe lasted only two rounds with Jeffries in the following year; and in 1905 Jeffries retired, but only temporarily. Jack O'Brien vanquished Fitzsimmons at San Francisco in twelve rounds that same year, and in 1906 Tommy Burns, who was the recognized successor of Jeffries, defeated Marvin Hart in twenty rounds. Twelve months after that Burns defeated Jack O'Brien in a twenty-round bout at Los Angeles and knocked out Bill Squires in a single round at Colma in 1907, where two years later Stanley Ketchel was knocked out in twelve rounds by Jack Johnson. The last of the big bouts was that between Gunboat Smith and Arthur Pelky, last January.

December 7, 1914

WILLARD VICTOR; JOHNSON RETIRES FROM PRIZE RING

Special Cable to THE NEW YORK TIMES.

HAVANA, April 5.—"It was a clean knockout and the best man won. It was not a matter of luck. I have no kick coming."

Such were the words of ex-champion Jack Johnson when he had recovered from Jess Willard's terrific left jab to the heart and right swing to the jaw in the twenty-sixth round of the championship fight that restored pugilistic supremacy to the white race and made Willard champion this afternoon at Oriental Park.

To those who watched the battle and longed for the white man to win the day looked dark in the earlier stages because the negro outgeneraled the younger man and appeared to hit him as he willed. As Johnson's terrific blows rained on Willard he appeared to be suffering, but as the fight continued and Willard found that the champion's blows were not able to put him out he appeared to gain confidence, which he had seemed to lack when the battle started, and, under the coaching of Tom Jones, he began to look more cheerful.

Johnson's old-time ring smile continued throughout these early rounds, but as time sped and he found that, although he landed his blows, they never appeared to have much effect, the smile disappeared, and from the tenth to the twentieth round Johnson exercised every art in his power to put out the challenger. After that twentieth round there was little doubt among those at the ringside as to how the fight was going. It was too plain that once more youth was showing. Johnson was tiring so fast that he tried to hold Willard in clinches, but his strength, which was able to do that earlier, was unable then, and Willard always got the best of the infighting, continually landing terrific blows to the body.

Sent Word to Wife to Leave.

Johnson realized in the twenty-second round that his hold on the championship was growing short and asked for Jack Curley. The latter was at the gate at the time, but appeared shortly before the last round.

"Tell my wife I'm tiring, and I wish you'd see her out," said Jack. Curley understood and carried out Johnson's wish.

It was only a little time after that when Willard landed his terrific body blow, followed by the blow to the jaw that spelled defeat to Johnson and turned bedlam loose among the thousands of spectators, who could hardly realize, so quickly did it happen, that Johnson was prostrate in the ring and that Jack Welsh was counting the fateful ten. The decisive blow landed about the middle of the round.

At the end Johnson made a movement as if to grab Willard, but the latter stepped back and Johnson fell full length upon the floor and lay there until his seconds had assisted him to his feet.

At first after his defeat Johnson appeared dazed, but he quickly recovered, and his smile reappeared as he explained that the best man had won.

Willard played a game in the ring that was declared necessary to beat Johnson, namely, to make the latter act as aggressor. Both realized the necessity of caution. Johnson showed skill and cunning in blocking his more husky opponent.

Youth Must Be Served.

As the fight wore on and Willard had received all the blows in Johnson's collection and had found their capacity to do damage grow less, he became more and more aggressive, while despair began to dawn on the countenance of the champion. Willard's blows were not so numerous and Johnson clearly outpointed him, except toward the last, but these early blows that the Kansas giant did land would have spelled a knockout for almost any one but Johnson.

When the fight ended there was no doubt as to which was the better man. Willard had fought his own fight and overcome the older master by the sheer force of youth; the thirties had to retire in favor of the twenties.

Willard appears to be a most unassuming champion. There was no boastfulness on his part afther the fight. The same quiet modesty was in evidence which he displayed for days before the fight while training in Havana, and which won for him many friends and caused the Cubans to look upon prizefighters in an entirely different light from that to which they had been accustomed.

The scene of the fight was a picture. Squadrons of Cuban cavalry sat their horses in perfect alignment near the ringside, while the great grandstand was filled with a crowd representative of the Cuban Republic, including Cabinet members, army officers, Governors of provinces, and Ministers of various nations. Many women, mostly American tourists, but with quite a sprinkling of Cubans, added color to the scene, while many other women, members of Cuba's aristocracy, from the seclusion of the racetrack clubhouse trained their glasses on the battling gladiators.

Women as Enthusiastic as Men.

The tremendous enthusiasm which the Cubans displayed over the match is thought generally here to augur well for the sport, and, as one prominent Cuban official said, causes Cuban boys and even men to yearn for skill in the manly art of defending themselves with their fists instead of with knives and pistols.

The enthusiasm of the women present grew as it became apparent that Willard probably would win. They groaned as Johnson appeared to outclass the white man, but as Willard's chances improved they grew wildly excited and vied with the men in striving to make their shouts of cheer reach the man who was battling for the pugilistic supremacy of their race.

Hardly any disorder occurred during the match, except when the great crowd charged into the ring as Johnson laid prostrate. The rural guards beat back the intruders with their machetes flat. One man was painfully, although not seriously, hurt.

Citizens of Havana will tender a reception to Willard tomorrow night, at which either the Governor of the province or the Mayor of Havana will present a gold watch as a souvenir to the victor. Willard had planned to leave Havana tomorrow, but yielded to requests to remain another day.

April 6, 1915

Jess Willard, the New Heavyweight Champion.

NEW WEIGHTS FOR BOXING CLASSES

New National Association Proposes Change in All Divisions to Meet Eastern Promoters.

Special to The New York Times.

CLEVELAND, Ohio, Aug. 22.—Fifteen boxing promoters and managers, representing as many sections of the country and almost as many more promoters, today formed the American Boxing Association of the United States. The purpose of the organization is to promote boxing in its best form, to exert control over the sport, to protect the public, the boxer, the manager, and the promoter. M. J. Hinkel of this city was elected President; Gene Melady of Omaha, Secretary and Treasurer, and Harry Edwards of Philadelphia, First Vice President.

A committee consisting of Sam Harris, Baltimore, Mike Collins, Hudson, Wis.; Tom Andrews, Milwaukee, and Harry Edwards, Philadelphia, was appointed by President Hinkel to meet with Eastern promoters who were unable to attend the convention here, at the Knickerbocker Hotel, New York, Sept. 12, the day after the Gibbons-McFarland contest.

The proposal to alter the weight limits for the various classes was passed. That means that henceforth the limits to be recognized by the A. B. A. are: Bantamweight, 118; featherweight, 125; lightweight, 135; welterweight, 147; middleweight, 160; light heavyweight, 175.

It was agreed to reduce the entrance fee for admission to the association from $25 to $10. It was decided that the larger sum would prevent small clubs from becoming allied with the organization.

It was feared at first that the New York promoters especially would show only a lukewarm, if any, interest in the association. But, in view of the fact that three Gotham promoters have signified their intention of joining, it seems probable that others will follow suit. Billy Wellman of the Madison Square Garden, New York; John Finneran and Hugh Shannon of Erie, Ed Thatcher of Toledo, and one or two others applied for admission into the organization.

Every officer in the new American Boxing Association donates his services. There are no salaries. The dues of both promoters and boxers are so low as to provide only enough money to conduct the affairs of the organization.

August 23, 1915

In order to do away with the practice of boxers adopting the names of men whose reputations have already been gained in the ring, the Athletic Commission at its weekly session in 41 Park Row yesterday passed a resolution to the effect that no boxer shall be permitted to usurp a name in current use by another ring performer. To accomplish this end, the committee, after first consulting the Attorney General's office to ascertain whether it has power to enforce the rule, will compel all boxers competing in this State to register their family names and their assumed names with the Secretary. The committee has taken up the task of a Solomon, for already it is confronted with the task of solving whether Al McCoy, so-called middleweight champion, or New Al McCoy, formerly Al Thiel, is entitled to use that name. Also whether Frankie Callahan, the Brooklyn lightweight who has been boxing under this title for years, shall have precedent over Frankie Callahan, a Manhattan featherweight, who boxes under his proper name.

The McCoy question is practically settled, because the New Al McCoy some time ago received permission from a Brooklyn Judge to change his name from Thiel to McCoy and apparently there is nothing for the commission to do but permit both to employ the title. Their decision in the Callahan matter will be announced at next week's meeting at which both boxers have been requested to appear.

Complaint was received by the athletic board that, in spite of the rule against boxers selling tickets for clubs, this practice is flagrantly carried on at present. The commission made a formal request for any evidence of this nature to be presented at its next meeting and promised drastic action against any club or boxers found violating the rule.

Chairman Wenck officiated at the open meeting yesterday, and announced that as yet he had nothing definite to say regarding decisions. Whether referees will be permitted to render verdicts in New York depends on the attitude of Governor Whitman, whose position is expected to be reflected by the man who will be appointed to succeed James R. Price, who resigned last week. The license of the Vanderbilt A. C. was renewed, and the Sharkey A. C. received two weeks' grace to produce a year's lease on its present clubhouse.

October 19, 1915

THINKS FULTON WILL GIVE WILLARD BATTLE

Tex Rickard Says Former Will Develop Into Worthy Foe for Champion— Mourns Decadence of Boxing and Boxers.

At a time when the boxing game in this State is apparently about to be put away on the shelf, along comes that breezy Western miner, cattleman, and promoter, Tex Rickard, to sing a swan song about the waning pastime of fisticuffs. It is a good word that Rickard has for the ring sport, for he thinks boxing should be encouraged and not suppressed. "What the youths of this country need," says Rickard, "is more boxing to help fit them for the work they may be called upon to do if this country goes to war. What's the sense of trying to teach people that it is wrong to put on boxing gloves and in the next breath ordering them to put a rifle on their shoulders and go out and fight? Boxing would do more to make good soldiers than anything else I know of."

Rickard has put up the largest purses and promoted the biggest pugilistic contests in the history of the ring. The Jeffries-Johnson fight at Reno, for a purse of $121,000, and with a gate of $270,000, marked the largest venture in the annals of the squared circle. It was Rickard, in staging the Nelson-Gans fight at Goldfield, Nev., who brought more fame to that camp for the time being than the precious metal which was taken from its mines. Also, it was the same Rickard who gave New York the greatest boxing spectacle this city ever witnessed, when he put up $71,250 to bring champion Jess Willard and Frank Moran together at Madison Square Garden last year.

His High Standing as Promoter.

Rickard is qualified to speak for the best interests in the boxing game, because every bout he has ever had anything to do with has been conducted in the proper way. Rickard says that the day when boxing was a sport only for the plug-ugly element has long gone by. There is no reason, he says, why the boxing club of today should not be conducted just the same as a theatre, where gentlemen may go and join an orderly gathering to see a sport which is admired by every healthy, vigorous man in the land. "Why shouldn't we have clubs here like the National Sporting Club of London?" asks Mr. Rickard.

"I think that boxing should be taught in the public schools," says the Western promoter. "It brings out all those manly qualities which a boy will need in after life. It is a mistaken idea that boxing is brutal. It is no more dangerous than many other branches of strenuous sport. Boys and men rejoice in rough sports. We don't want young America brought up on ping-pong, do we?"

Rickard is not primarily a boxing promoter. He has never taken up a fight venture save when he saw that there was a tremendous public demand for it, and because of his ability to anticipate the public's likes and dislikes he has made the biggest ten-strikes on record in the game.

"I realize that the boxing game here now is all wrong," said Mr. Rickard, "and I am sorry to see that matters have come to such a pass. It is doubly unfortunate because there is now a good boxing law in this State and boxing had won its way back to popularity. If we had a Boxing Commission which would uphold the boxing code as it is written and keep aloof from the promoters, the game would be carried on here under ideal conditions. The cheap, rough element which has always been a bad influence in the game, should be cut adrift from boxing. If the sport was kept clean and free from the contaminating influence of an undesirable crowd, it would occupy the high place it deserves to hold in public favor.

Boxing as Aid in Preparedness.

"At this time, when there is an impending national crisis, we hear the cry on every side for our young men to shoulder a rifle and get ready to fight," said the aggressive little Westerner, "and we also hear from the Governor of this State that it should be against the law for young men to put on boxing gloves and box. Such inconsistency as that to me is ridiculous. I tell you, boxing would be the greatest aid imaginable in preparedness. It is a sport which appeals to all red-blooded men and brings out courage, skill and physical power.

"When they kill a sport like boxing for the American youth, they are subduing a spirit which should be encouraged in every way. If you teach young men that self defense and fighting are all wrong, what will be the result? Why, you'll have a nation of chicken-hearted youths who will lose that independent, pugnacious spirit which has always characterized the stout-hearted American.

"If I had my way," said Mr. Rickard, "I'd have boxing in the public schools—yes, Sir, teach the lads to box from the time they are able to put on gloves. It would bring out the best that there is in the boys; it would teach them self-reliance and encourage bravery. You observe the lad who can take care of himself in the little scraps in the school yard and you will find that he makes a pretty good citizen in after life. More than anything else, boxing teaches youths not to be afraid. I simply cannot understand the attitude of some prominent men on boxing. Can't they see that the very things which make a successful boxer are the same things that make a good soldier?

Would Have Boxing in Schools.

"If they had boxing in the public schools along with the other games they play we would have stronger and healthier young men. No man admires another who will not fight for his rights or in self-defense, and yet this is the very spirit they are trying to kill in this State when they talk of doing away with boxing.

"I'll admit, as I say," remarked the promoter, "that the game as it has been going in this city is all wrong. But that is not the fault of the game of of the present boxing law. The trouble is that the sport is not conducted properly. It ought to be ruled with an iron hand. Keep the cheap, rough element out of the boxing game and it would be all right. Like everything else, boxing has changed. Unfortunately there are many boxers and promoters who think that they must cater to the 'rough-neck' element, which was such a strong factor in the game 'way back in the John L. Sullivan days. Men do not want to see boxing conducted that way nowadays. It should be conducted the same as a theatre.

"There is no reason why the boxing clubs here could not be run along the same lines as the National Sporting Club of London. There are now too many of the cheaper clubs with irresponsible management. The present law in this State is satisfactory, and I don't see where it could be improved upon. It is a good thing to limit the bouts to ten rounds, for this eliminates the possibility of danger which attended the long bouts of the old days. The boxers are really better prepared for the ten-round bouts, because they are keyed up to show all their skill in a short time.

"It had been charged that the ten-round bout with no decision had tended to develop stalling and playing safe in the bouts, but this is the fault of those who control the game," continued Mr. Rickard. "The commission could regulate this by compelling the boxers to put forth their best efforts while in the ring on penalty of forfeiting their shares of the purses. Leave it to the judgment of the referee; they can tell always whether or not the boxers are stalling. The methods around here have been too lax. Out in Wisconsin the boxing commission makes the boxers toe the mark. The game out there is kept clean and it could be kept clean here.

Control of the Game Lost.

"The game has become so popular and so many second-rate boxers and promoters have been receiving large purses that the authorities have lost control of them. If the present boxing law was properly enforced in this city we would not hear the cry against boxing that is now in the air. Politics is another thing which has hurt boxing, for the two can never get along together.

"Big bouts," went on Rickard, "for large purses, which attract nation-wide attention, like the Willard-Moran bout, are all right once in a while. But the conditions have to be just right, as they were for that bout. A bout of that kind must be demanded by the public and not forced upon it. Conditions may never be the same again as they were last year for the Willard-Moran bout at the Garden. Moran had twice knocked out Coffey, and was in the public eye. Willard had never been in a bout since he won the championship at Havana, and there was a real demand to see him in action. The game was clean at the time, and the promoters and boxers were conducting their affairs in a way which attracted no criticism. So the time was ripe for a big affair.

"But many of the men—I mean the substantial business men downtown—who attended that bout would not think of attending a bout today because the game has received too much adverse comment. They know that there is something the matter with it, and do not want to be seen at ring matches. This isn't because they have lost interest in the game, but because it is not being conducted properly. I doubt if you will ever again see a representative gathering like that at a bout in this city unless conditions change considerably. The undesirable element which follows the boxing game was not present at that bout. A woman was just as welcome there as at a theatre.

The Jeffries-Johnson Bout.

"Conditions will never be the same again, either, for a repetition of the Jeffries-Johnson fight at Reno," said the Westerner. "That was such a huge success because it was held at the psychological moment. The public wanted to see Johnson lose the title. The whole country believed that Jeffries was the one who could bring the championship back to the white race. The purse for that fight, $121,000, and the receipts of $270,000 form the high-water mark for a pugilistic contest and will probably never be approached again.

"Every so many years conditions are right for a big affair of this kind, but it is only after the public has had a long rest and circumstances are favorable. You must judge the public interest in these things and offer the attraction just when the public demands it."

Rickard talked interestingly of his first experience with the boxing game at Goldfield, Nev., in 1906.

"Out there everybody had plenty of money," he said, "and some of the men came to me and asked me to get up some kind of a celebration for Labor Day. Right away I suggested a boxing bout. I had been to New York some time before and had seen McGovern and Britt box. So I wired to McGovern, offering him $15,000 to box Britt at Goldfield. Just to show you what a great surprise an offer like that was in those days, McGovern thought that I was crazy and didn't even answer my telegram. Nobody had ever heard of me, and I guess they all thought that I was looney.

"Not thinking for a moment that it would attract much attention I wired to Nelson offering him $25,000 for a bout at Goldfield with Gans. Nelson wired back that he would come to Goldfield for $30,000. Well, the first thing I knew, newspaper reporters were flocking into Goldfield and papers were wiring for my pitcure, so I went to the leading men in the town and suggested that this was a pretty good way to advertise the mining town.

Flood of Money for Club.

"Then I started in and organized an athletic club to run the fight, and that athletic club broke all records for quick organization. The first man I went to put up $2,500 to go toward forming the club and the next man put up $5,000. In two days we had $52,000 subscribed and the bout was assured. So the little affair which was started as a Labor Day celebration became a matter of nation-wide interest and Goldfield became a pretty important place on the map.

"It marked an unprecedented occasion in the history of pugilism. One of the most surprising things about it to me was that outside of the arena on the day of the fight there were forty or fifty baby carriages, left there by the women who took their children in to the bout. The time was right for a big bout, with a championship at stake, and there was a real public demand for it. You can't force a big attraction like that on the public unless it wants it."

The next big bout that Rickard went after was the Jeffries-Johnson fight. Boxing had been slumbering for a long time, and the boxing public demanded that Jeffries come out of retirement and fight the big negro. Again Rickard did the theatrical thing at the right moment. The promoters met the managers of Jeffries and Johnson in Hoboken, because the proceeding was not legal in this State.

Promoters came from all parts of the country with their certified checks to land the bout. While the bids were being made Rickard stayed in the background. When the bids were about to close Rickard came forward and took everybody's breath away by offering $101,000 for the fight, with a bonus of $10,000 for each of the principals. To cap the climax he walked up to the long table around which the managers and promoters were seated and dumped $20,000 in gold on the table to bind the bargain. When Sam Berger, acting for Jeffries, and Jack Johnson saw the money before them their eyes almost popped out of their heads, and without any hesitation the bout went to Rickard. That's the way Rickard does things.

Next Match for the Title.

Some day, Rickard believes, the time will be ripe for another big heavyweight bout. "I think," said the promoter, "that this man Fulton will develop into a good enough opponent for Willard. But a ten-round bout would be too short for the big fellows. It will have to be a longer bout than that to satisfy the public demand. Willard is a marvel, but I think that some day Fulton wil give him a good battle.

"There has not been a big lightweight match for a long time, and a long bout for that title will be a great attraction at the proper time. With conditions as they are now, however, there seems to be little chance of an important bout."

Tex Rickard doesn't believe that the boxers nowadays are as good as the fighters of other days. "Of course, Willard is an exception," says Rickard. "His physical equal was never seen in the ring, and as long as he is able to train to the proper condition, he will be able to hold the championship. But the other heavyweights do not class with men like Corbett, Fitzsimmons, Sharkey, Jeffries. You can't name any of the present crop of heavyweights who can class with those fellows.

"It's the same with the lightweights. None of the men in that class today, in my opinion, is as good as the former lightweight stars. Of course, conditions change, and under the present system the second-rate boxer has a chance to show his skill and hold his own in the limited round bouts. If longer bouts were permitted, perhaps better and hardier fighters would be developed, but the fast, clever boxer who can give a good account of himself answers the requirements in the ring. It's a question, though, if these pugilists of today have the stamina that the old-time fighters had.

Considers Present Law Adequate.

"There seems to be a bigger demand for boxing in this State than in any other State," said Rickard, "and I think the New York State law on boxing is satisfactory in every way. There is no reason why this State should not lead all others in boxing. All that is necessary is for the commission to keep the sport clean.

"By keeping aloof from the promoters, by forcing the boxers to do their best, and insisting that the clubs be conducted in an orderly manner, the outcry against the sport could be prevented. It all depends on the Boxing Commission. New York's plan in having three Commissioners is a good one, for all the authority should not be invested in one man. The different sections of the State require different conditions, and it is advisable to have a Commissioner in each section. It is deplorable, however, to permit the sport to fall under political influence, for it is bound then to come to a bad end. There can be no monkey business in the conduct of the sport.

"Boxing is not brutal," went on Rickard, "as the agitators would have the public believe. Of course, in a strenuous sport of this kind, as in others, there will always be accidents, but a boxer is trained to take punishment and does not mind being hurt. The fact of the matter is that a boxer is not hurt half as much as he appears to be. There are other sports which are more punishing and cause a greater strain on an athlete's physical make-up than boxing.

Strong Appeal of Boxing.

"Boxing always had and always will have a strong appeal to lovers of strenuous sport. Few things so command the admiration of men as a smashing good boxing bout between evenly matched boxers. At a time when physical manhood is expected to come to the front and when bravery and courage are traits to be admired, it is deplorable that boxing, which brings out these very traits, should be in such a bad way. Many of the people who are loudest in their protests against the sport know the least about it. It isn't because the

TEX RICKARD.

game hasn't a host of defenders among our best classes of men that little is now heard in praise of it, but it is because the men who most admire the sport are sick and tired of the publicity and agitation which a controversy over the game involves.

"The day is past when boxing clubs have to cater to the rough element which has been associated with the pugilistic game in the past. It can be conducted in just as orderly fashion as other affairs which attract large crowds. If there are clubs which continue to allow undesirable spectators to mar their shows, why doesn't the commission revoke the licenses of these clubs? It is deplorable that a few should be permitted to kill a sport of such interest and value.

"I would like to see boxing conducted properly and established in public favor, especially at this time, when the physical courage of the youths of this country should be encouraged in every way. A young man who takes hard, strenuous exercise like boxing is sure to make a better soldier than the one who looks upon the sport as brutal and degrading. The hardiness which boxing develops, it seems to me, would be a valuable asset for the boys who enlist.

"Take one example, for instance, Kid McCoy," said Mr. Rickard. "What more typical soldier could be found than this athlete, who only recently returned from the border. McCoy was able to stand the rough life of the soldier better than the majority of the men because he had been a boxer. He was the picture of a robust, hardy fighting man when he came back."

March 25, 1917

TITLE TO LEONARD; KNOCKS OUT WELSH

New Yorker Wins World's Lightweight Championship from Britisher in Ninth Round.

FINALE IS UNEXPECTED

Welsh, Strong as Last Round Starts, Is Floored Thrice, Then Collapses on Ropes.

LEONARD ALL THE WAY

Briton's Defense Futile Before Harlemite's Sk ll—Turbulent Crowd Hails New Champion.

Benny Leonard became the lightweight champion of the world last night when he knocked out Freddie Welsh in the ninth round of their bout at the Manhattan Athletic Club. Boxing enthusiasts who crowded the big hall were wild with excitement as they saw the passing of the British titleholder, who had been so proficient in defense that it seemed almost as if his downfall would never be brought about. Loud acclaim greeted the new champion while the defeated Welsh was hanging over the ropes unconscious.

Three times in the ninth round Welsh was brought to the canvas before the finishing blow was delivered by the aggressive and confident Leonard. Once the Briton was down on all fours, but struggled to his feet, only to meet the blow that was to end his championship career.

The result came almost like a clap of thunder. From the second round on the honors were with Leonard, but the spectators in this city have so often seen Welsh outpointed, even severely punished at times, that Leonard's supremacy in the early rounds perhaps did not carry the weight which would ordinarily have been the case.

About fifteen seconds after the tap of the gong which sent them on their way in the ninth Leonard, with his never-ceasing, relentless offensive, landed a hard overhand right swing just back of Welsh's left ear. The effect of the blow was manifest immediately, for Leonard's right glove had hardly left his mark before Welsh tottered, and went halfway down to the canvas. The youthful Harlem boxer, seeing fame and fortune within his grasp, and urged on frantically by his friends and handlers about the ring, who no doubt saw more clearly than Leonard himself the effect of his blow, seemed flustered for a flash, but quickly went after to the Briton to complete his job.

He followed Welsh to the ropes in a neutral corner, and there the vanishing champion, reeling but instinctively trying to put up a front, was made the target of a shower of right and left hand blows which beat about his protecting gloves until he was forced finally to lower his famous guard. Then Leonard sent over a right-hand blow, and followed with a light left which landed cleanly on the "button," that part of a boxer's jaw which usually means unconsciousness when it has been hit. Welsh reeled badly and staggered to Leonard's corner, where he fell to one knee.

Before a count could be started over him the Briton was on his feet again, but he was in no condition to defend himself effectively against the onslaught of the fiery little Harlemite, who saw at the end of his punishing glovetips the ambition of his life.

No sooner had Welsh regained his feet after his first knockdown than Leonard was on top of him, raining blow after blow on his face and jaw. Some of them were warded off by the feeble guard the Welshman set up about his face, but enough of them landed to make the tottering champion fall to his knee again. The Britisher, game to the core and egged on with a dull vision of the loss of his crown, raised himself to his feet again, but this time there was a certain alacrity about his rising that was absent from the way in which he lifted himself up the first time.

Referee Billy (Kid) McPartland, himself one of the leading featherweight boxers of his day, looked appealingly to the falling champion's corner, as if seeking to have the Welshman's handlers throw a towel or other token of defeat into the ring. There was no answering response.

Welsh Goes Down Again.

Leonard, keeping just at arm's length from his opponent, where he could get in his effective blows with their greatest force, continued an avalanche of blows on the head, face, and jaw of the now beaten champion until Welsh, out of sheer exhaustion, finally went to the canvas a third time, the last blow struck before he collapsed being a right to the jaw. Once again Welsh doggedly grasped the ropes of the ring in Leonard's corner, and pulled himself to his feet, but this time he was unconscious of anything that was happening about him.

He did not even have sense enough to try to put up his gloved hands in an effort to ward off Leonard's blows, but just raised his arms until they were atop of the uppermost rope of the ring, and, holding himself in an erect position in this manner, stood there taking Leonard's relentless blows, while McPartland was watching Welsh's corner carefully to see if any sign was made to throw in a token of defeat. It was not forthcoming, however, and after Leonard had sent Welsh's head bobbing from side to side with numerous right and left hand blows, while the champion kept himself from going down under them by holding the ropes, McPartland finally brushed Leonard aside, and taking hold of Welsh's arms wrenched them from the ropes. The count of four had been reached when the falling title holder staggered in a half circle away from his position, eventually to collapse over the middle rope of the ring just above the timekeeper.

It was in this manner that Freddie Welsh went down in defeat and with the realization of Leonard's achievement there was a scene of wild enthusiasm perhaps never before equalled in a local boxing club. Admiring friends of the newly crowned king of the lightweight ranks burst from their seats in various parts of the house, past the restraining arms of special policemen and officials of the club, and swarmed to the ring, carrying with them all who stood in their path. Reaching the ring they crowded everybody out of their places, and those who did not move quickly enough were trampled while the admiring throngs climbed to the scene of battle and congratulated Leonard. This scene of joy finally ended with the crowd taking Leonard on their shoulders to his dressing room.

With Welsh things were different. He was the recipient of condolences and sympathies from those who clustered about him. But as a matter of fact the outpouring of feelings by his friends fell on deaf ears, for it was fully fifteen minutes before the rough usage his handlers gave him brought him around to a normal state where he even faintly became cognizant of where he was. Then his first action was to protest feebly to the referee that he was not defeated, but he was finally led from the ring a downcast boxer indeed.

It was rumored that one admiring friend of Leonard's grabbed the new champion's hand as soon as he reached him and pressed a check for $1,000 into his gloved hand. Billy Gibson, Leonard's manager, said after the bout, when questioned, that Leonard, who is billed to box in Philadelphia next week, will enlist in the army after that engagement.

It was the first time in about a decade that a lightweight title has changed hands in a ring in New York State. There were many among the boxers of the country, who could gain decisions over the Welshman in no-decision bouts, but none, until last night, could accomplish anything effective against him, because of his almost impenetrable defense. This defense gained him nothing against Leonard, however, for from the start the Harlem boxer set out to beat down this obstacle.

Cheers for Leonard.

Leonard was the first to enter the ring, and, when his almost diminutive form was first seen coming down the aisle, crowded with late-comers, who were unable to get their seats, a tremendous cheer was sent up. For fully ten minutes this outburst was continued, even as Welsh entered the ring, three minutes after his rival. Before the boxers were called to the centre of the ring by Referee McPartland, the weights were announced: Welsh, 136¾ pounds; Leonard, 133 pounds.

From the very starting bell Leonard set a fast pace. He danced in and about the Welshman, stinging him at every opening with left and right hooks, jabs, uppercuts, and crosses. Even as early as the first round Welsh was forced to seek refuge in a clinch, for he found the Harlem boy's attack to the face and stomach too strenuous. Welsh, on the defensive all the way, tried to reach Leonard with a left-hand jab. But only occasionally succeeded, and then without effectiveness.

Dazzled by his younger opponent's speed and cleverness, Welsh missed awkwardly and showed poor judgment of distance. In the second round Leonard continued his style of attack, principally to the face, and at times came in wide open in utter contempt of Welsh's blows. The latter, however, did not take advantage of these openings, for he was too busy covering up and was willing to hold whenever the opportunity presented itself.

Starting the third round, Leonard shifted his attack to the stomach, and it was here that he reached Welsh's vulnerable spot. The heavy left and right hand blows which he repeatedly rained in weakened Welsh noticeably. In the fourth and fifth rounds it was the same story, the only difference being that Leonard seemed to tire in the fifth from his exertions, but through it all Welsh smiled grimly, it seemed.

In the sixth session Welsh's smile left him for a while, but it was soon seen again, until near the bell, when Leonard almost doubled him up with a stiff left to the body. When hurt, however, Welsh covered up effectively and was able to ward off most of Leonard's damaging blows. In the seventh and eighth rounds the boxing was comparatively slow, although Leonard continued on the aggressive. Welsh contented himself with retreating and covering up, and seldom did Leonard reach his face effectively. Then came the ninth round with its disastrous results and the crowning of a new champion.

May 29, 1917

BRITTON KNOCKS OUT LEWIS.

Welterweight Champion Takes the Count in Ninth Round.

CANTON, Ohio, March 17.—Jack Britton of New York tonight knocked out Ted Lewis, welterweight champion of the world, in the ninth round of a scheduled twelve-round bout here.

The end came after two minutes and ten seconds from a long swing to the jaw. The veterans fought at catch weights. Lewis did not land five clean blows. The bell saved Lewis in the sixth round, when he was knocked down three times.

Britton, through his knockout victory, regains the welterweight championship title, which he lost to Lewis in a bout at Dayton, Ohio, June 25, 1917. This contest went to twenty rounds, and the English boxer received the award of Referee Lou Bauman. Previously Britton had advanced, through a process of elimination which included bouts against the leaders of his class in all parts of the country, to a position where he was universally accepted as the welterweight champion.

Britton and Lewis have been opponents in the ring on at least twenty occasions. Many of their matches have been of the no-decision variety, where one or the other received the popular newspaper verdict. The popular decisions were about equally divided between the boxers. Their most recent local performance was at a boxing benefit held in Madison Square Gorden last year for the war charities. Lewis received the popular verdict in this contest, and scored a clean knockdown over Britton.

The knockout will come as a complete surprise to those who are familiar with the styles of the two boxers. Britton has never been regarded as a heavy hitter against boxers who approach him in ability. His chief offensive weapon is a snappy left hand, which he consistently employs to jab an opponent. Lewis has demonstrated ability to hit harder and more effectively than Britton. The English boxer has been noted for his aggressive and effective style.

March 18, 1919

DEMPSEY WINS RING CHAMPIONSHIP IN THREE ROUNDS

WILLARD BEATEN IN EASY FASHION IN TOLEDO ARENA

Smashing Attack by Young Challenger Nearly Ends Battle in First Round.

SIX KNOCKDOWNS AT START

Special to The New York Times.

TOLEDO, Ohio, July 4.—Jack Dempsey won the heavyweight championship of the world this afternoon in an affair which was not a battle, but a slaughter. Never in the history of the American ring has a heavyweight champion offered such a spectacle in defense of his title as that of Willard today. From sixty seconds after the fight began Dempsey punched Willard virtually at will.

The end of the fight came thirty seconds after the finish of the third round, when Willard's seconds threw two towels into the middle of the canvas, signifying that their man was unable to come up for the fourth round. While Willard was not actually counted out by Referee Pecord, the result constitutes a technical knockout, and will be so recorded.

When the towels flashed through the air Willard's face was a mass of blood, while Dempsey was spattered on his breast and his back with the blood of his opponent. Jess's right eye was completely closed, there was a freely bleeding cut beneath this eye, his mouth was bleeding profusely, six teeth were out, and the whole right side of his face was swollen to almost twice its normal size. Dempsey had not one mark.

So terrific was the punishment which Willard received, so weak was he, so incapable of defense, that during the third round shouts of "Stop it! Stop it!" rose from many parts of the arena, in which were 45,000 spectators of one of the poorest fights in the history of boxing, the onlookers including 500 women. It was a fight which was unpleasant to watch, which brought none of the thrills of fine strife, and which gave no satisfaction to any one except those who had bet on Dempsey, and even these thought little of the spectacle except as a kind of pugilistic murder.

Mrs. Willard Happy.

Mrs. Jess Willard arrived in Toledo yesterday without the news being made known. She was in the arena and saw her husband beaten. Tonight she declared herself entirely happy because of his announcement that he is through and will never fight again. This was the first time she had seen her husband in action in the ring.

The spectators, indeed, were rather dazed with the complete collapse of the champion and the amazing speed with which the beginning of the end came. The battle opened with a feeling-out process by both men. Willard managed to get two punches to Dempsey's face. Then Jack let out. He put over a smashing right to the jaw and a left to the stomach. Willard's 245 pounds of weight crashed to the canvas. His title was gone right there.

A roar rose that could have been heard out in Lake Erie. Willard was near the edge of the north side of the ring, and struggled to a sitting posture. He seemed utterly dazed, but there was a fatuous smile upon his lips. At the count of six, he staggered to his feet. The remaining two minutes of the round saw the champion knocked down five more times, and battered twice to the ropes, helpless. He could not defend himself; he could not hit back; his immense bulk was almost as helpless as if he had been a child.

It was the whistle which saved Willard in this round from a knockout, for

at this fight a whistle was used, military fashion, instead of the time-honored gong. Seven seconds before the round ended Dempsey knocked Willard down for the sixth time. The champion was in the southwest corner of the ring, having landed on the floor from the ropes. Pecord began to count, "one, two, three, four, five, six, seven," he counted, amid bedlam. Then the whistle, inaudible except to those at the immediate ringside, sounded. Jess was saved for a few minutes longer.

Willard a Chopping Block.

As Willard was taken to his corner the Dempsey crowd shrieked in ecstacy, not having heard the whistle and thinking that the fight had ended by a knockout. Some enthusiasts burst over the sixty-dollar seats and clambered into the ring to shake Jack's hands, but they were waved back and shooed out of the ring. "It's not over," the officials yelled, and then the whistle blew for the second round.

Dempsey backed Willard into the ropes almost at once and began to pump his deadly left into Willard's countenance. In a few seconds the Dempsey heavy artillery showed its effect, and Jess's right eye became completely closed. Then came the opening of the cut on Willard's right cheek. Willard made a feeble attempt to fight back, but had nothing. He was too weak and tried to save himself by hanging on in the clinches. Pecord kept prying the men apart.

Fighting Face of the New Champion

Jack Dempsey, World's Champion
Wins the Title at 24.

The Smile That Came Off

Jess Willard Ex-Champion
Outclassed by a Younger Opponent.

Dempsey himself seemed rather tired in this round from the effect of the constant hitting of Willard's bulk and from the heat, which was 110 degrees at the ringside during the fight. The round ended without Willard having been kocked down, but he was one of the worst battered champions ever beheld.

When the third round began Willard showed the least iota of an attempt to fight back, but he could not land on Dempsey. Then Jack opened up the artillery again. He made nothing more or less than a chopping block of the champion. He punched Willard four times in succession in the face. These blows smashed up Willard's mouth pretty badly and knocked out some of the six teeth which Jess lost during the fracas. Willard's face could hardly be seen for blood. Dempsey continued to uppercut Willard with his left, and cries of "Stop it! Stop it!" rose in ever-increasing volume. But Willard weathered the round without being knocked down. If it had not been for his immense reserve of strength he would have been knocked out in the first round. In the third round Dempsey again showed fatigue from his own exertions.

Seconds Give Up Fight.

Then came the whistle for the end of the round. In another thirty seconds Ray Archer threw one towel from Willard's corner, followed at once by another towel thrown by Monahan. The crowd shrieked. Dempsey's friends rushed toward the ring, and the world had another heavyweight champion.

The spectators had two different views of Willard's behavior as far as pluck is concerned. Some gave him praise for coming up for the last two rounds in the condition he was in and taking the frightful beating which Dempsey gave him. Others declared he showed lack of heart by not coming up to the scratch for the fourth round and losing his title by standing on his feet until the last.

"How did he ever beat Johnson?" was the general question. Certain it is that Willard was in no condition to enter a ring. When he first stepped on the canvas it was noted that he showed not one trace of pink. His skin had a peculiar olive-drab hue. Dempsey was as brown as an Indian. Willard's paucity of fighting since he won the title from Johnson in Havana in April, 1915, his age, and his lack of hard training for the bout tell the story of his poor condition. The fight he made was pitiful for a world's champion. The Jamaica Kid, Dempsey's sparring partner, undoubtedly could have put up an infinitely better battle than did Big Jess.

For their nine minutes of fighting the battlers received a fortune. Willard drew down $100,000 from Tex Rickard, the promoter of the bout; something like $20,000 from admissions to his training camp, and a percentage of the moving picture receipts. Dempsey received $27,500 from Rickard, about $20,000 from admissions to his training camp, and a percentage of the movie receipts.

$500,000 Profit for Rickard.

The crowd which witnessed the sad affair was not up to expectations. Along the upper sides of the great hectagonal arena, where were the $10 seats, there was but a mere sprinkling of spectators. The $15 seats, that come in next toward the ring, were not occupied any better than the cheaper locations. Even the choicer seats were not all taken, and, just before the start of the bout those in the cheap seats, in mass formation, plunged into the better seats.

The arena, which has a total capacity of 80,000, was not much more than half filled. Tex Rickard could not give an accurate estimate tonight, but he thought that the attendance was 45,000. The total receipts are estimated at about $1,000,000. If this estimate of receipts, which is the best obtainable, is correct, this leaves the promoter a net profit of about $500,000, as the expenses of the bout reached half a million.

What the crowd lacked in numbers, according to these estimates, it made up in quality. There were sporting men and club men and society men and business men and hotel men there who are known from one end of the country to the other. The visitors came from all the big cities, from as far south as New Orleans and as far west as San Francisco. There was a big contingent of New Yorkers.

Probably more women saw this fight than have ever witnessed a heavyweight battle in the United States. There was a section on the southwest side of the arena reserved for them. It was well filled. There was also a scattering of women throughout the arena.

$2,000,000 Placed in Bets.

The betting on the fight was light for a championship battle. Early this morning the odds were at even money. Then came the New York and other contingents with Willard coin, and Willard again became the favorite. The prevailing odds when the men entered the ring were 5 to 4 on Willard. It is estimated about $2,000,000 was wagered in all.

The day's proceedings at the arena started at 11 o'clock, when the first preliminary, of which there were six, was staged. The amusement ended at 4:20½, when the towels acted as a curtain to the event. The main bout started at 4:09, the fighters having entered the ring shortly before 4 o'clock. Dempsey was the first to appear, climbing into his corner, the northwest, at 3:57. He got a big cheer. At 3:58 Willard took his corner, the southeast. His reception was not quite as uproarious as that for his rival.

The champion wore blue trunks, with a belt of red, write and blue. Dempsey wore white trunks, with a belt also of red, white and blue. Both men entered the ring with their hands already bandaged. Dempsey sat down on a stool beneath a big umbrella in his corner. He looked slightly worried. Willard stood up in his corner, also under an umbrella, and seemed much at his ease. He waved his hand to friends near the ringside and shouted greetings to some of them.

The champion walked across the ring to Dempsey's corner. He shook hands with Demsey and said: "Hello, Jack, how are you, Jack? All right?"

Dempsey grinned, and responded: "You bet."

In Willard's corner were Ray Archer, Jack Hempel and Walter Monahan. In the Dempsey corner were Jack Kearns, Jimmie De Forest and Bill Tate.

At 4:07 o'clock the fighters went to the centre of the ring. They were photographed shaking hands and then were cautioned by Referee Pecord. Tex Rickard, one of the judges, took his place in the press seats, at the north side of the ring, while Major A. J. Drexel Biddle, second judge, was seated in the press stand on the south side of the ring. Then the fight began.

One Thermometer at 120.

The moving picture machines were installed to the west of the ring on a platform about thirty feet high. The day was clear and excessively hot throughout. At 1:20 P. M. a thermometer at the ringside registered 120 degrees. A slight breeze occasionally stirred, and every time it did it was greeted by cheers from the fans. Once a cloud obscured the sun for a minute and it was also applauded. Nearly every man in the arena had his coat off and his handkerchief tucked under his hat. It was a white crowd sartorially, and to look over the shimmering masses of silk shirts, with the sun beating on them, was to risk eye trouble from the reflection.

One hundred enthusiasts reached the arena as early as 5 o'clock in the morning, although the gates did not open until 8:30. These were holders of ten-dollar tickets for rush seats, who were afraid they would not get their choice, but they need not have worried.

At 11 o'clock there were 8,000 persons in the arena. The best of the preliminaries was the semi-final, a bout of eight rounds, between Frankie Mason of Fort Wayne, Ind., and Carl Tremaine of Detroit, bantams. Billy Rooks of Detroit gave the decision to Tremaine, a verdict which was roundly hissed.

Another preliminary which attracted some attention was the eight-round go between Jock Malone of St. Paul and Navy Ralston of Joliet, Ill. They fought at 146 pounds, and the decision went to Malone.

Although there was not as great a crowd at the arena as had been expected, Toledo was jammed. Many persons slept last night in their automobiles and in hotel rotundas. It was difficult to get anything to eat this morning, because of the crowds in the hotels and restaurants.

Willard and Dempsey spent a quiet day until they left for the ring. Dempsey was up at 6:30 o'clock and had a breakfast of oranges, poached eggs, and coffee. He ate dinner at noon. Willard got up at 9 o'clock, and at 10 ate a heavy breakfast, his only meal before the fight.

Tonight Toledo is wild with joy over the result of the fight, as Dampsey has made himself extremely popular here. Enthusiastic rooters are parading the town, and jollification is in the air.

July 6, 1919

DEMPSEY WILL MEET ONLY WHITE BOXERS

Special to The New York Times.

TOLEDO, Ohio, July 5.—In the first statement he has made since becoming the heavyweight champion of the world, Jack Dempsey announced today that he would draw the color line. He will pay no attention to negro challengers, but will defend his title against any white heavyweight as the occasion demands. Dempsey said tonight that he would not fight again for seven or eight months at least.

The challenger and his manager, Jack Kearns, left at midnight for Cincinnati, where Dempsey will open a vaudeville engagement. It is stated that he is to receive $7,000 for his week's appearance. Kearns received several telegrams today making theatrical offers to the new champion.

The largest of these offers came from a vaudeville agent in Los Angeles, who offered the champion $10,000 a week for twelve weeks. Kearns stated that this sounded very attractive, and Dempsey may accept the offer. The tour will include all the leading cities on the Pacific Coast.

After Dempsey finishes his engagement in Cincinnati he will accept a week's engagement with a circus now showing through the Middle West. After that he may accept the coast offer. Eventually Dempsey will arrive in New York, where he expects to be a theatrical attraction. Almost all the other champions have made a lot of money through theatrical engagements and Dempsey does not propose to let the grass grow under his feet.

August 25, 1920

DEMPSEY KNOCKS OUT CARPENTIER IN THE FOURTH ROUND

DEMPSEY PROVES PROWESS

Jack Dempsey is still heavyweight champion of the world—it might almost be said that for the first time he is really the champion. Georges Carpentier, in many respects the most serious opponent Dempsey has ever met, stood up against him yesterday afternoon in Tex Rickard's stadium in Jersey City and could not last through the fourth round. And at that, Carpentier fought better than most American critics believed possible.

His end came at a few seconds after 3:30, when the fourth round had been going on one minute and sixteen seconds. Dempsey found the Frenchman's face with his left and followed it up with a hard right just in front of the ear. Carpentier went down, but on the count of nine leaped to his feet and seemed in shape to give the champion more trouble. But he never had the chance.

Dempsey led a light left to the face, and then as Carpentier swayed aside from the blow Dempsey drove a tremendous smash with his right hand into Carpentier's ribs, below the heart. This was quickly followed by a smashing right to the jaw.

The blow to the body was a hard enough blow in itself, because that spot had already been hammered and weakened by a score of fierce short-arm jolts in the desperate in-fighting of the previous rounds, but at the blow to the jaw Carpentier dropped again—dropped on his right side and lay there while Referee Harry Ertle swung his arm above him and counted. At the count of eight Carpentier stirred and made a desperate effort to rise; but he could not move. Nine, ten—and Dempsey's championship was secure.

Witnessed by 90,000 Persons.

So ended the "battle of the century," fought before 90,000 people—a fight which had aroused more interest, in all probability, than any other in all history.

Perhaps this interest had been enhanced by the futile efforts of moral reformers to stop the fight, but there were other elements which made it unique.

When the New World met the Old in the persons of Heenan and Sayers, when Jim Jeffries's gallant effort to come back against Jack Johnson roused the slumbering bitterness of racial feeling, millions of people who had never hitherto paid any attention to prizefighting found themselves roused by a new stimulus and found in the meeting of two boxers an interest such as they would never have supposed could be attached to a mere sporting event.

Yesterday's fight was international, too; it drew a bigger crowd than had ever seen a prizefight. It brought forward for the first time a real heavyweight contender from the Continent of Europe in a sport where heretofore the English-speaking world has had no serious competition.

There was novelty not only in the size of the crowd, but in the composition of it. The throng included thousands of women and a considerable number of public officials such as have rarely been seen in this country at a professional boxing bout. The fight aroused an intensity of interest that would have been impossible but for the still living emotions roused by the war.

No Accidental Champion.

Dempsey was in many ways the most unpopular of white champions. Those who know him best say that this unpopularity is largely undeserved; but the fact remained that millions of people in Dempsey's own country were hoping that the foreign challenger could beat him. The crowd, though it gave the champion a vociferous welcome, seemed to prefer Carpentier by a considerable majority—before the fight. Its speedy end found thousands cheering the winner who, ten minutes before, had been shouting for Carpentier. Dempsey had shown that whatever else might be said about him, he was no accidental champion. He can fight.

He had, to be sure, a big advantage in size. He had a reach longer by an inch than the challenger; he weighed 188 pounds as he stepped into the ring, while Carpentier weighed only 172. To the eye the difference was greater than this. Carpentier seemed fragile, a thing of mere nerves and desperate determination against Dempsey's huge bulk.

But Dempsey was no slow-moving leviathan. At long-range Carpentier had the better of him, but from half-way through the first round, when the in-fighting really began, Dempsey had been steadily hammering the Frenchman's body, and occasionally his face, with short but terrifically violent punches which broke Carpentier's defense all to pieces and left him a ready victim to the final blows.

So long as the fighting was at arm's length Carpentier had the advantage. His right, flashing with incredible speed, found Dempsey's jaw once in the second round, and shook him badly. Dempsey said after the fight that he couldn't remember being hit hard enough to unsettle him. But to the eyes of spectators at the ringside he looked unsettled through all the rest of that round: and the blow was hard enough to break Carpentier's thumb and sprain his wrist.

Carpentier's Right Failed.

Yet this one fierce smash was the only one that seriously disturbed the champion. He was able, after this shock, to drive Carpentier away from him with one or two fierce swings. The challenger's deadly right—the right that had knocked out most of the men who stood between Carpentier and the championship of Europe—never landed after that.

Again and again Carpentier swung—long, fast, powerful swings—with his right hand; but Dempsey always kept out of the way. Sooner or later he always brought Carpentier to close range; and once clinched, Dempsey began again the terrible pounding that a man of Carpentier's build could not long withstand.

No doubt the much-discussed moral factor had its effect on both fighters. Carpentier could not fail to be buoyed up, perhaps set on edge, perhaps even somewhat overstrained, by the knowledge that not only everybody in his own country and in England, but millions of men and women in the strange land where he had come to contest the championship with a native son, were hoping he would win.

Dempsey perhaps was settled into a fierce sullenness by the knowledge that his victory would be bad news to most of the world. But whatever the moral factor may have done to the dispositions of the fighters, it had nothing to do with the outcome of the fight. Carpentier lost because he could not keep Dempsey from hitting him and because he had not the strength to endure Dempsey's blows.

JACK DEMPSEY

Heavyweight Champion of the World, Who Knocked Out Georges Carpentier Challenger, Yesterday in the Fourth Round.

16 Minutes Late in Starting.

Rickard, the promoter, had promised the crowd that the big fight would start at 3 o'clock, daylight saving time, and, so far as was humanly possible, he kept his word. It was, in fact, sixteen minutes past 3 when the fight actually began, and to get it away as promptly as that it was necessary to defer the last of the six preliminaries, a match between Billy Miske and Jack Renault, until the big fight was over. It served as a sort of after-dinner consolation for the late comers, who had missed the other preliminaries, or for the exigent persons whose demand for action had not yet been satisfied.

Most of the women spectators, it was observed, came in rather late, filing through the alleys and aisles of the huge wooden arena during the fifth preliminary, between Gene Tunney and Soldier Jones.

Few of the masculine spectators were so deliberate as that. At 8 o'clock in the morning, when the arena was opened to the ushers and to the 1,600 Jersey City police and firemen, who kept excellent order throughout the day and were always vigilantly on guard against accidents that never happened, there were already hundreds of spectators gathered outside the ropes surrounding the stadium.

At 9 o'clock, when the doors were opened to the public, the hundreds had become thousands, and all through the rest of the morning more spectators were pouring in—across the ferries, from the tube stations, by surface cars, in automobiles and by train. Before the first preliminary bout began, at 12.50, the arena was almost full.

Not an Untoward Incident.

Any number of mishaps might have occurred, and with ninety thousand people gathered in a hastily-constructed lumber arena a mishap might have meant a catastrophe. But nothing untoward happened.

The arena had been soaked in water every day during its construction. The boards were still damp. The ground underneath—Boyle's Thirty Acres, in a dismal, unprepossessing section of Jersey City just below the eastward slope of the hill crowned by the Boulevard—was an almost stagnant pool. At every exit, at every gate opening into the various sections of the huge enclosure, firemen were stationed, alert for the first spark from a cigar stub or a carelessly discarded match. But though a blue haze of tobacco smoke hung over the arena all day, a fire would have had no chance to get started.

Policemen, two, were everywhere. Thanks to them the crowd was kept moving, ushered to the proper seats, and held pretty well in the seats. Conflicts over tickets which had been duplicated by forgers were few, and only here and there developed into sufficient importance to call for the subduing appearance of a policeman. Airplanes flew over the arena throughout the fight and some of them flew dangerously low; but by good luck none of them met with accidents.

Even the weather was surprisingly favorable. All day long gray clouds hung low over Jersey City, but only once, for a few minutes during the second preliminary fight, did rain fall, and then only a few scattering drops which had no more effect than to make thousands of perspiring men fight their way into raincoats which they presently discarded.

Breeze for the Big Fight.

A hot sun would have been as bad as rain, or worse, but the sun stayed behind the clouds except for a minute or two just after 2 o'clock, and during the big fight there was a light breeze which made the arena unexpectedly comfortable.

It might have been expected that, since a crowd which had been gathering all day would want to go away all at once, there would be some disorder. But there was none, nor any serious congestion. Thousands walked out after the big fight was settled, and the other thousands which waited for the postponed fight between Miske and Renault were able to get away at their leisure, for the afternoon was not yet ended and there was plenty of time to get home for dinner.

It was a rather apathetic crowd that sat through the preliminaries, eating the sandwiches and drinking the soft drinks that were distributed at two or three times the Polo Ground prices. What the price might be nobody cared, for it was a long wait while the early comers sat on their damp benches and watched the unimportant battling of minor fighters. The lunches were at least sufficient to sustain life in thousands of men who had dashed away from home after an early and hurried breakfast and had spent most of the middle part of the day in wishing that the Volstead act had not suppressed those corner dispensaries of first aid.

Crowd Patiently Waits.

The crowd seemed but little interested in the band and the song "pluggers," and its hopes of excitement from incipient fights over seating were disappointed. Its enthusiasm began to awaken, however, with the first knockdown, and the hard fighting in some of the later preliminaries whipped up the appetite of men and women who had come to see somebody damaged, and were beginning to be rather bored with the wait.

The fifth preliminary was ended at 2:50 by the referee's decision that ended by the referee's decision that Gene Tunney had given Soldier Jones as much punishment as was good for him, and the crowd was rather impatietly waiting for Miske and Renault, who stood, wrapped in towels, just beyond the ringside waiting their turn. Then Joe Humphries, the scarlet-faced announcer, who has been introducing champions, challengers and any extraneous celebrities who might be present at all the championship fights of recent history and who had been exercising his cracked voice through the amplifier on the unimportant names of the fighters in the preliminary, took up the transmitter, not unlike a desk telephone, connected with the three big megaphones that stood in the press seats just below the ring.

"Everybody sit down!" he shouted. The crowd, standing as it had stood after every bout to stretch weary muscles and ease aching bones, responded to this order in rather half-hearted manner. Everywhere men were still standing up in spite of the irritable entreaties of those behind them, while officials crowded into the ring and attendants sprinkled rosin over the dampened corners where fighters in earlier bouts had been sponged between rounds.

"Everybody sit down!" Humphreys repeated. And then, when his appeal seemed to have only partial effect, he added, "The big bout is next."

Then everybody stood up. Down an eastward aisle there was a confused swirling, and a thin blue thread of policemen, marked out sharply in the gray mass, tried desperately to clear the corridor. All about men stood on seats looking down for the entrance of the combatants. Humphreys was shouting again into the megaphone, announcing that a collection would be taken for St. Francis's Hospital in Jersey City—"the hospital that does good without any money," he added in an aside to those near the ring—and that there were only ten minutes left for the collection as the big fight began at 3.

But the collection got rather inadequate attention. The eyes of the crowd were drawn to that corridor where the police were trying to clear a passage to the ringside, where other police were pushing back the principals and seconds of the last unregarded preliminary, forcing out the hangers-on who had no right so near the ropes, compelling the telegraph messengers and the miscellaneous functionaries of the fight to sit down and clear the view for those behind them. Above two airplanes swung over the arena, lower than those which had circled about it earlier in the day.

Into the ring came a huge floral horseshoe—red roses, red and white carnations, and gladiolas—with the word "success" picked out in red letters. It was for Dempsey, from friends in Jersey City.

A swarm of photographers and movie camera men poured into the ring and began to take pictures of the horseshoe and the crowd, tearing the air with their cries of "Sit down!" flung fiercely at one another.

A Picture of Carpentier.

Then, while the ring was still crowded with photographers milling evcitedly and falling over one another's tripods, Carpentier suddenly appeared, followed by his seconds. Wrapped in his gray dressing gown, bordered in midnight blue, he came lightly into his corner—the southeastern one—and then as the crowd stood up and cheered with a flutter of waving straw hats he went to the ropes on each side of the ring and held aloft his clasped hands, shaking them in greeting, while the band played the Marseillaise.

A moment later he was back on his stool, talking to his manager and chief of staff, François Descamps. Carpentier has muscles, and formidable muscles; but it was hard to pay attention to the muscles or to remember that this was the man who had knocked out heavyweights who outweighed him thirty or forty pounds.

For those who were near enough to see them, the centre of attraction was his eyes—gray eyes, rather eager, rather excited, in a gray face with blond hair brushed back above it; a face that had more than ever the curious girlish quality that would hardly be looked for in an aspirant to the heavyweight championship. Eagerness and enthusiasm were there, but more than all an apparent realization of the fact that he represented France; that he represented millions of soldiers who had fought in the trenches as well as inside the ropes; and that this day was the climax of his whole career. His eager intensity, his fiery slightness, gave to some of the onlookers a curious sense of resemblance between Georges Carpentier and another French champion of old. He suggested Joan of Arc.

Descamps Is All Excitement.

And over this slender, eager, almost devout personage hovered the crafty Descamps. A fat, excitable man, wrapped in a gray sweater trimmed in a dark cream color, a light brown cap on his head and a pink-striped towel swinging from his belt, he talked to the champion, then passed about the ring and chatted with the officials, then came back to Carpentier once more.

A new focus of interest. At 3 o'clock exactly, four minutes after Carpentier had entered, Jack Dempsey came in. He, too, had come up the crowded aisle almost unseen, except by those just beside him; and his entrance into the ring brought a much louder cheer than the challenger had evoked.

Dempsey nodded and smiled slightly, but only for a moment. His famous scowl, the scowl that has entered into tradition as part of a personality, was on his browned, unshaven face. Under black eyebrows and curling black hair he glowered stolidly, sullenly.

Underneath his old maroon sweater showed his white trunks, and the end of a red, white and blue ribbon, which for some reason he had put on in place of a belt. He, too, sat down, but in a moment he was up, standing in front of the floral horseshoe for a photograph, and then crossing the ring to shake hands with Carpentier under fire of the movie cameras.

Object to Dempsey's Tape.

They stood there a moment, the eager gray-eyed blonde and the scowling dark fighter who had come out to defend his right to the championship before a public which seemed inclined to give him no credit for anything but ability to fight. Then they separated, back to their corners once more, and Dempsey, with a sombre, preoccupied air, danced up and down lightly on his tiptoes. Then he sat down and held out his hands to be wound with bandages and adhesive tape.

In a moment the vigilant Descamps was in Dempsey's corner.

"No, no, no!" he shouted, and tore the rolls of tape out of the hands of Dempsey's seconds. The belief that Dempsey's terrific pounding of Willard had been made possible in some degree by his tape-wound hands was strong in the Frenchman's camp, and Descamps was determined that only the soft gauze bandages permitted by the New Jersey Boxing Commission should be used. He thrust one of Dempsey's seconds aside rather roughly, and after a brief but bitter argument gained his way. Dempsey held out his hands to be wound with the strips of gauze, with Descamps leaning against the ropes, almost over him, and following every movement with the vigilance of suspicion.

Meanwhile Jack Kearns, the man behind Dempsey, was showing no interest in Carpentier's hands, nor very much in Dempsey's. Coatless, with a long dark four-in-hand tie over his white shirt and his thinning hair brushed up from his forehead, he could have posed better than Carpentier for a shirt advertisement, and would not have seemed wholly out of place as an illustration of what the well dressed man will wear.

Introducing the Principals.

Then there was an interlude while Humphries introduced the distinguished guests—first Mayor Frank Hague of Jersey City, then Governor Edward I. Edwards. Each in his turn shook hands with both fighters and both managers, and then the two shook hands with each other, outside the ropes, before they climbed down out of range of the cameras. Then followed introductions of the State Boxing Commissioners—Robert Doherty, Charles McNair and Charles Lyons—and of Bill Brennan, who was indulging in the popular outdoor sport of challenging the winner.

Referee Harry Ertle, looking rather strained and careworn, but resplendent in white shirt and flannel trousers, was next introduced.

Then a browned man in blue serge, carrying a light stick and a half-burned cigar in an amber holder, came in and allowed himself to be introduced as "the world's premier promoter, Tex Rickard," which he undoubtedly is.

The weights were announced and the public was informed that Joe Bannon was timekeeper.

Meanwhile the seconds of each fighter had been solicitously inspecting the big eight-ounce gloves and had found them satisfactory. The principals had sat silently in their corners; Dempsey glum and grim, Carpentier glancing about him alertly—at his antagonist, at the crowd, finally, with the interest of a veteran military aviator, at the gray airplanes circling against the gray sky overhead.

The gloves fitted on, Carpentier shed his dressing gown and stood out in white jersey trunks, with a light blue stripe down the side. He sat down and let his seconds fan him, while Dempsey, the gloves securely fitted, once more danced on his toes and then spat with an air of satisfaction.

Greater Cheer for Georges.

Once more Humphreys got the attention of the crowd. Going over to Dempsey's corner, where Descamps still stood alertly watching the champion, the announcer drew Dempsey out and presented him to the crowd as "the champion, Jack Dempsey, on whom every redblooded American pins his hopes this day." A cheer, a bow, and then Carpentier came forward to be introduced as "the heavyweight champion of the Old World, the idol of his people, and a soldier of France."

The roar that came from the crowd at that made its cheer for Dempsey seem like nothing but a hoarse whisper. All over the arena men stood on their seats and waved their straw hats while they shouted frantically. Through it all Dempsey glowered, as before, preoccupied and sombre.

Carpentier bowed, shook his clasped hands and then turned to the centre of the ring where principals and seconds gathered for the final instructions of the referee. Now Kearns stepped to Dempsey's side and let his arm linger across the champion's bare brown back, his fingers pinching Dempsey affectionately.

Back to the corners once more, where both men were sponged and Carpentier sank, then rose, flexing his knees. Then the seconds tumbled out of the ring and at 3:16 the gong signaled the beginning of the fight.

Starts for Dempsey's Head.

To the surprise of the experts, Carpentier rushed in, leading for Dempsey's head. It had been supposed that he would hold off and fight as much as possible at long range, where his greater agility would give him the advantage; that he would let Dempsey hunt him out. But he came in with fierce eagerness, as of a man who has a long-neglected duty to perform, landing lightly with a left, missing a long right swing that came with startling speed, and then coming into a clinch where he caught Dempsey's chin.

They broke away, Dempsey's hairy brown bulk moving with apparent slowness. But this was illusory; beside the lighter and more agile Frenchman Dempsey seemed slow, but he was fast enough to keep out of the way of Carpentier's fists, and in a moment his big brown arm had slipped under Carpentier's guard and landed a jolting blow on the body. They came to a clinch again.

Carpentier's slight figure hung lightly on Dempsey's huge body. The champion's heavy arm swung over Carpentier's shoulder and his right hand found Carpentier's head five times in quick succession. Carpentier could not stop it; he could not pin down the champion's big arms nor keep off that huge hand that moved with amazing speed and certainty.

Broken apart by the referee, they faced each other for an instant, and then Carpentier lashed out again with his swift and powerful right. It missed, and the two came into another clinch.

Infighting Punishes Georges.

Once more, while all Carpentier's energies were occupied in neutralizing Dempsey's left hand, the right pounded three short jolts into Carpentier's face. Short, but terribly powerful. Most of Dempsey's weight was behind them, and with sudden alertness he shifted and drove two jabs with the same hand into Carpentier's back. Carpentier's hands moved about in vain efforts to reach Dempsey as the champion's right pounded him steadily, now in the body, now in the face. As they broke apart both Dempsey's hands hammered into Carpentier's face and the Frenchman's nose was scarlet with blood.

Carpentier drew off, but Dempsey was now following him, steadily keeping him at work and looking for another chance for the infighting which has always been the champion's strength. Carpentier's right flashed out and grazed Dempsey's face. Dempsey also swung, but missed. They came together again, and while Carpentier hung on Dempsey's shoulder the champion's right landed four quick, hard punches in his face.

Again the breakaway; again Carpentier tried a right swing—a terrible blow, but it hit only the air. The ponderous Dempsey was fast enough for all practical purposes, and as he evaded the blow he cuffed Carpentier twice on the head.

Carpentier backed away and Dempsey followed. He forced the fighting, came up within the Frenchman's long sweeps, caught him again and hammered his stomach viciously. Carpentier's eyes were duller now; they were still full of determination, but he was plainly getting more than he expected. Against Dempsey's fierce jolts at a six-inch range he had no defense; it was as much as he could do to cover one hand, and the other kept pounding him.

Almost Through the Ropes.

As the referee's white figure came between the two they broke apart and Carpentier, slipping, fell against the top rope, then against the middle one, and almost tumbled out of the ring. Dempsey's supporters had been roused to volubility by their champion's success; they roared a demand that he be finished now. Carpentier could not prevent another clinch, and another battering; Carpentier seemed helpless, waiting for the end. But just as the referee threw the two men apart the bell rang and the round was over.

So was the fight, in the opinion of most of the onlookers. Kearns hurriedly dabbled his sponge over Dempsey, whispering solicitously in his ear while Teddy Hayes fanned the champion and Bernard Dempsey, Jack's brother, handled the water bucket back of the stool.

In the other corner Descamps was busy with the sponge while Gus Wilson, Paul Journee and Charlie Ledoux, Carpentier's other seconds, fanned him with nervous haste. Carpentier sat grimly on his stool, his face more grimly determined, now—more than ever the face of a man who has a great duty to perform and who is desperately determined to do it. So when the second round began he changed his tactics. He backed away, and Dempsey followed.

Joy as Carpentier Lands.

Still Carpentier backed away, and those of the onlookers who are always ready to rush to the rescue of a winner began once more to clamor for the finishing blow. Suddenly Carpentier leaped and his left hand flickered toward Dempsey's face. It landed, but from such a distance that the blow was light.

Nevertheless, Dempsey realized that there was still work ahead; and he pursued Carpentier relentlessly, allowing no more opportunity for long-range attack, till they were clinched again, and again Dempsey's right was hammering Carpentier's head.

The referee separated them, but Carpentier's inability to protect himself had been so evident that for the first time Dempsey's face was lightened by a momentary smile. He walked in again, driving Carpentier before him and looking for another chance to drive in some of his deadly short-range blows.

Then something happened. Carpentier's left hand shot out in a brown streak and hit Dempsey's face—not very hard, it seemed, but hard enough to throw the champion off his guard for the fraction of a second. In that flash Carpentier's long right had struck in and caught Dempsey on the jaw. The champion's head went back sharply and there was a roar of joy from the crowd. However he felt, Dempsey seemed badly unsettled. But he was still able to let go a couple of fierce swings that landed nowhere, but prevented Carpentier from following his advantage. Then Dempsey managed to close with Carpentier once more, but this time the champion's deadly right was idle.

Carpentier had had enough of clinches; he pulled away and swung again, fast and fierce, with his right. But Dempsey dodged it; and, when Carpentier landed with his left a moment later, Dempsey had ducked so that the blow slid harmlessly off his head. Dempsey waded in fiercely, the scowl back on his forehead once more. Rather lumberingly, but with a good deal of speed and deadly certainty, he moved around the ring trying to force another fight at close quarters. Carpentier swung again and still again with his right, but the sullen black face was never there. And before the round ended Dempsey had managed to get to close range once again, so that Carpentier went to the corner bleeding under his right eye.

Still, it had been Carpentier's round. Descamps chattered unceasing encouragement as he passed his sponge over his principal's body, dabbled it on his tongue, wiped away the blood that reddened the cheek and then dashed the

Heavyweight Champions.

John L. Sullivan	1882 to 1892
James J. Corbett	1892 to 1897
Robert Fitzsimmons	1897 to 1899
James J. Jeffries	1899 to *1905
Marvin Hart	1905
Tommy Burns	1907 to 1908
Jack Johnson	1908 to 1915
Jess Willard	1915 to 1919
Jack Dempsey	1919

*Retired.

sponge in water to cool the body once more. Carpentier's expression was still doggedly resolute, but he was evidently feeling the effect of the fierce hammering of the first round.

Kearns was silent now, busy with assiduous care in cooling and refreshing the champion, but wasting no more breath in whispering encouragement into his ear. He seemed to feel that from now on Dempsey's morale would have to be self-made.

The gong once more. Dempsey moved with soft-footed swiftness into the middle of the ring, his face well protected, and marched forward toward the challenger. A wild drive with his right, that missed; Carpentier had ducked under it. Carpentier's right hand slid over Dempsey's face, then came back again with eager rapidity and landed twice on the jaw—but lightly, too lightly to do much damage.

Fails to Punish Dempsey.

Dempsey pressed forward, driving his man about the ring, pushing on with all the dogged persistence of the German army marching on Paris—and for a time with about as much effect. Carpentier dodged out of an attempted clinch, almost thrusting his head between Dempsey's legs, and once more let fly a series of right swings at long range. They were just as fast and just as powerful as the one that had shaken Dempsey in the previous round; but none of them landed.

There was not a moment for rest or for change of strategy. Dempsey kept coming on, kept pressing in closer and closer, and he could not be hit. Carpentier's right landed again on the face, but once again from too far away. And then they were breast to breast, Carpentier's worn face looking over Dempsey's left shoulder, Carpentier's two hands trying desperately to get around the barrier of Dempsey's left arm. And the champion's right was once more at work, driving five uppercuts in quick succession into Carpentier's bleeding face.

As they drew apart Carpentier came in again with a furious right. Once more he missed, and then the old game began again. Carpentier backed away, backed around in a circle, while the hairy brown body pressed on and the black hairy face, chin on chest, scowled down at him. Dempsey was cautious, he kept coming, but he was not to be caught again by that dangerous right. So this time it was Carpentier who suddenly came in closer. Dempsey landed a right to the stomach and Carpentier staggered with his eyes rolling. This time it was he who had to force the clinch as the only way out.

For a moment it seemed that Carpentier was going to have the better of it. He caught Dempsey's face with one hand and landed two short blows on the body with the other; but in a moment Dempsey's right arm was on guard, and Carpentier could not get past it.

The men still hung on each other, and now it was Dempsey's left that was doing the work. The old story—six inches of room to hit, but a fierce succession of deadly blows delivered in incredibly rapid sequence, and with incredible force. Five times his left caught Carpentier's chin with uppercuts; a swift shifting of his shoulders and Dempsey's right beat past Carpentier's hands and caught the Frenchman in the ribs; then as Carpentier, exhausted and bewildered, guarded his body the left was at his chin again, pounding in and sliding back, pounding in and sliding back, four times.

The gong stopped the slaughter that time, but as Carpentier sank back on his stool his left eye and cheek stood out red and swollen. He looked, not beaten, but pounded to pieces. From his gray eyes there still shone the same fierce resolve, but the physical force behind it was obviously gone. He leaned back languidly as the solicitous Descamps put a bottle of smelling salts to his nose. Another second was on hand with another bottle, of mysterious character; this went to Carpentier's mouth.

Carpentier got up promptly with the gong, and once more began his retreating fight, evidently still in the hope of keeping out of range until he could land another of those right swings that could shake even Dempsey—when they hit.

Georges Takes Count of 9.

But Dempsey was still able to keep them off, and they no longer had their old swiftness. Moreover, Dempsey was closing in; pushing forward, crouching chin down on his chest, and gradually drawing closer and closer. Carpentier could not keep out of his way, nor could he hit him. Dempsey landed a right on Carpentier's body and in the clinch that followed he used his left on the Frenchman's face.

They broke and the retreat and pursuit started again. Dempsey was landing now at longer range as Carpentier weakened. A right to the body shook the Frenchman still more, but he hung on. There came another clinch. Again Carpentier managed to control Dempsey's right hand, but only by leaving the left free to drive a hammer blow to the nose and follow with two more in the ribs.

Carpentier broke away and struck desperately with his left; it caught Dempsey's mouth, but there was no longer any force behind it. And then Dempsey was on him again, driving his left to Carpentier's face, and then suddenly whipped out a right which caught the Frenchman on the cheek just forward of the ear.

Carpentier fell—on his hands and knees, first, and then collapsed prone on the canvas. There was a yowl of fierce satisfaction from the crowd as the referee's pump-handle arm swung up and town, but Carpentier came up again—at the count of nine. He came up with an effort at a smile.

Now Dempsey called in his reserves for the final assault. Carpentier struck out, but vainly; Dempsey's left reached his face, and the Frenchman's hands went up to guard. Dempsey's right shot forward and hammered fiercely into the spot just below the heart, where all through the fight he had been pounding. Carpentier staggered, and a swift right to the jaw brought him down again.

He fell full length, on his right side, and lay outstretched, a forlorn gray figure, while the referee counted over him. At the count of eight he stirred; he tried to rise; his legs moved spasmodically, then subsided. Two seconds more and the fight was over.

The crowd, that loves a winner, was cheering for Jack Dempsey louder than it had cheered for his opponent fifteen minutes before, and the champion was staring out with the same half-puzzled, half-resentful frown.

A swarm of enthusiasts was already pushing forward to shake hands with the winner, but a swarm of police was ahead of them. By Mayor Hague's orders the police took prompt possession of the ring at the close of the fight, and succeeded in keeping the crowd out.

All over the stadium people were on their way to the doors, but they paused, three minutes after the knockout, when Carpentier had been revived and Dempsey shook hands with him before the movie camera. And then, while the champion and the beaten challenger slipped out of the ring under police guard and pushed out toward their dressing rooms, Joe Humphreys took up the transmitter and announced that the last preliminary would then take place.

July 3, 1921

BOXING

Out of the involved mess which at present surrounds the world's middleweight title, the one thing that stands forth conspicuously is that the practice of title-holders carrying with them over the country their own hand-picked referees should be abolished. As long as this condition exists the sport will be jeopardized. It is a practice developed almost to the state of being a habit.

This practice created a controversy at Benton Harbor just before the Dempsey-Miske battle; again at Jersey City it cropped up until the New Jersey Commission stepped in and dictated just who was to referee the Dempsey-Carpentier bout, and now it manifests itself again, more odorous than ever, in the Wilson-Downey bout. These, just to mention a few important instances.

Of course, the argument might be advanced that title-holders, traveling about the country in defense of their honor are in danger of suffering from dishonest or unscrupulous officials. This excuse, on the very face of it, is ridiculous, particularly in cases where boxing is conducted under Commission rule. And if, by any chance, there are localities where unscrupulous officials would lend themselves to or countenance plots such as are feared by latter-day champions, then boxing in that particular locality should be abolished.

There is no excuse for the existence of a sport in a community wherein the highest ideals of sportsmanship and honesty are not observed. By the same token, it is a highly undesirable travesty to alter Commission rules relating to the selection of referees, no matter how important the individual boxer may regard himself. The condition has been curbed to a great extent, and if boxing is to continue in its present flourishing condition the practice must be entirely abolished.

Wilson finds himself today a champion whose right to the crown is clouded. Reports from Cleveland indicate clearly that Downey won the late bout. Downey has been proclaimed champion by the Cleveland Boxing Commission, which is a member of the National Boxing Association, and it is possible that the complete N. B. A. membership will recognize the ruling of the Cleveland board. The New York State Athletic Commission is prepared to adopt an attitude of accord with the Cleveland officials just as soon as the official details of the much-discussed bout are received.

The Massachusetts State Boxing Commission, standing alone, is reported staunchly back of Wilson in recognizing the decision of Referee Gardner that Wilson won on a foul. The Bay State officials take the view that the referee is supreme in ring bouts. This is so, except where Commission rules empower a governing board to reverse a referee's decision, a provision which is said to be embodied in the Cleveland rules.

As long as this unsatisfactory condition prevails the title will be surrounded by confusion. Downey appears to have the greater support in his title claims, but Wilson, too, will be regarded as champion—in some quarters. A remedy for the dilemma would be a return bout between the pair, over a championship distance, to a decision, and without tolerance of either boxer dictating who shall or who shall not referee.

August 1, 1921

TUNNEY CAPTURES LEVINSKY'S TITLE

Gains Decision Over Holder of American Light-Heavyweight Crown at Garden.

VICTOR BY A WIDE MARGIN

Greenwich Village Boxer Has Philadelphia Veteran in Distress in Sixth Round.

A new American light-heavyweight champion was crowned last night in Madison Square Garden before one of the largest crowds of the season. While a gathering of more than fourteen thousand people looked on Gene Tunney of Greenwich Village, a pugilistic product of the late war, hammered his way to victory over the veteran and venerable Battling Levinsky, survivor of more than three hundred battles in a brilliant career, which extends over a period of twelve years. The victory for Tunney carried with it the American title at 175 pounds, a championship Levinsky has held for the last five or six years. Tunney received the decision when the final bell clanged on the bout.

It was a manifestly just verdict, as was indicated in the approving shout that was sent up by the capacity crowd. In addition to the title, Tunney received the diamond-studded light-heavyweight championship belt offered by Promoter Tex Rickard.

The result was not unexpected. Levinsky, aged in ring activity and in years, assumed too great a task in the effort to overcome the youth and vigorous strength of the aspiring Tunney. It was another of those examples of the ring: A victory for youth and strength over age and experience.

There was nothing spectacular about the contest, which held an element of tragedy in the passing of a veteran of Levinsky's years and ability. The veteran Philadelphian's remarkable defensive ability was conspicuous by its absence. He was surprisingly ineffective against the rushing Tunney. Through the battle Levinsky fought strictly on the defense, while Tunney plunged in recklessly.

Champion in Retreat.

Levinsky had no time for an offensive. He was forced before the flailing arms of his ambitious rival throughout the contest. The result was that Levinsky was subjected to a withering fire and was in full retreat more than once during the contest. Levinsky failed to carry a single round. He weakened under the body hammering to which he was subjected, and as the battle progressed held continually and tenaciously, so much so, in fact, that the crowd several times openly voiced its displeasure at these tactics.

Several times in the course of the battle Levinsky was stung with the power back of Tunney's clean punches. Notable illustrations were furnished in the second, sixth and seventh rounds. Levinsky recovered in each instance, however, holding until his head cleared and his legs became certain again. In the eighth session Levinsky landed twice with rights to the jaw as Tunney was tearing in, but the blows had no effect.

It was announced officially that the gross receipts were $40,468.

Levinsky entered the ring one and one-half pounds over weight. The contest was signed at 175 pounds, the cruiser weight standard. Tunney, who was three pounds under the prescribed weight, declined to take Levinsky's weight forfeit. Tunney weighed 172 pounds and Levinsky 176½. The failure of Levinsky to get down to the required weight, however, did not interfere with the title aspect of the match, since Tunney was under the standard notch.

Tunney carried the first two rounds. The challenger pressed a spirited offensive from the time the opening bell sent the men on their journey and forced Levinsky steadily before him. The champion assumed a strictly defensive battle program and confined his work to short arm jolts at close quarters. In the last ten seconds of the second round Tunney crashed over a right to the jaw which sent Levinsky, stung, into a neutral corner. Here Tunney plied the champion with rights and lefts to the face and body until the bell.

Through the third, fourth and fifth rounds, the action was comparatively slow. Levinsky clung to his defensive program and seldom took the initiative. Tunney pressed his rival about the ring willingly and was on the aggressive, but the Greenwich Village boxer's assault, while steady, was ineffective. Clinches marred the stage of the contest to a considerable extent. Tunney's untiring work gave him a shade in the honors for the three rounds.

Levinsky weathered a trying storm in the sixth session. For a time it appeared that the bout would end there in a knockout for Tunney. Tunney, forcing Levinsky before him conntinuously, crashed over a left to the jaw which sent Levinsky up against the ropes. When the battler rebounded Tunney sent home a left and right to the jaw and quickly crashed past Levinsky's defense with a left hook to the jaw which staggered the champion. Tunney continued his assault until the bell ended the round. As he went to his corner Levinsky was bleeding from a cut over the left eye, a bruised mouth and a banged-up nose.

In the seventh Levinsky was hard pressed and held repeatedly in the clinches. The body punches of Tunney, no less than the fast pace set by the west sider, showed their effect on Levinsky and he utilized every opportunity to hold. Tunney had Levinsky's face a bloody smear, and in the last minute had the champion again shaky on his legs. A right to the jaw and a following right under the heart made Levinsky wince and dive into a frenzied clinch.

Levinsky Stages Rally.

When the men were parted Tunney hooked a left to the jaw and Levinsky again clinched.

Through the eighth and ninth rounds Levinsky rallied momentarily and for a time fought back in a spirited exchange. The veteran soon tired, however, and again resorted to clinching and holding.

In the tenth and eleventh rounds, Tunney forced the fighting steadily and had Levinsky in full retreat. Repeatedly at long range Tunney sank his left to the stomach and crashed over the right to the face in an assault which had the crowd yelling wildly.

Tunney gave his rival no time to set in the twelfth round. Following his systematic plan of battle, the West-sider forced Levinsky before him and the weary battler clinched with each exchange at long range. Tunney had all the better of the milling and had a clear lead in points at the final bell.

January 14, 1922

BRITTON DEFEATS LEONARD ON FOUL

Lightweight Champion Is Disqualified for Hitting While Opponent Is Down.

BOUT ENDS IN THIRTEENTH

Referee Declares Welterweight Titleholder Victor After 2 Min. 42 Sec. of Round.

Jack Britton, 37-year-old ring veteran, still is the world's welterweight champion. In his bout against Benny Leonard, world's lightweight champion, at the Velodrome last night, Referee Patsy Haley awarded the decision to Britton in the thirteenth round on a foul.

The end came 2 minutes 42 seconds after the round had started when in a swirling attack Leonard landed a left to the stomach. With the blow Britton went down on one knee, his face distorted in pain and supporting himself with his right gloved fist. Referee Haley thereupon stepped to the side of the fallen champion, as if to count over Britton. Before the referee could proceed, however, Leonard, eager and excited, hopped around Haley and swung a left to the face as Britton was on his knee. Then Referee Haley stepped between the boxers, waved them to their corners, and caused it to be announced that Britton was the winner of the contest on a foul.

When the decision was announced by Joe Humphreys, the boxers stepped out of the ring amid the mingled shouts of the crowd that was partly acclaiming and partly voicing dissatisfaction. Referee Haley stepped to a neutral corner of the ring, and, in explanation of his decision to ringside critics, said:

"I awarded the bout to Britton on a foul. Leonard floored Britton with a left hook to the stomach. Britton claimed the blow was foul, but I disagreed with him. I was preparing to start a count over Britton, when Leonard stepped up and struck Britton while the latter was down. It was this foul that I disqualified Leonard on and awarded the bout to Britton."

Decision Stuns Crowd.

The sudden, unexpected ending to the contest stunned the crowd. Ringside spectators stormed to the side of the ring and clamored for an explanation. The sentiment of the gathering was divided. Many thought that Leonard had been disqualified for striking the left to the stomach. thers thought there was no excuse for disqualifying Leonard at all. While the gathering was loud in its vocal demonstration, there was no indication of concerted disorder. After the excitement of the sudden finish had simmered down, the crowd left slowly and orderly. Urged by the special policemen, the crowd poured from the arena in a steady stream and the Velodrome soon was emptied.

The finish came as an unwelcome climax to a contest which provided a brilliant exhibition of skill by two past masters of the art of boxing. In a sense the contest was disappointing, however. The unsatisfactory finish was not the only disappointing element in the battle. Leonard failed to show up to expectations, in fact, failed to show up to the form he has exhibited in many of his previous local bouts.

Britton, on the other hand, showed surprisingly good form, and appeared to be an easy winner on points up to the time of the foul. Leonard, who was the favorite in the betting before the battle at odds of as high as 3 to 1, failed to show any form which would warrant these odds. The lightweight champion was careful and cautious throughout the contest, almost to the point of timidity, and lost many glowing chances to demonstrate his hitting power at the expense of Britton.

There were times when Leonard stung Britton noticeably with powerful right crosses or left hooks to the jaw which sent the welterweight champion reeling about the ring. But invariably Leonard hesitated in following what appeared to be an advantage, or he missed with punches which carried damaging power. Under the circumstances Britton was enabled to recover his equilibrium whenever danger threatened.

Seven Rounds for Britton.

Of the first twelve rounds Britton appeared entitled to the honors in seven sessions. These were the second, third, fourth, fifth, ninth, tenth and twelfth.

Leonard apparently discarded his caution, went in and outboxed Britton in the sixth, seventh and eighth rounds. In the eleventh round Leonard, concentrating his efforts in a determined effort to knock out his rival, almost succeeded in crushing Britton under the power of his blows in a furious two-handed assault which had the welterweight champion reeling like a drunken man and the crowd in a frenzy of excitement.

The lightweight champion, however, deliberated too long in what course to pursue in the situation, and Britton quickly recovered. The welterweight champion recovered so completely that he came back and outpointed Leonard in the twelfth round. In the thirteenth session, or that part of it that transpired before the unwelcome climax, honors were about evenly divided.

A crowd which taxed the capacity of the great arena turned out for the bout. Every nook and cranny of the huge bowl was occupied when the two champions entered the ring. The capacity of the arena is said to be 26,000. If so, this many persons made the journey to the battle centre. They came in droves from early evening until after dusk. Subways, surface cars and elevated trains were jammed with humanity headed for the fight. Automobiles pulled up to the arena entrance in steady streams and were parked by the hundreds in the seats.

In the battel as it progressed Britton appeared the complete master of his rival. Calling on all the ring wizardry at his command, the welterweight champion outboxed and outfought his contemporary of the lighter ding division. On the attack Britton was active with an assault which smothered Leonard's blows at times and had the lightweight champion missing repeatedly with his hardest punches.

Veteran's Offensive Consistent.

Making sporadic outbursts, Leonard outpointed the welterweight champion in brilliant boxing exchanges at long range, while the lightweight champion worked a stinging, accurate left jab to the face with effect. But the exhibitions by Leonard were flashes which, when measured against the consistent, untiring offensive of Britton, suffered by the comparison. It was through his relentless forcing, with its superb though light attack, that Britton gained the honors over Leonard in seven of the rounds.

In the four rounds he won, however, Leonard gave the gathering an indication of his real ability. The trouble with the lightweight champion was that his work was not sustained. This difference in aggressiveness swung the tide of battle in Britton's favor.

The first round was evenly divided. Both boxed cautiously and with the utmost regard, obviously, for each other's ability. The round was spent for the most part in the "feeling out" process, wherein both boxed at long range in the common endeavor to detect a weakness or to develop a method of forcing an opening.

In the second round, however, Britton cut loose a notch and outboxed and outfought Leonard. A stinging right to the jaw early in the round made Leonard seek the shelter of a clinch. At close quarters, however, Britton pumped rights and lefts to Leonard's stomach until the lightweight champion was forced to break. After shaking off the effects of the right, Leonard jabbed with his left in an effort to keep Britton at bay, but Britton bored in continually, and in the last minute grazed the jaw with another right. Just before the bell Leonard almost upset Britton with a hard right cross to the jaw.

Leonard started flashily in the third round, jabbing Britton repeatedly with the left to the face and upsetting Britton's attack. The welterweight champion, kept trying, however, and, forcing matters, peppered Leonard with both hands to the face and body. Before the bell Leonard was bleeding from the mouth, the result of a left hook.

A sharp left hook, followed by a hard right cross to the jaw early in the round, stung Britton in the fourth round and made the welterweight champion extremely cautious for awhile. Britton quickly recovered, however, and fought back valiantly. In a clinch Britton fought himself clear with a succession of rights and lefts to the jaw which drew a complaint to Referee Haley from Leonard. The men were ordered to box and Britton outfought Leonard to the bell.

In the fifth, too, Leonard started well, but was soon on the defensive as Britton forced matters, leading with both hands in a varied assault. In a clinch Leonard almost wrestled Britton down.

Leonard Shows Improvement.

Leonard went on the offensive in the sixth round and through this session, and in the seventh and eighth outboxed Britton. The lightweight champion's attacks, however, were light because of the caution he displayed in leading at his rival. With persistent left jabs, occasional left hooks and intermittent right crosses, Leonard made Britton miss repeatedly through this part of the battle. In the seventh round Leonard befuddled Britton with a crushing right which sent the welterweight reeling off balance in the last minute of the round, but Britton protected himself against assault until the bell.

Through the ninth and tenth rounds Britton, returning to the attack, carried off the honors. His work, as in his previous favorable rounds, was consistent and untiring while Leonard fought only in flashes.

Leonard had his best round in the eleventh, which, by the same token, was Britton's worst. The lightweight champion, with a succession of left hooks to the jaw, started soon after the bell beginning the round to hammer Britton into submission.

Leonard almost succeeded. Three sharp left hooks in rapid fire order sent Britton staggering and back against the ropes in a neutral corner. The welterweight champion was in distress, on the verge of a knockdown and possibly a knockout, and the crowd was in an uproar urging Leonard on to a knockout victory. Leonard leaped into the attack willingly, but as Britton covered instinctively, the lightweight champion was wild with a shower of swishing rights and lefts aimed at the jaw of the almost helpless welterweight champion.

Leonard stepped back suddenly and began boxing at long range, but the lightweight champion was too cautious in this situation and Britton recovered quickly. Just before the bell Leonard suddenly leaped in with another vicious outburst which carried Britton before it to the ropes, but the bell sounded without any damage being accomplished by the lightweight champion.

Britton Recovers from Attack.

Britton's seconds worked industriously over the welterweight champion during intermission between rounds and Britton responded to the bell for the twelfth apparently fully recovered. Leonard reverted to his cautious style in this session and was outboxed and outfought by Britton. The welterweight champion forced matters continuously and landed several times with rights and lefts which grazed Leonard's jaw. Leonard missed the majority of his punches while others were blocked by Britton or thrown off the the welterweight champion's attack.

In the thirteenth round honors were about evenly divided, until the sudden ending almost in midring. Britton was forcing matters. Leonard was holding his own with a retaliatory assault in which he gave blow for blow with the welterweight champion. Catching Britton's guard up, Leonard suddenly leaped in during the last half minute with a ripping left hook for the body.

The punch landed and Britton went down on one knee with pain written on his face and his left arm signalling wildly to referee Patsey Haley, who stood shaking his head negatively, apparently preparing to count. Then Leonard leaped in with a left to the face, and the disqualification followed.

In the semi-final bout scheduled for twelve rounds, Eddie Fitzsimmons, Yorkville southpaw, knocked out Sam Mossberg, former international amateur lightweight champion, in 1 minute 9 seconds of the first round. Johnny Coney and Jack Stark, local featherweights, boxed a draw in a six-round bout. In the first bout, a four-round contest, Joey Leonard, brother of the lightweight champion, won the decision over Sammy Marco.

June 27, 1922

LYNCH KNOCKS OUT BUFF IN THE 14TH

Former World's Bantamweight Champion Regains Title in Velodrome Before 18,000.

TOWEL THROWN IN THE RING

Round Lasts Only Six Seconds When Jerseyman's Seconds Acknowledge Defeat.

LOSER SEVERELY BEATEN

Puts Up a Game Fight, Refusing Referee's Plea to Give In at End of Thirteenth.

Joe Lynch regained the bantamweight championship of the world at the New York Velodrome last night when Johnny Buff's seconds threw the towel into the ring after six seconds of fighting in the fourteenth round. It was just a year ago this month that Lynch had returned the title to Pete Herman only to have the latter lose it last September to Johnny Buff.

The end was not unexpected. Lynch had had the better of every round. He had jabbed and punched Buff all around the ring until the champion's face was bruised and swollen and blood was streaming from his mouth and nose. Several of his teeth had been knocked out and his left eye was closed.

From the fifth round on it was simply a question of how long his handlers would defer acknowledging defeat by throwing in the towel. That he was game and that he assimilated a world of punishment will be attested by the 18,000 who were in the Velodrome to see the fight. At the end of the thirteenth round Buff was led groggy to his corner, but refused the referee's plea to have the fight stopped.

Lynch's victory was not treated with the wild acclaim that was anticipated should he succeed in his quest of the title. There was some cheering and a few of his more enthusiastic followers tried to climb into the ring to shake his hand, but it was scarcely the demonstration that would be expected following such a remarkable come-back.

It seemed that many in the crowd, even many of those who had backed Lynch to win, could scarcely find the spirit to cheer the newly-found champion in view of the game but hopeless battle that Buff had waged from the clang of the first round.

As the result of the bout Lynch's name will go down in pugilistic history along side of Stanley Ketchel, Pete Herman and the few others who have succeeded in regaining their championships once the crowns had been lifted from their heads.

It was the history of nature repeating itself last night. It was the case of a good little man losing to a larger one. Lynch had all the physical advantages. He weighed 117¼ pounds against Buff's 113½. He is three inches taller than his opponent from Jersey City, but the difference seemed even greater when they met in the ring.

The advantage in reach, too, was Lynch's. And last, but far from being least, there was a great difference in age. It was a young man of 23 fighting against a man of 34, and 34 is old as they measure age in pugilism. It was the old story of youth being served.

Lynch is Buff's Master.

That Lynch is Buff's master he convincingly demonstrated. He is a much superior boxer and a far more finished ring general. He fought a cool, well planned battle from the start. He was deliberate in his actions, and never once made a mistake of trying to finish the battle in a hurry. It seemed that after the first he realized that he was Buff's master, and he elected to fight a waiting battle rather than to take unnecessary chances.

It was his dazzling left hand jab that won the fight for Lynch. It had Buff completely baffled. The New Jersey boxer had no defense for it, and as a result he was subjected to merciless jabbing throughout every round he was in the ring. All that Buff had were two wild swings—his left and his right. He tried repeatedly to score with them, but except on rare occasions he was unable to land on his rival.

Lynch repeatedly ducked or blocked or retaliated with the damaging straight left and right crosses that continually had Buff in distress.

There were no clean knockdowns until the one in the fourteenth round. Lynch staggered Buff in the sixth round and Johnny slipped to one knee in the tenth, but he was up quickly without taking the count.

When the boxers left the ring Lynch did not carry a scar of the battle. Buff on the other hand was compelled to sit in his corner for several minutes before his weary legs could carry his bruised body to his dressing room.

The first preliminary was between

Murray Bresner, who weighed 113¾ pounds, and Willie O'Connel, who weighed 117. It was a four-round bout and the decision was given to O'Connell, who gained a clear lead on points.

The second preliminary was a six-round bout betw n Harry Brown of Philadelphia and Johnny Drummie of Jersey City. It went the limit, with Brown earning the decision by a clean-cut margin. Brown weighed 132¼ and Drummie weighed 134 pounds.

The semifinal was a scheduled twelve-round bout between Frankie Jerome of the Bronx and Jack Wolfe of Cleveland. Both boys weighed 120 pounds. Jerome was given the decision. He won by the proverbial mile. But it was a real battle that will be long remembered by those who saw it. After being floored eleven times during the bout, Wolfe was still fighting at the bell in the twelfth round. He was groggy and punch drunk, but the fighting instinct was still alive.

Wolfe was knocked down seven times in the first round. On each occasion he refused to take the count. He was floored again in the second and again and again he refused to take a count. In the seventh a glancing right to the chin sent the Cleveland boy to the canvas, but, as before, he refused to listen to a count.

In the ninth Wolfe once more was toppled over. The last time he went down was in the eleventh round, when a right swing dropped him for the count of seven. And yet he got in the last punch of the bout, driving a right to Jerome's body just as the bell sounded in the twelfth round.

Daylight When Crowd Begins to Arrive.

It was still broad daylight when the crowd began arriving. Thousands of motor cars were parked within a radius of a mile of the Velodrome but when the first preliminary was put on there were still nundreds of vacancies on the embankments and in the reserve sections. It was evident that the regulars who had purchased their reserved tickets in advance were delayed in getting into the Velodrome by the congestion outside. However, there was a steady influx of people, and by the time the main bout was on it was estimated that upward of 18,000 persons were in the Velodrome.

Most of the spectators were parked in the reserved section. Vacant seats were high up the track, where the cycle kings hold forth. There were blotches of these and it was evident that many who would have been at the bout had been frightened away, fearing they would have no chance to get seats at the last moment. They had figured without taking into consideration the vastness of the big arena.

Once more was Tex Rickard, the promoter, favored with fine weather. The temperature was such as to be just right for spectators and boxers. Fans were surplus luggage and the men in the ring were forced to extend themselves before working up a real sweat.

July 11, 1922

LEONARD OUTPOINTS TENDLER BEFORE A CROWD OF 60,000

Boxing Fans Pay More Than $450,00C to See No-Decision Bout in Jersey City.

CHAMPION HARD PRESSED

Challenger Wins First Five of the Twelve Rounds, but Victor Rallies Near End.

BOUT FINANCIAL SUCCESS

Rickard's Share of the Gate Receipts $153,750, Leonard's $191,-250 and Tendler's $90,000.

Benny Leonard is still lightweight champion of the world. In the big wooden arena at Boyle's Thirty Acres in Jersey City last night the champion outpointed the leading contender for his title, Lew Tendler of Philadelphia. It was a battle that will long be remembered by the 60,000 who witnessed Tendler's futile effort to try to pluck the crown that Leonard has worn since 1917.

Referees' decisions are not permitted in New Jersey and Leonard's victory was won by popular verdict.

The bout was one of the biggest money producers in the history of the American ring. Estimates show that about $450,000 was paid in admissions. Of this Leonard got 42½ per cent. or $191,250, while Tendler received 20 per cent. or $90,000. The expenses of Tex Rickard, who promoted the bout, are put at $15,000, exclusive of the fighters' shares, leaving a net profit to the promoter of approximately $153,750.

Leonard's victory was by the scantest of margins, so close, in fact, that had it not been for a whirlwind finish in the twelfth and final round, Tendler must have been accorded at least a draw, and might have been credited with the popular decision. Of the twelve rounds each had six. The first five were all Tendler's, and it seemed at that time as if the champion were doomed to lose by popular verdict if he were fortunate enough to avoid being knocked out. In the sixth he showed the first flash of the form that made him champion and has repeatedly turned back ambitious aspirants to the title. In the seventh it was the Leonard of old once again, but in the eighth Tendler crashed a vicious left to Leonard's jaw that caused Benny's knees to sag, and for a moment made it appear that the champion was about to be stretched on the canvas.

Leonard Gets Going.

That was the last flash in the pan for Tendler. It was the last time he could claim any superiority over his opponent for, starting in the ninth round through the tenth, eleventh and twelfth, Leonard treated the Quaker to a severe drubbing. At the end of the bout both boxers were bleeding profusely. Leonard's left eye was swollen and cut. He had lost a tooth in the fifth round and blood spurted from his mouth. He had a lump alongside of his right eye. It was a champion who had expended every ounce of energy in his perfectly trained body that returned to his corner when the final gong wrote finis to the affair. On the other hand Tendler's nose was bleeding and tiny crimson streams trickled from the corners of his mouth—mute but convincing attestations of the damage wrought by the viciously delivered lefts and rights with which Leonard had peppered him.

With the closing gong there was no wild demonstration. The thousands who sat in the inky blackness, that was lightened only by the glare of the lights over the ring, seemed stunned. A majority had gone to the fight convinced that Leonard was in a class by himself; that Tendler was little more than a lamb being led to the slaughter and sacrificed to the king. Those thousands were treated to a shocking surprise. They were treated to the same surprise that Leonard was, and that was the greatest surprise in Leonard's career. Benny met a tartar when he met Tendler. None in the vast throng that rose tier upon tier away from the ringside into the disappearing darkness of those top seats which seemed a mile away can declare that Tendler was unworthy of the champion's steel. Tendler fought a great fight. So did Leonard. Leonard had to. The easy romp that Leonard may have expected when he made the pre-battle prediction that he would knock out Tendler inside of seven rounds developed into a veritable beehive of boxing gloves. Never before in Leonard's career since he has been champion has he suffered as much punishment. He was battered about the body and about the head for the first five rounds. It was an extremely worried champion who struggled to solve the puzzling style of his southpaw opponent.

Tendler's Style a Puzzle.

Tendler's peculiar style of boxing with his right hand and right foot extended furnished a serious problem for Leonard. He could do nothing with his famous straight left jab, and the snappy right cross on which he was counting to lay Tendler low was practically useless. On the other hand, Tendler worked his left with great precision and effectiveness. He sunk it into Leonard's body and whipped it to Leonard's jaw repeatedly. These blows shook the champion from the top of his head to the soles of his boxing shoes. Then came the turning of the tide.

Leonard, realizing that he was being badly beaten, unleashed an attack he has seldom before been forced to display. He fought with viciousness that almost amounted to desperation. He rushed in and swung wildly, frequently missing with both left and rights, but landing often enough to pile up the points in his favor and to discount what Tendler had been able to accomplish during those early rounds.

It was this that made last night's bout in its picturesque setting at Jersey City one of the best lightweight battles that has been seen in the last decade. And battle is the word. It was anything but a boxing exhibition. It can better be described by calling it a slugfest, for throughout in the majority of the rounds these rivals of several years' standing stood toe to toe and traded blows.

Leonard Down and Up.

There were no knockdowns, but in the fourth round Leonard missed a vicious right swing and slipped to his knees. There was no count taken, for he was up immediately. In the first round Tendler had slipped to the floor without any persuasion from a blow. He, too, was up immediately and back into the fray, waiting only long enough to wipe the rosin from his gloves. While both boxers were frequently severely jarred by blows, at no time did a knockout seem imminent, unless it was in that eighth round when Tendler caused Leonard's knees to sag with a powerful left swing to the jaw.

Before the bout the consensus of opinion was that Leonard was much the superior boxer; that Tendler was chiefly a slugger, one who could assimilate punishment and a wicked puncher with his left hand. The bout proved that the estimation of Tendler was correct, but his peculiar style prevented Leonard from displaying any of the brilliant cleverness of hands and feet that usually features his work. Instead he was compelled to change his style and fight Tendler at Lew's style. He was compelled to slug, and slug he did. He literally slugged his way to victory.

As the two boxers entered the ring, Tendler first, clad in a greenish gray bathrobe, and Leonard a few seconds later in a faded old rose robe, the champion appeared to be drawn. It was evident that the effort of making the weight, 135 pounds, at 2 o'clock in the afternoon, taxed him sorely. There was a pallor on his fact that even outdoor training could not remove.

Tendler, on the other hand, appeared robust and in prime condition. How close was the shade for Leonard in the matter of making weight was shown by the fact that he weighed 134 pounds and 15 ounces, just one ounce under the prescribed weight. Tendler weighed 134¾. For weeks in advance of the fight, stories had been circulated about the ill-feeling that existed between Leonard and Tendler. This ill-feeling was evident throughout the battle.

Leonard repeatedly appealed to the referee about Tendler's blows being low and several times Harry Ertle, the third man in the ring, warned the Philadelphian to be more careful. Tendler made some very caustic remarks and invariably they drew a sharp reply.

These verbal passages became more brisk and were almost continuous during the closing rounds, but when the final bell sounded, they shook hands, patted each other on the back and stood talking for a full half minute in the centre of the ring. That was the end.

Unlike a year ago on a sultry July afternoon, when Jack Dempsey and Georges Carpentier met in this same arena before a seething mass of 88,000 human beings, the crowd which invaded the precincts of Jersey City was slow in arriving. There was no early rush on the stadium. Those who held reserved seats placed implicit confidence in the arrangements that Tex Rickard had made to assure each ticket holder of getting the seat his coupon called for.

Past experiences had taught them that there was no occasion to rush pell-mell to the scene. But those who were less fortunate—those who possessed admission tickets only—were early on the spot, and just as soon as the gates were thrown open to the vast reaches high up in the rear of the amphitheatre there was a mad rush.

But it was only for an instant, for the vastness of the arena soon swallowed its meal of humanity, and for the remainder of the time until the last preliminary had been staged the influx, while steady, was nothing approaching an onslaught. The fans came in groups—groups that numbered hundreds—but looked small in comparison to the bigness of Rickard's show place.

The drab twilight was still battling against the approach of the blackness of an overcast night when the arena began to fill up. Slowly, but nevertheless surely, the yawning blocks of vacant seats began to be transformed into living sectors of buzzing fans. The hours that preceded the first preliminary were spent by the populace in fighting the fight in advance with its chins. More vocal knockouts were scored than have ever been registered with leather-encased fists. There were arguments galore, but, for the most part, the crowd was orderly, and the hundreds of policemen stationed inside the bowl experienced little difficulty in maintaining order. It might easily have been a drawing room reception.

Women were liberally sprinkled in the vast throng. From the ringside back and up through the sharply rising tiers of seats the inevitable feminine lent color and tone to the gathering. In spite of the dire threats of the weather man to turn on his sprinklers and water the mushroomlike city, femininity came, as femininity always does, scintillating colors and sparkling with beauty. Thus has boxing progressed. But a few short years ago woman had no place at a boxing bout. If one or two condescended to attend their presence aroused almost as much interest as the principal bout itself. But now Mrs. and Miss Fan are just as much a part of the boxing melting pot as are fathers and sons. As one veteran ringsider remarked, "It's part of the equal rights movement and it's welcome."

By the time twilight had turned to murky dusk the most of those who held choice seats were in them, and the struggle for vantage points far upon the outer rim of the saucer had ceased. These vantage places were all gone, and late arrivals had no choice but to take the leavings.

It was just 7 o'clock when the big arc lights that skirted the back of the arena were turned on. They looked extremely pale and weak in the dwindling daylight, but as the shadows increased they sparkled forth and shed a welcome glare to help the police and ushers guide late comers to their places.

Four additional lights had been placed in each aisle, and dull red bulbs indicated the exits.

While battling went on in the ring, another battle was being fought aloft. Hovering threateningly above drab clouds frowned, and the presence of an umbrella gave a soothing feeling of preparedness. But clear weather maintained a grim fight. Jupiter Pluvius was mustering his forces, and many were the anxious glances that were turned aloft.

The bout preceding the Leonard-Tendler event, which had been scheduled for ten rounds, was ordered stopped at the end of the seventh round. This was done because of the threatening aspect of the weather and to get the lightweight champion and his challenger in the ring that much earlier to guard against the threatened rain putting a stop to the chief bout.

Mayor Hague and the Police and Fire Department officials had made elaborate arrangements for handling the crowd both inside and outside the stadium. Inside policemen were stationed around the ringside, in each of the aisles, at all of the runways leading from the entrances, at the entrances, and they were scattered around the rail fences that separated the different sections.

In addition Rickard had imported his usual staff from Madison Square Garden to act as ushers and guards and to assist the police in handling the crowds within the arena. There were 700 of them.

In spite of the alertness of the police and the ushers, shortly before the first preliminary was staged the thousands in the two-dollar seats crashed into the three-dollar sections. There was a rush for a moment or two, when the thousands that were in the dollar sections hurdled the fence into the five-dollar seats. But the rush was over by the time that the thirty-four big lights over the ring were turned on and Announcer Joe Humphreys introduced the principals in the first preliminary. As Humphreys was making his announcement the buzzing of thousands of throats ceased and a dead silence reigned. By that time all of the good seats were filled, and the only vacant bleachers that showed were far back in the cheaper sections. It was still daylight when the first preliminary started.

Just before Leonard and Tendler entered the ring Tex Rickard announced that he estimated the crowd at 60,000 persons and that he figured the total receipts would be in excess of $450,000. To those seated at the ringside it seemed that more than 60,000 were present, but, of course, in the darkness that blanketed the reaches beyond the pale of the glow of the ringside lights it was impossible to see just how many vacant seats there were away back.

July 28, 1922

DUNDEE WINS BY KNOCKOUT IN 9TH

Finishes Frush With Left Hook to Stomach in Bout for Featherweight Title.

END COMES SUDDENLY

Unexpected Victory of Italian Sends 13,000 at Ebbets Field Into a Frenzy.

LOSER DOWN IN EIGHTH

Takes Count of Nine in That Round —Out Fifty Seconds After Start of the Next.

Johnny Dundee, veteran of a dozen years of fighting and hundreds of hard ring bouts, surprised a crowd of about 13,000 persons last night at Ebbets Field, Brooklyn, when he knocked out Danny Frush, Cleveland featherweight, in the ninth round of their scheduled fifteen-round bout. A left hook to the pit of the stomach, a punch which carried all the driving power of Dundee's splendidly muscled body back of it, curled Frush up in a ludicrous position on the ring canvas just fifty seconds after the ninth round started.

The unexpected knockout by the supposedly weak-hitting Italian came with the suddenness of a clap of thunder. The victory sent the crowd into a frenzy and Dundee was carried from the ringside on the shoulders of an excited squad of admirers who fought each other for the privilege.

With the victory went the featherweight championship title of Johnny Kilbane, which was declared vacated by the State Athletic Commission on Kilbane's refusal to defend the title against Dundee, who had challenged. The championship atmosphere in this bout was similar to that which existed Monday night last in the contest between Dave Rosenberg and Phil Krug. There was this difference between the two matches, however —where Rosenberg hardly measured up to the standard of a champion, Dundee exhibited all the qualifications of a title holder.

His latest victory gives Dundee two titles. He holds the 130-pound championship belt, which he won when he was awarded a victory on a foul over George (K. O.) Chaney in a bout at Madison Square Garden last season. Through his latest triumph Dundee will be recognized by the State Athletic Commission as the featherweight champion. The Italian veteran now aspires to the lightweight title held by Benny Leonard, and has challenged for the last-named championship.

Nobody Expected a Knockout.

Seldom has such a ring surprise been witnessed in local boxing as this latest triumph of the battle-scarred Dundee. The Italian veteran, notorious for his weak hitting, was the favorite over Frush before the battle started. With his great store of experience, he was figured to outpoint and outbox the Clevelander, but not one in the great gathering, no matter how optimistic, anticipated a knockout victory for Dundee.

Dundee's knockout was presaged in the eighth round. The fiery little Italian in this session shocked the crowd when he floored Frush for a count of nine with a succession of lefts and rights to the jaw, following a wicked left hook to the stomach. The left to the stomach made Frush gasp, and must have paralyzed Frush, for the Clevelander could throw up no defense for the fusillade of blows which followed, and crumpled under a powerful right to the jaw.

Frush survived the storm after regaining his feet, but he got no chance for rest in the ninth. Dundee was on top of his rival with the clang of the gong and with a left to the mouth sent Frush's head back. Frush sought to throw up a defense as he retreated, but Dundee, with victory in sight, was not to be denied. Like an enraged bull, the Italian leaped in with a fiery assault and had Frush backing groggily about the ring under a shower of rights and lefts to the jaw.

Dundee suddenly stopped in his frantic assault and, stepping back, leaped in like a flash with a clean, powerful right to the jaw which made Frush stagger drunkenly about the ring. Frush backed uncertainly before Dundee's punching tirade, but when he got his rival near the ropes Dundee suddenly lurched forward and threw all his strength into a vicious left dig to the stomach.

Frush Sinks to Canvas.

Frush collapsed under the impact of the blow and sank to the canvas as lifeless as a soggy rag. The Clevelander took the count in a half sitting posture, resting on his left elbow, and with his gloved right hand hanging limply over the lower ring rope, as completely immovable as if he had been felled by a right from the fist of Jack Dempsey. Then the crowd let loose a roar which re-echoed through Flatbush.

Up to the knockout Dundee was complete master of his rival. Frush, reported to be a clever boxer and an accurate hard hitter, showed no indication of these ring essentials. Dundee, fighting almost solely with one hand—his left—left-handed Frush to death, to use the vernacular.

Frush was completely baffled by the speed, cleverness and ring generalship of Dundee and was overwhelmed when the Italian brought into play some of the spectacular stunts for which he is famous.

With his superb demonstration of boxing ability, Dundee earned every round of the battle, as far as it went, with the lone exception of the third. In this round Frush, in a short-lived recovery, outboxed and outhit Dundee. Frush's winning efforts, however, were confined to the third. The Clevelander was on the defensive for the remainder of the fight and was clearly excelled in every department of boxing by the wily Dundee.

In the first two rounds, and in every round after the third up to the ninth, Dundee's work was similar. He traded left jabs with his rival and invariably beat Frush to the punch. Tiring of this, Dundee, bounding in and out and catapulting himself off the ropes, would leap in with a left hook for the face, which seldom missed the mark. Occasionally Dundee would rip his left to the body, and in what little in-fighting there was Dundee outpunched his rival clearly.

Dundee Staggers Rival.

Dundee boxed like the veteran he is in the first, second and fourth rounds, and repeatedly landed past Frush's guard with a left hook to the jaw and face. In the fifth Dundee rocked his rival with a terrific left hook to the jaw, and the Italian leaped in with a furious assault in an attempt to finish his rival, while the crowd vociferously urged Dundee on.

Frush survived the storm, however, and was subjected to a continuance of the left-handed cuffing by Dundee until the eighth, when Dundee startled the crowd by driving Frush to the ropes with a wicked left hook to the stomach. Dundee followed this up with rapid-fire lefts and rights to the jaw, and Frush fell under the impact of the blows. It was the beginning of the end for Frush. Dundee applied the finishing touches in the next round, the ninth.

August 16, 1922

NEW WELTERWEIGHT KING IS CROWNED

Walker Gets Decision Over Britton in Furious 15-Round Battle at Garden.

CHAMPION THRICE DOWNED

Takes Count of Seven in Tenth Session and Another of Nine in the Twelfth.

CLOSE TO A KNOCKOUT

Victor Overwhelms Opponent in Last Six Rounds and Wins 12 of 15 —All Bets Declared Off.

A crowd of about 15,000 persons saw a stirring pugilistic drama enacted last night at Madison Square Garden when Jack Britton of Clinton, N. Y., was shorn of his world's welterweight title, after a spectacular fifteen-round bout, by Mickey Walker of Elizabeth, N. J., who only recently had attained a place of prominence in the ranks of Britton's numerous rivals. After a battle that was replete with thrills, crowded with exciting moments and tense situations, Judges Tommy Shortell and D. W. Dingey and Referee Patsey Haley cast the decision for the young New Jersey boxer, and thus crowned a new world's champion.

There was no doubt as to the winner, and, when the final bell clanged, the crowd was prepared for the announcement by Joe Humphries. Britton was beaten and beaten badly. He was entitled to only three of the fifteen rounds. Twelve went to Walker. Only indomitable will power, with a remarkable store of experience accumulated in his long years of ring service, saved Britton from the crushing humiliation of losing his title in a knockout defeat. Wildness in Walker's attack at critical moments also helped to save the champion from a knockout.

Britton went down with colors flying. He fought desperately to the last ditch. Floored three times for clean knockdowns in the course of the battle, Britton regained his feet on each occasion and arose only to be battered from pillar to post, under a furious onslaught by his younger, speedier and more strenuous rival. Britton was on the verge of a knockout in every round after the tenth. He had spent his strength in the futile attempt to forestall Walker's vicious assaults with his own superb boxing skill, but, distinctive as is this skill of Britton, it gained him nothing as far as results were concerned, save preventing his inglorious defeat by a knockout.

Youth Is Once More Served.

The battle brought forth one more proof that youth must be served. Britton is 37 years old and has been boxing for eighteen years in a career which started back in 1904, when Walker was just 2 years old. Britton won the world's title in March, 1919, when he knocked out Ted Kid Lewis in the ninth round of a battle at Canton, Ohio. Since that date Britton has defended his title on numerous occasions in various parts of the country. He was spending his energy and strength with each succeeding bout, and last night Britton showed that he had little but boxing skill with which to withstand the spirited, determined, two-fisted fire of his rival.

Walker impressed the large gathering greatly. He showed willingness, untiring aggressiveness and punching strength. But, without in the least detracting from the showing of the new champion he is no Jack Britton, considering Jack at his best. He has little cleverness, and depends on his natural strength.

Disquieting reports, circulated prior to the start of the bout, were proved, in the opinion of the majority, unfounded. Britton was a favorite in the afternoon at betting odds of 3 to 1, but the pendulum of speculation swung sharply to Walker's favor in the evening, until, before entering the ring, the Jerseyman was a favorite at odds of 2 to 1. This sudden switch in the betting, combined with the general knowledge of Britton's boxing skill and ring ability, overwhelming as compared with Walker's, caused suspicion to be cast on the genuineness of the contest. Before the bout started, and under instruction from Chairman William Muldoon of the State Athletic Commission, who was a ringside spectator, Joe Humphries declared all bets off in the following words: "If any person or persons have bet on this contest, I wish to announce, on behalf of the New York State Athletic Commission and the management of this athletic club, that all bets are hereby called off."

Cheers for Defeated Champion.

The crowd demonstrated, however, that it was thoroughly satisfied that Britton had met his conqueror in Walker. A tragic figure in his defeat, after the decision was announced, Britton was pulled to the centre of the ring by Announcer Humphries, who called on the hushed crowd for "three cheers for the greatest champion who ever lost a title." Even before Humphries had completed his request the cheers started, and gained in volume until the sides of Madison Square Garden trembled. Britton took the acclaim, as he had taken his ring laurels, modestly. He was assisted out of the ring and slowly made his way through the great crowd, whose every member seemed anxious to pat him on the back as a token of appreciation for a game stand. Walker, jubilant as a schoolboy, was carried from the ring shoulder high by enthusiastic supporters.

The demonstration for victor and vanquished was justified. Walker emerged triumphant from a stirring struggle. Britton gave of his best in a losing struggle for the greater part of the fifteen rounds.

Britton was floored in the second, tenth and twelfth rounds. The bell came to his rescue in the tenth session. Britton was on his knees, dazed and weary, taking the count, when the bell clanged as the count of seven was tolled off. The knockdowns in the second and twelfth came near the middle of both sessions and Britton was hard pressed to survive on both occasions.

Walker's terrific left hand assault won the battle for him. Walker ripped and slashed into Britton's stomach early in the bout with an attack which sapped the latter's strength, and the Jerseyman had the faculty of bringing the left up to Britton's face and jaw in a sustained attack which made Britton dizzy and dazed as the bout progressed, and for which the champion had no defense, despite his remarkable cleverness.

First Round Is Walker's.

The crowd was astonished and thrown into a frenzy in the very first round Britton missed repeatedly and was stung several times by Walker's terrific punches. Britton missed a left hook soon after the start and staggered under the impact of a return left hook from Walker. Again Britton missed with his left and then, for a third time, he fell short with this punch. On each occasion Walker connected with that wicked left hook to the jaw and rendered Britton groggy. A spirited fire of rights and lefts to the stomach contributed to Britton's unhappy state.

Walker landed his left hook to the jaw in a sensational exchange in the second round and floored Britton. The blow landed as Britton was partly off balance and spun him around and into Walker's corner. Britton rested on his hands and knees until Walker was pushed aside. Then Britton jumped up without the formality of a count.

Britton appeared like his old self in the third, fourth and fifth rounds. He boxed with consummate skill, evidently supremely confident, and had Walker missing continually. Britton took the honors of these three rounds, the only sessions he won. He made Walker fight the way he wanted him to, inveigled the challenger into leads which left him open for a crack from the right or left in a brilliant demonstration of boxing skill, but Britton was blowing plainly in the fifth round. He had quite evidently exerted his last bit of offensive strength. Walker went to the attack again in the sixth session and through the remainder of the battle pounded Britton almost at will. Left digs to the stomach and lefts and rights to the face and jaw forced Britton to the defensive in the seventh round, Britton's nose bled from the pounding, and several times in the eighth and ninth, Walker almost upset Britton.

Britton was getting wearier as the bout progressed and fell to holding in the clinches and taking every opportunity to create a clinch. He was frequently driven to the ropes and crouched low in an attempt to guard his stomach and jaw.

In the tenth round Walker pressed Britton hard. He had the defending champion on a steady retreat. In a closing rally in Britton's corner Walker drove his man to the ropes and crashed over a terrific right to the jaw. Britton crumpled in his corner and was on a bended knee, taking a count of seven when the bell ended the round. The gong saved Britton. He was weary when he toed the scratch for the eleventh, despite the frantic efforts of his handlers to restore his scattered senses. As Walker tore in Britton sought to outbox him, but the attempt was futile. Walker was not to be denied. Twice Britton slipped to his hands and knees as he missed leads with the left. A wicked left hook to the stomach in the twelfth session sent Britton down for a count of nine.

The champion, on the verge of defeat, was game and courageous. He struggled to his feet and clinched tenaciously, but Walker fought him off and strove mightily for a knockout. This was denied the Jerseyman, despite the terrific battering to which he subjected Britton in the three closing sessions, when the now thoroughly beaten champion, robbed of his last vestige of strength, fought solely on boxing resourcefulness and ring generalship.

Eddie Fitzsimmons, southpaw welterweight of Yorkville, and Sailor Friedman of Chicago were the combatants in the semi-final bout scheduled for twelve rounds. Friedman weighed 146 pounds and Fitzsimmons 137¾. Friedman knocked out Fitzsimmons in the sixth round after 2 minutes 5 seconds of action.

Following the knockout of Fitzsimmons, Rickard provided the crowd with an extra six-round bout before the championship event. Andy O'Boyle, former amateur, and Farmer Sullivan of Greenwich Village, welterweights, were the principals. O'Boyle got the decision.

Billy Mascott, California bantamweight, and Johnny Gannon battled on even terms in the opening encounter of four rounds. In the second bout, a six-round clash, Red Cap Wilson, Yonkers lightweight, and Jimmy Goodrich of Buffalo were the principals. Goodrich gained the decision after an exciting session.

November 2, 1922

DEMPSEY WHIPS FIRPO IN SECOND ROUND OF FIERCEST OF HEAVYWEIGHT BATTLES; 90,000 IN POLO GROUNDS, 25,000 RIOT OUTSIDE

FIRPO FELLED TEN TIMES

Champion Downed Twice and Punched Through Ropes at Outset.

CROWD IS SPORTSMANLIKE

Argentine Receives Striking Tribute of Cheers and Prolonged Handclapping.

RECEIPTS ARE $1,250,000

Dempsey's Share Is $468,750, and About $156,250 Will Go to the Challenger.

In the shortest and fiercest battle ever fought between heavyweights, Jack Dempsey last night knocked out Luis Angel Firpo before a crowd of 90,000 people at the Polo Grounds 57 seconds after the second round began.

But no champion ever had a closer call. In the first round, after Firpo had gone down seven times, one of his long, smashing rights caught Dempsey fairly and knocked him clear through the ropes. The champion's head disappeared over the edge of the ring, his white-clad legs shot up in the air, and it seemed that a new world's champion was about to enter into his glory.

On the count of nine, Dempsey managed to stagger back into the ring, but the end of the round found him obviously badly shaken, and staggering as he had never staggered before.

To the spectators at the ringside it looked as if Dempsey was all gone, but his heart and his head were still there, and enough punching power to carry him through to victory in the second round. Firpo's right was too slow to reach the champion, who was striking in with all his power. He caught Firpo with a right and put him down. Two seconds later the challenger was up but a moment more and Dempsey had him down again for the count of five.

Dempsey Instantly Upon Him.

Once more the "Wild Bull of the Pampas" staggered to his feet, but Dempsey was on him instantly, caught him with a left to the jaw and then toppled him with a right as he sank. Bleeding slightly at the mouth, the huge brown man from the Argentine turned slowly over, striving vainly to rise as the referee's pumping arm marked the counts of eight and nine, and stiffened helplessly as the tenth count ended his championship hopes for the time.

In less than four minutes of fighting the champion had been knocked down twice and the challenger ten times. From the first instant the fight had been a fight, a fierce exchange of wallops unbroken by any strategic manoeuvres. Dempsey won because he could hit faster and oftener, but above all because he could keep going and cash in on his advantages when he had them.

As for Firpo, he is not champion this morning by the slimmest of margins, but those who saw him fight last night were not inclined to predict that he never will be champion. He put up a terrific fight and at the end of the first round had ninety thousand more or less patriotic fans practically resigned to the loss of the championship. After the fight Firpo complained that he hadn't got an even break from Referee Jimmy Gallagher.

Firpo asserted that Gallahgher had warned the fighters before the bout began that after a knockdown the man on his feet must move away to a neutral corner. Dempsey, he protested, stood over him and was on him instantly when he got off the canvas.

Dempsey Fought With His Head.

Whatever the justice in this complaint, there is no doubt that Dempsey won because he fought with his head as well as with hands and Firpo had nothing but his hands and his courage. The question as to whether the Argentine fighter can "take it" is answered. He took a worse hammering even than Jess Willard took at Toledo, and if his brain had been as quick as his arm was powerful he would have survived it to win. He can also "give it."

But Dempsey outweighed by twenty-four pounds, shorter and with less reach, won because he had a super-fighting brain and a coolness which enabled him to hang on when everything seemed lost and to use all his powers in the desperate and successful effort to hold his time.

Firpo has at least a certain consolation in his 12½ per cent of the gate receipts. Promoter Tex Rickard, who always puts on a good show and always brings out the customers, reported that the ticket sale amounted to $1,250,000. Of this Dempsey got $468,750. and the challenger's share will come to about $156,250, not to mention the incidental profits of moving pictures.

85,800 Paid Admissions.

There were 85,800 paid admissions, and police, firemen, ushers, newspaper men, telegraph operators, refreshment vendors and so on will probably raise the total to 90,000, a figure surpassed only by the Willard-Firpo fight in the history of prize fighting. The receipts fell short of the $1,600,000 brought in by the Dempsey-Carpentier fight only because of the limit imposed in this state on the price of the ringside seats.

What might have happened had Dempsey utilized his superior boxing ability to stand off and take few chances until he had felt out Firpo no one can say. But he didn't do that. Realizing that most of his followers expected him to get in and fight he rushed in furiously at the sound of the bell, and partly slipping, partly caught by one of Firpo's smashes, he dropped to one knee before the round was five seconds old. Yet he still stuck to his aggressive tactics and thereby showed the crowd that both he and Firpo were better men than anybody knew. It is a rare fight which enables both victor and vanquished to feel that they have surpassed themselves all in the space of three minutes and fifty-seven seconds.

Good Sportsmanship Shown.

In one other respect the fight offered a pleasant surprise. The display of bad sportsmanship which had been feared, in view of the way a Polo Grounds crowd hissed Eugene Criqui and the obvious hostility to Firpo displayed by the crowds which came to see him train at Atlantic City, was not in evidence. There were a few, a very few, boos and groans when announcer Joe Humphreys told the crowd that Firpo weighed 216½ pounds, 24 pounds more than Dempsey, but when Firpo came into the ring he was greeted with considerable applause, and when Humphreys introduced him he received the tribute of prolonged cheers and handclapping.

It was exactly the note that comes from a college crowd when it gets up to give the conventional rah-rah for the visiting football team before the game begins. It was, of course, far surpassed by the roar of applause for Dempsey a moment later. But, at least, it may and should have saved the North American reputation for sportsmanship, which had seemed in considerable danger of being visibly and disreputably lost. The crowd was for Dempsey, of course, except for a tiny minority of Latin Americans, and it was tremendously relieved and delighted when he won. How it would have received a victory by Firpo no one can say, but at least it lived up to its opportunities and behaved much better than some other crowds of recent memory.

Forty Thousand Watts of Light

At half-past 7 the lights were turned on in the stands, and shortly afterward the great battery of thousand-watt lamps, thirty-six white and four blue, to give a scientifically blended synthetic daylight, flooded the ring and showed the long, unending lines of customers streaming into the tier of upper and lower stands. Ringside seat-bolders were coming in by that time, and the lights showed the first scattering arrivals of women near the ring, goodlooking women too, these early comers, as Meleager said of Sappho's poems, only a few but roses. They had to be goodlooking to stand the harsh revealing glare of those ring lights.

Yet, though the unending lines of ticketholders filed in at every entrance, the arena did not seem more than half full when the first preliminary fighters stepped into the ring at 8 o'clock. It was a relief to the veterans of the long wait when the bell-like voice of Joe Humphreys, world's champion announcer, rang out over the click of telegraph instruments and portable typewriters and the insistent shuffling murmur of arriving feet, and announced that 415 pounds of British Empire beef, almost equally divided between Joe Bright of England and Louis Brown of Australia, would mix it up for six rounds.

Inside of a minute, however, the mother country was vindicated when Joe Bright flattened the representative of the Dominions for the count and the bloodthirsty crowd roared with elation and the first casualty of the evening.

This entitled the spectators to an extra, and Frankie Koebele, who has been dodging Firpo's slow swings in his Atlantic City camp, came into the ring for a four-round struggle with Charlie Nashert. When Koebele went down half way through the first round it

THE KNOCKOUT IN THE SECOND ROUND.

Wide World Photo.

looked optimistic for those who expected an evening of one-round finishes, but he got up again and proceeded to demonstrate that being Mr. Firpo's sparring partner is not the best sort of boxing practice.

Mr. Koebele lost the decision, being saved twice by the gong; giving meanwhile an exhibition of club swinging that greatly amused the crowd. The ancient Greeks in their dramatic festivals liked a whole day of tragedy topped off by a swift knockabout farce. Spectators who come in time for the preliminaries of a big championship fight seem to prefer the comedy first, and they were much delighted with this bout. It probably was not so funny to Mr. Koebele.

Mike Burke from Greenwich Village stood up against Al Roberts of Staten Island in the next contest. This one really was a contest and the rapid thump-bump of gloves on bodies held the crowd's attention despite the distracting drumming of an airplane circling over the stadium on its groundward side advertising one of the big tax companies. By this time the seats were nearly all occupied and 90,000 people shouted their approval of the vicarious bloodshed. Roberts, though cut to pieces, stayed to the end of the rounds and drew much applause from the sporting populace.

Then came the semi-final between Leo Gates, the Mohawk Indian strayed off the reservation and now resident in Harlem, and Bartley Madden of the west side. Each of them, in contrast to the preceding fighters, fulfilled the Poet Herrick's ideal of beauty in being white and hairless as an egg. But before the first round was over Gates, the noble red man, was getting pinked up about the eye. The Mohawks have gone back since the days of Joseph Brant, for Gates took a good deal of hammering in the twelve rounds. The populace paid little attention to the last round of the fight, for just as it began Luis Angel Firpo with an escort of policemen came down to the ringside and diverted everybody's attention. Half a minute later Dempsey entered, and after that nobody paid much attention to the end of the semi-final, or the expected decision in favor of Madden.

Crowd Waiting Two Hours.

Most of the crowd had been gathered in the Polo Grounds for nearly two hours, watching a series of preliminaries, when the fighters appeared during the last round of the semi-final, at 9:55. A cold wave, the first of Winter or the last of this wintry Summer as the case may be, had not chilled their anticipations, which had been whetted by some bloody fighting in one of the earlier preliminaries and then allowed to slump during the long-drawn-out and slowly fought semi-final. In the centre of the baseball diamond was the ring in which Bartley Madden was working through the last of twelve rounds to a decision over Leo Gates, a ring flooded with light from forty big lamps overhead, blended into something that is supposed to be as near like daylight as possi-

ble, though it was not much nearer than near-beer.

The flood of light from these lamps, swung from a network of wires sixteen feet above the floor of the ring, spread out in a slowly dimming circle over the rows of benches placed in the playing field, falling on masses of upturned faces, glinting back in a hundred double reflections from pairs of eyeglasses. Around the field on all sides rose a great eliptical mass, buried in darkness—the double grandstand of the Polo Grounds, packed with people, pitch black save for the feeble red lamps marking exits here and there and the firefly flashes of smokers matches sparking out for an instant here and there all over the blank wall.

Firpo Appears With Escort.

Peering into the blackness, one could see here, too, the faint double flash of glasses, blinking this way and that as spectators tried to see into other portions of the crowd rather than watch the dull proceedings in the ring.

Suddenly, a rippling cheer began in one corner of the grandstand and slowly progressed down one of the diagonal aisles toward the ring side. A file of policemen was moving toward the ring, and a step behind the leader a towering figure, brown-faced, with matted hair, Luis Angel Firpo, coming up for the fight in which most of the experts, and even most unprofessional observers, among whom this writer to his shame must be included, thought he hadn't the ghost of a chance.

Firpo Fierce in Approach.

A few steps behind him came the portly hulk of Dan Washington, his negro rubber, and clustering in the rear his three seconds, Hughie Gartland, Guillermo Widmer and Horatio Lavalle, the wealthy Argentine sportsman, who has been his right-hand man in preparation for the fight. The cheering grew as Firpo neared his corner, the southeastern one, and all over the stadium people stood up, despite the protesting cries of those behind them, to get a look at the man who had been called "the wild bull of the pampas," and who, according to the experts, had nothing to entitle him to the name but his looks.

He looked fierce and dangerous as he approached the ring. He always does. But he was frowning with a faraway, nervous, almost wistful look—the sort of look that comes over the face of even the least wistful of men as he prepares to get into the ring with Jack Dempsey. As he stopped outside the ring the unconsidered semi-final ended, and there was another and louder cheer, coming down from the grand stand, heralding the progress of the champion toward the ring of light.

Firpo a Troubled Giant.

Firpo climbed into his corner and sat down on the swinging stool wrapped in a dressing gown of big checks of black and lemon yellow, with cuffs and collar of a deep pur-

ple. It was in character like all of this strange man's habits. Whether intentionally or not, it fits into the public character he has built up for himself, opulent, exotic, and contrasting boldly with the simple white sweater wrapped around the champion's shoulders.

Beside this troubled giant Dempsey looked slight and boyish as he came into the ring in white silk trunks and white sweater, boyishly simple against the other's splendor. The moment he entered the ring he crossed quickly, smiling, to the challenger's corner and shook hands with the opponent he had never seen before. It seemed a simple and spontaneous gesture, and was certainly an effective one. Firpo shook hands, of course, but he didn't smile. As Dempsey returned to his corner Firpo, still on his feet, moved his huge head about slowly and almost bewildered. He looked like a man who didn't know where he was. He certainly didn't look like the man who was about to give one of the best of heavyweight champions the hardest fight of his life.

Rituals of the Ring.

Then the usual formalities. Both boxers had put on their gloves before entering the ring, so that delay was obviated. But there had to be the usual poses of the two fighters, their managers and the referee before the cameras. There had to be the usual impassioned appeals of Joe Humphreys for sufficient quiet to enable him to tell the crowd that Johnny Gallagher was going to referee and that George Partrich and Billy McPartland would be the judges. This finished, the hardly repressed crowd began buzzing noisily again. Once more Humphreys appealed for quiet and announced that following the championship fight there would be another eight-round bout. A chorus of groans drowned out the names of the fighters. This crowd was in no mood for an afterpiece with the big fight still to come.

Firpo, seated in his corner, still looked about, frowning and puzzled, as Humphreys got Dempsey on his feet and proudly proclaimed him to the crowd, "The champion of champions, our own champion, Jack Dempsey."

Dempsey Small in Comparison.

The shouts that greeted the champion were partly, no doubt, the product of the natural tendency of most crowds to be with the man on top; partly to a genuine sympathy with the native son; partly, too, to the increased liking which Dempsey has won in the past few years. Then, stilling the crowd as best he could, Humphreys introduced "the pugilistic marvel of Argentine, the recognized champion of all South America, Luis Angel Firpo." A cheer adequate to the demands of courtesy; then the fighters were back in their corners for the last consultation with their seconds. Around Dempsey gathered Joe Benjamin, his brother John and his manager and dominant spirit, Jack Kearns; and by this time the champion, too, was serious, though even when frowning, even with his famous fighting face, he could

look like nothing but a small boy beside this sombre giant from the Argentine.

Strikes Up Firpo's Guard.

Final consultation of boxers and seconds with the referee, and then all but three men piled out of the ring as the gong sounded. Quick as a flash Dempsey rushed across the ring, struck up Firpo's guard or the place where his guard might have been and wasn't, but the challenger didn't go down. Instead, the champion, half slipping, half knocked over by Firpo's right-hand counter, was down on one knee, down for the first time since that ancient fight with Jim Flynn, the Pueblo fireman, long before he won the title. He was up again before they could more than start counting, and as he got up on his feet 90,000 people got up on their feet, too, and not one of them sat down before the round was over. Ninety thousand people realized in one breath that they were about to see one of the classic fights of all history.

They came into a clinch, and, breaking, Dempsey caught him on the jaw with his fierce left hook—a blow that looks hard and is in reality still harder. Firpo was jolted, but he lashed out with the famous pile-driver right. It must be feared that he was covering up that right, to some extent, in his training. Certainly last night it moved with none of the dismal slowness of those training punches at Atlantic City. It caught Dempsey in the ribs, caught him fair and square. The champion was apparently unshaken. Had the right been overestimated? Apparently, for a moment later, as they were breaking from a brief clinch, Dempsey again whipped a left hook to the jaw and the Argentine challenger tumbled to the floor.

Gets Dempsey Again.

But he, too, was up in an instant and once more that long right shot out and caught Dempsey in the body. Dempsey came back with a right to the jaw. Down went Firpo again. One, two, and again he was up. Dempsey's left struck his jaw and he went down again. One, two, three, and up again. The roaring crowd was beginning to think that here was another Jess Willard when that long right flashed out again. Dempsey, on the offensive, hadn't covered it. It caught him in the ribs. Another instant and it had caught him again.

The two huge fighters, huge and swift, double swift to the eyes of those who for an hour and a half had been watching the slow fighters of the preliminaries, closed again. In furious in-fighting Dempsey hammered a series of rights to the body. With a thump Firpo dropped again. This time he seemed to be gone, but on the count of seven he got to his knees and two seconds later he was on his feet. Dempsey kept at him. Three times in quick succession Firpo was hammered down, rising each time before the count was started. Jess Willard had never done this. The man could take it. He could take the best, the frantically repeated best, of the greatest heavyweight of the age, and still bounce back to his feet to go on fighting. Could he be beaten at all?

And then, as Dempsey came toward him again, his right toward the right field stands, Firpo's long driving right caught him on the point of the jaw, and head first, feet pointed in air, the heavyweight champion shot out through the ropes and to all appearance out of his championship. The referees arm waved while ninety thousand people howled frantically and inarticulately, but Dempsey, pushed back from the heads and shoulders of the sporting writers in the front row of ringside seats, crawled weakly through the ropes and was on his feet again with just one single second to spare. Leaning against the ropes for an instant more, he was an easy target, but Firpo, excited, swung that right again and again and missed.

Dempsey Falls Into Clinch.

Dempsey fell into a clinch and they were clinched against the ropes when the bell ended the first round. And out of 90,000 people about 83,000 thought that Dempsey was through. Jack Kearns, in his corner, rubbing his head, rubbing his body, patting him, constantly talking to him in an undertone, worried in all probability as he has never been worried before, did what he could for him, and Dempsey came up for the second round.

He came out a beaten man to all appearance, but his head and his heart were not beaten and he had enough strength left to fight through on the plan that his lightning-quick fighting brain told him was the only one that could win. Firpo came out slowly—too slowly to gather in that championship. He was worried for, after all, he had hit the canvas seven times in three minutes and had got such a pounding as no other man had ever received and kept on his feet. Dempsey came in, hooked over a left and put Firpo down; but in two seconds he was up again. Then a moment of in-fighting, always Dempsey's best game, and Firpo sank under a right to the body and a left to the jaw. This time he was down for four seconds, rising on the fifth as game as ever. But Dempsey lost no time. This was the decisive moment. The champion's left caught the Wild Bull on the jaw; the champion's right caught him as he was going down, and this time Luis Angel Firpo did not get up. He had lost. But he had lost about the greatest fight in the history of pugilism.

Though there was nothing to attract early comers except a program of run-of-the-mine music and the spectacle of sunset and nightfall over Washington Heights, a good many spectators insisted on arriving in the latter part of the afternoon. Naturally, those who meant to rush into the few unreserved seats in that small portion of uncovered bleachers left in the reconstructed stadium were on hand long before sunset, and the battalions of policemen, firemen, ushers, newspaper men and others whose early arrival might be regarded as an occupational disease increased the number of early comers. Those who held reserved seats, as a rule, stayed downtown for dinner before coming to the fight, yet even among these early arrivals were fairly numerous, and by 6 o'clock the long lines of men waiting their turn at the lunch counters in the rear of the grandstand were massing like a bread line of Japanese earthquake refugees.

Outside the stadium there were other spectators who had to come early to avoid the rush. Clinging to the rocky slopes of Coogan's Bluff, hundreds of hardy mountaineers peered anxiously through the narrow space between upper and lower tiers of the grandstand, which gave them a precarious and distant view of the ring. More distant still were the standees on the roof of a tall apartment house on Edgecombe Avenue, on top of the hill, who were able to look over both stands and down into the centre of the arena, though it seemed that they could hardly see anything but the network of wires supporting the forty lights hung above the canvas.

Inside, meanwhile, the crowd gradually increased by trickles, a fresh surge pouring through the gates with the arrival of each elevated train. In the great closed horseshoe of the double grandstand dark spots of spectators gradually took shape against the green slope of the seats. The yellow expanse of temporary board seats in the playing field, extending like the sands of a Roman arena inside the amphitheatre, was more sparsely populated in the early hours, for ringside seat holders were more apt to be of the type who dined well and carefully downtown before taking a taxi to the arena.

So the slowly gathering crowd amused itself by listening to the alternate offerings from a battery of three amplifiers at each corner of the ring. The sun went down, and for a period there was no light in the gathering dusk but the occasional golden reflection from one of Mr. Hedley's yellow elevated trains as it drew up into the parking space to the north of the Polo Grounds. Meanwhile the knots of yawning policemen and firemen clustered about the ring, more and more newspaper men and telegraph operators crowded their way into the narrow accommodations of the press benches, and clouds of tobacco smoke began to turn this outdoor arena into the semblance of an orthodox interior fight scene.

Resin Brought for the Arena.

The ropes were stretched and tightened, boxes of resin were emptied on the new canvas and trodden in. Various citizens, prominent or obscure, were paged from the ringside through the amplifiers and those who had come early tried to pretend that they were diverted by these pastimes, while newspaper men squeezed in tighter and tighter.

The British aristocracy, it will be remembered, was torn by dissension at the time of the Princess Mary's marriage because seats for Peers and Peeresses in Westminster Abbey had been assigned by a bony Scotch Duke who allowed no more than sixteen inches of seating space per lord and lady. British noblewomen protested loudly, but there was nothing for them to do but squeeze in.

This same Scotch Duke must have marked off the seating space on the press benches for Tex Rickard, and while the space might do for ordinary hard-run newspaper men, it was all too thin for the plutocratic and portly great men of the sporting page.

September 15, 1923

The Champion Invites the Ladies.

To the Editor of The New York Times:

I am taking the liberty of writing to you because I feel pretty deeply on a certain subject. Naturally, the subject is fighting; and since I spend most of my life at it, either in the ring or making movies, I feel mighty proud of my profession. But others don't always give it the respect that is its due. Of course, Bernard Shaw wrote a fine book about fighting called "Cashel Byron's Profession," and Jack London wrote one called "The Game." But somehow people like to think that fighting isn't polite, and that it is not the proper sort of entertainment for ladies. Thank heavens, the ladies are getting smart enough to decide this matter themselves. But I was mighty happy the other night when I went to a play and saw a real fight right on the stage. And the ladies were there, and they applauded the loudest of all, and no one seemed to think that they had been harmed by a little fierce fighting. I hope some day they'll get to the point where they'll even teach the girls a few smart blows.

BENNY LEONARD.

New York City, May 19, 1924.

June 2, 1924

FLOWERS IS VICTOR; LIFTS GREB'S TITLE

20,000 See Negro Beat 1 to 5 Favorite for World's Middleweight Crown.

WINNER GETS LEAD EARLY

Showers Veteran Opponent With Blows Throughout 15 Rounds in the Garden.

By JAMES P. DAWSON.

A new world's middleweight champion was crowned last night in Madison Square Garden when Tiger Flowers, Atlanta negro, slapped, slashed, cuffed and smacked his way to the decision over Harry Greb, Pittsburgh's human windmill that has become creaky and slow. Flowers slipped into the first world's title ever to be held by a negro in the middleweight division and the first championship to be held in any class by a negro since the days of Jack Johnson.

A crowd of 20,000 fight fans saw the spectacle, a crowd which was the second largest ever assembled for a fight in the Garden and which was as distinguished and representative as any ever attracted to the arena. It witnessed the passing of the champion after a reign of more than three years, and remained to cheer and acclaim a new champion and a just decision. The receipts totaled $105,134.70.

The men who voted the decision to Flowers were Judges Charles F. Mathison and Thomas Flynn. Referee William (Gunboat) Smith, one-time heavyweight fighter, was the other State Athletic Commission representative with voting power on the bout, and he cast his ballot for Greb. There was, however, no reason for this division of opinion. Flowers easily outfought Greb in the only style in which it is possible for any one to outfight Greb—by outroughing the Pittsburgher, who heretofore has been the marvel of the ring.

Not the Greb of Old.

The passing of his title marks also the passing of Greb. At least the Pittsburgh boxer left that impression on the great gathering of fans after a fight in which he showed he was not the Greb of old, while Flowers was better in every essential than he ever has been. Perhaps it was because of the fact that there is such similarity of style between the men that Flowers looked so good. But there is no accounting for the complete reversal of form by Greb other than that he has passed the crest, that even the wonderful physical powers that heretofore were his have weakened, as those of so many other fighters and athletes have weakened in the past under the stress of continued activity.

Greb fought like an athlete who is burned out. He had not the sustained speed and stamina and endurance which have carried him to so many glorious victories in the past.

Greb fought desperately to retain his title, but he was out-fought and out-thought at every turn of a bout which was mediocre because neither boxer could do anything but slap, cuff, maul, tug and pull. Of boxing finesse neither had even an elementary knowledge and as a consequence interesting boxing and brilliant action were conspicuous by their absence.

But ring combats are won or lost on the amount of work done by the principals inside the ropes and it was on his work that Flowers won the decision and the title. With the knowledge of Greb's style gained in that meeting two years ago in Fremont, Ohio, where Greb, as champion, experienced one of the hardest bouts of his career, the negro ripped and slashed at his rival with reckless abandon and, carrying the fighting almost uninterruptedly from beginning to end, won eleven of the fifteen rounds. Greb won only the fourth, fifth and twelfth. The eleventh round was even and in all the rest Flowers earned the points.

Result a Big Upset.

The result was one of the biggest upsets of recent years in pugilism and short-end bettors reaped a harvest. Greb entered the ring a prohibitive favorite. An hour before ring-time he was a favorite at odds of 4 to 1. These enticing odds failed to bring out any considerable amount of Flowers money and as the time for the gladiators to enter the ring approached, the odds went to 5 to 1 with Greb the favorite. There was little money to bet, even at these odds.

The contest was exciting because it was desperately fought by a champioon slipping into defeat and a challenger spurred under the lash of prospective victory. Greb tried to the best of his ability, but his best last night was not comparable to the best of the Greb of a past day. He lacked all his old fire and vigor and was off in his timing and hitting.

Flowers, on the other hand, fought the same steady battle from first bell to last. He was undeniably the aggressor, and scored countless points on this score. He also landed the greater number of punches, out-fighting Greb at all times.

Flower's greatest weapon on the offense was a right to the body. A southpaw fighter, who stands with the right leg and arm extended in unorthodox style, Flowers clubbed this blow to the ribs and to the region of Greb's heart until the defending champion's body was red and raw. To this blow Flowers added a slapping, cutting left which was neither a hook nor a swing. Flowers lands most of his blows with the side of his fists. He didn't show last night that he was capable of landing a straight jab or a swing of standard variety.

Flowers started on the attack with the opening gong and didn't relinquish the offensive thereafter, except at rare and short-lived intervals, when Greb fought desperately to stem the tide. As the battle progressed it developed into a struggle of trickery and all accepted rules of the ring were sidetracked. Holding and hitting were conspicuous, as was also wrestling. Each indulged, with Greb the greater offender. At one stage of the bout Flowers looked appealingly at Referee Smith and complained that Greb was using his thumb.

Greb gave a flash of the old Greb in the fourth when he swarmed all over Flowers and buried the negro under a hail of blows with both hands. Through the fifth session, too, Greb flashed some of his fiery assaults and for a time he caused Flowers no end of trouble, but the champion weakened under his own pace and in the succeeding five rounds Flowers showed to advantage. In the eleventh the action lagged, but in the twelfth Greb had another, and what proved to be his last offensive spurt, and out fought his rival. Through the closing three rounds, however, the Pittsburgher was plainly spent and he was beaten at every turn.

A more delightful middleweight exhibition was that furnished by K. O. Phil Kaplan, Harlem lad, in the scheduled ten-round semi-final, when he knocked out Mickey Rockson, Coast fighter, who was making his first appearance here, in the fourth round. Referee Johnny McAvoy stepped between the combatants after 1 minute 59 seconds of the fourth session and halted the bout to save Rockson from further punishment.

Kaplan, with clean, powerful and well-timed left hooks, twice floored Rockson in the first round, once solidly and again sending the Coast lad to his fingertips. With a variety of right hooks and swings he had Rockson wobbly and staggering through the second and third.

In the four-round emergency bout which followed Tommy Travers and Eddie McLaughlin, welterweights, boxed a draw. Dick Conlon, Altoona (Pa.) lightweight, won the decision over Joey Kaufman of Coney Island in the six-round preliminary, Kaufman substituting for Rubey Goldstein, who reported ill.

In their four-round bout Johnny Filucci, Harlem featherweight, won the decision over Frank Lagona of Philadelphia. Al Goldberg of Harlem won the decision over Jimmy Mendoza, Jimmy De Forest's young featherweight, in the opening bout of four rounds.

February 27, 1926

He Was Cheered by Men With Concave Profiles and Convex Ears.

PUGILISM CLIMBS UP THE SOCIAL LADDER

Literature, Art and the Drama Adopt the Fighter and the State Promotes His Once Outlawed Industry

By ALVA JOHNSTON

PRIZEFIGHTERS have reached the top after a social climb of two centuries. This season hundreds of battlers have been celebrating their rise in seven-fork dinners at the big hotels. Literature and art have taken them up. Boxers are replacing two-gun men in the films and supplanting saints in cathedral windows.

Memoirs of aged battlers outsell the confessions of passé statesmen. Bellows lithographs of the Dempsey-Firpo fight are offered in Fifth Avenue windows at $1,000 a copy. A prizefighter is the hero of the greatest dramatic hit next to "Abie's Irish Rose."

Prizefighters once boasted of Marty McCue, a boxer who became a first-rate Assemblyman. Legislators today boast of Monte Munn, an Assemblyman who has become a second-rate boxer.

Once New York laws were hostile toward pugilism. Today the State fosters it with an indulgent paternalism. All other arts and industries are left to their own resources, but prizefighting is the ward of the Commonwealth. Pugilism is one industry which the State compels to thrive.

The State orders fighters to fight. It tells them when to fight, where to fight and what promoter to fight for. The law used to punish men for battling. Today it punishes them for not battling. Dempsey and other champions have been suspended for not fighting. Their refusal to fight is, in effect, a breach of the peace.

By Virtue of Government

Once a week the fight-promoting machinery of New York State goes into operation, commanding this bout, canceling that one, and distributing dates among different promoters to avoid unprofitable competition. Boxing has thus achieved a unique distinction as the only field of private endeavor entitled to have direct State aid and guidance.

The State has never forced business combinations on individuals engaged in other callings. It has never, for instance, decreed the reunion of Gallagher and Shean. It has never ordered John Barrymore to co-star with Ben Turpin. It does not intermeddle and dictate in ordinary private business transactions, but it does regularly rise in its sovereign capacity to order one battler to trade punches with another. By a development of republican institutions that was not foreseen by Bryce or De Tocqueville, the State constantly acts as go-between and bottle-holder for assorted scrappers.

New York is a pioneer in the stimulation of prizefighting. It has taken pugilism under State direction through an extension of the processes of government by commission. New York's legal machinery for encouraging the industry has been imitated by other States. A sort of common law or system of precedents has also been established, the decisions of the New York commission being more or less accepted elsewhere. A few cases interesting from the legal point of view are Shade vs. Moody, Sharkey vs. Huffman and Walker vs. Milligan.

The case of Shade vs. Moody concerned a combat at Syracuse. The principals were two leading middleweights. Complaint was made after the fight that neither Shade nor Moody had exhibited the savageness which the spectators expected. The commission heard evidence. It decided that less than the legal minimum of viciousness had been manifested. It seized the gate receipts due to the prizefighters and ordered the men to fight again. This time they fought with acceptable ferocity and the State of New York returned their money.

Sharkey vs. Huffman was another leading case. The principals were Jack Sharkey, a large Lithuanian from Boston, and Sailor Huffman of California. Sharkey was the victor over Huffman, in a ten-round bout at Madison Square Garden. It was alleged after the fight that Sharkey had not beaten Huffman as badly as he might. The charge was made that Sharkey had violated the ethics of the profession by wantonly failing to knock Huffman unconscious.

The facts were gravely sifted. Sharkey was acquitted, but a general warning was issued that the State of New York would deal sternly with battlers detected in flagrant displays of humanity toward their opponents.

Doctrine of great importance was laid down in the case of Walker vs. Milligan. The parties were Mickey Walker, then welterweight champion of the world, and Tommy Milligan, the British challenger. New York State ordered them to fight at a charity show and to give half of their shares of the gate receipts to the charity. Walker excused himself on the ground that he had a sore toe. Later Walker and Milligan were matched again, no part of the receipts to go to charity. At the last minute the State ordered the bout to be canceled on the ground that Walker's toe was still sore.

Walker contended that his toe was perfectly healed and offered to exhibit it to the learned tribunal. The Commissioners declined to look at it. They informed Walker that the official ruling of New York State was that his toe was sore and that it would keep on being sore for sixty days.

The boxing profession has waited a long time to win its present governmental patronage and social recognition. For years fighters were outlaws. Fleeing from the authorities, they had to meet secretly in barns and ice-houses, on barges and in cornfields. Today the authorities threaten and coerce them into meeting in huge arenas for purses of hundreds of thousands of dollars.

Enshrined in Stained Glass

Ten years ago a boxer's place in ecclesiastical architecture would have been among the gargoyles. Today among the published designs for stained glass windows in the Cathedral of St. John the Divine is a boxing scene, one battler delivering a right chop to the head, while the other counters with a short left to the liver.

The modern boxing era is a little more than two centuries old. It dates from the beginning of the reign of Figg in 1719. The title-holders have been distinguished men for these 207 years, but it is only in the last five or six years that the whole profession has achieved a new social status.

Broughton, who knocked out Figg, became the pet of the Prince of Wales of his time. Nearly every subsequent H. R. H. has been the friend of the champion. John L. had hardly landed at Southampton when he was summoned to dine with the then current joy and pride of England. Hogarth and Hoppner did portraits of the eighteenth century champions. "Gentleman" Jackson was celebrated by Lord Byron and Tom Moore.

President Roosevelt, forgetting all his appointments on meeting George Siler, the referee, caused subcalibre reproductions of famous knockout punches to be executed on his own chin and solar plexus. Dempsey wrung the hand of Calvin Coolidge and illustrated affably how a left hook traveling less than two inches could cause a vacancy in the White House.

The social triumphs of the past, however, went only to the champions. Today the logical contenders, the forlorn hopes, the punchworn veterans and the preliminary boys are all distinguished personages.

The second-rater of a few years ago was a morose bird with a mud-colored sweater. Nowadays he is a languid patrician who holds court at exclusive watering places. In the old days when a manager lost contact with a battler he made inquiries among barkeepers and turnkeys. Today he seeks information from society editors.

Fully five years ago the battler discarded the brown sweater in favor of the purple shirt on all formal occasions. Recently he has graduated from the purple shirt. The fighter of standing is a severe dresser. The ones with the quagga stripes are veterans who have not caught up with the social revolution.

The new social level of the profession was fixed at a great public function in New York when Mayor Walker, Governor Moore of New Jersey and other public officials addressed between 300 and 400 eminent boxers. Every speech glorified the manly art. Every tribute was cheered by men with concave profiles and convex ears. There was no color line. Conspicuous among the diners were the noted black gladiators Harry Wills, Tiger Flowers and Kid Norfolk.

The first formal dinner of the profession was an all-around success. Not a knife was used for hoisting. Not a napkin was worn as a ruff. Jeweled flasks circulated to some extent, but the decorum was generally excellent. At one time a bellowing from a far corner interrupted the speech of Peter J. Brady, a banker, who shouted: "Hey, you battlers, if you must battle, battle outside."

Later Mr. Brady learned that he had committed an injustice. The bellowers were not battlers but managers. The deportment of the fighter was flawless, and he was admired for his confident bearing in a place which he could not have entered a few years ago without delivering a trunk.

One detail in connection with this dinner shows the polish of the modern boxer. Authorities differ as to the proper size of a hatboy's tip at these dinners. A dime may seem too little. a quarter too much. Fifteen cents is awkward. To aid a puzzled man in reaching a decision, the hat-boy keeps several quarters in view and removes coins of smaller denomination as fast as they are deposited. An inexperienced man usually heaves a sigh and puts down 25 cents.

A Test for Fighting Gentlemen

This night the plates were paved with decoy quarters. Here was a crucial test of the poise and the self-control of the fighting gentlemen, and they passed it with excellent marks. Some gave dimes, some nickels, some nothing. Bankers could not have done better.

New York is not peculiar in its glorification of the prizefighter. Chambers of Commerce and Boards of Trade in other parts of the country beg and plead for important fights to make their communities famous. In 1910 Governor Gillette of California threatened to call out the militia to stop the Johnson-Jeffries bout, on the ground that it would disgrace the State. In 1925 a strong faction in Philadelphia clamored for a Dempsey-Wills fight in order to help the Sesquicentennial.

A few years ago the earnings of the profession were small. For economy's sake fighters sometimes arranged with friendly magistrates for thirty-day sentences in order to be boarded and lodged at public expense while using the jail for a gymnasium. Through pull, Young Griffo, cleverest of all boxers, used to get himself incarcerated in roomy prisons, and there he wore circular paths in the courtyards as he worked himself into condition.

Today they train at fashionable shore and mountain resorts. They own race horses, strings of motor cars, country estates. They are moneyed men. Active practitioners like Stribling, Greb and Delaney have earned incredible revenues by toying with backward athletes. Tunney and Reynault, yachtsmen and country gentlemen, have grown rich by occasionally cuffing harmless giants. The most photographed tarpon fisherman in the United States is Paul Berlenbach. Dempsey, of course, is a millionaire mine and hotel owner.

Big business methods have lifted prize-fighting from its outlawed condition to its present prosperity. At one time an insult would make a champion fight. Today nothing less than half a million dollars will arouse him. Vengeance, love of battle and the thirst for fame play no more of a part in the fighting business than in the knit goods and the wood pulp industries.

A title is too valuable to be risked unnecessarily. The vaudeville, film and toothpaste rights of the world's championship are appraised at upwards of $100,000 a year. It is easier to embroil ten nations than one world's champion. There have been fully ten times as many wars as championship fights in the last twenty-five years.

With the business growing more complicated all the time, no fighter except Firpo has started on an important career in recent years without a manager to do the thinking and collect the money for him. Success in the boxing field calls not only for a punch, but also for capital for propaganda and other purposes, a familiarity with prizefight law, written and unwritten, and a working knowledge of referees, judges and boxing commissioners.

Prizefighting today is more like a chain-store business than like a sport. One manager—Leo P. Flynn—had at last accounts a string of twenty-eight performers. Max Hoff of Philadelphia has about the same number. Many other managers direct standing armies of pugilists.

The Flynn headquarters is like a

They Informed Walker That His Toe Would Remain Sore for Sixty Days.

Wall Street office. In the outer chamber is a velvet blackboard with the names of the twenty-eight Flynn boxers in white celluloid letters, like railroads, industrials, oils and specialties. After each name is quoted the fighter's weight and his open dates. By one glance at the blackboard a fight broker can see what members of the Flynn chain are available for match-making purposes. The big prizefight exchanges have all the Wall Street equipment except the ticker.

The modern manager buys and sells fighters. He trades in options on fighters. Not infrequently he takes them into court to clear his title to them. It is a routine procedure to invest $10,000 or $15,000 in a promising gladiator before he becomes an income-producing property. It is not unprecedented for a manager to maintain a good prospect in an unproductive state for two years, to keep him under the direction of high-priced tutors, and have his tonsils, adenoids, appendix and a few teeth out, before he is rounded into a fully improved and dividend-paying enterprise.

Three years ago Paul Berlenbach quit wrestling because the highest fee offered him was $50—and that to throw a match. Dan Hickey, once manager of Bob Fitzsimmons, took charge of Berlenbach and spent two years teaching him how to fight. Today Hickey's contractual rights over this fighter are worth between $500,000 and $1,000,000.

But prosperity, prestige and State patronage have failed to make great fighters, according to the best authorities. It is asserted that commercialization has ruined boxing as a fine craft.

"The manly art of self-defense is a lost art," says Mr. Flynn. "Prosperity has killed it. The apprentice earns as much now as the finished boxer of fifteen years ago. This is enough to satisfy the ordinary fighter, and he will not undergo the toil of learning his trade. The result is that the great majority of fighters remain crude beginners.

"The swarm of managers is another reason for the deterioration of boxing. They keep rushing untrained boys into the ring. Since they don't know how to defend themselves, the spirit and vitality is beaten out of them. Their fighting days are over before they have learned the first thing about fighting.

The New Trade of Boxing

"There are ten times as many professional fighters today as there were a generation ago, but not one-tenth as many good fighters. Formerly the boxer had to learn his trade. There was no public demand to see

scuffles between raw beginners. The fighter had to know his business to make more than half a dollar for his night's work. Most of them stuck to some regular trade, such as steam-fitting or truck driving, at least until they were near the top of the profession. This helped to keep them in condition and out of mischief. Today the poorest preliminary fighter earns enough in fights once or twice a month to enable him to loaf the rest of the time, and this is one reason for the early demoralization of the average boxer.

"The ambitious boys who make real progress do not become great fighters nowadays, but many of them become masters of the art of not fighting. They learn all there is to know about stalling, clinching and covering. They become adept at the science of keeping busy in the ring for ten or fifteen rounds without fighting.

"Still, few of them know the fine points of defense. The sidestep, for instance, is absolutely unknown today. The ring artist of a generation ago knew how to elude a punch and at the same time keep balanced and ready to hit back. Hardly a fighter in the ring today has any balance. Jack Dempsey is one of the very few exceptions.

"The present fighters do not understand feinting. They feint and feint all through a fight, but they do it just for the looks of the thing. Formerly a boxer feinted in order to open a hole in his opponent's defense. In all fine points of the game the modern boxer is a novice compared with the artists of twenty or twenty-five years ago."

Forgetting for the moment the decay of the art in his enthusiasm for the flourishing state of the business, Mr. Flynn estimated that under present conditions a contract with a brilliant fighter like Ketchel would be worth anywhere between $1,000,000 and $2,000,000.

While the profession never enjoyed such prosperity in the past as it has today, it at one time had much greater fame. The most cultured of all peoples made the greatest fuss over the battler. The Greeks dotted their cities with statues to the great maulers of their era. Homer inserted a full account of the Epeus-Euryalus bout in the Iliad. Pindar wrote an ode to the Diagoras boys. But the profession of today is not envious. The reward of the classic battler was a circlet of green leaves, and the manager's share was nothing.

June 27, 1926

TUNNEY WINS CHAMPIONSHIP, BEATS DEMPSEY IN 10 ROUNDS; OUTFIGHTS RIVAL ALL THE WAY, DECISION NEVER IN DOUBT; 135,000 PAY MORE THAN $2,000,000 TO SEE BOUT IN THE RAIN

TUNNEY ALWAYS MASTER

Challenger Bewilders His Opponent With His Speed, Accuracy.

AGGRESSIVE IN ALL ROUNDS

Sends Rain of Whiplike Lefts Which Champion Cannot Avoid.

OUTCOME IS A SURPRISE

Dempsey Lacks All Evidence of His Old Aggressiveness— Victor Is Acclaimed.

By JAMES P. DAWSON.
Special to The New York Times.

RINGSIDE, SESQUICENTENNIAL STADIUM, Philadelphia, Sept. 23.— Gene Tunney is the new world's heavyweight champion. The ex-marine fought like a marine here tonight in the Sesquicentennial Stadium, when he carried off the decision over Jack Dempsey, once known as the Manassa Mauler and the ring's man-killer, in a ten-round bout which saw the first passing of a heavyweight championship title on a decision.

Through every round of the ten, Tunney battered and pounded Dempsey. He rained rights on the tottering champion's jaw and he bewildered Dempsey with his speed and the accuracy of a whip-like left hand which Dempsey could not evade. When the decision was announced, the crowd let loose a roar of acclaim for "the man of destiny," who had conquered the man-killer, and the countryside sent the roar echoing back.

Confidence Aids Tunney.

The transfer of the title, the ascension of Tunney to the pinnacle in boxing, surprised the majority of those who witnessed the fight and experienced followers of boxing form. It surprised everybody, almost, but Tunney, whose confidence, more than anything else, perhaps, carried him on to a height which the vast majority thought unattainable for him.

He was complete master, from first bell to last. He out-boxed and he out-fought Dempsey at every turn. Where it had been expected that Tunney would break and run before the vicious attack of Dempsey, the tiger man, Tunney, the fighting marine, not only failed to back up, but he went forward all the time with the instinct of the true leatherneck and hammered Dempsey in a driving attack which brooked no restraining effort on the part of the champion.

There was no question of the victor at the finish. There was no question even of the winner of each round as the battle progressed, and Dempsey, instead of flashing the fighting fury which was expected of him, instead of surging forward with the tigerish, vicious rushes he has exhibited in previous and more favorable ring engagements, proved himself instead a floundering, weakened, almost helpless fighting machine from which the spark had gone.

All the evidences of the old Dempsey were merely that; only faint evidences, indications, unexpressive flashes save for their expression of futility of helpless hopelessness, of utter ineffectiveness.

They fought this battle in the rain— a driving, torrential downpour which started when the men entered the ring and which increased in fury as the fight progressed. The ring was flooded, the spectators drenched and the gladiators were drenched, but as the fury of the storm increased so did the fighting of Tunney, and Dempsey had nothing with which to meet this Marine attack.

Knockdown Is Lacking.

It was a disappointing transfer of a heavyweight title in one respect. The battle did not end in a knockout. Indeed, through its ten rounds the struggle held not even a knock down. This was due to the fact that Tunney is a weak hitter in the sense that he is not a finishing or destructive hitter.

He is not of the old Dempsey hitting school. But the New York lad is a punishing hitter, a cruel, tantalizing, tormenting puncher and a cool, unruffled boxer at all times. He did about everything else to Dempsey but knock the defending champion down and out. He battered Dempsey to a pulp, until the beaten champion at the finish was a close resemblance to the giant Jess Willard, whom Dempsey pounded and hammered into a helpless hulk out on the shores of Maumee Bay seven years ago when he won the title.

For the first time in his career Dempsey felt the sting and cutting pain of a rival's punishing blows. Not even in the long ago when he was knocked out by Fireman Jim Flynn for the only such set-back chalked against Dempsey's record, was the tigerish Dempsey subjected to such painful drilling from a ring foe.

At the finish Dempsey was a sorry, pitiful subject, the object of the sincere sympathy of the crowd as he slumped in his corner to which the clang of the final gong, welcome and a distinct relief, sent him. His mouth and nose spouted blood, his left eye, bruised and battered, was closed tight and bleeding. There was a cut under his left eye about an inch long. And he was all in, absolutely at the end of his tether, through as a fighter if ever a man was.

Like the true fighting man and sportsman, however, Dempsey dragged himself from his corner as the announcer ordered the decision flashed to the crowd through the giant microphones suspended above the ring. "The two judges have agreed on Tunney as the winner and new champion," and lurching forward on unsteady legs, embraced his conqueror for a few fleeting seconds, smiling through his painfully bruised and battered face, which was pounded out of all semblance of normal, and congratulated Tunney through bruised and bleeding lips.

Shakes Hands All Round.

The ring then was the scene of hand-shaking on all sides. Manager Billy Gibson and Gene Normile, for conqueror and conquered, clasped hands and so did the seconds, but Dempsey wanted nothing to do with this. He carried himself slowly, painfully away, slipped quietly through the ropes with the din of the rain-soaked crowd for the triumphant marine ringing in his ears, and made his way to his dressing room. In the privacy of his quarters Dempsey collapsed, utterly exhausted and completely crushed. It is believed here he may not fight again.

There was everything in this fight but the thrill of the knock down and the knock out. The suspense was sustained and the fight was fought fast and furiously, Tunney doing all the fighting and showing all the speed. The judges who rendered the decision were Mike Bernstein of Wilkes-Barre and Frank Brown of Pittsburgh. The referee was Tom Reilly of Philadelphia, but on the decision his vote was not needed. The judges did their work well. They had no other course, and their decision decided the issue under the Boxing law of Pennsylvania and to the complete satisfaction of the crowd.

Dempsey's time had come. That is the only way to account for this battle and its result. The man who had smashed and crushed all opposition, met his superior in Tunney, a fearless, confident, determined, stronger man, well equipped in every ring essential save finishing punching strength. Dempsey was not the old fighting machine, luxurious living and three years of idleness had done their work. You will hear tales of how this fight was not fought on its merits.

Such tales were circulated before the fight, but they are groundless and a rank injustice to Tunney, a true fighter who undoubtedly will take his place among the ring's greatest champions. Dempsey tried his best, but his best was not good enough. He was no match for the perfectly trained and strongly developed Tunney. He fought his battle. It was a losing one, but he fought on until the last bell sounded. He went down fighting.

Tunney excelled Dempsey in practically every department in which it had been expected that Dempsey would outdo Tunney. The fighting marine was faster, shiftier, more resourceful, more accurate in his fire, cooler at all stages of the fight, deliberate at all times, with an attack which was systematized and varied, but not methodical by any means, and thoroughly effective in its point producing and punishment inflicting propensities. Tunney's footing was steadier and surer. His timing and distance in punching were far superior to those of Dempsey.

In only one respect did Tunney fail to overshadow the defending champion. Dempsey was more aggressive, but with an offensive which was wild and misdirected, weak and ineffective and thoroughly harmless. The sting had gone from the Dempsey punch, the fear-instilling element had gone from the growling, scowling, glowering Dempsey, for these elements in Dempsey's fighting make-up were revealed here tonight in a rain-soaked ring as useless when flashed before a man who refused to be frightened.

Though Tunney failed to surpass Dempsey in aggressiveness the former marine nevertheless made capital by this very shortcoming, for he made Dempsey fight the fight he wanted him to fight—a rushing, tearing fight in which Dempsey was wild, floundered, missed awkwardly and wallowed about the ring.

Tunney, meanwhile, with the skill and precision of the expert fencer, countered this helpless fire with rapier-like lefts and lightning-like rights which cut and punished. Dempsey fooled everybody but himself and Tunney. He was successful in concealing his battle weaknesses in training from the public which watched him and from the critics who inspected him and took his efforts for their surface value. But he must have known him-

Jack Dempsey (left) became national hero when he held the heavyweight championship (1919-1926). He, along with Babe Ruth, Bobby Jones and Red Grange symbolized the golden age of sports in the 1920's. The boxer on the right is Gene Tunney, shown here in the process of detaching Dempsey from his heavyweight crown.

GENE TUNNEY, THE NEW CHAMPION

self that the spark was missing and Tunney must have known, too.

Dempsey came into the ring like a man bent on business, not like a fighter come to his doom. He even employed what was either a protection against tender eyebrows and a precaution against their bleeding under a hammering, or the age-old artifice of the ring, coming into the squared circle with both eyes decorated to give the impression of injury. Dempsey's eyebrows were covered with a white substance which was plain grease or zinc salve, not court plaster. There had been no evidence of cuts over either eye up to the time he left Atlantic City yesterday evening, so we must believe this foreign matter was employed as a sort of protection. It failed of its purpose.

Dempsey encountered a situation at the beginning of the fight which was new to him and which he could not overcome at any stage of the battle. He met an upright boxer, light and fleet on his feet, quick and accurate and cutting with his hands, who was unafraid of Dempsey and his rushes.

The defending champion charged as of old, leading to the body with a right and left and after a clinch he rushed again. But this time met the rush with a right, and another, and still another which rattled Jack's teeth and his whole body. Dempsey rushed again, this time landing a left to the body, but Tunney, instead of crumpling under the blow which sent the sent the giant Firpo down, countered with a staggering right to the jaw. Tunney tried another, dancing lightly about Dempsey, sharp-shooting and letting fly with the speed of a bullet. Tunney missed with this one but he landed twice with grazing bolws to the chin and then with a right to the head as Dempsey plunged in headlong, wide open and inviting attack.

It had been predicted and there was basis for the prediction on the strength of the previous records of the rivals. That Dempsey would do just this—invite attack with his corrugated steel jaw as the target, just to get home himself with a destructive blow. But the jaw which withstood the right of Carpentier in that second round five years ago, and the murderous right of the giant Firpo opening that memoriable battle three years ago, did not stand up so well tonight. Or, rather, the recuperative powers of the champion had deserted him, along with all his boxing effectiveness and fighting success. Tunney shot through an opening with another right to the jaw which staggered Dempsey and before the bell the former marine belted Dempsey with rights and lefts to the jaw until the defending champion was groggy as he went to his corner.

Here was something the vast majority of the spectators had not expected—Tunney not only standing fearlessly before the bull-like rushes of Dempsey, the killer, but meeting this attack flat-footed and dealing out his blows with a marksman's accuracy and with staggering force, or dancing away and pecking at the charging human in front of him. The crowd was awed; some of it was distinctly shocked, but the greatest shock was experienced by Dempsey himself.

Dempsey Keeps Up Rushes.

It was the same in the second round, Dempsey rushing and forcing Tunney about the ring, while Tunney, in strategic retreat, countered accurately and solidly with lefts and rights. Dempsey landed a left early which split Tunney's lip and he drove his left and his right to Tunney's body and ribs, but the blows did not disturb Gene, but, on the contrary, made the challenger fight all the harder to beat off this attack.

In the third round Dempsey continued to rush with the old fury, an indomitable will and spirit which commanded admiration, but which lacked direction and which was absolutely ineffective. Tunney's right crosses bounded off Dempsey's face and his right uppercuts smacked against Dempsey's head and face until the defending champion was spitting blood and his renovated nose was bleeding.

Two rights to the jaw staggered Dempsey again, but he survived the ensuing assault because in his eagerness Tunney himself became wild, and then, too, Gene lacks the punch of the true finisher. Dempsey plunged in with a right to the jaw, but, instead of crumpling or backing, Tunney went forward and planted a right uppercut to the face as Dempsey tore in wildly.

Dempsey's greatest exhibition of savageness came with the opening of the fourth round. The defending champion charged like an enraged bull and plunging across the ring, almost drove Tunney out of the ring near Gene's corner, with a swishing left hook to the jaw. Going in close Dempsey pounded the body and they wrestled across the ring to Dempsey's corner, where as they parted from close quarters Tunney wabbled weakly against the ropes. Here, it seemed, was the old Dempsey.

He had Tunney in distress, or so it appeared. But it developed into only a flash, a desperate effort by Dempsey to overawe his rival and instill in his pretender some respect for the monarch of the ring. Tunney didn't see it that way. He recovered his poise in a jiffy and began boxing. After a few stabs of his left Tunney opened a cut under Dempsey's right eye from which a crimson stream flowed and flecked the beautiful bronzed body which had been so liberally praised in song, story and picture. More, Tunney stepped in with a right to the jaw which staggered Dempsey and with a succession of left jabs and hooks and right crosses and swings with which he blinded Dempsey in a furious counter assault. Tunney had his rival navigating on unsteady legs and his face blood-smeared at the bell.

Dempsey Cowed at Last.

This treatment cowed Dempsey there and then. If he had had any doubts that he was facing his master, they had been dispelled. As he came up for the fifth round Dempsey, instead of ripping and plunging recklessly at Tunney, was cautious and apprehensive. He tried to box with Tunney, but he was not capable of doing so. Then he started forcing matters again while Tunney danced around, cold and appraising, looking for another opening for a smack with his right. And here it was seen plainly that the sting and force had gone from Dempsey's blows. With them had gone his chances for victory. For he landed to Tunney's jaw with a right as he rushed Tunney to a corner and Tunney came back with a right that was stronger. Again Dempsey lashed out with his right and grazed the jaw and he went close to the ropes and belted Tunney about the body, but Tunney came back with a succession of rights to the jaw which bewildered Dempsey.

Dempsey floundered awkwardly around the ring in the sixth round, but twice managed to hook his left solidly to the jaw, once forcing Tunney across the ring and again sending Tunney backward. But these blows were desperate lunges in a losing cause. The blows were widely separated and, most important of all, they lacked the old Dempsey crushing power. Against this wild attack Tunney set up a varied offensive, fighting all the time, hooking or jabbing with his left or hitting home with left and right to the face and jaw in a one-two combination punch. Under the pace, Tunney was tiring, but Dempsey was practically played out.

The Shift Only a Ghost.

Dempsey tried his shift in the seventh round, the ghost of the famous shift which once meant destruction and which heretofore invariably was well timed and accurate, but it was a pitiful effort last night; a dramatic gesture and nothing more. Against Tunney's jabs Dempsey came in with a left hook which brought the blood from Tunney's eye, the crimson showing as the men separated from a clinch. But Tunney went coolly and deliberately along and with a right to the jaw almost sent Dempsey down.

Tunney pounded home with his right to the face or to the body and Dempsey missed like a novice with a left and right. Tunney pecked away and Dempsey charged in with a left and right to the jaw, which sent Tunney backward on his heels. But Gene rebounded to the attack and clubbed Dempsey about the head with a right. At the bell Dempsey was a sorry looking spectacle, with his left eye blackened and swollen and a cut under his right eye, from which the blood continued to flow.

It was the same through the three succeeding rounds.

Tunney, the master, never overlooked a chance to send home a right to the face, head or jaw of the tottering champion, or a jab or hook with the left which stung and bruised. Dempsey floundered around, fighting doggedly, courageously, aye, recklessly, in the face of his opponent's withering fire, and Tunney fighting just as courageously, determinedly, but with not the recklessness which characterized the work of Dempsey.

Dempsey reached his rival's body with a left and he landed to Tunney's jaw with a right in the eighth round, but he missed more than he landed and the punches which went home had no sting in them. All the time Tunney was jabbing or hooking with his left and crossing his right whenever the opportunity presented for a crash to the jaw, or head.

Dempsey's Strength Ebbs.

Dempsey's strength was ebbing in the ninth round. He was weary when the session started, and he was discouraged, too. But he was desperate and he fought on though his task was hopeless by now. Tunney danced around his rival and he continued to dance even when Dempsey crashed home a solid left to the wind, the best body punch of the fight that Dempsey had landed, so far as accuracy was concerned. But Tunney retaliated with a clip of the right on the jaw and after each had missed in an exchange of rights for the jaw, Tunney suddenly started to be the pursuer instead of the pursued. He began chasing Dempsey around the ring.

Tunney closed this round fighting Dempsey in Dempsey's own corner, and battering the champion severely about the face and head with a fusillade of rights and lefts, while Dempsey tore blindly at the body with his right. The crowd sent up a terrific yell for the fighting marine at the end of the round. It was as if the gathering was practicing its shout of acclaim for the victorious Tunney; a sort of rehearsal for the greeting which was to come within the succeeding five minutes. Nobody minded the downpour, which drenched everybody and gave no indication of abating. Here was a new champion on the threshold of being elevated and the thrill overcame the inconvenience and discomfiture of unfavorable weather.

Dempsey Plunges Near End.

They merely touched gloves starting the tenth session and then Dempsey, with the urge of the old Dempsey still upon him, even if the effectiveness was gone, went on the offensive. He rushed blindly, although eagerly, it seemed, only to miss. Then he plunged again, ripping rights and lefts to the body, but Tunney, ignoring the blows, drove home a right which cut Dempsey over the left eye. Another right followed and Dempsey went staggering backward to the ropes.

With another right Tunney closed Dempsey's left eye tightly and the tottering champion clinched. He pawed the air and then suddenly sent a right to the head, but Tunney countered with a left and right to the face and Dempsey's blood smeared his face.

The rest was the picture of the finish of a once great fighter—a human hurricane petered out. Weary of body and mind, wabbling and staggering around, he cut and slashed, blinded and bleeding, his face battered, facing the foe, yes, but helpless. He commanded the admiration of the crowd to the end.

Tunney Appears, Smiling.

Tunney entered the ring first. He received a great reception as he stepped up smiling, wearing a dark robe with a marine insignia on his back. He was followed by his manager, Billy Gibson. Tunney smiled and bowed as he sat down in a swinging chair.

The referee was introduced as Tommy Reilly of Philadelphia, a medium sized but keen-eyed man of 50, wearing the conventional white sweater and white trousers. Then the judges were announced.

Dempsey, wearing a white towel over his shoulders and unshaven, stepped into the ring a few minutes later and received a mixture of cheers and boos. Dempsey wore a white plaster over his right eye. Gene Normile, wearing a white sweater and cap, entered the ring. Dempsey went over to Gene, said "How are you, my boy?" and shook hands. After this Tunney sat down and began wrapping the white bandages around his hands.

Philadelphia Jack O'Brien accompanied Dempsey, acting as his chief second. Jimmy Bronson, Lew Fink and Lou Brix were Tunney's seconds. After the cheering, which marked the entrance of the main bout contenders, quiet maintained over the arena.

As the boxers were bandaging their hands some light drops of rain began to fall and hundreds of the spectators stood up to put on raincoats. It was a tense moment, as it was a question of time if the big bout could go over before the rain began to fall in earnest.

The crowd began to cheer and whistle to hurry the fighters into action.

The boxers continued wrapping their hands as the pattering rain fell harder. Gibson finally began to slip Tunney's gloves on and Jerry the Greek put the gloves on Dempsey.

The weights were announced, Dempsey 190 pounds, Tunney 185½, and the fight was on.

September 24, 1926

WALKER DETHRONES FLOWERS IN CHICAGO

Captures Middleweight Championship Before a Crowd of 11,000 in 10-Round Bout.

DECISION CALLED WRONG

Critics Deplore the Verdict, Though It Appears Popular With Fans, Who Cheer It.

RECEIPTS PUT AT $77,000

Capacity Throng Pays Top Gate Since Recent Legalization of Boxing in Illinois.

By JAMES P. DAWSON.

Special to The New York Times.

CHICAGO, Dec. 3.—After ten rounds of sizzling, savage fighting before the largest crowd that ever witnessed a ring battle in this city, Mickey Walker of Elizabeth, N. J., won the world's middleweight championship from Tiger Flowers of Atlanta, Ga., tonight. A crowd of 11,000 thronged the Coliseum.

Referee Benny Yanger, old-time featherweight fighter, lifted Walker's hand in victory when the final bell ended hostilities after he had separated the contestants from a grim clinch.

Police swarmed into the ring from all sides and surrounded the victor and vanquished. Then the crowd let loose a roar of approval which left no doubt as to the popularity of the award. The former welterweight champion smiled happily as he realized he had won another title, which Flowers had won from Harry Greb.

Though the crowd was satisfied with the verdict, the same could not be said of the critics assembled at the ringside from all sections of the country. The decision was declared one of the worst rendered in recent years.

Flowers was the winner according to the majority opinion. The clownish champion, who disregards all accepted boxing procedure for a style which is now peculiarly his own, had beaten Walker so far in the opinion of some of the critics that there was no room for doubt.

Five Rounds to Flowers.

Among the dissenters was the writer. His score sheet showed five rounds for Flowers, four for Walker and one even. Even disregarding the round score, Flowers accomplished by far the greater work. Walker scored two knock-downs, it is true. He floored Flowers in the first round and in the ninth session he staggered Flowers with a vicious left hook to the jaw.

Flowers went down partly because he was off balance, and to show that he was unhurt he turned one of his favorite backsprings, regaining his feet, and then tore into Walker as Walker tore into him. He didn't take a count. But they were knock-downs even though Flowers regained his feet before one could be started. Perhaps these decided the issue in Walker's favor.

There is no other way for accounting for the decision of Referee Yanger. In view of the rumors and reports which preceded the fight the possible effect of the decision on Illinois boxing will be cause for speculation.

Commissioners John Reighemer, Chairman, Paul Phehn and O. W. Hunke were at the ringside, but got away before an expression of opinion could be obtained. Manager Walk Miller for Flowers, however, voiced his dissatisfaction.

"I must bow to the decision," said Miller after the fight. "The boxing commissioners had a good man as referee and he said Walker won and Walker must have won. At the same time, however, there is no denying that Flowers was fouled several times during the battle.

"I have an ironclad agreement which binds Walker to defend his title in a return bout with Flowers within three months in a city other than Chicago. Walker cannot fight any other challenger until he fights a return with Tiger. Of course the match will be held in New York City."

Gate Amounts to $77,000.

The paid attendance for the battle amounted to $77,000. The number of persons who paid for the spectacle was 9,127.

The five rounds which Flowers won were the second, fifth, sixth, seventh and eighth. Walker won the first, fourth, ninth and tenth and the third was even. The knockdowns scored by Walker in the first and the ninth were clean if not conclusive, but in the five rounds he won, Flowers overcame the point advantage which even these knockdowns gave to Walker.

It was expected that Walker would fight for a knockout as his only means of winning from Flowers. He did just that and failed. He was not expected to outpoint Flowers in ten rounds, although the challenger started admirably, and Walker didn't outpoint Flowers, the decision to the contrary.

At the final bell it was Walker who was the more tired of the two. It was Flowers who was carrying the fighting, as Flowers had done through the greater number of rounds. Flowers looked and acted the victor, not the vanquished.

Walker was blinded from the blood which flowed from a severe laceration over the left eye, a cut which Flowers opened in the second round and pounded at every opportunity through eight succeeding chapters until Walker's face was a crimson smear. Walker's lips were battered and bleeding. His nose spouted blood and the left side of his face was bruised by the club-like rights of Flowers. The champion, who was relieved of his title, on the other hand bled only slightly from the nose and mouth and was obviously fresher than Walker when the final gong clanged.

Walker Starts Fast.

Walker started the battle as if to make short work of Flowers. He ripped and slashed with tigerish fury and forced Flowers before him under torrid fire to the head and body. With a right to the jaw he deposited Flowers on the floor, and when the negro regained his feet immediately with a startled grin on his face it was to face a barrage of rights and lefts to the body and head.

Walker met with a surprise in the second round, and the battle took on a different hue. Flowers went into the challenger before Walker could get started, and blinded the New Jersey gladiator with driving rights and lefts as only Flowers can deliver them in his clownish style of fighting.

The punches carried no particular "steam," but they were bewildering blows and they upset Walker's battle plans. With a right to the jaw early in the round Flowers staggered Walker, and late in the session Mickey staggered backward under another right to the jaw, rebounding to face the fire again only to run into a smacking right which opened a cut over his left eye.

Manager Jack Kearns never could stanch the flow of blood from that wound and Walker went through the rest of the battle blinded partly at least. At times he had recourse to the thumb of his left glove in brushing aside the flow, which hampered his sight.

Flowers continued after his rival with the start of the third round, but Walker evened the round with a late rally, in which his furious fighting had the crowd, partial to the challenger from the start, yelling their encouragement. After being peppered and harried for half the round by Flowers, Walker launched an attack to the body, which hurt the negro.

In the fourth session Walker had his fighting fury of old. He battered Flowers freely with both hands to the head and body, staggering the champion with two hard rights to the jaw and almost bending Flowers double with two rights to the body. Against this Flowers was wild and flustered. But he recovered quickly and through the fifth, sixth, seventh and eighth rounds subjected Walker to such a fire as the New Jersey lad never before experienced.

Enough to Insure Victory.

This sustained offensive with its point scoring effect, was enough to clinch victory for Flowers unless Walker scored a knockout in the later rounds. The negro chased Walker, driving home to the head and body pitilessly, relentlessly, with both hands in a driving attack which had Walker plainly at sea and clinching at times to get a breathing spell from the drill fire.

Flowers protested he had been hit low in the stomach, and some at the ringside saw Walker's right for the body land low accidentally. The protest went unheeded. Later, in the eighth round, Flowers almost floored his rival with a wicked clubbed right to the jaw.

With the ninth round Walker launched a desperate attack, but for the time Flowers held his own in the torrid exchanges which resulted. Then Walker lashed a left hook to the jaw which staggered Flowers and a right which followed floored the negro, who regained his feet instantly and pitched into his rival.

The crowd was wild as Walker fought viciously for a knockout, but Flowers kept away from further damaging blows. In the tenth session the pair went after each other hammer and tongs. His reckless offensive gave Walker the round by a slight margin.

In the scheduled eight-round semifinal George Godfrey, local negro heavyweight, knocked out Cowboy Billy Owens of Texas in the eighth session, Referee Davey Miller stopping the contest to save Owens from further punishment.

Babe McGorgory, Oklahoma light-heavyweight, and Chuck Burns of Texas fought eight rounds to a draw. In another bout scheduled for eight rounds Walcott Langford, local negro middleweight, knocked out Jack Elkhart, Texas Indian, in four rounds.

Jackie Williams, local boxer, won the decision over Harry Robart, another local lad, in the six-round bout which opened the card.

December 4, 1926

Mickey Walker has just decked his opponent. Walker, a great crowd pleaser in the 1920's was known as *The Toy Bulldog*. He was the welterweight champion and later held the lightweight title.

Barny Ross (right) is shown here taking the lightweight title from Tony Canzoneri in 1933. Ross, who also held the welterweight crown, was the subject of a Hollywood film in the 1950's: *Monkey on My Back*.

DEMPSEY KNOCKS OUT SHARKEY IN 7TH BEFORE 80,000 IN THE YANKEE STADIUM; RECEIPTS EXCEED A MILLION DOLLARS

FOUL CLAIMED BY LOSER

Many at the Bout Insist Four Illegal Blows Were Struck.

DOCTOR IS NOT CERTAIN

Although No Indications Are Seen, He Says They Possibly Could Develop Later.

RESULT STARTLES CROWD

End Comes Although Former Champion Is Groggy and Bleeding—Triumph Popular.

By JAMES P. DAWSON.

The man they said couldn't come back made the grade last night in the ring at the Yankee Stadium, but his accomplishment was disputed by many who saw the test.

Jack Dempsey, the former heavyweight champion of the world, fighting for the chance to battle again for his lost crown, left the ring at the American League baseball park the winner by a knockout over Jack Sharkey, Boston's sturdy fighting ex-sailor, in seven rounds of what was to have been a fifteen-round struggle.

However, in the vast crowd of 80,000 men and women who witnessed this Homeric struggle and who had paid more than a million dollars for the privilege there were many—number undetermined because of the mingled cries which greeted the result—who always will hold the belief that Dempsey should have been disqualified on a foul.

Sharkey Grovels on Floor.

The contest ended after forty-five seconds of the seventh round with Sharkey groveling in the resin dust of the canvas-covered ring floor, his head burrowing a ridge there, his face distorted in pain, his hands twitching painfully as he feebly shook his head in protest of the progressing fatal ten-second count. He claimed a foul.

Referee Jack O'Sullivan, wise and experienced in his capacity, was undecided what to do in the circumstances. He hesitated, started to bend over the prostrate Sharkey, hesitated again, and finally picked up the count from the knockdown timekeeper, Billy (Kid) McPartland, at his station outside the ring.

Once he started, Referee O'Sullivan never stopped until he had completed ten seconds, and then he instructed Announcer Joe Humphries to raise Dempsey's hand aloft in token of a victory which was popular, even if its legality was and is questioned.

Not until Dempsey's hand went up did the stunned crowd know the result. Some thought the bout ended with Sharkey the winner on a foul. The traditional gesture of Announcer Humphries settled the doubt as to the official result, but it will be a long time before many of those who saw the fight, particularly those who were seated in the third base and left field sections away from the ring, will agree with the decision.

Dr. William H. Walker, State Athletic Commission physician, examined Sharkey in the latter's dressing room after the Boston heavyweight had been assisted from the ring and found no evidence of foul punches.

Signs Might Develop Later.

"There is no surface indication of foul, but this is not impossible," said Dr. Walker. "It is altogether possible that Sharkey received a foul blow or several of them. It does not necessarily follow that evidence of such punching would show immediately afterward."

Those who occupied seats on the third base and left field sides of the field were in the best position to see what occurred in the ring, and it seemed that it was this section of the crowd which raised the greatest hullabaloo as Referee O'Sullivan proceeded with his count despite Sharkey's painful protests.

This writer was among those in the best position to see what happened, and it is his verdict that Sharkey was hit low four times with a right. It was not deliberately or intentionally, for Dempsey is not that kind of a fighter. But Dempsey was fighting a desperate, savage battle last night, a losing last-stand encounter, in which he was rocked and shaken and groggy under the blows of his rival and the pace of the bout, and his attack probably became erratic under the circumstances.

The end of the bout came dramatically. Sharkey had boxed rings round Dempsey for six rounds, had surprised the great throng by disdaining a boxing offensive, electing to go into Dempsey and trade blow for blow where he might just as easily have stood off and peppered Dempsey. He had stood up under Dempsey's left hook to the jaw and was taking Dempsey's vicious digs to the body without cringing or crumpling until the seventh round.

They started the seventh round as they had started most of the previous rounds. Dempsey was digging both hands to the body and Sharkey was trying to stay the fire, until they worked to the centre of the ring. There Dempsey had his right hand loose while Sharkey locked his left, the former champion dug his right repeatedly into Sharkey, trying for the body, but they were unmistakably low punches, four of them, though concededly unintentional. Sharkey stood up under three of the low blows, but he sank under the fourth, protesting the illegal attack.

Dempsey, his faced smeared with blood which oozed from his mouth, nose and from cuts under and above his right eye, danced wearily to his corner after hesitating a moment over his prostrate foe. Referee O'Sullivan was temporarily bewildered and the crowd was stunned.

Cries of "foul" were mingled with cries of "quitter" and they were heaped upon Dempsey, the referee and Sharkey alike. Finally O'Sullivan picked up the count as knockdown counter McPartland carried it from the stop watch in his hand and Sharkey was counted out.

The result may lead Dempsey into a return fight with Gene Tunney for the heavyweight crown, or it may not. This depends entirely upon public opinion, but the chances are that Dempsey now will get the battle against Tunney, the man who conquered him last September, because this fight must be held in September and the time now is too short to stage a return meeting between Dempsey and Sharkey to see which is the better man.

Dempsey Only a Shell.

Dempsey certainly cannot be adjudged the better man on last night's battle. He was revealed as a shell of his former self, a man whose fighting spirit and effectiveness has left him. He has nothing now but the will to fight, minus even the desire. Of him it can truly be said that his spirit is willing, but the flesh is weak.

One of the greatest and most distinguished gatherings ever to witness a ring struggle viewed the battle and enjoyed every second of it up to the unsatisfactory ending. There were many who enjoyed this, too, for Dempsey carried the sentiment and hopes of the crowd as he sallied forth to battle, while for Sharkey there was mostly scorn and abuse.

Mayors and Judges held ringside seats. Millionaires rubbed elbows with just plain ordinary folks in the choice section under the glare of the huge incandescents which illuminated the battle platform. Actors and actresses, grand opera stars, captains of industry and kings of finance, leaders of the social world, were all there, thrilling to the spectacle as Dempsey fought in what many thought would be his last stand and Sharkey battled pluckily in what was to have been for him another step on the march to a championship fight.

It is estimated that the crowd paid $1,100,000 for the privilege of seeing this titanic struggle, for the Yankee Stadium was packed to capacity with a gathering of 80,000. Dempsey, in addition to his victory, collected about $375,000, for he was guaranteed 37¼ per cent. of the receipts. Sharkey signed for 22½ per cent., received about $250,000, and it is estimated that when everything is checked and paid, Promoter Tex Rickard will be in a position to count a profit of some $215,000 and the prospect of another success in Chicago around Sept. 10, when Tunney defends his title against Dempsey.

Spectacle Thrills Crowd.

All enjoyed this spectacle, though for some it was unwelcome, repulsive, for, almost from the first, Dempsey fought a losing, uphill battle. He fought gloriously, inspiringly, savagely, courageously, with a fighting heart that only a Dempsey can possess. But it was a lost cause in which he fought gallantly onward, for he tried to offset ring tradition and all the physical handicaps with which he entered the ring.

He was failing, even as he failed last Fall in Philadelphia's rain-soaked ring, slipping and skidding along to defeat if ever a boxer was facing defeat. It would have been a crushing, humiliating defeat for Dempsey, too, for there is grave doubt that Dempsey could have gone much beyond the seventh round.

Out of the fight, regardless of the disputed result, came one cold, undeniable conviction Dempsey is passé as a fighter. He has absolutely no chance against even the Tunney of today, with a year of soft living as champion behind him. For Dempsey has absolutely nothing with which to contend the boxing skill, accurate, precise attack and smart fighting head of the ex-marine who now rules the fistic roost.

Dempsey did not even have enough left to overcome the speed, skill, strength and boxing ability of Sharkey last night. He cannot hope to overcome the superior fighting qualities of Tunney.

Those who adjudged Dempsey below standards in his training had the satisfaction of having their deductions justified. Dempsey was nothing but the famous hollow shell he was described when he first started his comeback campaign back in late March in the Ventura Mountains of California.

He is slow and awkward, cumbersome, stiff and has not a remnant of his former fighting speed and agility left. His mind does not work with his muscles for there is a lack of coordination which was emphasized when the Dempsey of last night is contrasted with the fighting monarch of a few years back.

Most important of all, Dempsey has lost his punch. His mighty left, the blow which battered down the towering Willard, Carpentier, Firpo, and which for a time threatened so smart a boxer as Tunney, is absolutely gone now. Not even a semblance of its once destructive force remains.

Blows Fail to Shake Sharkey.

Dempsey hit Sharkey repeatedly and squarely with that left on the chin and Sharkey never faltered. On the contrary, Sharkey rallied under the blows and ripped and slashed into Dempsey, showing that he was unhurt, and what is more, that he was absolutely unaffected.

Without that left Dempsey is helpless. His right is and always has been just a gesture. His left held the dynamite and the destruction has left it. He is a machine burnt out through lack of activity and luxurious living.

There was a shower of straw hats into the ring and around the ringside section after the battle, but it was hard to determine whether they were in dispute of the result or acclaim of Dempsey. It is charitable to attribute this outburst to plain, ordinary enthusiasm.

Sharkey didn't show anything which would justify the assumption that he threatens Tunney's reign. If Dempsey was poor, Sharkey was just a little better, just a few degrees. Sharkey's plan should have been to step around Dempsey, box him, cut him and tire him.

Instead, he elected to fight Dempsey, not because he had to, but because he wanted to, for Sharkey could easily have escaped the floundering, awkward lunges of the Dempsey of last night and boxed rings about him as did Tunney last Fall.

As it was, Sharkey, fighting instead of boxing, did manage to cut and bruise Dempsey, and tired him, shook and rocked him, but he could not bring the shell of Dempsey down, although he drove his right and his left to the jaw in vicious, stout blows on numerous occasions. On the strength of this Sharkey is no world beater. At best he qualifies simply as the man who revealed Dempsey as a remnant of a once great fighter.

The best indication of the progress of the contest and the showing of Dempsey is the sway of the betting obtained from a layer after the bout. He said that Sharkey entered the ring a 3-to-2 favorite, contradicting a report that Dempsey went into the ring favorite at 11 to 10, and added that after the first round Sharkey was made a 3-to-1 favorite. That's how poorly Dempsey appeared from the very outset.

Jack Dempsey.

Jack Sharkey.

Runs a Poor Second.

The round-by-round description of the fight shows accurately the progress of the battle. It will show that Dempsey was running a poor second from the first bell.

The first note of the battle made by this reporter was, "Dempsey waits for Sharkey to come." It tells more clearly than anything else the extent to which Dempsey has disintegrated.

Dempsey never waited for any one. He was the first to leap in on the attack, the first to land a blow and the first punch invariably was clean and carried a salutary effect. But last night Dempsey stood half-crouched, waiting for Sharkey to lunge at him, instead of whipping out like the Dempsey of old. Sharkey came as Dempsey expected, with a long left hook, which missed, and they clinched twice, where Dempsey plied both hands to the body.

Dempsey Jarred by Sharkey.

Sharkey took this easily, without becoming excited. Then suddenly he whipped a short left and right to the jaw, and followed with another left, and Dempsey shook from head to heels, like a reed in the wind. Dempsey kept plunging in blindly and Sharkey forgot about his boxing. He had felt of Dempsey's blows and knew they couldn't hurt him.

He sailed in to fight Dempsey at close quarters. There he made a mistake, but it was not an irreparable one. He was outfought by Dempsey at close quarters, because that is where Dempsey is best—in the clinches.

But the best of Dempsey's blows didn't hurt Sharkey. Another left

hook to the jaw staggered Dempsey again, and a left and a right which followed sent Dempsey staggering giddily across the ring. He rebounded to the attack, however, and tried to fight his way to close quarters, but he was staggering at the bell.

It was much the same in the second round. Dempsey bored in to close quarters and became more confident with his success in a decidedly advantageous mixup. So confident did he become that he whipped two solid, accurate left hooks to the jaw, only to stand revealed in all his weakness. Sharkey, instead of crumpling under the blows, came right back at Dempsey with wicked smashes to the jaw, and actually outfought Dempsey.

It was just a flash from Sharkey, who seemed to be biding his time. He wanted, it seemed, to show that he could take the best Dempsey had to offer and not only stand erect but come back better than Dempsey. Then Sharkey started stabbing his left to the face and he had Dempsey looking foolish.

The ex-champion floundered around the ring, flat-footed, bewildered, not knowing where or when to start a counter-offensive of his own, and when he hid essay an offensive he simply pawed in the general direction of Sharkey, like a blind man feeling his way. Dempsey went to his corner at the end of this round with his nose bleeding and a cut under his right eye.

Dempsey had a good round in the third for he kept close to Sharkey, and the Boston ex-sailor seemed content to permit it, evidently to get a breathing spell for some long-range fighting. In one exchange Sharkey slipped to his knees in his own corner as his feet came in contact with the wet canvas there, but he came erect immediately, though the crowd

cheered, thinking Dempsey scored a knockdown.

Weakens in Legs.

That Dempsey's legs were becoming leaden weights was brought home to the observers at the ringside in the fourth round, for in an exchange the former champion's left leg apparently went out of control and his body swayed as Sharkey pummeled him. Sharkey peppered Dempsey hard in this round and opened a cut over the former champion's right eye, smearing Dempsey's face with blood.

Dempsey, however, fought gloriously onward in a stand that commanded admiration. Despite the buffeting to which he was subjected, Dempsey never stopped coming in, tearing at this opponent blindly, furiously, desperately, although his every rush invariably was met with a left jab and a left and high hook. Just before the bell Dempsey landed a solid left hook to the jaw and the populace went wild. But the punch didn't hurt Sharkey.

Dempsey continued to bore in blindly, savagely, in the fifth round, but he was being outboxed and out-generaled by a smarter ring fighter. A right and left to the jaw sent Dempsey backward on his heels, and it seemed he was being primed for a knockout. But when Sharkey's chances for a knockout seemed best the ex-sailor invariably stopped his assault. In this particular instance Dempsey covered his face and head with his two hands and Sharkey pawed fruitlessly at the crossed gloves, instead of hitting a blow to the body and bringing down the guard.

Sharkey brought into play a right uppercut to the chin in the sixth round which threatened to upset

Dempsey, but the ex-champion, courageous under fire, kept erect under the blow and pressed to close quarters. He pressed the retreating Sharkey about the ring, plodding home steadily with rights and lefts to the body until the pair were separated by the referee.

Sharkey ducked and bent under the blows and tried to tie his rival's hands, but Dempsey pressed onward to his own glory and to the satisfaction of those fans who had supported him when he entered the ring. After the bell in this sixth session Dempsey twice struck Sharkey in the face, but when Sharkey, starting for his corner, slapped a right to the face in retaliation he was roundly booed.

Then came the seventh, with its unsatisfactory, disputed finish. And it will always remain a question of doubt in the minds of those who saw the fray whether Dempsey won on a knockout or whether he fouled Sharkey.

Dempsey First in Ring.

A flock of photographers took possession of the ring after the last preliminary contest. A cheer from the crowd notified the ringside fans of the approach of Dempsey. He was first in the ring, attended by Leo Flynn, his manager; Sill Duffy, Jerry Luvadis and Gus Wilson.

Sharkey followed Dempsey into the ring, attended by Manager Johnny Buckley, Trainer Tony Pollozzlo and Harry Kelly. Dempsey, with a heavy white woolen sweater covering his shoulders, stepped across the ring to greet Sharkey.

Paulino, the Basque woodchopepr; Tom Heeney, New Zealand heavyweight, and Mickey Walker, the world's middleweight champion, were introduced from the ring.

When Sharkey and Dempsey were

introduced Dempsey got the greater reception. They stood posing before the photographers, looking each other in the eye, and it was Dempsey's eye that wavered.

Sharkey on the Attack.

Sharkey made the first offensive move, sailing into Dempsey with a left hook which missed. They clinched and Dempsey worked both hands to the body with good effect. In two more clinches Dempsey drilled rights and lefts to the body while Sharkey, stepping back, crossed several short lefts and rights to the jaw.

Sharkey drew blood from Dempsey's mouth with a left and right and Dempsey swung a light left to the jaw. Sharkey staggered Dempsey with a left to the jaw and then drove Dempsey across the ring grogy wigth a succession of lefts and rights to the jaw. Sharkey just grazed the jaw with a right at the bell. It was a delirious round for Dempsey and he was grogy going to his corner.

Sharkey leaped after Dempsey with the start of the second round and forced Dempsey to the ropes, landing a left and right to the jaw. Dempsey was inaccurate with two lefts to the body in a clinch. Sharkey drove a left to the face, which drew the blood from Dempsey's nose, and followed with a left and right to the jaw, which staggered Dempsey.

In a clinch Dempsey drove a short left and right to the face. Twice more he hooked his left to the jaw. Dempsey drove two lefts to the jaw, but Sharkey, instead of going down, came right back fighting, driving both hands to the jaw.

Sharkey then started to jab his left to the face and hooked a solid left to the body at the bell. Dempsey

was cut under the right eye as he went to his corner.

Dempsey Starts Boxing.

Dempsey started boxing in the third round, leading with a left to the body which missed. He pressed in close to Sharkey and gave a flash of the old Dempsey by clouting, throwing his right to the body and his left to the jaw. Sharkey never wavered under the punches, showing that the sting was out of the Dempsey blows.

Sharkey tried to box, but Dempsey kept on top of him, driving his right to the body at close quarters. Sharkey, too, worked a right to the body, and once Dempsey ripped a right uppercut to the face.

In one of the clinches Sharkey fought Dempsey off. Sharkey slipped in his o n corner as he retreated near the bell. It was a good round for Dempsey, because he pressed the attack.

Sharkey missed a vicious right for the jaw to start the fourth round and then put a left to the jaw. Dempsey was lost until he got to close quarters, where he drove both hands to the body. Sharkey hooked a short right and left to the face and kept repeating the blows as Dempsey came in wide open, leading for the body.

Has Dempsey Groggy.

Dempsey was groggy on his feet. His right eye was cut and bleeding, his nose was bleeding and his mouth was bleeding. He could hardly come in on his legs and he pawed the air, feeling for Sharkey. But he fought gloriously, coming in against Sharkey's lefts and rights to the face, lashing out with both hands to the body, and just before the bell hook-

ing a left to the jaw, which had the crowd on its feet yelling wildly.

Dempsey was short with a left hook opening the fifth round and Sharkey smothered him with rights and lefts to the face and jaw. Sharkey stuck his left jab in Dempsey's face repeatedly, but missed a right for the jaw as Dempsey drove a right to the body.

Sharkey grazed the jaw with a right hook and then jabbed his left to the face. In a clinch, he tied Dempsey up. A right and left to the jaw sent Dempsey back on his heels, but he came right in again, leading blindly for the body until Sharkey walked away from him.

Dempsey twice hooked his left to the jaw and crossed a right to the jaw. Sharkey retaliated by grazing the jaw with a right just before the bell.

Dempsey opened the sixth round boxing. He twice jabbed his left to the face and then ran into a right uppercut to the chin. Sharkey crossed a terrific right to the jaw and Dempsey's knees caved. Sharkey missed two more rights for the jaw and Dempsey missed a vicious left hook for the jaw.

Then, in a clinch, Sharkey tossed Dempsey aside like a sack of meal. Dempsey tried with a left to the jaw but it landed on Sharkey's shoulder. Sharkey rocked Dempsey from his head to his heels with a terrific right uppercut to the chin, but Dempsey bored in bravely, always working his hands to the body. At long range, Dempsey hooked a left to the jaw and they fought after the bell.

Crowd Finds Vantage Points.

The crowd which witnessed the struggle was one of the largest ever to witness a fight spectacle in this State. It certainly was one of the greatest ever to view a ring battle

anywhere. Not all the people were inside the ball yard inclosure. From the bill board fences of the field, from stalled subway trains on the structure, which is elevated at this point; from roof tops and from massive water tanks atop apartment houses offering a view of the field, the interested watched, some of those on the outside with better success than many who had paid good and sufficient money to get inside the park. Some of the more intrepid even scaled the park walls, making the rather dangerous drop inside the park with reckless success.

Promoter Tex Rickard said he had had 83,000 tickets printed for the fight. At 2 o'clock yesterday afternoon Rickard had some 900 pasteboards left in his box-office. The rest had been disposed of. Speculators did a thriving business, getting as high as $125 each for tickets whose face-value was $27.50. With the tremendous interest in the battle and the terrific demand for tickets, the brokers, who welcome just such occasions, experienced a pasteboard Klondike.

The crowd was orderly, good-natured and well handled. It came straggling into the park from the time the gates were opened in advance of the appointed hour. The bleacher section, where sat the purchasers of $3.30 admission tickets, filled first. This sale opened at 2:45 yesterday instead of 4 o'clock, because of the great crowd storming the box offices.

An hour later the park was thrown open for reserved seat ticket holders and they filed in slowly, but steadily into the arena, until the park was half filled.

July 22, 1927

GENE TUNNEY KEEPS TITLE BY DECISION AFTER 10 ROUNDS; DEMPSEY INSISTS FOE WAS OUT IN 7TH, AND WILL APPEAL; 150,000 SEE CHICAGO FIGHT, MILLIONS LISTEN ON RADIO

DISPUTE ON KNOCKDOWN

Challenger Went to Wrong Corner and Thus Delayed Count on Tunney for Few Seconds.

By JAMES P. DAWSON.
Special to The New York Times.
RINGSIDE, SOLDIER FIELD, CHICAGO, Sept. 22.—His refusal to observe the boxing rules of the Illinois State Athletic Commission, or his ignorance of the rules, or both, cost Jack Dempsey the chance to regain the world's heavyweight championship here tonight in the ring at Soldier Field.

By the same token this disregard of rules of ring warfare, or this surprising ignorance, saved the title for Gene Tunney, the fighting ex-marine, who has been king of the ring for just a year.

The bout ended with Tunney getting the decision, and the vast majority in the staggering assemblage of 150,000 people, who paid, it is estimated, $2,800,000 to see this great sport spectacle, approved the verdict.

The decision was given by Referee Dave Barry and Judges George Lytton, wealthy department store owner, and Commodore Sheldon Clark of the Sinclair Oil Company. It was announced as a unanimous decision,

but this could not be verified in the excitement attending the finish of the battle. But it should have been unanimous according to all methods of reasoning and boxing scoring, for Tunney won seven of the ten rounds, losing only the third, sixth and seventh, in the last of which, Dempsey made his great mistake. It is known that Judge Lytton voted for Tunney.

Dempsey's Furious Plunge.

In that seventh round Dempsey was being peppered and buffeted about on the end of Tunney's left jabs and hooks and sharp though light right crosses, as he had been in every preceding round, with the exception of the third.

In a masterful exhibition of boxing Tunney was evading the attack of his heavier rival and was countering cleanly, superbly, skillfully, accurately the while for half of the round or so.

Then Dempsey, plunging in recklessly, charging bull-like, furiously and with utter contempt for the blows of the champion, since he had tasted of Tunney's best previously, suddenly lashed a long, wicked left to the jaw with the power of old. This he followed with a right to the jaw, the old "iron mike" as deadly as ever, and quickly drove another left hook to the jaw, under which Tunney toppled like a falling tree, hitting the canvas with a solid thud near Dempsey's corner, his hand reaching blindly for a helping rope which somehow or other refused to

GENE TUNNEY, STILL THE CHAMPION.

be within clutching distance.

Then Dempsey made his mistake, an error which, I believe, cost him the title he values so highly.

Count Begun and Halted.

The knockdown brought the knockdown timekeeper, Paul Beeler, to his feet automatically, watch in hand, eyes glued to the ticking seconds and he bawled "one" before he looked upon the scene in the ring.

There he saw Dempsey in his own corner, directly above the prostrate, brain-numbed Tunney, sitting there looking foolishly serious, his hand finally resting on the middle ring strand. Beeler's count stopped. Referee Barry never started one.

It is the referee's duty to see to it that a boxer scoring a knockdown goes to the corner farthest from his fallen foe and it is the duty of the knockdown timekeeper to delay the count from the watch until this rule is obeyed. Beeler was simply observing the rule, which Dempsey either forgot to observe or refused to observe.

The challenging ex-champion stood there, arms akimbo on the top ropes of the ring in his own corner, watching his fallen rival, the characteristic Dempsey snarl o'erspreading his countenance, his expression saying more plainly than words: "Get up and I'll knock you down again, this time for keeps."

Dempsey Finally Moves.

Dempsey had no eyes for Referee Barry, who was waving frantically for the former titleholder to run to a neutral corner, even as he kept an eye on the fallen Tunney. Instead, Dempsey merely looked down at Tunney squatting there, striving instinctively to regain his feet and waiting for his whirling brain to clear.

Finally, Dempsey took cognizance of the referee's frantic motions. He was galvanized into action and sped hurriedly across the ring to a neutral corner, away from Tunney.

If he had observed the rule to the letter, Dempsey should, in fact, have gone to Tunney's corner, which was furthest removed from the fallen champion.

But three or four, or possibly five precious seconds had elapsed before Dempsey realized at all what he should do. In that fleeting time of the watch Tunney got the advantage. No count was proceeding over him, and quickly his senses were returning. When Referee Barry started counting with Timekeeper Beeler, Tunney was in a state of mental revival where he could keep count with the tolling seconds and did, as his moving lips revealed.

Slowly the count proceeded. It seemed an eternity between each downward sweep of the arm of Referee Barry and the steady pounding of the fist of Timekeeper Beeler.

Seconds are like that in a crisis, and here was one if ever one existed.

Tunney's senses came back to him. He got to his feet with the assistance of the ring ropes and with visible effort at the count of "nine." He was groggy, stung, shaken, his head was whirling as so many other heads have whirled under the Dempsey punch.

But Dempsey was wild in this crisis, a floundering, plodding mankiller, as Tunney, back pedaling for dear life, took to full flight, beating an orderly, steady retreat in the face of the plunging, desperate, vicious Dempsey, aroused now for the kill.

Dempsey plodded on so futilely and ineffectively that he tired from his own exertions. The former champion stopped dead in his tracks in mid-ring and with a smile spreading over his scowling face, motioned disgustedly, daringly, for Tunney to come on and fight.

But Tunney was playing his own game, and it was a winning game. He did not want to expose himself

to that deadly Dempsey punch again, and he would not.

Dempsey Wild in Eagerness.

Tunney backed steadily away from Dempsey, pecking and tantalizing with left jabs and grazing right hooks or crosses to the face or jaw. Which meant absolutely nothing to Dempsey. He brushed in against Tunney's blows but, in his eagerness, Dempsey was wild.

After motioning Tunney in, Dempsey backed the champion into the ropes near the challenger's corner and lunged forward savagely with a left and right to the jaw. But Tunney clinched under the blows and held Dempsey for dear life. And Dempsey never again got the chance that round to follow his advantage.

As the bell sounded the end of the round Dempsey was warned for striking low with a left for the body. He was hurling his punches in a blind fury, not particularly concerned over where they landed, so long as they did land.

The crowd which witnessed this dramatic fight, and particularly the critical moments of the seventh round, experienced varying emotions at the crisis. Some yelled themselves hoarse. The shrieks of women mingled with the howls of staid, old business men and the thousands of the purely sporting fraternity clustered about the ringside and extending backward from the battle platform in serried rows of faces.

Gripping Scene at Knockdown.

Society's bluebloods forgot decorum and yelled excitedly. Kings of finance and princes of industry were mingling their yells with those of Governors, mayors, Representatives in Congress, Senators, lawyers, doctors, theatre and movie folk and just plain ordinary people.

It was a scene to grip the observer, a situation to send quickening throbs through the pulses of those at the ringside and in the other sections of Chicago's memorial to her dead heroes. Here was a war hero, a ring hero, a champion, on the floor, and everybody was affected.

Out over the ether wastes some 50,000,000 people who listened to the fight broadcast by the National Broadcast Company over the greatest hook-up ever attempted for sport, had not the advantage of those actually watching the contest.

To those countless listeners it was plain that Dempsey was the victim of something, but just what only those who watched were aware. And there were some watching who did not realize the enormous consequences of this colossal mistake, because they are not versed in boxing rules. But it is safe to say that none among the 150,000 watching or among the 50,000,000 listening, will ever forget that particular elapse of time.

Flynn Will File Protest.

Leo P. Flynn, Dempsey's manager, made no effort after the fight to disguise or conceal his feelings or those of Dempsey. In plain words Flynn said that Dempsey had been robbed of victory because of that seventh-round situation.

"The watch in our corner showed fifteen seconds from the time Tunney hit the floor until he got up at the count of nine," Flynn said. "The legal count over a fallen boxer is ten seconds, not fifteen. Dempsey was jobbed. That's the way I look at it. But I'm going to appeal to the State Athletic Commission to reverse the decision, as is my privilege. Dempsey will fight him again and will knock him out if Tunney ever can be coaxed into meeting him again, just the way he knocked him out tonight."

In the final analysis, however, Dempsey was hoist on his own petard. The rule compelling a boxer to go to the corner furthest removed from a fallen foe is traceable to Dempsey himself. Its adoption followed the Manassa Mauler's battle in 1923 with the giant Firpo when Dempsey stood directly above the fallen Firpo striking the South American just as soon as his knees left

the floor without waiting for Firpo to come erect after a knockdown.

Dempsey was permitted to do this then. His attempt to do it tonight was the most expensive mistake he has ever made in his life.

Various Times on Knockdown.

Some watches at the ringside showed twelve seconds on the knockdown, others fourteen, and Flynn holds that Dempsey's corner watch showed fifteen seconds.

But a rule is a rule in boxing as in other big business, adopted to be observed, and the Illinois boxing authorities are to be commended for enforcing their rules without regard to victims or cost. It was unfortunate that Dempsey should have been thus penalized.

It would have been none the less unfortunate, however, if Dempsey had been permitted to remain standing within punching distance of Tunney to strike down the champion before Tunney had actually come erect.

On the strength of that colossal mistake of Dempsey's, it is hard, indeed, to say that Tunney was the better man in the ring tonight. Rather, the seventh round demonstrated what many have always contended despite assertions of Tunney and his associates to the contrary, that the real Dempsey would mow down the best Tunney like a cutting machine at work in a wheat field.

This is not said in an effort to detract from the victory of Tunney. He won and he won cleanly and clearly on points against the best Dempsey available today. But he was knocked down, had the closest call of his career, and, in the end, won only because of his superb boxing skill on defense and the little offense he attempted.

Dempsey Absorbs Tunney Fire.

Tunney peppered Dempsey with a cool, deliberate, two-fisted fire. He blinded him with flurries of punches, cut open old sores over the former champion's two eyes, drew blood from Dempsey's mouth and had Dempsey's face swollen. But it was revealed that Tunney could not hit hard enough nor often enough to keep Dempsey down.

True, Tunney floored Dempsey with a smashing right hook which curled over to the jaw in the eighth round, but Dempsey bobbed right up before a count could be started or before Tunney could be chased to a corner.

And Tunney shook and stung Dempsey times without number with solid right hand smashes to that corrugated steel jaw of the former champion, but, though Dempsey blinked under the punishment, shook from head to heels or went back on his heels, he always charged back in, tirelessly, relentlessly, savagely, viciously, desperately, on legs which were believed to be unsafe and unsound, but which carried him rapidly through ten rounds of persistent chasing in pursuit of the fleeting Tunney.

This Dempsey tonight was, after a manner of speaking, a reincarnation of the old Dempsey with the old spirit, the determination and the purpose. Greatest of all qualifications in this Dempsey of tonight was his courage and spirit.

Champion Fights Grimly On.

He fought a typical Dempsey battle to the great delight of his countless admirers in the vast throng. He was rough and foul at times. He hit Tunney low repeatedly and was warned, and he used the rabbit punch which is barred, and was warned.

In this respect Tunney deserves unstinted praise. He did not crumple like Jack Sharkey under a low blow, though they must have hurt. Instead, he kept grimly on with that determination and supreme confidence in his own ability which are his greatest ring recommendation aside from his superb boxing.

But all things considered, it cannot be denied that while Dempsey was defeated, he covered himself with glory. In the light of events it is charitable to attribute Dempsey's fouls to over-anxiety and wildness in his desperate bid for victory.

That seventh round was but one high light in a thoroughly exciting, thrilling, pulse-stirring battle. Each punch of Tunney's to Dempsey's jaw—and there were many of them—was a thrill in itself as Dempsey recoiled under the blow for a flash only to come charging in again. Those blows which floored Tunney were punches never to be forgotten, and the spectacle of Dempsey down squatting in the eighth round under Tunney's driving right to the jaw recalled the Dempsey-Firpo fight, save that the Tunney punch had not the power behind Firpo's.

Fight On After Final Gong.

And when Dempsey hooked a solid smashing left to the head in the tenth round and then went close and in trying to shake his rival off, wrestled Tunney down, the crowd got another thrill which surpassed that given it by the spectacular manner in which Dempsey piled into his rival fearlessly starting that tenth session. But Dempsey did so only to become exhausted and weakened by his own waning strength and Tunney's desperate blows and to finish the bout groggy, almost falling, but still with strength enough to keep fighting on and on with Tunney after the bell.

For the gong was heard neither by the principals nor the referee. Not until Tunney's seconds scrambled into the ring yelling wildly that the fight was over was the bout over. By then both champion and challenger had struck several blows at close quarters, as if for good measure.

In short, this was a fight worthy the crowd of distinguished men and women who graced it. It would well bear repetition, and possibly will.

Tunney won on his boxing ability alone and Dempsey lost because he could not keep up with the champion. That, in a nutshell, tells the story of the fight on results. Tunney was alert, resourceful, the cool ring general, the master boxer, hitting timely and accurately, and at times desperately in his own defense against the annihilating Dempsey with the revived punch.

Crowd Acclaims Fighters.

From the solid sea of faces which stretched from the side of the ring to the outmost rim of the Stadium on the sides and almost to the furthest row on the ends, came a mighty roar when Tunney and Dempsey were identified on their march to the battle platform.

Men and women arose as if pulled erect by some giant magnet, each cheering for his or her favorite while burly policemen and rugged handlers made passages for the champion and the ex-champion challenger through the mass of arms waving and trying to pat one or the other on the back.

Governor Small, Mayor Thompson, Promoters Tex Rickard and George F. Getz, President of the South Park Board, States Attorney Robert E. Crowe and Chairman John Richmeyer of the State Athletic Commission made a group in the ring before the champion and challenger entered and were introduced to the crowd.

Dempsey was the first one to enter the ring. He was wrapped in a white bathrobe. He was accompanied by Leo P. Flynn, Jerry Luvadis and Director Fred Tapscot. Gus Wilson also was in the corner, as was Bill Duffy of New York.

Dempsey Dances Around.

Dempsey danced around the ring, shook hands with the notables and waved greetings to friends as he recognized in the crowd while waiting for Tunney to appear.

Tunney climbed into the ring to the cheers of the crowd. He was seconded by Manager Billy Gibson, Trainer Lou Fink, Lou Brix and Jimmy Bronson.

The champion wore the blue and scarlet bathrobe with the Marine insignia on the back presented to him last year before the fight in which he won the title and which he refused to wear at that time.

Tunney was cool. He smiled and nodded quietly to friends at the ringside, while Jim Jeffries, Jack Sharkey and Paulino, the Spaniard, were introduced from the ring.

Dempsey got the greatest cheer when the introductions were made.

Record Figures for Receipts And Attendance at Title Bout

Attendance—150,000.	
Receipts—$2,800,000.	
Federal tax—$250,000.	
State tax—$225,000.	
Tunney's share—$1,000,000.	
Dempsey's share—$450,000.	
Preliminary fighters—$185,000.	
Rental of stadium—$100,000.	
Incidental expenses—$156,500.	
Rickard's profit—$250,000.	

Dave Barry of Chicago was the referee and Commodore Sheldon Clark and George Lytton, wealthy Chicagoan, were the judges.

It was 10:07 when the men were called to the centre of the ring for instructions. A minute later they were on their way.

The first round opened with Dempsey charging savagely and so did the tenth, but in the interval between the first and tenth so many things happened!

Dempsey missed a long left on his opening lunge and they clinched in the first embrace of many in which Tunney found refuge during the fight. Then Tunney started boxing and stabbing and crossing and hooking with lefts and rights and with one right to the jaw had Dempsey blinking.

Dempsey circled his man all the time, like a wild beast stalking its prey, but only in three rounds did Dempsey get close enough to take advantage of this circling, stalking style of his.

But his work in three rounds could not overcome the superb boxing of Tunney in the other seven. Boxing well and feinting coolly, Tunney peppered his rival for the first round until near the bell the champion crashed the challenger to the ropes under a left and right to the jaw.

Dempsey fought to get close and when in the clinches beat a drill-fire on Tunney's body whenever the champion was not holding his rival's arm against attack, which was seldom indeed.

Tunney Outgenerals Rival.

Early in the second round Dempsey hooked a left to the head with staggering power as Tunney missed a right to the jaw. Dempsey followed with a left to the body when Tunney left himself open and the punch did Tunney no good at all. But through the rest of the round Tunney outboxed and outgeneraled his rival in an impressive exhibition of boxing skill.

Dempsey was getting more vicious as the fight progressed and began hitting low with his leads at long range and his punches in the clinches in the third round. He was warned for these offenses. But he carried the attack so persistently, tirelessly, resistlessly, that he had Tunney in full flight, missing awkwardly as the former champion pounded the body and head with vicious drives of both hands.

In the fourth round Tunney drew blood from his rival with a right to the eye and with a pitiless fire drove Dempsey helpless in a neutral corner with savage lefts and rights to the jaw. Through the round Tunney battered his rival until the bell separated them, and it looked bad for the former champion.

Dempsey Piles in Again.

But Dempsey came charging back again in the fifth round to harass and worry Tunney with vicious drives to the body and head until the round was half completed, when Tunney again staggered his rival, after having shaken Dempsey with a right to the jaw, by repeating the blow.

Dempsey piled into Tunney in the sixth round with the same old rush, but with more of success in his execution. He was cut on the left ear and a swelling started under his

left eye from the blows of Tunney. But Dempsey persisted and hurt the champion with a savage fire of both hands to the body and when he shifted his left and right to the jaw. Tunney countered Dempsey's fire with a left hook, but was short or missed many of his blows.

Then came the seventh round and its tragic situation for Dempsey, but a round in which Tunney did the smartest fighting of his career.

It was followed by the exciting eighth session in which Tunney floored Dempsey for a fleeting second with a right to the jaw, and overcoming Dempsey's early fire, hammered the former champion relentlessly to the bell.

Tunney's Withering Fire.

Tunney had things his own way in the ninth round, subjecting Dempsey to a withering fire of boxing hands in snappy flashes of offensive work or outboxing his rival as the occasion demanded.

At the bell Dempsey's left eye cut was enlarged and the former champion was being blinded by the flow of blood. But he carried on and entered the tenth session with a rushing aggressiveness which for a time had Tunney worried. Dempsey hooked his left to the head and then going close, wrestled the champion down as Tunney sought to clinch and hold.

Tunney quickly regained his feet and his boxing poise, and then he went about hammering Dempsey pitilessly until in the last half minute it seemed that Dempsey must collapse from exhaustion as well as from the effects of Tunney's blows.

A light left and right to the jaw almost floored Dempsey just before the bell, which neither fighter heard, and then the pair went close and were hammering each other until the entrance of Tunney's corps of seconds, headed by Manager Billy Gibson, signaled the end of the fight.

Crowds Handled Without Hitch.

Chicago did itself proud for the occasion. Tonight's struggle was the third ring championship in the history of the city and the first for the heavyweight title, but the Middle West's leading city handled affairs as if it were used to the experience.

Elaborate plans were made long in advance for the accommodation and convenience of the largest crowd ever to witness a ring struggle, which was also one of the most distinguished and representative crowds of ring history. And the plans went through without a hitch.

Wonderful police arrangements kept congestion down to a minimum outside the city's memorial to its war dead and eliminated disorder entirely.

Police lines were established four blocks away from the scene of ring action and none was allowed to pass without exhibiting his or her ticket. Occupants of taxicabs and private cars were barred from the sacred zone maintained by the police unless they possessed a ticket and showed the pasteboard.

Approaching the arena were thousands who crossed the streets in solid waves when the police made passages through the seemingly never-ending flow of vehicles. Traffic in the city's main arteries, ordinarily heavy and slow, progressed at a snail's pace in what was the heaviest traffic Chicago ever experienced. Progress was just a little bit faster afoot.

Hawkers Do Thriving Trade.

Hawkers cried their wares outside the arena, greeting fans with such cries as "Get your lunch here, only 5 cents," and proffering an abbreviated bag of peanuts, or, "Get a ringside seat here, only a dime," and offering an imitation pair of field glasses.

Strange as it may seem, the hawkers did a land-office business. In such a vast throng there must needs be many gullibles. Cushions, too, of varying makes and indifferent appeal from the standpoint of practicability were offered for sale. And they sold fast, too.

TUNNEY AND DEMPSEY IN CHICAGO RING.

Times Wide World Telephoto.

The Champion and Challenger in a Clinch. This Telephotograph Was Taken in One of the Early Rounds of Last Night's Championship Battle.

Inside the arena an army of ushers, advantageously placed about the concrete plant, the accommodations of which had been increased by the addition of wooden stands, kept confusion down to a minimum and put the thousands of fans in a happy state of mind.

These ushers were recruited from the ranks of the Illinois Naval Militia, the National Guard and the colleges. They were well drilled in frequent rehearsals under the experienced direction of Bill Stillman, who has handled all of Promoter Rickard's important ring battles in late years.

The result was that this biggest crowd of ring history was almost one of the most easily handled. Courtesy was the watchword, satisfaction for everybody, an objective which was attained.

Radioed Over the Continent.

The gathering that saw the fight was only a small percentage of those who enjoyed it. Millions heard the bout described by Graham McNamee, veteran announcer, over a radio hook-up which included seventy stations, the largest undertaking of its kind known to sport.

For this important feature of the title struggle plans had been made in keeping with the importance of the occasion, and as a consequence, radio listeners from coast to coast and from the border to the Gulf, heard the fight graphically described from the ringside over wave-lengths which carried also through two stations in Canada.

Huge flood lights from the roof of the permanent stand on each side of the stadium illuminated the ring and the crowd so that those in choicest seats had a view which was emphasized by powerful incandescents, while those on the outermost rim of the plant found their field glasses more useful than they had hoped.

First Fighters Enter on Dot.

The fighters in the first bout entered the ring promptly on schedule, the principals, Big Boy Peterson and Johnny Grosso, being introduced at 8 o'clock by Announcer Al Smith, who addressed the crowd through a microphone transmitter attached to an extension wire permitting announcements from the middle of the ring to be heard clearly in all parts of the plant. A slight delay was occasioned by faulty wiring of the overhead ring lights, but this soon was corrected without any great loss of time.

By the time the opening bout got under way the stadium was more than half full with a crowd of men and women fans clothed in overcoats, fur coats, blankets, steamer robes, windbreakers, lumberjacks, leather jackets, mufflers—in fact anything that promised protection from the brisk breeze which blew over the arena.

But the weather was mild compared to what Chicagoans have experienced for the past few days. And in the glare of the ring lights, it was actually warm.

Two hours before the main bout entered the arena the ringside seats were occupied almost to their capacity by a collection of financial and social lights fortunate enough to get consideration from those in power on the advance ticket distribution.

Rain Causes Apprehension.

They came early and sat through cloudy, misty weather, proud of their ticket preferences but taking no chances, nevertheless. The booming of flashlights as celebrities were photographed in the ringside section and the constant babble of voices echoed over the arena while the crowd waited for the first pair of fighters.

Before this opening bout ended a light shower fell, causing apprehension among the thousands exposed to elements which threatened to become unfavorable.

The situation did not look any more promising when the telegraph wire chiefs at the ringside passed out rubber coverings for the instruments over which millions of words were being carried to all corners of the world.

Ugly rumors were circulating immediately preceding the fight, as is characteristic of all such major battles in this era of big business in pugilism. They were to the effect that Dempsey would foul Tunney and escape disqualification; that Dempsey would reopen the cut over Tunney's eye and that the bout would then be stopped because Tunney was bleeding too freely, which would, of course, involve some effort on the part of Dempsey; that Dempsey was to win by a knockout in five rounds. There were others, but they did not reach the ears of this reporter.

All these rumors, however, involved the necessity of collusion on the part of the principals or tampering with the bout officials. But none received especial attention.

State Commission Cautious.

The State Athletic Commission took every precaution to prevent tampering with the officials. Not until the bout was almost into the ring, did the names of the referee and judges become known, making it difficult to imagine any way in which officials could be approached.

Nor could it be regarded as probable that Tunney, with millions in his grasp and with his known umbrage at Dempsey following publication of the now famous open letter, would even permit himself to be approached with a traitorous offer.

But now that the fight is history it can be published that Tunney entered the ring to defend his title with every last spark of respect for Dempsey a forgotten thing. Publication of Dempsey's open letter led Tunney to a decision to discontinue saying nice things about the man he beat last year, after eight years of friendship and mutual admiration.

Another thing which indicated that these alarming reports were groundless was the fact that the odds in the betting remained with the champion, in accordance with ring tradition. As good as even money was reported in the early afternoon betting, with indications that Dempsey would enter the ring a favorite. But the prevailing odds at ring time were reported at 7 to 5, with Tunney the favorite.

September 23, 1927

LOUGHRAN WRESTS TITLE FROM M'TIGUE

Has Edge in 14 of 15 Rounds of Sensational Battling for Light-Heavy Crown.

LOSER RALLIES TOO LATE

Unleashes Crushing Attack in 15th, but Valiant Effort Fails to Offset Rival's Lead.

13,472 PAY TO SEE BOUT

By JAMES P. DAWSON.

The New York State Athletic Commission conferred Jack Delaney's vacated light-heavyweight championship of the world on Mike McTigue a few weeks ago, but Tommy Loughran, sprightly Philadelphian, knocked it off last night in fifteen rounds of spectacular, vicious and fast fighting in Madison Square Garden.

A crowd of 13,472 fight fans paid $72,562 for a battle which exceeded even the most optimistic advance expectations. Loughran weighed 175 pounds and McTigue a half pound less.

Mayor Walker was one of the interested spectators at the passing of the light-heavyweight championship, occupying a ringside seat, flanked on one side by James A. Farley, Chairman of the New York State Athletic Commission. Tommy Hitchcock, No. 2, on the International four, also witnessed the contest.

Through fourteen of those fifteen rounds, Loughran, the younger, more active and stronger of the two, hooked, cuffed, slapped and smacked McTigue with a hail of punches the like of which McTigue had seldom experienced.

In the fifteenth round, McTigue came through gloriously with a rally which had the crowd on its feet yelling and which had Loughran worried and tired. But the rally came too late to be of any great benefit to McTigue or to affect the award at the final bell.

Loughran had his hand hoisted in token of victory before a screaming, excited crowd, after Referee Lou Magnolia and Judges Charles F. Mathison and Harold Barnes had handed up their ballots.

Fourteen Rounds to Loughran.

Loughran won fourteen of the fifteen rounds going away. They weren't even close. McTigue won only one, the closing fifteenth in which the veteran Irishman threw aside caution and became a daring larruping fighter.

McTigue didn't succeed in his task, due only to the wise fighting head of Loughran. The pity of it, however, was that McTigue didn't throw some of that fighting into his earlier efforts. Then a different story might have been told.

This morning Loughran is champion of the world among the light-heavyweights, as far as our Empire State boxing authorities are concerned. He will not be accepted as champion by the National Boxing Association, which has eighteen States and several other boxing localities affiliated with it.

Loughran is determined to establish himself unqualifiedly as titleholder, and is absolutely sincere, for his first words after reaching his dressing room were:

"Now I want to fight Jack Delaney for the title if he cares to fight me."

And there were many in that throng who saw Loughran manhandle the wily old McTigue who expressed the belief the Philadelphian would outbox Delaney if they meet.

McTigue Is Outspeeded.

Loughran won from McTigue because the Philadelphian was too fast and clever for the veteran, too shifty and agile, too light on his feet and quick with his hands. It was a one-sided fight—the score on rounds reflects that. Yet it was a thrilling spectacle hard fought and bitterly contested. One couldn't help but feel the thrill offered by the cagy McTigue, his ringcraft gone, his heretofore puncture-proof defense swept aside, always pressing forward, never taking a backward step, even when Loughran's blows sent him off balance and rocking on his heels.

The best fighting came from McTigue in that stirring fifteenth round, when the Irishman went berserk. But one of the greatest boxing exhibitions ever seen in a Garden ring or elsewhere came from Loughran through the other fourteen rounds. He was like Tunney in his display of a fighting head, only Loughran's exhibition carried through fourteen rounds, not in one flash of a round.

McTigue Favored at Start.

Loughran showed himself a better fighter than he had heretofore been appraised. He entered the ring second in the acclaim of the crowd, which greeted McTigue with a salvo that drowned out the strains of jazz sent through the arena by the band of St. Monica's Naval Battalion, the protégés of the Philadelphian. But he left the ring a popular idol, more popular than ever he has been here before, because he made a greater fight than anybody expected.

He went on the offensive with the first bell and he never relinquished the attack. His one great fault is lack of punching strength. If he had possessed this desirable quality Loughran would have knocked out McTigue.

He hit McTigue with every conceivable punch when and where he pleased in the process of a boxing lesson administered to a veteran, thought one of the greatest boxers in the ring.

Philadelphians at the ringside noisily celebrated Loughran's victory, and they had just cause, for Loughran gave the city its first ring champion since the days when Philadelphia Jack O'Brien held the light-heavyweight title back in 1905.

A draw decision was rendered in the ten-round semi-final between James J. Braddock, Jersey City light-heavyweight, and Joe Monte of Boston. The verdict was greeted with cheers and jeers, but it satisfied the majority.

Yake Okun, east side light heavyweight, stopped Earl (Little Boy) Blue, Hoosier iron man, in nine rounds of their scheduled ten-round battle, Blue failing to respond to the bell for the tenth round. His handlers decided he had taken enough punishment.

In the opening bout of four rounds Murray Layton, east side featherweight, fought a draw with Al Ridgeway of Williamsburg.

October 8, 1927

Two Stretchers at Ringside Ordered by Illinois Solons

CHICAGO, Sept. 5 (AP).—"Take him out feet first, men!"

This may be the command at the ringside as a result of the order issued by the Illinois State Athletic Commission today requiring promoters to have two stretchers ready to remove knockout victims unable to walk out of the ring.

The usual procedure has been for the handlers to toss the losing fighters over their shoulders and carry them out through the crowd.

The commission has considered this a very ungentlemanly way to treat a boxer after he has been knocked out.

September 6, 1929

SCHMELING WINNER ON SHARKEY'S FOUL; 80,000 AT TITLE BOUT

Crown Goes to Europe for First Time as Stadium Match Ends in Fourth Round.

RECEIPTS ARE $700,000

Crowd Cheers the Decision of the Officials at Dramatic Closing of Fight.

AMERICAN AHEAD AT TIME

Boston Boxer's Shower of Lefts and Rights Kept German Rival on the Defensive.

By JAMES P. DAWSON.

One powerfully driven but erratic blow for the body, a conspicuously low, desperately powered left in a myriad of otherwise fair punches, cost Jack Sharkey, America's premier heavyweight, the world's heavyweight title last night.

Max Schmeling, Germany's like-ness of Jack Dempsey, succeeded to the mythical throne abdicated by Gene Tunney and will carry the title to Europe for the first time in modern ring history. It is, however, the second instance of an alien holding the championship since such title was established, in John L. Sullivan's time, as one must recognize the reign of Tommy Burns, a Canadian.

In the fourth round of what was to have been a fifteen-round battle at the Yankee Stadium, staged in the interests of the Milk Fund, Sharkey was disqualified on a foul.

It was estimated by Madison Square Garden officials that the crowd was 80,000 and that the gross receipts would be at least $700,000. Of this amount, each fighter, working on a percentage basis, would receive about $175,000.

Finish Is Dramatic.

The finish came dramatically, in a pulse-quickening contest, after 2 minutes 55 seconds of the fourth round, and at a time when Sharkey appeared well on the road to victory over the gallant lad from across the seas who disputed his right to the crown.

A low left hook, aimed for the body, but palpably a violation of ring ethics and code in the desperation with which it was driven, sent the German boxer groveling on the ring floor in pain.

Pandemonium broke loose in the ring among the officials and in the vast throng which crowded the three concrete tiers of the Stadium, the 17,000 ringside seats placed on the field and the serried rows of the bleachers in the far outfield of a ball yard converted for the occasion into a vast fight arena.

Referee Jim Crowley was in a quandary and hesitated in his action. He sought information from Judge Harold Barnes, who was in an excellent position to see the punch, since the action took place directly above him and the writer. Referee Crowley got the information he sought, for Judge Barnes vigorously shook his head in an affirmative indication of foul.

Still Referee Crowley hesitated, and the excitement of the crowd became intense. Crowley walked across the ring to Judge Charles F. Mathison on the opposite side of the square battle platform and was unrewarded, since Mathison was in no position to see the blow landing, because Schmeling's back was to him. A second time Crowley came over to Judge Barnes, and a third time. And then a fourth time. Always he received the same answer, an affirmative shake of the head, telling him that Sharkey had fouled Schmeling.

Confusion in Ring.

The bell ending the fourth round clanged and Schmeling's handlers, Joe Jacobs, Max Machon and Doc Casey, leaped through the ropes at a time when Referee Crowley seemed on the verge of starting a count. Timekeeper Arthur Donovan's arm was upraised outside the ring for an imminent count which never started because of the confusion.

Schmeling was writhing in pain, helpless, incapacitated by an illegal punch, and had to be carried to his corner. Sharkey was signaled quickly to his corner in the uproar, and for the minute's rest between rounds the confusion held sway. Manager Jacobs, strengthened by the decision of Judge Barnes on a foul, ranted all over the ring, and so did Manager Johnny Buckley for Sharkey, trying hard to convince Referee Crowley that no foul had been committed.

The bell rang to start the fifth round, and Sharkey leaped out of his corner and raced over to the corner in which the helpless Schmeling was writhing and groaning in agony. But he was restrained, and then Referee Crowley finally declared himself, advising Announcer Joe Humphries that he had disqualified Sharkey and given the victory to Schmeling on a foul.

The award stunned Sharkey. He was too overcome in the ring to say a word. But it was satisfactory to one of the greatest crowds ever to witness an outdoor fight, although it involved the winning of a heavyweight title on a foul for the first time in modern history.

The nearest approach to this result is furnished in the memorable Sharkey-Jack Dempsey battle, in which Sharkey's claim of foul was disregarded and Dempsey was declared winner by a knockout.

Last night I was advantageously seated to the left of Judge Barnes and the action was directly above me. And I can say that the left hook which Sharkey directed for the body landed foul and merited disqualification because of its obvious disabling effect.

Medical science supported the disqualification of Sharkey for Dr. William H. Walker, State Athletic Commission physician, examined Schmeling immediately after the bout and announced he found unmistakable evidence that a foul punch had been struck.

Decision Meets With Approval.

The opinion of the crowd, too, supported the disqualification, for it welcomed the delayed announcement with cheers.

Outstanding in this momentous situation was Judge Barnes, a medium sized, slim, quiet man who

JUST AFTER THE FOUL BLOW WHICH ENDED FIGHT AND GAVE MAX SCHMELING THE CHAMPIONSHIP.

Max Schmeling.

faced perhaps the most trying situation a modern ring has produced, and gave the decision as he saw it.

With 80,000 persons looking on, with the ring's richest prize, the heavyweight championship of the world, the stake, and an American the loser by an honest decision, Judge Barnes had the courage of his convictions, remaining adamant against the repeated interrogations of a confused referee in an international battle that has no parallel for result.

Sharkey was a pitiful figure in defeat. He was utterly crushed. He did not become emotional or excited. He was the other extreme, melancholy, morose, shocked to speechlessness and incapable of action. His handlers raved and ranted, and all Sharkey did was stand motionless in his corner permitting his handlers to drape him with his navy blue bathrobe with the navy insignia on its back. Then he walked dejectedly from the ring, a crushed, disappointed figure if ever there was one.

Low Punch Is Costly.

And he had reason to be overcome with his sorrow. He had flipped away a promising chance to win the heavyweight title which Tunney laid aside through one single, solitary punch whose course he could not guide truly in his desperation before a charging foe who backed him to the ropes with a gallant rush.

That the low blow was unintentional was patent. It could not have been otherwise, because Sharkey was in front on the action of the bout, as far as it went, by three rounds.

The first session was about even, but the second and third and the fourth, up to within the fateful five seconds of its conclusion, went to the Boston ex-gob, who was boxing coolly, calculatingly, methodically, unemotionally, a battle such as he had furnished three years ago against Dempsey, and was on the high road to success.

Sharkey was the boxer and the

sharp, true hitter last night against a foe whose courage was established, as was his resistance to punishment and his ability to survive in an emergency and be dangerous.

I am not prepared to say that Sharkey would have gone on to win the battle. He subjected Schmeling to every gun he had in those first three rounds and through part of the fourth. He had Schmeling in a precarious way in the third session when a barrage of rights shook and staggered the German boxer and sent him wobbling to the ropes.

Schmeling Equal to Emergency.

But in this emergency Schmeling was glorious, the true fighting man, pressing on and in, eternally on the attack, despite the buffeting to which he was subjected. And I have a well-grounded conviction that Schmeling would have taken everything that Sharkey had for perhaps half the battle and then came on to win against a discouraged Sharkey.

Schmeling gave early indications of the danger lurking in his powerful fists. He fought the fight of the challenger from the beginning, crowding, jamming, pushing in against the man he had to beat to win the title, in a manner which commanded the admiration of the crowd and the utmost respect from Sharkey.

He took Sharkey's jabs with indifference. He absorbed Sharkey's most powerful counters without weakening or cringing. His plan, quite obviously, was to crowd Sharkey until he had crowded him out of the title, and, though he was being subjected to a withering fire in his campaign, I believe he would have succeeded.

Schmeling had taken about the best Sharkey had to offer in the short time the bout lasted and he had given considerably of his own stock in trade. I doubt if Sharkey could have improved as the fight progressed, and I don't think Schmeling

who had weathered Sharkey's severe attack and continued to tear headlong, would have weakened.

Until last night there was a veil of doubt over Schmeling's ability to withstand punishment. He had never been forced to take punishment in his American ring appearances. But this doubt no longer has any justification. Schmeling cannot only take a punch but he can give one.

Schmeling Lands Right to Jaw.

He had Sharkey's lips dripping crimson from left hooks in the first round, and, pressing in against Sharkey's repeated left jabs, the German lad closed the first session with a smashing right to the jaw which stung Sharkey.

Sharkey's boxing carried the second session, and late in the round Sharkey drove a powerful right to the jaw which made Schmeling wince. Never, however, did Schmeling take a backward step. Always he plunged in, unmindful of the jabs which met him invariably, hooking short lefts to the head or pushing short rights for the jaw, and working both hands to the body in the clinches.

After outboxing Schmeling early in the third round, Sharkey suddenly brought a roar from the crowd when he shook the German lad with a powerful right to the jaw which sent Schmeling backward to the ropes.

Another right followed, and another and another as Sharkey fought to batter down his foe. But Schmeling came out of the danger in splendid fashion. Before the bell Sharkey smashed home a wicked left hook to the body.

German Fresh Starting Fourth.

Schmeling came up apparently fresh for the fourth, and his rushes, as had been customary, were met with Sharkey's well-placed lefts and a series of rights to the head. Schmeling broke through with a sharp right to the jaw and Sharkey countered with a similar blow.

Sharkey undertook to follow this advantage, but rained his blows on the head of a rival whose vulnerable point was protected with crossed arms and blocking gloves. The action was exciting and pulse-quickening, and the crowd was enjoying it. Schmeling was boring in repeatedly and backed Sharkey to the ropes with the attack. Then a left hook for the jaw drew a desperate left for the body which landed foul and ended the bout, giving Schmeling the title with the distinction of having his name inscribed on the Tunney-Muldoon championship trophy.

The result provided the climax to a series of eliminations which now end with Schmeling the champion. In these eliminations foreign and native born challengers, Victorio Campolo, Paulino, Phil Scott and Tommy Loughran, were eliminated, leaving Sharkey and Schmeling the survivors.

June 13, 1930

ROSENBLOOM WINS; DEFEATS SLATTERY

Gains Light-Heavyweight Title by Decisive Victory in 15 Rounds at Buffalo.

15,000 VIEW THE COMBAT

By JAMES P. DAWSON.

Special to The New York Times.

BUFFALO, N. Y., June 25.—Maxie Rosenbloom tonight won undisputed possession of the world's light-heavyweight championship which Tommy Loughran discarded when he entered the heavyweight ranks. The eccen-

tric ringman from New York overcame the only obstacle to the 175-pound throne tonight when he battered his way to the decision over Jimmy Slattery of Buffalo in fifteen rounds.

The decision which made Rosenbloom champion was a divided one and it was altogether unpopular, as could be expected, since the New Yorker figuratively came into Slattery's own backyard to battle the home-town pride. But no other decision was possible.

Haley Votes for Slattery.

Referee Patsy Haley constituted the minority in the vote. He gave his decision to Slattery. Judges George Partrick and George Kelly cast their ballots for Rosenbloom.

The decision was greeted with a round of hisses and jeers by an excited crowd of close to 15,000 which paid about $60,000 to view the spectacle, but there was no justification for the outburst, beyond local sentiment. Rosenbloom won eight of the fifteen rounds after a valiant effort.

Rosenbloom had to fight one of the best battles of his career to win the crown. The Slattery of tonight was not the Slattery of old, it is true, but he had trained steadily and conscientiously for this battle and entered the ring as near physical perfection as it is possible for him to be now, and prepared to make a gallant stand. He did and went down with colors flying, simply because Rosenbloom was not to be denied in the realization of his life's ambition.

Rosenbloom, getting off to a poor start in the sixth battle against a lad who had conquered him four times previously, started to make his efforts effective with the fourth session. He won this round and the fifth, sixth, seventh and eighth.

He annexed the eleventh, and then in a determined offensive to overcome the desperate, last-minute rally of Slattery to stave off defeat, overcame the local lad in the fourteenth and fifteenth rounds.

Slattery won the second and third rounds, and rallied to win the ninth, tenth and thirteenth. In the first and the twelfth sessions the action, always bitter with neither asking or giving quarter, found honors about even. Rosenbloom entered the ring the recognized champion of the National Boxing Association. Slattery was the recognized champion in this State, having won the title here last February in a battle with Lou Scozza.

When they weighed in in the afternoon Rosenbloom tipped the scales at 170½ pounds and Slattery at 166½.

June 26, 1930

FOULS ARE BARRED BY BOXING BOARD

Starting July 17 Fighters Must Wear Device to Guard Them Against Injury.

SINGER'S PLAN APPROVED

Pugilist Failing to Arise After a Low Blow Will Have Knockout Scored Against Him.

By JAMES P. DAWSON.

The commission of a foul in boxing was read out of the modern boxing code and regulations yesterday, at least in so far as New York is concerned.

At a meeting of the State Athletic Commission the three members, Chairman James A. Farley, William

Muldoon and Brig. Gen. John J. Phelan, unanimously adopted a regulation which permits no claim of an illegal blow. The regulation, which is to be incorporated in the commission's form of fight contracts, follows:

"The parties of the first and second part agree to equip themselves with an abdominal guard of their own selection, the type to be approved by the State Athletic Commission, which will obviate the necessity of any foul claim being made during the contest. It is expressly understood that this contest is not to be terminated by a foul, as the protector selected by the boxers is, in their own opinion, to be sufficient protection to withstand any so-called low or illegal blow which might temporarily incapacitate either or both of the parties."

The new rule is calculated by the commission to put a halt to the epidemic of fouls which lately have played conspicuous parts in important ring struggles.

Fans Welcome New Rule.

Boxing followers generally welcomed the new rule yesterday, although there were some who asserted it might tend to encourage indiscriminate indulgence in fouls by boxers. The provision will penalize a foul violator with the loss of the round in which a foul is committed, but if a boxer goes down under a foul blow and fails to arise he will be counted out and a knockout scored against him.

In its adoption of this measure the commission followed the suggestion of Al Singer, Bronx lightweight. Incidentally, it will be in Singer's bid for the 135-pound title against Champion Sammy Mandell at the Yankee Stadium on July 17 that the new order of things will be first applied.

Eddie Kane, manager of Mandell and Hymie Caplin, manager of Singer, appeared before the commission and approved the new regulation. If the proposed return bout between Max Schmeling, heavyweight champion, and Jack Sharkey, scheduled for Sept. 25 in the Yankee Stadium, is signed, as scheduled today, this new clause will be incorporated in the contracts for the match.

Few Fouls by Comparison.

Discrediting the idea that fouls have become the rule and not the exception, Chairman Farley announced he had caused an inspection to be made of the record of bouts in this State since the first of the year, and this investigation disclosed that of 1,500 matches only twenty-two ended in fouls.

July 2, 1930

CANZONERI STOPS SINGER, WINS TITLE

Knocks Out Defending Lightweight Champion in 1 Minute 6 Seconds of First Round.

LEFT TO MOUTH ENDS BOUT

Singer Aided to Corner After Being Counted Out—Fails in Attempt to Rise.

By JAMES P. DAWSON.

Tony Canzoneri, popular little Brooklyn boxer who formerly held the world's featherweight championship, hopped into the ring at Madison Square Garden last night at 9:23

a challenger for the world's lightweight crown and less than ten minutes later he left the battle platform the ruler of the 135-pound division.

In a still shorter period of fighting, one of the most startling upsets of modern times occurred, for Canzoneri knocked out Al Singer of the Bronx, the defending champion, in exactly one minute and six seconds of the first round in what was to have been a fifteen-round struggle.

A left hook to the mouth sent Singer down and out, and almost out of the ring, and brought a crowd of about 16,000 hysterically yelling men and women to their feet, rocking the Garden with their cries and cheers and exclamations at the ring drama.

That left hook to the mouth was one of perhaps a dozen blows Canzoneri unleashed in the short space of time consumed by the bout, and it sent Singer down as the powerful lefts and rights of Jimmy McLarnin had done last Summer.

It brought Canzoneri the crowning distinction, the goal of all boxers below the heavyweight division who aspire to hold the championship in one class and, outgrowing that, reign supreme in the class next highest—a distinction enjoyed by perhaps half a dozen boxers in all ring history.

More, that left hook to the mouth, following a grazing left hook to the jaw, brought Canzoneri the title in one of the quickest transfers of the lightweight title on record.

Gans Battle Recalled.

Back in the long ago Joe Gans regained the title from Young Erne in the first round of their battle at Fort Erie, and in the only other lightweight championship struggle to end in the first round, which comes to mind. Singer took the crown from Sammy Mandell last July 17.

But it required Singer less time to lose his bauble than it did to win it. Knocking out Mandell, Singer had to fight 1 minute 46 seconds. Canzoneri improved by forty seconds on this time in disposing of Singer and relieving him of the title the Bronx lad held for only four months.

The crowd which witnessed the fight was a distinguished gathering whose enthusiasm was excelled only by the shock of the sudden ending. Hardly had the battle begun than it was over, a new champion enthroned and an embryo idol crashed from his rising position before he had a chance to develop. But the better man won, despite the optimistic calculations of those fight followers who so rashly made Singer a favorite at odds as high as 3 to 1 before the combatants entered the ring.

Prominent among the spectators were Grover A. Whalen, former Police Commissioner; James I. Bush, Matt Brush, John Ringling, Walter Camp and Mrs. Camp, who was Ruth Elder; Charles A. Harnett, License Commissioner; James J. Corbett, former heavyweight champion; Sheriff Tom Farley and Gene Pope, contractor.

Singer Is Disappointment.

Singer was a disappointment as champion last night and has merited speculation as to his ability since the night Fernandez knocked him out. To the ringside after the bout came word that Singer left the arena in a taxicab for home, still dazed and in a haze. The blow with which Canzoneri accomplished the knockout and annexed the title was a powerful one, jarring in its force, but it would be an exaggerated testimonial to Canzoneri's punching strength to say that it was forceful enough to induce brain clouds ten or fifteen minutes after it struck.

Short and sweet was the bout indeed. Singer opened the contest sparring cagily, walking to his left, as is characteristic, leaving his corner with the opening gong and pecking lightly with his left. They clinched without striking a blow, and parted without striking a punch. At long range, they danced and sparred and Singer hooked a left to the head and drove a right to the face. They went to close quarters, where Singer drove a left and right to the body and they locked.

Canzoneri drove a right to the body and then, crouching, hooked a grazing left to the jaw. The punch flustered Singer, who floundered slightly and threw punches wildly in an effort to conceal the effect of the

Times Wide World Photo.
TONY CANZONERI,
Who Won the Lightweight Title by Knocking Out Singer.

punch. Canzoneri crouched and threw lightning-like lefts and rights to Singer's head, trying to land on the jaw. The crowd roared as it saw the champion tottering, and then went delirious as Canzoneri, jumping from his crouch, drove hard to the mouth with a left hook aimed at the jaw. Singer stiffened and tottered, falling almost flush on his face.

The fallen champion lay stretched there, immovable, not even a muscle quivering, as Referee McAvoy tolled off the fatal seconds. One, two, three, four, five, six went the rhythmic arm swing and the penerating drone of the referee's count. And Singer didn't move.

Singer Tries to Arise.

At "seven" the prostrate champion started to arise, got as far as his right knee, looked about dazedly, and fell back and over, landing on his back. He rolled over until he was outside the ring ropes and almost fell off the battle platform. And the count went on, eight, nine and ten, with Singer struggling to get back inside the ropes.

With the count over, the crowd was delirious in its demonstration for the new champion. Singer was aided to his corner. The bout was just twenty-one seconds short of the record lightweight championship knockout of Erne by Gans, thirty years ago. The paid attendance was 14,592. The gross receipts amounted to $69,728 and the net receipts were $58,757.

Singer weighed 134 pounds, one pound under the class limit, while Canzoneri scaled 132.

Rugged Ben Jeby, middleweight stablemate of Singer's, showed much more stamina in hammering his way to the decision over Harry Ebbets of Freeport in the ten-round semi-final which followed the title bout in the ring.

This was a free-swinging affair in which punches bounced off the chins of the rival boxers with monotonous regularity. But Jeby proved himself the better man at withstanding and dealing out these blows and was entitled to the award. Jeby weighed 157 pounds, Ebbets 163.

Solly Schwartz, English lightweight, furnished a surprise when he carried off the decision over Jimmy McNamara west-sider, in their ten-round bout. Schwartz weighed 136 pounds, McNamara 137.

Sid Lampe, Baltimore lightweight, won the decision over Frankie Carlton of Jersey City in the opening bout of five rounds. Lampe weighed 129½ pounds, Carlton 129.

Tony Canzoneri is 22 years old, according to his own statement, and was born at Slydell, La., a lumber camp near New Orleans. He has been boxing six years, having started his ring career back in 1925. His record includes 94 battles, including last night's encounter.

Canzoneri shares a unique record in boxing. His acquisition of the title witnessed one of the quickest

changes in division leaders known to the ring. The record was supplied in 1923 when Eugene Criqui knocked out Johnny Kilbane in June to win the featherweight title, only to lose it the following month to Johnny Dundee.

Another similar instance is the historic rivalry between Stanley Ketchell and Billy Papke back in 1908 for the middleweight crown. Papke won the title by knocking out Ketchell in twelve rounds on Sept. 7, 1908, at Los Angeles, but the Illinois Thunderbolt lost the title to Ketchell on a knockout in eleven rounds on the following Nov. 26.

Canzoneri enjoys an almost unparalleled record from the standpoint of popularity and earning capacity. He is one of the most popular boxers in the ring today as well as one of the most satisfactory performers. This is reflected in the fact that he has earned more than $250,000 in purses and has participated in bouts which, in the aggregate, have grossed more than $1,000,000.

November 15, 1930

CANZONERI VICTOR; RETAINS RING TITLE

Lightweight Champion Beats Chocolate in Stirring Bout Before 19,000 in Garden.

FIGHT DRAWS $83,408 GATE

Winner Is Master Throughout, Scoring Clearly in Eleven of the Fifteen Rounds.

UPROAR GREETS DECISION

Loser Roundly Cheered for Valiant Stand, Boos for the Conqueror— Kaplan Is Knocked Out.

By JAMES P. DAWSON.

The largest crowd Madison Square Garden has held in months gave itself over last night to one of the noisiest and most disorderly demonstrations the arena ever has witnessed after one of the greatest lightweight championship battles in local ring annals. The attendance was 19,000.

Tony Canzoneri, the world's champion, making his third defense of the title within the space of a year, battered his way to the decision over Kid Chocolate, his Cuban challenger, in fifteen rounds of hurricane fighting provoked almost exclusively by the titleholder, and then left the battle platform amid a demonstration of disapproval from the fans which was unjustified.

Referee Willie Lewis and Judge Joe Agnello voted for the titleholder, while Charles F. Mathison, the other judge, voted for Chocolate. The decision might well have been unanimous, so clearly had Canzoneri established his right to the award in a blazing offensive with which he swept Chocolate before him for eleven of the fifteen rounds.

Crowd Impressed by Rallies.

But the crowd, apparently carried away by spectacular rallies with which Chocolate closed most of the rounds, roared down the decision when announcer Joe Humphries raised Canzoneri's right arm.

From the balcony overhead and from the ringside sections and from the intermediate points in the vast arena, which held a crowd that paid gross receipts of $83,408, came an ear-splitting outburst of dissent.

Catcalls came from all parts of the building. Excited fans tossed papers and hats high in the air, some of the fans tossing cigarette and cigar stubs into the ring. One heaved an apple into the ring.

The writer had no disagreement with the award, save for its lack of unanimity. Canzoneri won eleven of the fifteen rounds by as tirelessly relentless an offensive exhibition as he has ever flashed in local competition.

Four Rounds For Chocolate.

Chocolate won four, the second, sixth, seventh and thirteenth sessions, when he made desperate, do-or-die stands in the face of the champion's otherwise sustained onslaught and fought Canzoneri to a standstill. For the rest, however, there could be no disagreement with the result.

Canzoneri never stopped tearing in on the attack. He was like a bulldog in ferocity and determination, piling into Chocolate for most of every one of the fifteen rounds, only at times to be sidetracked by the counter-offensive of the desperate Cuban.

He floored Chocolate in the fourth session when the champion's right to the jaw sent Chocolate off balance and to his finger-tips. He fought the only fight he could against the cagy, springy little Cuban, whose defensive skill is his greatest ring asset.

And in waging this battle Canzoneri subjected Chocolate to the most severe body-drubbing the Cuban ever has experienced, piling up points with his fearless offensive and his unstoppable rat-a-tat-tat of gloved left and right fists against Chocolate's body.

Against the consistent fighting of the champion Chocolate fought a fitful battle. The challenger fought only when the champion made him fight under the sting and lash of his blows.

In the second round Chocolate's jabbing cut the lips of Canzoneri, and a savage attack, as he rallied from five successive solid left hooks that Canzoneri sank in his body, found Chocolate forcing Canzoneri to the ropes. Near the bell, however, Canzoneri landed a right uppercut to the chin that staggered Chocolate.

Chocolate Stages Rally.

In the sixth and seventh rounds Chocolate also flashed bold offensive moves which showed Canzoneri at a disadvantage because he was too eager to return blow for blow to be effective. Chocolate harassed and punished the champion in the seventh with left hooks to the body and to the face from a crouching position as he ducked to avoid Canzoneri's vicious rushes.

Under the pace and the battering both tired in the thirteenth round, but Chocolate's fire had the greater accuracy and his boxing was best, notwithstanding a furious rally by Canzoneri near the bell.

But through every other round Canzoneri took the honors. He fought as a champion should fight, fearlessly and savagely in a superbly executed offensive which swept his challenger before it. He started rushing Chocolate about the right with the clang of the first gong, and never stopped his forward march.

In the fourth Canzoneri gave the crowd its nearest approach to a knockdown thrill when he keeled Chocolate off balance and to his glove-tips with a right to the jaw.

Canzoneri came through Chocolate's desperate flurry of the sixth and seventh rounds to press forward again with his tireless attack in the eighth and through the ninth, despite Chocolate's frenzied efforts to keep the champion at bay with straight lefts or an occasional right to the jaw.

Furious Exchange in Ninth.

The ninth ended with a furious exchange in which each whaled away at the body and head. Through the tenth, eleventh and twelfth rounds it was the same, Canzoneri pressing forward eternally, pumping left hooks to the body at long range and working both hands to the body at close quarters, while Chocolate tried unsuccessfully for one shot on the jaw as Canzoneri raced in.

In the thirteenth Chocolate rallied strongly and won the session, but he delayed his recovery too long in the fourteenth to overcome the good earlier work of Canzoneri.

The fifteenth was a torrid, wild affair in which Canzoneri, though palpably tired from the pace and his foe's counter-fire, nevertheless pressed onward and fought viciously from bell to bell. Indeed, Chocolate in the heat of a furious slugging bee which closed the battle and found Canzoneri backed to the ropes, did not hear the final bell, and landed two rights to the champion's jaw before they were pried apart.

The weights were 132 pounds for Canzoneri and 127½ for Chocolate.

Ran Knocks Out Kaplan.

Eddie Ran, 146½ pounds, Polish welterweight, knocked out Louis (Kid) Kaplan, 138¼, Meriden, Conn., veteran, in the first round of the scheduled eight-round semi-final. A right to the jaw finished Kaplan in a surprising ending which came after 2 minutes 24 seconds of the first round had been fought.

Kaplan had gone down previously under a right to the jaw, but regained his feet in the absence of any official count.

Chick Devlin, 159 pounds, California middleweight, won the decision from Vincent Sireci, 153, Yorkville, in their eight-round struggle. Devlin floored Sireci in the second round for a count of nine with a right to the jaw and thereafter proved too rugged for the local boxer.

Al Rowe, 153 pounds, Philadelphia, boxed a draw with Ray Rivera, 133½, Porto Rican, in their four-round encounter.

In the opening bout, scheduled for four rounds, Harry Oberman, 131 pounds, east side lightweight, knocked out Lester Robinson, 133, Brooklyn in 1 minute 34 seconds of the first round.

Jimmy Massera, 127½ pounds, won the decision from Petey Burns, also 127½, in a four-round battle of featherweights which served as an emergency match.

November 21, 1931

70,000 SEE SHARKEY OUTPOINT SCHMELING TO WIN WORLD TITLE

Boston Heavyweight Triumphs Over German in 15 Rounds in New Bowl.

OFFICIALS VOTE 2 TO 1

Many in Crowd Voice Disapproval of Decision—Majority of Experts Favor Loser.

$500,000 GATE ESTIMATED

Milk Fund to Receive 25 Per Cent of Net Profits—Many Notables at the Ringside.

By JAMES P. DAWSON.

The heavyweight boxing championship of the world came back to America last night. Jack Sharkey, disappointed in his quest of the title heretofore, won the crown when he received a fifteen-round decision over Max Schmeling, the methodical German, who entered the ring as the pugilistic king of the universe and left it an ex-champion.

On a divided ballot Sharkey won the title, the vote which gave him the honor being 2 to 1 among three officials, two judges and a referee assigned by the State Athletic Commission.

But among the ringside critics, and in the crowd as well, the ratio did not seem to be maintained, judging from the reception which greeted Announcer Joe Humphries's declaration, carried out by amplifiers over the broad expanse of the Madison Square Garden Bowl in Long Island City.

Referee Gunboat Smith and Judge Kelly voted for Sharkey. The other judge, Charles F. Mathison, boxing critic for years, cast his ballot for Schmeling.

Referee a Former Fighter.

Smith, the referee, is a former fighter who is credited in the records with hitting Jack Dempsey the hardest punch the former champion ever received. Kelly long has been associated with boxing. He was a boxer in the amateur ranks thirty years ago, but, although he never fought professionally, he has always been a keen student of the game.

Kelly said last night to this reporter at the ringside: "Sharkey fought the best battle of his life tonight. The trouble is that few critics around the ringside recognized it." Smith and Mathison did not comment on the award.

There were many, however, who did not agree with the official decision, and boos were mingled with cheers when Sharkey was announced as the winner. Not only did the spectators voice strong disapproval, but a canvass of newspaper experts at the ringside showed the majority believed the German was entitled to the verdict. Radio announcers also were of the opinion that the laurels should have gone to Schmeling.

Near-Capacity Crowd Present.

A crowd of 70,000, which paid prices ranging from $2.30 to $23 for seats, attended the contest, waged under the direction of the Madison Square Garden Corporation, and partly in the interests of the Free Milk Fund for Babies, Inc., of which Mrs. William Randolph Hearst is chairman.

The receipts were estimated at $500,000, on the theory that the bowl could hold only 71,872, paid attendance, and the crowd was of near-capacity proportions. A sell-out crowd would have produced receipts of $561,482.

The Milk Fund will be enriched by 25 per cent of the net profits, and is guaranteed a minimum of $10,000. Its share is expected to exceed this figure by a considerable margin.

In the gathering were the Governors of two near-by States, Governor Wilbur Cross of Connecticut and Governor A. Harry Moore of New Jersey, Mayor Walker, Mayor Frank Hague of Jersey City, and Mayor Anton Cermak of Chicago also were present.

Bankers, brokers, diplomats, Senators, Congressmen, politicians of city, State and national reputation, leaders in the commercial and industrial life of the nation and of the professions, the stage and the arts all were assembled in this huge throng.

Gene Tunney and James J. Corbett, former holders of the title for which Sharkey and Schmeling fought, led a group of ex-champions in attendance.

Whether they agreed with the verdict or disagreed is not known. but there were enough present who did disagree to make this dissatisfaction apparent.

As late as twenty minutes after the battle came a demonstration of discontent, when some disgruntled fan back in the inky blackness hurled an empty bottle in the direction of the ring. The flying missile grazed the head of a worker at the ringside and fell to the floor.

Jacobs Criticizes Verdict.

To the wail of discontent and dissatisfaction was added the voice of Joe Jacobs, manager of Schmeling, who criticized the verdict in no uncertain terms from the ring immediately it was rendered and from the ex-champion's dressing room following the fight.

Contrasting to this was the overpowering joy of Sharkey, his manager, handlers and adherents. The happiness of the former sailor knew no bounds. He lurched forward excitedly when the decision was announced after a slight hesitation by Announcer Humphries after reading the three scorecards.

Hearing the announcement, he jumped high in the air. On his bruised face, with a left eye that was closed tight, was a broad smile as he jumped across the ring to clasp the hand of the man to whom he lost two years ago on a foul.

Similarly elated were Sharkey's manager, Johnny Buckley; his trainers, Al Lacey and Tony Polozzollo, and his adherents in the crowd. His handlers danced gayly about the ring, slapping each other on the back.

The more intrepid of Sharkey's admirers near the ring suddenly started crawling through the ropes, until the ring was a surging mass.

In the crowd men and women stood on benches to cheer the victory and jeer the vanquished, in whose behalf mute protests were offered, or to boo the decision and pay tribute to the loser.

Gallant Gesture by Schmeling.

Schmeling made the gallant gesture of the sportsman, the handclasp he raced across the ring to give Sharkey instinctively, though he must have felt sorely that he was overlooked unwarrantedly in the distribution of points by which the decision was reached.

NEW HEAVYWEIGHT CHAMPION.

Jack Sharkey.

An unofficial survey of critics at the ringside disclosed that fourteen out of twenty-two thought Schmeling won. One favored a draw and seven supported the official decision for Sharkey.

On the Schmeling side was the writer. I gave Schmeling nine rounds, Sharkey five and one even. The even round was the eighth. The rounds I credited to Schmeling were the third and fourth, the ninth, tenth, eleventh, twelfth, thirteenth, fourteenth and fifteenth. To Sharkey I gave the first, second, fifth, sixth and seventh rounds.

Schmeling won, in this writer's opinion, and notwithstanding the official verdict against him, because of a tireless, persistent, unswerving offensive he launched at the opening bell and never once interrupted, even in the face of Sharkey's best blows.

Bout Lacking in Thrills.

In a battle that was altogether lacking in thrills ordinarily associated with heavyweight title combat, a struggle that was of necessity a methodical, systematic encounter of almost unvarying style, because Schmeling forced all the fighting, the German fought as a champion is expected to fight and as he should fight.

Making the fight every inch of the way, punching more often than he was being punched, Schmeling plodded onward through the fifteen rounds, even when he was more or less thoroughly outboxed by Sharkey.

He missed many punches, to be sure, and there were times when he overlooked chances to score, so intent was he on landing one solid blow. But there can be no mistaking that Schmeling made all the fighting, and a steadily aggressive battle commands its reward in points.

In hitting Schmeling outscored his rival, as was apparent from Sharkey's battered appearance. There were times when Schmeling's defense even excelled that of Sharkey, who made his battle one almost exclusively of defensive effort.

Sharkey Fights Fairly.

Sharkey fought fairly, and, on the whole, evenly throughout. He wanted to vindicate himself for the foul which cost him the title two years ago, just as much as Schmeling wanted to demonstrate that, but for that illegal blow he would have won from Sharkey over fifteen rounds.

There was, as a consequence, a distinct lack of objectionable methods, although early in the battle, notably in the fourth round, the crowd groaned as Sharkey's left hook for the body landed on the waist-line. The blow, however, was fair.

Fighting a defensive battle, therefore, Sharkey won the title; not with an affirmative defense such as Tunney exhibited in his well-planned encounters with Dempsey and Heeney, but with a demonstration of protective tactics which at times appeared to be those of a desperate man.

Through fourteen rounds Sharkey went on the attack only when provoked by Schmeling's assaults, and when he did assume the attack his blows lacked the snap that was in Schmeling's.

In the last round Jack, obviously with a bid for victory, started an outburst of fighting that was reminiscent of the Sharkey of 1930. But after that opening flurry, Schmeling continued to press his foe about the ring and harass him with rapid-fire blows that were halted only by the final bell.

Return Bout Is Likely.

Because of the difference of opinion on the outcome, it is altogether likely a return bout will be arranged.

The next struggle, regardless of the champion's foe, will be staged by the Madison Square Garden Corporation, which has Sharkey under contract for the defense of the crown he wears now after eight years crowded with disappointment.

For two rounds Sharkey toyed with Schmeling in an exhibition of defensive boxing that frustrated the German's determined attack.

Jack opened the battle with a sweeping left hook to the jaw, and then proceeded to counter Schmeling's left jabs and high rights for the jaw with a cross-fire of stiff left jabs, hooks to the face and rights to the body.

Schmeling seemed hesitant at this stage of the battle. He acted as if he was trying to solve Sharkey's style, and could not find the solution.

But in the third and fourth rounds the German pressed in tirelessly.

Makes Sharkey Clinch.

A short right to the jaw early in the fourth made Sharkey clinch, and Schmeling smilingly called Sharkey's attention to erratic body fire in this session when the challenger's left for the body hovered about the danger mark.

Sharkey's best fighting came in the fifth, sixth and seventh rounds. He had Schmeling missing awkwardly in those three rounds, stabbing steadily with straight lefts to the face. In flurries at close quarters Sharkey scored with short lefts and rights to the face and head.

Sharkey boxed cautiously and calculatingly in the eighth, retreating steadily and pecking away with lefts which at times upset Schmeling's battle plans.

However, from the beginning of the ninth, there was nothing to the battle but Schmeling. He spun Sharkey half-way around with a solid right to the jaw early in the ninth, an attack from which Sharkey rallied with a left hook to Schmeling's jaw. But, before the round ended, Schmeling reached his foe's jaw with a left and right that drew shouts from the crowd.

Keeps Up Attack in Tenth.

Schmeling's bombardment of jolting rights to the head and jaw continued in the tenth. Four times he landed, and twice Sharkey went back on his heels. Infuriated, Sharkey let fly with a swishing right which went wide of the mark.

Schmeling's eleventh-round attack made more noticeable a swelling under Sharkey's left eye, a bruise which was started in the third. And through the rest of the battle Schmeling pressed his rival hard, closing his rival's left eye completely and jolting him with varied blows.

In the thirteenth Schmeling landed a right to the body and a left hook to the jaw in a one-two punch that almost bent Sharkey over, and near the end of the round the German jarred his rival with a right to the jaw, a blow that stopped Sharkey dead in his tracks as it landed flush on the face and for a second dazed the ex-sailor.

Sharkey continued his defensive style, fighting weakly through the fourteenth round as Schmeling pressed in tirelessly and reverting to the defensive in the fifteenth after an opening flurry.

June 22, 1932

U. S. ANNEXED TITLE IN OLYMPIC BOXING

Victories of Flynn and Barth and Three Thirds Gave America the Team Laurels.

---

5 COUNTRIES WON FINALS

Argentina and South Africa Took Two Individual Crowns Each— Canada, Hungary Also Scored.

By The Associated Press.

LOS ANGELES, Aug. 14.—Olympic boxing crowns rested today upon the heads of eight doughty warriors of the leathered fist, representing five countries. They are survivors of the greatest international tournament ever held to determine world's amateur champions.

When the last punch had been tossed and the final gong rang last night the reckoning showed the United States, the Union of South Africa and Argentina each listing two champions, and Canada and Hungary each having one.

For the third time in the last four Olympics, the United States claimed team honors, accounted for by two championships and three third places. Italy, winner of the team title four years ago, failed to gain a single individual title.

South Africa Takes Third.

Argentina, with two champions and a defeated finalist, finished second. South Africa took third place laurels with two firsts and a third, while Germany was in fourth position, listing three defeated finalists.

To the flying fists of Eddie Flynn, New Orleans welterweight, and Carmen Barth, Cleveland middleweight, belong most of the credit for the United States team title. Flynn boxed his way to a close decision over Erich Campe of Germany, while Barth drummed a victory tattoo on the body of Amador Azar, swarthy son of Argentina.

In reclassification bouts held previously between defeated semi-finalists to determine third and fourth places, additional points in the winning total were contributed through the efforts of Louis Salica, Brooklyn flyweight; Nat Bor, Fall River, Mass., lightweight, and Fred Feary, heavyweight from Stockton, Cal. Salica and Feary won by default and Bor took a decision from Mario Bianchina of Italy.

Enekes Flyweight Victor.

Stephen Enekes of Hungary, flyweight champion of Europe, claimed Olympic laurels in his division by defeating Francisco Cabanes of Mexico. Horace Gwynne of Canada outpointed Hans Ziglarski of Germany in the bantamweight final, and Carmelo Robledo of Argentina reached the top of the featherweight division with a triumph over Josef Schleinkofer of Germany.

Lawrence Stevens, South Africa's lightweight pride, took the measure of Thure Ahlzvist, Sweden, while his team mate, David Carstens, tossed too many punches for Gino Rossi of Italy in the light-heavyweight windup. Santiago Lovell, Negro heavyweight from Argentina, topped off the last evening of the five-day carnival with a decision over Luigi Rovati of Italy.

August 15, 1932

CHOCOLATE STOPS FELDMAN IN 12TH

Cuban Wins Featherweight Title by Knockout Victory Before 6,000 in Garden.

REFEREE HALTS BATTLE

Acts to Save Battered Loser From Further Punishment—Devlin and Battaglia Draw.

By JAMES P. DAWSON.

Kid Chocolate, Cuban boxer, is the world's featherweight champion as far as the State Athletic Commission is concerned.

Without being seriously extended, the Cuban won this title last night in Madison Square Garden. Before about 6,000 fans he knocked out Lew Feldman, Brownsville challenger, in the twelfth round of what was to have been a fifteen-round battle carrying the commission's stamp as a championship fight.

Referee Patsy Haley stopped the battle to save Feldman further punishment after the twelfth round had gone 2 minutes 45 seconds. At the time Feldman was badly outclassed.

It was their third meeting and Chocolate's third victory. By winning recognition as champion Chocolate succeeds to the crown which has been unclaimed here since Bat Battalino forfeited it last January through inability to make the weight.

As to the merits of the boxers, Feldman has a stout heart and a willingness to fight. He made the most of these essentials, wading in to Chocolate from the first tap of the gong. He had his big moment in the fifth when he caught Chocolate on the jaw with a swing which made the Cuban's knees sag.

Chocolate Starts Slowly.

But that was the only time Feldman appeared to have a chance. Chocolate, off to a slow start, outboxed and outfought his foe without unduly extending himself.

For four rounds it was a listless struggle. Then came the fifth, when Feldman thrilled his admirers with that lusty right to the jaw. Through the sixth, seventh and eighth. Chocolate cut loose only in spurts, but he opened the ninth with a right to the jaw which dropped Feldman for a count of nine.

Arising, Feldman tried gamely to fight back, but he was hammered about the ring as Chocolate sought for a knockout.

Through the tenth and eleventh rounds Chocolate redoubled his efforts to land a knockout. He had things all his own way and he was proceeding similarly in the twelfth when Referee Haley stepped between the combatants and called a halt. Chocolate weighed 125¾ pounds and Feldman 125½.

Tribute to De Forest.

The crowd paid tribute to the memory of Jimmy De Forest, veteran trainer, who died Tuesday at his home in Long Branch, N.J. Just before the main bout started, Jack Dempsey, with whom De Forest associated as trainer, jumped into the ring. He stood bare-headed while Announcer Joe Humphries asked the crowd to rise and join in prayer.

Frank Battaglia, Canadian, battered Chick Devlin, California, in the second of the ten-round middleweight championship elimination bouts, but received only a draw for his efforts.

Battaglia won eight of the ten rounds in the semi-final, though he was floored for a count of nine in the eighth. Both boxers weighed 160 pounds.

McPartland Halts Bout.

Ben Joby, 159¾, east side contender for the world's middleweight title, started auspiciously in the 160-pound championship eliminations when he knocked out Paul Pirrone, 160, Cleveland, in the sixth round of what was to have been a ten-round battle.

Referee McPartland stopped the battle after 2 minutes and 12 seconds of the sixth round to save Pirrone from further punishment. Pirrone was floored seven times during the bout.

In the opening bout of four rounds, Danny Rosen, 129¾, east side featherweight, won the decision from Harry Oberman, 124½, another east sider.

October 14, 1932

Times Wide World Photo.

Primo Carnera.

ROSS WINS TITLE FROM CANZONERI

Takes the World's Lightweight Crown in Furious 10-Round Bout at Chicago.

11,000 SEE THE STRUGGLE

Boos Greet Decision, Which Stuns Dethroned Boxer—Gate Receipts $46,305.

By The Associated Press.

CHICAGO. June 23.—Barney Ross waded through the merciless fists of Tony Canzoneri tonight to take the lightweight championship of the world from the New York title-holder.

In the sweltering heat of the Chicago Stadium Ross won the title in a savage ten-round battle. It was so close that the officials did not agree on the verdict.

Referee Tommy Gilmore, himself a former boxer, voted in favor of a draw, while the two judges. Edward Hintz and William A. Battye, cast their ballots in favor of the 22-year-old Chicagoan on the closest of margins.

The crowd of 11,000, at first stunned by the verdict, expressed its disapproval in boos and hisses when Ross's right-gloved fist was raised in victory.

Canzoneri Is Amazed.

Canzoneri, in whose custody the 135-pound title has rested since 1930, was amazed.

"The decision was the surprise of my entire boxing career, and I have had many of them." Canzoneri said. "Honestly, I thought I was so far ahead of Ross that I coasted in the eighth and ninth and did not extend myself in the tenth."

Ross was entitled to the verdict, in the opinion of the boxing experts, because he revealed himself as a superior and speedier boxer, and even held his own in trading punches with the fiery Canzoneri.

Setting a blistering pace, Canzoneri started as if he would knock out Ross within five rounds. But the youthful Chicagoan, boxing defensively, met Canzoneri's furious opening assault with a left-jab counter-fire that forced Tony to miss badly.

Canzoneri Changes Style.

Canzoneri, in the eighth and ninth, quit boxing almost entirely and started to punch, but Ross refused to deviate from his plan of battle, which was to keep pecking away with long lefts and taking no unwise chances of running into a knockout punch.

Once he brought the spectators to their feet when he banged Canzoneri with a sizzling left hook to the chin.

Ross weighed 134¾ pounds and Canzoneri 133½. The gate receipts totaled $46,305.

June 24, 1933

Carnera Knocks Out Sharkey; Wins the Title in 6th Round

40,000 See Giant Boxer Stop the Defending Champion With a Right Uppercut to the Chin in Long Island City Bowl— Victor First Italian to Capture the Crown.

By JAMES P. DAWSON.

Jack Sharkey's first defense of the world's heavyweight championship was his last. The Boston ex-sailor was knocked out in the sixth round of what was to have been a fifteen-round struggle last night in the Long Island City Bowl, by Primo Carnera, Italian giant.

As a result, for the first time in ring history, the crown which has come down from Sullivan, Corbett, Fitzsimmons and the rest of that illustrious line to Dempsey and Tunney, is worn by a son of Italy.

A terrific right hand uppercut to the chin which almost decapitated Sharkey brought Carnera the title in a bout held by the Madison Square Garden Corporation. The Free Milk Fund for Babies, Inc., of which Mrs. William Randolph Hearst is chairman, will share in the receipts.

The blow dropped Sharkey in his tracks and stunned some 40,000 men and women who had paid an estimated $200,000 for a view of the spectacle, which provided the thrill that all looked for but few really anticipated.

Under the impact of the blow Sharkey stretched limp and immovable on his face on the canvas, while a bewildered crowd looked on as the count proceeded. Referee Arthur Donovan, picking up the official count from Eddie Forbes who was the knockdown timekeeper, worked his right arm up and down, shouting his count from beginning to end into the ear of Sharkey.

But there was no movement on the part of the defending champion no quiver of a muscle to show that he heard or heeded. There was no recovery of jarred wits or numbed senses, not even when the count reached the fatal ten, which signified the crowning of a new ring champion.

Sharkey's crestfallen handlers leaped quickly to the side of their beaten idol and carried him to his corner.

Their first aid administrations quickly revived Sharkey and he was escorted from the ring. As he left he heard the clamor of the throng, the cries of the crowd for the winner. For there came welling up from the huge pine and asphalt bowl on the Long Island flats a tremendous shout of acclaim for this gigantic new champion of the world.

Exactly two minutes and twenty-

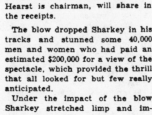

seven seconds after the sixth round started the fight was over. The ending came with a shock that was equaled only with that furnished in the recent knockout of Max Schmeling by Max Baer. None expected it.

There had been no indication previously that Sharkey would collapse, because Carnera had not struck such a blow as that terrific right hand uppercut.

And yet, the punch did not lift Sharkey off his feet. On the contrary, Sharkey slid gracefully to the floor.

After Sharkey had been lifted bodily from the ring, a scene of wild excitement ensued, aside from that ordinarily enacted when a new champion is crowned. Bill Duffy, Carnera's chief adviser and the man to whom credit must go for his scaling the heights, claimed that Johnny Buckley, Sharkey's manager, insisted on an examination of Carnera's gloves.

This aroused Duffy and he shouted commands to Carnera, apparently overcome to the point of helplessness, to remain in the ring until his gloves were removed.

Duffy even invited Bill Brown, recently appointed State Athletic Commission member, into the ring to remove and examine Carnera's huge gloves. But the excitement passed and the ring soon was cleared.

With his victory Carnera attained heights that perhaps he himself never even expected. But fight followers thought so well of him that for part of yesterday he was quoted favorite to win at odds of 6 to 5. Sharkey entered the ring the choice at 6 to 5 and 11 to 10, which was as it should be when past performances are considered.

Carnera Aroused to Fury.

Before he struck the fatal uppercut Carnera evidenced nothing that would lead to a suspicion of the result save a grim determination which became a raging fury on occasion as his efforts to wreak Sharkey with a blow were frustrated.

Of the five rounds completed before the knockout Sharkey won four, three of them beyond question, and lost only one. The Italian, towering close to half a foot above Sharkey, and outweighing him at 260½ pounds by 59½ pounds, proved the efficacy of size and strength, in the first round, and banged Sharkey around right merrily. But in the second, third, fourth and fifth rounds Sharkey had the advantage. There might have been a question over the fourth chapter, but in this Sharkey's boxing gave him the upper hand. In the other rounds Sharkey outgeneraled and outmanoeuvred the huge Italian, whose defeat he was seeking systematically.

Starting that sixth session, however, Carnera left his corner with the instructions of Bill Duffy ringing in his ears: "Take advantage of everything now. Overlook nothing. Go out there and win." He followed the instructions implicitly. Bounding at Sharkey, he started to cuff and maul the Bostonian, belaboring him with ponderous rights and sweeping lefts. These, however, carried no particular direction and, consequently, no devastating force beyond that contained in the fact that the blows were propelled by a veritable man-mountain of 260½ pounds.

Sharkey Retreats to Ropes.

Sharkey retreated and slid along the ropes. Carnera was after him, light as a featherweight on his feet for a man of his huge stature. Along the ropes they embraced in a clinch, and just as Sharkey, retreating, started to slip, Carnera crushed his chin with a right uppercut.

The crowd did not know whether it was a knockdown. Carnera's corner was alive with excitement. The Italian did not regard it as a slip, nor did his corner. The consequence was that, impelled by the frantic shouts of his advisers, Carnera leaped recklessly at Sharkey, who jumped to his feet before a count could be started. He

was more embarrassed at his own insecure footing than he was hurt by a blow.

Squaring away, Carnera continued to pile into Sharkey. The latter sought to stay his foe by dodging and weaving, and with spear-thrusts of his left in a jab or hook, or winging drives of his right.

Carnera, however, came in against Sharkey's most frantic effort, and jarred the titleholder with a right which grazed the jaw. Sharkey pulled erect after this blow. He put his hands together and a grim look came into his eye. With deliberation he seemed to be setting himself to retaliate. But he was forced backward to the ropes near his own corner, and there he left himself open for the finishing punch.

Out of nowhere Carnera pulled his right in an uppercut which curled to Sharkey's chin and dropped him in his tracks. In a round the complexion of the fight had changed. Sharkey, the charger for most of the journey theretofore, had become the man of flight. And, in a jiffy the title changed hands on Carnera's sweeping uppercut.

Finds Odds Insurmountable.

Sharkey gave his best against odds last night that were insurmountable. Two years ago they didn't constitute a hurdle worthy the description. But last night the size and weight of Carnera proved Sharkey's undoing.

Sharkey entered the ring at 9:30 o'clock, accompanied by his man-

ager, Johnny Buckley; Trainer Al Lacri and Tony Polozzolo and Gus Wilson. Carnera followed two minutes later, attended by Billy Duffy and Billy DeFoe.

Jack Dempsey and Gene Tunney, former heavyweight champions, and Tommy Loughran, former light-heavyweight titleholder, were introduced from the ring.

The referee was Arthur Donovan and the judges Jim Buckley and Charles Lynch.

Sharkey drew the larger amount of cheers when the boxers were introduced. It was announced that Sharkey weighed 201 pounds and Carnera 260½.

When the men were called to the centre of the ring for instructions Carnera towered above the group.

The championship bout was taken quietly by the public. There was none of the spectacle ordinarily associated with fistic title struggles, particularly heavyweight championship events. As a consequence there was little congestion or confusion.

A well-drilled usher corps and experienced special policemen under Captain Pat Gargan of the Garden staff, explained this in some measure. But there was also, as explanation, an undeniable public apathy.

What the gathering lacked in numbers it made up in representation. Women prominent in society, political leaders, stage and screen stars, industrial and professional leaders and sports celebrities were noted at the ringside.

June 30, 1933

Ross Defeats M'Larnin on Points For World's Welterweight Title

Chicago Boxer Adds 147-Pound Crown to Lightweight Honors by 15-Round Triumph in Garden Bowl—Referee's Vote Decides When Judges Disagree—60,000 Pay $225,000 Gate.

By JAMES P. DAWSON.

A new world's welterweight champion reigns in boxing today.

Last night in the huge Madison Square Garden Bowl in Long Island City, before a crowd estimated at 60,000 who paid about $225,000 to see the spectacle, Barney Ross, born on New York's East Side, but now from Chicago, captured the title. He hammered his way to the decision over Jimmy McLarnin, Oakland, Calif., defender of the crown, in fifteen sizzling rounds of fighting.

When he received the divided decision of the three bout officials, Ross, adding to his world's 135-pound title the 147-pound laurels, became the first fighter in modern ring history to rule the two divisions.

There was widespread approval of the award in the crowd which turned out to see the first ring struggle here between two champions in thirteen years.

The bout was staged in the interests of charity. The Free Milk Fund for Babies, Inc., of which Mrs. William Randolph Hearst is chairman, profited from the bout which reflected, temporarily, at least, a return of boxing to popular favor.

The crowd, which included persons prominent in many walks of life, saw a battle that was bitterly,

Times Wide World Photo.
Barney Ross.

systematically and, at times, savagely waged.

The fans waited expectantly as Announcer Joe Humphreys, at its conclusion, revealed a disagreement of the two judges, the veteran Tom O'Rourke and Harold Barnes. On the vote of Referee Eddie

Forbes the title changed hands, for Forbes cast his ballot for Ross. O'Rourke voted for McLarnin and Barnes voted for Ross.

The announcement of the disagreement between the judges attracted the only unfavorable outburst in connection with the decision. When this was broadcast through the amplifiers a solid section of the crowd rent the air with cries of amazement. But it was only for a moment.

Announcer Humphreys stilled them as he raised his hands and bellowed that "Referee Forbes awards his decision to the new champion, Ross."

Then bedlam broke loose. Cries of approval echoed from all over the arena, drowning out a minority shout of disapproval from the McLarnin adherents. Excited friends and admirers tore madly down to the ringside and some of them clambered over the backs of working newspaper men in their desire to get close to the conquering Ross, who donned his robe and shook the hand of the man he had just defeated.

Takes Reverse Quietly.

McLarnin took the reverse quietly, smiling bravely at the loss of his crown in what may be his last fight. His mentor, Charley (Pop) Foster, disagreeing mildly, as if for the record, with the result, declared from the ring after the battle, that this may be Jimmy's last fight. Foster would not authorize a definite announcement until he talks with his boxer.

Part of the joy of victory was shared by the mother of Ross, who came on from Chicago to watch her son in the greatest battle of his life. Part of the disappointment of defeat was the lot of Samuel McLarnin, father of Jimmy, who came from the Coast to see his son in action here for the first time.

The disagreement between the judges was distinctly wide. O'Rourke, on his score sheet, gave McLarnin the honors, nine rounds to one, with five even. Barnes called twelve rounds for Ross and only two for McLarnin, with one even. Referee Forbes's slip gave McLarnin only one round and held one even session, the remaining thirteen going to Ross.

The writer had Ross the winner at the final bell. Eight rounds to seven was the score in this unofficial tally, with Ross coming on in the last session to win the nod by a fiery attack that swept McLarnin before it.

Overtaken By Bugaboo.

McLarnin lost, overtaken by the bugaboo that has beset eight world's welterweight champions before him. He was defeated in his first defense of the title, as were Pete Latzo, Joe Dundee, Jackie Fields, Young Jack Thompson, Tommy Freeman, Thompson again, Lou Brouillard and Young Corbett 3d, his predecessors.

Almost a year ago, to the day, McLarnin won the 147-pound crown from Corbett in slightly more than two minutes of fighting on the Coast. He had not defended the title until last night.

Perhaps the long lay-off—McLarnin had only slightly more than two minutes of action in close to a year and a half—will be set up as an explanation of his dethronement, and it can very well be advanced. He was not the McLarnin with the pulverizing punch, the cool, crafty, vicious fighter of other local battles. He was far from the baby-faced fighter with the disarming smile and the disabling punch.

He had the disarming smile, all right, more a grin of grim determination than a smile of quiet confidence. But the disabling punch was conspicuous by its absence, even making allowances for Ross's ability to survive a blow.

In a final analysis McLarnin lost because he faced a better man last night. Ross respected him; he made that evident many times through the fighting. But he had no fear of the Californian. He showed this after the first two rounds, when he threw caution aside and waded into McLarnin through the succeeding six rounds to pile up an advantage that McLarnin could not possibly shake off.

Sweeps Attack Aside.

McLarnin rallied to take the ninth and tenth, but Ross came back to win the eleventh. Fighting desperately McLarnin won the twelfth, thirteenth and fourteenth, but he was frustrated in a bid for the fifteenth as Ross swept his attack aside and punched and pummelled him over the greater part of the round to clinch victory.

The hollow distinction of scoring the only knockdown the fight held went to McLarnin. It furnished a faint reminder of his punishing punching power to which local fight fans have become more or less accustomed. He upset Ross cleanly in the ninth round with a solid left hook.

Under the blow Ross went backward and down for the first time in his career. He hit the canvas as he tried to avoid stretching at length on the floor.

But the Chicagoan was up in an instant, before a count could be started, ripping into McLarnin whole-heartedly and forcing the Californian backward to a neutral corner. There McLarnin, avoiding a straight left, tripped and fell without being hit by the blow aimed at him.

Both were bleeding at the final bell. Ross from a bruised and battered mouth, which more than once felt the sting of McLarnin's rigid straight lefts or solid left hooks, and McLarnin from the nose which early and often felt the banging impact of the fiery outbursts for which the Chicagoan is noted.

Ross Discharges Obligation.

Ross looked the winner at the finish of a battle in which he justified the confidence of his admirers. The betting as the battle started was 6 to 5, take your pick, and Ross lost no time discharging the obligation this confidence implied.

Ross was reluctant to take the offensive for the first two rounds, and as a consequence McLarnin's work stood out. Thereafter, however, Ross threw aside his cloak of caution and willingly entered punching exchanges with his heavier foe, generally outpunching and outsmarting McLarnin.

So startled and desperate was McLarnin that on no less than four occasions was he warned for erratic body fire. In the fourth, ninth, eleventh and thirteenth rounds Referee Forbes found occasion to caution McLarnin for leads to the body that were unintentionally erratic.

The accidental violation in the thirteenth was the most glaring, and McLarnin promptly showed his realization of the offense by touching gloves with his foe in the time-honored apology. But these lapses, more than hurting Ross, brought home to onlookers the desperate situation in which McLarnin probably found himself.

McLarnin had close to a ten-pound advantage when the battle started. He weighed 142 pounds against Ross's 137¾ yesterday at noon, and he undeniably had heavier punching power. These disappeared soon after the battle got under way, and Ross's opening caution was replaced by a confidence that was almost reckless at times.

Ross didn't rush blindly at his foe, swinging punches, as the struggle started. Instead, he adopted a defensive style for the first two rounds. McLarnin tracked him, like a panther after its prey, jabbing and hooking in measured punches to the head and trying to bring Ross's guard down with body punches.

McLarnin never got Ross's guard down long enough for a solid shot. He never dislodged Ross's protecting gloves for a clean, decisive blow to the jaw. He grazed the jaw repeatedly; more often his blows landed jarringly on the head. After the second round Ross seemed to gain confidence and he ripped into McLarnin in fiery flashes through the succeeding six sessions. Times without number he pressed McLarnin to the ropes. He outpunched McLarnin in a body fire at close quarters and had the heavier champion slipping and sliding on uncertain feet. At times Ross twisted his rival in a manner that was altogether foreign to the Coast Irishman.

McLarnin plodded in as each round started, pecking and stabbing with his left and keeping his right poised. At times he held his fire hesitatingly, off balance or out of range. But Ross never held his. Whenever McLarnin halted or faltered, Barney leaped in eagerly, lashing out with both hands, driving home blows that didn't jar or bruise, but were, nevertheless, completely upsetting in their relation to McLarnin's plans.

Ross's Head Snaps Back.

Ross's head snapped back as if on a pivot at times, but it always bobbed back into position again as he rushed in with an avenging offensive for any stinging blow McLarnin landed.

The encouraging roars of the crowd echoed over the neighborhood as Ross backed his foe around the ring and McLarnin became cautious. With his fiery, two-fisted attack Ross drew blood from McLarnin's nose as the third round ended and the flow never was stopped. The fifth, sixth, seventh and eighth rounds were all Ross's as he charged in against McLarnin's desperate attempts to nullify these outbursts with a damaging punch.

The ninth brought some vicious fighting from McLarnin, whose left to the jaw upset Ross after a spirited exchange. But the cries of the crowd encouraging McLarnin were stilled when Ross leaped quickly to his feet and tore madly after his foe.

The Chicagoan worked McLarnin to a neutral corner and there led a left for the face. Jimmy backed away from the blow and tripped, going down in a sitting position without being hit.

Many in the gathering thought Ross had floored McLarnin and cheered him wildly. This was unnecessary, for he was after McLarnin anyhow until the bell ended the round. A warning for an erratic left for the body cost McLarnin this round, his best.

In the tenth McLarnin pressed the attack and once jarred Ross with a stinging blow to the head, a blow aimed at the jaw that went high. McLarnin was penalized again in the eleventh, although he did some good fighting against the furious, spasmodic flashes of Ross.

Presses the Attack.

McLarnin pressed the attack against a tired foe through the twelfth, thirteenth and fourteenth, but a warning in the thirteenth discounted his work, and at no time could he nail Ross with a finishing punch.

On the contrary, Jimmy had to protect himself as best he could against the furious fighting outbursts of Ross, and was more often than not in difficulty without being hurt. In the fifteenth round Ross started slowly but gradually launched a desperate attack which swept McLarnin before it.

May 29, 1934

COMMISSION RULES ON ROSS'S TITLES

Holds He Can Risk Only One at a Time—Must Specify Which Is at Stake.

Barney Ross won his lightweight and welterweight championships in separate fights, and that is the only way he can lose them. The New York State Athletic Commission yesterday made the ruling that Ross could sign to defend only one crown at a time and could lose only the one specified in the contract.

When Ross outpointed Jimmy McLarnin to add the 145-pound crown to the 135-pound laurels that he had previously wrested from Tony Canzoneri, the commission was confronted by an unprecedented situation. In the event that Ross lost to a lightweight, would he also drop his welterweight championship? That was the question that has had the boxing world agog since Monday.

The commission settled it, so far as this State is concerned, with a formal resolution. "A boxer who is champion in two or more divisions," said the resolution, "can defend only one title at a time. The title defended must be clearly

Times Wide World Photo.

McLarnin and Ross Sparring in the First Round.

47

specified in the contract, and should the champion be defeated, only one title can pass."

Although the National Boxing Association suspended Ross for failing to go through with a contract to fight Tony Herrera in Fort Worth, Texas, on April 20, the New York body refused to join the N. B. C. in its suspension.

The commission declined to regard Frankie Klick, San Francisco lightweight who held Ross to a draw in an over-the-weight match on the Coast, as the No. 1 challenger for the 135-pound crown. He was told that he would have to defeat Tony Canzoneri in Brooklyn on June 27 before he would receive such recognition.

The commission gave Jim Browning until Wednesday to accept a challenge from Jim Londos for the heavyweight wrestling championship.

June 2, 1934

Baer Knocks Out Carnera To Win Heavyweight Title

Referee Stops Fight in Eleventh Round After Italian Is Floored for Twelfth Time in Bout—56,000 Pay $428,000 Gate.

By JAMES P. DAWSON.

The world's heavyweight championship came back to the United States last night after an absence of a year.

Max Baer, the new Jack Dempsey in every respect save seriousness, knocked out Primo Carnera, Venetian ring giant, in the eleventh round of their scheduled fifteen-round battle in Madison Square Garden's Long Island City Bowl. He triumphed in one of the most sensational encounters ever waged for the ring's richest prize.

The finish came after 2 minutes 16 seconds of the eleventh round when Carnera could not possibly go any further. He had been floored twelve times through the fight, three times in the first round, as many times in the second, once in the third, three times in the tenth and twice in the eleventh.

He fell once under his own weakness and the drive of a languid right he pushed to Baer's face.

Carnera could go no further and he looked appealingly at Referee Arthur Donovan, murmuring a request to the arbiter that the bout be stopped for his own safety. Referee Donovan acted promptly.

"Carnera asked me to stop the fight, just at the second when I was going to stop it anyway," said Donovan after the fight. "He didn't know where he was. He could not have continued, and there was no use letting it go on when he was so helpless."

There was some confusion at the close of the tenth round. Just as the bell rang to terminate the session, Donovan leaped between the men and separated them. Many at the time thought the bout had been stopped.

"I didn't stop the bout in the tenth round," said Donovan. "The bell ended the round just as I stepped between them, and I heard it distinctly."

Notwithstanding, Donovan's action in the closing seconds in the tenth round was interpreted by many at the ringside as an official ending to the fray and surprise was expressed when he announced through the ropes that the bout would proceed.

This surprise was particularly manifest in Baer's corner, where the Californian's seconds had clambered through the ropes before the bell ended the round, in the mistaken belief that Baer had won the fight.

Some 56,000 persons turned out for this combat between two of the biggest men ever to fight for the crown. The gross receipts were were $428,000, that sum being paid by a gathering that came from near and far, and represented all walks of life.

One member of the President's Cabinet was in attendance—Postmaster General James A. Farley, who was there with Mrs. Farley. Governors and Mayors from nearby States and cities, including Mayors LaGuardia of New York and Frank Hague of Jersey City, and members of Congress were at the ringside.

The stage and screen were represented, as was the business world, all drawn thither by the promise of an exciting combat that was fulfilled, and the chance to do something for charity. For 10 per cent of the receipts from the show to to the Free Milk Fund for Babies, Inc., of which Mrs. William Randolph Hearst is chairman.

Ex-Champions in Crowd.

Five former wearers of the crown that Baer brought back to America were conspicuous in the gathering. Tommy Burns, Jack Johnson, Jack Dempsey, Gene Tunney and Jack Sharkey thrilled to the spectacle. Undoubtedly they were proud of Baer's achievement.

Certainly Dempsey was. He saw in the ring, triumphant, a man that is nearer to himself than any other heavyweight in existence. It had to be a reminder of the old Manassa Mauler—that was the title of Dempsey at his best—who crushed Carnera in defeat in a battle that rivaled Dempsey's well-remembered duel with Luis Angel Firpo in 1923.

Dempsey, incidentally, has a financial interest in the new champion. He was the first to leap through the ropes and greet this devastating champion, whose padded gloves are mailed fists, piston-like in action and loaded with punching TNT.

He fights in flurries, does this new titleholder, with a style that has made him heretofore unreliable. Outside the ring he is of an easy-going disposition that belies his primitive, fighting fury.

Inside the ring he is tolerant and, to an extent, indulgent. That is why many thought he could not become serious enough to crush the 6-foot, 6½-inch, 263¼ pound giant who held the title until last night.

But when aroused he glories in fighting punch for punch. With him it is a question solely of the survival of the fittest. He demonstrated this amply when he battered Carnera into a figure of abject helplessness with a pitiless, furious assault.

In defeat Carnera crowned himself with the glory of the vanquished fighter who sticks to his guns until he is helpless. Those who said the mammoth Italian could not withstand punishment—could not "take it," in the parlance of the ring—were confounded as the oak-like figure stood up under a battering that would have felled a less determined man.

A Record in Knockdowns.

No heavyweight title defender in the modern history of boxing has been a victim of so many knockdowns in a championship struggle. Even the beating that Jess Willard took at the hands of Dempsey in Toledo back in 1919 paled against that absorbed by Carnera in his desperate but futile attempt to retain the title he won a year ago.

He proved to everybody who saw his losing fight, a battle that was an uphill struggle for him from the outset, that he is thoroughly game and fearless.

Baer, of course, is not the one-punch finisher that Dempsey was. And he does not fight as intently as Dempsey did when he had a foe on the downward path. But he is a terrific hitter, and every serious punch he let fly at Carnera was loaded with dynamite.

The Italian took every blow until he could take no more. Going down twelve times. He also fell once while delivering a punch. And twice in the first round he stumbled drunkenly against and almost through the ropes, helpless and on the brink of defeat.

But he rallied from this harrowing experience and outboxed Baer when the latter became playful in the fourth, seventh, eight and ninth rounds. And he was doing all right until Baer suddenly turned in the tenth round, as he did a year ago against Max Schmeling, and became vicious in the wink of an eye.

Then came what many thought was the end as the bell finished the tenth. At any event, it was unmistakably the finish of Carnera in the eleventh.

Carnera denied after the bout that he had appealed to Referee Donovan to stop the fight, but he could have made his appeal without discredit to himself. He had gone further than anybody expected he would after those three knockdowns in the first.

More, on none of the knockdowns did Carnera take advantage of the nine-second count to which he was entitled and which an experienced fighter would use. Maybe this hastened his downfall, but it is doubtful.

Greater even than his survival of the early knockdowns was Carnera's self-confident rally through the fourth, seventh, eighth and ninth rounds. Cumbersome he was, but he fought on gloriously in his own awkward way, waging what he must have felt was a losing battle, but sticking to his guns until he could not go on.

It matters not whether he asked Referee Donovan to stop the fight—the intervention was imminent anyway—but none can dispute that Carnera went down to defeat gloriously, a Spartan to the last.

Baer fought an admirably clean fight, a fact which should be mentioned in view of the widespread suspicion in advance of the battle that he would wage the battle differently. Only one offense was charged against him in the State Athletic Commission's book of fouls, and this was accidental. In the eighth round the Californian was erratic with a sweeping left for the body.

Baer didn't have to resort to objectionable boxing. He tagged Carnera vitally three times in the first three minutes of fighting and from there on knew in his heart that Carnera was his victim whenever he elected to go after him.

Instead of rushing in and finishing the giant, the tolerant husky from California fought and coasted, charged and rested, was furious and easy in changing moods as the fight progressed. But he never withdrew the power from his punch, though at times he withheld the blow.

It followed as a consequence that Carnera was a pitiable sight at the finish. Baer was smiling and unmarked. He leaped over the ropes when his hand had been raised in victory, lithe as a panther and with a broad grin on his face.

"I'm not in condition," he said good-naturedly as he pounded his perfectly formed body on the ring platform.

The fight opened cautiously enough, a surprise for those who had expected Baer to tear out of his corner like a tiger. Carnera was cagey and Baer backed away, sizing up the giant. Short left leads were but feeble forerunners of what was to follow, and a harmless clinch was merely a disguise.

Suddenly, however, Baer leaped in on the attack, transformed in the wink of an eye from the cool strategist to a fighting fury. He led with a left for the body that was merely a feint, and then drove a right to Carnera's huge girth. The Italian winced under the blow and looked startled.

But he had no chance for counter or defense, for like a jiffy, Baer was upon him, lashing out wickedly with a roundhouse right which landed on the jaw, and toppled the giant in his tracks.

Carnera was only slightly more dazed than the crowd that witnessed the fall and the punch that precipitated it. Excitement ran high. Deep-throated words of advice and counsel came from the corner of Baer, clashing with words of encouragement and entreaty from the corner of Carnera.

In the general excitement the giant drew erect before a count could be started or heard above the din. Then Baer leaped after him and the downfall of the giant was under full headway.

In the six-round semi-final Charley Massera of Pittsburgh, 183½, pounded out a decision over Al Ettore, 184, Philadelphia.

James J. Braddock, 180, Jersey City, stopped Corn Griffin, Fort Benning, Ga., in 2:37 of the third round of a scheduled six-rounder.

In a five-rounder, Lou Poster, Pottsville, Pa., defeated Al White, 177½, Greenpoint. Dynamtie Jackson, 208 Los Angeles, defeated Willie McGee, 198, Tampa, Fla., and Eddie Hogan, 216½, Waterbury, outpointed Chester Matan, 208½, Brooklyn, in the other five rounders. The opening four was won by Don Petrin, 177¼, Newark, who turned back Ed Karolak, 188, Peekskill.

June 15, 1934

M'LARNIN IS VICTOR OVER ROSS IN BOWL

Regains World's Welterweight Title by Winning Decision in 15-Round Bout.

REFEREE'S VOTE DECIDES

Donovan Gives the Fight to Coast Boxer After Split Verdict of Judges.

By JAMES P. DAWSON.

The world's welterweight championship last night returned to Jimmy McLarnin, the fighting little Irishman who has never failed to come back.

In as glorious a battle as he ever waged the warrior from the Coast fought his way to a decision over Barney Ross, Chicago's double champion, before 25,000 fight fans in the Madison Square Garden Bowl, Long Island City, and regained the title he lost to Ross last May 28 in the same ring.

On the vote of Referee Arthur Donovan, who based his ballot on boxing and fighting ability combined, McLarnin gained the honors in this battle which bristled with fighting fury and boxing brilliance.

The two judges, Tommy Shortell and Charles Lynch, disagreed when the final bell clanged finis to a head-to-head skirmish, in which Ross, fighting furiously, was hammering with both hands a McLarnin who was blind in one eye.

Lynch Votes for Ross.

Lynch voted for Ross, calling eight rounds for the lad who was the ring's first to hold both the world's lightweight and welterweight titles at the same time. Six he gave to McLarnin and one he called even.

Shortell voted six rounds for McLarnin, five for Ross and four even. The voting slip of Referee Donovan gave McLarnin ten rounds and Ross five.

Through his superb boxing on the attack and the defense as well, McLarnin carried off the honors and kept clean a record which is a ring legend—he has never failed to conquer a fighter who beat him.

This record goes back to his days as a bantamweight. It encompasses such redoubtable fighters as Bud Taylor, the Terre Haute terror; Ray Miller, the Chicagoan; Sammy Mandell, ex-lightweight champion, and last, but by no means least, the marvelous old war horse of the ring who has since retired, Billy Petrolle. Now they can add Barney Ross to the list, without the stigma of disgrace.

More, this battle held true to ring tradition in other respects. The hoodoo that has followed the world's welterweight title since the reign of Pete Latzo dogged the footsteps of Ross as did the jinx of the bowl ring. Every welterweight championship fight since Latzo's days saw the champion losing his crown in its first defense, and there have been eleven of them, including last night's.

Jinx of the Bowl Holds.

No champion who has entered the bowl ring has departed with his championship prestige intact. And this goes down the line through Max Schmeling, Jack Sharkey, Primo Carnera, McLarnin and Ross. It is strange, but it is true.

Donovan leaned to the superb boxing of McLarnin in arriving at his award. He said as much in explanation of his decision when the excitement over the result had died in the vast recesses of the bowl.

"McLarnin won on his boxing," said Donovan. "He outboxed Ross at almost every turn. At least that is the way I looked at it. Ross fought only in flurries, and you can't win fights fighting only in spasms."

The battle, waged in the interests of charity, attracted a gate estimated at $115,000. The turnout of 25,000 was remarkable in view of the disappointments experienced in staging the contest. Four times rain forced its postponement and over eleven days this delay spread, affecting interest, gate receipts, and, no doubt, the fighters.

Last night the weather was forbidding. Dark clouds hung ominously in a starless sky following a morning of torrential rain and mist-like drizzle.

Eager to See Struggle.

But the fans wanted to see this struggle as they wanted to do a bit for charity. The consequence was a gate that is expected to provide a rich harvest for The New York American's Christmas and Relief Fund and a battle that thrilled with its suspense, its exciting moments and its exhibition of a boxing skill that was thought to be a lost art.

Not all who witnessed the skirmish agreed with the award. Some there were who jeered and booed openly, but these derisive cries were drowned in a salvo of cheers for a conquering hero who toppled a foe the bettors held the favorite at odds of 2 to 1.

This disagreement extended to the ringside section holding the critics. Many saw the battle differently. Many disagreed with the decision, though they resented it not too strongly. It was a close battle. The score sheets of the three bout officials reflect that.

Keenly waged and bitterly fought at a pace that was steady and at times electrifying, the contest progressed from its opening gong to its final bell with cheers for first one and then the other battler. And at the finish the acclaim for McLarnin overcame the cries of the dissenters.

Gives McLarnin Nine Rounds.

The writer was in complete accord with the verdict. He gave McLarnin nine rounds and Ross six, recognizing the superior combination of fighting and boxing that characterized McLarnin's work in the earlier rounds, and his cool, calculating boxing in the closing sessions.

McLarnin took the first, third, fourth, sixth, seventh, eighth, tenth, thirteenth and fourteenth rounds. Ross fought steadily in the six rounds he won. In these he fought desperately to fulfill that promise of his most enthusiastic admirers—a knockout triumph. But his sporadic boxing was a detracting influence and he suffered accordingly.

The Chicagoan won the second, fifth, ninth, eleventh, twelfth and fifteenth.

In one of the rounds credited to Ross, McLarnin actually had the better of the fighting. This was the fifth, in which McLarnin was penalized for striking foul unintentionally with a long left aimed at the body. McLarnin saw the illegal direction of the blow in time to still its power, but not soon enough entirely to recall its momentum. It landed and one of McLarnin's best rounds was charged against him as a consequence.

McLarnin proved the contention that his long lay-off cost him heavily in his first meeting with Ross.

Jimmy McLarnin.

Contrasting with the floundering, slippery-footed, erratic punching fighter of last May 28, last night there was in the ring a cool, deliberate marksman, whose timing was accurate, judgment sharp, boxing skillful, and whose punching power on what few occasions he exhibited it was awe-inspiring.

More, however, for the manner in which he scored his victory than for the victory itself did McLarnin deserve unstinted praise. A head-on collision in the very first round grew a slight lump over McLarnin's left eye, almost above the nose. A blow opened a cut over the left eye in the eighth round.

Eyes Completely Closed.

Ross's rat-a-tat-tat of lefts and rights gradually increased the swelling until the forehead was abnormal and, in the twelfth round, McLarnin's left eye was completely closed. He fought on, nevertheless, to win the thirteenth and fourteenth rounds on boxing skill alone, an almost unbelievable feat under the optical handicap. And his iron courage and heart carried him through a punching gale in the last round to the final bell, when he turned the familiar hand-spring, an acrobatic reflection of conserved McLarnin strength which preceded the raising aloft of his hand as champion again.

Ross was not unmarked as he left the ring. His two eyes were cut and bleeding, his mouth was bruised and his left side was red and raw about the ribs, grim testimony of the punching power that McLarnin boasts.

Ross's start was slow, and that cost him heavily. On the other hand, McLarnin profited by a snappy early start. He speared the Chicagoan with a left jab that was swift, sharp and snappy, and with powerful left hooks to the face counted often. Near the end of the first round McLarnin staggered his foe with a left hook to the jaw followed by a right that carried equal power and brought joy to the McLarnin adherents in the throng and dismay to Ross's followers.

Ross Returns to Fray.

Ross, nothing daunted, bounded back at his foe and was fighting furiously at the end of the round, although he missed repeatedly.

The second saw Ross fighting furiously after overcoming an early bombardment of left hooks which McLarnin unleashed. Countering this fire, Ross sprang at his foe and drove both hands to the head tirelessly in punches which were more bewildering because of their speed than they were effective with power.

McLarnin used a short chopping right smartly in the third and fourth rounds, in combination with a ceaseless fire of straight lefts and left hooks, which had Ross fighting in desperate flurries, unsuccessfully seeking to counteract or discourage this onslaught. Through the fifth it was the same, but the one foul punch he struck during the bout cost McLarnin the round.

In the sixth, seventh and eighth rounds McLarnin's boxing was superb and at times he stung Ross with right crosses to the jaw. The blows, however, never threatened a knockdown, nor did any punches of the fight.

Earns Cheers of Crowd,

Ross seemed to take a grip on himself and fought furiously and steadily in the ninth, driving McLarnin before him with a two-fisted fire of rights and lefts to the head, face and jaw which brought the cheers of the crowd to the defender's ears and consternation in the McLarnin camp.

In the tenth McLarnin began to be handicapped by his swelling left eye, but he continued to spear his foe with accurate left jabs and left hooks and made Ross miss awkwardly.

Ross fought furiously in the eleventh, hammering McLarnin steadily in a blazing fire of lefts and rights. And the same was true of the twelfth, when McLarnin's injured eye closed completely.

Through the thirteenth and fourteenth, however, McLarnin was the master boxer, with just enough of fighting fury at times to forestall an attempted recovery by Ross.

But in the fifteenth nothing McLarnin had to offer could offset the desperate, furious fighting of Ross, who threw every ounce of his remaining strength into a closing bid for victory.

McLarnin weighed 146¼ pounds and Ross 140¼ pounds.

September 18, 1934

NAZI PAPER HITS JEWISH MANAGERS

Munich Journal Is Angered by the Refusal of Schmeling and Neusel to Discharge Pilots.

Wireless to THE NEW YORK TIMES.

MUNICH, April 1.—The refusal of Max Schmeling and Walter Neusel, after years of warning, to discharge their Jewish managers "in the interests of Germanhood," has angered the Nazi newspaper, the Fraenkische Tageszeitung.

The paper particularly scores Joe Jacobs, Schmeling's American manager, for recently giving the Nazi salute with a "smoking cigar between the fingers of his saluting hand." The Tageszeitung calls for an immediate reform of these "shameful conditions in the German sport world."

Neusel not only ignored the official application of the Aryan clause of the third Reich to the boxing world, but followed his manager, Paul Damski, to Paris, where he has since trained.

April 2, 1935

Crowd of 40,000 Sees Ross Regain the World's Welterweight Championship

ROSS WINS TITLE; DEFEATS M'LARNIN

Regains Welterweight Crown by Scoring in 15-Round Bout at Polo Grounds.

DECISION IS UNANIMOUS

But Many in Throng Voice Disapproval — Encounter Draws $140,480 Gate.

By JAMES P. DAWSON.

A sizzling pace and an accompanying rapid fire of punches brought back to Barney Ross of Chicago, who only recently gave up the lightweight title, the world's welterweight crown last night at the Polo Grounds in fifteen rounds of spectacular fighting against Jimmy McLarnin, Vancouver veteran, before 40,000 fans.

Tired and weary, cut and bruised Ross had his hand raised in victory after fifteen rounds of the most grueling fighting he had ever encountered.

The unanimous decision of Referee Jack Dempsey and Judges George Lecron and Abe Goldberg restored to Ross the title he lost to Jimmy last September. Last night, incidentally, was the anniversary of his first meeting with McLarnin, when he won the crown for the first time to become the only lightweight and welterweight champion the ring has known.

But if the judges were unanimous, the crowd, which paid estimated receipts of $140,480 for the privilege because it was staged by the Twentieth Century S.C. partly in the interests of the Free Milk Fund for Babies, Inc., of which Mrs. William Randolph Hearst is chairman, was not.

When the announcement came from Harry Ballagh, substituting for the ailing Joe Humphreys, there came an echoing roar of disapproval which was deafening while it lasted. The crowd didn't agree with the verdict, particularly those who occupied seats in the upper and lower grandstands, removed from the ringside.

Some of the ringside observers disagreed and added their cries to the clamor which came when Ross was led to the centre of the ring, a smile on his battered face, to have his hand raised aloft in victory.

But there was little reason for this demonstration. Ross won by a margin of ten rounds to five, won not as a great champion but he won nevertheless on any basis on which boxing is scored.

Fighting Days Are Over.

He won so thoroughly that Charley (Pop) Foster, gray-haired old manager of McLarnin, announced after the fight, even as he protested the award which took from his boy the title he prized so highly, that McLarnin was through with the ring.

"I disagree with the decision," he said. "I think Jimmy won but I won't let him fight any more. He's through with the ring."

Gene Tunney was among those who disagreed with the verdict, going contrary to an old foe as he did eight years ago in Chicago.

But a gray-haired woman paid no attention to the derisive shouts. She heard only the cheers that greeted Ross as she rushed to the ringside through a crowd divided in its reception of the verdict, but preponderantly for the vanquished, judged by its cries.

She was the mother of Ross, here to see her son fight in New York for the first time. Ross spied her as she pushed forward. He dashed over to climb through the rope and greet her.

A Great Ring Warrior.

If McLarnin fulfills his promise to retire the ring will lose a mighty warrior, one of the greatest. But few will dispute that the move would be wise.

Jimmy is wealthy. He is unscarred after thirteen years of ring warfare through five ring divisions beginning with the flyweight.

In two of three battles he has bowed to Ross. The welterweight ranks do not hold opponents of a calibre to warrant McLarnin purses. A fourth meeting with Ross is unnecessary. It could only establish Barney's supremacy more clearly. The division of opinion among the spectators was not reflected in the voting of the judges. The decision was unanimous and justly so, although there was a wide variance with the number of rounds each official gave.

Dempsey, protested as referee by Manager Foster before the bout began, worked flawlessly, smoothly and unruffled through the encounter and at the finish voted five rounds for Ross, three for McLarnin and seven even.

Judge Goldberg gave Ross eight rounds, six to McLarnin and one even. Judge Lecron voted nine rounds for Ross, four for McLarnin and two even. The writer scored ten rounds for Ross and five for McLarnin.

McLarnin just came back to the ring once too often after another of his extended layoffs and paid the price. He suffered the consequences of inactivity in a battle that demanded that he be at his fighting best and which saw him weak in ring essentials.

Profited By Experience.

He was wrong in letting Ross sweep him before a succession of whirlwind rushes that carried no physical danger beyond what is ordinarily associated with a light-hitting fighter who herds and rushes a harder hitting foe for effect. He was wrong in his battle plan which saw him trying to outbox the speedier Ross when a furious attack might have produced results.

Ross, on the other hand, fought just the kind of battle he could calculate to be the most effective against McLarnin after the experience of two previous engagements. He knew better than anyone else the force of McLarnin's blows. It was his task to break this power and avoid as many blows as possible.

Ross captured the first three rounds, the sixth, seventh and eighth, the eleventh, twelfth, thirteenth and fourteenth. The schedule shows how perfectly he gauged his fighting in concentrated rallies, reflecting more clearly than anything else the measure of his steady march to regaining the 147-pound throne.

McLarnin won the fourth, fifth, ninth and tenth rounds, and in a furious, vicious, desperate fifteenth-round rally that saw him fighting like a fiend, he captured the last session, and did everything but knock out Ross. At the final bell Ross was wearier than the Vancouver lad.

Ross came out of his corner at the beginning jabbing and pecking with his left, protecting his jaw from that dangerous McLarnin left hook.

He led at McLarnin through the first three rounds, outjabbed Jimmy at long range and in the exchanges that came at close quarters outpunched McLarnin.

Ross Is Jarred in Fourth.

In the fourth a left hook to the jaw jolted and jarred Ross. But in the fifth Ross was back on the attack until McLarnin's left proved superior and in an exchange of rights McLarnin's was heavier.

The sixth, seventh and eighth rounds found Ross swarming all over McLarnin and Jimmy at a loss to discourage his foe's whirlwind attack.

McLarnin feinted like the master he is in the ninth, made Ross miss repeatedly and awkwardly and twice jarred Barney. In the tenth McLarnin was even greater as he outboxed and outfought Ross at every turn.

But in the eleventh a snappy left from Ross cooled Jimmy's ardor.

Ross charged on to win this round and carried on through the twelfth, when he bent McLarnin double under a wicked smash of the left to the body. In the thirteenth he fought toe to toe with McLarnin and kept up the pace in the fourteenth.

Came the fifteenth and McLarnin threw all caution to the wind. But the trouble with the recovery was that it came too late. Ross, by that time, had the fight won so far that only a knockout could keep him from the title. And the knockout never came.

In the semi-final Sixto Escobar, 119, Puerto Rico, stopped Joey Archibald, 118¾, Providence, in 1:36 of the sixth and final round. The other six rounders saw Paulie Walker, 149, Trenton, and Mickey Serrian, 143¾, New York, fight a draw; Lou Camps, 128, New York, defeat Jackie Sharkie, 129½, Chicago, and Frankie (Kid) Bruno, 139½, Brooklyn, knock out Calvin Reed, 137½, Philadelphia, in 1:09 of the second round.

The opening four-rounder went to Ralph Vona, 138¾, Asbury Park, who outpointed Andy Miritello, 137¾, Brooklyn.

May 29, 1935

Braddock Outpoints Baer To Win World Ring Title

New Jersey Heavyweight, on Relief Within Last Two Years, Caps Great Come-Back by Victory in Bowl—Takes 9 of 15 Rounds.

By JAMES P. DAWSON.

The wholly unexpected happened last night under a hazy moon in the Madison Square Garden Bowl, which spreads over Long Island City's acres.

James J. Braddock, born on New York's West Side, but now a resident of New Jersey, won the world's heavyweight championship from Max Baer, the playboy of the ring, who could not be serious even while a fortune was slipping through his fingers.

In fifteen rounds of fighting that was surprisingly easy for him as it started, but grew more painful and more grueling, Braddock, man of destiny, who was regarded as a has-been no longer ago than the Fall of 1933, scaled the ring's heights on his lion-hearted courage and a grim determination.

He hammered his way to the decision over Baer to the complete satisfaction of some 30,000 wild-eyed fight fans who paid estimated gross receipts of $200,000 to see one of the worst heavyweight championship contests in all the long history of the ring.

Referee Johnny McAvoy and the two judges, Charley Lynch and George Kelly, voted unanimously for Braddock as the new champion without a dissenting voice from the throng. It was impossible to obtain a round-by-round detail of the officials' vote, but none was necessary.

Hardly a critic at the ringside disagreed with the award. Certainly none in the crowd, not even the enthusiastic friends of the playboy, who is now an ex-champion, could disagree.

There was no room for doubt, because Braddock won by nine rounds to six. That is the writer's score, and it is also the general score of critics who viewed the battle from their close-up chairs in the glare of the ring's strong lights.

Braddock wanted to fight and did to the best of his ability. Baer, ever the clown, didn't want to fight, or just simply couldn't. That is the answer to this battle that was poor from a competitive standpoint and so stunningly amazing in its results.

And, simply because he wanted to fight, Braddock, truly the ring's man of destiny if ever there was one, today has the world at his feet.

Was on Relief Rolls.

Within the past two years he was on the New Jersey relief rolls for the unemployed. He could get no fights and there was no manual labor for him. He tried his hand at longshore work on the Hoboken

docks, but even this wasn't steady, and he had a wife and three youngsters to provide for.

When he beat Baer last night he not only furnished a ring upset that has no parallel in modern times but he supplied the climax to one of the greatest comebacks known to boxing, or any other sport for that matter. Courage with a determination spurred by desperation is responsible for the transformation which finds Braddock the world's heavyweight boxing champion today.

A year ago he started his comeback when he knocked out Corn Griffin in a preliminary on the card which saw Baer pounding huge Primo Carnera into defeat to win the crown. Braddock was called off the Hoboken docks without benefit of training for this scrap. Encouraged, he did a little training and conquered John Henry Lewis when that Coast fighter was heralded as a title threat. Then, last March, Braddock beat the highly touted Art Lasky and cleared the path to his chance at the title.

Match Was Ridiculed.

Even in the face of these conquests Braddock received scant consideration as a title prospect. Baer guffawed when it was announced he had been matched with the Jerseyman. Fight followers ridiculed the match.

Baer was made a prohibitive favorite. Odds of 6 to 1 generally were quoted and there were isolated cases of betting at odds as high as 8 to 1 and 10 to 1.

Only one heavyweight match since the days of the great John L. Sullivan caused such long odds. That was when Tunney, the favorite at 6 to 1, defeated Tom Heeney.

Sullivan was held a favorite at 4 to 1 when Gentleman Jim Corbett beat him in New Orleans in 1892. Jack Dempsey was the favorite at odds of 14 to 5 when he bowed to Gene Tunney in the rain at Philadelphia in 1926. These three fights hold the longest betting odds of any title struggles in the modern history of heavyweight championships.

Tunney's conquest of Dempsey was a mild surprise in comparison to what happened last night. Indeed, in retrospect, it is doubtful if even the triumph of the dancing young bank clerk who cut Sullivan to ribbons was as distinct a shock as the crowning of Braddock.

Bowl Jinx Scores Again

No single heavyweight championship bout since the bare knuckle days was so disappointing, so utterly lacking in competitive appeal, so absolutely unadorned by anything spectacular, as last night's battle, which saw upheld the tradition that no ring champion can successfully defend his title in the Madison Square Garden Bowl.

The size of the crowd was one of the most amazing off-shoots of the

fight. Every walk of life was represented in the throng, a tremendous attendance in view of the one-sidedness expected as reflected in the betting.

John Roosevelt, youngest son of President Roosevelt, was at the ringside. Postmaster General James A. Farley was there. Mayor La Guardia, Jack Dempsey, Gene Tunney, stars of the stage and screen, leaders in the professions, the arts, were present. It was a crowd that presented a cross-section of American life, gathered from near and far, not record-breaking in its numbers, but representative in quality.

They booed and jeered and yawned at the fight, because Baer clowned when he should have been fighting. For sentimental reasons they rooted for Braddock as the struggle started. Quietly their emotions swung to the underdog, as is inevitable. As the fight progressed and Braddock in his clumsy, awkward, but determined and desperate way piled up points, the cheers were for Braddock and in the champion's ears rang the derisive cries of a throng thrilled at the sight of a new champion in the making.

No Thrills During Bout.

The crowning of a new titleholder was their only reward. They had no satisfaction, absolutely none, from the fight as a spectacle. It ended with a champion on the throne who showed none of the accepted qualifications of a champion as these titleholders are appraised, say, by the Dempsey or Tunney standard.

The battle also maintained Madison Square Garden's grasp on the exclusive disposition of the world's heavyweight title. This ring crown has been at the disposal of the Garden since the days of Dempsey. It faced its first serious threat in last night's battle, for Baer had proclaimed his intention of campaigning independently after the Braddock match.

Instead, if Baer follows his post-battle announcement, he will go into retirement and forsake the

ring, diverting his attention to raising cattle in Oakland, Calif.

In the disappointment of his unexpected defeat Baer made this declaration sincerely in his dressing room after leaving the ring. His manager, Ancil Hoffman, pooh-poohed the idea, though. So it remains to be seen what Baer will do.

Poor Showing by Baer.

If he can fight no better than he fought against Braddock, however, Baer had better go into retirement. Preliminary boys who supported his first defense of the crown were better than Baer last night.

But as a cold matter of fact, Braddock showed little more. He is willing. He is game. He is fearless in a determined way. But he is slow-footed, awkward and stiff. He is an improvement on the Braddock of old, to be sure. But, at 29 years of age, and after ten years of ring service, the new champion is ordinary as titleholders are weighed and measured.

In extenuation of Baer's sorry showing his manager announced before leaving the ring that both Baer's hands were injured early in the fray. Manager Hoffman said the injuries came in the fifth round. But even this didn't explain the mediocre fighting of Baer in the round preceding.

Manager Hoffman had to fight his way through an exciting scene to make his statement. The echo from the announcement of Al Frazin, introducing the fighters and calling the results in place of the ailing Joe Humphreys, was still mingling with the roar of the acclaiming crowd.

Friends Pour Into Ring.

Inside the ropes the ring was a bedlam. Braddock, the new champion, was swallowed up in a flood of humanity which swept aside policemen and ring attendants just as soon as the decision was announced. His friends clamored about him. Those who didn't know him when he had recourse to the relief rolls of New Jersey wanted to pat the new champion on the back. Joe Gould, pint-sized manager of the

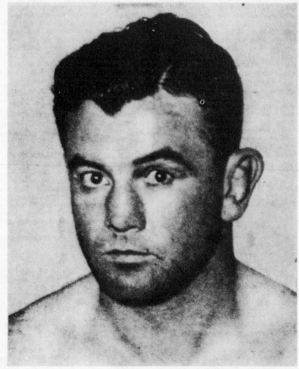

Times Wide World Photo.

James J. Braddock.

new champion, perhaps the only one who believed Braddock could outlast Baer, was wildly excited.

It was with difficulty Braddock was escorted out of the ring and to his dressing room, knowledge of his victory assuaging the pain of the drilling he had taken as Baer belatedly launched a bid to retain his title and pelted his foe viciously about the body and head with an attack that failed.

Baer was alone and unnoticed. He greeted his conqueror with an affectionate embrace in Baer's corner when the result was announced. Then he disappeared quietly, quickly, as if he wanted to get away from it all.

Baer had no complaint with the result. He could have none. He not only failed to fight as a champion should but he transgressed the rules of ring warfare more than once—accidentally, without a doubt, but the transgressions were there.

Baer lost three rounds because of fouls, chiefly backhand punches, which are barred all over the country. He was erratic, too, with body blows, which merit no disqualification here, but carry an automatic penalty of the loss of a round in which they occur.

Fouls Prove Costly.

Baer drew cautions for fouls in the fifth, ninth and twelfth rounds. He lost two sessions that might otherwise have gone to his credit. In the fifth round Braddock had the honors anyway. But in the ninth and twelfth Baer appeared to advantage, save for his fouls.

But these penalties had no bearing on the result. Even giving the ninth and twelfth rounds to Baer, the decision would still go to Braddock, who did most of what little actual fighting the battle held and was almost tirelessly on the offensive.

The most damaging blow of the fight was landed by Baer. It was the one punch that came near producing a knockdown. But it was an isolated case of Baer's hitting superiority, and it was an absolute accident.

It happened in the seventh round. Baer, after six rounds of idling, clowning and everything else but fighting, suddenly let fly with a wild right and Braddock actually walked into the blow. The Jersey man's knees sagged, his vision clouded, and he was in distress. But with opportunity thus beckoning, Baer was lethargic, indifferent.

Where he might have gone in, following his advantage, and at least floored his foe, he failed to grasp the chance. He never had another so bright.

A Withering Fire.

True, he wore Braddock down. He wearied and pained the Jersey man with a withering body fire through the closing stages of the battle, battering Braddock with a two-fisted fire that had James J. in palpable distress. But Baer never once, after that seventh round, landed a blow to the jaw that carried rocking force. And he couldn't knock out the determined, desperate Braddock with body blows.

In the final analysis, the story of the fight is this: Braddock was bad, but Baer was worse.

The defending champion made not one definite move in defense of his crown for six rounds. He posed, he clowned, he sneered or grimaced or smiled, but he did little or no punching. And, for these first six rounds, Braddock, with everything to gain and nothing to lose, plodded on, always forging in on the attack, while Baer played the actor.

Not until the seventh round was a staggering blow struck. Then came that accidental punch.

In the eighth, Baer still played the clown, instead of trying to land a blow without aid from a stumbling foe. He feigned grogginess when a

Times Wide World Photo.

Braddock driving a hard left to Baer's jaw in the first round.

wild right-handed swing from Braddock knocked him partly off balance. Baer's knees buckled and he swayed in mock distress. But, instead of roaring its approval of the act, the crowd voiced only resentment and urged Braddock on.

After that eighth round, the battle became a grim task for Braddock. His nose was bloodied in the sixth when Baer, stung to action by the penalty of the fifth, popped his foe with a right uppercut as Braddock came in head down.

Max Fights in Flurries.

Through the ninth round and for the remainder of the fight, generally, Baer fought in savage outbursts in which he pounded Braddock's mid-section with strength-sapping blows that would have crushed a less hardy, less determined foeman.

Braddock not only stood up under the battering, but never once stopped his attempts at return fire. He beat an orderly retreat at times, but he was always stabbing with a left that landed flush on Baer's face despite Max's longer reach. He had Baer's left eye swollen and discolored and his lips bruised and bleeding.

An unscheduled outburst of excitement came at the close of the twelfth round, after Baer had committed a third penalty-producing foul. Stung by body blows, Braddock didn't hear the bell, and neither did Baer, who was intent on crushing his foe with his two-fisted onslaught to the mid-section.

They fought after the bell in a livelier exchange than was furnished at many turns of the legal fighting time, and the trading didn't halt util Referee McAvoy stepped between the embattled pair. Then Manager Gould, incensed at the foul which cost Baer the round, climbed through the ropes and advanced half-way across the ring to

Times Wide World Photo.

Braddock's hand raised after victory. Baer is in lower right corner.

Baer's corner, as if to test his own punching prowess on the Californian.

A policeman jumped after Gould and pulled him back, threatening to toss him from the ring until he learned he was the manger of Braddock. The crowd was in a frenzy and the outlook was for a small-sized riot. But Referee McAvoy prevented this and the policeman who grabbed Gould supplied the quietus to the aroused manager.

Through the thirteenth, fourteenth and fifteenth rounds Braddock lived through a terrific storm of punches with a resistance to punishment that was amazing. Though worn and weary, he withstood the drilling to get his reward when he was crowned champion at the finish.

Galento Wins by Knockout.

Tony Galento, Orange (N. J.) heavyweight, turned in the most sensational performance in the preliminaries. He stopped Anthony Ashrut, better known as "Young Hippo" of Philadelphia, in 1 minute and 5 seconds of the first round in a scheduled six-rounder. He floored Ashrut once with a right to the jaw before putting him down for the count with the same punch. Galento weighed 221½ and Ashrut 219½.

Steve Dudas, 183½, Edgewater, N. J., pounded out a decision over Terry Mitchell, 186¾, Boston, in a hard-fought six-rounder.

In the other six-rounders, Eddie Hogan, 217, Waterbury, Conn., outpointed Jack McCarthy, 191½, Boston, and Don Petrin, 182, Newark, defeated Paul Pross, 207, New York.

The opening four-rounder between George Turner, 185, Tulsa, and Nick Masters, 173, Far Rockaway, ended in a draw.

June 14, 1935

LOUIS KNOCKS OUT CARNERA IN SIXTH; 60,000 SEE FIGHT

Detroit Heavyweight Sensation Stops Former Champion in Yankee Stadium.

LOSER FLOORED 3 TIMES

Helpless When Referee Stops the Bout, Which Draws a Gate of $375,000.

By JAMES P. DAWSON.

Joe Louis, sensational young Detroit Negro fighter, scored a technical knockout over Primo Carnera of Italy, former world's heavyweight champion, in the sixth round of their scheduled fifteen-round bout last night in the Yankee Stadium. Knocked down three times, Carnera was helpless when Referee Arthur Donovan halted the battle after 2 minutes 32 seconds of action in the final round.

A crowd of 60,000 paid about

$375,000 to see the encounter. It was the largest New York fight throng in eight years, or since 1927, when Jack Sharkey and Jack Dempsey fought at the same arena for the chance of meeting Gene Tunney in Chicago.

Referee Donovan's intervention was timely. Another blow on the unprotected jaw of Carnera might have sent the former champion to the hospital. Another punch would not have made Louis's victory any more decisive. He had Carnera knocked out standing on his feet, a figure of utter helplessness, clinging feebly but grimly to the top rope of the ring at a place near Louis's corner.

Demonstrates His Superiority.

To the satisfaction of one of the largest crowds ever to witness a heavyweight battle here, Louis had demonstrated his complete mastery over the huge Italian who outweighed him sixty-four and one-half pounds, towered over him in height, reached several inches further and boasted seven years experience on his opponent, who has been boxing for less than a year.

Those who contributed to the spectacle enjoyed one of the greatest heavyweight battles in local history and contributed to charity at the same time. The Free Milk Fund for Babies, Inc., of which Mrs. William Randolph Hearst is chairman, shared in the profits.

In the gathering were leaders of all walks of life in the city, State and nation. Postmaster General Farley watched the proceedings, as did John and James Roosevelt, sons of the President. Mayor La Guardia was one of four city executives present. The others were Mayors Hague of Jersey City, Ellenstein of Newark and Kelly of Chicago.

Four former holders of the title which Louis seeks were there and were introduced from the ring—Dempsey, Tunney, Max Baer and Jack Johnson. James J. Braddock, current titleholder, was present as were lesser ring champions. Baseball, golf, tennis and yachting were represented in the gathering.

Great Figure of Ring.

And they all saw one of the greatest fighters of modern times in action. They left convinced, as was the writer, that there was no exaggeration in the awe-inspiring names which have been hung on Louis. He is the Brown Bomber, the Alabama Assassin, the Detroit Destroyer and anything else that has been said of him. He punches like Dempsey. He is a reminder of the one and only Sam Langford.

He has sloping shoulders, powerful arms with sinews as tough as whipcords and dynamite in his fists. A slim, perfectly modeled body, tapering legs, an inscrutable, serious face that reveals no plan of his battle, gives no sign whether he is stung or unhurt—these are his characteristics.

In his shuffling, plodding style of advance he was Carnera's master at every turn. He never threw a punch unless he knew it would land with effect. He didn't take any more punches than he had to, and that was precious few. He knows the art of feinting, something that

Times Wide World Photo.

Primo Carnera down for the second time.

few boxers know today or take the trouble to learn. And when he starts a foe on the downward path little time is lost in finishing him.

He did a neater job than did Max Baer when he won the title from Carnera last year. He did a quicker job. Carnera, lightly regarded from the real fighting standpoint heretofore, is relegated out of the picture entirely now. Whether he will overcome the effects of the blows that rendered him helpless last night is a decision only he can make. But, whether he does or not Carnera will never again be the same.

This youngster, who is only 21 years old, impressed not so much with what he did but how he did it. He was far and away superior as a hitter to Carnera. In his own peculiar way Louis was faster and surer of foot.

Willing to Be Rough.

More amazing still, Louis proved he could actually out-rough Carnera. In addition, Louis has about the most savage, two-fisted attack of any fighter of modern times. He doesn't punch alone with one hand. He destroys with either or both.

It was tentatively announced following last night's bout that Louis is to be matched with Baer for a heavyweight elimination bout in September. If this is true Baer is in for a stormy evening. Right now there appears nothing on the fistic horizon to keep the world's heavyweight title away from the Detroiter.

Louis spent five rounds trying to get the range of Carnera's jaw. He attained perfect marksmanship in the sixth and the bout was over. Like any intelligent fighter would, he foreswore early any desperate attempt to beat past the huge arms of the giant in front of him. Rather, Louis threw just enough swings for the jaw to let Carnera know he was in for a hammering if the blows

Associated Press Photo.

Joe Louis.

connected as he led up to the paralyzing blows which ended the fray.

In the first round Carnera was all right while he pecked the air with a rigid left and sparred and danced cautiously. But when he whipped a left to Louis's ribs it was the signal for a savage counter fire that soon had the Italian giant bewildered.

Attack Astonishes Carnera.

Louis let fly with a right for the jaw but missed. He was wide with two others, but a fourth landed as Carnera retreated, a grazing blow that made Carnera wide-eyed with astonishment.

Another left and right followed,

then a right which split Carnera's lip as the Italian backed into a corner for protection. And when Carnera sought to rush Louis to the ropes, Joe went back willingly enough, but as Primo rushed the Detroiter brought up a short right uppercut that sent his foe's head back.

In the second Carnera kept away from his rival's vicious stabs, and his boxing alone gave him the round, because Louis deliberately withheld his attack.

But after that it was all Louis. He stalked Carnera like a panther. He feinted the giant into knots. He dug his left and he prodded his right to Primo's generous mid-section to bring down the Italian's upraised arms and so pave the way for a deadly drive to the jaw.

Desperately, Carnera tried every punch at his command without success. But Louis just plodded on all the time, gradually attaining his goal—reducing Carnera with body blows and occasional jarring drives to the head to a state where the Italian would be compelled to drop his guard.

Stung By Left to Body.

Carnera moved gradually to his own finish. He was stung by Louis's left to the body soon after the sixth round started and desperately tried a vicious right-hand swish for the jaw that missed. Louis countered with a right that was wild, but grazed the chin with a dynamiting left and Carnera was jarred to his toes.

A right to the jaw dumped the Italian head first in the centre of the ring, but he regained his feet at the count of four while Referee Donovan was showing Louis to a neutral corner.

Primo was rubber-legged, weary and almost defenseless turning to face his foe as Louis leaped at him, raining with blows from both hands until a right hand drive, clean on the jaw. again deposited Carnera on the floor.

Again Carnera came erect at the count of four. Without knowing what he was doing, he turned to face a relentless foe and what was in store for him. Under a fusillade of lefts and rights, which ended with a right and left to the jaw, Carnera went down for the third and last time. He regained his feet at the count of three. But he was helpless and Donovan ended hostilities.

June 26, 1935

LOUIS UNDEFEATED IN PRO RING CAREER

Detroit Boxer Has Won Every Bout Since His Debut on July 4 Last Year.

ALSO AN AMATEUR STAR

Success Is Attributed Greatly to Teaching of Blackburn, a Former Fighter.

Joseph Louis Barrow is the full name of the latest star on the fistic horizon. He was born May 13, 1914, in Lexington, near Montgomery, Ala., the fourth in a line of children born to a humble cotton picker who was deep in debt

Referee Arthur Donovan halting contest and waving Louis away. Carnera, helpless, is holding on to rope.

Times Wide World Photo.

and whose health was fast failing when his fourth child was born.

His father died when Louis was 2 years of age. Then Louis's widowed mother moved the family to Detroit when Joe was 6 years old, and there he has made his home ever since.

He was working in Henry Ford's plant at River Rouge, just outside Detroit, when the ambition to be a fighter seized him. Thereupon he launched a career that is almost unparalleled in fistic annals.

In the Spring of 1932 Louis—he has long since discarded the Barrow for brevity—launched a career as an amateur. He had been attending trade school when he first donned the gloves in a gymnasium with a classmate. Ignorant of methods, Louis naturally was the recipient of a boxing lesson. But he continued to visit the gymnasium until he attained that degree of perfection which justified his entering the amateur ranks.

Bowed in First Amateur Bout.

Forthwith Louis met with adversity. He suffered defeat in his first bout, but, undeterred, he persevered and in no time at all went through fourteen straight knockout conquests.

He continued to star as an amateur, and before deserting the simon pure ranks for the quest of fame and fortune, Louis engaged in fifty-four amateur bouts, winning forty-three by knockouts, seven on decisions and losing only four. He was runner-up for the National Amateur Athletic Union light-heavyweight championship in 1933. In 1934 he won the crown before turning professional.

As a professional Louis has been fortunate in one important essential. He has had the advice and experience of one of the greatest Negro fighters of all time at his disposal. Jack Blackburn, whose name is written indelibly on the pages of pugilism, has been chief

adviser to the youngster, and it is to Blackburn principally that many attribute Louis's amazing success.

Knocks Out Kracken.

Louis's first professional fight was staged on July 4 last year and he knocked out Jack Kracken in a single round. Going on from that encounter through a professional career of twenty-two engagements, he has yet to experience defeat.

Eleven battles followed the Kracken engagement last year and in nine of them Louis knocked out his foes. His terrific punching power claimed Stanley Poreda, Charlie Massera and Lee Ramage as victims. These were the better known fighters who lost to Louis in 1934.

He had ten fights this year leading up to the Carnera battle and won eight of them by knockouts. Ramage, knocked out in eight rounds last year, bowed in two in a return meeting this year. Only Patsy Perroni and Natie Brown survived ten rounds with the Detroiter. Hans Birkie was among his knockout victims in a campaign that stamped Louis as one of the greatest colored fighters in ring history and a threat to the world's heavyweight champion.

June 26, 1935

LOUIS STOPS BAER IN 4TH AT STADIUM AS 95,000 LOOK ON

LOSER IS DOWN 3 TIMES

By JAMES P. DAWSON.

Joe Louis, the sensational Detroit Negro heavyweight, hammered his way into a match for the world's heavyweight championship last night at the Yankee Stadium when he knocked out Max Baer, the Californian who formerly held the title, in the fourth round of a scheduled

fifteen-round bout that brought back to boxing a gate close to the million-dollar mark. The official gross receipts were $932,944.

While a crowd of 95,000 fight fans jammed the huge Bronx baseball park to the very limit of its capacity, the serious-faced, emotionless young Negro, who has been boxing professionally only fourteen months, floored Baer twice in the third round, and knocked him out in the fourth, when the round

Times Wide World Photo.

The Detroit boxer's arm being raised in victory.

lacked just ten seconds of completion.

A volley of right-hand drives to the jaw in the third round gave Baer the novel experience of being on a ring floor for the first time. A rat-a-tat-tat of vicious, solid, crushing left hooks toppled him again when he arose, and he was down at the count of four when the bell came to his rescue, ending the round.

Jack Dempsey, former champion, who had been one of Baer's staunchest supporters, had to leap through the ropes and assist the Californian to his corner.

Baer Sinks to Floor.

It was a destructive right for the jaw which landed high on the temple that crushed Baer finally in the fourth round. Under the impact of the blow, startling in its rapidity, crushing in its force, Baer sank like a toppling tree, slowly, gradually, his brain awhirl, his muscles limp.

He squatted there on the ring floor, not knowing where he was, while off at a safe distance stood the man who had rendered him helpless. As a count proceeded over him, Baer struggled to one knee. But he gave no indication he could arise as Referee Arthur Donovan continued counting until he had completed the fatal ten.

Then Baer, struggling erect with the referee's assistance, protested feebly, awkwardly. He didn't really know where he was. He didn't know what he was doing. He didn't realize that this first knockout for him had written finis to his championship hopes as long as Louis is around.

A Dramatic Finish.

There was drama in the finish and sensation in the fight that lived up to the best traditions of the ring from every viewpoint. It was the kind of battle the occasion demanded, the ultimate in competition for the most talked-about mixed match since Jeffries and Johnson met at Reno in 1910.

The crowd, coming from all parts of the country and from distant parts of the world, taxed the capacity of the stadium. A total of $932,944 in gross receipts was counted when a final check-up was made by Promoter Mike Jacobs of the Twentieth Century S. C., former associate of the late Tex Rickard, who conducted the affair as Rickard used to conduct his.

Profiting from this epochal struggle was the Free Milk Fund for Babies, Inc., the charity of which Mrs. William Randolph Hearst is chairman. The fund will collect 10 per cent of the gross receipts, less the Federal and State taxes.

The out-of-town visitors who flocked to the city in special trains, special planes, regular trains and by motor enriched the city's hotel operators and merchants by an estimated $1,000,000.

Their presence lent dignity to a gathering that was a record for any sport in this city, the third largest crowd ever to witness a ring battle with receipts the sixth largest in history.

Governor Lehman sat quietly in the fourth row ringside, so close that he was conspicuous in the glare of the ring's powerful lamps, the first chief executive of this State to grace an outdoor boxing event here with his presence.

Governors of five other States attended, together with the Mayors of half a dozen cities, nearby and distant. Diplomats, Congressmen, lawyers, doctors, members of the clergy, bankers, merchants, brokers, figures of sport, stage and screen, former ring champions and present title-holders—all were there, and they must have thrilled to a spectacle that was a pulse quickener as it ran true to form. Some who saw the fight paid as high as $125 for the privilege. But they were satisfied.

Has Won Twenty-five Straight.

They saw Louis win like the favorite he was entering the ring. They saw this amazing Negro, hero of twenty-one knockout triumphs in an unbroken string of twenty-five professional ring victories, knock down Baer for the first time and knock out Baer for the first time. And they saw him catapult himself into a position where it seems only a freak of fate can keep him from the title only one Negro, Jack Johnson, ever held before.

Jack Doyle, Broadway betting commissioner, estimated that $5,000,000 changed hands on the result in the wagering throughout the country, which found Louis the favorite from the time the match was signed.

Doyle's book yesterday quoted Louis at 1 to 2, the odds it quoted right along, but shortened the odds on Baer from 8 to 5 to 3 to 2. At the ringside the betting was reported to favor Louis at 9 to 5, with little Baer money in sight, although the shortening of Doyle's odds was explained on a show of Baer money.

Marries Chicago Girl.

Louis, incidentally, sprang a surprise by marrying ten minutes before leaving for the scene of the contest. His bride, the former Marva Trotter, 19-year-old Chicago secretary, was at the ringside. The ceremony took place shortly before 8 P. M.

The Negro boy, who was a laborer two years ago, won like a 1 to 10 shot as he crushed the fighting spark that was in Baer and caused the Californian to announce his retirement from the ring. Louis had no contention worthy the name. He faced but few offensive moves from Baer, who quailed under an opening-round fire that drilled home with startling suddenness and lacked, it seemed, just a few punches of bringing a first-round knockout.

Baer's boxing thereafter was a futile gesture. He must have known he was facing his master. He acted as if he realized this, with a full appreciation of Louis's paralyzing hitting power.

Now perhaps Max Schmeling, another former titleholder, will be imported to act as barrier to Louis's title threat. There is talk of this match as Louis's next engagement. He will receive well over $200,000 for last night's effort of less than twelve full minutes.

In all likelihood he will realize as much from a Schmeling match, for people undoubtedly will flock to see if the uhlan from the Rhine can withstand the punches that have crumpled Primo Carnera, King Levinsky and Baer in Louis's three most important matches.

There is no reason to suppose Schmeling, who collapsed before Baer, can withstand the murderous force of the Louis punch. Indeed, there is little reason to suspect that Champion James J. Braddock can escape the fate that overtook the ring's playboy, Baer.

Having Dempsey in his corner didn't mean a thing to Baer. The old Manassa Mauler, it is suspected, tried to instill some of his own effective fighting ideas in the head of Baer, but without success. Baer had his own special make of gloves on his fists, but they didn't mean a thing either. The fists they encased were powerless and the muscles that propelled them were cramped with the fear-instilling influence of the heavier guns of the Negro who has been so aptly termed the Detroit Bomber.

The ring clown who refused to take boxing or life seriously had nothing but a contemptuous grimace when the end came. He faced the end fearlessly. That can be said of Baer. But he was so helpless before his younger, more capable foe, that his finish was forecast almost as soon as the men squared off.

No Match for the Bomber.

Baer had nothing with which to withstand the tigerish assault of Louis. The easy life that has been his since he tamed Schmeling a few years back, the indifference with which he regarded his fighting implements and his haughty contempt for seriousness, even inside the ropes, all figured in the easy triumph of the Negro lad.

For the vicious, powerful, short-arm digs of Louis to the body, Baer had not the requisite recuperative powers. For the bone-crushing short hooks and long, sharp, unerring rights and lefts that Louis rained on it, Baer's chin had not the concrete foundation it was popularly supposed to have.

Good hitters tagged Baer's chin in the past, but none of them hit like Louis. No fighter since Dempsey hit with the paralyzing force of the Negro.

As he established this fact, Louis satisfied curiosity in another respect. He can take it. There can be no more doubt of this.

Baer, in one desperate, furious flash of the old fighting Baer, a frantic move that sought without success to discourage Louis's crushing fire, hit the Negro his best blow. More, in a fiery exchange that thrilled the vast throng, Baer fought with the fury of a man possessed. But he fought against a fighter who was tougher than himself, who disregarded Baer's blows as Max used to disregard the blows of a rival, and who kept punching after Baer stopped.

Louis can take it. This latest ring sensation is what has been said of him. He is a combination of Joe Gans, the Old Master, and Sam Langford, the Boston Tar Baby.

The wish was father to the thought with many who looked for a Baer victory before the battle. Those who outspokenly predicted Baer would win and sought by facts and figures to support their selection knew as early as the first round that Max was gone.

Almost at the outset the die seemed cast. Baer didn't rush pell-mell, as had been expected. He didn't undertake to make a longshoreman's brawl of it, as many thought he would. Maybe it was because Max changed battle plans and wanted to clown a little. If he did, he made a great mistake. Or it might have been that Max suspected Louis would be his equal in knock-down-and-drag-out fighting, thanks to the tutoring of that master of another day, Jack Blackburn. If the latter was his conclusion, Baer was right.

Whatever the reason, Baer came slowly out to face his foe and advanced cautiously. Louis, alert for any move, pecked and stabbed with a left as he circled and sized up Baer. For a time the crowd was breathless.

Then cheers echoed out over the Stadium as Baer suddenly and unexpectedly discarded his caution and leaped forward eagerly, looping his favorite long sweeping right to Louis's jaw.

Still Boxes Cautiously.

Louis shook his head under the blow but didn't blink an eye. He boxed as cautiously as he had been, moving slowly, catlike, ever alert, his fists always in position for the kill that would come when Baer presented an opening.

The chance came when Baer rushed in with a wild right that missed. Louis pelted him with two rights and a left to the face and a smile of contempt spread over Baer's features as blood trickled from his nose.

The sting of the blows spurred Baer to action, but blindly, wildly. He unloosed another right for the jaw and was awkward as he missed and exposed himself to fire. Louis calmly walked in and in a flash there came a mix-up of vicious blows that hammered home as Baer rushed his foe to the ropes, evidently seeking to awe the Negro.

Instead Louis volleyed rights as Baer volleyed them, threw lefts as Baer tried to throw them, and, fighting Baer better than blow for blow, suddenly cracked home with a terrific right to the jaw. It made Baer's knees buckle. Instinctively he clinched.

Louis had Max at his mercy, then and there. But Baer, with that clown's laugh, backed into a corner. There he had to take a drubbing of sense-numbing blows to the head, muscle-stiffening drives to the arms and strength-sapping digs to the body that paved the way for his later downfall. He still had the contemptuous look for Louis at the bell, but not much more.

Fails to Find Opening.

Through the second session Louis sought an opening for a finishing blow, but never had it. He sprang in with a jarring right to the jaw shortly after the round opened, and pounded steadily to the head and body.

Then Baer launched a short-lived counter-move that started with a right to the body as the gong clanged. It was followed by a right to the jaw as Louis, backed to the ropes, stood motionless, having heard the bell. The overtime blow was powerful but Louis never blinked. Nor did he seek to return the illegal fire.

In the third, however, Louis claimed his revenge. Baer started the round with a wide left hook to the head and then tried to master Louis in a clinch. But the Negro showed equal strength and more skill at smothering a foe in close, as he held Max helpless.

In a jiffy they were at arms' length and Louis was going seriously about the task of cutting his foe down. A sharp right to the jaw made Baer blink and go wild with a left for the body that merely grazed the Negro's midsection. Suddenly Louis shot another powerful right to the jaw and Baer's impulse was to clinch.

The ex-champion's knees sagged under a third right and when this rendered Baer a wide-open, flighty target, Louis leaped in for the kill, raining a succession of rights on the ex-champion's jaw which finally brought Baer down, to the consternation of the crowd.

Nine seconds were tolled over Baer before he laboriously pulled himself erect. But he was help-

The loser on his knees in the fourth and final round of last night's fight.

less and his finish was in sight. The dynamite in Louis's fists exploded full in Baer's face again. This time from another angle. Louis shifted to the port side and with a succession of left hooks crashed Baer down again.

This time it did not seem Baer could arise. He was in a pitiable condition. He was a sorrowful figure there on the ring canvas, striving instinctively to regain his feet, his face bloody from bruised nose and lips.

The bell came to his rescue. It sounded the end of the round when Referee Donovan reached "four" in the count that has a maximum of ten. Baer sagged awkwardly. Dempsey rushed to his side and half-dragged, half-carried him to his corner.

Frenzied work during the rest period brought Baer up looking all right for the fourth. But it was patent he would last only as long as it took Louis to hit him again.

Louis wasted no time. He sank a left to Baer's body and Max bent double. A left hook to the jaw, another to the head, a left and right with vicious power, followed in blinding succession. Baer didn't know where the blows were coming from.

Fists Speak for Joe.

Out of a clinch Baer unconsciously slapped a right back-hander to Louis's face and was promptly warned. The foul would have cost Baer the round but that was superfluous. From the expressionless face of Louis it could not be learned whether he had a resentful reaction to this breach. He simply let his fists show the way he felt, and without ceremony.

Suddenly stepping out of a crouch after feinting his foe into position, Louis cracked his right with all the force of his body, all the snap of his powerful arms, behind the blow. It landed high on Baer's head, on the left temple. Baer

stiffened momentarily, then sank slowly.

It seemed an eternity until the ex-champion hit the deck, as the saying is in boxing. He came down in a squatting position, a tragic figure. Referee Donovan skipped quickly to his side. The fatal ten-second count started. Louis stood off, doubting Baer could arise, knowing he would finish the ex-champion if he did.

Slowly Baer tried to rouse himself.

from the deadening influence of that lethal wallop. He struggled to one knee and rested. He was resting when Donovan finished the count, and aroused himself too late to the realization that the fight was over, that he had met his master.

Louis weighed 199¼ pounds for this most important fight of his career and Baer 210½.

September 25, 1935

SCHMELING STOPS LOUIS IN TWELFTH AS 45,000 LOOK ON

Hammers Foe to Canvas With Barrage of Rights to Jaw and Scores Major Upset.

BOMBER DOWN IN FOURTH

By JAMES P. DAWSON

In one of the greatest heavyweight battles of modern ring history Max Schmeling, sturdy, stolid German who formerly held the world's heavyweight title, last night provided one of the ring's biggest upsets when he knocked out Joe Louis, Detroit's famed Brown

Bomber, in the Yankee Stadium.

Under a murderous fire of desperate rights to an unprotected jaw, Louis went down to be counted out by Referee Arthur Donovan and Knockdown Time-keeper Johnny McAvoy in the twelfth round of what was to have been a fifteen-round battle.

Exactly 2 minutes 29 seconds of the fatal twelfth had gone into history when Louis, hailed as the king of fighters entering the ring, was counted out, his invincibility as a fighter a shattered myth, his vulnerability convincingly established and his claims to heavyweight title distinction knocked into the discard.

Louis Staggers Out of Ring

Louis had to be carried to his corner while the shouts of a crowd of 45,000 delirious fight fans rang in the ears of his battered, bruised and bleeding conqueror. And, when his handlers got him to his corner, Louis required several minutes of resuscitating before he was able to stagger on shaky legs out of the ring—unnoticed.

The crowd—estimated early in the evening by Promoter Mike Jacobs.

That left to the jaw is being thrown by Max Schmelling in 1932. Following his knockout of Joe Louis in 1936, the Nazis tried to make him a symbol of Aryan supremacy. This ended abruptly in 1938 when Louis finished him off in the first round of their second fight.

Henry Armstrong (left) has just avoided a right hook thrown by Jimmy Garrison in their 1939 fight. Armstrong was the only boxer to have ever held three titles simultaneously: featherweight, welterweight and lightweight.

to number 60,000—witnessed a form reversal that was greater even than that in which James J. Braddock lifted the heavyweight title from Max Baer last year. And it saw Schmeling, with the might of his right fist, his chief weapon of attack, hammer his way into another chance at the title he lost to Jack Sharkey.

Schmeling was the under dog in betting odds of 8 to 1 as the fight started. Bettors were offering even money he wouldn't come up for the fifth round. Without naming the round, they were offering 3 and 4 to 1 Louis would score a knockout.

But Schmeling, ignoring the contempt in which he was held as a foe for the Bomber with the latter's unbroken string of twenty-seven victories that held twenty-three knockouts, fulfilled the promise he made that he would fight his way into another crack at the title.

September Bout Likely

The German is now undisputed challenger for Braddock's crown. If he has his wish Schmeling will get his chance in September. None who saw last night's upset would contradict the German's bold assertion that he will be the first man in all ring history ever to regain the heavyweight championship.

The crowd that saw last night's struggle was smaller than was expected in aggregate and in box-office receipts. But it was thoroughly representative, including leaders in the life of the city, State and nation. A gathering assembled from the far corners of the country, it was rewarded with one of the greatest heavyweight battles since the days of Jack Dempsey.

Overcoming not only the mental discouragement of the betting odds that held him so cheaply and the almost complete unanimity of expert opinion that gave him little or no chance against the paralyzing puncher Louis had previously proved himself to be, Schmeling also overcame the shock of seeing a man die at his feet in his dressing room before the fight.

A report reached the ringside early in the night that the veteran Tom O'Rourke, former manager of fighters, promoter of boxing and State Athletic Commission attaché and judge, had dropped dead as he visited Schmeling to wish him luck.

Schmeling, it was said, was upset by the sight of the stricken man toppling at his feet, although he was allowed to think it was merely a fainting spell.

Max a Great Puncher

But he came into the ring shortly after with one set purpose in mind and didn't leave it until he had achieved his goal. He hammered Louis into defeat simply because he refused to believe that Louis was a superman of the ring, because he had plenty of the courage the ring calls "heart," because he never let himself be swayed from a set line of battle and because he is, on the record, a greater puncher than the man whose hitting prowess hitherto struck fear to the hearts of foemen.

Schmeling's one weapon of attack was his right hand. He seldom used his left. But with his resourcefulness, adaptability to different ring situations and his crafty ring work, he had Louis beaten on points when the knockout occurred and he must have won the decision had the bout gone the limit.

Under the punishing influence of the right-hand bombardment to which he was subjected, Louis lost all the ease and grace of motion that were associated with his previous bouts here. Stung and shaken, he was erratic when he shifted his attack to the body, trying to weaken Schmeling. Twice he hit low and was warned, losing the rounds. Louis struck foul in the eighth and again in the twelfth, the round that saw his finish.

Battle After the Bell

No quarter was asked in this fight. None was given. The boxers fought cleanly, save for Louis's two accidental lapses. They battled craftily, savagely, from the first bell. And they fought after the bell, too.

Schmeling's right hand was futile for the first three rounds, but when the German floored his foe for a count of two with a sharp right to the temple in the fourth round bedlam broke loose. After that it was difficult to hear the gong sounding the end of each round as Schmeling continued to hammer a foe who never afterward regained his equilibrium.

The bells ending the fourth, fifth and sixth rounds were unheard and the rivals fought through the din of the crowd. After the sixth, however, Referee Donovan was alert for the bell and took the precaution to step between the fighters.

One of the punches Schmeling landed in these overtime outbursts of fighting aided no little in his victory. It was a murderous right-hand drive clean to Louis's jaw as they fought near Louis's corner after the bell ending the fifth. The blow hit the mark with the full power of Schmeling's body back of it, and sent Louis to his corner in a state of collapse.

To say that this technically illegal blow brought about Louis's defeat would be stretching a point. The right-hand punch to the temple which floored him in the fourth round and enabled the knockdown timekeeper to toll off two seconds as the Bomber tried to arise started him on the downgrade.

Louis never recovered from that blow, nor from the countless other right-hand punches Schmeling rained on his jaw with the unerring accuracy of the true marksman through each succeeding round until the finish.

Leading up to that finish Louis tried with all the tricks of the trade at his command to live up to the excessive pre-battle confidence placed in him as a fighting man. But nothing he had, nothing the astute Jack Blackburn could tell him or do for him in the rests between those tortuous rounds after the fourth, helped him against the sense-numbing influence of Schmeling's right-hand punch.

Despite it all Louis stood up gamely as far as he could go. The Schmeling who fought the Bomber last night was not the Schmeling who fought Jack Sharkey in their second battle and let countless chances slip to score a knockout victory.

Schmeling was cagey to an extreme; he lost much valuable ground and many priceless seconds through his ultra-conservative style when he might have gone in and pressed advantages, perhaps for a quicker knockout. But in the end his plan was proved effective as it was safest.

Wears the Bomber Down

Gradually he wore Louis down through the savage fighting until the twelfth round saw the weary, punch-deadened Bomber commit his second foul with an erratic

Times Wide World Photos.

Referee Arthur Donovan has just counted Joe Louis out as Max Schmeling, in a neutral corner, leaps in elation. On top at left—The Brown Bomber hanging on ropes just before sliding to floor for the count.

powerful left for the body. The blow hurt Schmeling and he danced backward as Referee Donovan for the second time warned Louis. Ignoring this painful blow Schmeling uncorked a right to the jaw that jarred the weary Louis to his heels. Another high right banged Louis against the ropes, shaken and groggy, almost to the point of helplessness.

Schmeling now was like a jungle beast intent on the kill. The crowd was delirious with joy, hoarse with shouting as its sentiment turned to the German after the amazing knockdown of the fourth round. The Bomber was tottering drunkenly on unsteady legs, careening aimlessly about the ring.

Like a panther, Schmeling leaped after his foe, wasting not a split second, not a motion. He punched and punched and punched with his right to Louis's head, to Louis's jaw, to Louis's face, and with each succeeding drive of his rival's fists Louis came closer to disaster.

Finally as he veered backward desperately, knees knocking, eyes blinking, head shaking from side to side, Louis went down under one terrific right to the jaw into the first professional defeat he ever experienced. He struck the canvas on his haunches, stiffened in a reclining position, and struggled to get his feet under him as Referee Donovan and Timekeeper McAvoy carried the count as one man. But he could not make it.

At "five" Louis's shoulders were off the floor and at "seven" he was resting on his left elbow. He was still resting on this prop, shaking his head to clear it of the cobwebs, when the completed count sealed his first defeat, a knockout that may prove disastrous in its consequences with respect to Louis's future.

In the dressing room after the fight Louis said he hurt the thumb of his left hand in the fourth round and that of his right hand in the ninth. Those who saw the battle will testify that the numbing qualities of Schmeling's unerring punches really had more to do with the Bomber's downfall.

Schmeling, of course, was wildly elated. He had succeeded where practically none gave him a chance. More, he had knocked out the feared Brown Bomber and now was facing the goal he has set himself, another chance at the title.

Forgotten were the bruised and swollen left eye which testified to Louis's punching force and the swelling right eye he suffered as the bout progressed. Schmeling said he never was happier in his life. It was easy to believe this.

Schmeling made it plain from the outset that it was his hope to bring Louis down with a right-hand punch for the jaw. And Louis made it just as plain he knew this, for he speared the German with a blinding succession of powerful, snappy lefts to the face for the first three rounds. Undismayed, Schmeling cocked his right and let it fly repeatedly, but he never quite hit the mark. Louis, too, tried with rights for the jaw, but found Schmeling a difficult target.

Max Hits the Target

In the second round Schmeling first hit the mark, a right over Louis's left. Its force was spent when it reached the jaw and Joe only blinked. Later another right grazed the jaw as Schmeling countered Louis's jolting fire of stiff lefts.

Max was nearer the mark in the third, yet not quite to the point with the necessary force. Two early rights sent Louis back on his heels, but unhurt. And as Louis pumped left after left in the German's face, Schmeling missed rights that were desperate in their aim and wicked in their force.

A puffiness came under Schmeling's left eye to handicap his vision as the fourth started, mute testimony to the accuracy and snap of the Louis jab. But still Max had the one object in view. He wanted to hit Louis on the jaw with his right.

Twice the German shot for the mark and twice he grazed the chin. Then when he tried again, with all the power of his body back of the blow, Schmeling landed high on Louis's temple and the Bomber, cool, calm and collected before, staggered backward, groggy, his eyes blinking.

Timekeeper Counts Two

In a jiffy Schmeling was after his foe. The German pelted the Bomber with a succession of desperate rights to the face, head and jaw, until suddenly one right landed cleanly on the jaw and Louis collapsed near a neutral corner. He was stung and hurt and his brain was awhirl, but the Bomber came erect instinctively, a foolish move, while Timekeeper McAvoy counted two.

It seemed that he was up before a count could be started, so fast did Louis regain his feet, to face a gale of punches that continued even after the bell rang the end of the round.

After that every time Schmeling drove home with his right, Louis rocked and lurched. Early in the fifth the German cracked his right to the jaw and Louis was jarred to his heels.

The sting was out of the Louis jab and this blow was ignored by Schmeling as he kept winging away with his right.

Two terrific rights to the jaw stung Louis and had the roars of the crowd echoing over the ball park before the round ended. So great was the ear-splitting din that neither of the boxers heard the bell nor did Referee Donovan. They belabored each other as seconds climbed into the ring and just before they were separated Schmeling staggered his foe with a powerful right to the jaw. Louis lurched toward his corner and fell on his stool almost in a state of collapse.

Cracks Home With Rights

Five times during the sixth round Schmeling's right cracked home to Louis's jaw or head and carried staggering force. Yet Schmeling took nothing for granted. Instead, he watched craftily, and at times even backed to the ropes, seeking to draw his rival's fire for one finishing blow.

This hesitancy cost Schmeling dearly in the seventh, for he was stung when Louis dug his left to the body several times. These blows forced Schmeling to retreat, and before the round ended the German shook under a barrage of lefts and rights Louis rained on his head and jaw.

Schmeling came in against his foe's body fire in the eighth and reached Louis's jaw with several rights, staggering the Bomber in mid-ring. Rejecting the shelter of a clinch, Louis countered with a right to the head, but a moment later was warned for an erratic left for the body which reflected plainly that Schmeling's blows were taking their toll.

The left side of Louis's face was swollen as the ninth started. Schmeling's left eye was almost closed. Yet the German was the fresher of the two, surer of his punches. A right to the temple, a right to the face and a right to the jaw befuddled Louis's brain before bell time approached and then three successive rights to the jaw sent Louis shaken to his corner.

Late in Leaving Corner

The weary Louis was late getting out of his corner for the tenth. He was weary and pained and was all at sea. Schmeling was almost above him before the Bomber was heaved to his feet by the seconds who worked furiously over him. And when he started firing Louis was erratic with a left for the body. But the blow did no damage for, Schmeling leaped quickly in and staggered his foe, driving him to the ropes with merciless rights to the jaw.

Instead of pressing his advantage Schmeling parried punches, but the German was the master and knew it. He must have felt he could afford to take his time.

Through the eleventh round Schmeling never let slip a chance to fire at Louis's jaw, although at times his fire was delayed. The punches, however, carried enough power to aggravate the weakened condition of the Bomber and set the stage for the dénouement that came when the twelfth round was 2 minutes, 29 seconds old and Louis was counted out.

Louis weighed 198 pounds and Schmeling 192.

Al Gainer, New Haven Negro, scored a knockout over Tony Galento, Newark heavyweight, in the semi-final, scheduled for six rounds. Gainer was returned the winner in 1:04 of the fourth, when the referee intervened because of a bad cut over Galento's right eye. Gainer weighed 168½ pounds and Galento 220.

In a bout originally listed for six rounds but cut to four to allow the feature to get started on time, Jorge Brescia of the Argentine outpointed Abe Feldman, East Side. The victory was not popular with the crowd. Brescia weighed 208 and Feldman 181½.

Bob Pastor, 186, of Washington Heights, defeated Steve Dudas,

190½, Edgewater, N. J., in a dull six-round battle.

Steve Carr, 174, Meriden, Conn., survived a first-round knockdown and earned a draw with Dave Clark, 170¾, Detroit, in a six-rounder.

In another six, Sandy McDonald, 198½, Dallas, beat Jack McCarthy, 187, Boston. Bud Mignault, Brockton, Mass., defeated Mickey Patrick of Chicago in the four-round opener. Mignault scaled 171½ and Patrick 171.

June 20, 1936

SCHMELING GUEST OF HITLER AT LUNCH

Boxer, His Mother and Wife Are Present at Chancellery —Max Praises Louis.

VICTORY IS HELD POLITICAL

Nazi Daily Claims Hero Showed Supremacy of White Race in Beating Negro Opponent.

Wireless to THE NEW YORK TIMES.

BERLIN, June 27.—Max Schmeling lunched today with Chancellor Hitler in the Reich Chancellery. The mother and wife of the heavyweight boxer also were guests of the Fuehrer.

The German press today carried interviews with Schmeling in which he states that his winning match with Joe Louis was by far the hardest in his career. He again expressed his conviction that Louis struck below the belt mistakenly and asserted that the Negro was a great boxer with a perfect eye that never misses an opening.

Angriff, the afternoon organ of the Nazi party, gave its interview a political character, presenting the bout as a fight for white supremacy. It concluded, "Schmeling, the German, did that for the Americans, for the same people who did not want to give him a chance, who mocked him, derided him. He succeeded against world opinion. And he says he would not have had the strength if he had not known what support he had in his homeland. He was allowed to speak with the Fuehrer and his Ministers, and from that moment his will for victory was boundless."

June 28, 1936

Braddock Fined and Banned but Is Allowed to Keep Title

By JOSEPH C. NICHOLS

Max Schmeling's "one-man fight" was held yesterday at the New York State Athletic Commission meeting, and after a bruising session that had its repercussions long after he left the board's headquarters, the German ex-heavyweight champion admitted himself a beaten man.

The commission, convened ostensibly to examine Schmeling and James J. Braddock, the titleholder, for the fight scheduled in the Madison Square Garden Bowl last night, had only half that duty to perform. For Braddock, to the surprise of no one at all, failed to show up. He is in training at Grand Beach, Mich., to fight Joe Louis in Chicago on June 22 and had only academic interest in what was going on in New York yesterday.

Schmeling, however, was highly concerned. He had done everything asked of him since he signed last December for last night's fight that never came off, and there remained only the weighing in, at the time prescribed by the commission, for him to fulfill all clauses in the con-

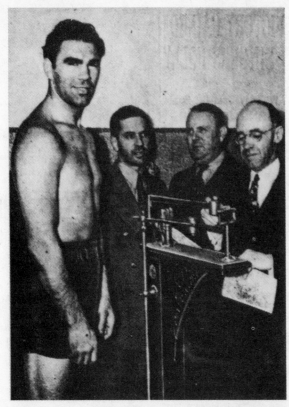

WEIGHING IN FOR THE "ONE-MAN FIGHT"
Max Schmeling at the State Athletic Commission's office yesterday

Times Wide World Photo.

tract that he had with the Madison Square Garden Corporation.

He Found Out His Weight

So, with the attitude of a man about to come into an inheritance, the German jauntily stepped on the scales of the commission shortly after 1 o'clock and was told he weighed 196 pounds. That, together with the findings of Dr. William Walker, who submitted him to the customary physical examination, seemed a point of great satisfaction to the fighter, for it proved he had been working sincerely in his training camp at Speculator, N. Y., where he spent a month getting in shape.

The weighing-in ceremony concluded, Schmeling looked eagerly for the next step. Surely, for having done everything asked of him, he was to gain some boon. That Braddock neglected to appear was no fault of his. He would receive some reward for his good faith, and the champion would suffer meet punishment for violating an agreement.

He stepped into the sanctum that the commission reserves for its more serious pronouncements and confidently anticipated hearing a verdict that, if it would not raise him to the status of champion, would, at least, divest Braddock of the title the German seeks so tenaciously.

Phelan Reads Decision

His feeling underwent a sudden, black transformation, however, when Major Gen. John J. Phelan, chairman of the commission, read the board's decision. "This body," solemnly proclaimed the chairman, "after due and lengthy consideration of the matter, finds James J. Braddock and his manager, Joe Gould, in violation of the commission's orders and hereby imposes a civil fine of $1,000 apiece on Brad-

dock and his manager. In addition, this board suspends Braddock from fighting in this State, or in any State affiliated with the New York commission, for an indefinite period. Also, any fighter meeting Braddock will be suspended automatically. Gould is also suspended.

"The forfeit money of $5,000 put up by the Madison Square Garden for Braddock shall be divided in equal parts by the Garden and by Max Schmeling, who is ready, willing and able to fight tonight."

The effect of all this was to leave Schmeling visibly stunned. His face belied the consternation that was seething within him, and after shaking hands peremptorily with General Phelan and the other two commissioners, Colonel D. Walker Wear and Bill Brown, he made a hasty departure.

He repaired immediately to his headquarters in the Hotel Commodore, where he was found an hour later bitterly deploring the turn of events. Eloquently, despite his thick accent, the frustrated boxer told all within earshot of his reaction to the verdict and his thoughts of the commission.

Deplores Neglect of Himself

"The ruling is a joke," he kept saying, over and over. "It practically legalizes the fight in Chicago and leaves me out in the cold. What does it mean to suspend Braddock? He's going to fight Louis anyway, and certainly the title will pass to Louis if he wins."

When asked what disposition would have been satisfactory to him, Schmeling replied that Braddock should have been stripped of his title. "The commission should have declared the championship vacated," he explained. "I certainly did not expect them to name me champion, and I would not have had it that way. But I do think that they could have declared for a tournament, with the winner to

fight me for the championship. As it is, I'm left with nothing and am out about $25,000 in traveling and training expenses."

The German, when asked what his immediate plans were, replied he would visit his attorney today. He would not reveal what further steps would be taken, except to say he would stand up for his rights. Questioned as to whether he would be in Chicago for the Braddock-Louis fight, the disappointed fighter fairly shrieked a violent "No!"

While in the midst of his excoriation of the commission and its treatment of him, Schmeling received a telegram. He opened it slowly, intent on what he was saying. Then he perused the message and seemed to explode. "What is this, a joke?" he demanded. The telegram read:

Must receive at once tax return for period you were at Speculator. Otherwise penalty will be imposed.
JOHN J. PHELAN.

Joe Jacobs, his manager, informed Schmeling the wire was no joke. "We have to pay it," Jacobs said, "it amounts to $18.75."

Suddenly, through it all, Max smiled. A bit ruefully, he vouchsafed, "It's all my fault. That's what I get for knocking out Joe Louis."

So incensed was the German at the treatment handed him by the solons that he was forced to forego making a coast-to-coast broadcast over the National Broadcasting Company's network last night. Schmeling had his script prepared but it contained references to the commission of so caustic a nature that the radio officials would not permit the speech to be aired, according to Joe Jacobs. The German refused to accept a substitute script.

Colonel John Reed Kilpatrick, president of the Garden Corpora-

tion, had no comment to make on the commission's action. He said he preferred to await the finding of the United States Circuit Court of Appeals regarding the Garden's plea for an injunction against the June 22 fight before committing himself.

Schmeling was not the only one to weigh in. All the contestants in the preliminary bouts arranged by James J. Johnston, in charge of boxing at the Garden, had their moment on the scales. They, along with Schmeling, were informed there was no need to make the trip to the Long Island City bowl in the evening.

General Phelan sent a notice of the board's decision to the Illinois State Commission and other bodies affiliated with New York. The action, however, was expected to meet no favorable response from Joseph Triner, chairman of the Illinois group. And as for Louis, the automatic suspension that will be his when he fights Braddock will hardly prove a deterrent to the Brown Bomber's seeking the chance at the title.

CHICAGO TO IGNORE ORDER

Braddock's Suspension Will Not Interfere With Louis Fight

CHICAGO, June 3 (AP).—Chairman Joe Triner of the Illinois State Athletic Commission declared his board "will not recognize the suspension of Champion Jim Braddock" by the New York State Commission for the titleholder's failure to appear for the scheduled title bout with Max Schmeling tonight.

June 4, 1937

LOUIS KNOCKS OUT BRADDOCK IN 8TH, WINS WORLD TITLE

Detroit Boxer's Right to the Jaw Ends Two-Year Reign of Veteran Heavyweight

60,000 SEE CHICAGO BOUT

Loser Carried Unconscious to His Corner After Being Pounded to Canvas

RECEIPTS ARE $700,000

Bomber Is First Negro Since Johnson to Hold Crown— Time of Last Round 1:10

By JAMES P. DAWSON
Special to The New York Times.

CHICAGO, June 22.—Joe Louis is the world's heavyweight champion, the first Negro boxer to hold the title in twenty-two years, or since

the days of Jack Johnson.

The Brown Bomber from Detroit knocked out James J. Braddock, New York's West Side-born Irishman, who was making his first defense of the title tonight in Comiskey Park before a crowd of about 60,000 fans who came from all over the country and from distant parts of the world. They paid about $700,000 for one of the greatest heavyweight battles in ring history.

The finish came in the eighth round of what was to have been a fifteen-round struggle. Under the impact of Louis's terrific right-hand punch to the jaw, Braddock, battered, bruised and bleeding, crashed limply to the canvas in the center of the ring to be counted out when the session had progressed only 1 minute 10 seconds.

Defeated Boxer Helpless

After Referee Tommy Thomas had completed the ring's traditional ten-second count, Braddock had to be carried from the ring floor where he lay still and inert.

The fallen champion's handlers, their white faces wearing a startled expression under the glare of the ring lights and the shock of Braddock's collapse, leaped quickly through the ropes, lifted the dethroned ring monarch bodily from the floor and carried him to his corner.

The spot from which Braddock had been lifted revealed a crimson stain about a foot in diameter, where Braddock's head rested as

AS WORLD'S HEAVYWEIGHT TITLE CHANGED HANDS LAST NIGHT IN CHICAGO

Wired Photo—Times Wide World.

Just after the eighth-round knockout, with Louis's hand raised in triumph and Braddock prone on the canvas

the count, which took from him the title he won two years ago, proceeded over him. He had suffered a hemorrhage under the bruising force of that one right-hand smash, driven like the fencer's rapier, sharp and true to the chin, with all the power of Louis's compact, muscular body behind it.

That one punch, the finishing blow, was one of hundreds with which Louis pelted and hammered Braddock in a bout whose ending early was forecast in reverse. Braddock, fighting grimly, fearlessly and willingly, as he had promised, unafraid of the destructive Brown Bomber and confident in his own strength, had knocked Louis down cleanly in the opening round.

A Temporary Vision

For many there came a vision of ascendancy for the 31-year-old champion, who came into the ring tonight weighted down under the burden of his age and twelve long years of ring service. But it was only a temporary vision—a mirage in a situation where the wish was father to the thought. Like chaff

before the winds, it disappeared under the cool, calculating, crafty boxing and the savage, vicious punching of a man who, at 23, has a boxing span of only three years.

That first - round knockdown buoyed Braddock's hopes for a while, as it did those of his handlers in his corner and his admirers in the distinguished gathering which viewed the battle. They were false hopes, in contradiction of all accepted appraisal of physical condition and ring warfare.

The situation made for a battle that was far above the ordinary, which held pulse-throbbing moments as have few heavyweight championships of recent years and thrilled this large crowd as, in a measure, had the famous long-count battle of ten years ago here between Jack Dempsey and Gene Tunney.

Foreign Diplomat Attends

Vladimir Hurban, Czechoslovak Minister to the United States, was a spectator. So, too, was Attorney General Cummings, the lone member of President Roosevelt's Cabinet to attend. The other fight fan mem-

ber, Postmaster General Farley, was prevented from attending because of the dedication of a post office in Fredericksburg, Va.

There were present also Governors of nine States, Mayors from many cities and Councilmen from numerous near-by hamlets; figures of prominence in the commercial, industrial and professional world, in society as well, stars of stage and screen in profusion, baseball players and magnates of the national sport.

Every walk of life was represented, drawn to Chicago's first heavyweight championship bout in ten years; Braddock's first defense of the title he won two years ago from Max Baer, and the first bid by a Negro for the title since Jack Johnson sank beneath the boulder-like fists of the giant Jess Willard in sun-baked Havana in 1915, his hands raised in protection from the sun's glare.

The tremendous gathering was rewarded with a fight that was a thriller, sentimentally and competitively, a fight that will take its place alongside the greatest ring battles of pugilistic history. It was a struggle whose finish was indicated one way in the first

round and was forecast in the opposite direction inevitably thereafter as the younger, stronger, more highly developed Bomber from Detroit worked by easy stages and gradual degrees in accomplishing the downfall of the greying veteran, whose greatest recommendation was, as it had been emphasized before the fight, his lion-hearted courage.

Braddock had blind faith in his own supremacy, though that supremacy came late in his life to lift him from the nation's relief rolls to an estate that has been strange and perhaps never really was expected—the world's heavyweight championship.

Champion in Fine Condition

Braddock entered the ring in the best physical condition that was possible for him. He looked better, trimmer, more compactly developed, more ruggedly set up at his 197 pounds than he had ever looked before in all his fighting life. He worked hard for this fight. He wanted to hold that title that came to him so late in life and he never really had a chance.

Braddock never had a chance for a number of reasons. An "old man" as athletic age is counted in the strenuous sports, he was making his stand against the youngest challenger to bid for the title. He was making his stand after two years of inactivity—of soft, luxurious living to which he had never been accustomed.

The defeated champion had never been knocked out—the only such defeat charged against him in the records is a technical knockout because of a cut eye. He had been knocked off his feet only twice before tonight.

The loser's spirit was high. He was determined, courageous and game. His handicaps were emphasized by the cool, crafty boxing of Louis, who turned primitive with the savage instinct to kill when the great chance opened before him. All Braddock's war implements were as nothing compared to those of Louis.

Lives Up to Promise

Braddock came out fighting as he had promised he would. He wanted to convince Louis he was not afraid. He desired, further, to impress upon Louis that he was the champion, the master, and meant to bludgeon his way through the defense of his title accordingly.

He had the Max Schmeling knockout of Joe as an encouragement in this plan, and a suspicion that a few good punches on Louis's chin would enable him to supply an upset that would be even more startling than was his defeat of Baer two years ago.

But Braddock's execution was inadequate, as might be expected, all circumstances considered. In the end he wound up on the ring floor, then in the arms of apprehensive handlers, while Louis's hand was raised aloft in victory, the conqueror and champion, besieged on all sides, protected by a cordon of policemen in a ring scene that was typically wild and incoherent.

When the battle started Louis was favored to win. He had been all along. But the odds had shortened from 1 to 3 to 1 to 2½ because of that mysterious condition that attaches inevitably to heavyweight championship bouts of recent years—rumors and reports of discontent in training.

Louis might just as well have been a 1-to-10 shot. He fought like one. He won like one. He is a worthy champion, whose one desire now is to get into the ring again with Schmeling, the man who knocked him out last year and put on a marvelous record the only blemish it contains in thirty-five fights.

Louis Stalks His Foe

The Bomber fought his usual fight. He was cool and calm, the counter-puncher, stalking a foe who charged willingly and eagerly, but wildly. Louis was sure-footed. He let few punches go without knowing their direction and their destination.

The Detroiter used a rapier-like left jab when he thought it met the situation confronting him. He clubbed lefts and rights to the head in short hooks when openings presented. He battered and pounded at every opportunity, puffing Braddock's eyes, ripping them open, splitting the defending champion's lips, with the punishing, cutting force of his punches.

With his bewildering left, Joe made Braddock look like a novice. And with this blow and following rights and lefts in hooks, swings and uppercuts, the Brown Bomber gradually reduced his opponent to a state of helplessness, ready for the finishing punch.

The victor had Braddock staggering and bleeding in the first round, the round in which the champion scored a clean knockdown with a surprising right-hand uppercut that was short and true, though it carried no paralyzing power.

The Bomber had the defending

Wired Photo—Times Wide World.

The old champion and the new sparring in the first round

champion tottering and reeling in the second round, when Braddock's fate was sealed. The titleholder rallied encouragingly merely because Louis was biding his time, boxing through the third and fourth rounds as Braddock fought gamely on with a blind courage that was practically all he had to offer.

Obviously feeling the tide turning against him, mindful of his own limitations under the jarring force of Louis's blows, Braddock fought recklessly in a blind, furious bid to halt his dancing tormentor. The veteran wanted to spike Louis's guns with one pile-driving blow, but he had to depend on chance against a rival who was perfection in marksmanship and adept in avoiding fire.

The first round presaged a hurricane encounter. Braddock leaped out of his corner, swept clear across the ring and in a jiffy winged a right for Louis's jaw. The blow didn't land. Joe saw it coming, ducked and was out of range and the blow landed on the challenger's head. Braddock charged, he never stopped charging in fact, and Louis stepped nimbly back. The Bomber was boxing and Braddock was plodding with bull-like rushes.

Suddenly Louis leaped in, discarding his cautious style as they manoeuvred about the ring, and pressed close to Braddock with both hands swinging for the head. They locked and as they were parting the champion suddenly ripped a short, right uppercut cleanly to the chin, and, as cleanly, Louis went down. He was unhurt and up before a count could be started.

The challenger subsequently was roundly criticized for this by Trainer Jack Blackburn. The punch aroused the fury in Louis and he slammed into Braddock, shaking and staggering the champion with a vicious fusillade which also drew blood, before the bell ended the round.

Starting the second, Braddock acquitted himself well. He apparently had recovered from those jolting blows of the first round and was jabbing well and also swishing his right through the air more menacingly than effectively. He slipped some of the challenger's blows, until Louis suddenly crashed over a staggering left and right to the jaw. This attack opened a furious assault by Louis in which he pounded his rival mercilessly.

Through the third and fourth rounds Louis gave his attention almost exclusively to boxing. He was taking his time.

Braddock's Eyes Puffed

Braddock came up for the fifth with his eyes puffed and his forehead ripped above the left optic. He jabbed jab for jab with Louis for a time, drawing a crimson smear from the challenger's nose, and keeping up the menace of attack from right-handers which were nothing more than threats. Joe, however, did the boxing and the solid punching. After that it was only a question of time.

In the seventh Braddock staggered under a right uppercut that was driven cleanly and solidly to the chin when he leaped in fighting his limited best. Then, in the next round, Louis leaped in for the kill. After a few preliminary gestures, the Brown Bomber ripped a left hook to the body. He brought a left hook to the jaw and Braddock tottered on uncertain legs, his guard down. Joe followed with a pile-driving right that dropped Braddock in his tracks, bruised and battered, his title gone, his gameness an imperishable memory.

It was fully ten minutes before the beaten champion was able to leave the ring under his own power.

Loses on Foul Claim

In the semi-final, scheduled for six rounds, Harry Thomas of Chicago received credit for a knockout triumph over Jorge Brescia, Argentine heavyweight. Brescia was hit after the bell ended the third round and his handlers claimed foul. They refused to let him come up for the fourth, with the result that Thomas was declared the winner. Brescia weighed 212¾ pounds and Thomas scaled 196½.

Arthur Godoy of Chile outpointed Tony Galento, Newark, in a slambang six-rounder. The winner weighed 194¾ pounds and the loser 220.

In other six-rounders Nathan Mann, 187¼, New Haven, Conn., defeated Charley Massera, 184¾, Pittsburgh, and Abe Feldman, 180, New York, held Hans Haverlick, 187½, to a draw.

In four-round bouts Max Roesch, 192, Dallas, beat Steve Carr, 182½, Meriden, Conn.; Jack McCarthy, 190, Boston, defeated Bernie Bowman, 225, Chicago; Henry Cooper, 186½, Brooklyn, turned back Al Kettles, 198, Chicago, and Max Zona, 202, Chicago, triumphed over Bill Irby, 180¼, Eufala, Ala.

June 23, 1937

Crowd of 14,000 Sees Armstrong Knock Out Sarron for Featherweight Title

ARMSTRONG STOPS SARRON IN SIXTH

Long Right to Jaw, Finishing Blow, Nullifies Loser's Early Lead in Fast Bout

---

PETEY STUNNED AT CLOSE

All 126-Pound Title Claims Settled—Victor Recognized by State, National Boards

---

By JOSEPH C. NICHOLS

Henry Armstrong clinched his claim to the world featherweight championship last night by stopping Petey Sarron, courageous battler from Birmingham, Ala., in the sixth round of their scheduled fifteen-round battle at Madison Square Garden.

A long, looping right-hand punch to the jaw sent Sarron to the canvas in 2 minutes 36 seconds of the sixth, and though Sarron managed to get up on his knees, he remained stunned in that posture while Referee Arthur Donovan tolled ten over him.

The outcome entitles Armstrong to recognition by the New York State Athletic Commission and the National Boxing Association as king of the world's 126-pound boxers. Previous to last night Sarron was regarded by the N. B. A. as champion, while the board in this State recognized Mike Belloise. The latter, however, waived his claim to the crown because of ill health, leaving the field clear for Armstrong.

Over $34,000 in Receipts

A crowd of 14,000 persons, of whom 11,847 paid $34,708, sat in on the battle and saw a thriller.

Although he was thought to have weakened himself by making 124 pounds for the fight, Armstrong entered the ring the choice to win, but Sarron tore into the Los Angeles Negro with both hands flying and easily outscored Armstrong through the first round.

As a matter of fact, the Alabama fighter clearly won the first four rounds of the sizzling battle by eagerly inviting Armstrong's attack and cleanly beating the Negro in counters. Neither fighter paid heed to the so-called finer points of boxing. They merely rushed at each other time and again, both arms swinging, and the encounter was one long succession of thrilling exchanges to the head and body.

The knockdown at the end was

the only one of the bout, but Sarron twice touched the canvas with his knees as the result of slips in the earlier sessions.

Sarron stepped after Armstrong and through the first round pounded him with good left hooks to the head and body. The Negro landed only two hard punches in the first, a right and left to the head, but these blows plainly shook his foe.

In the second, which was filled with action, Sarron again outpunched his rival with a fast left. Armstrong seemed to get the range in the third and bounced a number of rights off Sarron's jaw, only to lose the round officially because of a low right.

The Birmingham battler landed the more punches in the fourth, but seemed to be losing strength under the force of Armstrong's steady body blows. And in the fifth the Negro took complete command, forcing Sarron to the ropes and battering him without cessation.

Southerner Takes Cover

When the sixth started Armstrong sprang at his adversary and drove both hands to the body. One punch, a heavy right, apparently robbed Sarron of all his strength, for he was able to do nothing except cover up while Armstrong belabored relentlessly with lefts and rights to the mid-section.

Recovering somewhat, Sarron jumped at Armstrong and traded willingly with him in mid-ring until the latter, releasing his long right, crashed it squarely against Sarron's jaw.

Sarron slumped to his knees and elbows and slowly lifted himself. Referee Donovan picked up the count from the timekeeper at six and shouted the remaining seconds in Sarron's ear while the beaten fighter looked at him in wonder.

The loser quickly recovered from the effects of the punch and waved to the gallery as he left the ring. He scaled 126 pounds exactly for the battle.

October 30, 1937

Times Wide World

REFEREE DONOVAN COUNTING OUT SARRON LAST NIGHT

TELEVISION AT THE RINGSIDE

THE prize ring has always been looked upon as an ideal setting for television because there is plenty of action confined to a comparatively small area which the radio cameras can cover easily. Now, as the result of several boxing matches on the television in London, it is reported that whether the telecast is interesting all depends upon who is in the ring. If the fight is poor the radio spectator is bored exactly as if he were at the ringside.

Observers agreed that the television camera men must speed up their work, sacrifice the size of the image and show a wider view. For example, to get the boxers as large as possible on the screen only a head and waist view was shown most of the time. Occasionally the telephoto lense was focused on the footwork.

A sports commentator's description accompanied the telecast. This is what a critic in The Listener, journal of the British Broadcasting Corporation, said about his work:

"Boxing on television provides the commentator with a rather unusual task because it is no use for him simply to tell us, as he would in an ordinary sound commentary, that boxer A has just succeeded in hitting boxer B on the jaw. We can see that perfectly well for ourselves. Neither can he confine himself to saying that he thinks boxer A is getting the best of the round. Most of us who take an intelligent interest in boxing prefer to work that out without being told. The commentator got over the difficulty with conversational remarks of the 'that was a nasty one, wasn't it?' category, and added pleasantly to an enjoyable evening."

February 27, 1938

HEMINGWAY WINS BOUT

Enters Key West Ring as the Referee, Winds Up as Fighter

KEY WEST, Fla., March 13 (AP).—Ernest Hemingway, author, entered the ring as referee of a Negro boxing match here last night and left it winner of the decision over a second.

One of the fighters was floored in the last round and Hemingway started counting. The fighter's second threw in a towel. Hemingway promptly kicked it out and continued to count. In came the towel again and again it was kicked out.

Then the second himself leaped into the area with fists flying against Hemingway. The writer ducked and caught the second with a blow that left him groggy. Then he twisted the Negro's ear and held him until a policeman appeared.

"The kid lost his head," Hemingway grinned. "He asked me today to referee a fight in which he will be one of the participants next week and I agreed."

March 14, 1938

30,000 Watch Armstrong Easily Outpoint Ross for World Welterweight Title

ARMSTRONG GAINS UNANIMOUS VERDICT

Becomes First Boxer to Hold Welter and Featherweight Crowns at Same Time

ROSS TAKES BAD BEATING

But Refuses to Allow Referee to Halt the Bout—Notables Present at Garden Bowl

By JAMES P. DAWSON

He's a great little fighter, this Henry Armstrong from Los Angeles.

He beat a great little fighter in true fighting style last night in the Madison Square Garden Bowl in Long Island City to become the first ring warrior in pugilism's long history ever to hold the world featherweight title and the world welterweight crown at the same time.

Armstrong was the world featherweight titleholder entering the ring. He became the welterweight monarch too when he lifted the crown from the furrowed brow of stouthearted Barney Ross of Chicago, the defending champion, in fifteen rounds of vicious, savage fighting that was so one-sided as to make the result a foregone conclusion midway in the battle.

Like a human tornado, Armstrong cut down Ross. There was no resisting force. Henry just pounded the gallant Ross tirelessly, pitilessly through every one of the fifteen rounds, winning thirteen and losing one of these thirteen on a technicality, until at the end awarding the decision that made a new, unparalleled champion, was a mere formality.

Referee Arthur Donovan and Judges Billy Cavanagh and George Lecron collaborated in the decision, which was unanimous. No other verdict was possible. And there was none in the gathering of 30,000,

Times Wide World

ARMSTRONG BATTERING ROSS IN THE FOURTEENTH ROUND

paying $160,861 for the privilege of witnessing the battle, who disputed the award.

It was announced from Promoter Mike Jacobs's office that the paid attendance was 26,430 and the net receipts $136,016.

Lacking in Reserve Strength

An examination of the three official balloting slips gave Armstrong a lopsided score which reflected clearly by what a wide margin the Californian earned his twin title brackets. The lowest vote gave him ten rounds. The highest gave Armstrong twelve. The other gave him eleven.

In a word, Ross had not a chance, because he was unsuited to the style of the young Negro who hammered him out of his title and because he had not the stamina, the resistance, the reserve strength to come on against youth.

Referee Donovan's voting slip showed twelve rounds for Armstrong, two for Ross and one even. Judge Lecron voted eleven rounds for Armstrong, two for Barney and two even. Judge Cavanagh gave

Armstrong ten rounds, Ross four and called one even. And one of the rounds on which all three bout officials agreed on for Ross was the seventh, a session which Armstrong won off by himself but in which he was penalized under the State Athletic Commission rules for an unintentional foul.

The battle, in its change of ring titles, ran true to Garden Bowl tradition. No titleholder ever has successfully defended his crown in this jinx-ridden ring, an experience with which Ross was familiar before last night, since he lost the welterweight crown to Jimmy McLarnin there on Sept. 17, 1934, under conditions somewhat similar to those which obtained last night.

Professional Start in 1929

When he relinquished the welterweight crown to McLarnin on that occasion, Ross underwent the experience of four postponements in eleven days. Last night's battle was originally scheduled for last Thursday night and was postponed twice because of rain. When it went through to completion, another champion was shorn of his laurels,

and the champion was, for the second time, Ross.

After the battle was over and he had the relaxation of his dressing room, where there was mourning instead of celebration, Ross's retirement from the ring was announced. He has been through ten years of ring campaigning, dating back to the start of his professional career in 1929. Judged strictly off his performance last night, Ross is "through."

None in the crowd which saw last night's slaughter—and it was that on a moderate scale—will dispute the fact Ross has reached the end of his fistic rope. And in that gathering were Federal, State and city officials who must have sympathized with Barney as he made his futile defense of the title he had defended twice before.

Postmaster General Farley was among the notables present. Past and present champions of the ring were there, including Joe Louis, the ruling monarch of pugilism; baseball players and club executives, polo players, representatives of the race track, bankers, financiers, commercial and industrial leaders.

None to Dispute the Award

There were also figures of society, representatives of the arts and of the professions. And there was none among them, as there was none in the distant reaches of the vast bowl where sat the $1.15 admission ticket-holders, who disputed the award for Armstrong.

There was no room for doubt. Armstrong saw to that. He was the hero of a betting upset that should have been no upset at all. Because he demonstrated, almost at the opening gong, that his style, his strength, his inexhaustible supply of stamina, perseverance, his grim determination, in short, his singular fighting stock in trade, were too much for Ross.

It had been thought in advance that the man who withstood the punches of McLarnin, Petrolle, Garcia, Canzoneri and such hitters, would have the resistance and the counter-offensive to withstand and offset the awkward style of Armstrong.

The new champion is not the finishing hitter that were some of those named. Indeed, Armstrong is a sloppy hitter—a punishing puncher, and nothing more. If he were a finishing hitter, he would have knocked out Ross in ten rounds last night. After the tenth, it would have been merciful to stop the contest.

Ross plugged along on his nerve alone. Referee Donovan, seeing the plight of the defending champion, his right eye closed tightly, his nose battered and bleeding, his lips bruised and gory, his spirit wilted, his resistance practically gone, queried Ross's corner apprehensively from the tenth round, wondering if the fading champion's handlers wished to call it quits.

Protect Hollow Distinction

Before the start of the eleventh session, then before the twelfth round got under way, the arbiter stepped to Ross's corner and asked him how he felt. He intimated to the Chicagoan's handlers that he wanted to relieve Barney of the punishment he was taking. But Ross had never had the stigma of a knockout charged against him and it was plain his advisers wanted to protect this hollow distinction even though the sacrifice might be great.

Through the thirteenth, fourteenth and fifteenth rounds he fought spasmodically, feebly, instinctively, as if to demonstrate to Referee Donovan that he was "all right" as he claimed. But his best was but a gesture against the attack of Armstrong.

Davey Day, Chicago lightweight, won the decision over Norment Quarles of Hendersonville, N. C., in the eight-round semi-final. Each weighed 136½ pounds.

In the six-round bouts, Dem Wakerlis, Boston, 153¾, outpointed Frankie Blair, Camden, N. J., 155½, and Phil Siriani, Bronx, 135½, took the award over Young Chappie, Albany, 134¾. Sammy Julian, Brooklyn, 138¼, won from Johnny Rinaldi, Bronx, 138, in one of the four-rounders and in the other Jimmy Liddell, Los Angeles, 130¼, and Frankie Aiello, East Side, 128¾, fought a draw.

June 1, 1938

LOUIS DEFEATS SCHMELING BY A KNOCKOUT IN FIRST; 80,000 SEE TITLE BATTLE

FIGHT ENDS IN 2:04

Rights Drop the Loser Thrice and Trainer Tosses In Towel

1936 SETBACK AVENGED

Challenger Says He Was Fouled With a Kidney Punch —The Gate Tops $900,000

By JAMES P. DAWSON

The exploding fists of Joe Louis crushed Max Schmeling last night in the ring at the Yankee Stadium and kept sacred that time-worn legend of boxing that no former heavyweight champion has ever regained the title.

The Brown Bomber from Detroit, with the most furious early assault he has ever exhibited here, knocked out Schmeling in the first round of what was to have been a fifteen-round battle to retain the title he won last year from James J. Braddock. He has now defended it successfully four times.

In exactly 2 minutes and 4 seconds of fighting Louis polished off the Black Uhlan from the Rhine, but, though the battle was short, it was furious and savage while it lasted, packed with thrills that held three knockdowns of the ambitious ex-champion, every moment tense for a crowd of about 80,000.

A Representative Gathering

This gathering, truly representative and comparing favorably with the largest crowds in boxing's history, paid receipts estimated at between $900,000 and $1,000,000 to see whether Schmeling could repeat the knockout he administered to Louis just two years ago here and be the first ex-heavyweight champion to come back into the title, or whether the Bomber could avenge this defeat as he promised.

As far as the length of the battle was concerned, the investment in seats, which ran to $30 each, was a poor one. But for excitement, for drama, for pulse-throbs, those who came from near and far felt themselves well repaid because they saw a fight that, though it was one of the shortest heavyweight championships on record, was surpassed by few for thrills.

With the right hand that Schmeling held in contempt Louis knocked out his foe. Three times under its impact the German fighter hit the ring floor. The first time Schmeling regained his feet laboriously at the count of three. From the second knockdown Schmeling, dazed but game, bounced up instinctively before the count had gone beyond one.

On the third knockdown Schmeling's trainer and closest friend, Max Machon, hurled a towel into the ring, European fashion, admitting defeat for his man. The towel sailed through the air when the count on the prostrate Max had reached three.

Ignored in Boxing Here

The signal is ignored in American boxing, has been for years, and Referee Arthur Donovan, before he had a chance to pick up the count in unison with knockdown time-keeper Eddie Josephs, who was outside the ring, gathered the white emblem in a ball and hurled it through the ropes.

Returning to Schmeling's crumpled figure, Donovan took one look and signaled an end of the battle. The count at that time was five on the third knockdown. Further counting was useless. Donovan could have counted off a century and Max could not have regained his feet. The German was thoroughly "out."

It was as if he had been pole-axed. His brain was awhirl, his body, his head, his jaws ached and pained, his senses were numbed from that furious, paralyzing punching he had taken even in the short space of time the battle consumed.

Claims Blurred Vision

Following the bout, Schmeling claimed he was fouled. He said that he was hit a kidney punch, a devastating right, which so shocked his nervous system that he was dazed and his vision was blurred. To observers at the ringside, however, with all due respect to Schmeling's thoughts on the subject, the punches which dazed him were thundering blows to the head, jaw and body in bewildering succession, blows of the old Alabama Assassin reincarnate last night for a special occasion.

Louis wanted to erase the memory of that 1936 knockout he suffered in twelve rounds. It was the one blot on his brilliant record. He aimed to square the account and he did.

Because of the excitement attending the finish, Louis, in the records, will be deprived of a clean-cut knockout. It will appear as a technical knockout because Referee Donovan didn't complete the full ten-second count over Schmeling. But this is merely a technicality.

No fighter ever was more thoroughly knocked out than was Max last night.

Thrilling to the spectacle of this short, savage victory which held so much significance was a gathering that included a member of President Roosevelt's Cabinet, Postmaster General James A. Farley; Governors of several States, Mayors of cities in the East, South and Middle West, Representatives and Senators, judges and lawyers, politicians, doctors, figures of prominence in the professional world, leaders of banking, industry and commerce, stars of the stage and screen, ring champions of the past and present, leaders in other sports and other fields—all assembled eagerly awaiting the struggle whose appeal drew them from distant parts of the country and from Europe.

Millions Hear the Fight

In addition to those looking on at the spectacle, there were millions listening in virtually all over the world, for this battle was broadcast in four languages, English, German, Spanish and Portuguese, so intense was the interest in its outcome.

Louis, hero of one of the greatest stories ever written in the ring, owner of a record of thirty-eight victories in thirty-nine bouts spread over four years, entered the ring the favorite to win at odds of 1 to 2. He won like a 1-to-10 shot. The knockout betting was at even money, take your pick. It could have been on Louis at 1 to 10, for Schmeling never had a chance. His number was up from the clang of the opening gong.

Schmeling, 32-year-old campaigner over a period of fourteen years, aspired to the unparalleled distinction of being the first man to regain the heavyweight crown. He suffered, instead, the fate that overtook Jim Corbett, Bob Fitzsimmons, Jim Jeffries and Jack Dempsey, ring immortals all, who tried and failed.

The fury of Louis's attack explains the result in a nutshell. The defending champion came into the ring geared on high. He never stopped punching until his rival was a crumpled, inert, helpless figure, diving headlong into the resined canvas, rolling over there spasmodically, instinctively, trying to come erect, his spirit willing to return to the attack, his flesh weak, for mind and muscle could not be expected to function harmoniously under the terrific battering Schmeling absorbed in those fleeting two minutes.

Max Throws Two Punches

Emphasizing the savagery with which Louis went after this victory was Schmeling's feeble effort at retaliation. The German ex-champion threw exactly two punches. That is how completely the Bomber established his mastery in this second struggle with the Black Uhlan.

With the opening gong, Louis crept softly out of his corner, pantherlike, eyes alert, arms poised, fists cocked to strike from any angle as he met Schmeling short of the ring's center. Max backed carefully toward his own corner, watching Louis intently, his right, the right which thudded so punishingly against Joe's jaw and temple two years ago, ready to strike over or under a left guard. At least, that was Schmeling's pre-arranged plan.

But Louis wasted only a few seconds in studying his foe, menacing Max meanwhile with a spearing left, before quickly going to work.

65

Like flashes from the blue, the Bomber's sharp, powerful left started suddenly pumping into Schmeling's face. The blows tilted Max's head back, made his eyes blink, unquestionably stung him. The German's head was going backward as if on hinges.

Max's face was exposed to a lefthook attack and Louis interspersed his onslaught with a few of these blows, gradually forcing Schmeling back to the ropes and preventing the German from making an offensive or counter move, so fast and sharp and true was the opening fire of the defending champion.

Schmeling suddenly shot a right over Louis's left for the jaw, but the blow was short and they went close. At long range again, Joe stuck and stabbed with his left to the face and head, trying to open a lane through Schmeling's protecting arms and gloves for a more forceful shot from the right.

Again Lunges Forward

But the opening didn't come immediately. Instead, Schmeling again lunged forward, his right arching as it drove for Louis's jaw, and it landed on the champion's head as the Schmeling admirers in the tremendous crowd roared encouragement.

Louis, however, only scowled and stepped forward, this time with a terrific right to Schmeling's jaw which banged Max against the ropes, his body partly turned toward the right from Louis.

Schmeling shook to his heels under the impact of that blow, but he gave no sign of toppling. And Joe, like a tiger, leaped upon him, driving a right to the ribs as Schmeling half turned—apparently the blow Schmeling later claimed was foul—swinging with might and main, lefts and rights that thudded against Schmeling's bobbing head, grazed or cracked on Max's jaw and swishing murderous looking left hooks into Schmeling's stomach as the crumpling ex-champion grimaced in pain, his face wearing the expression of a fighter protesting "foul."

Shaken when he first landed against the ropes, Schmeling was rendered groggy under the furious assault to which Louis subjected him while he stood there trying unsuccessfully to avoid the blows or grasp a chance to clinch.

Suddenly the Bomber's right, sharp and true with the weight of his 198¾ pounds back of it as well as his knack of driving it home, landed cleanly on Schmeling's jaw. Max toppled forward and down. He was hurt and stunned, but gamely the German came erect at the count of three.

Louis was on him in a jiffy, with the fury of a jungle beast. After propping the tottering Schmeling with a jolting left to the face, the Bomber's deadly right fist again exploded in Max's face, and under another crack on the jaw, Schmeling went down. This time, however, the German regained his feet before the count progressed beyond one.

Crowd in an Uproar

But Schmeling was helpless. He staggered drunkenly for a few backward steps, the crowd in an uproar as Louis stealthily followed and measured his man. Max was an open target. His jaw was unprotected and inviting. His midsection was a mark for punches. The kill was within Louis's grasp. He lost no time in ceremony.

Spearing Schmeling with blinding straight lefts, numbing Max with powerful left hooks that were sharp, true and destructive, Louis set the stage for one finishing right to the jaw, released the blow and landed in a flash, and the German toppled over in a headlong dive, completely unconscious.

The din of the crowd echoed over the arena, cheers for the conquering Louis, shrieks of entreaty and shouts of advice for Schmeling. But this thunderous roar was unheard by the befogged Schmeling and was ignored by the Bomber, intent only on the destruction of his foe.

In routine fashion, Eddie Josephs, a licensed referee converted into a knockdown timekeeper, started the count over the stricken Schmeling. He counted one, then two, as Referee Donovan went about the duty of signaling Louis to the farthest neutral corner.

Machon Hurls Towel

At "three" a white towel sailed aloft from Schmeling's corner, hurled by the ever-faithful Machon, who realized, as did every one else in the vast gathering, that Schmeling was knocked out, if he was not, indeed, badly hurt.

The towel fell in the ring a few feet from Schmeling. It is the custom in European rings to recognize this gesture as a concession of defeat. It used to be recognized here. But for many years now it has been banned, and Referee Donovan, disregarding the emblem of surrender, tossed it through the ropes and out of the ring.

When he returned to the prostrate figure of Schmeling, moving convulsively on the ring floor doubtless with that instinctive impulse to arise, the count had reached "five." One look was enough for Donovan. Instantly he spread his arms in a signal that meant the end of the bout, although Time-keeper Josephs, as he is duty bound to do, continued counting outside the ring.

This led to confusion at the finish. Some thought the third knockdown count was eight. Actually, the bout was ended at the count of five, the three seconds beyond that time being a gesture against emergency that was superfluous. Schmeling could not have arisen inside the legal ten-second stretch. His hopes were blasted. He was a thoroughly beaten man.

In a few moments, however, as police swarmed into the ring and his handlers worked over him in the corner to which he was assisted, Schmeling returned to consciousness. He was able to smile bravely as he walked across the ring to shake the hand of the conquering Louis, a gesture that carried the impression, somehow, that Max realized at long last that Louis is his master now and for all time.

June 23, 1938

20,000 See Armstrong Annex Lightweight Title by Beating Ambers in Garden

ARMSTRONG TAKES VERDICT ON POINTS

Victory Over Ambers, 2 Votes to 1, Makes Him First to Hold 3 World Titles

DECISION ROUNDLY BOOED

Fans Demonstrate Despite 2 Knockdowns by Henry and His Battering of Rival

By JAMES P. DAWSON

Henry Armstrong did it last night! The doughty little Negro from California became the first fighter in all ring history to hold three titles at the same time when he hammered his way to the decision over stout-hearted, courageous Lou Ambers in fifteen rounds of as fast, furious and savage fighting as has ever been seen before a gathering of 20,000 frenzied fans in Madison Square Garden.

Entering the ring with the signal distinction of being the world featherweight and welterweight champion, Armstrong annexed the world lightweight title when he battered his way to a divided, disputed decision over Ambers after doing everything but knock out the defending champion.

Homicidal Henry or Hammering Henry, whichever you will, because he is a combination of both, won a 2-to-1 verdict from the bout officials. He left the ring with the derisive shouts of noisy protests ringing in his ears, victim of a sad demonstration after a glorious bout.

Drops Three on Fouls

Why the ballot slips on the decision should have been divided is a mystery. Henry won ten of the fifteen rounds, and three of the five he lost he dropped through accidental fouls.

As mysterious was the noisy demonstration of disapproval which came when the verdict was announced. Even making allowances for the possibility that Ambers might have been heavily backed as the short-ender in odds that went to 17 to 5 at ring time, taking into consideration, too, the rise and flow of emotional reaction to a glorious effort on the part of the tottering Ambers, not even discounting the tremendous popularity manifested for Ambers as the battle started—still it is hard to understand or explain the terrific din of jeers, boos and catcalls, the storm of torn papers, flying straw hats and cigar butts, which rained on the ring when the new champion, the youth who today has an unparalleled record of championship conquest, was crowned.

Referee Billy Cavanagh and Judge George Lecron voted the decision to Armstrong. Judge Marty Monroe, as capable, experienced and honest an official as the State Athletic Commission has on its roster, voted for Ambers. The margin by which Cavanagh declared Armstrong the victor was seven rounds to six, with two even. Lecron gave Armstrong eight rounds, Ambers six, and declared one even. Monroe gave Ambers the majority on his sheet, with eight rounds against Armstrong's seven.

The writer gave Armstrong ten of the fifteen rounds. Ambers received only the seventh, ninth, eleventh, twelfth and thirteenth. Only two of these rounds did Ambers actually win—the ninth and thirteenth. In the other three, as in the other ten Armstrong won, Ambers had been badly battered, but because of accidental fouls, inaccurate body blows, principally stout lefts which went awry in the heat of battle, Armstrong was penalized the seventh, eleventh and twelfth.

This margin in Armstrong's favor reflects the flow of battle. He was a perfect little demon, a human cyclone, a frenzied destroyer who did not encompass destruction as it is known in the ring only because he tired when the crucial moment came.

Armstrong had Ambers down in the fifth round under a crushing right to the jaw, but the knockdown, with Lou obviously hurt, came just a flash before the bell rang the end of the round and, at the count of one, Ambers was saved.

Ambers went down again, and again was obviously hurt and apparently on the road to a knockout, in the sixth round, under a fusillade of punches, a final left and right to the jaw accomplishing the knockdown. This time Lou remained down until eight seconds had been counted over him. He arose with his head still awhirl, but in a remarkable demonstration of ring generalship fended off Armstrong's furious bid for a knockout.

Becomes Wild Under Pressure

Armstrong became wild under the forced pressure of his knockout bid, which made him more furious and also ineffective. Ambers was emboldened under the circumstances to counter-fire in abbreviated gestures that upset Henry's designs without painfully hurting him.

In the ten rounds he won Armstrong did everything but knock out his foe. He had Ambers so weary at times that it seemed Lou could not go on.

Lou did survive, and, more, he came back. He came back gloriously, desperately, by living through a veritable inferno until the thirteenth round, when he came near turning the tables on his foe. In this round Ambers fought Armstrong to a standstill, hammering Henry, whose hammering blows seemed to lose their sting and force as the fight progressed, and even his amazing store of energy felt the strain.

But that thirteenth round effort took a lot out of Ambers. He was practically out on his feet in the fourteenth and fifteenth when he again essayed rallies, only to be brought up short by the California Negro, who would not be denied.

As a matter of fact, Henry looked the vanquished instead of the victor as the conquered and conqueror left the ring, Ambers to the ear-splitting cheers of partisan admirers; Armstrong to a demonstration of disapproval that was as unsportsmanlike as it was unjustified.

The ring's first triple champion finished the bout on wabbly legs. His lips and mouth were bruised and bleeding, and there was a gash an inch long on the lid of his left eye. He found his protective rubber mouthpiece an annoyance rather than an aid as early as the eighth round, when the crimson flow from his battered mouth became something more than a rivulet.

Ambers, on the other hand, was almost unmarked. His left eye was cut and there was a knob swollen above the optic. His lips and mouth issued blood. Those were the surface indications. How he felt under the surface can only be surmised after about the toughest battering he or any other lightweight has absorbed in the glowing history of this ring title.

Save for the rounds Ambers won, each succeeding session was a repetition of the preceding one. Only the knockdowns of the fifth and sixth interfered with the sequence.

Even in the rounds awarded to Lou on fouls, the seventh, eleventh and twelfth, there was no interruption to the sequence, because in these sessions Armstrong hammered and pounded Ambers tirelessly.

The California Negro started like a whirlwind. He was slowed almost to a zephyr at the finish, but this could only be natural after the terrific ordeal to which he subjected himself.

Whether Armstrong will remain long as the ring's only triple champion is a moot point. The understanding is that Eddie Mead, on behalf of the doughty little Coast Negro, will appear before the commission and surrender the featherweight title, concentrating on the lightweight and welterweight crowns. Supporting this belief is the fact that Armstrong is a legitimate lightweight, weighing 134 pounds to Ambers's 134¼ pounds last night. Further support is found in the fact that the commission, at a meeting yesterday, launched tentative steps for a tournament among featherweights to determine a champion, apparently against the day when Armstrong surrenders the title.

August 18, 1938

Louis Knocks Out Galento in 4th After Challenger Drops Him in 3d

Champion, Near Defeat, Comes Back to Pound His Foe Into Submission—Referee Stops Bout Seen by 34,852 at Stadium

By JAMES P. DAWSON

In a heavyweight battle that will take its place among the ring's outstanding title struggles because of its savage fury and methodical butchery, Joe Louis last night knocked out Two-Ton Tony Galento, barrel-shaped Orange (N. J.) challenger, in the fourth round of what was to have been a fifteen-round struggle at the Yankee Stadium.

The end came in 2 minutes 29 seconds of the fourth session, but only a short time before the Brown Bomber's hand was raised in victory he had been close to being dethroned.

Galento, the despised, the rolypoly, unorthodox, uncontrollable heavyweight who was not conceded a chance in advance of the bout, thrilled 34,852 wild-eyed, shouting men and women by knocking Louis down in the third round for a count of one. He missed the title only because in his awkward, heavy-footed way he could not muster the accuracy to uncork another left hook to the jaw such as the blow that floored Louis.

Failing in this unexpected emergency, Galento went the way of most Louis foes. He was butchered into submission under the paralyzing power of the champion's blistering blows, rendered helpless before a crowd that paid receipts of $283,303 for a battle which, in advance, promised to be ridiculously one-sided and developed, instead, into a bid for the title that was heroic, albeit futile.

Galento lived up to practically all his pre-battle forecasts before he went down after a gallant fight. He failed only in his prediction that he would knock out Louis. And the fans who viewed the bout will testify that he missed that goal—one that would have provided an unparalleled upset in boxing history—by only the slimmest of margins.

He rocked and shook and staggered Louis in the first round. He himself was pounded ruthlessly through the second, when he went down for a count of two. But he came back fighting with grim determination in the third and, pressing in against the blows of Louis, brought the champion down with a left hook to the jaw that landed in grazing fashion. Its full force was spent before it connected because of Tony's shorter reach and the fact that Louis was going away from the punch.

Louis hit the ring floor solidly, but was up at the count of one, careful, cautious, respectful of his foe's punching prowess. He was taking no chances against a challenger so many persons had held in contempt before this eye-opening exhibition of determined fighting.

Every last man and woman in the vast crowd was on his or her feet with the spectacle of Louis down, a sensation the champion had experienced only thrice since he started his climb to fistiana's heights—twice at the hands of Max Schmeling and once at the hands of James J. Braddock.

In the vast throng were representatives of every walk of life, drawn to the bout because of its championship significance more than through any expectation of viewing what was unreeled there before their eyes.

Postmaster James A. Farley was in a front row. Governors from many States, near-by and distant, were scattered through the crowd. Representatives and Senators, judges and lawyers, bankers and brokers, merchant princes and industrial kings, doctors, college professors, stars of the stage and screen—all thrilled to the stirring title bid and the amazing spectacle of Louis on the floor, even as did the obscure fight fan perched up in the last row of the top tier in the three-decker stand.

Challenger's Doom Is Sealed

But Louis came out of this emergency, gliding gracefully before his lunging foe, avoiding, parrying, blocking all of Galento's lustiest punches, driving in counters that punished his foe's nerve centers. And in no time at all, Galento's doom was sealed.

Starting the fourth round, Louis lost no time, took no chances. Galento, on the other hand, obviously inspired by his success of the third session, beside himself with the

Louis down in third round for a count of one after a left hook to the jaw by the challenger

AS JOE LOUIS RETAINED HIS HEAVYWEIGHT CHAMPIONSHIP LAST NIGHT

Times Wide World

Referee Donovan stopping the fight as Galento sinks to his left knee after a succession of rights and lefts by the titleholder

possibility of winning the world heavyweight title with its wealth, disregarded all instructions from his corner. He said he would go in there fighting, unafraid, because he had never before been knocked down, and it was live or die. He "died."

Louis drilled him unmercifully with left hooks and right crosses. Galento tried to fight through a veritable shower of punches. Every punch Louis landed hurt. No punch Louis unleashed missed, because New Jersey's fighting tavern keeper was an inviting target, becoming more helpless and harmless with each succeeding blow.

Galento tried to fight on and couldn't. Louis was punching himself arm-weary, but he couldn't again floor the gallant fighter from across the Hudson. Referee Arthur Donovan was alert to the emergency in a battle that had been transformed into butchery.

Under the nerve-deadening punching to his head, to his face, to his jaw, to his generous mid-section, Galento's resistance gradually lessened, his vision became fogged, his nerves became paralyzed.

He clinched for relief and then was subjected to more strength-sapping fire. Donovan stepped between them and, with a careful look at Galento, permitted the fight to continue, above the shouts of "Stop it, stop it" that came from ringside fans who feared tragedy.

A Louis left hook to the jaw signalized a resumption of the slaughter. Galento lurched under the blow. A right to the jaw spun Tony halfway around, a fusillade rendered him helpless and sent him into another clinch and then Dono-

van stepped between them. He clasped Galento in his arms to signalize the end of the fight which made Galento the victim of his fourth technical knockout in a career that extends over ten years.

Galento was so thoroughly battered when the intervention came that he collapsed completely as Donovan sought to half-carry, half-lead him to his corner. Like a sack of meal Galento slipped through the protecting arms of the arbiter.

Joe Jacobs, his manager, and Trainers Jimmy Frain and Whitey Bimstein plunged through the ropes to the side of their fallen charge. Dr. William H. Walker of the State Athletic Commission climbed through the ropes for a medical examination. A cordon of police stepped into the ring to keep out clamoring fans. Louis was escorted out of the ring after having had his hand raised aloft in the sport's traditional victory gesture.

Rapid first-aid was being administered to Galento in the meanwhile as he sat there on his stool, an inert hulk. His eyes were closed, his nose bashed, his lips split, gushing a crimson flow that spattered over the canvas.

For fully five minutes his seconds worked over Galento with industry and not without a bit of alarm. White-faced, their eyes mirroring their concern, they rubbed his numb muscles, shook his head, bathed his bruised and bleeding face, forced him to inhale smelling salts. Finally they brought him back to consciousness.

Surprises were many in this battle that stirred the emotions. And they

came principally from Galento, so that their shock was greater. Two-Ton forgot his clownish antics, discarded his unorthodox tactics and fought cleanly, gallantly, fearlessly.

He was beaten but not disgraced, because he fought Louis as far as his strength and his limited boxing skill would permit. Never did he turn his back to the foe, not once did he break ground, until he could stand no more. Then he collapsed.

Galento supplied his first surprise in the opening round. Coming out of his corner following instructions to crouch and hook with his left for the body or jaw, he brushed aside the punishing stabs Louis made with a cautious left, shook the champion with a left hook to the jaw and drove him into a neutral corner.

There Galento leaped on the titleholder, trying to belabor Louis with drives for the body or head. But Louis parried most of the blows, although some got through to his midsection and one left landed high on his cheekbone to cause a small swelling.

Warned through this first round, Louis sought to finish Galento in the second—and couldn't. Two-Ton Tony stood up valiantly against a battering that would have crushed a less hardy, determined foe. Countless times Louis stabbed and hooked his left to the jaw and head. He followed invariably with his right, with stunning force. Painful digs to the stomach hurt Tony when he clinched or charged bullishly.

His face was cut and bruised and swollen.

A left and a right to the jaw knocked Two-Ton's feet out from

under him for the first knockdown of his career.

But the globular Galento bounced erect at the count of two and charged bullishly again, right into the teeth of a punching gale that all but finished him. That he did not go down and out in that second round is a tribute to his remarkable resistance and unquenchable fighting spirit.

Came the third and Galento's near-approach to championship status. He was being liberally sprinkled with a two-fisted fire when, about midway in the round, he whipped a left hook to the jaw and Louis went down cleanly, solidly, but unhurt, in mid-ring.

The champion bounced up as the timer's arm dropped on the count of "one" and cautiously stayed away from Galento until Tony's wide-open rushing invited further paralyzing fire from Louis's right and left.

Tony shot his bolt in the mad bid for victory inspired by the knockdown of the champion. With the opening of Louis's assault in the fatal fourth it was patent the end was in sight, that even Galento couldn't stand much more of the hammering that came his way.

This victory was Louis's seventh since he won the crown two years ago and his third in 1939. A fighting champion, he has set a record for activity.

With the gross receipts $283,303.68 and the radio rights having been sold for $25,000, the gate was well over the $300,000 mark.

June 29, 1939

29,088 See Ambers Win From Armstrong and Regain World Lightweight Title

AMBERS TRIUMPHS IN SAVAGE FIGHT

Referee Takes Five Rounds Away From Armstrong for Fouls at the Stadium

VICTOR BADLY BATTERED

Has Claim to Welterweight Title—Defeat First for Negro in 47 Bouts

By JAMES P. DAWSON

A novel chapter was written in boxing last night by Lou Ambers in circumstances that were—and doubtless will be for a long time—highly controversial.

The doughty little Herkimer Hurricane gained the decision over Henry Armstrong, tireless little bit of fighting machinery from Los Angeles, in fifteen rounds of savage punching at the Yankee Stadium, to regain the lightweight title Armstrong lifted from Ambers just a year ago almost to a day.

With his victory Ambers gained distinction as the first fighter in all ring history to regain the lightweight crown from the man to whom he lost it. He also is the second fighter in the long annals of lightweight activity to regain the 135-pound crown. Tony Canzoneri was the other.

And with this victory, too, Ambers entered a claim to the welterweight title that Armstrong also held when he entered the ring specifically to defend his world lightweight crown, notwithstanding the fact that by contract and with the State Athletic Commission it was expressly understood the men last night were fighting only for the lightweight crown.

Dissension in the Crowd

But there was dissension in the crowd of 29,088 fight fans over the decision at the end of the battle that drew gross receipts of $137,025 and was crowded with thrills from first bell to last. There was undisguised doubt that Ambers is the master of the man over whom he won a verdict that brought the first defeat to Armstrong in forty-seven battles, over a span of three years.

Strangely enough, it was a unanimous decision on which Ambers rode home again to the title he first lifted from Canzoneri. Referee Arthur Donovan and Judges Bill Healy and Frank Fullam were in perfect accord on Herkimer Lou as the winner. Healy by the widest margin of the three. He gave Ambers eleven rounds, gave Armstrong three and called one, the thirteenth, even. The rounds Healy gave to Armstrong were the fourth, twelfth and fourteenth.

Referee Donovan and Judge Fullam, who is also a licensed referee, both gave eight to Ambers and seven to Armstrong, although their distribution of the rounds varied widely, if not strangely.

Donovan gave Ambers the second third, fifth, sixth, seventh, ninth, eleventh and fifteenth rounds. The rest he awarded to Armstrong. Judge Fullam gave Ambers the first, second, fifth, seventh, ninth, eleventh and fourteenth, and gave the remaining seven to Armstrong.

The dispute concerning this highly exciting struggle will come over the penalties imposed upon Armstrong for infractions of the ring's rules.

Applying the law more severely than ever before, and certainly more painfully than ever it has been applied in a championship event, Referee Donovan penalized Armstrong no less than five rounds for foul punches. These were the second, fifth, seventh, ninth and eleventh.

Four of these rounds Armstrong won on competition beyond question. Ambers, without the foul that was called, carried the second. But there were times when the fouls were not visible, notably the second one which cost Armstrong the fifth round.

On this observer's score sheet Armstrong was the victim of an injustice, even taking into account the penalties of which he was the victim. Giving Ambers the benefit of the doubt in the five rounds he won by the ring's law enforcement, Armstrong still won the battle eight rounds to seven in the writer's opinion.

Score Sheet on Bout

This observer's score sheet gave Hammering Henry the fourth, sixth, eighth, tenth, twelfth, thirteenth, fourteenth and fifteenth rounds by wide margins. To Ambers this reporter gave the first, second and third rounds on action, together with the remaining four Donovan penalized Armstrong on fouls.

So it can be seen that this title was decided not on competition, but on fighting rules and ethics. Armstrong lost his title on fouls—the first time the crown has been involved in such an award since the day back in 1906 when Joe Gans retained his title on a foul in forty-two rounds of fighting with Battling Nelson at Goldfield, Nev.

Last night's encounter was decided as clearly on fouling as if Donovan had halted proceedings and tossed Armstrong from the ring, as happened in the case of Nelson. And it was regrettable, too, that such an ending should come to such a slashing battle.

The backwash of the decision started immediately Armstrong reached his dressing room. His manager, Eddie Mead, protesting that his fighter had been jobbed, had been the victim of a plot he had suspected as long as three weeks ago, declared he intended pressing a protest that would repeal boxing in this State. Of course, allowances must be made for excitement in this declaration by Mead.

Summing up, Ambers this morning is the world lightweight champion because, as the saying is, they pay off on decisions. And he has a substantial claim on the world welterweight title if one is to proceed on the old-fashioned theory that a title changes hands any time a challenger is at weight and conquers the champion, regardless of contracts.

Ambers weighed 134½ pounds, half a pound under the lightweight limit. He certainly was well under the 147-pound maximum for the welterweight class, in which Armstrong also was champion entering the ring. And, when Armstrong bowed to Ambers by decision, he lost both titles by any method of reasoning on old ring lines.

But whether Ambers will be uni-

AS LIGHTWEIGHT CHAMPIONSHIP CHANGED HANDS AT STADIUM LAST NIGHT

Ambers resting on one knee after slipping to the canvas while retreating from his rival in the fourth round   Associated Press

versally recognized as a double champion is open to dispute. He was compelled to enter into a contract, posting a $2,000 forfeit as guarantee, that he would fight Armstrong within ninety days for the welterweight title, to clarify any confusion that might surround the 147-pound crown. Meanwhile, Ambers has agreed not to fight any one else.

As to the bout, it was one of the greatest lightweight struggles seen here in years. In advance it had figured to be a primitive, savage, furious slug-fest. It was all of that.

After three opening rounds in which Ambers surprised everybody

by fighting exactly to Armstrong's style and beating Hammering Henry in the bargain—taking into account even the penalized second session—Armstrong went hot on the pursuit and chased Ambers all over the ring.

Nothing Ambers could do affected Armstrong. A gallant, determined warrior himself, Ambers lashed out after the third round with desperate rights and lefts to the face, head and body, trying to keep Armstrong away. Failing this, he tried to fight blow for blow with Henry at close quarters.

But the Coast Negro pressed on and on. He paid no attention to

blows which repeatedly dislodged his mouthpiece, which cut and bruised his tender lips and mouth, which caused a cut over his right eye and a swelling under his left. He waded in from first bell to last, rebounding always when Ambers's frenzied blows drove him backward before they lost their power, as they did in the closing five rounds.

And all the time he was pressing in Armstrong was flailing away with both arms, until it seemed Ambers must collapse.

Indeed, Ambers gave indications of crumpling in the last three rounds. He was unable to get away from one spot in the ring, a point

near Henry's corner, in the fourteenth round, and it seemed he would drop if only Armstrong stepped away. And when Armstrong finally did cease firing momentarily Ambers sidled along the ropes, weary and sick.

The most that can be said for Ambers is that he fought gallantly. He waded in recklessly as the bout opened and before he was forced into a desperate retreat. But he wasn't entitled to the decision. He isn't Armstrong's master.

August 23, 1939

Armstrong Loses Title to Fritzie Zivic on Points in Stunning Boxing Upset

PITTSBURGH BOXER WINS DECISIVELY

Zivic Dethrones Armstrong as Welterweight Ruler in Garden 15-Rounder

LOSER BLINDED BY BLOWS

12,081 Thrill to Savage Fight —Kogan Outpoints Scalzo in Non-Title Match

By JOSEPH C. NICHOLS

Fritzie Zivic did what the rank and file of boxing followers deemed impossible at Madison Square Garden last night. The 26-year-old Pittsburgh fighter, member of a family that has had representation in the ring for the last score of years, crushed the heretofore invincible Henry Armstrong into decisive defeat to win the welterweight championship of the world in a savage fifteen-round struggle that thrilled a crowd of 12,081 frenzied fans.

Pacing himself splendidly and standing up under Armstrong's hardest punches, the durable Zivic made his way to the championship by exhibiting a willingness to trade with his foe when such strategy seemed expedient and to stay away and stab effectively with a long left hand when that course appeared the better one to pursue.

Rallying after a start which seemed to indicate that Armstrong was on the way to another of his easy triumphs, a triumph that would justify the odds of 1 to 5 against the Los Angeles Negro to retain his title, Zivic won the onlookers over almost to a man by the excellence of his performance.

Collapses Near Close

Where he was expected to sag under the force of his opponent's whirlwind, ceaseless attack to the body, Zivic conserved his strength surprisingly, and in the final round it was Armstrong whose strength flagged, who found himself so ex-

DURING TWELFTH ROUND IN GARDEN TITLE BOUT
Zivic driving a left at Armstrong in last night's battle
Times Wide World

hausted that he collapsed to the canvas under a half-push, half-punch just before the bell.

Coming when it did the fall spared Armstrong the humiliation of having a count tolled over him, something that has never occurred to the deposed champion in all his splendid efforts in this city. But the fall, ruled a legitimate knockdown, sealed the victory in Zivic's favor. Going into the fifteenth round, Armstrong still had a chance to win. Referee Arthur Donovan and Judge Marty Monroe had the round count even, at seven apiece.

In going down to defeat Armstrong exhibited a brand of courage that will cause him to be long remembered even if he had not in the past held the featherweight, lightweight and welterweight championships of the world simultaneously.

The steady impact of the clever Zivic's sharp left to the face gradually caused a swelling about Armstrong's eyes, and in the eleventh round the defending titleholder was blind, to all intents and purposes.

In that session and through the

following ones, Zivic, aware of his foe's plight, kept the battle at long range and ripped both hands to the head at every opportunity. The pitifully handicapped Armstrong had trouble even locating his tormentor, and as he returned to his corner at the end of each round he would murmur prayerfully, "Oh, if I could only see."

When hostilities got under way, Armstrong moved forward in his characteristic manner, but his fire was wild, and Zivic clipped him with short punches through the first and second rounds.

In the third Armstrong managed to find the range and, resting his head on the Pittsburgher's left shoulder, proceeded to belabor the body a two-handed tattoo. He kept up this line of attack in the fourth and fifth, but at the end of the fifth it was apparent that his eyes, if the fight went the limit, would give him trouble. It was then that the swelling was evident.

Zivic capitalized on Armstrong's wild eagerness by stabbing the champion repeatedly in the sixth

and seventh, but the next two rounds saw Armstrong more than hold his own.

Furious Pace in Tenth

The tenth round, though, was the one in which every spectator in the house went delirious. The boxers stood toe to toe and each fired his heaviest artillery at the other's head.

Armstrong scored with body punches in the eleventh, and, after taking a beating in the twelfth, came through in the thirteenth to gain the edge with another body attack.

So worn was Armstrong in the final round that a knockout victory for Zivic seemed imminent. The Pittsburgh fighter trained a steady, long-range fire on Henry, but the latter took all his foe had and kept advancing courageously. At the final second, seeking to close in on Zivic, Armstrong tried to seize the challenger's right arm. Zivic gave him a long shove and Henry went to the floor just as the battle ended.

This observer awarded eight rounds to Zivic and seven to Armstrong. But Zivic had a clear margin of superiority in the rounds he won. He weighed 145½ pounds, as against 142 for Armstrong. The receipts were $29,212.

Julie Kogan, hard-hitting lightweight from New York, scored two knockdowns over Petey Scalzo of the West Side to win the decision in the semi-final, an eight-round clash.

Scalzo, recognized by the N. B. A. as featherweight champion of the world, was not risking his title as his foe weighed 132½ pounds. Scalzo scaled 128½.

Joey Iannotti, 129¼, of New Haven, survived a second round knockdown to earn the decision over Curley Stangelo, 128½, of the Bronx in a savage six-round bout.

Al Bernard, 151¾, of Greenwich Village scored an upset over Jackie Donovan, 151½, of Buffalo in a six-rounder.

Ray Robinson, 134½, Harlem Negro, who won the Golden Gloves lightweight crown last Spring, made his professional debut in the opening four-rounder and stopped Joe Echevarria, 132, Puerto Rican, in 1 seconds of the second frame.

October 5, 1940

Louis Wins in Seventh Round When Buddy Baer Is Disqualified by Referee

35,000 SEE BOMBER TRIUMPH ON A FOUL

Baer, Floored After Bell in 6th, Loses When His Pilot Stays in Ring Protesting

LOUIS DOWN FOR 4 IN 1ST

Sent Through Ropes, He Comes Back to Punish Buddy, Who Is on Canvas 3 Times

By JOSEPH C. NICHOLS
Special to THE NEW YORK TIMES.

WASHINGTON, May 23 — Joe Louis was successful in the seventeenth defense of his heavyweight championship of the world when he defeated the ponderous Buddy Baer in Griffith Stadium tonight.

The mere statement of the champion's victory, however, leaves no room to express the drama, excitement, surprise and uncertainty in a contest that contained more thrills than any heavyweight title bout since the oft-referred-to classic between Jack Dempsey and Luis Angel Firpo in 1923.

Arthur Donovan, who refereed tonight's clash, named Louis the winner on a foul in the seventh round, but before the bell sounded for that last official session of the scheduled fifteen-round encounter the 35,000 fans in the ball yard had been treated to the spectacle of Joe Louis on the floor, Joe Louis out of the ring, Joe Louis holding, Joe Louis clinching, and Joe Louis bleeding.

Baer Absorbs Punishment

In addition, they had also seen the towering Baer absorb an unbelievable amount of punishment in his own right, a punishment that reached its culmination in the sixth round when he was sent sprawling to the canvas three times.

It was as the result of Baer's final trip to the floor in the sixth that the fight had its unique ending. Louis, after taking a pretty bad beating in the fifth, launched a savage, merciless attack on his foe in the sixth, pounding him without let-up about the head.

The accumulation of those punches wore down Baer, and he went down the first time under the force of a right to the face. The challenger pulled himself to his feet at the count of seven, but Joe sprang at him quickly and soon had him down again with a lightning left and right to the jaw.

Challenger Gets to Feet

Baer appeared to be completely out on this knockdown and the fans were hailing Louis with a thunderous roar of acclaim, but, miracle of miracles, the doughty Baer, whose courage in the past

CHALLENGER DOWN FOR THIRD TIME IN LAST NIGHT'S BOUT

Buddy Baer has just been dropped by Joe Louis with a right to the jaw in the sixth round
Wired Photo—Times Wide World

has been questioned, climbed to his feet just before the count of ten was tolled. Just as the challenger reached his feet the bell rang, but the contestants did not seem to hear it, and neither did Donovan.

Sensing a knockout triumph, Louis let fly with a long right to the chin, and down went Buddy again.

The challenger's handlers, Ray Arcel and Izzy Kline, rushed to the fallen fighter and hauled him to his corner. They, together with manager Ancil Hoffman, worked over him through the rest period, but Baer seemed far from recovered when the signal sounded for the seventh round.

With the bell, Hoffman placed himself in front of his fighter, who remained perched on his stool, while Louis advanced to midring to continue, or conclude hostilities. Donovan waved, then shouted at Hoffman to leave the ring and allow matters to proceed. Hoffman refused, insisting that the blow that felled Buddy the last time was a foul one, delivered at an illegal time, and that his charge deserved the award.

Reason for Disqualification

Once more Donovan ordered Hoffman to leave, and again the man-

ager refused. As a point of observation, it may here be stated that the presence of a fighter's handler in the ring after time is called is a foul and reason for disqualification. Donovan invoked this rule after Hoffman's refusal, and announced that Louis was the winner on just that technicality.

The unusual ending and the award were satisfactory to the fans, and they applauded roundly. They seemed to realize that the fight could produce no further thrills comparable to those that they already had seen.

As a matter of fact, the fight was hardly two minutes old when the spectators found themselves beholding the wholly unlooked for spectacle of the mighty Joe Louis falling through the ropes under the force of a punch and landing on the ring apron. Incredible, but true.

The scorned challenger, who was given little chance to last five rounds, and practically not at all to go the limit, found himself on the threshold of the championship that his elder brother Max once held, and the Stadium was bedlam.

Baer Is Undaunted

Louis's contretemps came about after he himself had enjoyed some success in the opening minute by landing several lefts to the head.

The punches seemed to shake Buddy, but his reaction to them might be compared to the sensation experienced when one first encounters something dreaded, finds it's not so bad and then goes on to smother it.

Finding Joe's punches far from the crushing weapons he expected, Baer assumed the aggressive, moved toward his foe, and let fly with a long left hook to the head. The blow landed on the side of Louis's face and the champion reeled backward to the ropes, fell between them and landed outside. He managed to avoid falling into the working press row and got to his knees, his back to the ring.

At the count of four, delivered by the knockdown timekeeper, Charley Reynolds, Louis was back in the ring and trading lefts with his opponent.

From the manner in which Louis handled Baer in the second, the latter's success might have been considered a fluke except for after-developments. Buddy took considerable punishment in the second, as Joe trained his powerful left hook on his jaw. Buddy stood up well enough under these blows and came out for the third with a rush. He forced the titleholder to the ropes under a barrage of rights to

71

the head and the punches had their effect when a swelling appeared over Louis's left eye.

No Sign of Wilting

The champion outscored his foe in the close exchanges in this round and also in the next, but Baer showed no sign of wilting. In fact, he was ever dangerous and forced the champion to hold once in a while as he unleashed a series of heavy right-hand blows to the head.

And in the fifth Buddy came into his own with an attack so effective that he actually had things his own way.

He started the session by sampling two of Louis's choicest left hooks to the head without flinching. Then he ripped his own left to the face twice in quick succession, and the puffiness around Louis's eye was accentuated by a trickle of blood. The champion rubbed his thumb across the wound often, while Baer pounded him with both hands.

After clinching several times, Louis suddenly found himself consumed by fury, and he rained a shower of lefts and rights on his tormentor's head. This late rally caused Baer to sag, but he succeeded in remaining on h' feet.

The champion's fury did not abate during the minute of rest, and he sprang at Buddy with the next bell. He pounded the challenger about the head with both hands, but his shots with the left had greater accuracy.

After withstanding this early assault, Baer lashed out with an attack of his own, and the pair traded punches at a furious clip until Louis held. When they were parted, the champion resumed his aggressions, worked Baer into an opening and exploded a cannon-ball right that landed squarely on Buddy's face.

Down toppled Buddy, but he clambered to his feet and got up at seven. Stalking his adversary, the Bomber let fly with a lightning two-hand fire to the head, and again Baer collapsed.

As Baer hit the canvas, Timekeeper Reynolds arose at the side of the ring and commenced his count, which seemed superfluous right then and there. As the seconds were tolled off, with Donovan counting in unison with Reynolds, Baer showed signs of life.

His limbs writhed, he rolled over on his hands and knees, and he struggled mightily to arise.

As this was going on, through the din, Donovan counted nine and was about to start the count of ten when Baer made it. Then the bell rang, but all that Donovan, Louis, and probably Buddy, could hear was the tumult of the crowd.

It was then that Louis launched the right that floored Baer a third time, to bring about the action by Hoffman that caused Donovan to decide matters as he did.

Louis weighed 201¾. Baer, in exceptionally fine condition, weighed 237½.

In Baer's dressing room after the fight Hoffman announced that he would protest the outcome with the District of Columbia Athletic Commission tomorrow.

May 24, 1941

LOUIS, NEAR DEFEAT, STOPS CONN IN 13TH AND RETAINS CROWN

Bomber Suddenly Turns Tide, Hammering Foe to Floor With Furious Attack

CONTEST THRILLS 54,487

Polo Grounds Bout Marks 18th Successful Defense of His Title by Champion

By JAMES P. DAWSON

Joe Louis still is world heavyweight champion, after his eighteenth defense of the title he won four years ago from Jim Braddock in Chicago.

The famed Brown Bomber sank Billy Conn, former world light-heavyweight champion, with a depth-bomb in the thirteenth round of their scheduled fifteen-round battle before a crowd of 54,487 wildly excited fight fans, who paid $450,000, in the Polo Grounds last night.

But the Bomber will never come closer to being toppled from his throne than he did before Conn collapsed under the paralyzing power of nerve-deadening blows. Thus Joe escaped crashing into the category of the ring's ex-champions.

In a battle that was thrilling and highly spectacular to a degree not generally anticipated, Conn came within the proverbial eyelash of upsetting predictions as he stirred the emotions of the great crowd with a brand of battle few had dared expect, Louis least of all.

Frail in Comparison

The doughty Pittsburgher, 25½ pounds lighter than Louis, frail in comparison and with none of the heavyweight fighting experience the champion boasts, held his rival even in action and on rounds, through twelve sessions while men and women, envisioning a transfer of the title, yelled themselves hoarse, encouraging the challenger as he seemed about to succeed where few had given him a chance.

Then the fight ended, as it had been predicted it would end. Conn left himself open for one dangerous blow to a vital point. A desperate, harried Louis, fighting with savage fury, whipped home through the opening with a right to the jaw.

The blow landed high, but it was a powerful one. Conn, a few seconds before on the high road to fame and fortune, tottered backward. His knees buckled. The Brown Bomber was the Alabama Assassin. He leaped in savagely, thudding home with both hands with a crushing fire. Conn fell under the barrage, a right to the jaw, as a final thrust, sending the brave challenger careening and crumpling.

The challenger, who gave promise of becoming the champion, was counted out by Referee Eddie Joseph in 2 minutes 58 seconds of the thirteenth round, amid a scene that was veritable bedlam.

That is the way of the ring. One second you are on top. The next you are down in despair. Conn came to the realization of this painfully.

Only Six Minutes More

Billy was within two rounds of what appeared a victory. Actually, the battle had only six minutes and two seconds more to go. And the way Conn had performed there was every reason to believe a new champion would be crowned.

Perhaps it was his own contempt for the punching prowess of the champion that led Conn into the fatal error. He had felt the Louis blow and survived. More, he had outboxed and, at times, outslugged the devastating puncher who has established himself as one of the greatest heavyweight champions of all time and without a peer as defender of the throne.

Perhaps Conn had come to the end of his endurance. His energy may have been burned up with the slashing battle he gave Louis through the eighth and up to and including the twelfth round, when the challenger treated the amazed onlookers to the spectacle of Louis being pounded steadily about the ring by a lighter, fearless foeman.

Whatever it was, the battle started as it had been predicted it

Conn doubled up on the canvas and Louis standing over him at the end of the fight

would start, and it ended as it had been predicted it would end. Because, in advance, it had been said that Conn must rely on his speed if he were to survive and defeat Louis. It also had been told that Conn would drop the first time Louis hit him with a powerful punch to a vital spot.

Avoids Bomber's Punches

The surprise, in addition to the wonderful battle Conn made, came in the delay before Louis connected. This was a tribute to the ability of Conn, not only to avoid the Bomber's wallops, but his ability to withstand those that Louis landed. More, it was a testimonial to the surprising manner in which Conn fought in retaliation and sometimes on the attack, against the man every one else has feared since he ascended the throne.

One of the greatest heavyweight battles of recent years, the struggle was waged in an atmosphere reminiscent of older and better times in boxing. In the double-decked concrete and steel stand, in the temporary wooden chairs that had been placed on what is ordinarily the Giants' baseball playing field, men and women sat, in rows extending back as far as the eye could reach in the darkness.

They came from all sections of the country and from every walk of life. They came early and stayed late to thrill to a really great battle for the championship, one that will take its place alongside the best in ring history, from the standpoint of surprise, excitement and competitive appeal.

A sportsmanlike battle, it was cleanly fought, bitterly and cagily waged. It was tense with the element of the unexpected to a high degree.

Governors of near-by States were in the gathering. There were Mayors of cities, national leaders in politics, Representatives, Senators, State lawmakers, bankers, merchants, leaders of the country's commercial and industrial life, members of the clergy, stars of the stage and screen. They were drawn by the championship magnet and that uncertainty about whether the title would change hands, the majority, wishing it would, but feeling that it couldn't.

Fights True to Style

This great gathering saw Conn fight a battle that was true to his style, of necessity, but better than usual, though it proved inadequate. And the crowd saw Louis fight as a champion should, a champion who refused to become discouraged though he was buffeted about outlandishly at times.

Naturally, the greatest thrill came from Conn. The finish by Louis was an anti-climax. Most of those in the vast throng expected Joe to knock out the challenger, as he had done to challengers in fifteen previous defenses of the title. Few, however, expected of the frail-looking Conn the battle he flashed—least of all Louis, if the truth is known.

Unmistakably Louis has slipped. Even making allowances for style—the contrast in styles was inescapable—the champion is not the champion of old. He was not sure of himself last night, a fact which might be explained by the circumstance which found him in the ring with a veritable wraith for speed. But the speed that Louis once boasted himself is gone, the accuracy behind his punch is slipping. He is becoming heavy-footed and heavy-armed, weaknesses which

The champion ducking under Conn's guard in one of the early rounds   Times Wide World

were reflected as he floundered at times in his quest of the target that was Conn.

One thing remains undiminished with Louis and that cannot be denied. He still is an annihilating puncher. His right hand claims a victim when it lands. His left hook jars a foe to the heels and props him for the finishing potion that is in the right hand.

Surprises Most Onlookers

Conn, almost exclusively, boxed Louis through the first seven rounds. Having gone so far, Billy became confident. He became overconfident in the eighth and surprising most onlookers, was hammering his way past Louis in grand style.

The challenger started the fight on treacherous feet. He slipped coming out of his corner soon after the opening gong and, before the first round ended, he went down while pivoting to escape Louis's rush. Neither time was Conn struck a blow.

Through the first three rounds Conn sparred cautiously and skillfully, dancing before the shuffling, plodding Louis who moved steadily, stealthily in on the attack. Billy's plan was to stay away; Louis's was to get close and strike home with short jolts to the body and head. Louis struck a number of these blows in the first three rounds,

picking most of Conn's left hooks off in midair the meanwhile. The champion's blows, however, had no deterring effect on the sprightly Conn, who only once, in the third round, resorted to a covering stance as a defensive move. But the challenger ended the third with a flurry in which he drove Louis to the ropes under a fiery volley of lefts and rights to the head and body, amid the roars of the crowd.

Conn outdid himself in the fourth when he started making the champion's jaw the target for a succession of rights. They were blows driven home at long range, but, reflecting the lack of power in Conn's fighting armor, they only made Joe blink.

Shoots Home Left Hook

The challenger was proceeding with a daring attack in the fifth, when Louis suddenly shot home a left hook to the jaw. Conn staggered under the blow and sought retreat. But Louis was upon him, drilling lefts and rights to the head and face s Billy, lurching and staggering, covered against attack. The blows opened a cut over Conn's right eye. Another cut appeared on the bridge of his nose.

But Billy survived the storm and managed to keep out of harm's way in the sixth and in the seventh. Then, with the eighth, Conn launched a thrilling attack of his

own. He parried most of Louis's lunges early in the round and began making a target of Joe's jaw for right-hand smashes that went home straight and often. The blows lacked steam and merely flustered the titleholder. More important, however, is the fact that the success of his offensive lifted Conn's confidence.

This was reflected as the ninth started and Billy added a verbal assault to his fistic fire. "You got a tough fight tonight," it developed later, was what Conn said, although the words were indistinguishable at the time above the roar of the crowd. "That's right," replied Louis, who continued shuffling into a rival who was banging him around scandalously.

Trades Blows Willingly

Repeatedly Conn drilled home with his right to the jaw in the ninth. He ripped full-arm rights to the body. Left jabs brought blood from Louis's nose. A left hook to the body hurt Joe before the bell. All the time Louis was helpless to counter the fire.

Infuriated in the tenth, Louis pressed his foe hard. Once Conn slipped on the wet canvas in his own corner in escaping a fierce lunge. Billy traded blows with the champion, giving as good as he received and sometimes better.

Through the eleventh Conn

fought gallantly as he hammered the titleholder from all angles, beating Louis about the face and jaw with rights at long range and about the heart and body at close quarters. Louis winced under some of these blows. He was infuriated under others. But he could do nothing about them.

In the twelfth Conn, after an exchange in which one of Louis's lefts cut him under the left eye, suddenly rocked Louis on his heels with a full-arm left hook to the jaw. Staggering, Louis dived into a clinch to keep from falling while Conn fought furiously in a bid for a knockout.

Maybe this shot that went true and staggered the champion made Conn overconfident. At any rate, he was the pursuer instead of the pursued as the thirteenth started and he made the mistake of going too close to Louis too often.

Battered by the desperate champion's powerful lefts and rights about the head, Conn suddenly emerged from close quarters flailing furiously for Louis's jaw with lefts and rights in an outburst that electrified the crowd.

Lands Flush on Jaw

Suddenly Louis's right shot out on an opening with a blow that landed flush on Conn's jaw. The challenger's knees buckled. He swayed backward. He was hurt, and Louis knew it. And Joe thundered in with that savagery that is his characteristic when he has a foe in distress.

About the head and face Louis fired countless rights and lefts while Conn sought to cover and retreat. Some of the blows missed, but many of them landed, carrying force even against Billy's defense of raised gloves. The Bomber shifted his fire to the body. Blows there hurt Conn, sapped the speed from his legs, took the last ounce of his endurance. Billy was slipping about uncertainly when Louis drove over the right-hand blow to the jaw that toppled him in defeat within two seconds of the end of the round, and shattered a dream of a championship.

The police detail was the largest ever assigned to a boxing event in this city. A total of 2,250 of New York's finest patrolled the Polo Grounds, inside and out, and the streets of Harlem.

Chief Inspector Edward M. Butler was in charge of the detail inside the park. Deputy Chief Inspector John J. DeMartino was in charge of the outside detail.

Seven hundred police, some of them carrying the old-fashioned night sticks, patrolled Harlem streets from 8 P. M. on. More than 300 others were on reserve duty between the East 126th Street and the West 135th Street stations. There were 200 detectives, sixty-six mounted police, thirty-three motorcycle men and two emergency squads on the job.

Trouble was not expected. It has been characteristic of Louis battles hereabouts that they have been taken in stride, with a minimum of disorder in the Harlem district, regardless of whether he won or lost. But the Police Department, at the same time, wanted to take no chances.

Plenty of Betting

Betting on the fight was active, with no change in the odds. Louis was the favorite at 1 to 4 to win and the price on him to score a knockout was 5 to 11. Trick bets on the number of rounds were numerous but inconsequential. The volume was reported on decision. The 1-to-4 odds appealed to many Conn supporters and others who inevitably "invest" whenever odds are better than 1 to 2 or 3.

Among those seen at the ringside were James A. Farley, John F. Cur-

ry, former Mayor John O'Brien, Mayor Frank Hague of Jersey City, J. Edgar Hoover, George Ruppert, Edward G. Barrow, Leo Bondy, Bob Hope, ex-Governor James Cox of Ohio, William F. Carey and George Weiss.

Lending a note that was in keeping with the time was the presence of many soldiers and sailors in their olive drab and their navy blue. They were sprinkled through all sections of the arena.

June 19, 1941

N. B. A. REAFFIRMS 'FREEZING' OF TITLES

Rights of Champions in Armed Forces Will Be Protected for Duration, Says Greene

DUTY OF BOXING STRESSED

Head of Association Urges Civilians in Sport to Fan Interest in the Ring

PATERSON, N. J., Oct. 16 (AP)—Freezing of titles for champions in the armed services today was pronounced as a National Boxing Association policy for the war's duration.

"A man in the service is entitled to complete protection of his championship under all circumstances until he is able to defend; this is the N. B. A. policy announced early in the conflict," Abe J. Greene, head of the association, said in commenting on a proposal by Jerry Giesler, chairman of the California Boxing Commission, that such action be taken.

In classes where champions are not in the service, Greene declared, boxing owes it to the public to keep active.

Entertainment Value Cited

"Frozen titles mean frozen interest," Greene remarked. "If boxing is to continue during the war as a means of providing entertainment on the home front, then everything possible must be done to maintain it on a lively and active plane."

The civilian champion ought "to carry the ball for his comrade champions in uniform," Greene continued, "because if he is a fighting champion he can keep interest in the sport alive for the day when the other fellow comes home and can fight."

Greene took up the situation in the heavyweight division, of which Champion Joe Louis and two leading contenders, Billy Conn and Melio Bettina, are soldiers.

"All any boxing authorities could hope to do to maintain even a tepid interest in the class would be to set up the outstanding contend-

ers and keep them fighting among themselves with the hope of extracting from the potpourri the best of the lot," Greene commented.

Clearer Viewpoint Expected

"By that time the government authorities will have either relaxed their policy of restricting service men's boxing or will have tightened it so that no one in the service will be fighting except for Uncle Sam.

"Under such circumstances the best that civilian contenders could hope to attain would be some designation like sub-champion or 'pretender,' but at all times it would be understood that the service man champion would be unquestioned titleholder with full claim to every right that goes with a title, recognition, major share of purses, etc."

October 17, 1942

RETURN TITLE BOUTS OPPOSED BY N. B. A.

Ruling Adopted in Move to Give Logical Contenders Chance

PATERSON, N. J., Nov. 23 (AP)—The National Boxing Association announced today a move to end "shotgun" championship return bouts and "chain-store" fights not "based on championship merit."

President Abe J. Greene said the organization would deny championship recognition to any contest unless the proposed match first had been submitted to the N. B. A. for approval.

The ruling was adopted, Greene said, "to avoid the see saw game such as is now operating between Bob Montgomery and Beau Jack, in which first one, then the other, gets a return bout.

"If a man loses a title, and there is public demand or a sportsmanlike reason for a return bout, naturally the N. B. A. would approve," Greene said, "but the very managers and fighters who cry for a championship opportunity resort to all kinds of ruses and subterfuge to avoid giving other contenders the same chance."

He cited as another example the return contest between Phil Terranova, featherweight champion, and Jackie Callura, the man he dethroned.

"Callura accepted Terranova as a challenger in New Orleans almost at the expiration of his time limit for title defense. Apparently, however, he exacted from Terranova a new contract for a return engagement, which the champion's manager now insists was wrung from him. This is not our problem, however. It is for the New Orleans commission to pass on. Now Terranova objects to meeting Callura again on the ground that he has defeated him twice."

Greene said the N. B. A. declines "to recognize a third Callura-Terranova contest as a title defense. We do not regard Callura as a logical contender."

Greene explained that Terranova stands suspended in all N. B. A. States until he fulfills a contract to fight Callura in New Orleans,

or until the Louisiana commission lifts his suspension.

November 24, 1943

Soldiers Overseas Will See Louis Box

By The Associated Press.

WASHINGTON, July 10—Sgt. Joe Louis is going back to boxing—in exhibitions at Army posts around the world.

Whether he will go back to professional fighting after the war, the heavyweight champion said today at the War Department, will depend on how long the war lasts.

Details of his world tour, on which he also will give lessons in physical conditioning, remain to be worked out, Louis said. He expressed the hope that he can take his old sparring partner, Sgt. George Nicholson, along. Joe also wants Ray Robinson and Sgt. Jackie Wilson, boxers, with him.

Now on furlough, Louis said he expects to play in a golf tournament in Chicago beginning July 19, adding that as a golfer "I'll just be one of the crowd."

Last year Secretary of War Stimson canceled a projected title fight between Louis and Corp. Billy Conn. There is a chance they might meet in the exhibition tour. Conn was said by the Army to be now at Camp Campbell, Ky.

July 11, 1943

LOUIS STOPS CONN IN EIGHTH ROUND AND RETAINS TITLE

Rights and Lefts to the Head End Yankee Stadium Bout After Slow Start

45,266 ATTEND CONTEST

Receipts of $1,925,564 Also Are Short of Predictions— Billy Retires From Ring

By JAMES P. DAWSON

With a volley of thunderous rights and lefts to the head and jaw, a succession of blows that

THE CHAMPION SUCCESSFULLY DEFENDING HIS HEAVYWEIGHT TITLE LAST NIGHT

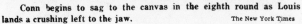

Conn begins to sag to the canvas in the eighth round as Louis lands a crushing left to the jaw.
The New York Times

Referee Eddie Joseph orders Louis to a neutral corner before starting to count over the fallen Conn.
Associated Press

came suddenly, with flashing speed, unerring aim and paralyzing power, Joe Louis last night knocked out Billy Conn, his Pittsburgh challenger, in the eighth round of their scheduled fifteen-round world heavyweight title battle in the Yankee Stadium.

Striking with the speed and accuracy of a cobra, Louis crushed his foremost rival in defeat after the eighth round had gone exactly 2 minutes 19 seconds, bringing to a close in dramatic manner a battle that had been marked for the most part by purely perfunctory gestures through seven previous rounds as a crowd of 45,266, which paid receipts of $1,925,564, looked on expectantly.

For seven rounds Louis had stalked his rival before unloosing the murderous fire that ended the battle. For seven rounds the champion had pressed hard on a rival who was in full flight, his one aim the destruction of the smiling-faced challenger whose desperate retreat seemed to taunt the titleholder in this first post-war battle between two ex-soldiers for which boxing followers waited five years.

End of a Career

And, when he finally administered the coup which a majority had predicted in advance of the battle, Louis wrote finis to the career of Conn. For, in his dressing room after the fight, Conn announced his retirement from the ring. "I'm convinced I haven't got

it any more, so I'm quitting. This is my last fight," said Conn.

Louis made his twenty-second defense of the title he won back in 1937 with this latest victory, his thirtieth ring triumph in an unbroken string. He added a fresh chapter to a career which stamps him as one of the foremost titleholders in point of competition and ring earnings.

He wrote this chapter with greater ease than he had experienced in many of his previous battles, certainly with less trouble than he encountered five years ago when he required thirteen rounds to knock out Conn after staggering under the punches of the challenger in the twelfth.

Declines to Vary Plan

Last night Conn landed only one clean, telling blow. It came early in the second round, a smashing right to the jaw which shook Louis noticeably. But, determined not to vary a preconceived battle plan, Conn did not follow the momentary advantage this punch gave him. Instead, he resorted to a back-pedalling defensive style that, obviously, was calculated to enable him to survive and at the same time wear Louis down.

This plan overlooked the fact that Louis is a determined fighter and a capable boxer. It followed as a natural consequence, therefore, that Louis, forcing the fighting and doing most of the punching, had things more or less his

own way. Conn's boxing was discounted by the stiff, straight left jabs with which the champion tilted the challenger's head back not once but often.

In flashes Louis rushed close as he pinned Conn along the ropes or backed him near a neutral corner, delivering rights to the liver and ribs and jolting, short lefts and rights to the head, which lowered Conn's resistance as they shook his confidence.

Louis was pressing forward as he had been doing from the clang of the first bell, when the punch that won the battle arched through the air. It was a solid right-hand smash that landed with stunning, bruising effect on Conn's face.

Cut Under Left Eye

Coming shortly after the eighth round opened, Conn went back on his heels under the impact, a smile on his face, an open acknowledgment it had been a good punch and had stung. Blood trickled from a cut under the left eye opened by that one smash.

Louis knew he had his man and acted with the assurance that is concealed under the expressionless mask he wears. He stalked Conn, shuffling forward, alert, fists raised, arms poised to strike at the slightest opening. Conn retreated, pecking and pawing with his left, futile, feeble blows which Louis brushed aside. Conn's aim was to gain time, to shake off the effects of the blow. Louis' plan was to strike again before Conn's head cleared.

Backing his foe near a neutral corner, Louis crashed home a left and a right to the jaw under which Conn spun around, shaken and staggered. Another left and a right to the jaw and Conn crumpled to the feet of the Brown Bomber, collapsing like a deflated balloon, stretching out finally at full length on his back, while Referee Eddie Joseph crouched above him, tolling off the count.

As the ten-second count proceeded, Conn made as if he would rise. The muscles of his legs flexed, his arms moved, his body worked convulsively as the count reached "seven." The crowd which had been disappointed earlier, the fans who had been heard to boo as early rounds ran their course without exciting action, were afoot raising a noisy din, above which it was hard to distinguish the count.

Referee Assists Challenger

At "eight" Conn's convulsive movement was almost imperceptible. He was getting to a sitting position at "nine." He was still striving for that position when Referee Joseph said "ten and out," and stooped to assist the beaten challenger to his feet as a sheepish grin spread over Billy's bleeding face.

Watching this latest spectacular victory of the boxing-fighting marvel that is Louis was a crowd that made up in distinction what it lacked in numbers. It was a disappointing gathering in the sense that it fell far short of the 70,000 spectators and the $2,250,000 gate Promoter Mike Jacobs had forecast. On the evidence of the statistics, it could hardly be termed what is inelegantly called a "flop."

It was not announced whether the receipts included the $225,000

The end came in 2.19 of the eighth round, with Referee Joseph tolling the fatal ten over the challenger as Louis looks on

The New York Times

Promoter Jacobs received for the radio and television rights. The addition of these items would explain the $2,000,000 gate the Twentieth Century S. C. head announced more than a week ago.

The widespread, unseen crowd, coupled with the record-making prices charged for the battle, may explain the fact that, while the bout fell into place as the eighth million-dollar gate of boxing history, it fell far short of the record receipts of $2,658,660 which 104,943 fans paid under a more moderate price scale back in 1927 to see Jack Dempsey's famed battle of the long count against Gene Tunney in Chicago.

Last night's gate was the second largest in ring history and set a record for New York City.

Promoter Jacobs placed a $100 ringside charge on this fight, the heaviest impost to be found in all the history of boxing. His intermediate prices for reserved seats were $50, $30 and $20. His lowest price for a reserved seat in the bleachers was $10. He placed 10,-000 standing-room admissions at $5 on sale a few hours before the title struggle started.

Apparently the prices didn't appeal to the masses. The fight was broadcast to all corners of the country on a nation-wide hook-up, short-waved to distant parts of the world, televised through Washington, Philadelphia and the local area on the most elaborate undertaking of its kind in this latest development of the ether waves, and the fans had ample opportunity to follow the progress of the battle without digging into the exchequer, even in this day of cheap money.

Nevertheless the bout attracted its measure of prominent persons. Delegates to the United Nations, some of them with their staffs,

Bout Finances at à Glance

Paid attendance—45,266.

Gross Receipts—$1,925,564.

Federal tax—$385,113.

State tax—$96,278.

Louis' share (40 per cent of net) —$577,669.

Conn's share (20 per cent of net) —$228,834.

Promoter's share (from which estimated expenses of $300,000 must be deducted)—$577,669.

were reported at the ringside, along with figures of prominence in the nation, State and city.

Stars of the stage, screen and radio, leaders in finance, commerce, industry, in the various sports fields, doctors, judges, lawyers, past and present champions of the ring—all were gathered in the crowd which filled the field seat section, the $100 circle, as it were, solidly, but hardly filled the three decks of the permanent stands.

Some Given Away

Not all of the $100 seats were sold, although the heaviest part of them disappeared under pressure of an early rush which was responsible for the price maximum in the first place. Some of those which were sold on a no-refund basis were given away at the last moment. Others were sold independently, it was reported, at marked down prices. No section of the huge plant was completely sold out. Empty seats were gaping holes all over the stands.

Those who saw the bout witnessed a struggle that lacked the spectacular elements of the fight these rivals furnished before they went off to war, yet it was tense

with expectancy from the opening bell. Its dramatic finish provided the excitement, revealing Conn as a hollow shell of the daring, reckless, ambitious challenger of 1941 and Louis as the expressionless, shuffling, plodding tower of human dynamite before whom heavyweights of all sizes and varying descriptions have crumpled since the Brown Bomber started one of the longest title reigns the ring has known.

Conn fought the battle that had been forecast in his long training siege. Since he was faster afoot than the champion, the Pittsburgher had to try to capitalize on this speed and what shiftiness it gave him. He could not undertake to punch with Louis. He had to try to stab and peck with his left, keeping out of range of Louis' murderous blows as he sought to reduce the titleholder's stamina and put pressure on thickened legs which some thought could not go fifteen rounds.

Circles Louis' Right

Conn followed that style religiously for seven rounds and survived. He circled to Louis' right, back-pedaling furiously all the time, although experts were agreed in advance that Conn's best plan would be to circle to Louis' left and keep the champion off balance.

The desirability of this move seems to have substantiation in the events unfolded as the battle ended. It was a right that split his eye which started Conn on the path to defeat. He was circling right into the blow, increasing its power. Had he been circling in the opposite direction he would have been going away from such a punch, with his right guard high against possible left hook exposure.

In the final analysis, however, Louis called the turn in a training interlude a week or so ago. "He can run, but he can't hide." said the champion, and he proved the truth of this assertion as speedily as conditions warranted.

Louis also proved he had his old punch, the sharpness that makes that punch more effective and the alertness which enables him to drive like a piston through the slightest opening. And he proved once again he is a great champion, a gentleman, a sportsman.

Louis twice stepped back to avoid taking an unfair advantage of Conn when the challenger slipped. Conn slipped first in the fourth round. Louis stepped back, allowed his foe to regain an erect position, then touched gloves in the ring's gesture of fairness. Again, in the sixth round, Conn slipped, this time to his right knee as he stuck a straight left in Louis' midsection. Again Joe backed off and permitted his rival to come erect before making a move to resume hostilities.

Far Below 1941 Form

These slips demonstrated that Conn's legs were not the springy legs that carried him through twelve rounds against Louis in 1941. The battle action proved, too, that Conn, in the best condition possible for him, was far below the fearless, confident challenger Louis faced five years ago.

The score sheets of the three bout officials spoke eloquently of this, too. Whereas Conn was ahead on points at the end of the twelfth round in their 1941 fight, Louis was far out front in the scoring of last night's fray. Two voting slips had the champion in front, five rounds to one, with one even. This is what the majority of ringside critics had, giving the first round even because of lack of action, and awarding the third to Conn. Judges Jack O'Sullivan and Frank Forbes were in agreement on this.

Referee Joseph, however, had Louis in front, five rounds to two. He gave Louis the first round, doubtless on the score that the champion made the fighting. He gave Conn the second and third, attaching particular significance to that right-hand drive Conn landed on Louis' jaw shortly after the second opened. In the third round

Conn outfought and outboxed Louis. But, in the rounds he won, Louis was far and away the master.

Louis' success with a left jab against Conn must have been a revelation to those who had seen the 1941 battle and to others whose appraisal of Louis' boxing ability had dimmed because of the champion's mighty punch. It came as a surprise to camp followers who, after watching Louis in training, concluded the years of ring in-

activity had dulled the titleholder's boxing capabilities.

Billy Takes No Chances

After a dull first round, Conn aroused the excitement of the crowd in the second when he cracked a right solidly to Louis' jaw. The champion shook under the blow and the crowd roared. Neither the success of the punch nor the encouraging roar of the crowd, however, could lead Conn into another daring move. He had steeled himself against making

the mistake through which Louis exploded his fists in their first meeting and he was taking no chances.

Conn opened the third round with a solid left hook to the head and followed with a combination left hook to the body and head. He made Louis miss awkwardly in what little action the round held. After that, however, Conn never had a chance.

June 20, 1946

39,827 See Zale Knock Out Graziano and Retain World Middleweight Honors

LEFT HOOK TO JAW ENDS FIGHT IN 6TH

Zale Records a Spectacular Triumph Over Graziano in Yankee Stadium Ring

SAVAGE BATTLE IS WAGED

Champion, Near Defeat, Comes Back With Great Courage to Conquer East Sider

By JAMES P. DAWSON

Tony Zale, a fighting champion who refused to crumple before the mighty punches of one of the most devastating hitters the ring has developed in recent years, retained his world middleweight title last night by knocking out Rocky Graziano, doughty east sider, in the sixth round of a scheduled fifteen-round battle at the Yankee Stadium.

A crowd of 39,827 fight fans, who paid $342,497, transformed into a joy-crazed, wildly yelling mob at the spectacle of one of the greatest middleweight title struggles since Stanley Ketchel ruled the class, saw Zale dispose of his most dangerous challenger in 1 minute 43 seconds of the sixth, bringing to a close a contest that was savagely and furiously fought from the very first second of the first round.

Floored with a left hook to the jaw, Graziano squatted on the ring floor as the count proceeded above him in unison between referee Ruby Goldstein and the knock-down-timekeeper, Johnny Burns. Rocky, trying to pull himself erect, grabbed the ring ropes, first the lower one, then the strand in the middle. He seemed perfectly aware of what was going on about him, although the din of the crowd was terrific. He must have heard the count as referee Goldstein stood above him, yelling into his ear and Burns immediately be-

MIDDLEWEIGHT CHALLENGER GOES DOWN TO STAY

Rocky Graziano after being floored by Tony Zale in the sixth round of their bout at Yankee Stadium Referee Ruby Goldstein is coming around from behind the champion to pick up the count. The New York Times

neath him, outside the ring, shouting the count at the top of his voice.

Clings to the Ropes

The count went on through "five, six, seven, eight, nine." Then Rocky was astir. He had a grip on the middle rope. He was rising. He wanted another chance at that precious title.

He was getting up as Goldstein's arm descended with the stroke of "ten," but, he wasn't quite erect as Goldstein's arm spread in the time-honored motion that means "and out." But just at that moment Rocky was up and ready for battle.

Goldstein had counted him out,

however, and despite Rocky's frenzied efforts, he clasped the beaten challenger firmly in strong arms that used to throw lethal punches when Ruby was a contender for the world welterweight title.

Struggling desperately, Graziano tried to free himself and resume the battle. But, Goldstein clung to him, shouting into his ear that he had been counted out, as his handlers hopped through the ropes to lead the struggling Graziano to his corner.

Apparently unhurt, in full possession of his faculties, Graziano, with a sheepish grin of resignation, finally desisted, and, while handlers were ministering to the conquering champion in the corner,

under protection of a police cordon, the beaten challenger quickly left the scene amid the cheers for Zale which echoed through the vast arena.

Cheers for the Loser

There were cheers, too, for Rocky, the thunderous puncher who had gone down to defeat so gloriously against a champion who had lived up to every tradition of this title division, a class whose greatness has now been restored.

Zale came back from the brink of defeat to score his sensational knockout. And he did it with a right hand that was injured in the second round. Graziano survived a near-knockout in the first session and came crashing back in a furious bid for the triumph. He failed only because Zale is a better fighter, a greater ring general, a sturdier man under punishment. Moreover Tony is better equipped to deal out the finishing blow, though he is eight years older than Graziano, has been boxing eight years longer, and after four years in the Navy, was making the first defense of the title he won in 1941. Zale enlisted before he had a chance to defend the crown he won from Georgie Abrams just before Pearl Harbor.

In the final analysis, it was the body-battering to which he was subjected that beat Graziano, robbed him of victory when he had the champion rocking and tottering. But Zale found the weakness in Graziano's armor and battered it until it burst at the seams.

After the battle Rocky said a right to his mid-section hurt him more than the left hook to the jaw which was the final blow.

Heard Final Count

"I heard 'eight, nine, ten,' and it seemed to come quickly," said the beaten challenger. "But it was a right to the body that hurt me more than anything else."

Zale had to be a great champion to win. He had to pace himself expertly, had to weather a storm of blows that would have crushed a man with less courage, less stamina. His foe was a crude, primitive fighting type, a younger man with only a little boxing skill, but a Stone Age man when stung—throwing punches furiously, recklessly, viciously, from all angles, with crushing, paralyzing power.

Tony seemed weary and sorely hurt just before he came on to score his knockout. Notwithstanding the result, Graziano was the fresher of the two at the finish. But this is only a testimonial to a fighting spirit which has carried Zale to the top and will keep him there for a while.

The champion left the ring with a right hand that may be fractured, according to Dr. Vincent Nardiello of the State Athletic Commission, and an upper lip which will require stitching. The beaten challenger had only a bloody nose in addition to the jar his pride suffered at this first knockout of his career.

Graziano went to the floor, under a solid, short left hook to the jaw half-way through the first round, and took a count of four before arising. Zale tried hard for a knockout then and there. But, Rocky covered well against the champion's fire, retreated until his head cleared and, before the bell, was battering Zale with a succession of right-handers to the head and jaw that had the crowd yelling wildly. Zale was teetering under the punching as the bell sounded.

The Volcano Erupts

Encouraged by the effect of his punches in this display, Graziano was a human volcano in action in the second round, when he charged Zale all over the ring, battering and staggering the champion with rights and lefts to the head and jaw despite Zale's courageous counter-fire with hands to body and head. During this assault Zale's lip was split. The danger increased as the round progressed, until, finally, four successive rights to the jaw toppled Tony amid a deafening roar from the amazed onlookers.

Referee Goldstein had counted.

"three" over the fallen titleholder when the bell sounded the end of the round. The champion was able to go to his corner unassisted.

In the third round Graziano was again the fighter of maniacal fury. He hammered the champion all over the ring with rights and lefts to the head, face and jaw until it seemed Zale must drop. But Zale survived the storm, though in distress and apparently near the end. But Graziano could not land that finishing punch.

When Zale came up for the fourth he was amazingly fresh. He shifted his fire to the body and kept it going, occasionally making Rocky wince with left hand smashes to the face and jaw. It was evident that the body fire was hurting Rocky as he retreated through most of the round. Rocky was wilting.

Presses the Advantage

Early in the fifth Zale pressed.

his advantage, concentrating mostly on the body with both hands and for a time Rocky backed away. Then he suddenly charged furiously with a tigerish recklessness that is his greatest characteristic and began again to hammer Zale.

Many observers thought Zale was through as he staggered and backed away from the ponderous rights and lefts which rained on his head and about his face.

But the champion came up fresh again for the sixth and, weathering Graziano's early, desperate attack, finally crashed over a right to the stomach which banged Graziano over near the ropes. A left hook to the jaw, and Rocky sank on his haunches. And, in a few seconds a blazing battle for the middleweight title was a glorious chapter in ring history.

September 28, 1946

Doyle Dies of Injuries Suffered In Cleveland Bout With Robinson

Brain Operation Is Unavailing and the Los Angeles Boxer Is Unconscious to the End— Coroner Plans Investigation

CLEVELAND, June 25 (UP) — Jimmy Doyle, Los Angeles fighter, died today of injuries caused "largely by blows to the jaw and face" suffered in his welterweight championship fight last night at the Arena with Ray (Sugar) Robinson.

County Coroner Samuel Gerber ruled that Doyle died of a cerebral hemorrhage and said that "the greater damage was done by blows to the jaw and face, although his head striking the ring floor may have added to the damage."

Gerber said that "despite unholy pressure" to stop the investigation, he would continue his questioning of all connected with the tragedy. He refused to disclose the source of the "pressure" but said he had informed those "unidentified persons that no power whatsoever will prevent me going through with it." He said that no one connected with the Robinson camp brought such pressure on him.

Gerber said that after he finished his questioning and a final and complete autopsy report was in he would decide whether or not he would ask for Grand Jury action.

Doyle died at 3:25 P. M. in St. Vincent's Charity Hospital where he had been taken unconscious from the Arena last night after he was technically knocked out in the eighth round by Robinson. He never regained consciousness.

Autopsy Shows Hemorrhage

Gerber said an autopsy of Doyle's body showed the hemorrhage was largely in the rear part of the brain.

The 22-year-old fighter died after a game, but losing, seventeen-hour battle for life. A delicate brain operation failed to save him.

Jimmy Doyle
Associated Press

The Cleveland Boxing Commission's examining physician, Dr. A. F. Hagedorn, said that Doyle was in good health before the fight. He told a hearing called by Mayor Thomas Burke that he believed the fighter's death was caused by a new injury because X-rays taken before the fight showed Doyle was in good shape.

Dr. Hagedorn also testified that Doyle had been approved for fighting in New York State on April 11 by Dr. Vincent Nardiello of that state's Athletic Commission.

Doyle's Purse Held Up

Chairman Andy Putka of the local commission held up Doyle's purse of $11,841. He said the money would go to Probate Court where the fighter's relatives could claim it. Robinson's purse of $25,000 was not held up.

The Californian was sent to the canvas by the champion's left hook last night. His head hit the floor and bounced twice. Doyle tried to rise but sank back.

With the young challenger when

he died was Father James Nagle, chaplain of the hospital.

Funeral arrangements were to be made by Doyle's brother, Edward, who was flying to Cleveland from the West Coast.

Doyle's death was the first resulting from injuries in a championship fight in modern ring history.

Other ring deaths included those of Ernie Schaaf, who died from injuries received at the hands of Primo Carnera of Italy in New York's Madison Square Garden in 1933, and of Luther McCarty, who died from a neck broken when knocked out by Arthur Pelky at Calgary, Alta., Canada, in 1913. Twelve fighters died from ring injuries throughout the world last year.

Dr. Hagedorn, who attended Doyle in the Arena's first aid room immediately after the fight, said it appeared to him that the most damage had been done by Doyle's head bouncing off the ring floor, rather than from Robinson's hook.

Out of Ring Nine Months

Doyle was near death fifteen months ago from a concussion suffered in the same ring at the hands of middleweight Artie Levine. He stayed out of the ring for nine months before attempting a comeback.

In the hospital last night Doyle was placed under an oxygen tent. He never once took an unaided breath because of a paralysis caused by brain injury.

Dr. Spencer Braden, a brain specialist, operated on Doyle at 3 A. M. to release pressure caused by a blood clot.

Dr. Braden said that "extensive" damage had been done to the boxer's brain.

Robinson, who joked with reporters after the fight, later learned that Doyle was in critical condition and went to the hospital before dawn.

He said he was "sure sorry" but that he "didn't have any idea he was seriously hurt when I left the ring. He was a great kid and a swell fighter."

Started Boxing in 1941

Jimmy Doyle was born Jimmy Delaney in August, 1924, in Los Angles and was of French-American parentage. He launched his boxing career in 1941. Including the fatal bout against Ray Robinson, Doyle's career encompassed fifty-two ring engagements in six years of activity. He suffered only seven defeats, three of the losses by knockouts, including the Robinson knockout, and four on decision.

In his early days Doyle was tutored by such ring greats of the past as James J. Jeffries and the late Jack Johnson, two former heavyweight champions who took an interest in the youth and undertook to develop his boxing capabilities. Most of his career Doyle spent fighting in California rings. It was not until late in 1944 that he came East. He was a clever, scientific boxer, whose style lacked appeal, although it was effective.

June 26, 1947

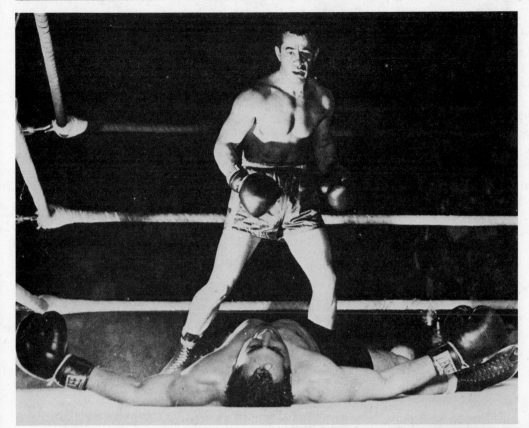

Rocky Graziano (standing) briefly held the middleweight championship in the late 1940's. He is remembered especially for his three gruelling fights with Tony Zale. Like Barney Ross, he was also the subject of a film biography: *Somebody Up There Likes Me.*

"Jersey" Joe Walcott (right) is shown here retaining his heavyweight title against Ezzard Charles in 1952. Walcott, who lost two close fights to Joe Louis in the late 1940's, eventually surrendered his championship to Rocky Marciano.

Graziano Knocks Out Zale in Sixth Round to Take World Middleweight Title

18,547 SEE REFEREE STOP CHICAGO FIGHT

Graziano's Blows Drape Zale Helplessly Over Ropes at 2:10 of 6th in Stadium

---

RALLY LAUNCHED IN FIFTH

New Yorker Pounded in Early Rounds, Floored in Third— Receipts $422,918

By JAMES P. DAWSON
Special to THE NEW YORK TIMES.

CHICAGO, July 16 — Rocky Graziano is the new middleweight champion of the world.

The doughty Brooklynite with the devastating punch fought back from the brink of knockout defeat tonight in the Stadium to thrill a sweltering crowd of 18,547 that paid record receipts of $422,918 for an indoor boxing show to view the spectacle, with a six-round knockout of thirty-three-year-old Tony Zale, Gary (Ind.) veteran who has held the title since 1941.

A thunderous shower of full-arm rights and lefts to the head, face and jaw draped Zale over the middle strand of the ring ropes when the sixth round had gone 2 minutes 10 seconds. Under that fire, Zale was rendered helpless, though his stout, fighting heart refused to let him go down.

It was patent, however, that Zale was through when he sagged against and then collapsed over the ropes. Referee Johnny Behr, hesitating only a moment to pull Graziano off the back of the helpless Zale, waved an end to the fight, a signal which made Graziano world's champion.

Wise Move by Referee

It was announced officially that the fight ended with a "technical knockout." No fighter, however, ever was more thoroughly knocked out than Zale. Had Referee Behr permitted resumption of the battle, he would have invited disaster. Zale, who looked like a winner in the second round, was hopelessly beaten at the end, his brain awhirl, his senses numbed, his legs wabbly, unsteady things which supported him not so much as his ring bravery.

A thunderous roar welled from a distinguished crowd as a gladiator who had appeared on the verge of a knockout earlier hammered back to a glorious triumph. Every walk of life, political, judicial, professional, business, financial, stage, screen, radio and religious, was represented in the crowd which

AS THE CHALLENGER BECAME CHAMPION LAST NIGHT

Tony Zale crumples on the ropes under rain of blows landed by Rocky Graziano in sixth round of their bout in Chicago.

Associated Press Wirephoto

literally melted in the humidity of the indoor arena, to be rewarded with a battle that was to all practical purposes a repetition of the September encounter in New York between these rivals, but with a different result.

After the battle, Zale said the enervating heat had sapped his strength. That may be true, but the paralyzing punches of Graziano unquestionably had more than a little influence in the champion's complete collapse.

Thrilled with victory immediately after the battle, Graziano, over the radio from the ring, shouted above the din of the crowd: "Mama, the bad boy done it."

Barred in New York State

He was winging a message to his mother in Brooklyn, letting her know that a fighter barred in his native New York State was going

home with a ring title rich in tradition and financial production.

He will go back to a curious situation which finds him ineligible in New York because his license last winter was revoked, following an investigation there by the District Attorney's office and the State Athletic Commission, of charges Graziano had failed to report a bribe offer. New York State, therefore, has a world middleweight champion, just about the most spectacular since the days of the late Stanley Ketchel, who is barred from appearing in New York rings and from whom, consequently, official recognition must be withheld.

This unprecedented state of affairs, however, does not affect in any way the fact that Graziano is king of the ring's 160-pound fighters. He won that title cleanly, decisively, bravely, in a typically

vicious demonstration of the fighting style which has made him one of the sport's spectacular figures.

That he came from behind to batter his way to the crown is officially a part of the Illinois State Athletic Commission's records. Referee Behr's voting card had Zale in front by 28 points to 22. Cards of both judges, Art Oberg and Harold Marovitz, scored 27 points for Zale and 23 for Graziano.

A Spectacular Fight

This point distribution was justified in just about the most spectacular middleweight fight this city has seen. The writer had Zale in front, four rounds to one. Not until the fifth did Graziano appear to advantage. Then it was he uncorked the recovery which presaged Zale's doom.

That was the turning point. For

the first time, it became evident Zale lacked the spontaneity on attack that had been his unforgettable characteristic last September.

That admirers expected Zale to repeat was evident from the betting odds as the battle started. He was favored at 10 to 13 and the general expectation was that victory would go the champion's way by a knockout.

For that matter, Graziano's supporters expected a Graziano victory by a knockout. They cashed dividends on the courage of their convictions.

They had some apprehensive early moments, though. Zale, ripping and slashing with more accuracy and effect than Graziano as the battle started, leveled his fire repeatedly at the mid-section, where he knew from experience that Rocky was weakest.

Through the first round, Graziano rushed in accustomed style, swinging wildly, daringly, full-arm with lefts and rights for the jaw, trying to score a quick knockout. Three successive rights thudded against Zale's chin and his knees buckled.

A left and a right sent the champion reeling, but nobody thought that particularly dangerous. It had happened before Graziano had floored Zale and the champion had got off the floor to win. It was expected, more or less, that he might go down again.

That Zale didn't crumple was both a testimonial to his steel-like jaw and indomitable fighting spirit and a reflection on Graziano's marksmanship. Not only did he refuse to topple, but he fought back blazingly, drilling solid lefts and rights to Graziano's body and staggering Rocky with occasional short rights to the jaw which sent the challenger reeling against the ropes.

A right ripped open a cut over Rocky's left eye. Thudding left hooks started a swelling about the right optic. Steady application of punishing blows had Rocky's face a crimson smear thereafter, with his right eye closing gradually until the dramatic finish.

Hammered steadily through the late stages of the first round, Graziano rushed out with a sweeping left hook for the jaw opening the second, but a few short lefts and rights reopened the cut over his left eye and body fire had the challenger retreating and covering. Intermittently Graziano fought back, but he was wild with most of his blows and Zale hammered steadily, cautiously, solidly, with lefts and rights, shifting his attack from head to body or body to head, as openings presented. For the most part, Graziano missed desperate thrusts calculated to stem this battering tide.

Graziano Floored in Third

Graziano went down under a short right to the jaw early in the third round, toppled cleanly by a powerful punch which glanced off his chin with momentary numbing power. He was up, smiling sheepishly through a crimson-smeared face, before a count could be started.

Zale hammered his rival all over the ring, dealing out solid smashes with both hands to the body which had Graziano doubled, shifting to the head and face and grazing the jaw with wallops which rocked Rocky back on his heels. The champion ignored Graziano's occasional desperate lunges as the challenger retreating, sought to turn the tide with one blow. The

end of the round found Graziano weary and shaken and there was a feeling the challenger was on the way to defeat.

In the fourth, however, Zale appeared weary and contented himself with boxing Graziano. The challenger, of course, was wary in the face of this transition, but swung savagely with round-house rights for the jaw in retreat.

One of those blows glanced off Zale's shoulder and provoked a light counter by the champion. Zale missed like a novice, sprawling on his hands and knees. The spectacle was eloquent in the light of what followed, for the fifth round saw a complete change in the battle.

Rocky Leaps to Attack

Graziano leaped to the attack in the fifth, starting with three rights to the head and a left hook to the jaw which shook Zale to his toes. Encouraged by this show of his foe's weakness, Graziano tore after the champion like a man possessed, battering Zale with savage lefts and rights to the body and head in a furious assault which had the crowd yelling wildly.

Zale "rode" with some of the punches, stepped out of range of others and ducked under more, but Graziano knew no frustration. He just piled into his foe, letting fly with both hands indiscriminately, unleashing thunderous right uppercuts which missed awkwardly, but finding the target with more blows than he missed.

When the sixth started Graziano reached the jaw with a short right out of an exchange at close quarters. The blow made Zale's knees buckle.

The crowd roared in amazement and encouragement. The beginning of the end was unfolding as Graziano leaped in for the kill. All the fury of his fighting nature was unleashed at the sight of his foe weakening. The championship was within his grasp. He was not going to let it slip, as he had last September.

No Counter-Attack Possible

Pitilessly, tirelessly, savagely, Graziano slashed at Zale, driving rights and lefts to the head, face and jaw. Zale was rendered helpless to protect himself; he couldn't summon a counter-fire.

Fighting instinct led the tottering champion to sway and duck and flounder away from or under some of the paralyzing punches aimed at him, but only a precious few. Graziano blazed away with both barrels, sending Zale reeling across the ring, into the ropes, eyes glazed, arms leaden, legs like rubber, incapable of supporting his lurching body, save when he was backed against the ropes.

Graziano piled into the falling titleholder with both hands, until Zale sank into the ropes in a neutral corner. The strands braced him for one final volley of lefts and rights, a pulverizing right spinning him around unconscious on the middle ring rope near his own corner.

Zale weighed 159 pounds and Graziano 155¼.

Rocky Struggles With Handlers

In the first flush of his victory, Graziano acted strangely. As if he didn't know the fight had been halted and he declared champion, the Brooklynite struggled furiously with his handlers in the few seconds immediately following the dramatic finish. Then, however, he

calmed and leaped across the ring to shake the hand of his battered foe, pose for pictures and step to the radio.

After the battle it developed Zale and Graziano had an agreement for a return bout within ninety days should the title change hands. This third meeting now is in prospect. There is no question that Graziano wants it, because, when Zale visited his conqueror in the dressing room after the battle, Graziano said: "You'll get your return bout; you're the guy I want to fight."

Every walk of life was represented in this crowd converging from all parts of the country to view a battle originally scheduled as the year's outstanding outdoor ring attraction. Difficulty in obtaining material for installation of temporary seats at one of the local major league baseball parks forced the fight indoors.

Following tradition, local merchants made the bout something of a social occasion. Dinner parties were arranged, along with cocktail sessions, with attendance at the bout part of the entertainment.

Governors of many states were in attendance, several having flown from the convention in Salt Lake City. Gov. Dwight H. Green of Illinois was in that group.

Stars of stage, screen and radio were scattered about the ringside, some having flown from Hollywood. Financiers, industrial leaders, doctors, lawyers, figures prominent in the political life of the city, state and nation, past and present champions of the ring, administrators of boxing laws, promoters, matchmakers, managers and boxers from far and wide were assembled for a battle which transformed this city into the mecca of boxing because of Graziano's ineligibility in New York.

The license of the eccentric Brooklynite was revoked last winter following investigation by the district attorney's office, as well as the New York State athletic commission of his failure to report a bribe attempt.

First Meeting a Thriller

That disciplinary action followed the spine-tingling struggle in which Zale knocked out Graziano in six rounds last September, in the champion's first post-war defense of the title. It was the first knockout suffered by Graziano in a highly spectacular career and a return match in one of New York's

ball parks was in prospect until Rocky fell afoul of the authorities.

Evidently with that in mind, Commodore Sheldon Clark, chairman of the Illinois State Athletic Commission, directed his remarks principally to Graziano at noon following the weighing of champion and challenger.

The fighters were found to be in tip-top shape by Dr. J. J. Drammis. Pulse and blood pressure reading showed Graziano calmer of the two, Dr. Drammis said, without attaching importance to that condition.

Weighing of the boxers was delayed when examination revealed a discrepancy of one-quarter pound in the Stadium scales.

Chairman Clark, flanked by Commissioner Fred Tuerk and Chief Inspector Harold Ryan, supervised the weighing. He instructed the boxers at length before the medical examination.

Chairman Clark said: "This is an important fight, particularly important to you, Graziano. If anything happens contrary to our rules, you are just out of luck. We belong to the National Boxing Association and if you are suspended here you will be suspended all over the country. We want this fight to be as clean as a whistle."

Obviously from his experience as one of the judges in the "long count" heavyweight title battle between Jack Dempsey and Gene Tunney at Soldier Field here twenty years ago, Clark was explicit in his instructions about knockdowns, particularly when counting should start over a prostrate boxer. "No count can start while a man is going down," he said.

Dempsey Broadcasts Fight

Dempsey and Tunney were at the ringside, with Dempsey broadcasting and Tunney a spectator. Bernard Gimbel, New York merchant, accompanied Tunney.

Al Jolson, Joe E. Brown, George Raft, Tony Martin, Harry James, Marvin Schenck and Frank Sinatra were some of the cinema and theatrical celebrities present. Bob Hannegan, Democratic National Committee chairman, was on hand, as was J. Edgar Hoover, FBI chief.

Sol Strauss, director of New York's Twentieth Century Sporting Club during the illness of Promoter Mike Jacobs, Matchmaker Nat Rogers and Harry Markson, director of publicity, viewed the reissue of the battle Jacobs promoted last September.

July 17, 1947

PROSECUTOR'S AIDES QUESTION LAMOTTA

Jake LaMotta, Bronx middleweight, and five others, including Frank P. Carbo, reputedly a major although shadowy figure in the behind-scenes manipulating of boxing bouts, visited the District Attorney's office yesterday for questioning about last Friday's contest in which the fighter was knocked out in the fourth round.

Neither Carbo nor Frank (Blinky) Palermo, manager of the victor, Billy Fox of Philadelphia, would answer questions put by Assistant District Attorneys Alfred

J. Scotti, head of the rackets bureau, and Andrew Seidler.

Carbo, Mr. Scotti asserted, would answer only "certain questions," and Palermo said he would reply to inquiries about the fight only in the presence of his attorney. Both refused to sign waivers of grand jury immunity.

LaMotta was accompanied by his father, Joseph, and younger brother, Joseph Jr., when he arrived at the prosecutor's office, 155 Leonard Street, at 10:30 A. M. It was learned that the elder LaMotta and his younger son had been questioned and allowed to leave early.

When asked by reporters about reports the match had been "fixed," LaMotta replied: "I have nothing to say. We know nothing." He insisted, "All I know is I fought

AT BOXING INQUIRY HERE YESTERDAY

Jake LaMotta

Frank Carbo
The New York Times

the best I knew how and I was in fine shape."

To questions about reports of a pre-fight conference between himself and his opponent's manager,

the boxer declared: "I read about that. All I can say is it's a dirty lie."

November 21, 1947

Louis, Floored Twice, Beats Walcott on Split Decision

Bomber Keeps Title on Two Judges' Ballots, Though Referee Votes for Challenger— Many of 18,194 Fans Boo Verdict

By JAMES P. DAWSON

Joe Louis is still the world heavyweight champion today because he won a split, unpopular decision over Jersey Joe Walcott, Camden (N. J.) Negro challenger, last night in a fifteen-round battle in Madison Square Garden.

By the same token, Walcott is not the heavyweight titleholder simply because never in the history of the ring has a boxer won a championship running away without attempting a defensive counter-fire.

Though he retained his title, Louis was nearer dethronement than he ever had been through his ten-year reign as the world's premier boxer.

He was knocked down twice— in the first round for a count of two and in the fourth round for a count of seven. He was battered, bruised and bleeding; he was out-maneuvered, at times outboxed, always out-thought and generally made to look foolish.

The Brown Bomber, who left a share-cropper's acreage to become one of the greatest heavyweight champions of all time, is past his peak. At thirty-three years of age Louis is ripe for defeat at the hands of a courageous boxer with a good right hand and a fearless disposition. The Louis who had achieved fourteen straight knock-outs in twenty-three title defenses before last night, the dark destroyer who completely removed all opposition through the longest and most active reign of any heavyweight champion, the dread punch-er whose very presence in the opposite corner often "froze" a rival before hostilities began, definitely is on the downgrade.

No longer is Louis the death-dealing, sure-fire puncher of old.

His reflexes are bad. His defense, never air-tight because it consist-ed chiefly of attack, is conspicuous by its absence.

More than ever is he a mark for the right cross with which Max Schmeling knocked him out in 1936 for the only defeat of his career. He is an open target for a left hook to the head or jaw, because his reflexes momentarily delay his counter-fire.

All that was revealed plainly to 18,194 fans who paid record re-ceipts for the Garden of $216,477 to see a battle considered so one-sided in advance that Louis was a 1-to-10 favorite. The receipts eclipsed the twenty-year record of $201,465 established by Jack De-laney and Jim Maloney in 1927, and the result not only stunned the tremendous crowd; it provoked from a noisy majority an outburst of disagreement that echoed through the Garden rafters with deafening volume when it was announced.

Referee Ruby Goldstein, veteran of welterweight fighting days and one of the best arbiters in boxing, actually voted for Walcott, credit-ing the challenger with seven rounds to Louis' six, while calling two even. Marty Monroe, one of the judges, gave the decision to Louis by nine rounds to six. Frank Forbes, the other judge, called Louis the winner by eight rounds to six, with one even.

The writer scored eight rounds for the champion to seven for his rival, giving the third, fourth, fifth, sixth, seventh, eighth, ninth, tenth and eleventh rounds to Louis in a sweep that was uninterrupted after Walcott had been frustrated earlier in his bid for a knockout that would have been one of the most stunning upsets in the long history of boxing.

Louis Appears Clear Winner

Sentiment might explain the dis-approval which greeted Harry Balogh's announcement of the de-cision. Certainly by any standard of evaluating boxing points, there was no reason for it because Louis made all the fighting, did most of the leading and, his two knock-downs notwithstanding, landed the greater number of blows. Except for Louis, there would have been no fight.

By inverse ratio, except for his back-pedaling, Walcott might be enjoying more than the distinction of being the third man to survive fifteen rounds with Louis in a title fray. Tommy Farr, Welsh heavy-weight long since retired, was the first. Arturo Godoy, still-active Chilean, was the second, a feat that was dimmed somewhat in a return bout when Louis knocked out Godoy in eight rounds.

Louis said following the battle that he had hurt his right hand in the fifth round. First reports were that he had broken the extremity. Later it was announced the cham-pion would determine by X-ray whether the hand was broken. That may account for perhaps the sorriest bout of Louis' entire career, not excepting even the knockout he suffered in twelve rounds at the hands of Schmeling before he scaled the championship heights.

That it was a disappointing exhibition even to the champion was indicated im-mediately after the final bell clanged. In an

excess of disgust (it couldn't have been bewilderment because he had not been touched by a forceful punch immediately before) Louis climbed through the ropes before reaching his corner and was out on the apron of the ring before his handlers hastily forced him back through the ropes to await announcement of the decision.

Walcott Earns $25,000

Besides the distinction of surviving fif-teen rounds against what is left of the Brown Bomber, a not inconsiderable feat for a 34-year-old veteran who found himself thrust into a championship battle originally scheduled as a mere exhibition, Walcott earned a purse of about $25,000, the largest of his career, for a bout that truthfully can be said to have attracted at-tention to him for the first time.

Louis, with a 45 per cent share of the net receipts in addition to a share of the movie, radio and television rights, will receive close to $100,000. That should have an assuaging effect upon the wound to his feelings and pride and the physical marks of battle with which, amazingly for him, he left the ring. The purse should console him, too, for the embarrassment of having been dumped on a ring canvas for the first time since Tony Galento was so close to knock-ing him out in their title struggle.

The crowd which attended was a testimonial to the tremendous popularity of Louis. The prospect of it being Louis' last fight may have influenced the atten-dance, too; that and the ever-present chance that, no matter how lightly held the challenger, the title can change hands when a heavyweight champion enters the ring.

It may well prove this was Louis' last bat-tle. John Roxborough, associated with Julian Black in the management of Louis since the Bomber left the amateur ranks back in 1934, said before the fight Louis' ring future, if any, was to be determined not so much on whether Louis won or lost against Walcott as on how the champion looked in action.

Walcott's Style Puzzles Joe

There is no gainsaying the fact that Louis looked bad. Making allowances for an awkward Walcott style doesn't altogether account for Joe's inferior showing, based on Louis' standards.

The champion said over the radio im-mediately following the bout that he had been worried throughout, but that he thought Walcott entitled to another chance at the crown, and that he was eager to give it to him. That, along with the important question of whether Louis will continue in the ring, probably will be decided today.

Louis has admitted realization that he is slipping. If he makes up his mind he has lost his devastating ring effectiveness, he may be expected to announce his retire-ment. It is significant he has no plans for a future battle.

Not a particularly torrid heavyweight championship bout, the struggle packed thrills that overrode the lack of continued competitive thunder for the distinguished gathering. The throng, incidentally, was thoroughly representative of the financial, commercial, industrial, professional, social and entertainment worlds.

The first thrill occurred with startling suddenness in the first round. After subjecting Louis to a baffling succession of left jabs and hooks in a blinding display of early defensive speed, Walcott suddenly whipped a solid, short right to Louis' jaw and, amid a roar from the crowd, floored the champion unceremoniously for a count of two.

Louis Bewildered by Blow

More than the crowd Louis was bewildered by the unexpected turn of events. He was pressing forward against the dancing challenger when the blow struck and he keeled over like some of the victims his mighty fists had claimed, though not with such permanence. The fact that Walcott had shaken under a grazing right to the jaw shortly before the knockdown intensified the surprise.

The delivery of the blow and its consequences, bringing into bold relief a weakness that Schmeling had discovered back more than eleven years ago, transformed Louis from a solemn, expressionless fighter into a raging maniac. When he drew erect blazing, it was to run blindly into a cuffing of lefts and short rights to the head as the champion missed all his paralyzing array of vicious lefts and rights aimed at the immediate destruction of Walcott.

Through the second round the enraged Louis continued wild as he forced the fighting. Sticking left jabs at Walcott's face, hooking short rights at a fleeting target, he was missing virtually all his blows, while Walcott stabbed in return and three times drove his right to the head, aiming at Louis' jaw.

The third saw Louis jabbing better, sending Walcott back on his heels several times with stiff thrusts as the challenger sought to dance out of harm's way. Louis even seemed eager for an exchange of rights to the jaw, but Walcott never exposed himself, although he three times lashed out with short rights which landed high on the head.

Bomber Takes Count of 7

The fourth was not a minute old before Walcott again crashed his right to the jaw, toppling Louis in his tracks for a count of seven. Then the Garden vibrated with the thunderous roar for the challenger whose chances had been so thoroughly despised before this all-revealing battle.

On his hands and knees Louis listened as the count went to seven and when he arose the Bomber, for one of the rare occasions of his career, fell into a clinch. He was hurt. Louis wanted time for his ringing head to clear, but Walcott fought like a demon, first to shake himself free, then to hammer the champion.

For a fiery few seconds Walcott hammered at the jaw and head of Louis, but the Bomber was bobbing his head out of range, while seeking ineffectively to counter the fire and stop the eager charges of his foe. Seeing the futility of getting another solid shot at Louis' chin, Walcott withheld his fire and contented himself with out-boxing Louis through the rest of the round.

Through the next four rounds, leading up to the ninth, Louis pressed his challenger tirelessly, sticking left jabs in Walcott's face, digging lefts for the body, curling an occasional right to the head.

Walcott fought defensively exclusively. He almost fell more than once back-pedaling before the plodding champion, whose fists were poised, ready for the strike that might achieve a fifteenth straight knockout for Louis.

Several times straight lefts almost upset the retreating Walcott, but the challenger occasionally halted his retreat to cross a short right. Those blows added to the swelling about Louis' left eye and drew blood from his nose.

Not until the ninth did the enraged Louis catch up with his foe. Then a succession of left jabs tilted Walcott into position for a right cross and when the blow landed high, the challenger sagged into the ropes.

Like a maniac Louis was upon his rival driving thunderous rights and lefts to the head. Walcott was pinioned on the ropes near his own corner, staging a desperate counter-offensive which was ignored by Louis, so intent was the champion on the destruction of the man who had twice floored him.

The crowd sensed a finish for a fighter who had made a glorious stand. It seemed Louis must crash through the web of flailing arms with a decisive thrust, or at least a punch that would expose Walcott to a finish flurry. The roars were deafening as Louis plied left and right, left and right, aiming at the jaw, landing mostly to the head. Though the punches carried jarring force Walcott not only withstood them, but lashed back savagely with poorly directed lefts and rights calculated to stop the champion's fire.

Above the din it was impossible to hear the clang of the bell ending the round. They might have fought on had not referee Goldstein leaped between them. With the bell, Louis' best chance for a knockout disappeared. For thereafter Walcott was on a bicycle, determined to stay the fifteen rounds and fighting back only in spasms.

Walcott Misses and Falls

In one desperate offensive lunge that interrupted his back-pedaling in the thirteenth round, Walcott missed a round-house right for the jaw and fell forward on his face. He was too busy racing madly away from Louis to start more than an occasional desperate right for the jaw, landing chiefly on the head.

In the fifteenth round, however, the challenger, still in full flight, checked his mad race often enough to fluster Louis with occasional left jabs. When the crowd jeered, it was hard to decide whether the demonstration was aimed at Louis for his futility or at Walcott for his sprinting.

Louis weighed 211 pounds and Walcott 194½.

December 6, 1947

Jacobs to Quit Boxing 'Forever' After Louis-Walcott June Fight

MIAMI BEACH, Fla., Jan. 22 (AP)—Michael Strauss Jacobs, for nearly twenty-five years one of the world's leading fight promoters, announced today that "win, lose or draw," he will "retire from boxing forever" after a return match this spring between heavyweight champion Joe Louis and Jersey Joe Walcott.

Jacobs, now 67, who has owned Louis' contract since 1935, said in an interview that "when Joe announced he was retiring after this fight, I decided it was time for me to bow out, too."

"We'll see this return match through together and then take it easy."

Jacobs, better known in boxing circles as "Uncle Mike," said that Felix Boccicchio of Camden, N. J., owner of Joe Walcott's contract, will be "down sometime next week to work out a contract for the return match and that will be the last fight contract I'll ever sign."

His long career in the fight game was climaxed yesterday when Louis surpassed John L. Sullivan's record of holding the title 10 years and 212 days. It also marked the longest period of time a single promoter has held a champion's contract.

Looking back over the years as a promoter, Jacobs recalled that his biggest moment came when Louis, in 1935, then a virtual unknown in big-time boxing, knocked out Max Baer before a crowd that spent almost a million dollars for seats.

"That was when I was wondering if he really was championship material. After that fight I knew I had hit the jackpot."

It was just 10 years and 214 days ago that Jacobs deserted Madison Square Garden and took Louis to Chicago to win the title from Jim Braddock. In the intervening years the Brown Bomber has defended his title twenty-four times before a combined gate that grossed approximately $30,000,000.

Jacobs said he planned to remain in Florida to "fish, loaf and raise my daughter." He and his wife, Josie, adopted Joan three years ago when she was only a year old.

As far as he is concerned, there's no dispute about the decision of the recent Louis-Walcott fight.

January 23, 1948

STRICT RING RULES ADOPTED BY N. B. A.

Thorough Physicals and Long Rests After Knockouts on 21-Point Safety Code

PHILADELPHIA, March 20 (UP)—The National Boxing Association, in a sweeping revision of its rules, today adopted a 21-point safety program designed for the protection of all fighters under its jurisdiction.

The wide-range program stressed thorough physical examinations for all boxers, and long lay-offs after knockout defeats. It directed that a physician supervise the movement of knocked-out fighters, and also gunned for fight managers found to be persistent rules' breakers.

Abe Greene, N. B. A. president, said that all affiliated commissions, including those of Great Britain, Canada and Mexico, would be notified immediately of the rules changes and that their adoption today was tantamount to quick passage. He predicted they would be in effect within a month.

Urge 8-Ounce Gloves

Specifically, the new legislation advocated by the N. B. A. to its fifty-six member commissions, asked for eight-ounce gloves to be used in all contests, and withheld approval of any badly beaten fighter for a match until he went through a thorough examination.

In a move which would cull consistent losers and washed-out fighters from boxing, the committee decided that in case of repeated knockdowns and beatings, the boxer shall be retired.

The drastic changes demanded that a minimum of six weeks elapse before a knocked-out boxer can be permitted to fight again, and then only after a complete examination by commission physicians.

A knocked-out boxer in the future can not be touched nor moved except by the direction of the ringside physician, the committee ordered, and added that the physician personally shall attend the fighter.

The eight-count knockdown, recommended by the Pennsylvania commission and requiring a boxer cleanly knocked down to take a count of eight whether or not he has regained his feet, also was written into the new regulations.

Blood Tests Desirable

Boxers who receive severe concussions will not be permitted to fight until they have been examined and passed by a board of at least three commission doctors, the committee ruled. Physical examinations will approximate those required by life insurance companies, and will include all blood tests and the use of the electro-encephalograph, wherever available.

Pointing a finger at the potential punch drunk boxer, the N.B.A. ruled that any boxer who has suffered six straight defeats shall be subject to investigation, examination and a national report to all members.

The committee spoke its piece on boxing's "undesirables" when it ruled that any applicant for a license must certify as to whether he ever was convicted of a felony. It voted to bar for life any promoter, manager or matchmaker who conspires to break commission rules.

Better padded gloves, the use of ten yards of bandage and two feet of adhesive tape on each hand, and approved padding for rings also received committee approval in the first session of a two-day meeting.

March 21, 1948

Zale Regains Middleweight Title by Knocking Out Graziano in Third Round

VETERAN PUMMELS RIVAL FROM START

Zale Drops Graziano for 3 in First and 7 in Third Before a Left Ends Bout at 1:08

UPSET STIRS 21,497 FANS

Savage Fight Culminates With East Sider Unconscious on Floor of Newark Ring

By JAMES P. DAWSON
Special to The New York Times.

NEWARK, N. J., June 10—Tony Zale, sturdy Gary, Ind., ring veteran, regained the world middleweight title tonight.

He knocked out Rocky Graziano, doughty warrior from New York's East Side, in three blazing rounds of what was to have been a fifteen-round bout at Ruppert Stadium, before a crowd of 21,497 yelling fight fans who paid gross receipts of $335,646 to see another primitive installment of this ring feud.

Under the paralyzing punches of the 34-year-old Hoosier, fighting a grim battle to regain the title he lost last July 16, Graziano sank unconscious after 1 minute 8 seconds of the third round, to be counted out, flat on his back, by Referee Paul Cavalier.

The flamboyant Graziano, fighting here because he is ineligible in his native New York, favorite to win entering the ring at odds of 5 to 12, was an easy victim of the remarkable Zale. The East Sider was floored for a count of three in the first round, he was rocked and staggered in a stanza in which the action became so torrid neither heard the bell ending the round.

Graziano Hits Canvas

Shortly after the third round opened, Graziano sank for a count of seven, arising game, instinctively, his face to the foe, his scattered senses dictating he must fight to defend himself, not cover up. Rocky tried to fight. But he was incapable of the effort and with a left hook to the jaw and a volley of vicious, sense-deadening rights and lefts to the body and head, the final poke a smashing left which stiffened Rocky on his heels and sent him toppling like a falling tree, Zale finished his foe.

Scoring this sensational victory, Zale went back forty years to rip a glittering page from ring history. He became the second middleweight champion to regain the crown, and he had something

Rocky Graziano falling to the floor for a count of seven after Tony Zale landed a left hook followed by a right cross in the third round at Newark last night.

The New York Times

of the slashing, destructive, battering style of his predecessor in this respect to carry him to victory. For only Stanley Ketchel, who retrieved the title by knocking out Billy Papke in 1908, ever came back to win the middleweight crown and Ketchel is one of the ring's immortals.

Scoring one of the biggest upsets of recent years, Zale pounded out his second knockout victory over Graziano in half the time it took him to score the first and lose the title in the second. Zale knocked out Graziano in six terrific rounds at the Yankee Stadium in New York, in 1946, and was knocked out in six rounds himself in Chicago last July, when Graziano ascended the throne. In this first defense of the title he held so short a time, Graziano never had a chance.

Victor Is Unmarked

Zale was unmarked leaving the ring, conquering hero in a battle on which many of his friends and admirers looked with apprehension. Graziano was bleeding from nose and mouth and from a slight cut over the left eye, and he left the ring on shaky legs. He looked the beaten fighter.

It may be maintained, and not without justification, too, that illegal blows helped Zale on the road to his marvelous triumph. One of the most effective punches of the battle was a murderous right to the heart that Zale drove sharp and true to the target after the bell ending the first round.

This was but one of a fusillade Zale drove to the head and face and body in a tornadic outburst of punching after a left hook to the jaw sent Rocky staggering backward to sag against the ropes, just before the bell clanged the end of the round. Referee Cavalier didn't hear the bell, or was slow in his reaction. For in a brief, fiery assault, which ended with that damaging right to the heart, Zale rendered Graziano helpless before they were separated.

That this extracurricular punching had an effect on Graziano is unquestionable. It is likewise unquestionable, it was accidental, and not deliberate. Neither fighter

heard the bell. Some at the ringside didn't hear it for the roars of the crowd urging Zale on, pleading with Graziano to counter.

Graziano tried to fight back but couldn't. He was being battered helpless as Zale pressed his advantage. But, even without this overtime onslaught, Zale must have won tonight. He was the master. There was no escaping that at any stage of the battle.

Rocky Tries "Weaving"

A shouted instruction, an ear-splitting tempo, to "weave," sent Graziano out to battle—and to his doom. Rocky tried "weaving" as they exchanged long left hooks to the head before the bell's echo died away.

But, in a jiffy, Graziano was rushed to the ropes under a left to the body and to the head, and, backed to the ropes, Graziano had to withstand a two-fisted battering to which Zale, who seemed like a man possessed, subjected him.

Coming away from this situation, Graziano was pressed across the ring under a fire of stinging left jabs to the face and head. Trying to counter this assault, Rocky left himself open for a solid left hook to the jaw and a right which dropped him in his tracks.

He started up at the count of "two," but the count of knockdown timekeeper Nat Fleischer went to three before the defending champion was erect and the battle resumed on signal of Referee Cavalier.

Rocky was through then and there. Zale knew it would be only a question of time. Rocky must have known it, in his heart, too. For through the rest of the session Zale battered Graziano with a pitiless, two-fisted fire that raked the East Sider about the body and head alternately. .

Sags in Own Corner

Near the end of the round, a smashing left hook to the jaw made Graziano sag against the ropes in his own corner. Quick as a flash, Zale leaped in with paralyzing rights and lefts to the head and body as Rocky tried to fight back. The bell clanged, but neither heard it. Zale ripped and slashed with both hands, driving at any opening that presented, seeking to batter Graziano helpless, intent only on that as the crowd roared.

Graziano's head rolled under a left hook and a sharp right and his knees sagged as his arms went up protectively. And, when the covering from the body was lifted, Zale sent a crushing right to the heart, cleanly, powerfully, with all the weight and strength of his body behind it, before Referee Cavalier belatedly stepped between the combatants. Rocky's body sagged under the impact. His handlers leaped through the ropes and propped him on his corner stool.

Through the second round Zale sparred cautiously for perhaps a minute, sticking and stabbing Rocky with unerring, snappy left jabs to the face and head, and upsetting Graziano's attempts to return the fire. Rocky lunged wildly, viciously at his foe, lashing out with both arms, flailing rights and lefts for the jaw which, for the most part were wide of the mark. When Rocky did land, it was in glancing fashion because Zale was either going away from or leading in under the blows.

Zale Parries Lunges

A right to the jaw staggered Graziano midway of the round and he sank back to the ropes, to rebound like an infuriated bull and, with a blazing, ill-directed fire of lefts and rights, forced Zale about the ring.

Several times Rocky crashed his right to the head. A long left banged against Zale's right eye and the crowd roared when Graziano grazed the jaw with a powerful, full-arm right. But, Zale, stepping nimbly back to a neutral corner, parried Graziano's lunges, picked off Rocky's desperate blows, and, smilingly, danced out to ring center and proceeded to batter Graziano through the rest of the round.

Zale was on the attack as soon as the third round opened, sticking and stabbing and punishing with his powerful, straight, accurate left to the head, hooking his left to the head and driving Graziano to the ropes under a withering body-fire for which Rocky had no defense and less of counter-fire.

A left hook to the jaw rocked Rocky to his heels. A right and left to the head followed. Rocky

staggered backward drunkenly. Zale was after him cat-like. A right to the body and Rocky cringed. A left hook that landed solidly on the jaw sent Rocky down to be counted out after the third round had gone 1 minute 8 seconds.

Dr. Vincent A. Nardiello, New York State Athletic Commission physician, examined Graziano after he had been assisted to his dressing room, and diagnosed a slight concussion. It was all of five minutes after he reached the dressing room, before Graziano became aware of his surroundings, or those about him. A report spread Grazi-

ano had been rushed to a hospital from the Stadium, but this could not be confirmed at the ringside.

While the gross receipts were $335,646, a total of $405,646 was realized, including the radio and motion picture rights.

June 11, 1948

The champion down in the third round when Walcott smashed a right to the cheek-bone. However, Louis was up after a count of one.

JOE LOUIS RALLIES TO STOP WALCOTT IN ELEVENTH ROUND

Trailing on Points, Champion Turns Tide With a Right to Jaw and Keeps Crown

42,667 AT THE STADIUM

Jeer Early in Bout Because of Lack of Action—Bomber Says He Is Retiring

By JAMES P. DAWSON

Because he has the punch that has made him one of the greatest heavyweights ever to hold the title, Joe Louis, the ring's Brown Bomber, still is the world champion.

He knocked out Jersey Joe Walcott of Camden, the challenger for the title, in the eleventh round of an ordinary championship battle last night in the Yankee Stadium, and plucked glorious, spectacular victory from threatened defeat.

Trailing the 34-year-old challenger through ten rounds of fighting which more than once drew jeers from the crowd of 42,667, Louis turned the tide of battle with one punch. It was a right to the jaw which shook Walcott to his toes. It was delivered as the shifty challenger was boxing in the confusing style that had baffled Louis last December and was baffling him again before a great crowd which paid $841,739 for the spectacle.

The blow provided the opening which Louis had sought from the start. The champion lost no time pressing his advantage. A savage, furious flurry of short-arm lefts and rights drilled against the head of Walcott as the challenger backed to the ropes and sought to throw up a defense of crossed arms.

One Right—and It's All Over

Louis' punches drilled home to the head, however, and they jarred. A right to the jaw shot through a brief opening, and the fight was over.

Walcott pitched forward on his face, rolled over on his back, lay with arms outstretched as the count was tolled over him by Referee Frank Fullam. He struggled to his knees at "seven," but was bewildered, befuddled. He knelt there apparently listening to the count, but probably hearing it not at all.

At "ten" he was struggling to get erect. But he was beyond the effort. He didn't know where he was, though he made as if he would resume fighting.

Referee Fullam clasped the beaten Walcott in his arms and guided him to his corner, knocked out after the eleventh round had gone 2 minutes 56 seconds.

Doctor Leaps Into Ring

Dr. Vincent A. Nardiello jumped through the ropes to examine the beaten veteran. His examination apparently showed Walcott had suffered no ill effects from the brief ordeal which brought about his downfall just when it appeared he was on the road to the heavyweight championship of the world.

Walcott was able to step to ringcenter and clasp the hand of his conqueror and pose with Louis in wordless acknowledgment of the master's superiority. He was able, too, to talk into a radio microphone, and it was Walcott who led the procession from the ring when the excitement had subsided.

After the battle Walcott was critical of Referee Fullam. The arbiter had found it necessary several times to step to the corners of the rivals and urge them to greater action. The crowd more or less demanded this official move by booing and jeering at the lack of excitement.

It was this with which Walcott found fault in his dressing room. He claimed that Referee Fullam's repeated exhortations had veered him from a planned style of fighting and indirectly, at least, brought about his downfall.

The fact remains, however, that Fullam was within his rights in moving as ne did. He not only urged Walcott, but he demanded greater action of Louis.

It is not for a referee to concern himself about a fighter's style. His responsibility is to see that the boxers, whether they be champion or run-of-the-mill fighters, provide a clean, honest, interesting contest in accordance with the law and it was in discharge of this responsibility that Referee Fullam acted as he did.

Perhaps the warning did disconcert Walcott, although there was nothing in his actions to support this conclusion. Rather, the inescapable fact was that Louis hit his foe just once with a good right-hand punch and it was the beginning of the end for the veteran Walcott. He was thoroughly knocked out. He was far from disgraced.

He must have known entering the ring that it was a question whether Louis could "tag" him. Every experienced follower of boxing knew or felt this, even those who had picked Walcott to win off his battle of last December.

Bomber Says He's Through

Louis repeated his previously announced intention of retiring from the ring.

"I will definitely retire from boxing," were his words. If he sticks to his determination, and there is no reason at the moment to believe he will not, Louis will join Gene Tunney as a retired undefeated world heavyweight titleholder.

That Louis was on the verge of losing his title was disclosed after the bout, when the official ballots of the referee and the two judges were disclosed.

Two of the officials had Walcott in front. Referee Fullam had Louis in the lead. The arbiter's card showed five rounds for Louis, with only two for Walcott and three even.

Jack O'Sullivan had the bout five rounds for Walcott, four for Louis and one even. Harold Barnes, the other judge, had Walcott in front, six rounds to three, with one even. Of course, on all ballots the voting involved only the ten rounds preceding the eleventh.

The writer had Walcott in front by a margin of six rounds to two,

with two even. The first two rounds were adjudged even because there was no action to consider, no points to distribute. There just wasn't any fighting.

Louis won only the eighth and ninth in a brief outburst of determined offensive work when his left jab was his best weapon. All the other rounds went to Walcott.

Louis Down in the Third

Louis had to come off the floor to win this one, as he did last December. He was knocked down in the third round with a right that landed on his cheek-bone, for a count of one. The knockdown was significant only in that it reflected Walcott's power to upset the Bomber with a well-driven punch. Louis was unhurt by the blow, unless his pride suffered further damage for this indignity, which followed the two knockdowns he suffered in the battle of last December.

The champion bounced up from the experience without difficulty, but his sullen, expressionless face was a bit darker, indicating a seething fury.

Louis' rage grew in the fifth when his knees sagged under a right to the jaw in a brief exchange that interrupted a slow process of thinking which seemed to stymie the champion when he appeared to have Walcott propped for a telling blow.

His success with rights emboldened Walcott as the bout progressed and, more frequently than he had done last December, the challenger discarded his retreat to let fly with occasional rights for the jaw. No more landed, however.

Trainer Seamon Protests

Indeed, the action became so

annoying to Louis, as Walcott kept out of range and bedeviled the champion with stabbing lefts and body and arm-feinting, that Trainer Mannie Seamon rushed excitedly across the ring at the end of the eighth round to protest to Referee Fullam that Walcott was striking with an open left glove. The referee brusquely ordered Seamon to Louis' corner, ignoring the protest.

As a championship battle it was not much to view. But for the suspense, it must have been taxing on the patience of the onlookers to sit through the ten rounds that preceded the knockout.

It is a testimonial to the drawing power of Louis that the crowd and the gate were so large. Two postponements had put the million-dollar goal beyond reach. It had been set last December when Walcott survived fifteen rounds with Louis, knocked the champion down twice and furnished such a surprising showing many thought him the victim of an injustice in the decision that went, rightfully, to Louis.

In representation, the crowd lived up to heavyweight title tradition. Men and women of prominence were to be seen clustered about the ringside in serried rows that extended back almost to the concrete and steel stands.

Stanton K. Griffis, Ambassador to Poland, headed a list of distinguished guests. Even royalty had been invited to this fistic spectacle, for the Count and Countess Hohenlohe were on the list.

Present, too, were college professors, newspaper and magazine publishers, Senators and Representatives, merchant princes and kings of finance, leaders of the industrial, commercial and profes-

sional worlds, stars of the stage, screen and radio, and members of the clergy.

But for the fact that a flood of refunds had followed the second postponement on Thursday night, the receipts would have exceeded the million-dollar goal. More than $100,000 was refunded to disappointed fans yesterday, when tickets were offered also at cut rates in private sales by those who could not adjust their schedules to the two delays the battle suffered.

Louis Provides the Answer

The magnet, of course, was Louis. The curiosity was about whether Walcott could repeat—more impressively—the showing he had made last December. Louis supplied the answer, in typical manner, as he scored his twenty-second knockout triumph in his twenty-fifth defense of the crown he lifted eleven years ago from James J. Braddock in Chicago.

It was unfortunate that the curtain fell on Louis' unparalleled record in a dismal battle. By the same token, it would be unreasonable to expect the 34-year-old Louis, after eleven years of championship activity, to have the verve and fire, the snap and dash, that shone through his earlier career. His reflexes are not what they used to be. The fact that Walcott went as far as he did demonstrated this.

Louis reached a stage where he could not afford the luxury of a careless moment. He had a shifty, elusive target at which to toss punches and a hitter of established ability as well. The Bomber, despite his paralyzing punching power, could not afford to take unnecessary chances.

Walcott on the floor when he was counted out in the eleventh round after Louis scored with a right to the jaw. Fullam is the referee.

A Matter of Style

Nor could Walcott expose himself unnecessarily, aware as he was of the punching strength of the champion. Walcott could have regarded Louis as on the wane, as indeed he is. The challenger was confident of his own ability to avoid this punching strength long enough to out-skip Louis in fifteen rounds. He had the style he thought would accomplish this end and therein lay the explanation for the desultory firing of the night: style! Walcott couldn't, and Louis wouldn't —until he was reasonably certain of success.

When the moment came, Louis, with the neatness and dispatch that have always been among his greatest characteristics, with that master's stroke of authority that had made him supreme, demonstrated his reflexes are still in good working order.

Louis looked trim as he stripped for action, contradicting the suspicion that the forty - eight - hour delay would result in excess poundage. He was trained to the minute.

It had been more or less expected that Louis would come charging out of his corner in raging fury, intent only upon avenging the wound to his pride suffered last December. He had followed this course in the return match with Max Schmeling, battering into defeat the German who knocked him out in twelve rounds for the only defeat Louis has suffered.

"I'll finish him quick," was Louis' oft-repeated promise when queried on his battle plans.

Champion Stalks His Man

But there was no blazing opening charge by the champion, no reckless, headlong, do-or-die bid for quick victory.

Instead, Louis stalked his man from the first bell until the opening presented itself for that right-hand punch which turned, and quickly finished, the battle.

He stalked Walcott through rounds in which hardly a blow was struck by either, through periods when the jeers of the crowd must have made him wonder why the people were yelling at him and at Walcott, when they were up there fighting for boxing's richest prize, fighting as best as they could under the circumstances.

Two rounds of wasted effort opened the battle. Hardly a blow was struck as Louis plodded onward and in with his shuffling gait and Walcott retreated, decorously, boxing and feinting and shifting and swaying and sparring—doing everything calculated to befuddle the champion.

Not until the third round did Louis bestir himself. Then he started reaching for Walcott with wicked rights for the jaw. He missed one by almost a foot and another by a scant margin, as Walcott retreated, boxing coolly and cleverly.

It was after missing the second that Louis exposed himself to the right-hand punch that bounced him off the ring canvas. It crashed against his left cheekbone, leaving a pink mark, and Louis went down in his tracks, to arise almost with the same motion.

Walcott displayed an offensive flurry as Louis came erect at "one." The challenger rushed close and sought to land with a more vital punch. But a clinch followed, and in this Walcott had no time to throw punches. He had to protect himself.

Walcott Gets Bolder

Emboldened, Walcott shot a right for the head after sparring for a while in the fourth. He regretted the blow almost immediately. Louis cut loose in a flurry with which he rushed Walcott to the ropes and about the ring, volleying lefts and rights furiously, trying to make an opening for a shot to the jaw. The opening never presented itself, and Louis missed most of his blows.

The lack of coordination which handicaps Louis was manifest in the fifth when, after absorbing Walcott's right to the head in an exchange, and tolerating a succession of light left jabs from the challenger in retreat, Louis pressed in swinging short-arm blows for the head which backed Walcott into a neutral corner.

There, while Louis was contemplating a move, Walcott curled over a right to the jaw and Louis' knees buckled under him. He fell back against the ropes, but before Walcott could follow the advantage the bell ended the round.

More cautious in the sixth, Louis pressed the action carefully in this round and the seventh.

Left jabs earned Louis the eighth and ninth, and what seemed like smiling acknowledgement from Walcott of his foe's marksmanship. Near the end of the ninth, however, Walcott shook the champion with a right to the head and in the tenth Walcott made so bold as to launch four rights for Louis' jaw while the champion stood flustered. Three landed on the head.

But they were the last fearless moves undertaken by Walcott. The challenger was boxing defensively in the eleventh, when Louis shot through a right to the jaw which made Walcott's knees buckle. It was the beginning of the end.

Walcott tried to back to the ropes and sagged as Louis ripped into him, firing solidly with both hands, against Walcott's desperate attempts to throw up a protective curtain of crossed arms. Lefts and rights to the head drilled home and Walcott almost went through the ropes. A right to the jaw toppled Jersey Joe, and from that there was no coming back.

Louis left the ring the conqueror, the champion, looking forward to retirement.

The weights announced for the championship were what the boxers scaled last Wednesday, Louis at 213½ pounds and Walcott at 194¾ pounds.

June 26, 1948

LOUIS TELLS WHY HE IS RETIRING

Says That He Has Been 'Around a Long Time, and It's About Time I Quit'

Joe Louis has had his last fight. That is what the Brown Bomber declared in his dressing room immediately after his conquest of Jersey Joe Walcott.

Surrounded almost to the point of suffocation by the customary throng that visits the winner's quarters after an important bout, Louis made his farewell statement several times, and each time with conviction, despite the fact that a good many skeptics in his presence positively refused to believe the news.

"That was my last fight," was Joe's declaration. "I've been around a long time and I think that it's about time I quit. And I'm glad to quit with the title still mine."

In announcing his withdrawal from competition the Brown Bomber took occasion to thank all concerned with the boxing game for the treatment accorded him. The public, officials, opponents and promoters all came in for a word of gratitude from the fighter who ruled the heavyweight division since June 22, 1937, when he stopped Jimmy Braddock in Chicago.

Champion Queried Often

The champion was not allowed to make his farewell announcement without interruption. He was asked often whether he would not extend his career until September, to box either Gus Lesnevich, holder of the world light heavyweight championship, or Ezzard Charles, Cincinnati boxer whom Louis himself has called the most dangerous heavyweight extant.

To all these questions, though, Joe had but one answer, "I'm retiring. Tonight's fight was my last fight."

His manager, Marshall Miles, and his long-time adviser, John Roxborough, seemed just as certain of Joe's retirement as was the Bomber himself. Asked what Louis' plans may be, once out of the ring, Roxborough replied than an announcement would be forthcoming soon.

Until the announcement Louis will rest preparatory to getting down to work with a soft drink company in which he has a considerable interest.

Referring to his tussle with Walcott, Louis said that he was not surprised at the way the fight went. "We knew that Walcott was going to try to keep away as long as he could and we knew that we would catch him in time," he explained.

Seamon Praised By Louis

By "we" the Bomber meant his trainer, Manny Seamon, and himself. Louis gave every credit to Seamon for his victory, saying that he followed his trainer's orders as closely as possible.

Said orders were to stalk Walcott regardless of how things seemed to be going, with the certainty that the opportunity to apply the coup de grace would make itself apparent sometime during the fifteen rounds.

At the end of the tenth round, according to Louis, Seamon told him that he was trailing on points, but that the succeeding round should be the final one. The observation was based on Seamon's perceiving that Walcott was carrying his arms much lower than he had been in the earlier stages, an obvious indication that the challenger was tiring.

"Waited for the Chance"

"I didn't take too many chances in the eleventh, either," said Louis. "I waited for the chance to hit him solid, and when I did he went down. And when he went down, I knew he wouldn't get up."

Sol Strauss, acting director of the Twentieth Century Sporting Club, was one of the few on hand who was inclined to accept Louis' retirement announcement without a grain of salt.

"If he says he's retiring, there's nothing I can add," he said. "I have no reason to doubt him, nor do I have any reason for pressuring him into fighting again. He's been a great champion, and he's certainly entitled to do what he wants to do now."

June 26, 1948

CHAPTER 2

BOXING FIGHTS FOR ITS LIFE

Rocky Marciano, the only undefeated heavyweight champion, has just snapped Archie Moore's head back with a hard right in their 1955 fight. Moore, who was really a light-heavyweight, had trouble getting his due in his own weight class because other boxers feared him and avoided giving him a shot at the title he finally won in 1952 at the age of 36.

Cerdan Captures World Middleweight Title by Knocking Out Zale in Twelfth

DEFENDER IS DOWN AS ELEVENTH ENDS

Zale Collapses Under Cerdan's Left Hook and Is Unable to Continue Fighting

AMERICAN BADLY BEATEN

French Boxer Subjects Rival to Ceaseless Battering in Annexing World Crown

By JAMES P. DAWSON
Special to THE NEW YORK TIMES.

JERSEY CITY, N. J., Sept. 21—The world middleweight championship in boxing, an exclusive American property since Ruby Robert Fitzsimmons gave up the title, went to foreign lands tonight when Marcel Cerdan, doughty French gladiator from Casablanca, knocked out tough and rugged Tony Zale of Gary, Ind., in the twelfth round of their championship battle in the Roosevelt Stadium.

Before a crowd of 19,272, paying receipts of $242,840, Zale collapsed after one of the most futile battles of his glorious career. He had gone as far as he could in a pitifully weak defense of the crown he regained so spectacularly when he knocked out Rocky Graziano in Newark last June.

His strength sapped, his resistance at an ebb, his face battered and bruised, his body wracked and pained from an almost uninterrupted battering to which he had been subjected from the time the bell started the fighters on a journey scheduled for fifteen rounds, Zale collapsed under a left hook to the jaw just as the bell rang the end of the eleventh round.

Onlookers Are Stunned

His collapse stunned the onlookers, most of whom had backed him at odds of 5 to 8 to retain his title. He sank slowly, like a balloon deflating, alongside the ropes, near his own corner. Zale had to be assisted to his corner by Art Winch, one of his managers, and his trainer, Ray Arcel. A glance showed the helplessness of his condition, the impossibility of his going farther, and Winch signaled a halt to Referee Paul Cavalier. The referee stepped to Zale's corner and, while his handlers were still working frantically over the beaten champion, swung his right arm in a horizontal stroke, for the ring's ten-second count, which made the ending of the battle officially the twelfth round. This is in accordance with the rules governing boxing in New Jersey.

The finish came dramatically after a feeble, desperate effort by Zale to retain his crown against a fighter who fought furiously but gallantly and methodically to win a battle which brought for Cerdan the realization of a lifetime's ambition.

Regarded by the majority in advance of the struggle as an inviting target for the paralyzing blows of Zale, Cerdan surprised everybody with a style of fighting on which he rode to easy triumph in the most important fight of his career against the most dangerous foeman he has ever faced.

Eight Rounds to Cerdan

Cerdan was a leader on points by a one-sided margin when the dramatic finish came. Referee Cavalier had Cerdan in front with eight rounds and had scored two for Zale, calling one even. Only in the third and fourth rounds did Cavalier vote for Zale.

The writer gave Zale only the fourth session, a round in which he rocked Cerdan with the one good punch he landed in defense of his title, a smashing right to the jaw.

In every other round Cerdan swarmed all over Zale, gradually reducing him to a state of exhaustion, where the Hoosier collapsed more because he had run out of steam than from the effects of the left hook to the jaw which was the final blow of the fight.

In his dressing room after the battle, Zale was examined by Dr. Harry F. Cohen, New Jersey State Athletic Commission physician. Dr. Cohen verified the exhausted condition of the beaten champion.

Zale's reflexes were found to be normal, as was his coordination. His pulse was said to be rapid, but Dr. Cohen said he simply was exhausted. Zale agreed with this.

Couldn't Do Anything

"I just wasn't there tonight," said Zale. "I just couldn't 'get off.' I knew what he was doing; I knew he was throwing all those right hands at me. But, I just couldn't do anything about it."

That, too, sums up the battle. Zale never looked more pitiful. Not even when he was swaying and staggering under the pile-driving blows of Graziano, in the first battle in which he knocked out the East Sider; in the second encounter when Graziano knocked him out, and in the recent Newark battle in which Zale so spectacularly regained the crown.

This is not to say Zale didn't fight his best. Rather, his best was inadequate. He had no counter for the furious fire of his foeman. He had no defense for the tireless fusillade of punches Cerdan unleashed at a pace that was amazing for a ring veteran of 32 and thirteen years of campaigning.

His unquestioned punching power a nebulous quality, Zale was as putty in the hands of the determined, irresistible Cerdan, whose fire knew no check or restraint.

The defending middleweight titleholder landing a right uppercut on Cerdan's face in first round

The New York Times

For gaining one of the ring's richest titles, Cerdan was guaranteed $40,000. Zale was guaranteed $120,000 as the defending champion. However, Cerdan's guarantee is steeped in conditions designed to assure an American locale when he defends his new-found honors.

An official of the Tournament of Champions, under whose auspices the battle was held, made known after the bout that Cerdan would collect only 20 per cent of the guarantee, after taxes. The rest will be held in escrow until Cerdan defends the championship in New York, Chicago or New Jersey, against a rival to be selected.

Cerdan's triumph created an unprecedented ring situation, which finds three Europeans in possession of world championships for the first time. Freddie Mills, the light-heavyweight titleholder, and Rinty Monoghan, flyweight champion, are the other class leaders.

Cerdan's triumph was attended with a scene of the wildest disorder, a tableau which gave Chief Charles J. Wilson's Jersey City police a busy half-hour or so in the excitement of the finish.

Wild-eyed countrymen of Cerdan, who had stood at attention while the French National Anthem was played and the "Star-Spangled Banner" was sung before the bout started, streamed like grasshoppers into the ring from all sides, stepping on writers, cameramen and officials in their mad dash to get to the side of their hero and congratulate Cerdan.

This demonstration of popularity exposed Cerdan to more danger of injury than he faced at any moment in the battle he so richly deserved to win. A blue-coated cordon finally went into action to beat off the advances of some who attempted to jump into the ring, and gathered up the ineligibles already there so that Cerdan could be escorted to his dressing room—a hero.

Battered and bruised and bleeding, Zale was the undeniable epitome of a beaten gladiator in his corner. His handlers worked furiously to restore his scattered senses and get him into a physical state where he could be pulled erect to

execute the ring's traditional acknowledgment of the vanquished for the victor, a shake of the hands, a forced smile through battered lips, and the time-honored expression, "good luck to you." It is doubtful if Zale's words were audible above the terrific din, or that Cerdan's response was heard.

As a fight it was a satisfactory spectacle, a bruising battle that was one-sided and yet held the possibility for drama. The expectation through most of the fight up to the eighth round was that Cerdan would tire through the combination of pace and the occasional body punching to which he was subjected, and that Zale's paralyzing punch would claim another victim.

That the drama came from the other direction only made the finish more exciting, but it was a nat-

ural consequence of what had been produced in the ring.

As he so expertly put it, Zale "never got off." This means he never really got started. He didn't get started because he never had a chance. Cerdan saw to that.

Cerdan started the battle leading a looping right to the jaw, and never thereafter relinquished the attack. He swarmed all over Zale from the first bell until Zale collapsed, from the strength-sapping combination of punch, pace and the inescapable drain on his physical and nervous reserve.

Gesture Is Ignored

Early in the third round Zale crashed through with a terrific right to the heart which made Cerdan's knees sag as the French fighter sank toward the ropes. Cerdan looked appealingly at Referee Cavalier with the clinch

that followed, but the gesture was ignored. It was a legal blow. Later in the round Zale shot another right to the heart, and again Cerdan looked, again to be ignored.

A right to the jaw rocked Cerdan in the fourth, and in the first minute of the fifth Zale sank another mighty right to the heart which hurt Cerdan.

That just about sums up Zale's damaging effort in this struggle. For the rest, Zale was a human shock-absorber. He was bounced around the ring on the end of blinding rights and lefts which came in full-arm swings, short-arm hooks, decisive, tantalizing, annoying thrusts in an assault that was unstoppable.

September 22, 1948

Saddler Wins World Featherweight Title by Knocking Out Pep in 4th Round

VETERAN FLOORED 3 TIMES AT GARDEN

Saddler Pins First Knockout on Pep, 1-3 Choice, in 2:38 of Fourth Before 14,685

LEFT TO JAW LIFTS TITLE

Down Twice for 9 in Third, Willie Suffers Only Second Defeat in 137 Pro Bouts

By JOSEPH C. NICHOLS

Sandy Saddler became the featherweight champion of the world last night by knocking out Willie Pep of Hartford, Conn., in four rounds. In one of the biggest ring upsets of the year, the spindly Negro from Harlem stretched the defending titleholder on the canvas for the full count with a left hook to the jaw after the round had gone 2 minutes 38 seconds.

Just before the fighters entered the ring Pep became a 1-to-3 choice to retain the crown that he won clearly in June, 1946, but Saddler confounded the pricemakers by doing a workmanlike boxing job on Willie in the first two rounds. He floored Pep twice for counts of nine in the third before putting the crusher on the favored one in the fourth.

In going down to defeat, the 26-year-old Pep definitley lacked the quality from which he took his ring name. The veteran of ten years of amateur and professional battling had little spring in his legs, no sharpness to his punching and an inability to get away from

a tantalizing, and at the same time punishing, left to the face that Saddler constantly threw at him.

Veteran Fights Cautiously

In addition, the defending champion fought what for him was a cautious battle. Accustomed, in the past, to carrying the action to his rivals with the sound of the bell, Willie was all caution in his joust with the 22-year-old Saddler. It was the latter who did all the forcing, who advanced toward his foe without reck and who seemed every bit superior even in the first two rounds. A fairly good puncher with either hand, Pep reached his challenger once or twice with a solid left or right to the chin in those sessions, but Saddler showed no ill effects from them and went about carving up Willie with sharp lefts to the face and short rights to the body and head.

A crowd of 14,685 paid a total of $55,751 to sit in on Saddler's surprising success. The new champion was probably the least surprised person in the whole place at the end. He knew, as did most of those in attendance, that the fight was surrounded by "fix" rumors in which he was supposed to win, but the manner in which he disposed of Willie made it clear no collusion was necessary, that he had enough guns at his disposal to take care of Pep on his own. The battle simply proved that Willie didn't have enough to hold off the eager young Negro.

Veteran Has Weight Edge

Saddler weighed 124 pounds, as against 125½ for his victim. When they went out for the first round, the impression arose that the more compactly built Pep would have no trouble with his rangy rival, but Saddler quickly dispelled that belief by stepping into Willie and driving both hands to the body.

Returning a left and right to the head, Pep sought to carry the fight to close quarters. Saddler wrestled the champion, though, and twisted him around so that both were looking in the same direction before Referee Ruby Goldstein could untangle them. After the separation the challenger reached Willie with

several left hooks to the body.

In the second round Pep shot a straight right to the head, but Saddler moved forward to jab his left to the face repeatedly. The Harlem boxer again wrestled Willie out of position and received a solid right to the head after Goldstein had parted them.

Saddler continued to wade into Pep in the third, absorbing Willie's punches and sending a steady two-handed attack on his own account. Midway through the round Saddler let fly a straight left to the face and the punch carried so much force that it spilled Pep for a count of nine.

Bell Saves Pep in Third

On arising, Pep walked into a left hook and a right to the jaw, and went down again, once more taking nine. The bell ended the round before Saddler could resume his attack.

The challenger sprang at Pep in the fourth, belaboring him with rights to the jaw as Willie made only feeble returns. Suddenly, in a neutral corner, Saddler released a smashing left hook to the jaw and down went Willie for the full count.

The defeat was only the second and the first knockout suffered by Pep in 137 professional fights, of which he won 134. He was outpointed once by ex-lightweight king Sammy Angott and was held to a draw once by Jimmy McAllister.

The fight was the ninety-fourth of Saddler's pro career and his sixty-fourth knockout victory. A native of Boston, he moved to Harlem as a child. He has been boxing in the paid ranks for four years.

In his dressing room the new champion said he felt he would win after sampling what Pep dealt him in the first round. The Hartford fighter offered no alibi, except to say that the over-confidence of his handlers might have affected him.

Touching on the "fix" angle, Chairman Eddie Eagan of the State Athletic Commission told the fighters at the noon weighing that rumors of that nature attached themselves to every fight. He add-

ed: "I am holding you responsible to uphold the good name of boxing. There are rumors of a 'fix' before every fight, but we don't pay any attention to them. You are two honest athletes fighting in a great class for a great championship. You will represent boxing tonight."

On leaving commission headquarters, Pep said to reporters: "Don't worry about me. I'll be in there to win."

Saddler said nothing. He just won.

After the bout, Chairman Eagan declared the fight was a "good scrap." "Both boys did their utmost," he added.

C. P. Powell, another member of the commission, said, "it was a good, hard-hitting fight."

October 30, 1948

Pep Outpoints Saddler at Garden and Regains World Featherweight Crown

HARTFORD FIGHTER SCORES DECISIVELY

Pep Takes Unanimous Decision Over Saddler in 15-Round Contest Before 19,097

BATTLE SAVAGELY WAGED

Crowd Is Thrilled as Willie Avenges 4-Round Knockout by Negro Ace in October

By JAMES P. DAWSON

A precedent was set in the featherweight ranks last night when Willie Pep, the redoubtable little battler from Hartford, Conn., became the first boxer in the history of the 126-pound class to regain a lost world championship.

Pep swept tradition aside as he battered Sandy Saddler, Harlem Negro star into defeat in fifteen rounds of savage fighting at Madison Square Garden.

Another record was set as 19,097 fans paid $87,563 to see the struggle, the first defense by Saddler of the crown he lifted from Pep by a four-round knockout last October and they witnessed one of the most startling upsets in boxing annals. The previous indoor record for a featherweight title scrap was the $71,869 established here by Pep and Chalky Wright back in 1942.

Pep regained the title on the unanimous ballot of the three State Athletic Commission officials, and by a margin which could only have been improved upon with a knockout. The referee, Eddie Joseph, who more than once had to warn one or the other of the principals against roughness, voted ten rounds to Pep and five to Saddler. Frank Forbes, one of the judges, gave Pep nine rounds, Saddler five and called one even. The other judge, Jack O'Sullivan, gave Pep nine rounds and Saddler six. The writer gave Pep the decision by a margin of twelve rounds to three, voted Saddler only the fourth, tenth and fourteenth sessions.

Finest Fight of Career

To regain the title to which he first laid claim after beating Wright in 1942, but which he did not win outright until he conquered Sal Bartolo four years later, Pep put up the greatest battle of his career. He called on every ounce of strength within his compact little body, and all the guile he has accumulated through

eleven years as amateur and professional fighter to gain the triumph.

First, he had to avoid the smashing blows to which he fell victim less than five months ago, then he had to force the attack and keep forcing. How well he succeeded is reflected in the tabulation of the officials. And in riding to victory he proved to be one of the greatest featherweight champions the ring has known.

The fans who wager on boxing had installed Saddler a favorite at 5 to 7 when the rivals entered the ring. The odds had fluctuated through the day, with Pep the choice for a time at 5 to 7 shortly after the weighing at noon. The consensus before the battle was that Saddler would win again, and again by a knockout, on the generally accepted boxing theory that what has been done once will be done again.

But Pep is no believer in theory or tradition. He is a fighter of wind-mill style, tireless and with resourcefulness and baffling speed. He is champion again today because he has all these ring essentials, with unflagging courage as well.

Cuts About Both Eyes

He didn't look like a champion as he left the ring. He had nasty

cuts above and below the right eye and under the left eye. He was weary. He had just enough strength left to gallop through a terrific fifteenth round, fending off the desperate bid of his rival for a knockout that would turn impending defeat into glorious victory. He had enough to do this and his rival, too.

He had the championship and that made amends for all the bruises and pain.

None disagreed with the award at the final bell. None could. There was no disputing the decision, so well had Pep baffled and bewildered and beaten the man who a few short months ago had inflicted the only knockout in a long and glorious career.

Saddler had his greatest chance for victory in the tenth and fourteenth rounds. He almost finished Pep with a terrific right to the jaw in the tenth. This blow had Pep teetering as if to fall.

In the fourteenth a right to the jaw rocked Pep, and a left hook to the jaw shook the Hartford gladiator to his toes. But he rallied quickly from these punches and was alert and strong. The blows served only to arouse his fury.

Stung by Straight Left

A straight left to the face by Saddler was his best punch in the

fourth round and he cracked a right to the jaw solidly in the ninth that stung Pep. But the lad from Hartford was in top condition; he was out to win and there was no stopping him.

The fight was sensational because it was so unexpected; few in the gathering thought the Pep who crumpled last October could come back from that harrowing experience.

But Pep fooled them and he fooled the confident Saddler camp with an exhibition that was little short of amazing. In the first round he actually jabbed Saddler thirty-seven successive times in a demonstration of blinding speed that had Sandy looking like a novice. He neither gave quarter nor asked for it.

Pep was warned for wrestling in the first round and for "heeling," in the third. He prevented Sandy from landing his heavy punches at close quarters.

Giving Saddler a boxing lesson through the first three rounds, Pep appeared to weaken in the fourth, when Sammy plastered him with savage digs to the body and grazed the head with dangerous swings, almost upsetting Pep once with a left jab.

Punches From All Angles

A right opened a cut under Pep's

Willie Pep smashing a hook to Sandy Saddler's body in the first round of championship fight

The New York Times (by Edward Hausner)

left eye in the fifth, but the Hartford lad ignored the wound and out-boxed his foe through this session and those that followed up to the tenth. In fitful bursts Pep hammered Saddler with lefts and rights from all angles and in tireless fashion, while Saddler missed most of his blows.

Pep electrified the crowd with his boxing and fighting through the eleventh, twelfth and thir-

teenth rounds. He pelted Saddler with every blow known to boxing. But he gave his greatest thrill in the fifteenth when, after weathering the jarring fire of the fourteenth, he came back to fight Saddler all over the ring with a strength that few, if any thought he possessed.

Pep weighed 126 pounds, Saddler 124.

Eddie Comp, 130½, New Haven,

won a verdict over Eduardo Carrasco, 131, Peru, in the eight-round semi-final. Del Flanagan, St. Paul, 133¼, knocked out Walter Kolby, 138, Blasdell, N. Y., in 2:52 of the fourth round in their scheduled six-rounder. Referee Berle halting the battle because of a severe cut over Kolby's right eye.

Charley Angelee, 153½, Kings Mountain, N. C., outpointed Fran-

kie Cordino, 152½, Toronto, Canada, in six rounds. Sonny Luciano, 141¼, Paterson, N. J., received the verdict over Mel Goldsmith, 142, Bronx, in four rounds. Larry Mujica, 133, Yorkville, defeated Nick Darby, 132½, Jamaica, L. I., in four.

February 12, 1949

LaMotta Wins Title by Knockout as Cerdan Is Unable to Answer Bell for 10th

BRONX MAN VICTOR DESPITE HANDICAP

LaMotta Breaks Left Hand in Second, but Wrests Middleweight Title From Cerdan

22,183 SEE DETROIT UPSET

Frenchman, Nearly Floored in First, Badly Outfought and Unable to Start Tenth

By JAMES P. DAWSON
Special to THE NEW YORK TIMES.

DETROIT, June 16—Jake LaMotta is the new world middleweight champion. The rock-ribbed, steel-jawed little warrior from New York's Bronx, won the title tonight at Briggs Stadium, where before 22,183 wildly enthusiastic fans he knocked out stout-hearted Marcel Cerdan from French Morocco in the tenth of a scheduled fifteen-round struggle.

In his corner, unable to respond to the bell which rang to start the tenth round, sitting on his squat little stool, pained and near the point of exhaustion, Cerdan let pass the title he had won last September by blazing his way to victory over a shop-worn Tony Zale.

The gallant French fighter was complaining of pain in his left shoulder. Lew Burston, Cerdan's American representative, told Referee Johnny Weber at the end of the ninth round that the defending champion had found it difficult to raise his left arm ever since the second round.

Referee Weber summoned Dr. Joseph L. Cahalan of the Michigan State Athletic Board of Control to Cerdan's corner, where superficial examination disclosed no fracture or dislocation. Dr. Cahalan ordered the bout to proceed.

Cerdan Fights Gallantly

The bell rang for the tenth round to begin while Cerdan's handlers were still ministering to a worn and weary, pained and sickened fighter. Though he fought gallantly every inch of the way, Cerdan nevertheless was no match for the

sturdy oak that was LaMotta in this bruising struggle.

Jo Longman, manager of Cerdan, declined to let his protégé go out for the tenth round, so LaMotta received credit for a knockout in ten rounds. It is ring tradition that a boxer who refuses or is unable to respond to a bell starting a round is "knocked out of time" in that session.

Scenes of ecstatic joy and darkest gloom attended the finish. The joy was in the camp of LaMotta, whose handlers rushed to his side as the announcer clarioned "the winner by a knockout and the new champion, Jake LaMotta," and smothered him with caresses and good-natured thumping.

Joe Louis, director of the International Boxing Club, which promoted the fight, stepped into the ring and presented to La Motta a solid gold and jewel-studded championship belt, a $5,000 creation of Ray Hickok made especially for the occasion, which must be won three times to become the personal property of the champion. It is an attractive design, constructed with at least a pound of gold and studded with diamonds, sapphires and rubies.

Reign Lasts Nine Months

The gloom was in the Cerdan camp, where the French warrior was a dethroned king after a reign of nine short months, one of the shortest in the history of the division. The first defense of his title resulted in the most crushing defeat of Cerdan's career. In this blazing battle, postponed from last night and rushed into the ring almost one hour ahead of schedule tonight to beat a threatened rain storm, Cerdan was punched into oblivion cleanly and decisively through seven of the nine rounds completed.

LaMotta exhibited a left hand which had a notable swelling on it. He broke the second knuckle of the hand in the second round and was robbed of this weapon for hooking or swinging purposes. He had to jab with it for the most part or swing cautiously.

Dr. Vincent A. Nardiello, New York State Athletic Commission physician, here in the role of spectator, and Dr. Harold A. Robinson of the Michigan State Athletic Board of Control staff, examined Cerdan in his dressing room after the battle. They said it appeared he had torn the supra spinatus muscle, known as the elevator muscle, of the left arm. Burston planned to take Cerdan to a hospital.

From a betting standpoint, the result was an upset. Cerdan, at one time a 5-to-13 favorite, entered

the ring a 5-to-8 choice despite reports that there was little support for LaMotta.

To the student of boxing styles and fighting form, however, the result was more or less expected. Cerdan couldn't match LaMotta in strength, either in administering or absorbing punishment. Six years older, at 32, than LaMotta, with six years more of ring wear and tear after fourteen years of campaigning, Cerdan went as far as he could against a huskier, stronger, more savage foeman.

Following the fight, Chairman Eddie Eagan of the New York State Athletic Commission, visited LaMotta's quarters and significantly congratulated him as the "new middleweight champion" after a clean battle.

It was a thoroughly decisive battle, too, from the outset. In the first round LaMotta almost knocked out his rival. A long left hook to the jaw drove Cerdan against the ropes midway through the session, the champion's knees buckling under him.

So furious was LaMotta in his bid for victory that he wrestled Cerdan across the ring, trying to shake off the desperately holding defending champion. Finally he flung Cerdan down with a vicious thrust that many thought was a knockdown. Referee Weber refused to start a count and helped a stunned and surprised Cerdan back to his feet.

The psychological effect, however, sank home. Cerdan never reached the expectations of his supporters, though he fought valiantly in a recovery sustained through the second and third rounds, jarring LaMotta to his heels with successive short choppy rights to the jaw, head and face.

Bleeding from a cut over the right eye sustained in that boisterous first round, Cerdan suffered a cut on the bridge of the nose in the second as LaMotta jabbed repeated lefts to the face when he wasn't sinking intermittent rights and lefts to the ribs and wind. In

the third round Cerdan's left hooks and short arm jolts ripped open an old cut over LaMotta's right eye. Incensed, LaMotta was wild with his attack and was warned for an erratic left aimed at the body.

After the third round, however there was nothing to the battle. LaMotta swarmed all over Cerdan, weakening him with a two-fisted body fire, shifting to the head with short arm lefts and rights and jabbing at will. These jabs were the contest's only approach to boxing skill.

For a battle of bruisers, it was amazingly clean. LaMotta was warned for a low left in the third round, and a low right in the fourth. Cerdan was warned for a low right in the sixth. No penalty was imposed.

Cerdan was so weakened he didn't know where his corner was as the seventh and eighth rounds ended. Indeed, the eighth round found Cerdan in a disorderly retreat that indicated clearly he would not last.

Though he suffered no particular battering through the ninth, Cerdan would have fallen at the bell had not his handlers eased him gently on to his stool.

Cerdan has an agreement for a return title bout with LaMotta within ninety days. Jim Norris of I. B. C. wants it for this city, but Harry Markson seeks it as a New York attraction, perhaps in September.

Cerdan would be advised wisely to forget all about it, though. He is flirting with disaster even entertaining the thought of facing LaMotta in a ring again.

Gross receipts amounted to $159,762. Net receipts were $127,810.

It was announced LaMotta weighed 159½ pounds and Cerdan 158. These were for yesterday's original weighing before last night's postponement, but at a reweighing which flaunted precedent this morning LaMotta scaled 158¼ and Cerdan 159¼.

June 17, 1949

Charles Wins NBA Heavyweight Title by Beating Walcott

CINCINNATIAN GETS UNANIMOUS VERDICT

Charles Defeats Walcott for a Partial Claim to World Title Vacated by Louis

25,932 FANS PAY $246,546

Slow Chicago Fight Justifies New York Refusal to Accept Winner as New Champion

By JAMES P. DAWSON
Special to THE NEW YORK TIMES.

CHICAGO, June 22—In a bout that bore not even a faint resemblance to the twenty-five title struggles in which Joe Louis engaged during his twelve-year reign, Ezzard Charles, 28-year-old Cincinnati Negro, tonight gained partial recognition as successor to the world heavyweight championship Louis relinquished when he retired from the ring.

Charles became the National Boxing Association's titleholder when he carried off the decision over aging Jersey Joe Walcott of Camden, N. J., at Comiskey Park, in a fifteen-round bout witnessed by 25,932 fans who paid receipts of $246,546.

Radio and television rights increased receipts to $281,546.

Referee Davey Miller and the two judges, Harold Marovitz and Frank (Spike) McAdams, were unanimous in their verdict favoring Charles at the close of a bout that was notable principally for the patience demonstrated by the onlookers whose sentiments were revealed in frequent demands for action.

On an aggregate basis, as points are weighed under the rules of the Illinois State Athletic Commission, Charles won by 233 to 217. The judges were agreed on scorecards of 78 to 72. Referee Miller scored the battle 77 to 73 for Charles, who won by eight rounds to six, with one even, on the writer's sheet.

Not Recognized in New York

Despite this victory, Charles has yet to establish himself as a universally recognized champion. The New York State Athletic Commission, of which Edward P. F. Eagan is chairman, declined to recognize the battle as a championship affair, preferring a series of eliminations to establish clearly a successor to Louis' vacated title.

A feeling that Charles and Walcott did not represent the best in a class never before so barren of capable performers explained the hesitancy reflected in New York's decision. After the battle, observers felt the justification for New York's action was inescapable.

It is proposed to pair Charles with the winner of a meeting between Lee Savold and Bruce Woodcock in London Sept. 6. The survivor doubtless will merit universal recognition, for the international flavor will be a strong consideration.

Perhaps such a champion will be determined under more exciting and satisfactory circumstances. For this meeting of Charles and Walcott appeared no better than a good preliminary on previous championship cards to which fans had become accustomed through the reigns of Louis. Gene Tunney and Jack Dempsey, to mention only the moderns.

Wild Post-Battle Scene

The real excitement was crowded into a post-battle scene. Only two of the ballots had been announced, certifying that Charles could not lose, when many of Charles's friends and Walcott's sympathizers, jostled by photographers and radio microphone bearers, swarmed into the ring along with a detail of burly policemen assigned to keep order during a modified good-natured riot.

At the height of this confusion Jake Mintz, manager of Charles, suddenly went into a swoon near a neutral corner. His wife became hysterical and climbed recklessly over seats and working press benches trying to fight her way into the ring.

She was restrained by a strong-armed reporter who counseled calmness while Dr. J. M. Houston, of the State Athletic Commission staff at the ringside, rushed to Mintz and restored him with an application of smelling salts. Then Jake, pale but laughing, was aided out of the ring yelling wildly he expected Charles to be "a fighting champion."

In his dressing room following the eminently fair and tremendously popular decision, Charles paid tribute to Walcott as a rugged foeman. He added his only immediate plan was always to be in condition to defend the title.

Left Hand Hurt, Says Charles

"I didn't think the fight was close," he said. "I thought I was far in front, but I wasn't sure until the final bell.

"I hurt my left hand in the fourth round but didn't realize it until the fight was over. I didn't chase Walcott more than was necessary because he hits hard with his right hand and I wasn't exposing myself to unnecessary danger."

Walcott, disappointed, said he was ready to fight Charles again next week to prove his mastery.

"I thought I won nine rounds," said the beaten veteran of nineteen years in boxing. "I thought I was ahead all the way and so did my handlers."

Asked why he hadn't chased Charles more and let fly with more punches, as he had in flashes against Louis in two bouts, Walcott said: "I hurt my right hand in the third round and had to be careful. Charles don't take a punch good but he moves away fast. Louis was easier to hit, but he hit back harder."

Izzy Klein, who seconded Walcott, said: "I told Joe after the seventh round to go out there and stop backing away, to go forward and be the boss, but I guess it didn't turn out that way."

Charles left the ring with five minor cuts about his left eye, the visible evidence of Walcott's stiff left jabs and occasional right crosses. Walcott had a split upper lip.

As a competitive spectacle, the struggle left much to be desired. This is offered as a critical appraisal rather than a complaint, for it had been said in advance that Charles and Walcott merely were the best of a poor lot, as measured by N. B. A. standards. Under the circumstances, only a knockout could have redeemed the affair, but at no stage was such a result even approached.

ACTION DURING FOURTH ROUND OF TITLE BOUT IN CHICAGO

Jersey Joe Walcott, right, swings a vicious right at Ezzard Charles in NBA championship match

Associated Press Wirephoto

The nearest approach to a knockdown was in the seventh session when Charles, low with a sweeping left hook aimed at the body, landed the punch on Walcott's right thigh. Off balance with the direction of the blow, Charles pitched forward on his left shoulder in a neutral corner as Walcott backed to the ropes, pointing, for Referee Miller's benefit, to his right thigh. Miller refused to recognize the tumble as a knockdown and ordered Charles to rise, which the Cincinnatian did, slowly.

In a tedious exhibition, Charles carried the attack through most of the rounds and won the first, second, third, fourth, seventh, ninth, tenth and eleventh. In the fifth, sixth, twelfth, thirteenth, fourteenth and fifteenth, Walcott appeared to have the advantage, principally because he out-boxed his foe. The eighth was about even.

Both Fighters Draw Warnings

Four times Charles was warned for low punching. He drew the first caution in the opening round, two more in the fourth and another in the sixth. Walcott was warned for holding and hitting in the fourth and twice in the eleventh, when one of Charles' rights split his upper lip.

Charles didn't rip and slash at his rival as a capable contender for a heavyweight title might be expected to do. Walcott didn't tear and thunder at Charles either. In fitful bursts, Charles grazed his aging rival's chin with damaging rights, which, however, lacked the power to topple.

After dropping the first four rounds, Walcott drove Charles to the ropes with a left hook to the jaw in the fifth, grazing the chin with a left and a right before the bell. In the sixth Walcott smacked his foe off balance with a left hook to the body and stirred Charles to such excitement the Ohioan ripped low with a left for the body and was warned. Referee Miller notified the judges he was taking the round from Charles, but Walcott had won the session without the penalty.

Charles pummeled Walcott in the seventh after he had risen from his tumble. A left and a right to the jaw shook Walcott to his heels and Charles battered the Jersey man mercilessly through the round until Walcott lashed a long left hook to the jaw and the attack stopped immediately.

Rivals Cautious in Eighth

The eighth was a cautious round with little action. In the ninth a puffed eye Charles had sustained in the fourth started dripping blood under Walcott's occasional left jabs in retreat, but Charles was the aggressor through this session as he was in the tenth when he twice rocked Walcott with rights that grazed the jaw and pounded the veteran's body with solid left and right-hand smashes. Even so, Walcott near the end of the round drove Charles back with a full-arm right to the jaw.

In the closing four rounds Walcott assumed the offensive. Outboxing his rival, he forced Charles about the ring, lashing out in spurts with desperate rights for the jaw, obviously in a grim bid to turn the tide. The only distinguishing feature of this period of battle occurred in the thirteenth when Walcott rocked his foe to the heels with a right to the jaw and missed another before the bell.

Walcott weighed 195½ pounds and Charles 181¾.

June 23, 1949

Robinson Retains Welterweight Title by Outpointing Gavilan Before 27,805

CHAMPION RECEIVES UNANIMOUS VERDICT

Robinson, Weighing 147-Pound Limit, Outboxes Gavilan in Philadelphia 15-Rounder

---

RECEIPTS REACH $175,754

Harlem Veteran Indicates He May Drop Title and Seek Middleweight Crown

By JAMES P. DAWSON
Special to The New York Times.

PHILADELPHIA, July 11—In a masterful exhibition of combined boxing and fighting, Ray Robinson of New York's Harlem tonight retained his world welterweight championship by outpointing rugged Kid Gavilan of Havana in a fifteen-round bout that attracted 27,805 paying fans to Municipal Stadium and receipts of $175,754.

By unanimous decision of the referee and two judges, Robinson won a stirring battle which, strangely enough, held little or no danger from the gallant Cuban regarded as the outstanding challenger. This was Robinson's fourth successful defense of his title wrested from Tommy Bell in 1946.

Pacing himself perfectly, adjusting his fighting to situations provoked by Gavilan's awkward style, parrying blows, slipping and swaying with them, blocking punches and picking them off in mid-air, Robinson won as he pleased in a demonstration of ring perfection which has established him as one of the best welterweights ever.

Referee Charley Daggert called nine rounds to six for Robinson. So did Harry Lasky, one of the judges. The other judge, Frank Knarsborough, voted twelve rounds to Robinson and three to Gavilan. The writer scored it as did Knarsborough, giving only the third, fourth and eleventh rounds to the Cuban Negro.

Cuban's Stamina Not Enough

Gavilan just is not in the same class with the Harlem Negro, though the Cuban has more endurance, determination and fearlessness than any other in Robinson's limited field of challengers. What Gavilan lacks is the boxing skill and paralyzing punching power of the champion.

Robinson admitted after the battle he was taking no chances, though he might have in the eighth round when he staggered Gavilan. Robinson's play was to win and that he did without exposing him-

Sugar Ray Robinson driving a blow to Kid Gavilan's head in the sixth round at Philadelphia's Municipal Stadium last night. The referee is Charley Daggert.   Associated Press Wirephoto

self to any more danger than a slight cut over the right eye sustained in the fourth round.

Gavilan sought with his reckless rushing and steady punching to the body to wear down a champion he, like so many others, had suspected must be nearing the end of his tether after nine years of professional boxing. However, this line of reasoning overlooked Robinson's superlative style and the strength Sugar Ray retained even though he just did make the 147 pounds to his rival's 144½.

Following the battle a contradiction developed in the champion's quarters. Manager George Gainsford said from the ring that Robinson would be ready again to defend his welterweight title Aug. 24. Robinson, however, indicated he might surrender the welterweight crown and seek the middleweight title, now held by rugged Jake Lamotta.

At His Best, Says Robinson

"I was in the best shape of my career for this fight," said Robinson. "I never tired and he never hurt me. I don't know if I will fight any more as a welterweight. If I can get a crack at the middleweight title I'll give up the 147-pound title."

Gavilan, crestfallen, nevertheless had little complaint to offer. "I didn't see too many rounds for Robinson," he said in his broken English. "The judge who gave him twelve rounds, he crazy. He hit me hard several times, but I was surprised at the decision and would like to make one more fight with heem."

Spectacular and altogether satisfying the battle was, despite its one-sided nature. Gavilan made it so because he fights only one way and that way is advantageous to Robinson.

The Cuban ripped and slashed at the champion from first bell to last. In many plunges, Gavilan's marksmanship was affected by his own recklessness and Robinson's consummate cleverness, but he did land at times and never stopped trying.

After opening a cut over Robinson's right eye early in the fourth, Gavilan made the wound a target for occasional lefts. He rushed Robinson to the ropes and worked him around to a neutral corner with his fiery lunges, hammering at the body all the time.

Robinson Takes Command

After Gavilan's opening flurry in the fifth, Robinson took command, although, near the bell in the seventh, Gavilan let fly a sweeping right for the jaw which caught Robinson off balance and spun the champion partly around. Early in the eighth, too, Gavilan pressed forward fearlessly, hooking lefts to the body and sweeping rights which grazed the jaw, but near the end of the round Robinson staggered his foe with a crashing right to the jaw followed by a flurry of lefts and rights to the head.

In every round thereafter, save for the eleventh, when the champion took a breather, Robinson was in absolute command. He hurt Gavilan with wicked right digs to the ribs when the Cuban crouched, wearied the Kid with solid rights to the heart and jarred him off balance repeatedly with sharp left hooks, singly or in two-fisted volleys.

In the fourteenth round the

champion backed to the ropes and slipped or swayed with countless punches the Cuban missed. Then Robinson broke out in a two-fisted assault which battered Gavilan about the face and head until Robinson tired of the drilling.

July 12, 1949

Dempsey Voted Greatest Fighter In 50 Years, With Joe Louis Next

Jack Dempsey, the Manassa Mauler, has been named the greatest fighter of the past fifty years. Not boxer but fighter was the word for this restless man with the cracked-in nose and the brine-soaked fists.

Always a merciless stalker inside the ropes, Dempsey parlayed a punch and a dream into more than $5,000,000 earnings after a hungry start in the jungle camps of the Far West.

Now comparatively sleek and comfortable but once raw as life itself, Dempsey outdistanced all opposition in the opinion of sportswriters and broadcasters in The Associated Press mid-century poll.

It was strictly a two-man race between Dempsey and Joe Louis, with Dempsey a runaway winner. Of the 393 votes, Dempsey drew 251 and the Brown Bomber 104.

Henry Armstrong, a great triple champion, polled 16 votes. Gene Tunney, who dethroned Dempsey, drew only six votes for fourth place.

The Dempsey of the broiling July.

4 afternoon, 1919, at Toledo, has been called the perfect fighting machine of all time. Certainly there have been few to compare with the weaving, crouching terror who cut ponderous Jess Willard to ribbons that sizzling day and won the world heavyweight championship.

After flooring the massive Willard seven times in the first round, Dempsey climbed out of the ring and started for his dressing room. He didn't know the bell had rung while the referee was counting out Willard. Hustled back to the ring, he went two more rounds before Jess' seconds threw in the towel.

His end of the $27,500 purse must have seemed like a fortune to the ex-bouncer in the red sweater and tattered cap who left home after the eighth grade and took to the rails.

The record books go back to 1915 on Dempsey, who was born at Manassa, Colo., June 24, 1895.

But he was fighting long before 1915. Moving from town to town, picking up whatever work he could get and fighting for small change, Dempsey learned the trade the hard way.

Long before Jack Kearns ever saw him, he came to New York. Nobody rolled out a plush carpet. He returned to the West and was knocked out by Fireman Jim Flynn, his only knockout loss, at Murray, Utah, in 1917. Shortly after that Kearns came into the picture.

Hit Jackpot at Toledo

The team of Dempsey and Kearns, the old ballyhoo merchant, rocketed to the top. They hit the jackpot at Toledo. From that time on, they were in the big money. Georges Carpentier, Luis Angel Firpo and the two Gene Tunney fights were ahead, but before the Tunney bouts, Dempsey and Kearns parted.

With the help of Promoter Tex Rickard, the Dempsey-Kearns team made boxing's first million dollar gate in 1921. Carpentier, a French war hero, was the bait. The crowd paid $1,789,238 to see Dempsey win easily on a knockout in four rounds.

The Firpo bout, most dramatic of all time, followed closely a dreary Dempsey performance against Tom Gibbons at Shelby, Mont., on July 4, 1923. It was a financial fiasco that plunged Shelby into bankruptcy, and Dempsey failed to hurt Gibbons in a bout that went the full fifteen rounds.

All that was forgotten after the Firpo battle at the Polo Grounds on Sept. 14, 1923. Knocked down seven times in the first round, the Wild Bull of the Argentine Pampas knocked Dempsey through the ropes to touch off one of the wildest scenes in boxing history.

A HIGHLIGHT IN JACK DEMPSEY'S FIGHTING CAREER

Battering his way to the title as he had Jess Willard on the ropes in their match at Toledo, Ohio, on July 4, 1919.

With the help of newspaper men, Dempsey barely scrambled back through the ropes at the count of nine. They still argue about that one. Could Dempsey have climbed back by himself? Was Dempsey really knocked out? Was Dempsey pushed or punched?

Victor in Second Round

Dempsey quickly flattened Firpo in the second round. That fight drew $1,188,603 and Dempsey's share was $470,000.

Not until he met Tunney in the rain at Philadelphia, Sept. 23, 1926, did Dempsey risk his title again. He lost it to the ex-Marine boxing master before the largest crowd ever to see a fight, 120,757. Dempsey received $718,868, his biggest purse, of the $1,895,733 house.

A ring-rusty Dempsey who hadn't had a real fight in three years explained this loss to Estelle Taylor, his wife.

"I just forgot to duck, honey," he said. Those were the days when Dempsey had discarded the sweater and the cap for the fine silk shirts of a gentleman.

A "warm-up" fight for the second Tunney match, a knockout victory over Jack Sharkey, July 21, 1927, produced another million dollar gate, and Dempsey collected $350,711.

Discounting exhibitions and an ill-fated comeback, Dempsey wound up his active career in his second bout with Tunney. In keeping with his character, it was a tumultous ending.

Dempsey lost again but not until he had floored Tunney for the famous "long count" of 14 by Referee Dave Barry in the seventh round. While Barry tried to persuade Jack to retreat to a neutral corner, the seconds flitted away and Tunney came around.

In those fleeting seconds Dempsey lost his chance of becoming the only man in history to recapture the heavyweight championship. He did collect $425,000 as his share of boxing's richest gate, $2,658,660.

Following is the result of the poll:

	Votes.
1—Jack Dempsey, heavyweight	251
2—Joe Louis, heavyweight	104
3—Henry Armstrong, 126-147 pounds	16
4—Gene Tunney, heavyweight	6
5—Benny Leonard, lightweight	5
6—Jack Johnson, heavyweight	4
7—Jim Jeffries, heavyweight	2

One Vote Each—Bob Fitzsimmons, heavyweight; Sam Langford, heavyweight; Mickey Walker, middleweight; Ray Robinson, welterweight; Joe Gans, lightweight.

January 29, 1950

Pep, Shoulder Injured, Loses Featherweight Title to Saddler in Eighth Round

DOCTOR HALTS BOUT WITH WILLIE AHEAD

Pep Dislocates Left Shoulder in 7th-Round Clinch, Goes to Hospital for X-Rays

SADDLER GETS KNOCKOUT

Hartford Man's Superb Boxing Dominates Fight, Though He Is Down for 9 in Third

By JAMES P. DAWSON

An injured left shoulder last night ended Willie Pep's reign as world featherweight champion, and gave to Sandy Saddler, Harlem's string-bean former champion, the distinction of regaining the title on a knockout in the eighth round of what was to have been a fifteen-round battle in the Yankee Stadium.

Finishing the seventh round with a magnificent exhibition of the boxing skill that has been his characteristic for ten years of ring warfare, Pep could not respond to the bell when it rang starting the eighth round because of a dislocated left shoulder, sustained in the wrestling action of a clinch on the ropes near a neutral corner in the last few seconds of the seventh.

Dr. Vincent A. Nardiello, summoned to the ring by Referee Ruby Goldstein when Lou Viscusi, Pep's manager, notified the arbiter of the injury, diagnosed the injury as a dislocated left shoulder and authorized the announcement Pep could not continue.

Saddler Eager to Continue

Saddler sprang across the ring eager to resume fighting, as Dr. Nardiello ministered to Pep in the latter's corner. But Referee Goldstein met the furious, eager charge of Sandy, clasped him in his arms, turned him and led him back to his corner—victor and champion in a battle in which he was trailing, and badly, at the time of the interruption.

Referee Goldstein authorized the announcement the bout ended in the eighth, dispelling the controversy usually associated with a fight here when a boxer fails to respond to the bell starting a round. The rule here is that in such cases the ending reverts to the last completed round.

In the jurisdiction of the National Boxing Association the ending is recorded in the round the affected boxer fails to start. But any dispute on the finishing round was obviated because the bell rang starting the eighth round, Saddler leaped from his corner, eager to resume milling, and Pep was unable to heed the bell's call.

The knockout followed automatically since it is the time-honored routine that when a boxer, through any cause whatsoever, fails to respond to the call of "time," he is knocked out.

Three Doctors Attend Pep

Mystery surrounded the Hartford (Conn.) veteran's condition immediately following the bout. Writers clamoring for admittance to his dressing quarters were rebuffed while three physicians, including Dr. Nardiello, attended the dethroned fistic king. Indeed, one of Pep's retinue failed to break past the barrier for ten minutes until he had identified himself thoroughly.

It was a dramatic, though disappointing, finish to a tense, spectacular battle, in which Pep was moving steadily to a one-sided victory on points. The tenseness arose from the uncertainty about the veteran Pep's ability to avoid and/or withstand the battering blows of the heavier hitting Saddler. The spectacle was wrapped up principally in the bewildering speed with which Pep baffled his younger foe and his blinding rapidity, in the use of his piston-like arms.

At the time of the unexpected ending Pep was in front on the score sheets of the two judges, Arthur Susskind (Young Otto), and Frank Forbes. Susskind had Pep in front, five rounds to two. Forbes had Pep leading, four rounds to two, with one even.

The writer had Pep in front, six rounds to one, giving Saddler only the third session. This was the most sensational round of the battle, when Saddler dropped his rival for a count of nine with a sharp left hook to the jaw, as the climax to a vicious outburst the Harlemite launched.

X-Ray Examination Made

Pep was removed to St. Clare's Hospital for X-rays following the bout.

Drs. Nardiello, Alexander Schiff and Charles Muzzicato, acting chairman of the State Athletic Commission's Medical Advisory Board, collaborated in the following statement after an extensive examination of the ex-champion in his dressing quarters:

"Pep complained of severe pain in his left shoulder and inability to move it in any direction. Examination in the ring by Dr. Nardiello showed he sustained a sub-luxation, a dislocation of the left shoulder, which was immediately reduced by Dr. Nardiello.

"Examination in the dressing room also disclosed a soft tissue swelling and immediate X-ray has been ordered. Pep will be removed to St. Clare's Hospital."

Pep complained bitterly of the unexpected ending and charged Saddler with wrestling tactics instead of fighting. "He got a double arm lock on me in that last clinch on the ropes in the seventh round and that is what did it," said Pep. "I felt a crack in my shoulder and couldn't raise the arm when I went to my corner."

It was unfortunate the bout ended as it did; unfortunate from the spectator's standpoint because it finished abruptly a bout that was proceeding at a blazing pace between a marvelous little boxer and a slugger who was stalking his prey waiting for the kill he so confidently had predicted in advance; unfortunate, too for its effect on Pep's status. For, the defending champion undeniably was on the road to victory. The only question was whether he could maintain the terrific pace. Indications were that he could.

The 38,781 spectators who turned out for this third meeting of Pep and Saddler, paid receipts of $262,150.41, a record for featherweight title contention. The question of whether Pep could retain the title he had regained from Saddler in February last year, together with the promise of a spectacular bout, produced this record crowd.

Underdog in the betting entering the ring, although the odds shortened from 9 to 5 to 7 to 5, Pep amazed most of the onlookers with a charateristic battle in which he out-thought, out-maneuvered, out-boxed, and, at times, outfought the dashing, crashing Saddler.

Pep Makes Difficult Target

One of the most difficult targets the ring has ever known, Pep made the most of his boxing superiority, contravening the admittedly heavier hitting power of Saddler. He jabbed Saddler dizzy in the first two rounds, hooked his left to the body, swung his right occasionally to the head and had Saddler all at sea, though Sandy never stopped pressing forward.

Tiring of this treatment, Saddler tossed caution aside with the third round. Turning on the fury he had been expected to flash from the opening bell, he ripped and tore at Pep regardless of the Hartford boxer's jabs, cuts, hooks and slaps.

A left hook to the jaw dropped Pep for nine. Arising unhurt, Pep ran into a blazing volley with which Saddler opened an old cut under Pep's left eye, bloodied his nose and battered Pep generally.

Counter-firing, Pep blasted away with desperate left jabs and hooks and an occasional right swing. Enough of these swings landed, along with jabs, to cause a swelling over Saddler's left eye.

Eager to follow what he though was his advantage, Saddler ripped and slashed at his foe early in the fourth round, bidding for a knockout, jarring Pep with a grazing left hook to the jaw. Pep proved he was unhurt by fighting back furiously, outpunching and outjabbing Saddler as he avoided Sandy's most devastating blows.

In the fifth round Pep was so much the master that at one stage he ducked under a left hook, backed to the ropes, grasped Saddler's left elbow and, with a slight twist, sent Sandy sprawling down and almost out of the ring.

Saddler Becomes Wilder

Desperate with his futility against a will-o'-the-wisp target,

A classy featherweight who held the title several times, Willie Pep (left) is shown here in one of his several fights with Sandy Saddler.

Kid Gavilan (left), middleweight champion for four years, was one of the finest fighters active in the 1950's. In this photo he is shown with an opponent he faced several times: Billy Graham.

Saddler became wilder in the sixth, as Pep leaped in, sticking left jabs to the face, stepped back and leaped in again. Ducking under his foe's blows, cracking an overhand right to the face or head, or swinging a left to the body in combination with a right to the head, Pep had Saddler bewildered and helpless to stop or counter this fire. Saddler at one stage of the sixth almost wrestled Pep down in a clinch.

Pep was proceeding smoothly through the seventh, boxing as he had through the preceding six rounds, when Saddler lashed out with a left hook to the body. Three others followed in quick succession.

Pep continued to pepper and stick and stab with lefts that were accurate and frequent, and to swing with rights or hook with lefts that found the target on body or head until near the bell. Then, in a clinch on the ropes near a neutral corner, Saddler bent Pep's left arm backward in a move Pep said produced his injury.

It was announced each boxer weighed 124¾ pounds. But this followed a repair job on erratic scales which first had champion and challenger weighing 120 pounds, and the authenticity of the official weights was measured accordingly.

An injury ended the scheduled eight-round semi-final, similarly with the prospective winner transformed into the loser by a knockout. Fabela Chavez, 125, Los Angeles, received credit for a six-round knockout over Tom Collins, 125½, Boston, in the sixth round of this encounter, when Collins sustained an injury to an abnormally swollen left eye which impaired his vision and Dr. Nardiello refused to let him go out for the seventh round. At the time Collins was far ahead on point, having

won every round except the sixth.

Tony Cimmino, 146¼, Bayonne, N. J., won a six-round decision over Manouk Markarian, 145, Argentine. Massimo Sanna, 135½, West Side, outpointed Jackie Blair, 132, Dallas, in another six.

Bobby Fenty, 124, Harlem, earned the award over Charley Debow, 120½, Springfield, Mass., in four rounds. In another bout scheduled for four rounds, Georgie Flores, 141, Brooklyn, knocked out Fred Maybe, 136, Brooklyn, in 2:38 of the second.

CALLS IT WRESTLING BOUT

Pep 'Praises' Saddler's Mat Tactics, Which Sandy Admits

Though disconsolate after the fight, Willie Pep had nothing but praise for Sandy Saddler—as a wrestler.

"He beat me with a double armlock," was Willie's explanation of his downfall. "I couldn't use my arms the way he did, but if I could I'd have won."

Besides his reference to Sandy's grappling ability, Pep said that his rival did a fine job with his head. He indicated a welt under his left eye and explained, "He butted me here early in the fight."

The ex-champion was in considerable pain in his dressing room interview, and had to be eased by a sedative. He was proud of his showing up to the end, and expressed himself as eager for another fight with his two-time conqueror.

Saddler took his victory calmly. He admitted to wrestling, saying that's how Willie wanted it.

As far as the fight was concerned, Saddler said, "I know I had him in the third, but I was in no hurry."

September 9, 1950

Charles Outpoints Louis In Bruising 15-Round Bout

Proves 'They Never Come Back' in Winning Unanimous Decision for Heavyweight Title—Bomber Says He's Through

By JAMES P. DAWSON

A great champion went into the discard last night at the Yankee Stadium, the fightingest world heavyweight champion boxing ever knew, as Ezzard Charles pounded Joe Louis into a bleeding, helpless hulk to become undisputed holder of the heavyweight crown, at least as far as American boxing authorities are concerned.

Charles won the recognition through fifteen rounds of bruising fighting, in which he hammered Louis as he pleased, punched Joe around the ring as if he were an inanimate punching bag, outboxed, outfought, outmaneuvered what was once a great champion in a manner that proved, once again, the truth of the ring legend,

"they never come back."

By unanimous decision Charles ascended to the ring's highest pinnacle. He won the undivided vote of the three officials, Referee Mark Conn and the judges, Joe Agnello and Frank Forbes. None at the ringside disputed the verdict, for the progress of the battle left no room for disagreement, because Charles did everything except knock out Louis, and was perilously near doing just that in a blistering fourteenth round.

A crowd of 22,357, paying receipts of $205,370, saw the fall of the man who, until he retired in March of last year, was king of the ring. In the gathering were Gov. Thomas E. Dewey, Lieut. Gov.

Joe R. Hanley, Acting Mayor Vincent Impellitteri, Supreme Court Justice Ferdinand Pecora, Gen. Lucius D. Clay, and a giant from the Argentine who once bid for the title, Luis Angel Firpo.

They went to see whether Louis could succeed where some of the ring's illustrious before him had failed: Fitzsimmons, Corbett, Jeffries, Dempsey. They watched a battle in which the wish was father to the thought, a struggle in which sentiment overbalanced sound judgment as Louis was made a 1-to-2 favorite. And they saw a great fighter crushed ignominiously into a defeat that was only the second in a career dating back to 1934, a defeat that lacked only the finishing punch to parallel the only knockout Louis ever suffered, at the hands of Max Schmeling, back in 1936, a year before he became champion.

Desperately Louis fought with his limited, current best to thwart the fate that sent him down the road with other champions who had failed. Just as desperately did Charles fight to prove once again they never come back and, the Cincinnati Negro had his reward in a victory that was so one-sided there was almost no competition.

By a vote of thirteen rounds to two, Judge Forbes said Charles won. Judge Agnello gave the fight to Charles by twelve rounds to three. Referee Conn voted ten rounds for Charles and five for Louis. The writer gave Louis only three rounds, the second, fourth and tenth.

Louis didn't have a chance, not necessarily because of the fact he had been idle for more than two years and had been officially in retirement since March 1, 1949. He didn't have a chance because his marvelously muscled body and his nervous system responded to the natural disintegration that comes with age.

At thirty-six years of age, Louis was a shadow of the Brown Bomber, the Dark Destroyer who had boomed out of Detroit as a stripling in 1934 and, battering past all heavyweights in an unparalleled, almost uninterrupted surge forward, had fought his way to the title in three years. Everybody knew his reflexes must have suffered. That's inevitable. Few suspected his coordination would be what it was, so amazingly lacking that it was non-existent.

Stalking Style Still There

There is the story of the battle. Louis, fired with an admirable determination to regain the crown he voluntarily had surrendered on retirement, plodded forward with his old irresistible, stalking style.

But there the similarity between the old Louis and the Louis of last night ended. He wanted to do things. He wanted to strike out with paralyzing left or pulverizing right, as he had so often before in a brilliant career. He set himself as he shuffled forward in the old, familiar way, but he never quite got around to throwing the punches.

He wanted to block, dodge or pick off punches as used to be his custom, and strike with lightning-like speed and with savage finality, but, he never quite could do it. He didn't have the coordination, that irreplaceable element so necessary

to boxing which vanishes so rapidly as you grow old.

Truly it may be said in Louis' case, the spirit was willing, but the flesh was weak. He fought gallantly, grimly, desperately, recklessly at times, but the communication system between nerves and muscles was faulty—and Louis went down to defeat, without, however, being disgraced.

His face battered out of shape under the pummeling of his 29-year-old rival, his left eye closed, his right eye sporting a lump, his nose bleeding, his lips cut and bruised, Louis announced his retirement from the ring in his dressing room following the battle.

No Note of Regret

He said nothing about regretting this return bout, arranged primarily, it was announced, so the Bomber that once was could get money to pay back income taxes. But, he did say "positively" when he said this au revoir, and it can be believed this time Louis means it. He is like the old Louis, only in appearance.

In the conqueror's dressing quarters the scene was typical. Joy ran to pandemonium measure as well-wishers clustered about Charles, led by his manager, Jake Mintz, and his financial backer, Tommy Tannas.

They were celebrating with a conqueror who was not unmarked. Charles' face was battered out of shape, too. His left eye was puffed to the closing point. A swelling was noticeable about his right eye and cheek bone.

His nose was bashed and bleeding and his lips were bruised, all evidence of the battering power remaining in the few punches Louis managed to land, but these wounds will go unnoticed. Now that Charles is world heavyweight champion, he has achieved the goal of every boxer who ever drew on a glove.

True, his claim to the title is not universally certified. He is a ring king without honor in the jurisdiction of the British boxing board of control, which recognizes Lee Savold of Paterson, N. J., because he knocked out a harmless, inoffensive Bruce Woodcock.

A Confusing Situation

Nor does the International Boxing Union recognize Charles as champion, perhaps in sympathy with the British authorities. Still Charles need worry little about this conflicting and confusing situation since he is the ring monarch in America, boxing's mecca.

In true boxing tradition, Louis paid tribute to his conqueror in the ring after his own farewell to boxing had been sealed by the first decision ever given against him as a pro. Then he wished Charles luck in his reign.

Afterward, in his dressing room, Louis, always honest in his actions and statements, admitted he had been beaten, but refused to become extravagant in his praise of Charles. This was not because he begrudged Ezzard his victory, but because it always has been his characteristic to be moderate in everything—except the ring warfare he waged when he was The Louis.

Charles' boxing skill, agility, resourcefulness and unerring marksmanship against a ponderous, floundering foe won the battle. To the surprise of many this over-

Joe Louis blocks a long left in the fourteenth round of the heavyweight championship fight at the Yankee Stadium

The New York Times

grown light-heavyweight, held more or less in contempt as the best of a bad lot of heavyweights, flashed a battle plan and grim determination which brooked no interference, even from Louis.

Charles only briefly evinced respect for his rival's punching prowess. It was as if he realized more than anybody else the feeble nature of Louis' fighting maximum and he acted accordingly.

He ripped and slashed at Louis for the entire fifteen rounds. He outjabbed Louis, who once had boasted a rapier-like and destructive jab. He outslugged this Louis, who outweighed him by more than thirty pounds and towered and bulked above him. He outthought Louis, which was easy.

In short, Charles did everything that could be expected of him, and he had an easy time doing it. He left only the suspense that goes with the feeling that sooner or later Louis must "nail" him with a destructive punch. That feeling was always there, right up to the final bell.

When Louis did land his most damaging blow of the fight in the tenth round, a solid left hook to the jaw which made Charles' knees sag, the ebony-hued fighter from Cincinnati charged right back. Fighting superbly to skirt danger, he frustrated Louis' most savage outburst of fighting as the Brown Bomber sought to press a momentary advantage.

Two-Fisted Attack Erratic

The real highlight developed in the fourteenth round and Louis was the victim. A right to the jaw

sent the fuseless Bomber staggering against the ropes near a neutral corner. Blinded and buffeted, weary of arm and leg, harassed with the punishing punches of his foeman, Louis was primed for a crash to the ring floor.

Charles was after him in a flash, fighting his wearied best to score a knockout. The crowd was roaring its encouragement.

But Charles' desperate fire was erratic, though he plied Louis with blows to the head and body from both hands. Louis had the instinct to sway and "ride" with, or duck, the punches which might have sent him tottering to the canvas.

Through the round Louis was battered like a human punching bag. He shook off the effect of the staggering right and resumed shuffling, pressing, plodding forward, but aimlessly.

Just as the bell clanged, Louis hooked a solid right to the jaw, but Charles responded with a left hook to the head that landed after the bell. Referee Conn had to separate them.

Charles was warned, for two violations as the battle started. The first was for hitting on the break. The second was for sweeping low with a left hook for the body at long range. These punches, however, were not intentional fouls.

Louis had his big chance in the tenth because an early left hook to the jaw jarred Charles to his toes. Louis pressed in recklessly and pounded his foe in a stirring bid for a knockout. Charles fought back spiritedly, but craftily and cau-

tiously, though battering body blows and stinging drives to the head and face hurt him.

That Charles was hurt was revealed as his handlers pushed him up for the eleventh. "Get close and hold," was the last instruction shouted into his ears. Every round before that had started with a final warning: "move around; hands up."

Bomber Misses Awkwardly

Early in the eleventh Louis crashed a wicked right to the body, but Charles responded with a left and right to the head and jabbed and hooked and cuffed Louis at will. The Bomber pressed in, trying to follow his body blows with more damaging punches, but missed awkwardly.

Charles weighed 184½ pounds and Louis 218.

Gates to the arena were not opened until 6:30 P. M., when the sale of 15,000 admission tickets, priced at $3 each, started. These tickets did not sell as quickly as had been anticipated, despite a favorable turn in the weather from the conditions existing over the week-end.

Those close to the situation attributed this condition to television. Complaints were heard in advance about the advertising methods in connection with this medium. The rights were sold for $140,000 and the telecast was conducted through fifty-eight C. B. S. stations on a basis and for the benefit of remote fans never before paralleled in connection with boxing.

September 28, 1950

ROBINSON DEFEATS OLSON IN TWELFTH

Knocks Out Honolulu Fighter to Keep His Pennsylvania Middleweight Crown

PHILADELPHIA, Oct. 26 (AP)— Ray (Sugar) Robinson shattered the dreams of another ambitious youth tonight as he methodically chopped down Honolulu's Carl

(Bobo) Olson and then knocked him out in 1:19 of the twelfth round in defense of his Pennsylvania middleweight championship. Robinson weighed 158 and Olson 159 for the scheduled 15-rounder at Convention Hall.

Robinson, the master ring craftsman, had everything his own way against the 22-year-old Olson, but rightfully claimed, after the bout, that it was one of the toughest in his long and illustrious career.

Olson brought an unusual style with him in his 5,500-mile jaunt from Hawaii. He kept his gloves high and his elbows protruding, thus presenting a difficult target.

Trains Fire on Body

It was easy to see what the islander had in mind. He was making Robinson work, hoping to tire him and finish him in the late rounds. But Bobo was mixing in the wrong league.

Robinson, following the instructions of his manager, George Gainford, whacked away at Olson's body and occasionally smashed a vicious right high on the nose and head.

The Pennsylvania 160-pound champion and world welterweight ruler never had to worry about receiving any punches. Olson was too intent on defense. The pace through the early rounds was slow

and the crowd of 5,034—they paid $16,912—clapped their hands for some action.

Robinson gave it to them. He shook up Olson in the eighth and hurt him again in the ninth with pile-driving rights.

Robinson, beaten only once in 121 fights in the eleven years he has been fighting as a professional, lost the eleventh round because of a low blow. It apparently angered him, because he came out with a determined glint in his eye for the twelfth.

The champion lashed out with a sweeping right hand to the side and Olson hit the canvas as if felled with an axe. He couldn't get

to his feet even after Referee Charley Daggert counted him out.

Victor Has Big Edge

In a post-fight count, it was revealed that Judge Frank Knaresborough gave Olson the sixth round and, of course, the low-blow eleventh, with the balance going to Robinson. Judge Harry Lasky and Referee Charley Daggert called the sixth even, gave Olson the eleventh and the rest easily to the champion. On The Associated Press score card Olson didn't get a round, except the one awarded him by Daggert.

In his dressing room after the battle, Robinson issued his usual lamenting cry, "Well, Jake, how's

about it?" He referred, of course, to the middleweight champion in the other 47 states, Jake La Motta.

In the preliminary bouts, Santa Bucca, 140, Philadelphia, outpointed Ermando Bonetti, 135½, New York, in six rounds; Danny Womber, 145½, New York, outpointed Lloyd Tate, 148, Philadelphia, over six stanzas; Terry Moore, 161, Baltimore, knocked out Lou Pompey, 153½, Scranton, Pa., in the second, and Dan Bucceroni, 177, Philadelphia, knocked out Shamus O'Brien, 190, New York, in the second.

October 27, 1950

Robinson Knocks Out La Motta in 13th Round for World Middleweight Title

GRUELING BATTLE ENDED BY REFEREE

He Acts on Signal of Doctor as Robinson Slugs Away at a Helpless La Motta

BRONX BOXER COURAGEOUS

Hangs On Grimly Until 2:04 of 13th — Victor Abdicates His Welterweight Title

By JAMES P. DAWSON
Special to THE NEW YORK TIMES.

CHICAGO, Feb. 14—Ray Robinson battered Jake La Motta into submission in thirteen rounds of gruelling fighting at the Stadium tonight and won the world middleweight championship.

Hammering the famed Bronx Bull into a state of utter helplessness in a struggle that developed into a slaughter, Robinson won the 160-pound title when the referee, Frank Sikora, stepped between the combatants and ended the battle after the thirteenth round had gone 2 minutes 4 seconds.

Referee Sikora acted upon a signal from Dr. J. M. Houston, physician for the Illinois State Athletic Commission, who was in charge of the battle from a medical standpoint. Through the thirteenth round, the referee had been watching for the signal, aware of the distressing condition to which La Motta had been rendered by the damaging blows of one who is recognized as the greatest boxer in the ring today.

Pummeled in Corner

When the referee intervened, La Motta was being pounded into a human bulk on the ropes near a neutral corner, helpless to defend himself and powerless to fight

back. Only his indomitable courage kept him from toppling to the canvas for the first time in his career.

Under Illinois boxing rules, the finish will go into the records as a "technical knockout." They make the distinction here between a knockout where the victim is counted out, and a knockout where intervention comes from the referee.

But, to the crowd of 14,802, which paid gross receipts of $180,619 and net of $138,938, no cleaner knockout ever was scored than the triumph of Robinson here tonight. It ended the middleweight reign La Motta started on June 16, 1949, when he stopped the late Marcel Cerdan at Detroit, and brought the second knockout charged against the Bronx Bull, who, even tonight, a pitiful excuse for a fighting man under the bludgeoning blows of a savage foe, left the ring with his boast untarnished—that he has never been knocked off his feet and has never been counted out.

Sixth Meeting of Foes

Never in his life has the Bronx strong-boy been subjected to such a hammering. In this sixth meeting of these bitter ring rivals, Robinson, the master craftsman, did everything short of battering La Motta unconscious as he registered his fifth triumph of the series.

That La Motta did not collapse will always be a testimonial to the amazing resistance to punishment that has always been his greatest recommendation; this, and a grim determination to go down fighting with his face to the foe.

When it was over, and frantic ministrations of his handlers had restored his faculties, a disillusioned La Motta disdained the willing hands that reached up to assist his descent from the ring. Instead, he went down the steps under his own power, stopping several times with a wide-open gesture of the hands which spoke louder than words of his keen disappointment and the complete futility he felt through the vital part of the night.

La Motta Receives Oxygen

It was one hour 55 minutes after the fight before La Motta was able to leave the stadium, and he was

assisted by a trainer under each arm. He gave the customary interview after the bout and then, near collapse, received oxygen for nearly forty minutes.

With his victory, Robinson abdicated the world welterweight throne he has occupied since Dec. 20, 1946, when he pounded out a victory over Tommy Bell. This was a condition of the battle when contracts were signed, since boxing's ruling bodies have frowned upon double title-holders since the confusion produced by Henry Armstrong's triple championship reign in the featherweight, lightweight and welterweight classes.

Combining superlative skill with damaging punching power, Robinson excelled La Motta in every boxing essential.

Robinson permitted himself to be outrushed by a bull-like La Motta in the first round. He proceeded to outbox and outpunch La Motta through the second, third and fourth rounds. Then Robinson held back through the fifth, sixth and seventh as La Motta plunged and swung from all angles with his best blows to the body and head in what looked like a resurgent La Motta in action against a tiring Robinson.

But only briefly did the illusion last. For with the eighth Robinson went back into action with a clever exhibition of boxing skill against an overeager adversary who was like a pupil against the master.

With the eleventh, Robinson cut loose with a savage fury that

proved the beginning of the end. Through most of the round he hammered La Motta all over the ring. He did the same in the twelfth. He was on the verge of battering La Motta down and into an unqualified knockout when the thirteenth had gone 2 minutes 4 seconds.

It was a sudden spurt by La Motta which hastened his own downfall. He had gone through ten rounds of bruising fighting in which his own face was puffed under the sting and stab of his foe's blows, and Robinson's nose and mouth were bloodied under the drive in the La Motta jab and swing and hook. The tenth ended with the count six rounds to four in Robinson's favor.

La Motta had been the aggressor all through the mill. He walked in fearlessly, foolishly, it seemed, at times, against the stinging jabs and left hooks, the right-hand uppercuts and sharp right crosses of Robinson, blazing away with both hands for the body.

La Motta made the championship poundage of 130 right on the nose at the weighing this morning. Robinson weighed 155½, heavier than he ever has been in action against La Motta.

Bobby Bell, 124, New York, won the decision over Tony Spano, 129, Chicago, in the eight-round semi-final.

February 15, 1951

Gavilan Takes World Welterweight Title by Outpointing Bratton at the Garden

CUBAN BOXER GAINS UNANIMOUS VERDICT

Gavilan's Speed Proves Too Much for Bratton in Dull Fifteen-Round Contest

SOLID BLOWS JAR LOSER

But New Welterweight Ruler Fails to Score Knockdown as 11,747 Fans Watch

By JOSEPH C. NICHOLS

Kid Gavilan, the Cuban Hawk, became the welterweight champion of the world last night. The speedy battler from Camaguey in the Antilles easily outpointed Johnny Bratton of Chicago in a fifteen-round bout at Madison Square Garden.

It was by unanimous decision that Gavilan ascended to his lofty estate, the deed to which had a few flaws that the Cuban's cabinet hopes to clear up in time. Referee Ruby Goldstein's ballot had it eight, five and two even, but the other officials, Judge Arthur Schwartz and Judge Joe Agnello, had it eleven and four. This observer favored the winner, twelve rounds to three.

A crowd of 11,747, an unusually large turnout in these days of television, paid $55,531 to watch the bout, which followed a dull pattern. Gavilan was the 5-8 favorite to outspeed the Westerner. And that was exactly what he did.

Gavilan Lands Often

There were few electric moments during the contest, and no approach to a clear knockdown, although Gavilan landed enough solid punches to make Bratton think that he was in a revolving door made solely of projecting boxing gloves.

The match was a compromise one, arranged to provide a successor to Ray Robinson as ruler of the 147-pound division. Robinson has never been beaten at 147 pounds, but according to the dictate of the National Boxing Association and the New York State Athletic Commission, Sugar Ray

waived his claim to the welter crown when he won the world middleweight championship from Jake La Motta in February.

The N. B. A. decided, last March, that Bratton was the welterweight champion after he had outpointed Charley Fusari in Chicago. The New York board disagreed, but consented to extend its recognition to last night's winner.

There is an "if" connected with New York recognition, however. Gavilan has a $2,000 forfeit posted with the New York board, to insure his fighting Billy Graham of the East Side for the title, within sixty days. If he fails to go through with the match, he may lose the $2,000 and the title, or both.

Briton Also in Picture

Another flaw in Gavilan's claim to the world championship exists in Great Britain, where the British Board of Boxing Control will consider the title vacant until Eddie Thomas, the Empire and European champion, is involved in a competition for the world crown.

It is certain that the Cuban will have much more trouble removing the further obstacles to clear possession than he had with Bratton. The latter, a straight, stand-up boxer, was not able to cope with Gavilan's whirlwind style that called for punches to be thrown from any angle at any time. He learned that in the first round

when Gavilan, after catching Bratton with a right to the jaw that sent him to the ropes, closed in to batter away at the jaw with both hands for almost a minute.

These punches bothered Bratton no little, but did not carry enough power to send him to the floor. Still, they caused the Westerner to show great respect for his opponent in the subsequent heats. Gavilan had an edge in a tame second round but in the third Bratton sparred deftly to gain the advantage. He was outpunched in the fourth, but stepped around skillfully again in the fifth and sixth, beating Gavilan with straight left hands.

From there on however, there was nothing offered by Bratton except speedy retreat. He went backward so fast that Gavilan at one time had to run to catch up with him.

The Cuban raked Bratton with left hooks to the head, and whenever Bratton showed a disposition to mix, Gavilan stepped inside to rip both hands to the head. There was very little in-fighting in the contest, which Gavilan described as one of his easiest. He weighed 145¼ pounds against 147 for Bratton.

May 19, 1951

Sports of The Times

By ARTHUR DALEY

Larceny at Its Worst

BEAU JACK is a little fellow with a big heart. His courage and his eternal hustle carried him much farther than his physical equipment had any right to carry him. The Beau became the lightweight champion of the world. He pulled into Madison Square Garden alone more than a million dollars at the gate.

Beau Jack was the victim of a technical knockout in Philadelphia the other day, a battered, bruised and aged fighter plying the only trade he knows. It matters not that he has since announced his retirement. He never should have had to announce it. He never should have had to fight any more. Considering all the money he made, he earned a life of ease long ago. He never got it.

This is one of the most contemptible episodes in a sport that has had far more than its share of disgraceful actions by the thieves and hoodlums who infest its outer edges. Pugilistic authorities utter pious platitudes about the nobler aspects of the manly art and along comes a Beau Jack to show how empty their words can be.

At the age of 30 this admirable little fellow is broke. He's broke because he was robbed of his heritage, his earnings squandered away. He didn't squander them. The Beau's tastes were simple because he's essentially a simple fellow. There have been fighters who deserved what they got, their money tossed away in riotous living. Not the Beau, though.

No youngster ever had more delightful sponsorship in the beginning than Jack. He had

Beau Jack being carried to his corner in his fight with Tony Janiro on Feb. 21, 1947.

been a shoeshine boy at the Augusta National Golf Club, the site of the Masters. A group of millionaires watched him fight in a battle royal and became so intrigued by his windmill style that they decided to finance him as a fighter. They sent him up North and the Beau was on his way. Never did they dream, though, that they'd sent him on a cruel and torturous journey to nowhere.

The rise of the little Negro was a mite on the sensational side. He was never a heavy hitter but he never stopped trying or stopped hustling. He became a crowd-pleaser without a peer. Whenever the Beau fought, the spec-

tators were sure of action. He threw punches without a let-up and, so amazing was his stamina, that he never seemed to tire. His main attributes were youth and a boundless energy. They brought him to the championship.

Easy Mark

The Beau could neither read nor write when he first reached New York, the easiest kind of mark for larceny. Besides, he was naïve, gullible. Uncomplainingly he accepted a few dollars a week of spending money. The main wad was being invested for his future—or so he was told. He didn't care much, perhaps. He loved to fight and life was wonderful.

This reporter has a vivid recollection of one incident, so typical of the Beau in those early years of his career a decade ago. The fellow he was fighting has been forgotten but the punch he threw never can be forgotten. The flailing Jack was swarming all over his rival when the other guy got set. He threw his Sunday punch. It landed flush on the Beau's jaw.

It actually and visibly shook Jack to his shoe-tops. His knees grew rubbery and his legs trembled. Instinctively he clinched. A few seconds later his youth and inexhaustible recuperative powers had completely shaken off the effects of that devastating punch and he was immediately pouring leather at his foe once again.

There was one other incident that comes to mind. It happened four years ago when he was fighting Tony Janiro, who could have been the greatest of them all but never was or will be. In the fourth round Jack went down in his corner under the force of a half-punch, half-push, his first knockdown in a hundred fights. He grimaced in pain, his left leg strangely doubled beneath him.

At the count of eight he laboriously dragged

himself to his feet and hobbled one-legged at Janiro. He tried to place his weight on his left leg and it collapsed. Beau Jack had broken his kneecap. And still he strove mightily to fight on!

Yes, he was an admirable little fellow. His awakening came too late. Not until he was married and his wife got a look at his finances, however, did he start to work for himself. She severed him from all his advisers except Chick Wergeles, who had been his manager in name but never in fact. But this came too late. Already he was a washed-up fighter, his future behind him.

How could such a thing come to pass? The sport of boxing has to take the blame no matter how many disclaimers its apologists offer. The career of Beau Jack automatically points a guilty finger at the sport which permitted him to give so much and take so little. His youth is gone. His money is gone.

The Beau can read now and his favorite book is the Bible. Perhaps he can take some comfort from the passage relating to the man who fell among thieves. It's the only comfort he has left.

May 25, 1951

Ray Robinson Loses Title in Britain

By The Associated Press.

LONDON, July 10—Randy Turpin, 23-year-old British Negro who never before had fought a bout of more than eight rounds, scored the most amazing upset in twenty-five years of boxing history tonight when he defeated Ray Robinson to win the world's middleweight championship.

The fifteen-round bout was Robinson's first defense of the crown he won from Jake LaMotta in Chicago Feb. 14, and only the second loss in a career that stretched through eleven years of pro fighting and 133 bouts.

A sell-out crowd of 18,000 in Earl's Court Arena cheered wildly as Turpin opened a deep gash under Sugar Ray's left eye in the seventh, brought blood from the New York Negro's nose in the twelfth and had him on the verge of a knockout in the fourteenth.

A left hook to the jaw staggered Robinson in the fourteenth and the crowd yelled for Turpin to finish off the champion whose only previous defeat came on Feb. 5, 1943, when La Motta outpointed Robinson in Detroit. Sugar Ray made up for that loss by beating Jake five times.

Robinson, hailed as the greatest fighter of the generation, was stripped of his welterweight crown by the National Boxing Association and the New York Athletic Commission when he won the 160-pound title.

To many, tonight's result was the greatest upset since Gene Tunney outpointed Jack Dempsey in Philadelphia, Sept. 23, 1926 for the heavyweight crown.

There was no fluke about Turpin's victory. The confident, aggressive youngster, waded right in after Robinson from the opening bell. The Associated Press scoreboard gave Turpin nine rounds, Robinson four and called two even.

Robinson had been guaranteed a return bout in September. In New York, Jim Norris, president of the International Boxing Club, which holds an exclusive contract on Robinson's services, said the bout would be staged in New York. George Gainford, Robinson's manager, said it would be held Sept. 26.

Turpin's Face Unmarked

Turpin, holder of the British and European middleweight crowns, didn't have a mark on his face. There were no knockdowns although both fighters were rocked by hard punches.

The broad-shouldered Englishman from Leamington, who turned 23 last June, had scored twenty-nine knockouts in forty-six professional fights. He won forty-three, lost two and drew in one. He knocked out both of his previous conquerors, Jean Stock and Albert Finch.

Turpin, who outweighed Robinson 158¾ to 154½ pounds, had won all six of his fights this year by knockouts. He staggered Robinson just before the end of the first round, sending the American back on his heels with a left hook.

Referee Eugene Henderson, the only official, warned both fighters continuously through the bout. He called Robinson repeatedly for holding, admonished Turpin for the kidney punch and for butting and warned both for hitting in the clinches.

Turpin, confident after the opening round, swept the second as Robinson continued to miss. Sugar Ray stung Turpin with left jabs and scored with a fast right to the head in the third.

Turpin came back in the fourth with jabs, uppercuts and left hooks to the head.

The youngster continued to pile up points in the fifth, sixth and seventh rounds. Robinson came out of a clinch in the seventh with a deep gash under his left eye and later a cut on his left brow.

Robinson Shakes Turpin

Robinson rallied in the eighth, shaking Turpin with two hard rights to the head and the Englishman had to hold. But Randy rallied in the ninth with fine boxing.

Robinson dominated the tenth and eleventh rounds and the early part of the twelfth with a smashing attack to the body and head. Turpin, however, rallied at the end of the twelfth and from then on he couldn't be stopped. He belted the champion with both hands to the body and head and almost finished Robinson in the fourteenth.

After Henderson had raised Turpin's hand aloft, the jubilant, newly crowned champion told the crowd from the ring:

"I hope I'm able to keep this for you for a long time."

In his dressing room, Turpin said, "I thought I was winning all the way. He never hurt me once."

Turpin's first stop after leaving the ring was Robinson's dressing room where he told Robinson, "You were a real champion just like they told me." Robinson replied, "You were real good. Just like they said you were. I have no alibis. I was beaten by a better man."

The fans paid $224,000, Robinson receiving $84,000, the largest purse of his career, and Turpin collecting $24,000, a new high for him, too. The fight was a sell-out three days after it was announced. The promoter turned back more than $100,000 to disappointed customers.

July 11, 1951

Walcott Knocks Out Charles in Seventh, Wins Heavyweight Title

LEFT HOOK SCORES FOR JERSEY JOE, 37

Walcott, Oldest Fighter Ever to Annex Honors, Finishes Charles at Pittsburgh

By JAMES P. DAWSON
Special to The New York Times.

PITTSBURGH, July 18—In a boxing upset even more startling than the victory of Randy Turpin over Ray Robinson in London last week, Jersey Joe Walcott, Camden, N. J., tonight became the oldest fighter in ring history to win the world heavyweight championship, when he knocked out Ezzard Charles, Cincinnati, in the seventh round of what was to have been a fifteen-round bout at Forbes Field.

Walcott put an end to Charles' brief reign as titleholder with a terrific left hook to the jaw 55 seconds after the seventh round opened.

Under the force of the blow, Charles fell forward, his gloved fists under him, his nerves deadened, while the crowd of 28,-272 came to its feet with an ear-splitting roar for the man who scaled the heights at thirty-seven years of age and after four previous failures against Charles and the dynamiting Joe Louis.

Referee Buck McTiernan, in unison with Tommy Grant, the knockdown timekeeper outside the ring, tolled off the fatal seconds as Charles tried unsuccessfully to lift himself off the ring floor.

Charles worked his arms spasmodically, trying for leverage. At "six" he got his head up. At "eight" his arms came free. At "ten" the beaten champion got to his knees just as the referee spread his arms in a signal that the fight was over.

Falls Over Backward

Then Charles toppled over backward, apparently oblivious of his surroundings.

His handlers, led by his co-managers, Tommy Tannas and Jake Mintz, jumped into the ring to lift him off the floor and carry him to his corner. The round had gone exactly fifty-five seconds when Walcott's powerful left hook landed on the point of Charles' chin.

The late Ruby Robert Fitzsimmons is the closest approach to Walcott in the matter of age when winning the ring's richest title.

The gangling Cornishman was 35 when he knocked out James J. Corbett in fourteen rounds at Carson City, Nev., March 17, 1897.

In the emotional reaction to his amazing victory Walcott almost fainted after the ten second count certified the beginning of his reign as world champion. Friends, admirers and fans stormed into the ring to congratulate the new ruler of the heavyweights.

Police fought their way through the milling crowd to the ring to protect Walcott, whose handlers were trying to get the new champion away from the fans.

Walcott Is Speechless

Walcott, breathing heavily, dropped to his knees, trying to say something over the radio. He couldn't utter a word and even if he could he could not have been heard above the din.

Here was a man at a time in

life when the average boxer has long since retired, crowning a career that reaches back through twenty-one years, with a heavyweight title victory that is without parallel in ring annals in many respects.

A despised underdog in the betting, 6 to 1, and deservedly so, on the record, Walcott was conceded only an outside chance to win. Expert opinion was practically unanimous in the selection of Charles as the winner. Hadn't he beaten Walcott twice? Was it reasonable to suppose a thirty-seven-year-old boxer, whose career started back in 1930, could do anything to upset the clever Charles, who was defending for the ninth time?

The crowd of 28,272 paid $245,-004 to view the spectacle. This sum is in addition to $100,000 realized on the sale of the radio and television rights. The crowd was rewarded with a finish about which they can talk for a long time. For no fighter ever was more thoroughly knocked out than was Charles in this, the city's first heavyweight championship.

Mintz Is Suspended

Not all the action was confined to the battle itself. Preceding the encounter, Mintz, one of Charles' managers, objected so strenuously to the selection of bout officials that he was ordered from the ring by the local Commissioner, John Holohan, who was supported by John (Ox) Da Grosa. Mintz watched the from a second-row working press seat.

When it was over, he found he was under suspension by Pennsylvania's State Athletic Commission for an indefinite period, pending a hearing. Mintz was speechless, more at the result of the fight, than at the penalty for his objection to the selection of Charley Daggert of Philadelphia as one of the judges.

Mintz once ordered Charles out

of the ring, saying he would refuse to let him fight. On this point he was overruled. Mintz said in his protest it had been agreed none but local officials would be used for the bout. As it turned out, the officials could have come from Timbuctoo. All that was needed was a referee who could count ten.

It is ironic that Charles should lose his title in his first big bout here and one that was arranged principally in the interests of charity. The Dapper Dan Club, a charitable organization, was the sponsor of the battle, in cooperation with the Rooney-McGinley Club and the International Boxing Club. The charity organization was pledged 10 per cent of the receipts, less taxes.

Restored to consciousness in his corner, the beaten champion was escorted almost unnoticed from the ring while the crowd showered all its attention upon the emotionally stricken Walcott.

In his dressing room after the battle Charles attributed his defeat to a lucky punch. "It was a sucker punch," said the Cincinnati fighter. "Why I ever got in the way of it I'll never know."

It was necessary to take two stitches in Charles' lower lip and his handlers had to stanch the blood flow from a cut under his right eye as well as depress a swelling under his left eye. Walcott was unmarked.

Under the battle contracts Charles is assured a return bout within ninety days. Fulfillment of this contract clause will upset an elaborate promotion plan under contemplation by the I. B. C. It had been proposed to pair Charles with Joe Louis in September, in the expectation that Charles would emerge from the ring tonight with his title intact. Now the schedule must be revised to meet Walcott's plans.

It was a different Walcott who scaled the heights tonight after enough rebuffs to discourage a less determined man. Jersey Joe didn't beat an inferior Charles, either. He battered into helplessness a Charles who was trained to the minute, lithe, powerful, sure-footed in action against a foeman whose puzzling style was his greatest asset.

The Walcott of tonight did not slap and run, stab and hold. This was a cagey, alert Walcott who measured his blows carefully, and landed them, so much so that he was ahead on the official ring ballots at the finish.

Referee McTiernan gave Charles the first round and Walcott the succeeding five that were completed. Judge Daggert gave Walcott four rounds, calling the first even and giving the sixth to Charles. The other judge, Arthur (Red) Robinson, gave Charles the first, fifth and sixth rounds; the second, third and fourth to Walcott. The writer gave Charles the first two sessions and Walcott the next four.

Early Rounds Are Tame

It was not a spectacular bout up to the seventh and this made the finish all the more exciting.

Cautious sparring characterized the first two rounds, though it had been expected that Charles, eager to get Walcott out of his life, but definitely, would seek to overwhelm Joe with a whirlwind assault from the starting gong. It was felt that the Ohioan could not afford to take chances against Walcott, that he must try for a quick knockout.

Surprisingly, Charles waited for Walcott to carry the fight to him. Walcott fought shrewdly. He locked Charles' arms in the close-range action.

Charles landed oftener in the first two rounds, stabbing left jabs. Near the end of the second round,

Charles blocked Walcott's solid left hook for the jaw, and, driving close, battered Jersey Joe freely about the body and head with short rights.

In the third round, it was Walcott who became bold. He dug two left hooks to Ezzard's body and followed with several stabbing lefts to the face. Sparring carefully, wasting no move, alert to strike with either hand, Walcott bided his time as Charles pawed forward with several light lefts to the face. Suddenly, Jersey Joe hooked a left for the jaw that landed high.

The blow caught Charles under the right eye, ripping the flesh. This was followed by a right to the jaw as Charles stumbled in, head down, and the punch jarred Charles to his heels. Walcott leaped eagerly to the attack, driving a left and right to the head before the bell rang.

Walcott held command thereafter.

Four solid left hooks to the head stung Charles to a fiery, explosive bit of infighting in which he pounded Walcott savagely about the body near the end of the sixth round.

They were sparring at long range near the center of the ring in the seventh when Walcott lowered the boom—a lightning-like, paralyzing left hook to the jaw. Charles went down and out, his string of victories checked at twenty-four, knocked out for the second time in his career.

And the man who had quit the ring more than once because he couldn't make a living for himself and his large family was the new champion.

Charles weighed 182 pounds, Walcott 194.

July 19, 1951

Gavilan Keeps Welterweight Title by Beating Graham in Close 15-Round Bout

REFEREE'S BALLOT DECIDES FOR CUBAN

Vote Favoring Gavilan Brings a Storm of Protests From Many Graham Rooters

By JAMES P. DAWSON

Amid riotous scenes in Madison Square Garden last night Kid Gavilan, the cyclonic Cuban, retained his world welterweight championship in a tense fifteen-round battle with Billy Graham of the East Side.

On a split decision that went down to the fine features of a couple of points, the Cuban is champion today because Referee Mark Conn's scorecard, splitting the rounds even, gave Gavilan the

decision by three scant points, 10 to 7. One of the judges, Arthur Schwartz, had balloted for Gavilan, nine rounds to six. The other judge, Frank Forbes, split his vote even, seven rounds for each with one even, as did Referee Conn. But Forbes voted Graham the winner, 11 points to 10.

So keen was the fighting, so sharp the interest in this battle, although it drew but 8,137 fans paying receipts of $34,419, that each ballot announcement was received with mingled feelings by the noisy crowd. The majority, it was plain, thought Graham was entitled to the decision and the championship.

Debris Lands in Ring

When it was announced Schwartz's vote went to Gavilan a jeer, ear-splitting in intensity, went up from the crowd. A couple of cigar butts came sailing through the air to land in the ring, along with torn cigarette packages and paper. Announcement of Forbes' vote mollified the crowd somewhat.

When Referee Conn's vote was announced, the crowd went berserk. Fans tried to fight their way into the ring. Two made the grade unmolested, despite the special police guard, but they were hustled out of the ring after clasping a disconsolate Graham in fond embrace. Others about the Graham corner contributed their menacing gestures, while Conn, under instructions from a State Athletic Commission Deputy, remained in his neutral corner.

Finally, when the hubbub subsided somewhat, Conn crossed the ring and, surrounded by a bodyguard of city and special police, was escorted from the scene, his every step marked by jeers and a shower of miscellaneous articles from the overhead balcony.

The writer scored the battle, nine rounds to six, for Gavilan. The champion was entitled to the first four, eighth, ninth, tenth and eleventh and the thirteenth. Graham won the fifth, sixth and seventh rounds, the twelfth and, in a closing burst of brilliant boxing, the fourteenth and fifteenth.

Disagreement on Verdict

Perhaps it was this closing burst of boxing by Graham that swayed the opinion of the fans. Perhaps it was the fact Graham was solidly backed as the underdog in betting odds of 5 to 14. However, the disagreement with the verdict was not confined to the fans. The majority of critics at the ringside thought Graham entitled to the verdict as well.

Graham's superior boxing skill carried him through the rounds he won. In these sessions he outboxed the champion. After taking a drubbing through the first four rounds, Graham stung Gavilan to aimless fury with his clever boxing and sharp hitting through the three succeeding rounds.

Repeatedly Graham reached the jaw over this span with sharp right-hand drives. He made Gavilan miss awkwardly with long lefts and rights while getting under the fire with solid rights to the heart or left hooks to the head.

With the eighth round the tide of battle turned Gavilan's way. He forced the fighting, swarmed all over Graham, charging in against Billy's best blows and raked the East Sider about the head with rights and lefts. In the twelfth Graham's punches were cleaner and sharper and he grazed the jaw several times with rights.

Reaches Champion's Jaw

Through the fourteenth and fif-.. teenth rounds Graham, throwing all caution to the winds, reached the champion's jaw repeatedly with grazing rights and left hooks. He frequently beat Gavilan to a left jab to the face. However, the earlier lead accumulated by Gavilan could not be overcome by this closing rush of the challenger.

Gavilan weighed 145½ pounds, Graham 145.

George Flores, 28-year-old welterweight from Brooklyn, did not regain consciousness after being knocked out by Roger Donoghue of Yonkers in the semi-final and was taken to St. Clare's Hospital, where his condition was reported critical.

Flores went down on his back after taking a left hook to the jaw when the eighth round had gone 46 seconds and was counted out by Referee Barney Felix. He was attended by Dr. Nardiello and helped from the ring. He collapsed in his dressing room and Dr. Nardiello had him taken to the hospital. Donoghue weighed 152½ pounds and Flores 151.

August 30, 1951

Randy Turpin, dethroned middleweight champion, landing a punch to the face of Ray Robinson in the fourth round   *Associated Press*

Robinson Knocks Out Turpin In Tenth Round of Title Bout

American Boxer Regains Middleweight Crown When Referee Halts Action Before 61,370 at Polo Grounds

By JAMES P. DAWSON

Ray Robinson brought the world middleweight championship back to America last night.

With a savage attack in the tenth round, he knocked out Randy Turpin, gallant British fighter to whom he had lost the title in London two months ago.

Amid the roars of a crowd of 61,370 fans who had paid record receipts of $767,630 to see the spectacle at the Polo Grounds, Robinson battered Turpin into such a helpless state that the referee, Ruby Goldstein, stopped the battle after the tenth round had gone 2 minutes and 52 seconds.

At that time, Turpin was an open target, unable to defend himself from the blazing drives of a merciless foe who was smarting under the terrific blows the Englishman had landed in two previous rounds.

The British defender had been floored early in the round by a right to the jaw for a count of nine. When he arose, Robinson, going all out for victory, battered his rival to the ropes, ignoring blood which streamed from an old cut above his own left eye, intent only upon the complete destruction of the man who had dethroned him last July 10.

Loosing a barrage of rights and lefts, Robinson raked his foe about the head, face and body.

Randy tried to cover against the blows. He crouched behind upraised arms and gloved fists in an attempt to ward off the stunning punches to the head and jaw. Robinson then shifted his attack to the body and with wicked smashes of the right to the ribs, brought down his rival's guard. Then he pounded his head again.

It seemed that Robinson would fight himself out in this frenzied outburst. But he got home clean with a right to the jaw, and then another. Randy sagged. It seemed he would fall. Then Referee Goldstein stepped between them and Turpin was knocked out for the second time in a career that goes back to 1946 and through forty-five engagements.

Because he wasn't actually counted out this bout will probably go into the records as a "technical knockout," but that will be mis- leading. Actual counting over Turpin would have been a mere formality had Robinson withheld his fire long enough to let the defending champion fall. And Turpin would have gone down but for the fusillade of blows that pinioned him to the ropes, rendered him helpless and brought a dramatic finish to a bout that had attracted more international attention than any ring battle since Joe Louis polished off Max Schmeling in a brief round back in 1938.

Turpin was collapsing like a deflated balloon in the arms of Referee Goldstein, but he tried, instinctively, to protest the interference and fight his way clear. His legs buckled. Goldstein took a firmer grasp on the helpless fighter, holding him as he would a child until Turpin's handlers scrambled through the ropes to lead the beaten warrior away.

A squad of police moved quickly into the ring under Inspector Cornelius Lyons. They blocked the four sides of the ring against the possibility of intrusion by excited fans.

Turpin was soon restored to his senses and walked to the center of the ring where Robinson was acknowledging the thunderous roar of acclaim which rang out over the scene. Smilingly, gripping the hand of his conqueror, the hand that had battered him from under the valuable ring title he held so short a time, Turpin posed for pictures. This over, he was led out of the ring amid an ear-splitting cheer from a crowd which was paying its tribute to a fighter who went down giving his best.

The cheers for Turpin were followed by a mighty roar for Robinson, who had dissipated the idea that he was no longer the sparkling, capable boxer of yore with this thrilling, highly dramatic return to the heights.

Referee Goldstein said after the battle that when he stopped the bout he was certain that Turpin was a beaten fighter.

"He couldn't go on. The punches were coming fast and furious. He might have been seriously hurt had I let it go further."

Tribute to the Winner

George Middleton, Turpin's manager, was stunned by the knockout.

"I think it was a great fight," he said. "I'm disappointed at the result, of course. But I think Robinson showed he has the punch many people thought he'd lost. I don't want to make excuses. But, perhaps the humidity hurt Randy. It was kind of close after the mountain air we've been used to, you know. But that is not offered as an excuse. Randy lost in a great fight. Robinson is a great fighter. He beat a great fighter tonight."

All middleweight attendance and receipts records which finds Robinson the third man in the long history of the 160-pound division to regain the title. The crowd of 61,370 exceeded the 60,071 which turned out for the last heavily attended battle here, the first Joe Louis-Billy Conn heavyweight championship in 1941. It dwarfed the 44,266 which saw the second Louis-Conn clash in 1946, without, however, threatening the receipts for that match, which drew $1,925,564 at a $100 "top" ticket price.

The receipts, amounting to $767,-630, gross will send this fight into the $1,000,000 class, the ninth in ring history. To this box-office figure $250,000 will be added from the sale of motion picture and theatre-television rights. There will be the added income from a percentage of the picture which will accrue to the International Boxing Club, Inc.

Robinson will collect 30 per cent of all the net receipts for his vic-

tory. Turpin's wounds in defeat will be assuaged by 25 per cent of the net. In each case the boxers will receive the largest purses of their careers.

From all corners of this country, from Canada and England, boxing followers and sport adherents came to this battle, attracted by a struggle that captured the public fancy as had no international ring event since Tex Rickard's first $1,000,000 fight in the 1921 clash against Georges Carpentier in Jersey City's Boyles' Thirty Acres.

Turpin gave his best last night but it was not good enough. He faced a different Robinson than the shopworn tourist who went down to defeat in London. The Robinson who battered his way back to the heights was the Robinson of old, sharp as a razor's edge, master of boxing finesse, alert, and conditioned for the test of his life.

The great crowd left the arena convinced of the Harlem Negro boy's ring greatness. In the crowd were figures of international prominence, led by General of the Army Douglas MacArthur, innumerable stars of the entertainment world, leaders in finance, industry, the arts and professions, political leaders and society folk.

Champions, past and present, in many sports fields were among the onlookers. Gene Tunney, Joe Louis and Ezzard Charles were three former holders of the heavyweight title present, along with the current titleholder, Jersey Joe Walcott; Sandy Saddler, world featherweight champion, was there, as was Jake LaMotta, former world middleweight titleholder.

This gathering set attendance and receipts records for a ring championship below the heavyweight class. Until last night the mark was the 49,186 who paid $461,789 to see the light heavyweight championship bout between Jack Delaney and Paul Berlenbach back in 1926.

Only two other middleweight champions have lost and regained the title. Stanley Ketchel, the "Michigan Assassin," regained the crown from Billy Parke in 1908. Tony Zale did it in 1948 when he stopped Rocky Graziano.

There was some confusion outside and inside the arena before the fight. Fans arriving late had to fight a way through the struggling masses that blocked the entrance gates on two sides. Eighth Avenue on the east end of the ball park was almost impassable. The

ramp leading from the speedway entrance on the west side of the plant was blocked so thoroughly that mounted police were sent there to straighten things out.

There were several thousand fans trying to buy the last 200 tickets an hour before the title bout entered the ring and that added to the mix-up.

Inside everything was all right until the late-comers were jammed trying to get to the field, where there were 15,000 seats which sold at $30 per copy at the box-office and $130 per copy at the speculators.

Leap From Dugout Roof

Leaping upon the roof of one of the baseball dugouts, these fans started jumping down on the field in waves. This encouraged similar leaping by ticket-holders whose seats were in the stands. It was strenuous work for a hastily summoned group of special police to restore order.

But, when the main fight started, every seat in the place was occupied and the overflow was standing back of the ringside rows on the field and in the rear of the lower stands. Many were turned away for the first time since Jack Dempsey knocked out Luis Angel Firpo, the Wild Bull of the Pampas, twenty-eight years ago, in the same arena.

The ring battle was a thriller, as had been expected. It ended as the majority predicted it would. Robinson was the favorite at odds of 5 to 11.

Younger Man Beaten

Before the battle there was a disposition in some quarters to regard Robinson as past his peak and that he would be unable to withstand the attack of the 23-year-old Englishman, a warrior less used up in a five-year career than Robinson in eleven years of campaigning. Robinson is 31 years old.

True, Turpin had battered Robinson into defeat in fifteen rounds in London. But many thought that Robinson had taken the London assignment lightly and that his preparations for that bout were inadequate. They recalled, too his tour of the Continent, which was more or less a lark.

Before that London fight Robinson had been regarded as "the greatest fighter, pound by pound, the ring has ever known."

To all this, Robinson gave the answer last night. He was the old Robinson, trained to the minute, determined to prove that the

things they used to say about him were true.

He boxed skillfully. He was careful not to let Turpin swarm all over him, not to let the defending champion take the lead at any stage of the battle.

On this writer's score Robinson swept the first seven rounds. He seemed to tire after the seventh, however. In the eighth and ninth Turpin repeatedly beat Robinson to stiff, powerful left jabs, crashed right-hand drives to the head, hammered the body with solid rights.

Early in the tenth a head-on collision re-opened the wound Robinson suffered in the London battle. Like a wounded stag, Robinson ripped into his foe. Two minutes later he was champion again.

Official score cards on the bout varied. Referee Goldstein had the bout even on rounds at four, four and one even. Joe Agnello, a judge, had Robinson in front, five rounds to four, and the other judge, Harold Barnes, had Robinson leading, five rounds to three, with one even.

Elkins Brothers, Washington, D. C., heavyweight, and Aaron Wilson, Knoxville, Tenn., were the principals in the eight-round semifinal, in which Ray Miller was the referee. Brothers weighed 191½ pounds and Wilson 192.

A slugging match from the outset, the bout ended dramatically in 2 minutes 31 seconds of the eighth round when Wilson knocked out Brothers with a left hook to the jaw. The left hook pulled victory out of defeat for the Tennesseean, for at the time he was staggering from the effects of a left hook to the jaw which Brothers had landed.

Mike Spataro, Bronx featherweight, knocked out Johnny Caro, a borough rival, in 1 minute 42 seconds of the first round, in the opener. Caro went down and out under a left hook to the jaw. Spataro weighed 123½ pounds and Caro 128½.

In the second bout Billy Hazel, Harlem lightweight, disposed of Jay Parlin, Philadelphian, in 2 minutes 49 seconds of the third. Parlin sank several left hooks to the body and was through for the night when Referee Ray Kazak stepped in. Hazel weighed 137¾ pounds and Parlin 135¼.

September 13, 1951

Saddler Stops Pep in Ninth Round and Retains His Title

ROUGH BOUT ENDED BY REFEREE MILLER

By JAMES P. DAWSON

Sandy Saddler retained his world featherweight championship last night, stopping Willie Pep in the ninth round of a scheduled fifteen-round battle at the Polo Grounds.

For roughness, disregard of ring rules and ethics, and wild fighting, this surpassed anything seen in the three previous meetings of these bitter ring rivals.

Any resemblance to the accepted theory of boxing as a "fair, stand-up" exhibition of skill between two perfectly trained, well-matched, sportsmanlike individuals was purely coincidental in this brawl.

It ended at the end of the ninth round with Pep, badly bruised about the right eye, battered severely in the mid-section, telling the referee he couldn't go on, as he had in their last meeting a year ago.

Last year Pep was forced to quit because of a dislocated left shoulder at the end of the seventh round. Last night he told Referee Ray Miller at the end of the ninth that he was "unable to continue."

In an explanation to Dr. Vincent A. Nardiello, state athletic commission physician at the ringside, Pep said he felt unable to go on because his right eye, blinded by blood from the second round, was bothering him.

Over the protest of one of his handlers Pep decided to quit, evidently convinced in this fourth and, what many hope will be the last, installment of this ring serial, that the distinction of being the first to win the same ring crown three times is not for him.

REFEREE HITTING THE CANVAS AT FEATHERWEIGHT FIGHT

An unidentified second was heard to yell a countermanding order to Referee Miller as the arbiter left Pep's corner after getting the Hartford lad's surrender. But Miller continued to the other side of the ring, signaled an end to the contest, and summoned Dr. Nardiello to examine Pep. The former champion was found to be all right, though indisposed, and left the ring under his own power.

The excitement over the confusing finish was as nothing to the preceding events in the ring. For a world championship battle it was a sorry spectacle. Both fighters were guilty of the collar-and-elbow, rough-and-tumble style of fighting made famous on the waterfront.

By some oversight, they failed to bite each other or to introduce that quaint kicking game—la savate—at one time very popular in France. The crowd of 13,836 didn't like this exhibition at all.

The new chairman of the State Athletic Commission, Robert K. Christenberry, thus had an unpalatable introduction to his new duties.

Even Referee Miller hit the floor in the seventh round while trying to separate the combatants from a death-like embrace.

Saddler was twice wrestled down, at the end of the fifth and again in the eighth. Both hit the deck from body holds near the end of the sixth. They engaged in a mild exhibition of strangling in the eighth. But only one penalty was called. Pep lost the seventh for unnecessary roughness.

To the wild action of the battle and confusion of the finish was added some post-battle recriminations of the dressing rooms. Pep, in one burst, said, "I had to fight the other guy, the referee and City Hall."

Saddler frankly admitted that he was rough. "I figured to fight cleanly and started to do so, but Pep started it. He was heeling, thumbing, stepping on my toes and wrestling all night."

It is this writer's opinion that Referee Miller would have been justified in tossing both out of the ring. It was fortunate that the International Boxing Club had kept this spectacle from home consumption on television and radio.

It is amusing to recall that Referee Miller, calling the principals to the center of the ring for instructions, had greeted them with a courteous, "good evening, gentlemen." That was something new.

Saddler started the fight with a long left hook to the jaw. Pep gave the champion a boxing lesson through the rest of the round, drilling lefts and rights to the face, hooking solid lefts to the body. Saddler was cautioned for holding and hitting.

A left hook cut Pep's right eye early in the second round. In a clinch in Saddler's corner, the champion whipped a left hook to the body which dropped Pep for a count of eight. After this round the roughness started.

For the record Pep was ahead on the official ballots when he surrendered. Referee Miller had Pep in front five rounds to four. One of the judges, Arthur Aidala, had them even on rounds, four, four and one, but Pep ahead on points, 8 to 6. The other judge, Frank Forbes, had Saddler in front, five rounds to four. The writer had Saddler leading, six rounds to three.

Saddler weighed 125½ pounds and Pep 125.

September 27, 1951

Ray Miller falling on his knees as he attempted to separate Sandy Saddler and Willie Pep in seventh round of title bout at the Polo Grounds last night. *Associated Press*

PEP LOSES LICENSE, SADDLER SET DOWN

Commission Acts After Rough Title Bout—Champion Out for Indefinite Period

Featherweight Champion Sandy Saddler of Harlem was suspended indefinitely and Willie Pep, former ruler from Hartford, Conn., had his license revoked yesterday as an aftermath of their rough world title bout at the Polo Grounds last Sept. 26.

In announcing the decision on behalf of the State Athletic Commission, following an open hearing, Chairman Robert K. Christenberry told the two boxers, "You violated every rule in the book. It is the unanimous opinion that the punishment be affixed."

Saddler's manager, Charley Johnston, also was penalized for interfering with Dr. Vincent A. Nardiello, the commission physician. He received a thirty-day suspension and fined $100.

Veteran Pilot "Sorry"

Christenberry, who had attended the bout in his first official role, reminded Johnston that "it would have been better to call any action you disagreed with to the attention of the commission. In your behavior you displayed poor judgment before thousands in the Polo Grounds and millions on television." The veteran pilot replied, "I shouldn't have done it. I'm sorry."

Johnston, however, declared that the suspension of Saddler seemed to be "a drastic decision against my boy." He insisted that Pep did all the thumbing, while "Saddler was never suspended and never questioned about his behavior in the ring."

Lou Viscusi, Pep's manager, who had been asked to appear at the hearing, the first since Chairman Christenberry took office, was on hand. He waited to be heard but was not called as a witness.

Asked to Explain Tactics

Both fighters were asked to explain their roughhouse tactics in their fourth meeting, which ended with Pep, his right eye badly cut from the second round, sitting in the corner and giving up at the completion of the ninth. He said he was unable to continue. They were told that press reports indicated the fight had done much to "destroy the reputation of boxing and bring the game into disrepute."

Pep, a 29-year-old veteran battler who had endeavored to become the first man ever to win the same title three times, answered, "I didn't try to destroy the reputation of boxing. It is my livelihood and I want to continue boxing."

He was the first to appear before the commission. When asked to explain his failure to obey Referee Ray Miller's constant warnings, Pep replied: "It seemed there was no referee in the fight. He was getting in too late to break us up. The only way I could get away from him (Saddler) was to wrestle him. He was holding me by the head and banging away at my eyes."

The former champion was then sent out of the room and a conference among the commissioners followed. Pep was recalled and told that his license had been revoked. He asked for how long. "I expect to box again." He was told, "You can always come back to the commission. The door is not closed."

Saddler Is Called

Saddler was then called. The 25-year-old world titleholder said, "I thought I fought a clean fight." "You don't think the warnings of the referee were justified?" Christenberry asked him. "No," replied Saddler promptly.

The chairman then told him, "Your opinion is contrary to the opinion of the judges and other observers at the ringside. And since you have no explanation for the foul tactics you employed, holding, hitting and continually violating virtually every rule in the book, and conduct detrimental to boxing, I hereby suspend your license indefinitely."

Saddler is expected to seek reinstatement in thirty to sixty days, the usual "cooling off" period. He has figured in the International Boxing Club's plans this season. The I. B. C. must now await future developments. As for the revocation of Pep's license, "he can always appeal" said one of the commissioners. But it is doubtful that he will get any consideration in the immediate future.

The commission also adopted a rule providing that any boxer counted out be suspended for not fewer than thirty days and requiring that he have a medical examination, including electroencephalographic and neurological tests.

October 6, 1951

Marciano Knocks Out Louis in Eighth Round of Heavyweight Fight in Garden

THE FIRST KNOCKDOWN AND THE END OF THE BATTLE LAST NIGHT

Rocky Marciano watches Joe Louis sag to canvas after a left to the jaw in eighth round. The Bomber arose after a count of eight.

EX-CHAMPION LOSES TO BROCKTON BOXER

Louis Is Knocked From Ring by Marciano's Right to Jaw in 2:36 of 8th Round

REFEREE DISDAINS COUNT

Goldstein Waves End to Fight With Brown Bomber Lying on Back Outside Ropes

By JOSEPH C. NICHOLS

Joe Louis was knocked out last night.

The once incomparable Brown Bomber of the dreaded punch and the electric reflexes lost to Rocky Marciano, undefeated battler from Brockton, Mass., in the eighth round of a scheduled ten-round bout at Madison Square Garden.

At least, the record books will say that it was Marciano who beat Joe, but everybody knows it was age. The years, a half-score of them, were against the 37-year-old Louis, as he plodded through seven dreary rounds with his rival, ten years younger. There was little indication that Louis wouldn't be able to go the scheduled ten, but in the eighth things changed suddenly, and Louis showed his years.

In this round Marciano, adhering to his plugging style of moving inside and seeking to wear down the ex-champion with a barrage of punches to the head and body, managed to force Louis to the ropes, where he tagged him with a solid left hook to the jaw. Louis fell to the canvas, but almost immediately gained one knee, there to await the count of eight.

Joe seemed sure enough of himself on arising, but his appearance did not bother Marciano. Springing at the once invincible Detroit athlete, Rocky missed a fast flurry of punches intended for the head, suddenly slowed his overeager gait and levelled his punches directly at Louis' jaw.

Lands Two Sharp Lefts

Two lefts landed with sharp, authoritative impact, the second one forcing Louis back to the ropes. He was standing, but with his eyes glazed and his arms dangling at his sides. Here the younger man made no mistakes. He looked at his foe, ascertained his helplessness in a fifth of a second, and shot across a right to the jaw.

Through the ropes toppled Louis, landing on the ring apron. Ruby Goldstein, who capably served as referee, realized that there was no sense in undertaking a count, and waved his arms in signal that the fight was over, that Marciano was the winner by a knockout in 2:36 of the eighth round.

The fallen Louis was instantly surrounded by a solicitous group as he lay on the ring apron, with Dr. Vincent Nardiello in the lead. The ex-champion remained supine after regaining consciousness, but finally arose and climbed through the ropes to congratulate his conqueror. In the dressing room Louis was in good enough condition, considering, and expressed the opinion that the "best man won."

As a matter of fact, the best man didn't have to be too good against the Louis of last night. His armament was best described by Edmond Rostand when, in speaking of Cyrano, he lamented that he was "shod with marble and gloved with lead." Obviously the lead in Joe's instance was not calculated to aid the Bomber in administering punishment to his foe.

Loser Was 8-5 Choice

A crowd of 17,241 paid a total of $152,845 to see the fight, which was the thirty-eighth professional one for Marciano. The Brockton gladiator won all his previous encounters, but was the short ender in last night's betting at odds of 8 to 5.

The officials' sheets indicated that it was Marciano's fight even before the sudden termination. Goldstein had it four to two in Rocky's favor, with one even; Judge Harold Barnes favored Marciano four and three and Judge Joe Agnello voted for Rocky, five and two. This observer's score coincided with Agnello's.

Marciano did the greater damage through the evening with a wild right hand intended for the head. The punch missed its target just about as often as it landed, but when it hit Joe it bothered him considerably. As for Louis, his best punch was his ramrod left jab. This blow is as powerful as most heavyweights' solid right hand wallops.

On occasion Marciano seemed to walk right into this left and when he did it seemed only natural that Louis would whip across the finishing right to the jaw, as he used to do. But here the reflexes were noticeably lethargic, and Rocky was able to move away from blows that no man in the world could have avoided a few years back.

Louis weighed 212¾ pounds to Marciano's 187, but the younger man did not seem to mind this difference as he closed with the ex-champion in the opening round. Marciano willingly traded rights to the head in this chapter, and to his advantage. Late in the round he tagged Louis on the jaw with a right and staggered the veteran.

Rocky Hits From Crouch

In the second round Marciano went into a crouch, and the strategy worked in that Joe couldn't get a good shot at the jaw, while Rocky was able to "wing" long rights to the head. The same pattern obtained in the third, but Marciano, for some reason or other, forgot to duck in the fourth and Louis appeared to excellent advantage, using his jab almost exclusively.

The fifth was another good round for the Louis jab. In the sixth, though, Louis slowed down perceptibly. Once he had Marciano wide open for almost any kind of punch, in mid-ring, yet h pped in and patted his opponer on the shoulder, as if unaware of exactly what to do.

Marciano knew. He continued to move in and maul, and willingly exchanged with the one-time Hercules. In the seventh round the New Englander fired away at the head from all angles, and once more Joe's reactions were noticeably slow. Still, it looked as if he might pull the victory out when, near the end of the session, he shook Rocky with a solid left hook to the jaw.

Opening the eighth round Louis

shot a rare right to the ribs, but Marciano took the punch and moved in. He drove several lefts to the face as Joe attempted to shoot back right upper-cuts to the face. Then Rocky released the left hook that put Joe down the first time.

The old warrior, to whom a knockdown was not a novelty, had the awareness to take eight, and he looked as if he could survive with only a minute left to the round. But Rocky had ten years in addition to this minute on his side, and he flailed away, recklessly at first, then with purpose, and bat-

tered the whilom Bomber into defeat with the pair of lefts and the solid right.

The defeat was only the third suffered by Louis in a professional career of seventy-one fights. He was knocked out by Max Schmeling in twelve rounds on June 19, 1936, and was outpointed by Ezzard Charles on Sept. 27, 1950. He won the heavyweight championship of the world by knocking out Jim Braddock in 1937, and abandoned the title on March 1, 1949. During his reign as champion, he successfully defended his crown

twenty-five times. He was born May 13, 1914.

Wilding Stops Gambiano

For Marciano, with his streak of thirty-eight victories in as many ventures, the knockout success was his thirty-third. His most notable knockout victim before last night was Rex Layne, who once beat the present heavyweight champion, Jersey Joe Walcott. Marciano, whose real name is Rocco Francis Marchegiano, was born on Sept. 1, 1924.

October 27, 1951

Maxim Wins on Knockout When Robinson Fails to Answer Bell in 14th Round

BID FOR 3D TITLE FAILS AT STADIUM

Robinson Stunned, Weakened in 13th, Loses to Maxim in the 14th Before 47,983

REFEREE IS FORCED OUT

Goldstein, Affected by Heat, Leaves After Tenth and Ray Miller Takes Over

By JAMES P. DAWSON

Ray Robinson, world middleweight champion, had the world light-heavyweight title within his grasp in his battle with the defending champion, Joey Maxim, last night at the Yankee Stadium, but he didn't have the strength to carry through.

After battering and out-boxing the heavier Maxim through eleven of thirteen completed rounds, Robinson collapsed at the end of the thirteenth and, failing to come up for the fourteenth, went down to defeat by a knockout, the first knockout defeat in his brilliant career.

The bell had rung for the start of the fourteenth, so that there can be no disputing the round in which this battle of champions was ended.

Staggering drunkenly about the ring through the twelfth and sagging against the ropes at the end of the thirteenth, Robinson had to be helped to his corner. His seconds made every effort to clear his head during the one minute rest period.

Ice packs were applied to Ray's head and neck. Smelling salts were used. Physical therapy was attempted under the supervision of Dr. Alexander I. Schiff, of the State Athletic Commission staff. But all in vain. Then, while the stunned crowd of 47,983 stood in

amazement, the bell clanged for the start of the fourteenth.

A Victim of the Heat

Robinson made no move to get off his corner stool. Referee Ray Miller, in the ring on relief duty, stepped to Robinson's corner. Maxim leaped across the ring, only to be waved aside. Dr. Alexander Schiff had informed Referee Miller that Robinson could not continue and the battle was over.

"Robinson was a victim of heat exhaustion," said Dr. Schiff. "He was all in, absolutely unable to get up on his feet. I asked him if he could continue, if he wanted to go on. He replied that he just couldn't, and I told the referee when he came to the corner. I didn't stop the bout. Robinson stopped it when he said he couldn't get out of his corner."

Referee Miller had become the third man in the ring after the tenth round, when Ruby Goldstein, who had officiated up to that time, was so affected by the heat that he was ordered out by Dr. Schiff. When it was over Robinson had to be assisted to his dressing quarters. Thus Robinson failed in an attempt to match the records of Bob Fitzsimmons and Henry Armstrong, the only other fighters in ring history to win titles in three different classes.

Fitzsimmons held the middleweight, light-heavyweight and heavyweight crowns at different times. Armstrong held the featherweight, lightweight and welterweight laurels at one time.

Robinson surrendered his world welterweight title last year when he captured the middleweight honors and was prepared to drop the 160-pound championship under State Athletic Commission rules if he had won last night.

A Number of Surprises

The unexpected ending was only one of the surprises for the crowd. On top of the postponement from last Monday, because of rain, there was some confusion at yesterday's weigh-in when two scales were found to be faulty. Then, in 104-degree heat at ringside came the near-collapse of Referee Goldstein.

Goldstein's departure during the course of the bout was the first time such a thing had happened in local championship boxing. He said he felt dizzy at the beginning of the tenth, but was revived momen-

tarily by the smelling salts given to him by Dr. Schiff.

During the rest period, however, Goldstein staggered to the ropes and had to be assisted by Dr. Schiff. His retirement was immediately ordered and Miller replaced him.

Perhaps the heat did affect Robinson. Maybe he didn't have the stamina to go on, or that he decided his strength was ebbing and he was afraid of serious injury. Only Robinson can supply the answer to this question, which will be a long time leaving the minds of those who witnessed this surrender by a champion who was only two rounds away from another title and a life's ambition.

Robinson's dressing room was barred to visitors when the battle was over. Mayor Impellitteri was able to get past the guards, but no one else. Goldstein was resting in the same dressing room. His condition was reported satisfactory. A similar report followed on Robinson.

Scramble of $3 Customers

Fans swarmed to the ringside and some of them got into the ring at the finish. This scene was just an echo of events earlier in the evening when occupants of bleacher seats, in three successive waves, vaulted over the grill fence and dashed from the $3 section to the $30 locations without opposition. The park was inadequately policed. These scrambles and the roars of approval which accompanied them were only a prelude to the more startling developments in the ring.

From the outset Robinson demonstrated his mastery as a boxer. On this observer's score card he won every round but the twelfth and thirteenth. He gave indications of fading in the eleventh, however. And the change came soon after Robinson had staggered his rival with a mighty right to the jaw, his best punch of the fight.

Through the twelfth and thirteenth Robinson staggered and stumbled all over the ring. But Maxim was unable to take advantage of such an inviting chance for a finishing punch. Robinson missed awkwardly with punches he had previously sent home unerringly. He sagged into clinches and jabbed and swung aimlessly.

He almost fell through the

ropes early in the thirteenth, while in retreat. Ray missed a sweeping right for the jaw later in the round and fell flat on his face. But near the end of the round, when he appeared weariest, Ray crashed a terrific right to Maxim's jaw as Joey came in with lefts and rights to the body and head.

Robinson clung to the ropes in a neutral corner as the thirteenth ended. His handlers leaped in to carry the weary fighter to his corner.

Before that, however, Robinson had, with dazzling speed, dancing legs, consummate boxing skill, given Maxim a boxing lesson and a battering.

Fights From a Crouch

Fighting out of a crouch, ignoring a weight handicap of close to twenty pounds, Robinson blazed through eleven rounds, punching Maxim almost at will with left jabs to the body and face, with left hooks and right crosses, with solid lefts to the head and body. He employed a short, right uppercut to the chin in the clinches when he wasn't holding to avoid the fire of Maxim, the superior close-quarters fighter.

In the third, seventh and eighth rounds, Robinson jolted Maxim's head with straight lefts and hooks, kept up a two-fisted fire to the mid-section, shook Joey to his heels with a left hook to the jaw. Maxim was warned by Referee Goldstein in the seventh for using his forearm in a clinch.

Robinson jarred Maxim for the last time in the eleventh with a solid right to the jaw, but Joey bounded right back, going close and hammering the body. This round ended with Robinson going wearily to the wrong corner, a neutral one. It was the beginning of the end. Sugar was melting.

Maxim weighed 173 pounds and Robinson 157½. Gross receipts for the fight were $421,696.

June 26, 1952

U. S. FIGHTERS TAKE FIVE GOLD MEDALS

Lee of American Squad Wins Outstanding Boxer Trophy —Patterson Is Victor

By The Associated Press.

HELSINKI, Finland, Aug. 2—A twenty - year Olympic victory drought ended in a cascade of first-place medals tonight as America's boxers swept five championships, defeated Russia in the only face-to-face meeting of the two nations in the sport and won the unofficial team title for the first time.

In matching their perfect five-for-five performance in the semi-finals yesterday, the United States' boxers not only broke the Games record for individual victories but also romped off with the silver loving cup given to the outstanding boxer in the tournament.

This went to Norvel Lee, the 27-year-old fighter from Washington, who won the light-heavyweight crown and drew rave after rave from other boxers, officials, coaches and trainers for being the "perfect Olympic boxer."

Lee Takes Unanimous Decision

Lee, who boxes in the classic stand-up style, gracefully maneuvered to a unanimous decision over wild-swinging Antonio Pacenza of Argentina.

The United States victory parade was touched off by slender Nate Brooks, the 18-year-old flyweight from Cleveland. Light-Welterweight Charley Adkins of Gary, Ind., Middleweight Floyd Patterson of New York, Lee, and Heavyweight Eddie Sanders of Los Angeles scored for the Americans in that order.

Lee won the cup, but Adkins, a 20-year-old National Collegiate A. A. champion from San Jose State, beat Russia's Viktor Medkov in the bout that clinched the team championship.

The United States piled up 50 points on an unofficial 10-5-4-3 basis. There was no fight-off for third and fourth places and the beaten semi-finalists in each division received 3½ points apiece.

Russia's two finalists both were beaten and the once high rolling Soviet boxing brigade finished in a tie for second place with Finland, the host nation, each with 24 points. Finland had a champion to boast of, its second in the history of Olympic boxing.

Pentti Hamalainen sent Finland's colors fluttering up the center victory pole when he outpointed John McNally of Ireland for the bantamweight prize. The other four

titles were divided by as many nations.

Jan Zachara of Czechoslovakia outpointed Italy's Sergio Caprari for the featherweight crown. Italy's Aureliano Bolognesi rallied to whip Poland's Aleksy Antkiewic for the lightweight gold medal.

Poland's Ziggie Chychla conquered Russia's Sergej Scherbakov for the welterweight prize. Hungary's Laszlo Papp became the second man ever to win two Olympic boxing championships when he drubbed South Africa's Theunis Van Schalkwyk for the light-middleweight crown. Papp won the middleweight title in 1948.

The United States hadn't won a boxing championship since 1932 when Welterweight Eddie Flynn and Middleweight Carmen Barth slashed to victory.

All five American winners are Negroes. Adkins, the 20-year-old father of one child, entered the ring with a patch over and under his left eye to protect his cuts. The Russian had two heavy patches over his eyes. He had big gashes requiring seven stitches over the right eye and six over the left one. Adkins took the fight to the usually aggressive Russian. He ripped left hooks to the head to win the first round and knock the patch of Medkov's left eye. In the second, Adkins hammered the Russian all over the ring. He kept the barrage up in the third and made the Russian hold on. Twice the sturdy Soviet boxer was staggered and the blood flowed from his cuts.

Adkins Victor on Points

Adkins got only a split decision. The British judge voted for Adkins, 60—55, the French official gave it

to him, 60—57, but Poland's J. Neuding, the object of a bitter American protest yesterday, scored it even in points, 58—58, and cast his ballot for the Russian.

The only sour note of the night came in the heavyweight bout when Sanders won on a second-round disqualification of Ingemar Johansson of Sweden. The 19-year-old Swede just refused to fight. He ran and ran and ran. After two cautions and three official warnings, Referee Vaisberg of France ended the bout.

The officials were so disgusted with the Swede's actions — the cause of a piercing din of whistles and boos—that they declared there

would be no second place and Johansson would not get a silver medal.

The Swedish flag was not flown while the colors of South Africa and Finland, tied for third and fourth, were raised from the third place poles.

Behind Finland and Russia in the team race came Italy, 18½; South Africa, 15½; Poland, 15; Czechoslovakia and Hungary, 10 each; Rumania, Germany, Argentina and Sweden, 8½ each; Ireland, 5, and Korea, France, Denmark and Bulgaria, 3½ each.

August 3, 1952

Floyd Patterson (left) of U. S. eluding a right thrown by Omar Tebbaka of France in middleweight bout. The Brooklynite won the decision and yesterday captured the title.

Associated Press

MARCIANO ANNEXES TITLE IN 13TH BY KO OVER JOE WALCOTT

By JAMES P. DAWSON

Special to THE NEW YORK TIMES.

PHILADELPHIA, Sept. 23 — Rocky Marciano, undefeated Brockton, Mass., fighter, knocked out Jersey Joe Walcott, 38-year-old ring warrior from Camden, N. J., tonight to become the world heavyweight champion.

With a devastating right to the jaw, Marciano ended the reign of

the old champion after forty-three seconds of the thirteenth round. Until that moment it was a bruising battle that thrilled 40,379 fans from all over America in Philadelphia's Municipal Stadium. The receipts were $504,645.

Under the impact of that one terrific blow Walcott sank against the ropes, then slid head first to the canvas, while Referee Charley Daggert counted him out of the title he had won after much desperate effort slightly more than a year ago.

The knockout was the cue for a tremendous demonstration. Fans swarmed into the ring as the unbeaten Bay State boxer with the paralyzing punch stood in his corner, winner of the ring's richest, prize after a battle that he could have lost as early as the first round. He was the first white heavyweight to hold the title since Jim Braddock was stopped by Joe Louis in Chicago in 1937. Here was the new champion and nothing could halt the crowd in its eagerness to acclaim him.

Many Trampled in Rush

From all sections of the vast arena, where Gene Tunney had lifted the title from Jack Dempsey just twenty-six long years ago, fans rushed on the ring to greet the conqueror.

Many were trampled in the rush, which started in the lower-priced seats in the permanent stands and, under increasing momentum, moved across and through the seats at the ringside.

For a time a wall of police about the working press rows checked the rush. Police climbed into the ring. A straggler broke through the cordon back of the press rows. Then another. Then it was a steady stream of humanity climbing and clambering over the backs of the writers.

Then the crush became too much for the police. They gave up and let the demonstration run its course. Several telegraph instruments and typewriters at the ringside were kicked under the ring. A movie camera was broken.

Most of the demonstrators were young fellows with the reckless abandon that only youth can boast. They risked broken and bruised limbs to get into the ring.

When Walcott had been counted out his stricken handlers leaped through the ropes to the side of their fallen idol and carried him to his corner. It was several minutes before he could be revived sufficiently to leave the ring, with the assistance of Trainer Dan Florio and his brother Nick, and his manager Felix Bocchicchio.

Marciano, on the other hand, was virtually a prisoner in the ring, in more danger of injury at the hands of the crowd than he had been against Walcott through twelve bruising rounds of fighting.

It was at least fifteen minutes before the ring was cleared and order restored. Then Marciano was taken through the crowd under protection of a flying wedge of police and his handlers. Hundreds followed the conqueror to his dressing quarters, singing his praises, yelling themselves hoarse.

Marciano pulled victory from imminent defeat with that one paralyzing punch to the jaw. He didn't know it, but the three bout officials all had Walcott in front on a round basis for the twelve completed sessions.

Referee Daggert had Walcott leading, seven rounds to four, with one even. Zach Clayton, one of the judges, called it eight rounds for Walcott and four for Marciano. Pete Tomasco, the other judge, had Walcott leading, seven rounds

Associated Press Wirephotos

Marciano hits the canvas in the first round when Walcott landed a short left.

to five. The writer had it even at six rounds apiece, giving Marciano the third, fourth, fifth, sixth and seventh, and Walcott the first, second, eighth, ninth, eleventh and twelfth.

Suffers First Knockdown

Marciano came on to win after being knocked down in the first round, the first knockdown of his career. He rallied courageously, shook off the best punches of Walcott, and gradually wore down his 38-year-old rival with blistering blows. And, finally, to the stage where Walcott exposed his jaw for the finishing wallop.

Fighting before the largest crowd of his career, Rocky proved himself every inch a fighting man. He was crude and awkward so far as ring finesse is concerned, but amazing in his resistance to punishment and altogether destructive in administering it.

A less hardy soul would have been finished in the first round. Rocky took an unmerciful beating then, and went to the canvas under a short left hook to the jaw. It was with such a punch that Walcott had knocked out Ezzard Charles in July of 1951 to win the title.

But, whereas Charles, as champion, succumbed to the blow, Marciano, as challenger, arose at the count of three, infuriated, enraged at having been floored for this first time in an undefeated record of forty-two engagements that held thirty-seven knockouts. He was determined not only to avenge

the indignity, but to accomplish the complete destruction of his foe.

So Marciano plodded on, though buffeted about at times like a cork on an angry sea, until he had registered his thirty-eighth knockout. This was the big one.

Marciano was bruised and bleeding at the finish. He bled from a cut on the crown of his head, suffered in the sixth round when he accidentally bumped heads with Walcott. Joe got a severe cut over the left eye. Marciano had a puffed left eye and he bled from a cut above the right eye.

Walcott had only the cut over his left eye to show for the fifth knockout in a career that extends back over twenty-two years. His ribs must have been sore, his body must have been weary and his

nervous system certainly was upset under the pounding to which he had been subjected. But he had made a gallant stand, one that came near to completely upsetting the dope.

A Crafty Old Battler

Marciano entered the ring a favorite to take the crown, at odds of 8 to 5. It was forecast in advance of the fight that he must score a knockout to win. He won just as had the majority predicted, but with greater contention than had been anticipated. It did not seen possible that the aging Walcott legs could carry Joe on the long journey he traveled before going down for the count.

Walcott surprised all but his own supporters by the crafty, perfectly paced battle he waged until Marciano broke through with the crusher.

The finishing blow was a surprise. It was the first really clean punch of the fight landed by Marciano. Bewildered and confused earlier by the strategy of his more experienced and heavier rival, Rocky floundered badly through most of the battle, while winning some of the rounds principally through his fiery offense.

It was a short punch, straight and true to the mark, delivered as Walcott backed into the ropes near a neutral corner. Walcott appeared to be taking it easy at the time, boxing superbly, retreating cagily, letting Marciano fight himself out, as he had done earlier.

In the twelfth round, Walcott had befuddled by his clever defensive fighting followed by furious slugging. In the eleventh Walcott hurt Marciano with a right under the heart and, volleying furious lefts and rights to the head, face and jaw, had Rocky sagging.

The thirteenth had opened as had many of the rounds preceding, with Marciano pressing forward on the attack, half-crouched on his toes, boring in, fist and arms poised to strike. Walcott backed away carefully, pecking and pawing with straight lefts, circling about the ring. A rush by Rocky and a wild left and right sent Walcott to the ropes.

Walcott parried a left for the head and blocked a left for the body. Walcott swayed slightly. His left arm and shoulder was down. Marciano swung with a right that didn't travel more than eighteen inches, and the fight was over. Marciano, 28 years old, weighed 184 pounds and Walcott 196.

September 24, 1952

Moore Easily Beats Maxim to Take World Light-Heavyweight Title

COAST BOXER GAINS UNANIMOUS VERDICT

Moore's Steady Attack Opens Cuts but Maxim Fights On Gamely for 15 Rounds

THREE-YEAR REIGN ENDS

Clevelander, 30, Yields Title to 36-Year-Old Opponent —12,610 See Bout

Associated Press Wirephoto

REACHING FOR THE TITLE: Archie Moore throws a long left jab at Joey Maxim in the third round of St. Louis bout last night. He later won the light-heavyweight championship.

ST. LOUIS, Mo., Dec. 17 (UP)—Archie Moore, 36-year-old restaurateur of San Diego, Calif., gave Joey Maxim a thorough battering tonight and wrested the world light-heavyweight championship from him on a unanimous fifteen-round decision before 12,610 in the Arena.

Moore, who had been the scourge of the 175-pound division for nearly a decade without getting a title chance, made the most of his opportunity in a fight that set a new Missouri gate record of $89,487.

Moore drove the Cleveland fighter to the ropes in nearly every round and there gave Maxim a terrific battering again and again.

Maxim, scaling 174½ pounds to Moore's 172½, bled from gashes on both cheeks and from a cut at the corner of his left eye when the fight ended. Although 30-year-old Maxim suffered a bad beating, he amazed the crowd by his ability to absorb staggering blows to the body and head and then try to fight back.

At 36, Moore was the second oldest man to win the title in the 49-year history of the light-heavy division. Bob Fitzsimmons won it at 41 in 1903, when he took a twenty-round decision over George Gardner at San Francisco. Only the year before, Fitzsimmons had lost the heavyweight title to Jim Jeffries.

Referee's Vote Surprising

Referee Harry Kessler scored tonight's bout surprisingly close after taking the fourth round away from Moore on a foul for two low blows. Kessler gave Moore 76 points and Maxim 74. However, the judges saw it differently. Howard Hess registered 82 for Moore and 58 for Maxim. Fred Connell favored Archie, 87 points to 63. On a round-by-round basis, The United Press favored Moore, 12-1.

Maxim, making his third defense of the crown he won from England's Freddie Mills on Jan. 24, 1950, made his best showings in the third and sixth sessions. However, in most of the other rounds the action showed a champion going down to defeat because he had a poor right hand, while his challenger was explosive with both fists. A cracked elbow, resulting from an old break, prevents Maxim from throwing good, straight rights.

Maxim, an upright boxer but a weak hitter, tried to keep the bobbing and weaving Moore at a distance with left jabs. But Moore marched in steadily. He forced the Clevelander about the ring, always aiming for the ropes, where he could bend Joey back and rock him with lefts and rights to the head. During the forcing process, Moore battered Maxim's body until it was almost as red as his bloodstained trunks.

Moore's 103rd Victory

Moore, favored at 8-5, registered his 103rd victory in the 108 professional bouts of his sixteen years of professional fighting. It was his greatest victory. He has a return-bout contract for a defense against Maxim in sixty days. But whether the thoroughly beaten Maxim would demand the return was a question. His wounds certainly will not permit a bout in sixty days.

If Maxim does not demand the return, Moore may defend against Randy Turpin of England, former middleweight king. That defense would be at the end of six months, permitting Moore to pick up some money in Argentina fighting non-title bouts.

Although the bout was one-sided, it was interesting to watch until the closing sessions. The fans appeared to be delighted with the victory of Moore, who was born in Toledo, Ontario, but who launched his professional career in St. Louis sixteen years ago.

The gate of $89,486 broke the former Missouri record of $56,907 attracted at St. Louis on Jan. 16, 1950, by the Willie Pep-Charley Riley featherweight fight. Promotor Emory Jones, the St. Louis representative of the International Boxing Club, was delighted with the receipts of the seventh title fight in St. Louis history. It was the sixteenth and last world title bout of 1952 and the sixth title change this year.

Moore, who was evaded by the previous champions, Gus Lesnevich and Freddie Mills, and who didn't get the shot at Maxim until the New York Commission forced the fight, will be stepping into the footprints of some great light-heavy champions of the past. They include Fitzsimmons, Jack Dillon, Philadelphia Jack O'Brien, Battling Siki, Paul Berlenbach and Tommy Loughran.

In the dressing room, Maxim said he had not fought since his last defense against Sugar Ray Robinson on June 25, and that the lay-off of nearly six months was too long.

"I needed this fight under my belt tonight," he said. "I'll be in much better condition for my return bout with Moore. Sure I want it."

Moore said, "I made up in fifteen rounds what I had missed in sixteen years."

Maxim suffered a beating tonight, but he was well rewarded with a guarantee of $100,000. Moore will receive 10 per cent of the net proceeds, which will include $50,000 from television and radio.

December 18, 1952

Sugar Ray Robinson (right) was one of the most skillful and graceful boxers to ever enter a ring. He held the middleweight crown five times. Here he is shown defending that title against Carl "Bobo" Olson in 1952.

Carmen Basilio (right) is shown in this photo taking the welterweight title from a bloodied Tony DeMarco in 1955. Basilio was also a middleweight champion. In that division he fought a brutal battle with Sugar Ray Robinson in 1958 in which Robinson's punches closed one of his eyes for several rounds.

Gavilan Rallies After Being Floored in Second Round and Outpoints Basilio

CUBAN KEEPS TITLE ON A SPLIT DECISION

Gavilan Victory Over Basilio Arouses Ire of 7,500 Fans in Syracuse Auditorium

By JOSEPH C. NICHOLS
Special to The New York Times.

SYRACUSE, Sept. 18—Kid Gavilan encountered the most stubborn and unlooked-for opposition in the defense of his welterweight championship of the world against Carmen Basilio of near-by Canastota tonight. The Cuban from Camaguey gained the decision all right, after fifteen rounds of torrid battling, but the award was a split one and was unpopular with the bitterly partisan crowd.

The onlookers, some 7,500 in number, were virtually unanimous in the belief that their favorite had won, and for a time the referee, George Walsh, appeared in danger of an attack. Some of the more irate Basilio sympathizers in the Syracuse War Memorial Auditorium tried to "get" Walsh as he left the ring but he received excellent protection and was untouched.

Walsh's card had Gavilan in front by eight rounds to six, with one even, and Harold Barnes, one of the judges, favored the Cuban seven rounds to six, with two even. Walsh and Barnes are from New York. The other judge, Jim Kimball of this section, voted for Basilio, seven rounds to five, with three even. This observer favored Gavilan, eight rounds to seven.

Down for Count of Eight

The fight, the first world championship contest ever held in Syracuse, was a thriller that held action almost every minute. The challenger, scorned in the betting at odds of 4 to 1, waged a battle that had several highlights. The most important of these came early, in the second round. In this frame the local athlete electrified the spectators by whipping across a left hook to the jaw and flooring Gavilan for the count of eight.

Gavilan, patently affected by the blow, offered little aggressive opposition through the next four rounds as Basilio moved after him, shooting his accurate and power-packed left hand at the champion with little let up. Gavilan did not regain his sharp punching ability until the seventh round when he managed to outstab the charging Basilio with straight lefts to the face.

Even when he was back on the beam, Gavilan found that the task of catching up with Carmen was not an easy one. Basilio's strength was very much in evidence in the infighting, and the Cuban had to proceed with absolute caution, picking away at long range with his fast straight left and countering with rights before stepping inside where he held almost as often as he punched.

Champion Moves Deftly

Although the battle was uphill, it was definitely pro-Gavilan after the seventh round and through the fourteenth. He moved deftly, if not as speedily as he used to do, and his left was just the thing to keep the forward moving and courageous Basilio from getting set sturdily enough to be dangerous.

In the fifteenth, Basilio contributed a fine rally and his showing so moved the fans that they followed his every move almost hysterically. The challenger may have thought, a desperate bid was in order. Or again, he probably paced himself brilliantly, despite his never having gone fifteen rounds before.

Whatever the situation, Basilio fought with confidence and strength and his margin in this round, slight though it might have been, was clear enough. It was this stirring, fearless finish that led the fans to believe that Carmen deserved the award.

The challenger, at the start, did not seem to have much chance, and in the opening round his left eye became puffed as the result of Gavilan's sharp wallops. The picture changed completely in the second when Basilio, moving in on the champion, traded punches and then ripped the left hook to the jaw that felled the Cuban.

Through the middle rounds Basilio's advantage was so evident that Gavilan could not make the injured eye much of a target. Toward the close, though, the Kid got on the target and Basilio's eye was almost shut tight.

Easily Makes the Weight

The matter of the weights was another story in itself. The gladiators weighed in at noon, under the direction of Bob Christenberry of the State Athletic Commission. Gavilan, on the scales first, hit the beam at 146¾ and his handlers breathed with relief, for they feared that the Kid would be overweight.

In the Basilio camp there were no such concerns. The knowledge was general that Carmen was a legitimate welterweight and would have no trouble. Before he stepped on the scales, he gave Christenberry a blithe "146." The commissioner believed him and set the lever accordingly. He then peered at the figures in open disbelief, made Carmen get off and on the scales three times, then almost sadly intoned, "Basilio 148."

The commissioner, with the consent of all concerned, gave the challenger three hours to shed the necessary poundage. But Basilio, through violent exercise and brisk massaging, lost the pound in a little more than a half hour.

Basilio gave little evidence of weakness through reducing in the fight. Gavilan, though, must have been affected by theh weight-making regimen. It may even be that his reign as welterweight king will have to end against his own wishes, for it is doubtful if he can make 147 and still be strong against a first-rate foe.

The knockdown was the second suffered by Gavilan in his professional career of 112 bouts. His previous trip to the floor occurred in 1948 in a fight with Ike Williams.

The receipts were estimated at $79,000 by promoter Norman Rothschild.

September 19, 1953

Is Boxing on the Ropes?

Yes, says a veteran critic of the manly art who can remember Tony Canzoneri as a preliminary boy – and he blames it all on TV.

By ARTHUR DALEY

TEX RICKARD was the promotional genius who gave boxing its first million-dollar gate. The cold-eyed gambling man from the Klondike strove earnestly to attract a better class of people to his fisticuffing productions, preferably folks with blue blood or gold dollars. Those cold eyes glistened at the sight of bejeweled women in evening dress at the ringside.

Rickard didn't just seek class because he had no class himself. In his practical, down-to-earth fashion he realized it was better for business that way. Gentlemen in dinner jackets gave more tone to the Busted Beak industry than crum bums in turtle-neck sweaters ever could. "I never seed so many nice people," drawled Tex one night about thirty years ago. It was to become his favorite expression and he was to say it with ever-increasing frequency until the day he died.

Boxing never has drawn so vast a number of "nice people" as it draws today. Its steady spectators are in the countless millions. Is boxing therefore thriving as it never thrived before? Nope.

The television revolution has dislocated all sports in one way or another. But boxing has become its prize captive. No form of athletics reproduces on the video screen with the faithful exactness of boxing—unless you insist on including wrestling, which isn't a sport but a dramatic burlesque of consummate fakery. The TV camera can't begin to cover all the fringe happenings in baseball or football or basketball or hockey or any other sport. But boxing has no fringes. The ring is small enough to be always in focus. The contestants are the absolute minimum of two. It's the ideal arrangement because every seat in front of a video screen is a ringside seat. And the price is perfect—free.

THE sponsors don't give away their foaming glasses of beer or the sharpest razor edges ever honed. But they've made boxing a gigantic give-away program. There's a boxing show on TV practically every night in the week and it has created millions of new fans. But none of them ever got in the habit of digging into his jeans for the price of

ARTHUR DALEY writes "Sports of The Times" daily for The New York Times sports page.

PRE-TV—In the bare-knuckle days of 1889, Sullivan vs. Kilrain attracted a national crowd to the tiny way-station of Richburg, Miss. (John L. won in 75 rounds).

a ticket at the box office. Those free samples more than satisfy their wants. Amateur boxing is deader than Marley's ghost. The smaller fight clubs are dying off fast. Only a few big ones are left, most of them controlled by that pugilistic monopoly, the International Boxing Club.

By the virtually indiscriminate use of television, the major league baseball teams have been killing off the minor leagues. This is akin to eating one's young. But boxing devours its young even faster than baseball does. Once upon a time the Amateur Athletic Union and its various district associations received a high proportion of their revenue from amateur boxing. With considerable regularity, the simon pures drew capacity or near capacity crowds to Madison Square Garden. Even the "bootleg amateurs" (who were semi-pro fighters) did well in outlying sections of the country.

But when boxing fans could see genuine professionals for free in the comfort of their homes, they resolutely refused to inconvenience themselves and pay money to watch amateurs. So that phase of the sport is dead. Or if it's alive at all, it would take an expert coroner to detect the flicker of a pulse beat. Amateur boxing was the kindergarten for professional boxing. Then the small clubs were the grade school and the high school, graduating only the brightest, cleverest and best-

equipped students to college—Madison Square Garden, the Boston Garden, the Detroit Olympia, Chicago Stadium, the San Francisco Cow Palace and other such show places.

All the stars of yesteryear followed the same routine—amateurs, small clubs and then the big time. And they had many small clubs where they could learn their trade. New York City, for instance, was loaded with them. There were the Broadway Arena, Ridgewood Grove, Dexter Park, Fort Hamilton, Pioneer, Coney Island Stadium, Henderson Bowl, the Coliseum, Star Casino, Rockland Palace, Manhattan Casino, Lenox, Sunnyside, Queensboro, Eastern Parkway and St. Nick's, among others.

HOW many of those are left? Eastern Parkway is still in operation. St. Nick's is used by the Garden when the big arena has to yield time to the circus, rodeo, ice shows or some other major production. All others have closed down. This is not a situation indigenous to New York. It's the same the country over. The little fellow just can't compete with the big fellow any more, especially since the big guy is giving his away on nation-wide networks.

This reporter still can remember one of his earliest assignments for The New York Times more than a quarter of a century ago. He went to the Broadway

Arena in Brooklyn and found himself fascinated by a kid from New Orleans, a youngster just up from the amateur ranks. The kid could box, could hit and could take it. So the reporter assumed a proprietary interest in him, watching him move up to Garden preliminary bouts, Garden semi-final and eventually Garden final. There was a vicarious thrill for an awfully young and awfully impressionable reporter when his new hero, Tony Canzoneri, went on to win both featherweight and lightweight championships of the world. Canzoneri was a great little fighter, one of the best. He had been properly schooled in the small fight clubs.

IN boxing, as in life, there are few short cuts to success. Maybe there are fewer short cuts. Hard work is still the only sure road to the mountain top and only by toiling indefatigably at his job can a man learn it properly. Television has done a double disservice to boxing. It has helped kill off the kindergartens and the secondary schools. So they are uneducated folks who suddenly reach the pugilistic college these days. They've skipped so many grades that they flunk the big test as soon as it comes.

The story of Chuck Davey, television's darling, is the perfect illustration of what's happened to boxing. Davey had been on the boxing team at Michigan State, a top-flight intercollegiate performer. Then he turned pro. Davey was photogenic and he had flash in his style. He was an instant hit on TV. The guys and dolls went gaga over him and thought him the greatest thing the ring had seen since John L. Sullivan.

THE dolls loved him because he looked like the All-American boy. The guys loved him for the superficial class he showed. Not being genuine fight experts themselves, but only the synthetic TV brand, they couldn't recognize superficiality when they saw it. The Davey build-up was shrewd and well handled. He was artfully matched against men with styles that made him look better than he was. The big coup was matching him with Rocky Graziano, the one-time dread killer of the ring, but then an over-the-hill, washed-up fighter. Davey outdanced the lumbering Rock.

So he was matched with Kid Gavilan for the welterweight championship. The Kid from Havana is probably the best all-round ringman in the game today—which may be damning with faint praise. He started fighting in the Cuban canebrakes, as a tot and he learned his trade soundly. If you'll pardon a personal allusion, I wrote a column before the fight in which I said that the television experts expected Davey to beat Gavilan. "With what?" I asked. And then went on to say why I thought Davey didn't have a chance.

Oh, brother, how the mail rolled in! Most of the letters were of the Dear-sir-you-cur type. I was a dope, a rockhead, an ignoramus and so on. Yet I wasn't being uncannily prescient. I was merely stating an obvious fact, one that anyone who knew the slightest bit about boxing couldn't fail to see. Gavilan, of course, punched Davey's ears off.

When Jimmy Carter, the lightweight champion, bounced Tommy Collins off the floor as though Collins were a rubber ball, indignant TV fans almost demanded a Congressional investigation. So violent were their outcries that this fight actually became front page news. Collins, by the way, was just another of those synthetic TV fighters.

THINGS used to be different. When Tex Rickard was in charge of Madison Square Garden's fistic promotions, he didn't break his back to have a show every week. He'd rather wait until a good match came along. When radio took over Friday nights at the Garden, a weekly show was a must. Not all of them were good, but it was no undue strain. Then came television with Wednesday for suds and Friday for blades, both on a coast-to-coast basis. There just aren't that many good fights or fighters any more. Boys are brought up before they're ready for that quick dollar. They go down as fast as they rise.

Nor are there as many of them any more. One reason is the disappearance of the small clubs. Another is general economics. Boxing's most overwhelming appeal was to the underprivileged. It offered a chance to leap quickly over social and financial barriers. Joe Louis, a cotton picker, earned millions of dollars. So did Jack Dempsey, once a hobo. So did Gene Tunney, once a shipping clerk.

But the nation's economy and way of life are such these days that there are not many underprivileged left. If a kid can earn more than $100 a week as a truck driver or bricklayer or something better, boxing has little appeal for him. Why should he train endlessly and then fight once a month for a $50 purse he has to split down the middle with his manager?

ONCE upon a time, a good

manager was the key figure in the development of every fighter. Most of them had been fighters themselves and they knew every trick of the trade. What's more, they could teach it expertly. The few who couldn't, latched on to clever trainers.

They taught their pupils proper techniques and proper strategies. They taught them how to throw a punch with maximum power, how to roll with a blow, how to sidestep, how to maneuver in the clinches, how to stay in balance, how to piece their punches into telling sequences. There were a thousand and one things they taught them. Some even taught extra refinements—if that's the correct word—such as jabbing a thumb in the other guy's eye or giving him the laces across the face.

The main point is that they taught them. They might have been crude about it at times but they were effective. For instance, Jack Dempsey never used his left hand until Doc Kearns, his manager, angrily tied the Mauler's right hand to his side and made him practice fighting only with his left. That's how Dempsey developed

the most murderous left hook the game has ever known. Joe Louis had the big punch but little finesse in the beginning. But the wily Jack Blackburn taught him well. Before the Bomber's second fight with Billy Conn the experts wrote that it was a match between a slugger and a consummate boxer. That nettled the Jolter. "I kin box pretty good, too," drawled Louis.

However, the great teachers have almost all faded from the scene. The manager of today is anything but an ex-fighter. Some of them are merely fronts for far more sinister characters whose police records wouldn't permit them to manage fighters openly. And most of them are linked together in a tight cabal which almost amounts to a syndicate operation of sorts. They give nothing to boxing. They only take from it. Least of all do they give any instruction to their charges. Perhaps that's the most alarming aspect of the situation.

AT the same time, American youth these days is more inclined to seek security than that pot of gold at the rain-

bow's end. They also realize —they're better educated than yesteryear's fighters — that the odds are prohibitively against their winning a championship. Suppose they win a title? Will it pay off?

Champions reach such an economic saturation point these days that they can lose money once their income tilts over a certain figure. Please remember, though, that there are only eight champions of the world and even that is stretching matters as far as importance is concerned. The big one, of course, is the heavyweight title and a colorful performer can make it pay (although taxes nowadays take a big bite) fairly handsomely. But dull champions like Jersey Joe Walcott and Ezzard Charles couldn't. The middleweight crown can be a valuable asset if the right man wears it. So can welterweight and lightweight laurels. But the other four are not revenue producers of any particular consequence.

The lure of the ring just isn't as compelling for the youth of America as it once was. This, perhaps, is reflected in the roster of the champions of the present. Marciano's

TV ERA—Madison Square Garden was a "ghost arena" at a recent Graham-Young bout, although it matched the pride of Manhattan's East Side against a West Side boy.

place in history has yet to be determined. So terrific a hitter is he that he may yet rank with the great ones, although his crudeness as a boxer and his advanced age of 30 militate against him. Most of the other champions are second-rate. Maybe Gavilan would rank among the top ten in his weight division on an all-time basis, but none of the others would. Yet most of these champions dominate their divisions so utterly that there aren't even logical contenders in sight.

ALTHOUGH it may seem at the moment as though boxing is dying of pernicious anemia, that's a wrong conclusion. It's too primitive, too fundamental, too tough ever to die.

Perhaps it will get the infusion it needs if pay-as-you-go television should replace the give-away television of the present. The shoddy match-making of today would have to making. The small clubs might even get back into business, each shooting for the customer's dollar or quarter or whatever it is he'd put in the coin machine.

It could be a throwback, of sorts, to the past. The little clubs built up the fighters and matched them shrewdly with an eye toward the gate receipts. A hot attraction would draw a packed house. A dud would leave it empty. So there rarely was a dud. Pay-as-you-go television would be the same thing, except on a larger scale.

Rare were the nights when the Garden drew an attendance of less than 10,000 spectators. But the Garden has become a ghost arena on fight night. It's now an oversized television studio. Not long ago, for instance, a Friday night fight attracted—if that's the word—2,991 spectators.

And folks wonder what's happened to boxing? This was merely a fight to fill the provisions of the contract with the television sponsor. But if the Garden had to compete for the customer's dollar on a pay-as-you-go basis, there'd be no clinkers. With more fights in more clubs for more money, interest in ring careers might be revived among the youth of the land.

THE blight of give-away television is stunting boxing's growth and making it wither. The promoters, ostrichlike, refuse to admit what's happening. But there can be some significance in the fact that there is a new trend among promoters. Whenever there's an out-of-the-ordinary fight, the city where the show originates is blacked out to TV.

The professional football people discovered this first and made it work. Baseball is edging toward it until the day may come when all home baseball games will be blacked out. Only the away games will be televised, a policy that the Cleveland Indians will inaugurate next season.

It seems utterly ironical that there should be more fans and more interest in boxing than ever before in history while there is a shrinkage in sites, competitors and caliber of performance. Maybe pay-as-you-go television will be the ring's salvation. This give-away method of operation simply doesn't work.

January 31, 1954

Marciano Keeps Heavyweight Title With Unanimous Verdict Over Charles

47,585 SEE RALLY BY CHAMPION WIN

Marciano Takes Command in Savage Bout at Stadium After a Slow Start

By JOSEPH C. NICHOLS

Rocky Marciano successfully defended the heavyweight championship of the world against Ezzard Charles at the Yankee Stadium last night. The favored titleholder from Brockton, Mass., gained the unanimous decision over his Cincinnati opponent, who once was the ruler of the division.

The contest was a savagely waged one in which Marciano's greater strength and punching power enabled him to gain the award. Referee Ruby Goldstein had it eight rounds to five, with two even. Judge Artie Aidala scored it nine, five and one, and Judge Harold Barnes had it eight, six and one. This observer favored Rocky by nine rounds to six.

A crowd of 47,585 fans witnessed the fight, and the onlookers were pleased with both the action and the decision. Although he was plainly defeated, Charles made one of the best showings of his career. He gamely mixed with the ponderous-punching Rocky, and dealt out considerable punishment with his left hook through the first half of the proceedings.

Marciano's strong point was his right hand, and he landed the weapon quite often. Strong as it was though, it failed to knock down the challenger. This circumstance was in the nature of a surprise in that while Rocky was the betting favorite to win, at odds of 7 to 2, his supporters expected him to score by a knockout.

Marciano Absorbs Blows

It really was not through boxing that Marciano gained the award. It was more through his ability to take great punishment, to absorb everything that came his way until his opponent became tired of punching.

When Charles showed that he had little left, after tagging the champion, Rocky moved in and slammed away almost without let up. Only the fact that he was in the best of condition permitted Ezzard to go through the gruelling fifteen rounds without hitting the canvas.

For Marciano, the victory extended a string that is without equal in the history of modern boxing. It was his forty-sixth professional contest and his forty-sixth victory.

Nobody before him in the ranks of the heavyweight champions reached the top of the class with a perfect record. Only in the matter of knockouts did Marciano's average fall off against Charles. The champion has stopped forty of his rivals.

Charles Best Boxer in Division

Despite the decisive count in his favor on the ballots, Marciano did not have an easy time of it at all, particularly at the start. For Charles, probably the best boxer now in the heavyweight division, caused Rocky to make many mistakes and at the same time succeeded in scoring with excellently timed left hooks to the body and right counters to the head.

For the first four rounds Rocky could do little but lunge and seek to grab Charles, to make him stand still and serve as a target for his pile-driving right. Of course, Charles would have none of that. He moved in fearlessly on the champion, whipped away at the head and body until he felt that he had delivered enough punishment, and then stepped back to avoid Marciano's eager rushes.

This pattern gave the Charles followers much hope, especially when a cut appeared over Marciano's left eye after a clinch that was followed by a Charles right to the head.

The slow-starting Marciano probably needed this blood-letting to urge him into formidable action. At any rate, he took command in the fifth round when, after sampling some of Ezzard's right-hand punches to the head, he bethought himself of his own right, and applied it to Charles steadily.

Champion Hits After Bell

So eager was the champion to employ the weapon that he even landed after the bell. Charles, of course, hit him right back.

In the sixth Marciano dared everything in the hope of bringing about a sudden termination. Making little effort to avoid Charles' blows, the champion moved forward firing right-hand punches.

A good number of these wallops bounced off Ezzard's jaw, but the latter took them well and he thrilled the crowd by springing back at the close of the session to hurt Rocky with a well-placed left hook to the jaw.

Carrying over his attack to the seventh, Marciano found that Charles was willing enough to mix with him, so much so that the challenger had the better of the several exchanges, in which the left hook was the key drive. These blows made Rocky stop his attack several times, but beyond that they did not seem to carry enough force to spill him.

The great strength that Rocky possesses began to manifest itself at this point. He seemed to retain his freshness after every bitter exchange, whereas Ezzard, for all his courage, seemed slower and slower getting his punches across.

Marciano punched away with little concern for any return in the eighth. He evened the matter of cuts then by opening a small one beside Charles' right eye.

The ninth showed the tide strongly in Marciano's favor and he bounced right after right off Ezzard's chin. The latter seemed on the verge of "going" several times, but he thrilled the crowd by rallying toward the close and shaking Rocky with his left hook.

An exchange in the tenth round was one of the highlights. The pair waded willingly toward each other, Rocky matching his right against Ezzard's left, to the latter's advantage.

In the eleventh, the champion hit Charles with "everything." These punches shook the challenger often, but Ezzard took them and fought back. So well did he react, in fact, that he out

117

Champion Rocky Marciano, blood streaming from left eye, jars Ezzard Charles, challenger, in thirteenth round of title bout.

smarted Rocky in the twelfth with his left hook delivery.

From there on, though, the champion was in command. He had the better of every trade in the thirteenth and fourteenth, and in the fifteenth he swarmed over Ezzard in an effort to floor him.

The latter took many punches, but he showed that he was still in a fighting mood by tagging Rocky with two solid left hooks just before the end.

Charles' Weight Surprises

Marciano weighed 187½ pounds and Charles 185½. The latter figure was a surprise since Ez was expected to weigh 190, but there was no fault to find with his condition.

The gross receipts were $543,-092 and the net $469,653. Marciano gets 40 per cent and Charles 20 per cent of "everything," including some $200,000 theatre-TV money and $35,000 from the radio. The same split will be made on money received from movie rights.

Marciano was born in Brockton on Sept. 1, 1924. His right name is Rocco Marchegiano, and he is the oldest of six children born to Piecino and Pasqualina Marchegiano.

The father, an Italian immigrant, supported his family as a cobbler, and Rocky had the typical American town upbringing. Baseball and football were his main sports pursuits in the two years that he went to high school. It was not until 1943, when he entered the Army, that he took boxing seriously. He was a full-fledged heavyweight then.

In the service Rocky took part in camp tournaments and built up a fine record.

After the service Marciano, who had been a good enough baseball player to get a trial with the Chicago Cubs, decided to take up boxing in earnest and turned professional in 1947. He gradually gained renown in New England and presently came under the management of Al Weill. Charley Goldman became Rocky's trainer and Marciano made rapid progress.

His first "big" fight occurred in New York on March 24, 1950. He met Roland LaStarza, also previously undefeated and considered an exceptionally good boxer for a heavyweight. Marciano gained a split decision and became a top star. He continued to topple all opposition and was matched with Joe Louis, the erstwhile champion of the world.

Rocky knocked out Louis in eight rounds on Oct. 26, 1951. He stopped four subsequent rivals before getting into the ring with Jersey Joe Walcott for the championship, in Philadelphia, on Sept. 23, 1952.

Marciano knocked out Jersey Joe in thirteen rounds to become the titleholder. In his defenses previous to last night Rocky knocked out Walcott again and LaStarza.

June 18, 1954

24 BOXERS NAMED TO HALL OF FAME

Writers Pick Dempsey, Louis and Armstrong as Modern Fighters for Honor

Jack Dempsey, the fighter of the half-century in an Associated Press poll in 1950; Joe Louis, and Henry Armstrong, a former triple champion, led the modern pugilists into Boxing's Hall of Fame yesterday.

The list included twenty-four ring warriors of the pioneer era, the oldtimers' era and the moderns to the New York City institution, which will parallel its baseball counterpart at Cooperstown, N. Y.

Boxing writers for the world's major news services composed a board of directors to name fifteen boxers of the pioneer era going back to the eighteenth century.

The fighters selected were America's John L. Sullivan, Jack McAuliffe, John C. Heenan, John Morrissey, Tom Hyer and Nonpareil Jack Dempsey, middleweight; England's James Figg, Jack Broughton, Daniel Mendoza, Tom Cribb, Gentleman John Jackson, Tom Sayers, Arthur Chambers and Jem Mace and Australia's Young Griffo.

An oldtimers' committee that included writers, Dempsey and Gene Tunney, selected six stars who were active until 1919. They were former heavyweight kings James J. Corbett, James J. Jeffries, Bob Fitzsimmons and Jack Johnson; Joe Gans, lightweight champion, and Stanley Ketchel, middleweight titleholder.

Fitzsimmons, better known as Ruby Robert, was a champion of three divisions, middleweight, light-heavy and heavyweight, but not at the same time. Eleven votes were required for selection, and Ketchel received seventeen of the twenty.

After the first two groups were picked, ninety-one writers around the world voted for ten of the best boxers who fought after 1919 and who have been out of the ring for at least two years.

These moderns had to be selected on at least 75 per cent of the ballots. Sixty-nine votes were the minimum, and only Dempsey, Louis and Armstrong made it.

Dempsey received 85 votes, Louis 78 and Armstrong 74. Armstrong is the only fighter in history to hold three titles at once. He was featherweight, lightweight and welterweight champion at one time in 1938.

Other boxers in the balloting and their vote totals were: Sugar Ray Robinson, 66; the late Benny Leonard, 63; Tunny, 58; Mickey Walker, 57; Harry Greb, 55; Tony Canzoneri, 34; Barney Ross, 29; Jimmy McLarnin, 26, and Tommy Loughran, 18. In all fifty-seven boxers were named.

No Home TV of Bout

James D. Norris, president of the International Boxing Club, said yesterday there would be no home television of the heavyweight title fight between Rocky Marciano, the champion, and Ezzard Charles at the Yankee Stadium, Sept. 15.

Instead the I. B. C.-promoted bout, the second between Marciano and Charles, will be sent coast to coast over a closed theatre circuit. The first fight last June 17 was handled similarly.

However, the fight will be broadcast nationally by the Columbia Broadcasting System.

August 6, 1954

BOXING BODY BARS 'RETURN' CLAUSES

World Group Will Refuse to Recognize Title Bouts if Contract Is Restricted

LONDON, Nov. 16 (AP) — The World Boxing Championship Committee today banned the controversial "return bout" clause in title fights and said the group would not recognize a bout if the "return" was included in a contract.

The committee of four men representing New York, the National Boxing Association of the United States, Britain and Europe, also announced that no champion could defend his world title without the committee's approval; that no fight could be billed as a world title bout without the committee's approval and that if a promoter did so, the fight would not be recognized in the United States, Europe, Britain or the British Empire.

After the decision was announced following a two-day meeting of the group, it promptly drew the fire of Charley Johnston, manager of two world champions — Featherweight Sandy Saddler of New York and Light-Heavyweight Archie Moore of Miami.

Johnston to Ignore Ban

Johnston, who is president of the International Boxing Guild of Managers, said in New York that neither Saddler nor Moore would defend his title without benefit of the return bout clause.

"I had to give return bouts to Willie Pep (for Saddler) and Joey Maxim (for Moore)," said Johnston. "I want return bout contracts for Sandy and Archie. So does every other champion want one. Ask Rocky Marciano (the heavyweight champion) what he thinks."

Harry Markson, managing director of the International Boxing Club (I. B. C.) which has "exclusive" contracts for the title defenses of most of the United States champions, said in New York:

"The I. B. C. has always gone along with the ideas of regular constituted bodies and will continue to do so. Whatever decisions are made by boxing administrators in the states where we operate will be adhered to.

The world committee meeting was attended by Robert K. Christenberry, chairman of the New York State Athletic Commission; Livingston Osborne, chairman of the Illinois State Athletic Commission who represented America's National Boxing Association; J. Onslow Fane, chairman of the British Boxing Board of Control, and J. Edouard Rabret of France, representative of the European Boxing Union.

List of Champions Adopted

The committee also agreed on a list of champions and top contenders in each of the eight classes.

In explaining the listings, which will be made quarterly, Fane said "it does not follow that the committee would not recognize a fight between the champion and one of the contenders as for the world title.

He said that the group could approve a title bout, for instance, between the champion and the No. 3 contender instead of the No. 1 challenger.

The return bout clause has been insisted on by almost all champions for years. It guarantees the champion, if he loses his title, a return bout with his rival within a specified time, usually ninety days.

The committee ranked Cuba's Nino Valdes as the No. 1 heavyweight contender.

THE RANKINGS

Heavyweight Class (Champion, Rocky Marciano, Brockton, Mass.)—1. Nino Valdes, Cuba; 2. Don Cockell, Britain; 3. Bob Baker, Pittsburgh.

Light Heavyweight Class (Champion, Archie Moore, Miami, Fla.)—1. Paul Andrews, Buffalo, N. Y.; 3. Jimmy Slade, New York.

Middleweight Class (Champion, Carl (Bobo) Olson, San Francisco)—1. Joey Giardello, Philadelphia; 2. Pierre Langlois, France; 3. Rocky Castellani, Cleveland; 4. Charles Humez, France.

Welterweight Class (Champion, Johnny Saxton, New York)—1. Carmen Basilio, Canastota, N. Y.; 2. Kid Gavilan, Cuba; 3. Ramon Fuentes, Los Angeles.

Lightweight Class (Champion, Paddy De Marco, Brooklyn)—1. Jimmy Carter, New York; 2. Duilio Loi, Italy; 3. Ralph Dupas, New Orleans.

Featherweight Class (Champion, Sandy Saddler, New York)—1. Percy Bassett, Philadelphia; 2. Teddy Davis, Hartford, Conn.; 3. Ciro Morasen, Cuba.

Bantamweight Class (Champion, Robert Cohen, France)—1. Raton Macias, Mexico; 2. Willie Towell, South Africa; 3. Chamrern Sangkitrat, Thailand.

Flyweight Class (Champion, Yoshio Shirai, Japan)—1. Pascual Perez, Argentina; 2. Dai Dower and Eric Marsden, Britain; 4. Leo Espinosa, the Philippines.

November 17, 1954

Basilio Knocks Out DeMarco in 12th to Capture World Welterweight Title

DEFENDER DAZED AS BOUT IS HALTED

Basilio's Counter-Punching Decisive—DeMarco Floored Twice in 10th Round

By JOSEPH C. NICHOLS
Special to The New York Times.

SYRACUSE, June 10 — Carmen Basilio became the welterweight champion of the world tonight. The sturdy "onion farmer" from near-by Canastota knocked out Tony DeMarco of Boston in 1:52 of the twelfth round of a scheduled fifteen-round clash.

The clash was a savage one in which the favored Basilio wore his rival down by a succession of sharp counter-punches. He knocked Tony down twice in the tenth round, but the defending champion surprised by making a stand in the eleventh. In the twelfth, though, Tony had little left and was a standing target for Basilio's blows.

It was apparent to all that DeMarco had no chance of victory.

and Referee Harry Kessler stepped in to call a halt. The referee's action met with the approval of the crowd, most of whom were fanatically in favor of Basilio.

Local Boxer Favored

Until DeMarco went down in the tenth, he had made a strong stand against the local boxer, who was the betting favorite at 8 to 5.

Tony fought in the true manner of the champion, carrying the action to his rival and eagerly endeavoring to trade with the more experienced Basilio.

For a good part of the fight Tony had Carmen puzzled as he grazed the chin with long rights and reached the target solidly

with long lefts. This method had its effect on Carmen's face, for the Canastota fighter was cut across the nose and over his left eye before he took command in the tenth.

DeMarco's left hand was more accurate than Basilio's, but neither showed anything that resembled a left jab. It was their plan to step in and swing away, after each tried to get the other to lead.

Their willingness to trade blows rather than box made a big hit with the crowd, and the fighters' actions were accompanied by an almost continuous round of cheering.

In the opening session De Marco had a slight margin because of his lefts to the head.

Basilio took charge in the second and opened a cut over Tony's right eye in a close exchange.

Left Hook Jars Carmen

The defending champion ripped a left hook to the head in the third and shook Basilio, who seemed about to fall. Tony's over-eagerness was the only thing that prevented him from dropping Carmen, the New Englander missing any number of wild swings for the head.

Carmen made Tony miss considerably in the next two rounds and he took advantage of these mistakes to send heavy left hand punches to the head and body.

These wallops did not seem to have much effect on DeMarco at that stage, for he came back strong and in the next three rounds appeared to be building an advantage.

In the ninth round Tony threw his left hand wildly and Basilio was able to pick his spot, so to speak. He shot a long right to the head and the punch made Tony stop coming in. Sensing the reaction, Carmen sprang inside and punched the body with both hands, and also ripped short uppercuts to the face.

In the tenth DeMarco tried to rush his rival, but Carmen was strong and wrestled Tony into position for short lefts and rights to the head, a solid right sending DeMarco to the canvas.

He got up at seven and had little to offer Carmen, who dropped him again with a two-handed attack to the head. Tony arose just as the referee said eight, and there was no time left in the session for Carmen to register another knockdown.

One of the more dramatic things about the fray was the manner in which Tony faced Basilio in the eleventh. The tired champion punched steadily, even though his efforts lacked steam. Carmen knew that he had his man, though, and did not go wild.

Manages to Keep Feet

In the twelfth, though, Basilio fired away without let-up. Tony sagged and buckled and threatened to fall, but managed to keep to his feet. He was so helpless, however, that Kessler prudently halted matters.

Basilio weighed 145½ pounds and DeMarco 144¾. It was Tony's first defense of the title that he won from Johnny Saxton on April 1.

The fight was a financial success, 9,170 persons crowding into the War Memorial Auditorium to witness it. Governor and Mrs. Harriman were among the spectators. The receipts amounted to $119,794.

Kessler's card favored Basilio, eight rounds to two, with one even. Judge Bert Grant had it 7 and 4 for Basilio and Judge Frank Forbes scored it 8 and 3 for Carmen. This observer favored Basilio, 6 to 5.

June 11, 1955

Marciano, Floored in Second Round, Stops Moore in Ninth to Keep Title

CHAMPION DROPS OPPONENT 4 TIMES

Moore Down Twice in Sixth, Saved by Bell in 8th, Then Marciano Wins in Ninth

By JOSEPH C. NICHOLS

Rocky Marciano had the hardest time in his entire career beating Archie Moore at the Yankee Stadium last night. The Brockton Blockbuster, the holder of the heavyweight championship of the world, knocked out the 38-year-old Moore in 1 minute 19 seconds of the ninth of a scheduled fifteen-round bout, but before he did he was in desperate danger himself.

The contest, witnessed by a crowd of 61,574 fans, was one of the most savagely fought, thrilling duels in modern prize ring history. The heavily favored Marciano's superb condition, that and nothing more, enabled him to subdue his crafty and courage challenger.

Moore, the light heavyweight champion, gave an exhibition of boxing skill that, even in defeat, was almost as thrilling and moving as the display of awesome power that eventually brought the victory to Rocky.

The 31-year-old Marciano, undefeated in a career of forty-eight previous clashes, was the strong favorite to win, at odds of 4 to 1. Moore made a most commendable bid to upset these figures before the combination of Marciano's heavy wallops and sheer fatigue prevented him from going on.

Before he went out, Moore en-

joyed the satisfaction of cutting up Marciano with short sneak lefts and sneak rights, of befuddling him completely with adroit and clever feints and footwork, and of dropping him with a right-hand punch, a circumstance hardly expected by the sympathizers of the strong-jawed Marciano.

Moore contributed one of the great surprises of the fight by scoring the first knockdown. There were five knockdowns in all, Moore going down four times. In the second round Moore sent the champion to his knees with a beautifully executed right-hand sneak punch.

Marciano, plainly dazed, arose at the count of two. He walked

Challenger Moore stands over Champion Marciano after dropping him in second round

Official Scoring of Fight

	1	2	3	4	5	6	7	8
Kessler	R	M	R	R	E	R	M	R
Aidala	R	M	R	R	R	R	R	R
Barnes	R	M	M	R	M	R	R	R

R—Marciano.   M—Moore.   E—Even.

Champion Not Groggy

When Rocky resumed fighting, he was not groggy, but he was puzzled. Moore moved in and out on him and punished him with both hands, but could not get on the target again.

The challenger showed boxing skill in the highest degree in the third round. Depending on Marciano to force the fighting, the challenger moved competently and with virtuosity as he capitalized on Rocky's crude lunges by scoring with repeated counters.

It was evident in that session that Marciano was far from being a polished boxer. Moore just about made him do anything he wanted to.

In the fourth, Marciano's strength gave him the edge as he pounded Moore with both hands. Archie went into a shell in the face of Rocky's attack and did not absorb as much punishment as it appeared to the crowd. At the bell, Rocky smote Archie with a right to the face and the challenger returned in kind.

After giving another fine exhibition in the fifth, Moore took the two sixth-round knockdowns that preceded the "epic" exchange.

Going out for the seventh, Moore sought to pound the body, hoping to capitalize on the exhaustion shown by Marciano in the previous frame. But Rocky's splendid condition showed and the champion fought back ably. Midway in the session, Moore slipped to the floor, but it was not a knockdown.

Rocky had a big edge in the eighth, in which he landed frequently with his right. He scored a knockdown with a right to the jaw near the end of the round. As the count reached six, the bell rang.

In the ninth, Marciano again resorted to pure power in a successful attempt to end matters. He merely flailed away with both hands as Moore tried, weakly, to punch back. After a particularly heavy Marciano barrage, the challenger sagged to the floor and took the count.

Marciano bled from the nose and from cuts about his eyes. Moore was cut above the right eye, which was closed through the eighth and ninth rounds.

The fight was originally scheduled for Tuesday night, but was postponed because of the imminence of Hurricane Ione. The postponement only served to help the gate, according to Jim Norris, president of the International Boxing Club. He announced gross receipts of $948,117.95.

There was no home television of the fight, but the video rights

to the ropes, for no discernible reason, while Referee Harry Kessler counted to five. Strangely enough, the ring-wise Moore, a veteran of 144 previous skirmishes, did not avail himself of the opportunity of springing at the puzzled champion.

This was the high spot of Moore's offensive, but his fine skill and boundless courage served to force Rocky to his greatest efforts in the subsequent rounds. Moore was dropped for the count of four in the sixth, for eight in the sixth, for six in the eighth, and for the full count in the ninth. Before his strength wore out, Moore had his fans hopeful that the old magician of the ring could pull the victory out.

Abounding in highlights as the fight was, it contained one that will probably be referred to by this generation as comparable to any single round in heavyweight title history. That was the sixth round, when Archie was floored twice.

It started as a reasonably easy round for Rocky, as his powerful punches pounded Archie about the head. A right to the jaw floored the challenger, who arose at four—another surprise. A combination of rights and lefts sent Archie down again, this time for eight.

Rocky Springs to Attack

Sensing that this was his time, Rocky sprang at Archie, prepared to blast him into the ranks of the also rans. Moore was neither of a mood nor of a consistency to be blasted out, at least not then. He met the savage onslaughts of the champion bravely, and in kind.

For every punch Rocky threw, Archie threw one back. All semblance of boxing was forgotten as the tremendously strong athletes flailed away at each other with a fury that bordered on the heroic.

Most of the fans expected Moore to go down with every exchange, and some of them hoped that one of Archie's blows would find the mysterious "button" and put the champion out. Whatever the expectations were, the fact emerged that the warriors showed no inclination to terminate the exchange, and the wonder arose as to just how much they could stand.

The question was very nearly answered, at that, for when the bell rang the combatants stopped, automatically, and started for their corners. They could not walk steadily, out of sheer exhaustion, and it was almost ludicrous to see them wobble to their respective corners, Archie across the ring and Rocky along the side, helping himself by grabbing the top rope with his left hand.

Rocky of the crushing punch landed many of his "pulverizing" rights on his foe in this exchange and Archie took them all. It was this ability to absorb the wallop that gave Moore's followers the hope that was dissipated mainly through the cumulative effect of Rocky's punches.

Indeed, the final knockdown, the least spectacular of the fight from the standpoint of execution, was only the result of a series of belaboring lefts and rights that Marciano visited on Archie's head. The challenger slumped to the canvas, got to his haunches at the count of eight, attempted to rise, and then fell back, exhausted and beaten, but not unconscious.

Marciano, who weighed 188¼ pounds to Moore's 188, began the fight cautiously and with seeming confidence in the theoretical betting odds. He used his left to the head with surprising effectiveness and, after Moore jabbed him repeatedly with snaky lefts, returned enough strong rights to the head and body to insure himself the margin in the round.

In the second, "Old Archie" worked the magic. He tricked Rocky into a lead and cracked him on the jaw with a solid right. He feinted, Rocky moved in, and Moore sneaked over a pinpoint sneak right to the jaw and down went the champion.

were sold to more than a hundred theatres throughout the nation. It was estimated by Harry Markson, one of Norris' aides, that the receipts from theatre television, from radio, and from the moving picture potential would raise the total receipts to $1,125,000. Of this sum Marciano will receive 40 per cent and Moore 20 per cent.

There were four knockouts in the scheduled four-round preliminaries. Mike De John, 193½, Syracuse halted Jack Taylor, 214½, Newark in 1:35 of the first; Clint Bacon, 176, Chicago, stopped Hosie Boil, 178, Hempstead, L. I., in 1:08 of the second; Toxie Hall, 197½, Chicago, knocked out Bobby Biehler, 181½, Rochester, in 0:26 of the second and Ernie Cab, 208, Brooklyn, stopped Lou Benson, 220½, Baltimore at 2:59 of the first.

In other bouts. Warren Lester, 183, Philadelphia, beat Waddell Hannah, 173½, Philadelphia; Mickey Maye, 198, New York, defeated Johnny Orgen, 204, the Bronx; Frank Gioseffi, 192, New York, outpointed Bob O'Brien, 195, West Side, and Calvin Wilson, 197½, Philadelphia, fought a draw with Johnny Jenkins, 178, Harlem.

September 22, 1955

Robinson Knocks Out Olson in Second to Win Middleweight Title 3d Time

RIGHT TO JAW ENDS COAST MAN'S REIGN

In Full Command From Start, Robinson Drops Olson for 10 in Upset at Chicago

By JOSEPH C. NICHOLS
Special to The New York Times.

CHICAGO, Dec. 9—Ray Robinson is back on top of the heap. Sugar Ray of Harlem, once the welterweight and middleweight champion of the world, again became the middleweight ruler of pugilism tonight. He returned to that eminence by scoring a two-round knockout over Carl (Bobo) Olson of San Francisco.

Boxing as superbly as he did when he was rated as the best fighter ever, "pound for pound," Robinson flattened his foe with a right hand to the jaw. Olson lay stretched on the canvas while Referee Frank Sikora tolled the full count of ten at 2 minutes 51 seconds of the second round.

As far as the fight went, it was all Robinson. The Harlem wizard was in complete command, from the opening exchange of left-hand jabs to the final right-hand wallop that floored Olson.

Olson, a little cumbersome in his attempts to keep matters at close range, seemed constantly befuddled by the confidence and grace shown by Robinson. Bobo did little in the short time the fight went to indicate that he was the champion.

First Victory in 1951

The result was a surprise mainly because Robinson had been out of top-flight action for a long time. He became the ruler of the middleweight (160-pound) division on Feb. 14, 1951. On July 10 of that year he was outpointed by Randy Turpin, but he regained the title by stopping Turpin in ten rounds of Sept. 12, 1951.

In December, 1952, Robinson gave up the crown to go into show business. The footlights failed to interest him as much as he had hoped, and he returned to ring warfare early this year. Thus Sugar Ray tonight became the first man to win the middleweight crown three times.

Because of his long absence from top-flight competition, Robinson was the short-ender of tonight's fray, at odds of 3 to 1. But from the way things went, there didn't seem any evidence that Ray had ever been away from the ring.

He knew Olson, because he had beaten the San Francisco boxer twice in the past and so, knowing him, he was completely aware as to how to proceed against the defending champion.

Waits for Big Mistake

Ray, in effect, forced Olson to make all the mistakes, and, when the greatest mistake occurred, he belted Carl out of his title with a solid right-hand smash to the jaw.

The end of the fight, of course, was the most spectacular part of the whole thing. The crowd of 12,441 was resigned to long, fifteen-round exhibition, in which Olson was expected to wear down the ex-champion because of youth, if nothing else. Olson is 27, Robinson 35.

Olson fought along those lines, too. He crowded Robinson as much as he could and sought to overpower the former champion at close quarters. But, at close quarters through the first round, Robinson would have none of this bull-dozing.

Instead, Ray held judiciously at close range, resolved to save his strength for one of two things. They were: either the long uphill rigor of fifteen rounds against a bull-like opponent or the good chance of a one-punch shot against said bull-like opponent's jaw.

In the opening session Robinson exhibited the grace of a competent counter-fighter. He permitted Olson to lead, then struck back with neatly placed head punches, mainly delivered with the left hand. To emphasize that he was not a one-target fighter, Robinson kept Olson wary by driving a solid right-hand punch to the body.

Bobo Moves in Close

In the second round Olson showed his determination to fight in close. He grappled with Ray as often as he could, but Robinson met the moves by loosely dangling his arms at his sides and looking at the clock that indicated the time of the round.

Exchanges of this nature occurred two or three times before Robinson felt the situation was in his favor. Olson had just been pushed out of a crowding attempt by Sugar Ray and the defending champion sought to punch his own gloves together, in a sort of habitual gesture. But Robinson didn't let him finish.

Looping a long right, Robinson found the target and Olson sagged, bound for the floor. To aid Bobo in his downward flight, Ray delivered a left hook to the head, but the punch was a mere brush.

Olson landed on his back, and the question in the minds of the fans was whether or not Olson could get up.

Bobo, at the count of six, made a motion with his head and it appeared that he might arise. But this little gesture was too much for him, and he remained on the canvas as the count proceeded to the decisive end.

The crowd paid $128,462 to see the fight. Robinson weighed 159¾ pounds and Olson 159¼.

Robinson gained the middleweight title the first time by wresting it from Jake La Motta. After losing it to Turpin and winning it back from Randy in the same year, Ray ruled until he announced his retirement three years ago this month, leaving the title vacated.

But he showed tonight, in assuming the 160-pound toga for the third time, that he is the best of all the middleweights in the world. He is still Sugar Ray.

In the semi-final of six rounds, Russ Tague, 128¼, Eldridge, Iowa, defeated Gil Cadilli, 129, San Francisco.

December 10, 1955

Fencing Origin of Manly Art Spells Blow to Boxing Fans

By WILLIAM R. CONKLIN

Millions of fans who watch televised boxing bouts often are confused by the commentator's rapid-fire references to "left hook," "right cross" and other fundamental blows in boxing.

How did those punches originate?

John Broughton, boxing champion of England in the mid-Eighteenth Century, undertook to teach the gentry and nobility "the art of hitting without getting hit."

"Persons of quality and distinction," he advertised, "should not be deterred from entering into a course of these lectures, because they will be given with the Utmost Tenderness and Regard to the Delicacies of the Frame and Constitution of the Pupils, for which reason Muffers (gloves) are provided that will effectively secure them from the Inconvenience of Black Eyes, Broken Jaws and Bloody Noses."

Broughton, known as the Father of Modern Boxing, is credited with popularizing the

LEFT HOOK

RIGHT CROSS

LEFT JAB

LEFT UPPERCUT

The New York Times (by Ernest Sisto)

Ray Drake demonstrates, with his sparring partner, Bob Richter, four fundamental punches in the science of boxing

padded glove. Earlier, boxing techniques had been drawn from fencing. Both boxer and fencer found that the "on guard" position permitted any attack or defense at a given moment.

From the all-important stance, a straight right or left-hand punch can stop any blow coming from the side. Orthodox boxers use their left sides for defense, the right side for offense.

Footwork Often Identical

As in fencing, the leading arm and foot travel the same path. The fencer holds his right arm extended, while the boxer extends his left arm. Footwork in both arts is similar, often identical.

"In order to find the true position," wrote Capt. John Godfrey in 1747, "the left leg must be presented some reasonable distance before the right, which brings the left side toward the adversary.

"This the right-handed man ought to do, that, after stopping the blow with his left arm, which is a kind of buckler (shield) to him, he may have the more readiness and greater power of stepping in with his

right hand's returning blow.

"In this posture," the London fencing master continued, "he ought to reserve an easy flexion in the left knee, that his advances and retreats may be quicker.

"By this proper flexion his body is brought forward so as to have a just inclination over the left thigh, insomuch that his face makes a perpendicular or straight line with the left knee whilst the right leg and thigh in a slanting line, strongly prop up the whole body, as does a large beam an old wall."

The left jab is comparable to the lunge of a fencer. Left arm and left foot move out simultaneously. The right hand moves up to cover the chin, and the right elbow is tucked in close as a body defense. At the same time the boxer on offense drops his head slightly to the right to avoid an opponent's counterpunch.

Right-hand jabbing by a southpaw employs a similar technique.

Jack Dempsey is credited by several sources with developing the short left hook to knock-

out proportions. The blow is delivered with the left foot advanced and the left arm rigid and slightly bent at the elbow. The boxer hooks from his shoulder toward the opponent's jaw.

Left hooks to the body go in under the opponent's right guard. The man on offense exposes himself to a hard right counterpunch. He may avoid it by bending to the right as his blow is delivered.

On defense, the incoming hook may be blocked by the right hand or forearm. Against body hooks, the defender drops his right elbow.

The straight right to the head is the punch that starts many knockdown counts. It is thrown in a straight line with the right shoulder adding impetus. The body twists at the waist and the right heel comes off the floor. The left arm, meanwhile, must remain up.

Uppercut Hard to Land

The uppercut, traditionally one of the most difficult blows to land, may be either a right-hand or left-hand punch to the jaw. The opponent must be coming in head down. The blow

must be timed to the split second to register effectively.

In infighting to the body, the boxer tries to get his elbows inside those of his opponent. The side position means more effective punching. At the same time the opponent must punch to the outside, losing power and control. Uppercuts to the body are effective here as short-range blows.

Boxers use the fundamental punches in combinations, sometimes too swift for the eye to follow. One typical sequence is a left hook to the jaw, a right to the body, a left hook to the jaw.

Another employs a left jab to the head, left hook to the body and straight right to the jaw. A third involves getting away from an incoming left hook to the head by throwing a right cross inside the aggressor's hook.

By trial — and error — the boxer learns which sequence of blows is most effective against his adversary.

February 19, 1956

Marciano Retires From Boxing; Heavyweight Ruler Undefeated

Victor in All 49 Pro Bouts, He Wants to Devote More Time to His Family

By WILLIAM R. CONKLIN

Rocky Marciano, iron-fisted son of a New England shoe factory worker, retired yesterday as undefeated world heavyweight boxing champion at the age of 31 to devote more time to his family.

The comeback trail, Marciano said, will never feel the weight of his feet so long as his present prosperity continues. To a boxing world that has seen, numerous retirements-followed-by-comebacks, Marciano said:

"I thought it was a mistake when Joe Louis tried a comeback. No man can say what he will do in the future. But, barring poverty, the ring has seen the last of me. I am comfortably fixed, and I am not afraid of the future. Barring a complete and dire emergency, you will never see Rocky Marciano make a comeback."

Rocky's retirement was first disclosed by his wife, Barbara, yesterday morning in their home town, Brockton, Mass. A few hours later in New York, Rocky and Al Weill, his man-ager, confirmed the report at a Hotel Shelton press conference.

Rocky Marciano as he announced his decision to retire.

Forthwith, the nation's news wires buzzed with speculation as to who would succeed to the heavyweight title. Marciano named the light-heavyweight champion, Archie Moore, as having "as good a chance as anybody." He knocked out Moore in the ninth round last Sept. 21 in a sizzling bout at the Yankee Stadium.

In Vancouver, B. C., Moore said he would claim the title if Rocky was serious about retiring. He met the announcement with a skeptical laugh and said:

"Marciano won't quit, because he loves the jingle of the American dollar too much. He'll soon hie himself to the North Woods with an axe on his shoulder to get into condition to meet Archie Moore. But—if Rocky does retire as he thinks, then I'll claim the title."

April 28, 1956

Joe Brown Gains Split Decision Over Bud Smith to Take Lightweight Title

DEFENDER DOWN TWICE IN THE 14TH

Smith Beaten in 15-Rounder Though Brown's Right Is Fractured in Second

NEW ORLEANS, Aug. 24 (AP) —Joe Brown of New Orleans, a 30-year-old former carpenter with a buzz-saw left hand, floored Wallace (Bud) Smith, the defender, twice in the fourteenth round tonight and went on to win the world lightweight title on a fifteen-round split decision.

Brown weighed 133 pounds, Smith 134½.

Brown, the No. 8 ranked con-tender, unleashed a two-handed barrage in the fourteenth that sent Smith down for counts of seven and nine. The bell saved Smith from a knockout on the second trip to the canvas.

The 27-year-old Cincinnati boxer was bleeding badly from the mouth and nose and hung on through the fifteenth on wobbly legs.

The 9.200 fans that jammed the Municipal Auditorium let go with a deafening roar when the verdict was announced.

Referee Roland Brown had Brown in front, twelve rounds to three. Judge Charles Dabney had Brown the winner, nine rounds to three, with three even. Judge Frederick Adams had Smith ahead seven rounds to six, with two even. The Associated Press card had Smith ahead, eight rounds to seven.

Owen Confirms Report

Ringside reports after the fighters left the ring said Brown had broken his right hand in the second round. Promotor J. T Owen of the sponsoring Louisiana Boxing Club confirmed the report.

Brown fought almost exclusively through the latter part of the fight with a flicking left hand jab and an occasional hook to the midsection and head.

Brown set a fast early pace and outscored Smith with a steady stream of lefts and a few rights that discouraged Smith's potent left hand.

Smith regained his poise in the middle rounds and began to carry the attack to the fleeting New Orleans challenger, a polished performer at avoiding dangerous corner traps.

Waiting Game Futile

The margin for the challenger grew as Smith waited for an opening in the sixth and seventh rounds. Brown offered little opportunity, moving in quickly with pot-shot lefts to the head and retreating back to safer distances.

Smith was staggered in the second round when Brown scored with a straight right flush on the chin.

Smith recovered and started a counter-offensive that had Brown retreating again.

Brown, who entered the ring as a 2-to-1 favorite despite streaks of mediocrity in a ten-year professional career, ran into trouble in the twelfth round.

Smith successfully maneuvered his dodging opponent repeatedly into the corners and dished out heavy punishment with both hands.

The victory was Brown's sixty-first against fourteen losses and eight draws. Smith suffered his fifteenth setback against thirty-three victories and five draws.

Tonight's bout was Smith's second defense of the title since he won it from Jimmy Carter in June, 1955. He beat Carter's attempt to regain the crown last October.

The gross gate was $43,910.

August 25, 1956

Basilio Halts Saxton in Ninth Round to Regain Welterweight Title

By JOSEPH C. NICHOLS
Special to The New York Times.

SYRACUSE, Sept. 12 — Carmen Basilio became the welterweight champion of the world by blasting Johnny Saxton of Flushing, Queens, to a knockout defeat tonight. The strong fight-er from Chittenango, N. Y., stopped the defender in 1:31 of the ninth round of a scheduled fifteen-round bout in the War Memorial Auditorium.

The fight ended with Saxton on his feet. But he was a helpless, beaten hulk. Al Berl, the referee, halted the action when it was apparent that Saxton could do nothing except absorb punishment at the hands of his savage, incessantly punching challenger.

A crowd of 8,546 saw the scrap and enjoyed it immensely. Basilio is most popular here-abouts and his victory was hailed with an outburst of wild yells.

In battering Saxton, Basilio had a comparatively easy time. He carried the fight to Saxton all the way, and invited Johnny's most direct wallops in an endeavor to get in there and mix in accordance with Carmen's way of fighting. Basilio was eminently successful in that respect, too. For he just about spread-eagled the defender on the round count.

Round Count Unanimous

All three officials agreed that Basilio had taken every round except the second one. The judges working with Berl were Frank Forbes and Harold Barnes. This observer gave every round to Basilio.

Because Basilio was the short-ender in the betting, the crowd liked the outcome much more than it would have ordinarily. Basilio had been the favorite all week. But this afternoon, after the fighters weighed in, the odds moved in favor of Saxton at 6 to 5.

The weights couldn't have been the cause of the switch. Neither fighter had trouble meeting the requirements. Saxton scaled 145¾ pounds and Basilio 146¼. The limit for the welterweight division is 147 pounds.

It was through expert and excellent use of the left hook to the head that Carmen carved out his victory. He used that weapon unceasingly, firing it at Saxton even at times when it seemed that to punch at all would be a risky venture because of a possible counter.

Filling out the left-hand delivery to the head was a two-handed body attack that must have caused Saxton to wilt despite his excellent condition. At first Carmen's body punches didn't seem to do much harm. But as he continued that line of fire it became evident that Saxton was feeling the effects.

Saxton Changes Tune

Saxton seemed content to box through most of the early rounds. His manner seemed to indicate that he could turn it on whenever he wished.

But as time wore on, his attitude changed. He was truly a desperate fighter throughout the seventh and eighth rounds.

Basilio softened up his opponent in the fourth when he belted

Associated Press Wirephoto

DIRECT CONNECTION: Carmen Basilio landing a left to the face of Johnny Saxton in the fourth round of last night's welterweight bout in Syracuse War Memorial Auditorum.

him steadily with both hands while Saxton sought to hold. Carmen wrestled out of this clutch and banged his rival's body so wildly that he drew a warning from the referee.

The upstate athlete kept well ahead of Johnny in the succeeding sessions. In the seventh, he went at Saxton with both hands. He fired left hooks to the face and opened a big cut on Saxton's lip. He made the head the target in the eighth until Saxton tried to retreat. Then Carmen punched the body effectively.

In the ninth it was all Basilio. He ripped across a long right

to the head and drove Saxton to the ropes. After that Saxton faced Carmen with his hands at his sides, and Basilio belted away at the head until Berl stepped in to rescue Johnny.

Victor Avenges Setback

The fight gained revenge for Basilio. Last March 14, he was defeated by Saxton in Chicago, and the setback cost Basilio the welterweight crown. That verdict was a most unpopular one.

There was no question about tonight's outcome. "He fought like a man this time," Basilio commented.

"The booing upset me," said Saxton. The crowd had jeered him unmercifully when he was introduced and during most of the fight.

Frank (Blinky) Palermo, Saxton's manager, said that Berl should not have stopped the fight. He was virtually alone in that opinion.

Saxton will have ten to fifteen stitches taken in his cut lip tomorrow.

The gross receipts were $134,-939.

September 13, 1956

Patterson Knocks Out Moore in Fifth Round to Win World Heavyweight Title

LEFT HOOK SETS UP CHICAGO TRIUMPH

By JOSEPH C. NICHOLS
Special to The New York Times.

CHICAGO, Nov. 30 — Floyd Patterson became the heavyweight champion of the world tonight by knocking out Archie Moore. The 21-year-old former

Olympic boxer stopped Ancient Archie in 2 minutes 27 seconds of the fifth round of a scheduled fifteen-round bout.

The end came with dramatic suddenness, Patterson setting his man up with a left hook that was truly artistic in its delivery. This punch was landed about midway in the round. It dropped Moore flat on the canvas.

It appeared to the fans that Archie was certain to remain down for the full count. But

he stirred at six, and succeeded in dragging himself to his feet at nine. He was up, but he had nothing left. Patterson sprang at him—this time with no finesse, but with both hands swinging. The flurry had force. Again Moore went down.

Moore was not unconscious the second time. He was just tired. He followed the count of Referee Frank Sikora attentively and got up again at nine.

The referee was of the opinion that Archie was through. He

stepped between the men as Patterson was about to punch some more. There was a small protest made by Moore at Sikora's action. Some spectators also voiced their dissatisfaction.

It appeared to this observer that Moore was an easy target for Patterson and that Floyd would certainly have floored Archie once more.

The outcome was in the nature of an upset. Moore, who admits to 39 years of age, was the favorite at 2 to 1 on the basis of his experience of twenty years as a ringman. Patterson had engaged in only thirty-one professional fights previously, with thirty victories and one defeat.

The men were fighting for the right to succeed Rocky Marciano as the heavyweight champion of the world. Marciano retired last April with a record of forty-nine victories in forty-nine professional fights. His last ring appearance resulted in a knock-out triumph for him over Moore. This was in September, 1955.

Poise and Confidence

In disposing of Moore, Patterson gave an exhibition of poise and confidence that belied the betting odds. It was expected that Moore's skill and generalship would enable him to handle the youngster easily in the early going. Instead, Patterson boxed equally as well as Archie. On this observer's scorecard, Patterson took three of the first four rounds.

Because of the skill possessed by each man and the respect they had for each other, the fight was not especially productive of exciting action.

Still, the crowd followed proceedings tensely, aware that in a heavyweight fight a one-punch ending is always highly probable. Strictly speaking, while Patterson did not put Archie out with a single wallop, the left hook was the real finisher.

The fight got off on an amusing note when the opponents went at each other ahead of time. They confused a warning buzzer with the starting signal. However, Sikora was between them and held them off until the bell called for action.

In the opening round Moore tried to hold Patterson off with light lefts to the head. But Floyd moved toward his foe and reached him with several left hooks to the head. Late in the session Moore had to step backward briskly to avoid his eager opponent.

Unable to Find Target

Moore's inability to find the target handicapped him in the second round. The usually accurate Archie had trouble finding the target with right chops. Patterson scored with left hooks to the head and body after Archie made these mistakes. The youngster tagged Moore with both hands forcibly late in the round.

In the third Moore was a little more aggressive. He moved in to punch to the body. One of these blows was a mite low, and Sikora warned Archie.

Moore then tried to slug it out with Patterson, but Floyd was willing and he had much the better of the exchanges. Moore emerged from this trade with a cut over his left eye.

Moore was a business-like performer in the fourth round. He reached Patterson often. The manner in which Archie went about his work seemed to indicate that he was about to take charge, and that it was about time to put the youngster in his place.

Going out for the fifth, Patterson went at Moore with both

hands. He sent lefts to the head and rights to the body. Moore came through with a left to the head and then "he never knew what hit him."

The cool Patterson stalked Archie, saw the opening and shot across the left hook to the jaw. It was a perfect punch, neatly timed, speedily delivered and authoritative. Moore was not the same after that.

There was an excellent reason for Patterson to end matters quickly. Word arrived here just before the fight that Mrs. Patterson had given birth to a daughter earlier in the evening at Queens Memorial Hospital, Elmhurst, Queens. Patterson was told about it after the fight and he expressed a desire to see the baby as soon as possible. Patterson, reared in Brooklyn, now

lives in Mount Vernon, N. Y.

The new champion, who had intended to hold a press conference tomorrow morning, flew back to New York after the fight.

Patterson weighed 182¼ pounds, the highest of his career, and Moore scale 187¾. There was some small solace for Moore. He still has the light-heavyweight championship of the world.

Archie, who lives in San Diego, Calif., won the 175-pound crown from Joey Maxim in 1952. Maxim is the only man ever to beat Patterson. He got a decision over him in eight rounds in Brooklyn two years ago.

All three officials had different scores. Sikora gave Patterson three rounds and called

one even. Judge Jim McManus gave all four rounds to Patterson. Judge John Bray had it two for each fighter.

The fight, which was televised through the country except for a Chicago area blackout, attracted a paid attendance of 14,000. The gross receipts were $228,145 and the net $187,585. The rivals received 30 per cent of all receipts—gate, radio and television.

Patterson is the youngest fighter in history to hold the heavyweight crown. He was born on Jan. 4, 1935. When Joe Louis won the heavyweight crown, Louis was 23. Moore, who claims he was born on Dec. 16, 1916, is believed to be a year or two older than he claims.

December 1, 1956

AMERICANS GAIN 2 BOXING TITLES

Rademacher Stops Russian, Wins Heavyweight Crown —Boyd Also Triumphs

By ROBERT ALDEN
Special to The New York Times.

MELBOURNE, Australia, Dec. 1—Peter Rademacher, hard-hitting heavyweight from Grandview, Wash., scored a one-round technical knockout over the Russian champion, Lev Moukhine, tonight to win an Olympic gold medal.

A second American gold medal winner was Jim Boyd. He won the light heavyweight crown. Boyd, who had Gheorghe Negrea of Rumania on the canvas three times, earned the unanimous decision of the judges.

The only United States loser in the finals was Jose Torres of Puerto Rico. Torres dropped a decision to Laszlo Papp, the Hungarian light middleweight.

By winning, Papp became the first man in the history of the Olympic Games to win three gold medals in boxing. Papp won medals in London in 1948 and at Helsinki in 1952.

Duke of Edinburgh a Fan

But the fight of the evening as far as the fans (including the Duke of Edinburgh) were concerned was the match between Moukhine and Rademacher. The two boxers had registered impressive knockout victories in the tournament, and both got off the floor in their semi-final bouts last night to flatten their opponents.

Rademacher, with the United States Army, was Northwest Golden Gloves champion four

times and had won the all-Army and interservice titles. He punches with the force of a sledge hammer with either hand.

Moukhine is a body puncher with good boxing ability. He was no match for Rademacher, however. Rademacher, at the outset, jabbed effectively with his left.

The first time Rademacher connected with a right it left the Russian rubber-legged and glassy-eyed. For thirty seconds or so after that punch the balding 28-year-old Rademacher measured Moukhine with his left, and waited for his opportunity to clobber the Russian with another right.

When the opportunity arose, Rademacher bounced the Russian right onto the ropes with a hard right. Almost immediately a barrage of lefts and rights by the American put Moukhine down on the canvas. The Russian took the obligatory count of eight. Then Rademacher stalked him again. Moukhine made the mistake of trying to bang home a couple of punches of his own. But Rademacher caught him flush on the chin with another right.

A succession of lefts and rights drove the Russian to the ropes, where Rademacher pinned him and scored at will.

Moukhine was a helpless target and the referee stepped in and stopped the contest. It was the only thing that he could do. Not even the most ardent Russian fan could gainsay that.

In his bout Boyd, who hails from Rocky Mount, N. C., and who like Rademacher is based at Fort Benning, Ga., in the U. S. Army, met a willing but unskilled opponent.

Negrea wanted to mix it up with Boyd. He kept throwing punches. Boyd hit in flurries and then fell inside, where Negrea rained ineffective punches against the arms.

In his contest Torres fought on fairly even terms with the skilled Papp for the first two rounds. However, in the final stanza the 29-year-old Hungarian carried the fight to the tiring American.

At the final bell Torres looked like a beaten fighter. He was a beaten fighter.

In the other fights, the Russians won three gold medals, the British two, the Germans one and the Rumanians one.

At Helsinki, the U. S. had won five gold medals. This included one by the new heavyweight champion of the world, Floyd Patterson.

December 2, 1956

Robinson Knocks Out Fullmer in Fifth Round to Regain Middleweight Crown

LEFT HOOK TO JAW ENDS TITLE FIGHT

Fullmer Hits Canvas for Full Count as Robinson Takes Crown Fourth Time

By JOSEPH C. NICHOLS
Special to The New York Times.

CHICAGO, May 1—Sugar Ray Robinson flattened Gene Fullmer with a left hook to the jaw tonight and became the world middleweight champion for the fourth time. The splendid flash from Harlem knocked out the defending titleholder in 1:27 of the fifth round of a scheduled fifteen-round fight.

The end came with blinding suddenness, and was quite unexpected. The defending champion from West Jordan, Utah, was the strong favorite at odds of 3 to 1 at ringtime.

The major factors that made Fullmer the favorite were his comparative youth and the ease with which he relieved Robinson of the championship on Jan. 2. On that occasion Fullmer gained the unanimous decision in Madison Square Garden.

In carving his way to success, Robinson waged a crafty struggle. He let Fullmer carry the action to him at the start, he let the younger fighter rough him up in close, and he even let Fullmer make probing right hand attempts to reach Ray's face. And when he figured he had his man analyzed perfectly, Sugar Ray let fly with the left hook that spread Fullmer on the canvas for the full count.

Attempt to Arise Fails

There was no question as to the cleanness of the knockout. Fullmer was "dead" when he hit the floor, and could not make an attempt to stir until Referee Frank Sikora counted eight into his ear. Then the Westerner made an instinctive attempt to arise, but he failed, and the count ran through to ten.

It was the first time in a career of forty-four professional fights that Fullmer had been knocked out. The 25-year-old Westerner has been recognized generally as almost impervious to punishment. In their first fight he took Robinson's best punches without seeming to feel them at all.

Until Ray came through with the devastating left hook tonight, Fullmer seemed to show the same reaction to Robinson's wallops. Ray hit him sharply from the first round.

Full. just absorbed these

Associated Press Wirephoto

FIFTH (AND FINAL) ROUND: Victorious Sugar Ray Robinson standing over Gene Fullmer after landing the knockout punch in their title bout last night in Chicago.

blows and moved forward, intent on wearing down the 36-year-old New Yorker with body punches. But Robinson's condition was the best. He took Fullmer's best wallops, even the errant ones that landed low, without showing any signs of weakening.

Star-Studded Record

Those who favored Robinson's chances were prepared to sit through the fifteen rounds and see their favorite gain the decision. There were few indeed who had any hope or confidence that Sugar Ray could "take out" the hitherto armor-plated Fullmer with a punch. But he did, and thus added another sensational accomplishment to a sensational - studded professional record that began in 1940.

In the four rounds that were fought through to completion the rivals were on fairly even terms, with Fullmer taking the first two and Robinson the others.

The Westerner, in the early moments, waited for Robinson to come to him. When he did, Fullmer banged Ray briskly about the body with left hooks. Robinson did little but hold in the first round, until near the end. Then he shot a light left

to the body and, a little later, fired a right uppercut to the chin. Fullmer showed no expression at all as these punches reached him.

Fullmer's left hand was in almost continuous action through the second. He still awaited Robinson's forward movements, and he poured his left to the ribs and stomach of the advancing New Yorker. Robinson did little in the way of attack, remaining content to fire only one solid right to the head. Near the end of this round they engaged in a steady infighting trade with Fullmer landing more frequently.

There was a change of pattern in the third, a change that was not too discernible. Robinson, instead of moving forward, forced Fullmer to "make" the fight. He feinted Gene into advancing, and flashed left hands to the face. Still, Fullmer fired for the body, and one these punches was so wild that the referee warned him for hitting low.

Ray Becomes Aggressor

At the start of the fourth Robinson surprised the crowd and his opponent by springing forward and bouncing two fast right hands off Gene's jaw.

Fullmer once more applied himself to his set style of pounding the body, but this time Robinson willingly mixed with him, rather than to hold as he had done so frequently in the preceding rounds.

There occurred a tingling exchange at close quarters that had the fans roaring as the session came to a close. There was no indication of fatigue in the features of either boxer as they walked to their corners.

Fullmer beat Robinson to the punch when the bell signaled the fifth, and he drove several lefts to the body. They closed in to trade short punches, and the crowd jeered when Fullmer hit Ray on the break. That is, as they broke from a clinch.

This seemed to be the signal for Robinson to get going in true championship style. He was sharp with straight lefts to the face, making Fullmer lunge toward him to counter.

Robinson pounded the ribs, then stepped back to await another counter. Fullmer made a characteristic forward lunge, expecting to rip the body, but he never made it. The skillful Robinson calculated the lunge perfectly, and fired his lightning left to the jaw of the incoming

Fullmer. The latter fell straight down, no reeling or staggering, and he stayed down until he was counted out.

Robinson, in his dressing room, gave the best description of the crushing punch. Somebody asked him how far the left hook traveled, and he said, "I can't say. But he got the message."

Robinson weighed 159½ pounds and Fullmer 159¼. In their first clash Robinson weighed 160 pounds and Fullmer 157¼. The paid attendance was 14,753 and the gate receipts were $156,000.

All three officials had Fullmer ahead on points for the first four rounds. Sikora gave Fullmer, 5, 5, 5 and 4 for 19 points, and Robinson 4, 4, 5 and 5 for 18. Judge Jim McManus had it 5, 5, 5, 4 for Fullmer and 4, 4, 5, 5 for Robinson. Judge Frank Clark had it 5, 5, 5, 4 for Fullmer and 4, 5, 4, 5 for Robinson.

May 2, 1957

SUGAR RAY SHOWS WHAT'S IN A NAME

Robinson Borrowed Amateur Card of Friend to Start His Boxing Career

Ray Robinson has been on the professional boxing scene a long time, since 1940. And before that, he was nationally famous as an amateur performer.

Robinson was born in Detroit, and his real name is Walker Smith. There is some dispute about his correct age, though. Sugar Ray insists he is a year younger than the records show. And the records show he was born on May 3, 1921.

When he was about 12 years old, Robinson moved to New York with his mother and he quickly showed an interest in boxing. Taking the name and amateur registration card of a friend, Robinson entered the amateurs and competed in eighty-nine bouts.

He turned professional as a lightweight in 1940 and ran up a string of forty victories before meeting defeat. He served a short time in the Army, and on being released resumed boxing, this time as a welterweight.

The 147-pound crown was open because of the abdication of Marty Servo, and Robinson opposed Tommy Bell for the right to claim the crown. The fight took place in December, 1946, and Robinson won by a decision.

He retained the welterweight title until 1951, when he gave it up after beating Jake La Motta for the world middleweight crown. Robinson lost and won the 160-pound crown in the same year.

Randy Turpin beat him in London by decision in July and he stopped Turpin in ten rounds in September in New York. He tried for the light heavyweight championship but he was stopped by Joey Maxim in 1952, and then "retired."

He came back in 1954 and on Dec. 12, 1955, captured the 160-pound title a third time by knocking out Carl (Bobo) Olson. He dropped the title to Gene Fullmer on Jan. 2 of this year, but took it back last night. Robinson has won 139 of 148 pro fights.

May 2, 1957

LEGAL BLOWS TO THE BOXING GAME

U. S. Courts Demand More Competition

James D. Norris.

By JOSEPH C. NICHOLS

The boxing industry in this country has been dominated since 1949 by James D. Norris Jr. and Arthur Wirtz. Through control of some of the largest indoor arenas in the nation, Norris and Wirtz have been able to offer "big-time" presentation of the most attractive matches.

Norris inherited his fondness for sports, and a tremendous fortune, from his father. When the senior Norris died in 1953 he left an estate estimated at $200,000,000 to four children. Included were railroads, steamships, hotels, wheat, cattle and arenas. In one of these arenas, the Chicago Stadium, Jim Norris and his father's partner of many years, Arthur Wirtz, had promoted boxing immediately after World War II.

When Joe Louis gave up the heavyweight championship in 1949, Norris and Wirtz organized the International Boxing Club of Illinois, wholly owned by the Chicago Stadium Corporation of which Norris and Wirtz are the sole owners. They staged a fight between Ezzard Charles and Joe Walcott to determine Louis' successor, and Charles won. Norris and Wirtz then moved on New York, bought out the late Mike Jacobs' Twentieth Century Sporting Club, and set up the local I. B. C., in affiliation with Madison Square Garden. Norris and Wirtz together piled up 39 per cent of the Garden stock, enough to make Norris president

of the organization. The I. B. C. of New York is a wholly owned subsidiary of the Garden.

Enter Television

Among the other arenas in which Norris and Wirtz have title or controlling shares are the Chicago Stadium, the Detroit Olympia, and the St. Louis Arena.

Besides having the arenas, Norris and Wirtz have had the fighters. That is to say, they had contractual call for the exclusive services of many of the leading fighters in the world.

With television making such progress in the late Nineteen Forties, the entire picture of boxing promotion changed. Only

televised shows could make any big money for promoters and boxers alike. Sponsors were willing to buy long contracts, but they wanted assurance of regular shows and the presentation of several championship fights as climaxes to ordinary sequences of weekly bouts.

Norris has been able to provide the sponsors with what they want, in the matter of facilities and of fighting personnel. The TV people and the boxers have been eager to do business with him, the former because of assurance of performance and the latter because of sure pay. The I. B. C. groups have television contracts with national sponsors to produce boxing programs on Wednesday and Friday nights. The Wednesday night package brings $18,500 weekly and the Friday show $25,000.

Profits of Boxing

How many persons are concerned in the general operation of boxing, and how much money is involved, is difficult to venture. There are about 3,700 fighters in this country, but only a very small percentage get enough ring work to enable them to support themselves. Most of them are "part-time" boxers, with steady jobs. Unofficial reports of the I. B. C. operations of 1956 indicated that the groups handled about $3,-500,000 with a net profit of less than $100,000. The biggest I. B. C. operation of the year took place on Nov. 30 when Floyd Patterson knocked out Archie Moore to become the heavyweight champion. Although Patterson was not under

the control of the I. B. C. this fight took place in the Chicago Stadium, where 14,000 persons paid a gross of $228,145 at the gate. Augmenting the receipts was $180,000 for the television and radio rights.

The Government's monopoly prosecution of the I. B. C.'s began six years ago but was dismissed when the court ruled that professional boxing was like professional baseball which the Supreme Court had ruled as beyond the limits of the anti-trust laws.

The Government appealed and the Supreme Court said that boxing, unlike baseball, could be prosecuted under anti-trust laws. The case was sent back for retrial which began a year ago last April before Federal Judge Sylvester J. Ryan.

Court Decree

Last March 8 Judge Ryan found Norris and Wirtz guilty of violation of the Sherman Act. Also found guilty were the two I. B. C.'s and the Madison Square Garden Corporation. Last Monday Judge Ryan decreed that Norris and Wirtz were to withdraw from the Madison Square Garden Corporation management completely and were to sell all their stock in that organization. Also, they were ordered to dissolve the I. B. C. of Illinois and the I. B. C. of New York.

The Madison Square Garden Corporation, without Norris and Wirtz, will be permitted to promote two championship fights a year for the next five years. The Chicago Stadium may do the same, under Norris and Wirtz. This pair may also operate in the other arenas that they control, but not under I. B. C. auspices.

The purpose of this, according to Judge Ryan's decree, is to open the way for competition between Madison Square Garden on one hand and the Chicago Stadium, the Detroit Olympia and the St. Louis Arena on the other.

Norris and Wirtz said they would appeal Judge Ryan's decree. Kenneth Royall, chief attorney for Norris, said in court: "What we have done has been accepted practice in boxing. It has been our belief that sport does not come under the scope

of the anti-trust laws. We have no idea of wrong doing."

Effect of Ruling

The practical effect of the judge's ruling on Norris and Wirtz is difficult to predict. There is more to promoting a championship fight than having two men get in the ring and swing at each other. The general set-up of a plant is not a simple one. Publicity bureaus,

training camps, guarantees, advances, outright loans, staff salaries and printing require much more money than the neophyte promoter can command. And then there is the question of the very valuable radio and television contracts, which have as long as two years to run.

All concerned are agreed that Judge Ryan's decree has dealt a staggering blow to the business of boxing. It is generally

felt that a strong organization must operate the sport on a national scale, because of the guarantees demanded by television. And without the support of television, boxing could recede to the chaotic state of the days of John L. Sullivan and the barge fights.

June 30, 1957

Basilio Wins World Middleweight Title With Split Decision Over Robinson

Associated Press

THE CHALLENGER SCORES: Carmen Basilio lands right to the head of Ray Robinson in fourth round at Stadium

TWO JUDGES VOTE FOR UPSTATE MAN

By JOSEPH C. NICHOLS

Carmen Basilio won the middleweight championship of the world from Ray Robinson of Harlem last night. The durable gladiator from Chittenango,

N. Y., gained the split decision after fifteen rounds of the most savage fighting at the Yankee Stadium.

The two judges, Artie Aidala and Bill Recht, voted for Basilio, and the referee, Al Berl, cast his ballot for Robinson. Aidala's score card had it nine, five and one even, and Recht's had it eight, six and one. Berl voted nine rounds to six for Robinson. This observer had it in Basilio's favor, nine rounds to six.

The result was a surprise more in that the fight went the limit, than in anything else. Betting on the outcome favored Basilio until yesterday, when the odds receded to even money. But most of the wagers were based on the expectation of a knockout. Those who liked Basilio thought that Carmen would wear Sugar Ray down with a steady attack. Those who liked Robbie thought that he would take the upstate warrior out with one punch.

Calculations Are Upset

These calculations were sent awry as the rivals battered away at each other with bitterness and persistence through the gruelling championship route. Basilio succeeded in landing any number of wallops of all descriptions on his older rival, and Robinson withstood the blows surprisingly.

In his turn, Sugar Ray blasted Carmen with his best single shots, with either hand. On a couple of occasions, Ray's punches had enough power to cause Carmen to wabble, but the upstate gamester managed to hold his feet.

The outcome was a popular one and the result was made known by the announcer, Johnny Addie, in a dramatic sequence. First he called Aidala's vote and the crowd yelled. Then he announced Berl's and the crowd jeered. When Recht's ballot was made known, the crowd went wild, for Basilio was the overwhelming favorite fr. the standpoint of sentiment.

The fight was a meeting between two champions. Basilio went into the ring the holder of the world welterweight championship. His 147-pound title was not at stake, as Robinson weighed 160 pounds, the limit for the middleweight class. Basilio scaled 153½, a figure that many expected would slow him down.

While the weight was supposed to be in Robinson's favor, Basilio had the edge in years. He is 30 years old, while Robinson admits to 36 and is believed by many to be a year older. Whatever his age, Robinson revealed that he still had durability, as he showed a surprising surge of strength in the late rounds.

Basilio revealed almost awesome strength as he bulled his way into his bigger rival. Carmen was expected to center his attack on the body, but he fired away at the head quite frequently. Robinson, the master boxer, was supposed to stay away from his aggressive rival as much as possible, but Ray defied planning and fired away at the body many, many times.

Indeed, one of Robinson's most effective punches, in the fourteenth round, was a right to the body that Carmen about as badly as any other wallop thrown by the Harlem fighter.

Basilio went in to take charge at the start and he took the first two rounds by beating Ray to the punch and scoring with long rights. These gestures, at the time, didn't seem to bother Robinson much and when Ray found the range with sharp lefts to the face and short rights to the head in the third, the belief was general that Ray had his man.

In the fourth, when Basilio absorbed punishment in close and emerged from a clinch with a cut over his left eye, the Robinson stock was further in the ascendancy.

The upstate athlete returned in the fifth to outpunch Robinson, mainly in an exchange of right hands, but in the sixth Robinson treated the crowd to an exhibition of boxing that clearly earned him the session. Basilio's bulling tactics enabled him to take over in the seventh and he ripped away at his foe with hooks to the head and body.

Challenger Gains Edge

The challenger sailed along from there on, gaining a slight edge in the eighth and ninth. But it was not until the tenth that there was what any one could call a "big" round. Then Basilio just about overwhelmed Ray and bombed away at him with left hooks to the head and body. Only a few light right uppercuts were ventured by Robinson.

The eleventh round was the single most thrilling session of the night. Basilio shook Robbie with a left to the head. Robbie did some shaking of his own with a right to the head and seemed to have Carmen ready.

Then they closed and proceeded to whale away at each other in a savage exchange that saw each fighter putting his last ounce of effort forward. Robinson was first to hold and in so doing ceded the round. In the twelfth, the pace slackened until near the end, when Robinson popped Carmen with four left hooks. Carmen looked shaky, but he returned in the thirteenth to outrough his foe 'til near the end. Then Robinson got off a left hook that almost floored Basilio, who barely wobbled to his corner at the bell.

The Harlem gladiator was in complete charge in the fourteenth. When he ripped a savage right to the body, it appeared that Carmen would fall. He remained upright, but had trouble getting to the corner at the bell.

The fifteenth saw Robinson attempt to jab his way home, but Basilio pressed forward, punching away steadily and these tactics earned him the round.

The fight was witnessed by a crowd of 38,000, who paid an estimated $560,000 at the gate. These figures were eclipsed, though, by the television tally. There was a closed video broadcast into 174 theatres in 131 cities, the spectator potential amounting to more than 500,000.

Robinson, as the defending champion, will receive 45 per cent of the gross gate and $250,000 for television. Basilio's purse will be 20 per cent of the gate and his television take will be $110,000.

There is a return bout agreement between the fighters for a return bout within ninety days. Basilio said that he would wait a week before extending negotiations on this matter.

Basilio now will automatically relinquish his welterweight title, according to the rules of the New York State Athletic Commission.

September 24, 1957

Robinson Outpoints Basilio and Wins World Middleweight Title Fifth Time

CHICAGO OFFICIALS SPLIT ON OUTCOME

Judges Vote for Robinson, but Basilio Is Named Winner by Referee

By JOSEPH C. NICHOLS
Special to The New York Times.

CHICAGO, March 25—Sugar Ray Robinson beat Carmen Basilio in a fifteen-round bout at the Chicago Stadium tonight to become the middleweight champion of the world for the fifth time.

The famed Sugar Ray of Harlem registered a split decision over his smaller rival in a contest that just about matched their first clash for grueling action and savage exchanges.

The verdict that enabled Robinson to lift the crown from his Chittenango (N. Y.) rival was based on the votes of the judges. Boxing rules in this state call for scoring on a basis of five points maximum per round, with the winner of a round getting the maximum and the loser getting a proportionate lesser number of points. Judge John Bray scored it for Sugar Ray, 71 to 64, and Judge Spike McAdams voted for Sugar, 72 to 64.

Frank Sikora, the referee, favored Basilio by 69 to 66. The ballots, announced by Ben Bentley, had Sikora's vote in the middle. When it was made known, the crowd of 19,000 booed loudly. The fans quickly became quiet, though, for everything depended on the next announcement—of McAdams' vote. When it was announced, the spectators went wild.

This observer, scoring on the New York State system of rounds won, favored Robinson by a margin of eleven rounds to four. True, many of the sessions were exceedingly close, but any margin was Robinson's creation.

Throughout the bruising contest the fans showed a heavy sentiment for Basilio, as well they might. For the doughty former marine, fighting with his left eye closed almost tight from the seventh round, waded into his rangier rival with a willingness and persistence that at times threatened to discourage Robinson. At other times Carmen caused Sugar Ray to rip away with both hands in an attempt to bring matters to a sudden termination.

There was no knocking out Basilio, although for a time or two in the fifteenth round it seemed that Robinson would be able to knock him down. The Harlem flash tried with all the skill and power he possessed and he had Camen shaky once or twice, but he couldn't send him down. The Chittenango fighter is still proud in the boast that he has never been floored.

That pattern of the fight was that of the plodding, chunky Basilio moving forward steadily in an attempt to wear Robinson down with body punches. There was a substance to this strategy, in that Robinson, at the age of 37, was not expected to be too strong around the middle for the attack of his 31-year-old foeman.

Robinson had to go without food for almost twenty hours before weighing in at noon. He scaled 159¾ pounds and Basilio, a recent welterweight champion, had no trouble, weighing 153.

Basilio's board of advisers had the idea that the rigors of weight-making might also have contributed to a weakness about the stomach for Ray. And there were times when the Harlem boxer did show some fatigue under the pounding. But when things got too tough, he managed to hold until the referee stepped in.

Basilio was the first one to "rough it up" and drew a warning in the first round for hitting on the break. In this session, Robinson tried to box, but Basilio bulled his way inside and he outpunched Ray. They were so intent at their task that they slashed away at each other after the bell. This action infuriated a Robinson handler, who tried to climb into Basilio's corner, but the Stadium staff restrained him.

Robinson brought his boxing ability into play in the second round and speared Carmen with a variety of sharp punches. They didn't seem to have much effect as the Onion Farmer-as Basilio is known—moved ahead with his determined aim to strike the body. Robinson, though, succeeded in avoiding his punishment.

In the third and fourth, Robinson exhibited a willingness to trade and he landed more punches than his forward moving rival. Robinson again boxed at long range in the fourth and his left jab began to have its effect on Carmen's eye.

In the fifth, Basilio's body punches slowed Robinson, but Sugar Ray took charge in the sixth, mainly by use of his left. This weapon banged against Carmen's eye steadily and the

Chittenango boxer could not defend against it.

Basilio presented a sad picture in the seventh when his eye was shut tight. Robinson looked away at him as if a quick victory was to be his. But Carmen absorbed all the punishment and occasionally lashed out with left hooks to the head and body that indicated that he was still dangerous.

After Robinson built up a slight margin in the eight, Basilio staged a fine rally in the ninth and tenth. He dealt out considerable damage with his crashing left hooks to the body. Robinson changed his style after that

and boxed instead of trading.

Through each of the last five rounds Sugar Ray had at least one good shot a Carmen's jaw and some of these punches had enough impact to floor anyone except the iron-jawed Basilio. In the fifteenth round Basilio moved in and butted Robinson, for which he was warned by the referee. They shook hands and then Robinson tore after Basilio with a studied sharp right-hand attack, punishing Carmen quite a lot, but failing to floor him.

The odds on the fight favored Basilio at 2 to 1. When the pair met in

New York on last Sept. 23 Basilio gained a split decision over Robinson. Oddly, the referee in that fight, Al Berl, also voted for the loser.

The receipts tonight amounted to $351,955 contributed by 17,976 paying fans. The gladiators received 30 per cent of this sum, as well as 30 per cent of the television, radio and motion picture receipts. The video was sent off on a closed circuit for a minimum guarantee of $275,000.

March 26, 1958

Moore Stops Bassey in 13 Rounds and Takes Featherweight Title

LOSER'S MANAGER CALLS FOR A HALT

With Bassey Unable to See, His Corner Refuses to Let Him Out for 14th

LOS ANGELES, March 18 (UPI)—Davey Moore tonight won the world featherweight championship when the manager of Hogan (Kid) Bassey, the titleholder, stopped the fight after thirteen bloody rounds.

Moore took command in the sixth round and the Nigerian champion fought gamely for another seven rounds. But at the end of the thirteenth round, Manager George Biddles refused to send out the champion. The victory was recorded as a thirteenth-round knockout under California boxing laws.

"He couldn't see," Biddles explained. "I wouldn't send him out to be murdered—champion or not."

Thus the featherweight championship returned to the United States after an absence of more than a year and a half. Bassey won the title in an elimination tournament.

Punches Are Vicious

Moore gave a demonstration of sharp lefts and vicious rights rarely seen in a championship fight between little men.

There was a near-capacity crowd of 9,000 in the Olympic Auditorium.

The champion weighed 125 pounds, Moore 125½.

The challenger's sharp-shooting tactics had Bassey bleeding from above both eyes. In the final round Bassey repeatedly wiped the blood from his eyes with the backs of his gloves.

In the early rounds, it looked as if the champion would have an easy time of it. After an even first round. Bassey stung and hurt Moore in the following two stanzas.

It was the Bassey the fans here had seen when he successfully defended his title a year ago against Mexico's Pajarito Moreno, and he appeared on his way to another impressive triumph.

But after an even fifth round. Moore suddenly went to work. In a flurry of lefts and rights to the head and body, he drove Bassey to the ropes and appeared to have the champion on the verge of a knockout.

Bassey was so dazed that he could not find his corner for a moment. The champion's handlers worked desperately on him between rounds, but Bassey still was suffering from the punishment of the previous

round. Moore followed up his advantage with lashing lefts and rights that opened cuts above the eyes.

Bassey Cuts Easily

For all intents, that was the fight. Moore continued to pile up points, although he could not drop the champion, who fought like a lion from his native Nigeria whenever he could summon the energy—which became increasingly less frequent as the fight progressed.

In the twelfth round. Bassey called upon some hidden reservoir of energy and started strong. But after a few moments he ran out of steam.

Between rounds. Referee Tommy Hart examined cuts over Bassey's eyes but said they were not endangering the eyes themselves.

The champion was known to cut easily, so Hart let the fight

continue. But after the thirteenth, Biddles brought the action to a halt.

All three officials had the challenger well ahead on points. Hart and Judge Mushy Callahan scored it 126 to 119. while Judge George Latka had it 125-121 for Moore. The United Press International card scored it 128-119 for Moore.

The fight contract called for a return match within ninety days, here or in England.

For dropping his title. Bassey received $45,000 against 40 per cent of the gate, whichever was greater. Moore, as challenger, received a straight 20 per cent of the gate, which was unofficially estimated at more than $30,000.

Bassey also received a share of the proceeds from the national television.

March 19, 1959

Johansson Crushes Patterson With 7 Knockdowns in Third

By JOSEPH C. NICHOLS

Ingemar Johansson knocked Floyd Patterson down seven times in the third round at the Yankee Stadium last night and won the world heavyweight boxing championship.

The 26-year-old native of Goteborg, Sweden, struck with his right hand, and it was the same as striking with the Hammer of Thor. Down went Patterson time after time as the crowd of 30,000 gasped.

Thus did Johansson earn the greatest prize in professional sport. The Swede, underrated by American boxing writers,

became the first native-born Scandinavian to win the heavyweight title and the first non-American to hold it in twenty-five years.

Patterson, obviously overrated by American boxing observers, had climbed to the top of the division by stopping Archie Moore on Nov. 30, 1956.

It was while the defending champion was on the floor for the seventh time that Referee Ruby Goldstein stepped in to halt the proceedings. The time of Goldstein's intervention was 2 minutes 3 seconds of the third round. Termination of the bout was caused by the punch that

Ingemar Johansson drives Floyd Patterson to the canvas in the third round with one of a series of hard right hands

Johansson had boasted about, but which few people really thought he could throw. Early in the third round the Swede, who had been boxing carefully but with confidence, let fly with his right hand. It was everything that he had said it was.

The punch landed with force and precision on Patterson's jaw, and down went Patterson, flat on his back. He was out, and there were many who thought he would never get to his feet in time for the count of ten. He made it, though, at nine.

Johansson gave his opponent no chance when he arose, but sprang at him even while Patterson's back was half-turned to him. The Swede landed with a left and a right and down went Patterson again, for another nine.

Thereafter, the challenger did not rely exclusively on the strength of his right. He tossed a series of lefts and rights to the head and floored his opponent twice in a row for counts of six. He used the same offensive in flooring Patterson for

a count of seven, and also in dropping the American for another count of nine.

This swinging style, with both hands, was continued against the surprisingly willing Patterson after Floyd arose after the sixth knockdown. Indeed, the champion succeeded in landing several short punches to the head at close range, but they carried little force.

Johansson, just about as fresh as he was at the start of the round, employed a two-fisted attack to drop Patterson the seventh time. Although Patterson was aware of his surroundings, he was so dazed and helpless that there was no point in going on.

The result completely vindicated Johansson in his approach to the fight. In his training sessions in this country, he appeared awkward and even "left-footed" to most observers. By contrast Patterson "looked great" in his training chores, and he impressed almost everyone who saw him with the speed with which he delivered his combinations — series of

punches with two hands, to the head or body.

Free Advice From Many

Johansson, in his preparations, was told often that he was unimpressive and there were many who were free to offer him advice. Most of the advice had to do with the proper way of throwing his right hand. The Swede, an eminently gracious person, accepted all counsel quietly with a "wait and see" expression. He did say, on occasion, that he felt that he could knock out any man that he could tag with his right hand.

In knocking down Patterson so many times, Johansson equaled Jack Dempsey's mark, set on two occasions, but he did not equal the modern title record.

Dempsey knocked Jess Willard down seven times in winning the heavyweight championship on July 4, 1919. On Sept. 14, 1923, Dempsey floored Luis Angel Firpo seven times, but was flattened himself to the extent of having been

batted out of the ring.

The modern record for knockdowns in a title fight was set by Max Baer of California in June, 1934, when he floored Primo Carnera of Italy eleven times in winning the heavyweight championship.

As far as the action went, Johansson demonstrated boxing ability that was equal to Patterson's.

In the first round Ingemar moved forward a little at the time, pawing away with a left to the face and stepping just out of range of Patterson's lefts for the head.

The champion, fighting behind his characteristic arms-before-his-face stance, showed no inclination to rip away with the combinations that were supposed to be his chief stock in trade.

The fans sat almost silently through the first round until Johansson left go with his right hand. This was late in the session. The punch landed too high to do any damage. The crowd yelled when Ingemar threw the punch. The fact that the challenger even ventured the punch was enough to stir the crowd.

Seems to Find Range

Patterson's hardest punches in the first round were lefts to the body, one of which seemed to hurt the European. Still, on this observer's scorecard, Johansson had the edge in this first session.

In the second round Patterson seemed to find the range with his left, and he drove it to the face several times. There was a slight mark under Johansson's right eye, probably caused by several lefts reaching the same spot. For his part, the challenger did little except to throw light lefts and rights to the body at close range.

Patterson indicated that he had his man solved when they came out for the third round, for he showed little concern for his opponent while driving two straight lefts to the face. On delivering the second left, Patterson was guilty of what many experts thought was a big Johansson flaw. Floyd brought the arm down to his side.

This was the moment, the opportunity, the big chance for Johansson to throw his right. He threw it on a wide orbit, and everybody in the park saw it. Everybody that is, except Patterson. It knocked him down and opened the way to his going out.

In achieving his conquest of Patterson, Johansson extended his streak to two in a row over first-rate American heavyweights. On Sept. 14, 1958, against Eddie Machen of California in Goteborg, Johansson exploded his right hand to the jaw and scored a one-round knockout. It was this victory that earned him the right to fight Patterson.

The last previous time the heavyweight title left this country was in June, 1933, when Carnera took the championship from Jack Sharkey. Baer relieved Carnera of the crown in June, 1934, and it remained here until last night.

Johansson weighed 196 pounds for the greatest fight of his life. Patterson scaled 182. The fighters weighed in on Thursday morning, as the fight originally was scheduled for Thursday night but was postponed because of threatening weather. Each fighter was surprisingly light. Patterson had hoped to make 183 pounds and Johansson 198.

For Bill Rosensohn, 39-year-old comparative newcomer to the field of boxing promotion, the event was one of tremendous success. He had been quoted early in the week to the effect that he was gambling a half-million dollars on the fight. He explained that this sum could well be his if Johansson should surprise with a victory. Rosensohn then could promote the return bout "which should draw the million-dollar gate."

Gate About $450,000

There was little likelihood

Floyd Patterson is toppled by the attack of Ingemar Johansson in third round at Stadium

that last night's exhibition drew much more than $450,000. The promotion faced the prospect of a second postponement last night when rain fell until an hour and fifteen minutes before the scheduled 10:30 start for the big event, which was slated for fifteen rounds.

The judges for the fight were Bill Recht and Frank Forbes. Recht gave Johansson the first round and Patterson the second. Goldstein and Forbes gave both rounds to Patterson.

Johansson's record as a professional is now twenty-two victories in twenty-two fights. He is the fourth boxer in modern ring history to ascend to the title without encountering defeat as a professional. John L.

Sullivan, James J. Jeffries and Rocky Marciano moved to the top of the class without a setback.

Before opposing Patterson, a resident of Rockville Centre, L. I., Johansson had another title. He was regarded as the heavyweight champion of Europe, on the basis of a knockout victory over Franco Cavicchi in Bologna, Italy, on Sept. 30, 1956.

As professionals, Johansson and Patterson had only one common opponent, Archie McBride of Newark. Johansson outpointed McBride and Patterson knocked him out. Despite this, McBride last week said that the Scandinavian hit hard-

er, punch for punch, than Patterson.

Johansson now holds the unqualified esteem of his home folk, who at one time were inclined to question his courage. In the 1952 Olympic Games at Helsinki, Finland, Johansson was disqualified in the final round for not trying. He was shunned by many after that, but he won people over with his splendid professional performances. After he beat Cavicchi he was accepted, and now that he is champion of the world he is a national hero.

June 27, 1959

CARBO ENDS TRIAL WITH GUILTY PLEA

Admits 3 Charges in Boxing Case in Surprise Move —Faces 3 Years

By JACK ROTH

Frankie Carbo, reputedly the "boxing commissioner of the underworld," threw in the towel yesterday.

He pleaded guilty in the Court of General Sessions to three counts of a ten-count indictment. The three counts charged him with conspiracy, undercover managing and undercover matchmaking of professional boxers.

The counts are all misdemeanors, each punishable by a year in jail. Thus, the man described by the prosecution as the "prime minister of the boxing racket," faces a possible jail term of three years.

Carbo's plea came dramatically after an hour's conference between his lawyer, Abraham Brodsky; Assistant District Attorneys Alfred J. Scotti and John G. Bonomi, and Judge John A. Mullen.

Courtroom Crowded

On a table before the jury box was a loudspeaker. Mr. Scotti, who headed the prosecution team, was prepared to begin playing court-sanctioned wiretaps of conversations in which Carbo had participated.

The courtroom was packed with spectators and there were others outside waiting to get in.

Mr. Brodsky rose, and the thought was that the trial was about to resume.

There had been no hint that Carbo had been negotiating a plea. It was rumored that the conference with Judge Mullen concerned a delay that Mr. Brodsky was supposed to be seeking because he was not feeling well.

Suddenly Carbo rose and stood beside his lawyer.

"Your Honor," Mr. Brodsky began, "the defendant now

wishes to withdraw his plea of not guilty and plead guilty to the first, second and seventh counts of the indictment to cover the indictment." This meant Carbo would not be prosecuted on the seven other counts because they were incorporated in the plea.

Mr. Scotti rose and said: "I respectfully recommend the acceptance of the plea."

There was a note of victory in Mr. Scotti's voice. Carbo had been his main target since his office had begun its investigation into the scandal-ridden boxing field nearly two years ago.

Judge Mullen directed that the plea be taken. Carbo then admitted to the following charges:

¶That he had conspired with Herman (Hymie the Mink) Wallman, a prize-fight manager, that he, Carbo, would "act as an undercover manager for certain professional boxers whom the said Wallman was licensed to manage, and that the defendant * * * would use his influence to secure matches' for the said professional boxers."

¶That he participated directly and indirectly as a manager without having procured an appropriate license in the match between Jimmy Peters and George Chimenti on Feb. 21, 1958.

¶That he participated directly and indirectly as a matchmaker on March 21, 1958, in the bout between Virgil Akins and Isaac Logart without first having gotten the appropriate license.

Carbo, speaking in low tones, then gave facts about himself. He said he was 55 years old, lived at 970 Northeast 111th Street, Miami, Fla., and was married, unemployed and temperate.

Judge Mullen then set sentencing for Nov. 30 and the defendant was returned to Rikers Island Hospital, where he has been held since the trial began Oct. 5. Carbo was said to be suffering from diabetes and a heart condition. He showed no emotion as court officers led him from the court.

Judge Mullen, senior judge on the General Sessions bench, then discharged the jury after telling the panel:

"Your presence here has been a most effective lever to cause the defendant to be realistic. He has pleaded guilty."

This will be the second time that Carbo will be serving a jail sentence. His other conviction came in 1928, when he was found guilty of first-degree manslaughter in the killing of a taxi driver here. He was sentenced to serve two to four years in prison and was released after twenty-three months.

His police record shows truancy in his early years and arrests for petit larceny, for being a fugitive and a suspicious character, for robbery with a pistol, for murder and for disorderly conduct. He is now under a Federal indictment in Los Angeles on an extortion charge.

October 31, 1959

LaMotta Confesses He Threw '47 Garden Bout With Billy Fox

Tells Senate Group He Faked Knockout Loss — Testifies After Reported Threat

By United Press International.

WASHINGTON, June 14 — Jake LaMotta, once the world middleweight boxing champion, confessed to Senate investigators today that he had thrown a fight in 1947, two years before he won the title.

Testifying after a reported death threat from the underworld, LaMotta admitted that his light-heavyweight bout with Billy Fox at Madison Square Garden on Nov. 14, 1947, was fixed. He said he was only "play-acting" when the referee stopped the match in the fourth round and awarded a technical knockout to Fox.

" * * * 175 pounds of flesh was hitting me in the face but I wasn't hurt badly." LaMotta said.

LaMotta, who will be 39 years old next month, said he had lied about the fix to the office of Frank S. Hogan, the New York District Attorney, when it investigated the bout. He said he was telling the truth today because the statute of limitations had run its course and he could not be prosecuted by New York.

Reliable sources said racketeers had telephoned LaMotta and warned him he would be "hit in the head"—meaning murdered—if he implicated certain persons in his testimony before the Senate Antitrust and Monopoly subcommittee.

When the Senate investigators asked LaMotta if he or members of his family had been threatened with bodily harm, LaMotta hesitated, then said he hadn't been.

He looked down at the witness table and tore up a piece of paper as he thought more about the question.

"I'm not afraid for myself," he said quietly.

Then he suddenly became

angry. "And I'm not afraid of none of them rats," he shouted.

Rand Dixon, a subcommittee counsel, spoke sympathetically to LaMotta. "This isn't a healthy thing to know, is it?" Dixon asked.

"No, sir, I guess it isn't," LaMotta replied.

LaMotta said he took a dive in the Fox fight in return for a shot at the middleweight championship. He won the championship in 1949 from the late Marcel Cerdan, a French Algerian. But even with the rigging of the Fox fight, he said, he still had to pay $20,000 to Cerdan's manager "and representative" for the privilege of fighting Cerdan in Detroit.

Lew Burston of New York, one of Cerdan's two American representatives at the time of the LaMotta fight, denied to the subcommittee that he had received any part of the alleged $20,000 payment. Burston said he knew nothing about it until Senate investigators told him.

He said his total purse from the Cerdan bout was only $19,000. But he added that he had covered himself by betting $10,000 on himself at the 8-to-5 odds favoring Cerdan. He knocked out Cerdan in the tenth round and his bet returned $16,000.

The subcommittee, headed by Senator Estes Kefauver, Democrat of Tennessee, is trying to determine whether there has been and is now a conspiracy between underworld elements and others to maintain monopoly

control over major boxing contests.

Two Named in Deposition

In a signed deposition given to Senate staff investigators last month, LaMotta said he had received an offer of $100,000 to throw the bout with Fox. He named Bill Daley and Frank (Blinky) Palermo as the men who had put up the bribe money.

But in his testimony today, he said he didn't know who had put up the money. He said word of the bribe offer had been passed along to him by his brother "Joey" (Joseph LaMotta).

In any case, LaMotta said, he turned down the money, although he did agree later to throw the fight in order to get a crack at the championship.

Joseph LaMotta, who had served as Jake's trainer and sometimes as his manager, also testified. He invoked the Fifth Amendment in refusing to answer questions about bribe money. He said his answers might incriminate him.

Joseph, unlike his brother, brought along an attorney. A professional fighter himself from 1945 to 1947, Joseph testified he now distributed pinball and other vending machines in New York.

The examination at the hearing was directed by John B. Bonomi, a former New York Assistant District Attorney.

Jake said he also had been offered $100,000 to throw his Madison Square Garden fight with Tony Janiro of Youngstown, Ohio, five months before the Fox fight. But he said he rejected that because he had "a

Associated Press

'PLAY-ACTING': Photo showing Referee Frank Fullam stopping light-heavyweight bout between Jake LaMotta, right, and Billy Fox on Nov. 14, 1947, at Madison Square Garden. LaMotta admitted to Senators bout was fixed.

Jake LaMotta during hearing yesterday in Washington.

lot" of money at the time.

LaMotta said word of this offer also had come through his brother but that he didn't know "any names" of the persons putting up the money.

LaMotta said that in the early Nineteen Forties, when he was considered the uncrowned middleweight champion, he "carried" many of his opponents.

"I tried not to look too good, because I wanted better matches," he said. He conceded he overdid it in a 1947 split-decision loss to Cecil Hudson when he laid back too long.

"I thought I had it," LaMotta said. "One judge gave it to me. The two other bums didn't, though."

Sorry for 'Mistake'

As for throwing the Fox fight, LaMotta said he realized that he had "made a mistake and I'm sorry I did."

"I thought I was right then," he said. "I just wanted to be champion."

He said he had decided to go along with the fix while in training. He said his spleen had ruptured and he knew he would be in difficulty if Fox hit him hard there.

But he said that Fox did not hurt him seriously. He said he had just pretended to be "helpless" until the referee, Frank Fullam, stopped the fight.

The knockout of LaMotta drew a storm of criticism from New York sports writers. They called it a "phony" and the New York State Athletic Commission as well as the District Attorney's office investigated.

LaMotta had been a favorite before the fight, but the odds suddenly switched, making Fox a 3-1 choice and raising suspicion.

During the New York investigation LaMotta denied any wrongdoing. He did admit that he had failed to report the spleen injury to the commission. He said a blow by Fox to the left side had made him helpless early in the fourth round.

The commission suspended

LaMotta for seven months and fined him $1,000 for not disclosing the spleen injury. The commission chairman, Edward P. F. (Eddie) Eagan, said this had "perpetrated a fraud upon the public."

La Motta's first defense of the middleweight championship was to have been against Cerdan. But the Frenchman was killed in an air crash on Oct. 27, 1949, while en route to the United States to train for the bout.

LaMotta lost the championship to Sugar Ray Robinson on a thirteenth-round knockout in Chicago in 1951. He left the ring in 1952, tried an unsuccessful comeback in 1954 and then retired.

In 1955 he was refused a boxing manager's license by the New York commission. Jackie

LaBua, a boxer, testified that LaMotta had violated commission rules by acting as his undercover manager.

LaMotta told the Senate investigators he had earned about one million dollars in his thirteen-year fight career. He fought 106 matches.

James P. McShane, an investigator who formerly served on the staff of the Senate Rackets Committee, testified that he had studied changes in the gambling odds on the Fox fight.

McShane, who was a New York detective for almost twenty-one years, said that two days before the bout LaMotta was the favorite at 8—5. One day before the fight the odds were even, he said, and at fight time they were 3—1, with Fox as the favorite.

McShane said a "terrific amount of Philadelphia money flowed into the city and all of it being bet on Fox."

McShane later testified that

Palermo, Fox's licensed manager at the time of the fight, was the "numbers king of Philadelphia."

McShane's testimony also brought out that Fox was now a patient at Kings Park (L. I.) State Mental Hospital. In recent years, he had worked as a pinsetter in bowling alleys and sometimes sought accommodations at the men's shelter in the Bowery. He was hospitalized last April.

After their appearances today, the LaMotta brothers were excused from further testimony by the acting subcommittee chairman, Senator Philip A. Hart, Democrat of Michigan, who described Jake as "a keen and intelligent person."

June 15, 1960

Patterson Knocks Out Johansson in 5th; First to Regain the Heavyweight Title

By JOSEPH C. NICHOLS

Floyd Patterson last night became the first man in the history of boxing to regain the heavyweight championship of the world.

The 25-year-old fighter from Rockeville Centre, L. I., knocked out the defending titleholder, Ingemar Johansson of Goteborg,

Sweden, with a left hook in 1:51 of the fifth round of their scheduled fifteen-round fight at the Polo Grounds.

Patterson was clearly the master of the man who sent him to a humiliating defeat and deprived him of his title last June 26. He outboxed the Swede at almost every turn, withstood

Johansson's famed right hand, then showed power sufficient to bring him the triumph with two quick, sharp strokes.

The surprisingly large crowd of 31,892 fans thrilled to Patterson's conquest. Johansson, who weighed 194¾ pounds to Patterson's 190, had been the 8-to-5 choice to retain his

Floyd Patterson (left) is not executing a pirouette. He is falling to the canvas due to the heavy punching of Ingemar Johansson, who is about to claim Patterson's heavyweight crown. A year later Patterson returned the compliment and became the first man to regain the heavyweight title.

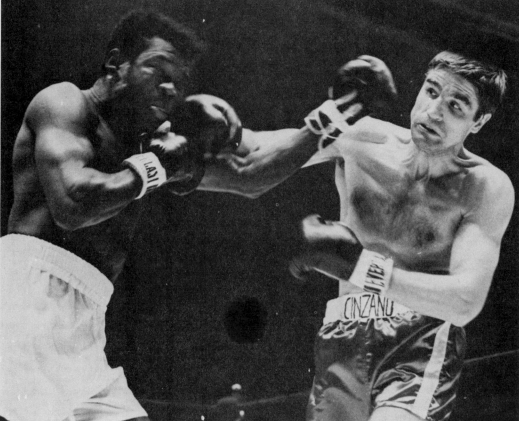

Emile Griffith (left) a fine middleweight and welterweight of the 1960's, is shown in this photo losing to Italy's Nino Benvenuti in 1968.

crown. A year ago Patterson had been the favorite at 5 to 1.

In bringing about Johansson's downfall, Patterson used a "picture-punch" left hook. He ripped the blow across to the chin early in the fifth and Johansson went down heavily. But it was plain that he was not senseless. He was certain to get up, and he did at the count of 9.

Patterson was unhurried now in the approach to his task. He stalked Johansson eagerly and even recklessly, as if aware that Johansson couldn't hurt him.

Johansson kept his eyes wide open, almost unnaturally so, as Patterson came at him. But he didn't have enough vision to pick off Patterson's next wallop.

This punch, like the earlier one, traveled in the perfect arc that makes the left hook the deadly blow it is. It hit the mark perfectly, right on the Johansson jaw, and down went the Swede.

Referee Arthur Mercante went through the motions of the full count, but Patterson knew his foe was out as soon as Johansson hit the canvas.

The new champion leaped for joy even as Mercante was tolling off 10. When the count was completed, Patterson was mobbed by his handlers and the many fanatics climbing into the ring.

Again A Surprise

The fight was the first for both boxers since Johansson beat Patterson. As in the 1959 encounter, the results confounded the majority of the experts. The fight followers were heavily in favor of Patterson last year. Last night they were much in favor of the 27-year-old Johansson.

Johansson's setback was the first in his professional career of twenty-three fights. Fourteen of his twenty-two triumphs had been knockouts.

Patterson's record before last night had showed thirty-five victories in thirty-seven starts, with twenty-six knockouts. The only one to beat him besides Johansson was Joey Maxim, who outpointed Floyd before the latter became the heavyweight king.

There was tension throughout the fight, most of it generated by the belief that Johansson's mighty right-hand punch—last year likened to the Hammer of Thor—could end matters whenever it hit the target.

Patterson was most careful in not presenting a target, but Johansson succeeded, at least once, in crashing his right to the jaw. When it landed, Patterson surprised the excited crowd, and the eager Johansson, by remaining on his feet. This was in the second round, the only one of the four complete rounds that Johansson won.

In the first round, Patterson, aggressive and confident, moved into his rival, firing left hooks to the head. These punches were more probing than potent. It was as if Patterson was trying to ascertain how to bring the Johansson chin into the left-hook orbit.

Johansson Also Waits

Johansson did little but send

United Press International

IT'S ALL OVER: Arthur Mercante, referee, ends his count over prostrate Johansson

light punches to the head and body in close through the first round. He, too, seemed to be waiting for the opportunity to crush once more the man whom his heavy artillery had felled so easily last year.

In the second round Johansson let go with the right hand, and his supporters were certain he was going to make it two in a row over Patterson.

Patterson had opened the round with his left hooks and jabs, and when he was short with one of these blows, Johansson countered. He fired a long right-hand punch. It landed on Patterson's jaw and Floyd was shaken.

Immediately Patterson went into reverse, releasing light, flicking jabs into the face of the steadily advancing Johansson. Johansson caught Patterson on the ropes and fired one more right. This one was a little high on the cheek and did not shake Patterson so much as the first.

In few moments the effect of these blows wore off. Patterson ceased retreating and stepped in to trade body punches.

Patterson did all the leading in the third round. He continued to pump his left to the face and, infrequently, to the body.

Patterson's boxing was excellent in the fourth. He moved in and out gracefully, peppering Johansson with lefts, holding his right out merely as a threat-

ening weapon, and agilely stepping away from Johansson's rigid moves.

The only punch of any consequence that Johansson landed in the fourth was a right to the head that connected at the bell.

Opening the fifth round, Patterson drove several lefts to the face. Johansson sank a right to the body and Patterson responded with the first left hook, the one that was just short of being the crusher, though it floored Johansson.

The crusher was not long in coming. After a few moments of measuring his man, Patterson had his sights properly set. He released the left hook and down went the foreigner, down and out.

Johansson had been cut and bruised over the left eye in the first round. And he bled freely from his mouth after the first knockdown.

Last week at his training camp Johansson had said, "When I hit him square with my right, the referee can count to a thousand."

Instead, it was Johansson who was hit square, and by a left. He was completely out, and he remained out for several minutes after his handlers had helped him to his corner.

Man in a Fog

He was still in a daze as he was escorted down the ring stairs.

Patterson's joy was something to see. Frequently in his training campaign he had said that he was eager for this fight for two reasons: One, to even matters with Johansson and two, to become the first man in boxing history to regain the heavyweight title.

A number of the best-known heavyweights, starting with James J. Corbett, had failed in the attempt to return to the pinnacle of pugilism. After Corbett, those who missed were Bob Fitzsimmons, Jim Jeffries, Jack Dempsey, Max Schmeling, Joe Louis, Ezzard Charles and Jersey Joe Walcott.

Last night's promotion was a highly successful one. The gross gate was announced as $824,814.07. But much more important than the local gate were the receipts from the ancillary rights of television, motion pictures and radio.

With the fight televised on closed circuit into 230 locations in 160 cities in the United States and Canada, and with the motion pictures and radio bringing guarantees of a half-million dollars, the final financial figures may approximate $2,500,000.

The pay-out commitments are complicated, but the general acceptance is that each fighter will receive about 35 per cent of all this money.

Neither Patterson nor Johansson has a manager. Cus D'Amato discovered Patterson and managed him to the title, but his license was revoked by the State Athletic Commission for violation of the local rules. Johansson does his own business, but works with an adviser, Edwin Ahlquist of Goteborg.

Patterson won the title for the first time on Nov. 30, 1956, by knocking out Archie Moore, also with a left hook. He and Moore fought for the crown vacated by the retirement of the undefeated Rocky Marciano and Patterson became the youngest to win the heavyweight championship.

Last night's fight was promoted by a group known as

Feature Sports, Inc. It was formed by Roy Cohn as the successor to an organization headed by Bill Rosensohn. The latter, who promoted last year's fight, lost his license for undercover dealings.

The new promoters were responsible for an amateurish operation. There was confusion and disorder in many parts of the Polo Grounds and the press arrangements were of the very worst. There was, however, adequate accommodation for a host of deputy commissioners in the working press section.

June 21, 1960

Neurosurgeons Study Knockout Physiology

No Lasting Changes in Brain Produced, Physicians Say

By ROBERT K. PLUMB

Knockout in the boxing ring occurs when the brain's organizing network is suddenly overwhelmed by nervous signals, two nerve specialists reported here yesterday.

The ring knockout does not produce lasting changes in the brain, the two asserted at a medical conference on injuries and deaths in professional boxing that was sponsored by the New York State Athletic Commission.

However, specialists at the meeting disagreed on the cause of the phenomenon known as "punch drunk." One held that a boxer could become punch drunk as a result of repeated knockouts; the other said that knockouts had nothing to do with the condition.

The physiology of the knockout was discussed in studies conducted by Dr. Jefferson Browder, Neurosurgeon of the Long Island College Hospital, and Dr. Harry A. Kaplan, Associate Professor of Neurosurgery at the State University of New York, Downstate Medical Center.

Long Study Made

Dr. Kaplan reported that he and Dr. Browder had long studied knockouts at ringside with a view to furthering medical understanding of unconsciousness common in many medical emergencies. They soon decided that boxing, unless a fighter fell and hit his head on the mat, produced only a temporary state of affairs in the brain. They maintained that it was different from being hit by an automobile.

Their opinion is that a strong blow on the side of the jaw can twist the head and neck and send a flood of nerve impulses into the reticular activating mechanism at the base of the brain.

This mechanism is a network of nerve tissue that sorts out incoming nerve signals from various parts of the body and directs them to higher levels of the brain.

The knockout punch that finished Ingemar Johansson

Associated Press

When the reticular activating mechanism is suddenly overwhelmed by nerve signals a person may become unconscious, Dr. Kaplan said. This can happen as the result of a hard blow in boxing. It also can happen when a person chances upon a horrible sight in the street. In either case, he maintained, the result is temporary unconsciousness, which has no lasting effect on the brain. Studies of 3,000 brain-wave records of boxers, some studies both before and after knockouts, supported this conclusion, Dr. Kaplan said.

"Boxing is not an innocuous sport," Dr. Kaplan asserted, "but much of the stigma associated with boxing because of belief that it causes permanent brain damage is based on impression and not on fact."

Others at the conference maintained that professional boxing did not have so many injuries or fatalities as other contact sports.

The chief medical examiner of New York City, Dr. Milton Helpern, reported on autopsy findings of boxers who died in this city after bouts.

Pacheco Death 'Unusual'

The second boxing death in eight years to reach the medical examiner's office was that of Tommy Pacheco, who died four days after a bout this month. Dr. Helpern reported that Pacheco died of complica-

tions following a torn brain blood vessel despite expert surgical treatment. He said that the New York City medical examiner's office studied more fatalities than any other place in the world and that the number of fatalities in boxing was "very small." He termed the Pacheco death "very unusual."

At the same time, Dr. Helpern cautioned that boxers who died did not have facial markings that would have indicated the severity of their injuries.

Dr. Helpern said that he agreed with Dr. Kaplan that the usual ring knockout was a temporary thing and that residual injury to the brain usually could not be established as resulting from blows to the head.

Dr. Abraham M. Rabiner, Emeritus Professor of Neurology at the State University of New York College of Medicine, discussed the punch drunk. He said he did not know what caused the condition. However, Dr. Rabiner speculated that repeated knockouts could injure the brain as a series of small strokes could injure it.

During the session a report from a physician who had just talked to the former heavyweight titleholder, Ingemar Johansson, was read. Johansson was allowed to postpone the required post-knockout electroencephalogram until tomorrow.

Johansson said that he did

not see the first left hook that knocked him down and that he did not remember the second blow or being knocked out. The last thing he remembered was being chased by his opponent, Floyd Patterson, he reported to the physician.

Dr. Marvin A. Stevens, chairman of the medical advisory board of the New York State Athletic Commission, and Dr. Ira A. McCown, the commission's medical director, were chairmen for scientific sessions that began Monday and ended yesterday at the New York University-Bellevue Medical Center.

Participants at the symposium went to the weighing-in ceremony before the fight Monday night and most attended the bout. At the conference were ring physicians and other medical specialists, former boxers and boxing officials.

Dr. John L. Madden, director of surgery at St. Clare's Hospital, said he believed that Patterson was lucky to have survived the beating he took in his earlier encounter with Johansson. He called upon officials to stop fights before someone was hurt and not to yield to the demands of a hysterical, bloodthirsty championship fight crowd.

June 22, 1960

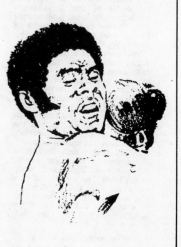

American Boxers Win Three Gold Medals at Olympics

178-POUND CROWN IS TAKEN BY CLAY

McClure Wins in 156 Class and Crook in 165 Before 16,000 at Rome Games

ROME, Sept. 5 (AP) — Cassius Clay, an 18-year-old Louisville light heavyweight, gave the United States its third gold medal in boxing tonight when he soundly whipped Ziggy Pietrzykowski, an experienced Polish Olympian, in the 178-pound Olympic final.

The other American winners were 21-year-old Willie McClure of Toledo in the light-middleweight (156-pound) class and 31-year-old Eddie Crook, a sergeant at Fort Campbell, Ky. in the middleweight (165-pound) division. They were the only United States finalists.

The Russians also sent three men into the finals but had to settle for one gold medal by Oleg Grigoryev in the bantamweight (119-pound) class.

Clay battered the Pole mercilessly in the last round with a flurry of left and right combinations that had his rival groggy. He opened a cut over the Pole's left eye and almost finished him.

It was a unanimous 5-0 decision by the judges. This one went down well with the crowd of 16,000, which also cheered the Pole.

The 25-year-old Pole, the bronze medal winner in 1956, who has had 231 fights, met his master. It took the American a little while to counteract his opponent's southpaw style but by the third round he had it figured out. There were no knockdowns.

Italy Also Triple Winner

Italy matched America's total of three boxing gold medals when Francesco de Piccoli knocked out South Africa's Daniel Bekker, a 28-year-old policeman, in the first round of the heavyweight final that ended the night's program.

McClure won the first American gold medal by beating Italy's Carmelo Bossi.

The rangy McClure rallied in the last round to pull the victory out of the fire after his shorter rival had used right-hand punches in the early rounds to build up a lead. The decision was 4—1 for McClure.

The Italian seemed to have it all wrapped up going into the final round, but McClure tore after him and shook him up early in the round with a left and a right to the jaw. He staggered the Italian midway through the round with a left and a right to the jaw. The Italian's knees buckled and his eyes were glazed as he fought on desperately.

An Unpopular Decision

Crook received a 3-2 decision over Poland's experienced Tadeusz Walasek. The decision drew hoots and jeers from the crowd, who thought the Pole clearly had outboxed the American. Walasek is listed in his country's record as having had 292 fights.

Crook put up a game fight, spotting the Pole three inches in height. Walasek was the better boxer to most expert observers and it was difficult to determine the basis for the decision. When the band played the Star-Spangled Banner at the presentation, the fans demonstrated noisily again.

Guyla Torok, a 22-year-old Hungarian, won the first boxing gold medal when he decisively outpointed 20-year-old Sergei Sivko, a Russian, in the 112-pound final.

The Russians won a gold medal in the bantamweight (119-pound) class when Oleg Grigoryev took a loudly booed 3-2 decision over Italy's Primo Zamparini, a 21-year-old soldier.

The big crowd got a chance to cheer when Italy's Francesco Musso, a 22-year-old soldier, won the featherweight title on a 4-1 decision over Poland's Jerzy Adamski, the 23-year-old European champion.

The lightweight (132-pound) final was so slow that the crowd hooted both Italy's Sandro Lopopolo and Poland's Kazimierz Pazdzior.

The Italian, fighting from a crouch, and the 25-year-old Polish locksmith were so wary of each other that little action took place for two rounds. For his superiority in the closing moments, the Pole won the gold medal by a 4-1 vote.

Bohumil Nemececk of Czechoslovakia won the light-welter (140-pound) gold medal with a decision over Clement Quartey of Ghana.

Giovanni Benvenuti of Italy won a 4-1 decision over Yuri Radonyak, a Russian, in the welterweight (147-pound) final.

September 6, 1960

Kefauver Proposes a Three-Year Federal Board to Clean Up Boxing

LICENSING POWER IS CORE OF PLAN

Hearings End With Proposal for a Commission—Carbo Pleads 5th as Witness

By TOM WICKER
Special to The New York Times.

WASHINGTON, Dec. 14 — Senator Estes Kefauver proposed today a temporary Federal boxing commission to eliminate racketeers from the sport.

The Tennessee Democrat put the plan forward as his Antitrust and Monopoly Subcommittee ended eight days of hearings on boxing, capped by the appearance of Paul John (Frankie) Carbo, the sport's underworld "ambassador of goodwill."

Carbo, silver-haired and chipper, was an affable but unproductive witness. He refused to answer any questions about his boxing associations or activities, and volunteered nothing except a cheery "congratulations" to Senator Kefauver on his recent re-election.

"The traveling salesman," as Carbo is also called by his boxing cronies, was brought here by two deputy United States marshals from the New York City Correctional Institution on Riker's Island. He is serving a two-year term for matchmaking and managing without a license.

In his thirty-five-minute appearance, Carbo was questioned by a former New York assistant District Attorney, John T. Bonomi. Bonomi, now the chief subcommittee investigator, is the man whose prosecution sent Carbo to Riker's Island.

Carbo gave positive answers to questions about his age (he is 56) and his out-of-prison address (970 Northeast 111th Street, Miami).

Role of Norris Decried

In his closing statement, Senator Kefauver said that James D. Norris, who was president of the now dissolved International Boxing Club, had "sought and made use of" Carbo and other "unsavory elements" to dominate boxing in the Nineteen Fifties.

Moreover, the subcommittee chairman said, Carbo's "influence with promoters, managers and matchmakers continues today" despite his imprisonment.

In particular, he said, there is evidence linking Carbo with the group "exploiting" Charles (Sonny) Liston, who is regarded as the No. 1 heavyweight contender. Senator Kefauver said these men, particularly Frank (Blinky) Palermo of Philadelphia and John Vitale of St. Louis, were "as vicious a group of racketeers as ever appeared on the boxing scene."

To eliminate such influences in boxing, the Senator proposed that the Federal commission have a life of three years, with power to license all participants, including television officials, in "interstate" matches. Any person participating in an interstate match without securing a license from the commission would be subject to criminal penalties.

The Senator also proposed that it be made a crime to "participate in a bribe offer in any interstate boxing match."

Court Ruling Recalled

A Supreme Court decision of Jan. 31, 1955, held that "the promotion of championship boxing contests on a multistate basis and the sale of rights to televise, broadcast and film such matches for interstate transmission" constituted interstate commerce.

Senator Kefauver has stated that he believes any televised match, and probably any major bout, would be involved in some way in interstate commerce. Thus the remedies he proposed apparently would affect all but purely local boxing promotions.

The Senator specified that television officials, "particularly in closed circuit TV," were par-

139

SILENT WITNESS: Paul John (Frankie) Carbo testifies before Senate Antitrust and Monopoly Subcommittee. He refused to answer all questions about his boxing activities.

ticipants in boxing matches, although they were not currently subject to license. They would have to obtain such licenses under his proposal.

"Some legislation," the Senator said, "must be passed in order to remove monopolistic influences in professional boxing and restore the integrity of the sport itself." Otherwise, he said, "the sport might very well pass from the American scene."

Action, Senator Kefauver said, should be taken "as quickly as possible." He hoped the commission could clean up the sport in three years. In that time, it would be paid for by taxes on licenses and boxing promotions. He said he would ask Congress to create such a commission.

Carbo's appearance was first on the subcommittee agenda. He was accompanied by his attorney, Abraham H. Brodsky of New York.

"Mr. Gray"—another Carbo nickname, justified by his well-kept silver mane—donned blackrimmed spectacles and read hoarsely from a slip of paper: "I cannot be compelled to be a witness against myself."

That was the answer—based on the Fifth Amendment to the Constitution—that Carbo gave to more than twenty-five questions designed to elicit information about his activities, acquaintances and opinions on boxing. Frequently he began reading his litany of refusal before a question was completed.

At the end of his testimony he addressed this remark to Kefauver:

"There is only one thing I want to say. I congratulate you on your re-election."

Kefauver replied, "You look like a pleasant man, Mr. Carbo."

But the Senator already had pledged to recommend that Carbo be cited for contempt as a result of his silence.

Carbo, who was reportedly a trigger-man for the executed Louis (Lepke) Buchalter of Murder, Inc., fame, has been arrested five times for murder and served time for manslaughter. A welterweight in stature and nattily attired, he appeared unabashed by the subcommittee or the marble columns of the Senate Office Building's caucus room.

After his "testimony," he asked immediately for orange juice. "I been trying to hold up," he complained, "but no breakfast yet." His attorney said Carbo was diabetic.

Brodsky said he had advised Carbo to invoke the Fifth Amendment because of an extortion and conspiracy charge pending against him in California. He said Carbo had been sincere in congratulating Senator Kefauver.

"He really thinks you're a great fellow," the attorney told the chairman.

December 15, 1960

GRIFFITH FINISHES PARET IN THE 13TH AND TAKES CROWN

New Yorker Uses 2-Fisted Surge to Capture World Welterweight Title

LEFT HOOK IS DECISIVE

Cuban Is Knocked Out First Time in His Career Before 4,618 at Miami Beach

By United Press International.

MIAMI BEACH, April 1—Emile Griffith, a 22-year-old boxer from New York, knocked out Benny (Kid) Paret in 1 minute 11 seconds of the thirteenth round tonight to win the world welterweight championship.

Griffith had been taking a beating from the Cuban. He ended the fight with a savage two-fisted attack to the head before 4,618 fans and a national television audience.

The fighters came out for the thirteenth round working furiously to the body. Referee Jimmy Pearless separated them near Paret's corner. Then Griffith threw a long left hook that caught Paret on the jaw. Paret reeled backward, badly hurt as Griffith followed with a solid right that spun Paret around. Another left hook dropped Paret near Griffith's corner.

Paret Stays Down

Paret remained on the canvas after Pearless had counted him out. He made no effort to rise. Paret's seconds assisted him to his stool, and it took them several minutes to get him into condition to leave the ring.

Griffith leaped and ran around the ring when the count reached 10. His seconds crowded in screaming. Griffith's mother climbed into the ring, hugged her son and then almost collapsed on her son's stool. Bystanders helped her from the ring.

The 23-year-old Paret had been battering Griffith with savage in-fighting throughout. Paret abandoned defense for his two-fisted body attack, and was the master in the early going. He beat Griffith to the punch frequently.

His whirlwind punching to the body kept Griffith off balance. Griffith scored rarely with long-range rights and lefts.

Paret's Face Cut

Until the thirteenth, Griffith's best rounds were the third and fifth. In the third, he cut Paret near the left eye and the mouth with hard overhand rights. He used the same weapon in the fifth.

But Paret, who had won the title from Don Jordan on May 27, 1960, pressed the challenger in every other round.

Griffith weighed 145½ pounds to 146½ for Paret. He seemed sluggish in the middle rounds and could not break away from his opponent's inside attack.

It was Griffith's twenty-third victory in twenty-five fights. Paret's record is thirty-four victories, eight losses and three draws. It was the first time that Paret ever had been knocked out.

A late surge of betting for Griffith dropped the odds from 7 to 5 in favor of Paret to even money.

April 2, 1961

CARBO, 4 OTHERS ARE FOUND GUILTY

Long Prison Terms Loom Over Boxing Extortion

LOS ANGELES, May 30 (AP) — Frankie Carbo, an underworld figure long reputed to be boxing's boss, was convicted today with four others of trying to cut in on a champion's earnings.

All face possible lengthy prison terms.

The special Federal prosecutor who obtained the convictions said more such prosecutions were likely.

A Federal jury, after a thirteen-week trial and three days of deliberations, found the five guilty of conspiracy and extortion charges.

The defendants were accused of trying to muscle in on the contract of a former welterweight champion, Don Jordan, by threatening physical harm to his manager, Don Nesseth, and Jackie Leonard, a Hollywood fight promoter.

Sentencing on July 20

Sentencing is set for July 20. The convicted men are:

Carbo; Frank (Blinky) Palermo, a Philadelphia fight manager and allegedly Carbo's front man; Truman Gibson Jr., who headed the now defunct International Boxing Club, and Joe

Sica and Louis Tom Dragna, Los Angeles men with police records.

Gibson, who admitted during the trial that the I. B. C. had dealt with underworld figures, remained free on bail during the trial. Bail was denied to the others.

For Carbo, the conviction was the second in less than two years. He was sentenced to two years in a New York jail for acting as an undercover manager of fighters.

Their possible prison terms. are: Palermo 125 years, Carbo 85, Sica 45, Dragna and Gibson 25 each.

They showed surprise at the verdict by ten women and two men.

Government attorneys tried to show during the trial that the defendants had taken over prominent fighters by threatening to halt matches because of powerful connections.

Leonard testified that in 1959 he was beaten up and his home set on fire.

Special Prosecutor Alvin H. Goldstein Jr. had charged that Dragna and Sica had been employed to carry out threats Palermo and Carbo had made on Leonard and Nesseth.

Victims Are Cited

"The prosecution also revealed collusion between Gibson, as head of a multi-million-dollar corporation, and the underworld." Goldstein said. "The choice which this big business

made was to use the underworld in order to obtain a monopoly in professional boxing and make millions of dollars at the expense of the poor fighters and the public."

Specifically, the defendants were convicted of conspiring to violate the Hobbs Act by using extortion in obstruction of interstate commerce and conspiring to use the telephone in interstate commerce to communicate threats.

In Washington, Attorney General Robert F. Kennedy issued a statement that said in part:

"Frank Carbo has been a sinister figure behind the scenes in boxing for more than twenty years. This verdict will be a great aid and assistance to the Department of Justice and local law enforcement authorities in taking further action against the attempts of racketeers to control boxing and other sports."

Senator Estes Kefauver, Democrat of Tennessee, praised the verdict as one that gives Congress "an unparalleled opportunity to effect a final and conclusive clean-up job in professional boxing."

Kefauver is chairman of the Senate antitrust and monopoly subcommittee that has investigated alleged racketeering in boxing. The committee starts hearings tomorrow on a bill to set up Federal regulation of boxing to drive out racketeers.

May 31, 1961

Louis, Calling New York Lax, Supports Bill on Boxing 'Czar'

Gangsters Here Get Chance to Control Fighters, Former Champion Testifies

WASHINGTON, June 1 (UPI) —Joe Louis, a former world heavyweight boxing champion, told a Senate committee today the fight game had become a disgrace that badly needed a czar to clean it up.

The soft-spoken Brown Bomber testified before the Senate anti-trust and monopoly subcommittee that is considering legislation to set up a national boxing commissioner and a federal licensing system to weed out crooked boxers, promoters and managers.

Louis, natty in a dark blue suit and a blue bow tie, endorsed the proposal. He said:

¶Ninety per cent of all fighters have shady managers. His manager was honest, he added.

¶New York has done the least to clean up boxing. "I know of no state that has given gangsters as much of a chance to get a hold on boxers as New York," he declared.

¶The criminal element definitely has invaded the sport.

Associated Press Wirephoto

Joe Louis as he testified yesterday in Washington.

"If your bill passes, and I hope it does, it will do the boxing game a whole lot of good," Louis told the committee chairman, Senator Estes Kefauver, Democrat of Tennessee.

Kefauver questioned Louis closely on his own career. He asked whether it was influenced by the underworld.

"No," the ex-champion replied. "I was lucky. I was lucky my managers could not be swayed by anyone."

Kefauver wanted to know whether some of boxing's troubles were caused by a lack of good new fighters entering the game.

"Clean it up and they'll come in," Louis replied.

Kefauver couldn't resist asking a question that wasn't exactly on the subject at hand.

"What was your hardest fight?" the Senator inquired.

"My hardest fight? The Billy Conn first fight was my hardest fight. I won in the thirteenth round. I was lucky."

Then Louis, cupping his big hands in front of a microphone, added that part of his ring success stemmed from something he had heard as a kid—"Hungry fighters make the best fighters."

"I guess I was hungry," said

the Alabama-born boxer, who grew up as one of twelve children in a poor Detroit family.

Representative William Fitts Ryan, a Democrat of New York, who preceded Louis, called boxing the "red light district" of professional sports. Ryan is a co-sponsor with Kefauver of the antiracketeer legislation.

Another witness was Melvin L. Krulewitch, chairman of the New York State Athletic Commission. He said he was in "agreement with the general approach and objectives" of the Kefauver bill. But he added: "I do not believe at the present time there is a taint of hoodlumism or gangsterism in the boxing game."

June 2, 1961

PARET REGAINS TITLE

GRIFFITH BEATEN ON SPLIT VERDICT

Paret, Bleeding With Face Swollen, Regains World Welterweight Crown

By WILLIAM R. CONKLIN

Benny (Kid) Paret of Cuba regained the world welterweight championship in Madison Square Garden last night by outpointing Emile Griffith.

At the end of fifteen hard-fought rounds, Paret gained a split decision from the 22-year-old Virgin Islander who had taken the title from him last April.

Referee Al Berl was the only official who decided for Griffith. Berl scored it for Griffith, eight rounds to six, with one even.

Judge Tony Castellano gave it to Paret, eight, six and one even. Judge Artie Aidala scored it for Paret, nine rounds to six.

A crowd of 6,072 paid $20,000 to see the bout.

Paret's Eyes Swollen

Paret bled from the mouth from the fifth round on. After the thirteenth, both his eyes were swollen with a cut under his left eye bleeding. Griffith stayed unmarked.

Paret's usual windmill body was hardly in evidence in the early rounds.

Griffith could not get the knockout blow in. Many of his shots to the head rocked Paret.

The challenger was successful with his body shots at close range.

Griffith mixed in close on occasion, but seemed to prefer long-range boxing with frequent pops at Paret's damaged eyes. This was his second defense of the title. He had stopped Gaspar Ortega of Mexico in the twelfth round at Los Angeles on June 3.

In a poll of boxing writers at ringside nine thought Griffith had won and three gave the decision to Paret.

Paret has no immediate commitments on future fights. In forty-seven starts he has won thirty-four, lost ten and fought three draws. He had been knocked out twice. Griffith has

Official Score Cards in Title Bout

By The Associated Press.

The official score cards of the Emile Griffith-Benny Paret welterweight title fight last night:

	1	2	3	4	5	6	7	8	9	10	11	12	13	14	15	Total
REFEREE AL BERL																
	P	G	G	G	P	G	P	E	P	P	P	G	P	G	G	8—6—1
JUDGE ARTIE AIDALA																
	P	P	G	G	G	P	P	P	P	G	G	P	P	P	P	9—6
JUDGE TONY CASTELLANO																
	P	G	G	G	P	P	E	P	P	P	G	G	P	P	G	8—6—1

P—Paret; G—Griffith; E—Even.

141

never been stopped in winning twenty-five of twenty-eight, with three losses by decision.

Paret apparently gained the decision through his more accurate punching inside. His close-in work was his major pattern, though he scored occasionally with solid head shots.

Griffith's preference for a stand-off, head-hunting style cost him points every time he missed. He never had Paret in serious trouble. The challenger fought strongly in the last five rounds.

Manuel Alfaro, Paret's manager, was asked afterward if

Paret would fight Griffith again. His answer was: "No-where, no how, no place."

After Griffith, the eldest of eight children, began boxing in 1958, he used his ring earnings to bring the family, including his widowed mother, here from St. Thomas, Virgin Islands. Emile works as a hat designer in Manhattan.

Griffith went into the ring a 3-1 favorite over Paret. In prior bouts Emile had won twenty-five of twenty-seven, with two losses by decision. He had won his first thirteen before Randy Sandy outpointed him in a Garden ten-rounder in October,

1959. His only other loss was to Denny Moyer by decision in Portland, Ore., Moyer's home town, on April 28, 1960. Earlier he had outpointed Moyer in the Garden.

Griffith won the 147-pound title from Paret by knocking out the Cuban in the thirteenth round at Miami Beach on April 1. A left hook to the head followed by a sharp right sent Paret to the ring floor for the count of 10.

Paret, 24, was born in Cuba and worked there as a sugar-cane cutter. He speaks no English.

Paret won the welterweight

title with a unanimous fifteen-round decision over Don Jordan on May 27, 1960, at Las Vegas. He had not fought since he lost the crown to Griffith last April.

At 147 pounds Griffith was one and one-half pounds above his weight for the April fight. Paret, 146, was half a pound lighter than for his first meeting with Griffith.

Each boxer expected to realize about $25,000 from the fight. Each was to get 30 per cent of the $60,000 television fee, plus 30 per cent of the net live gate.

October 1, 1961

PARET UNDERGOES BRAIN OPERATION AFTER DEFEAT

GRIFFITH IS VICTOR

Paret Knocked Out in 12th Round of Title Fight at Garden

By ROBERT L. TEAGUE

Emile Griffith of New York regained the world welterweight boxing championship from Benny (Kid) Paret last night at Madison Square Garden. Paret was knocked unconscious and underwent brain surgery at Roosevelt Hospital this morning.

Griffith stopped Paret after 2 minutes 9 seconds of the twelfth round. Paret was out on his feet. When he failed to regain consciousness in the ring, he was taken to his dressing room on a stretcher and later removed to the hospital by ambulance.

At the hospital, Dr. Harry Kleiman reported that the 25-year-old Paret was in serious condition. Dr. Lawrence Schick, a neuro-surgeon, then performed surgery to relieve pressure on the brain. Another doctor at the hospital said Paret's chances to recover were "poor."

15 Fans and Friends Wait

In a waiting room downstairs from the operating room, about fifteen fans and friends quietly awaited word of Paret's condition. This group included Garden officials.

Griffith was among those in the waiting room and said: "I'm sorry it happened. I hope everything is being done for him."

Griffith left before the operation began.

Before Paret left the Garden, the last rites of the Roman Catholic Church were administered.

Although Griffith had been down for an 8-count in the sixth, his triumph was anything but surprising. He had been in command most of the way, and there had been times when the punishment he in-

flicted on Paret seemed much more than any normal human could withstand.

What finally ended the stubborn Cuban's reign was a two-handed flurry that started with ten consecutive right uppercuts to the chin. The 23-year-old Griffith punched faster than most observers could count. All told, his winning assault consisted of twenty-five blows.

Long before Griffith had completed this cyclonic sortie,

many in the crowd of 7,600 were begging Referee Ruby Goldstein to intervene. Goldstein was not moved to pity until one fact became obvious: The only reason Paret still was on his feet was that Griffith's pile-driving fists were keeping him there, pinned against the post in a neutral corner.

Paret's eyes were closed. His hands dropped at his sides. His head snapped to the left and to the right as Griffith pounded away. The fact that Paret would not fall seemed to arouse the New Yorker to new heights of fury.

Perhaps he was remembering the split decision he lost to Paret here last Sept. 30. That was the bout in which Paret regained the crown he had lost to Emile on April 1, 1960, at Miami Beach. That fight ended in a thirteenth-round knockout.

Whatever it was that Griffith was thinking about last night, it certainly was translated into something akin to savagery. After the ten rights to the face had failed to do the job, he began alternating the rights with left hooks. All these blows were thrown from behind Emile's back, it seemed. Paret sagged but still would not go down.

Goldstein finally made his move but had difficulty restraining Griffith. When the referee finally pulled the attacker away, Paret slid slowly down the ropes and to the canvas. He lay on his back unconscious for about eight minutes while physicians worked on him. He still was unconscious when carted to his dressing room.

In a sense, it was something of a miracle that Paret had reached the twelfth round. Had he not possessed more courage than skill, he would have been knocked out in the tenth.

Paret Hits Below Belt

That round opened with Paret landing a left below the belt. Griffith winced and clutched his abdomen. Goldstein dutifully warned Paret, just as he had on two other occasions for butting.

Immediately following the foul, Griffith scored with four rights and three lefts to the head without a return. Paret was pinned against the ropes, and he was helpless. Emile waded in and threw another series of left hooks and rights to the head, but Paret merely sat on the ropes. That was as much as he would concede.

Although there still was about a minute left in the tenth, Griffith simply was too tired to finish what he had started. He coasted through most of the eleventh round while regaining his strength. Paret did most of the fighting in the eleventh and won the round easily. However, he was in no condition at that stage to mete out serious punishment.

Paret's best round was the sixth, in which he scored a surprising knockdown. Early in the round, Paret landed a right to the chin, followed by three stiff lefts to the jaw. Paret rushed into a clinch, apparently hurt.

Griffith Down for 8

As they broke voluntarily, however, the Cuban unleashed a right hook that caught Emile squarely on the jaw. Down went Griffith. He got up at 8, still shaken. The bell rang before Paret could follow up his advantage.

In building up his wide margin on the score cards, Griffith punched faster and harder than his opponent. Paret frequently made the mistake of allowing his foe to bore in under slow-motion jabs and pump both hands hard to the body. And at close quarters, Griffith invariably was the man who managed to work a hand free to throw a stiff uppercut.

Griffith weighed 144 pounds and Paret 146¼ for the scheduled fifteen-round bout. The gross gate was $27,000, and thousands more were paid for national television rights. Paret was guaranteed $50,000, and Griffith's purse was about $17,000. Griffith was a heavy favorite.

Goldstein's score card had Griffith ahead, 7 rounds to 3, with one round even. The two judges also had Griffith leading, 8—3 (by Tony Rossi) and 9—2 (by Frank Forbes).

The knockout was the fourth of Paret's professional career. His record now shows thirty-four victories, twelve losses and three draws. Griffith has won twenty-nine bouts and has lost three.

Soto Wins Preliminary

Left hooks were the principal weapons in the opening bout, in which Angelo Soto finished Angel Coloncito at 2:38 in the third round. Soto had downed his rival three times with lefts to the mouth and once with a right to the jaw. Both boys are from Puerto Rico and each weighed 127 pounds for the scheduled four-rounder.

In a pedestrian bout between willing but unschooled lightweights, Taco Gonzales, 136, of Puerto Rico, gained a majority decision over Sid Marcus, 136, of Brooklyn. Each was teddy-bear slow and puppy-clumsy.

A majority verdict was awarded to Willie Giles, 165, of Miami after his six-round fight with Dave Russel, 168¼, of Hempstead, L. I. This was a match between a boxer and a slugger, and it generated the most excitement during the preliminary program.

Many spectators accused the ring officials of rendering a "hometown" decision when they called the six-round semi-final a draw. The majority of spectators apparently believed that Andy Figueroa, 154½, of Puerto Rico, had outpointed Billy Bello, 152¼, of the Bronx.

Figueroa built up a sizable lead in the early rounds as he landed rapid fire combinations to the head. For the most part, Bello threw only one punch at a time until he rallied fiercely in the sixth.

March 25, 1962

Griffith Lives With Nightmare, Saying He Just Wanted to Win

Emile Griffith, two long nights after his greatest triumph, is still a fighter with a nightmare.

"They say how come a sweet little boy like you who designs hats can turn tiger and hurt a man's brain," he said. "They all say that. They're trying to get me to say I wanted to kill him. All I wanted was to be champion again. I didn't want to hurt him."

Griffith was encountered yesterday in a little room on the third floor of the New York State Athletic Commission offices. Seven floors above, the commission was readying a report to Governor Rockefeller on the savage beating that Emile had given Benny (Kid) Paret in their welterweight title bout Saturday night.

A crushing barrage of punches in the twelfth round had knocked Paret unconscious.

"I didn't know his head was through the ropes," Griffith was saying. "I was so excited. All I could think about was regaining the title. Now I can't sleep. And they won't let me see him."

Griffith acknowledged that there had been hard feelings between him and Paret. A fight almost started between them at the weighing-in ceremonies Saturday afternoon.

"He made some bad remarks to me in Spanish," Griffith said. "And he patted me on the back."

Griffith translated Paret's remarks to mean "anti-man."

Griffith said:

"I was afraid I'd hit him right there. 'Don't touch me, Paret,' I said. 'I beg of you to keep your hands off me.' But when I got into the ring I forgot all about it. Maybe he did that so I would lose my head in the ring."

In an earlier interview yesterday with Howard Cosell of the American Broadcasting Company, Griffith said he had no knowledge of Paret's condition as he smashed the fighter with blow after blow.

". . . all I was doing was punching," he said. "That's all I can remember. I didn't know that his head was through the ropes. I didn't know if his eyes or anything was closed. I was just punching until the referee stopped the fight."

Cosell asked him if he was sorry he had become a boxer.

"Yes," he replied, "I am sorry."

March 27, 1962

The Referee's Dilemma

A View That Goldstein's Critics Are Adhering to an Ancient Boxing Ritual

By ROBERT L. TEAGUE

Once again boxing suddenly has become an ugly word. Another man has been injured critically, perhaps fatally, in the ring.

This one just happened to be a young Cuban named Benny (Kid) Paret. His licensed assailant was Emile Griffith of New York. Their positions easily might have been reversed. That much must be admitted by any boxing buff whose memory extends beyond last Saturday night's tragic welterweight title bout at Madison Square Garden.

News Analysis

After all, the object of the so-called manly art is to hit one's opponent as hard and often as necessary to render him helpless or senseless. The inherent risks include blindness, madness, mutilation and death. Nearly everybody forgets that harsh fact, it seems, until some boxer is knocked into a deep coma.

Millions now are asking: Why didn't the referee stop it sooner? Couldn't he see that Paret's life was in danger? No satisfactory answer ever is given. Nobody really expects as much. Another popular adjunct to the ritual is the "complete investigation." Governor Rockefeller dutifully ordered same after the Paret affair. It undoubtedly will support the findings of the incomplete investigation: No one was at fault; Paret showed no sign of having a head injury before being knocked out in the twelfth round.

The Ritual Continues

By the way, exactly how does one indicate he has two blood clots in his brain while an aroused opponent is beating him about the head?

As usual, the responsible party is sorry. Griffith has cried and prayed. As usual, a sympathetic coterie of former boxing champions and ring officials has rushed to the defense of the referee in question, Ruby Goldstein.

And any day now, if history continues to repeat, somebody will propose another "safety rule," something like a complete physical examination for each boxer minutes before each bout. There may even be a benefit boxing card to raise money for Paret's family. Then everyone can relax—until the next prizefighter is critically or fatally hurt.

According to Dr. Charles P. Larson of Tacoma, Wash., the president of the National Boxing Association, boxing has killed an average of ten men in each of the last ten years.

The average boxing buff would be hard pressed to name five of the last ten victims. He is sorry about Paret, but remains eager to watch Floyd Patterson defend the heavyweight title against Sonny Liston this summer. He is extraordinarily curious about Griffith's scheduled bout with Jorge Fernandez of Argentina on June 9 at the Garden. He does not expect any of those four fighters to suffer serious injuries. He will be sorry if one does.

The First-Guesser

In the meantime, he asks: Why didn't the referee stop it sooner? The answer that follows here is an informed guess another adjunct to the ritual:

Goldstein has been stopping fights too soon or too late for the last twenty years. His critics always have the advantage of guessing second. Goldstein guesses first—in the ring.

Like most knowledgeable boxing men, Goldstein knew that Paret was the kind of fighter who sometimes absorbed a good deal of punishment early in a round, then rallied fiercely. In fact, Benny had demonstrated that faculty at least twice before the twelfth round.

Early in the sixth, he was pinned against the ropes and pummeled, but escaped and scored the bout's first knockdown. In the tenth, Griffith pinned him again. Benny appeared on the brink of oblivion. This reporter, perhaps more squeamish than most, would have stopped it right then.

Goldstein guessed differently and correctly—as things turned out. Paret won the eleventh round.

March 27, 1962

BENNY PARET DIES OF FIGHT INJURIES

Boxer, in Coma 9 Days, Had Developed Pneumonia

Benny (Kid) Paret, former welterweight boxing champion of the world, died at 1:55 A. M. today, nine days and three hours after he had lost consciousness under a rain of blows in a bout at Madison Square Garden March 24.

The collapse of the 24-year-old Cuban, in the twelfth round of a match in which he lost his title to Emile Griffith, had set off a state investigation and a clamor for a ban on prize fighting.

Unconscious with two blood clots on his brain, Paret had held his own against long odds until yesterday, when pneumonia set in.

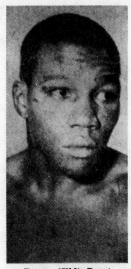

Benny (Kid) Paret

At his bedside in Roosevelt Hospital when he died was his manager, Manuel Alfaro. His pregnant wife, Lucy, arrived an hour later. Her 2-year-old son, Benny Jr., was left with friends.

The New York State Athletic Commission, in a report to Governor Rockefeller after the fight, absolved all officials concerned.

The referee, Ruby Goldstein, had been criticized by Paret's manager for not having stopped the bout sooner. But the commission held that Goldstein had "acted in good judgment in stopping this contest when he did."

The fight had been witnessed by a nation-wide television audience. Many observers thought Paret had lost consciousness early in that final flurry, but was pinned against the corner of the ring and could not fall.

Goldstein was defended on the ground that Paret had shown strong recuperative powers in previous fights, and might have been able to come back. It was also pointed out that a world title was at issue.

During the investigation that followed the fight, District Attorney Frank S. Hogan said that if Paret died, his office would investigate to learn whether any criminal negligence was involved.

He said that even if no evidence was found that negligence had caused the death, the case would be submitted to a grand jury as a matter of routine.

The 1962 Legislature, which closed its session Saturday, has set up a committee to investigate boxing and report back on whether professional bouts should be outlawed.

Hours after the fight, Paret underwent an operation. Surgeons drilled four holes to remove the clots and relieve pressure on the brain. This procedure is often effective, but in this case the damage proved too severe.

Hospital authorities said the cause of death would not be announced pending an autopsy by the medical examiner's office.

April 3, 1962

MANY FATALITIES LISTED FOR BOXING

Toll Since 1900 Put at 450 —Paret 4th to Die in '62

By ROBERT L. TEAGUE

Boxing has killed approximately 450 men since the turn of the century, according to the foremost authority on the sport. He is Nat Fleischer, editor of Ring Magazine and perennial compiler of "Nat Fleischer's Ring Record Book and Encyclopedia."

The death of Benny (Kid) Paret from injuries suffered in a welterweight title bout with Emile Griffith was the fourth of its kind this year. However, six other athletes will meet death under similar circumstances in 1962 if the current average of ten ring fatalities a year for the past decade is maintained.

A neurologist familiar with Paret's case said the damage to the fighter's brain had occurred during the Saturday night fight with Griffith at Madison Square Garden, not before it.

"But there is no way to establish what earlier damage he might have incurred," the physician added. "And it is virtually impossible to differentiate between old and new damage, even by autopsy."

Amateur a Victim

Blood clots, or "acute subdural hematomas," had formed on the left and right sides of Paret's brain, the neurologist said. He added that such clots did not occur frequently, but that fifteen of the twenty-one boxers who died in New York between 1918 and 1950 had succumbed to the effects of such blood clots.

A brain injury also caused the death of 19-year-old Cookie Ronan, who died on Nov. 19, 1961, three days after being knocked out in an amateur bout at St. Nicholas Arena in Manhattan.

Five months earlier, on June 3, José Rigores of Cuba, a 25-year-old featherweight pro, died four days after being knocked out by Anselmo Castillo of Puerto Rico at St. Nicks.

Rigores and Ronan were the last boxers to die after fights here—until the Griffith-Paret bo'.

Fleischer has been tabulating ring deaths since 1945, but his career as a boxing historian spans more than forty years. His records show that before the Paret fatality only two deaths had resulted from world championship bouts. The first occurred in 1897, when Jimmy Barry knocked out Walter Croot in a bantamweight title fight in London. Croot died of an injury to the brain.

22 Deaths in 1953

In 1947, Jimmy Doyle died after being knocked out by Sugar Ray Robinson in a welterweight championship match at Cleveland.

There are 194 boxing deaths listed in the latest edition of Fleischer's annual encyclopedia, covering the years from 1945 through 1961. The highest number of fatalities in one year was twenty-two, in 1953. Few of the victims were well known in the trade. One was a 21-year-old Nigerian named Homicide Illori. His was the third boxing death in Lagos, Nigeria, in an eighteen-month span.

Following is an excerpt from Fleischer's comment on ring deaths in his 1954 encyclopedia:

"A new record for world-wide ring fatalities was set during the past twelve months [1953] .....Ten amateurs and eleven money chasers [a twelfth was reported later] had the ten-count tolled over them ... It is interesting to note that only two professionals met their death in American rings..... Among the amateurs we were not so fortunate . . . six occurred in the United States.

In 1951, the New York State Athletic Commission instituted a compulsory thirty- day suspension for any fighter who was knocked out. The fighter must undergo a medical examination to be reinstated.

Such check-ups have not been foolproof, however. Paret had been pronounced in tip-top condition before the Griffith bout. And the ill-starred Cuban had passed an electroencephalogram test, which measured his brain waves, earlier this month.

The use of padded headgear, similar to those employed in college boxing, has been advocated for the pros. After the recent Garden tragedy, Paret's manager, Manuel Alfero, was reported to have called for a new regulation requiring the use of such headgear.

Others have simply criticized Referee Ruby Goldstein for not stopping the fight sooner. Still others have demanded that boxing be outlawed.

April 3, 1962

ORTIZ CAPTURES TITLE

Associated Press Wirephoto

UNEASY LIES THE HEAD THAT WEARS A CROWN: Carlos Ortiz of New York scores right to head of crouching Joe Brown of Houston in third round of their lightweight bout in Las Vegas. Ortiz won championship from Brown by a unanimous decision.

BROWN IS BEATEN

Ortiz Wins by Wide Margin in Taking Lightweight Title

By BILL BECKER
Special to The New York Times.

LAS VEGAS, April 21—Carlos Ortiz, an underdog to everybody but Carlos Ortiz, gave the more-experienced Joe Brown a fifteen-round boxing lesson tonight and won the world lightweight championship by a unanimous decision.

Ortiz, the Puerto Rican-born pride of New York's "Fighting 69th" Regiment of the National Guard, took control like the sergeant he is. The 35-year-old champion seldom was the aggressor. He earned just one or two rounds on the officials' cards.

A crowd of 5,881 saw the nationally televised bout in Las Vegas' Convention Center. Each fighter weighed 134¾ pounds.

. As the bell rang ending the fight, Ortiz danced a little jig, and most of the audience also sensed the result. Cheers for Ortiz mingled with boos for Brown before these official reckonings were read:

Judge J. H. (Bud) Traynor, 74—58, in favor of Ortiz; Judge Dave Zeno, 74—66; Referee Frankie Van, 74—60.

It was a case of youth being served, and generously, as the 25-year-old New Yorker kept left jabs and hooks in Brown's face most of the way. Only in the fourth and perhaps the twelfth did Brown cause any any trouble.

There was no knockdowns, although Brown slipped to the floor during an exchange in the twelfth. The accident caused the champion to unleash one of his few furious bursts, including a hard right to the jaw that slowed Carlos briefly.

But Ortiz regained control in the thirteenth, however, and kept Brown off balance the rest of the way.

Brown 8-5 Favorite

Brown thus lost the crown in his twelfth defense in almost six years. He had won the title from Wallace (Bud) Smith in New Orleans on Aug. 24, 1956. He was favored by odds of 8 to 5 tonight.

Ortiz won the championship in this forty-first fight, following a two-year stalk of Brown. He performed much as he said he would, keeping the pressure on the arm-weary champion for most, if not all, of each three-minute round.

He had accused "Old Bones" of being "a thirty-second fighter"—that is, a flurry man who put out for only one-sixth of each round. "Old Bones" was hard-pressed to do even that after the sixth round tonight.

Ortiz' handlers kept calling from his corner, "Keep cool, Carlos." The youngster did just that except for a closing burst of temper in the sixth round when both men continued fighting after the bell had sounded.

Referee Van stepped in to part the battlers. The enraged Ortiz looked as if he was about ready to throw all Marquis of Queensbury rules overboard and start a pier 6 brawl.

Ortiz Changes Tactic

The curly - haired Ortiz changed only one tactic. Whereas he had announced he was going to batter "Old Bones" body, he concentrated his main fire on Brown's face. He drew blood over Joe's left eye in the opening round.

By the eighth, Brown had nicked Carlos' right eye, but the damage was not serious.

At no time was Brown in major trouble. His defense was adequate against Ortiz' right, but he was obviously surprised by the speed with which the cocky Carlos snapped his left.

Ortiz merely stole Joe the Jabber's favorite weapon and speared him out of the throne room with it.

The fiery-tempered Latin had gotten his Irish up eight hours before the battle. He was nettled when he had to do some calisthenics for forty-five minutes to make the lightweight limit of 135 pounds. He finally made it on his third try at the scales.

The elated Ortiz revealed later in his dressing room that the body-attack talk was just propaganda to cross up the champion. "It worked too," he said with a smile.

A $100,000 Offer

He said Brown was "a fine champion" and he would be "glad to give him a return fight," although there was no such clause in the contract for tonight's scrap.

"I think I'll knock him out next time," grinned Carlos.

He said he had an offer of $100,000 from a New Jersey promoter to make his first title defense.

The coolness of Ortiz was apparent in his disclosure that along about the twelfth he had looked out and seen Joe Louis and Billy Conn sitting at ringside.

"That reminded me to be careful," said Carlos. Conn forgot that lesson once while leading Louis on points, and was knocked out in the thirteenth round of their 1941 meeting.

Brown said merely, "I just couldn't get going." His manager, Lou Viscusi, said Joe's tonsils still bothered him, although a Nevada State Athletic Commission doctor had given him a clean bill of health.

His tonsilitis had forced the postponement of the scheduled Feb. 24 meeting between Brown and Ortiz.

The crowd paid $62,535 into the gate, far below the $100,000 expected by the promoting Silver State Sports Club.

Television rights added $60,-000 to the gross receipts. Brown had been guaranteed $50,000 and Ortiz $17,500. Those figures undoubtedly will be reversed the next time they meet.

. April 22, 1962

JOHNSON DEFEATS JONES ON POINTS

Retains Light-Heavyweight Crown With a Unanimous Decision at Philadelphia

By FRANK M. BLUNK
Special to The New York Times.

PHILADELPHIA, May 12 — Harold Johnson of Philadelphia became light-heavyweight champion of all the world except the State of California tonight.

The 33-year-old craftsman achieved this distinction by taking a unanimous decision in fifteen rounds over 21-year-old Doug Jones of New York before a crowd of 5,137 in the Philadelphia Arena.

Before this stirring battle, Johnson had been recognized as world champion by the National Boxing Association members. New York, Massachusets, California and the rest of the world had withheld such recognition. All but the West Coast state had announced that the winner of tonight's bout would be their champion, too.

The N. B. A. acceptance of Johnson followed his victory over Jesse Bowdry in Miami Beach, in February, 1961. The title had been taken from the N. B. A. from Archie Moore of California for his failure to defend it.

Johnson left no doubt of his worthiness in his triumph over Jones. He boxed superbly and defended himself with great skill. When he found chinks in Jones' armor, he hurt him with well-directed punches.

It was a fight of unending action. Of Jones, it must be said that he never backed away from it. He displayed great courage; he was in fine condition, and he showed on several occasions that there was iron in his fists, especially the right.

Jones Displays Courage

But Jones is young and he had had only twenty professional fights before this opportunity came to battle for the world title. He should not be ashamed of his performance here tonight, for it gave promise of better days to come. This young man needs only experience to make him a fighter of the very top rank.

There were no knockdowns, though at one stage Jones was groggy on the ropes. He appeared ready to fall, but the bell saved him. He recuperated quickly and was never in such danger again.

Johnson's incessant jabbing and his well-executed combina-tions of lefts to the body and rights to the jaw piled up points round after round. There is a 5-point-a-round system in effect here.

The voting for Johnson was 74 points to 61 by Referee David Beloff, 73 to 64 by Judge Zachary Clayton and 71 to 63 by Judge Nick Spano. On The New York Times card, Johnson won, 72 to 62, receiving twelve rounds to two, with one even.

Receipts from the crowd amounted to $31,784, of which Johnson's share is 40 per cent. The champion also will get $20,-000 from television.

Johnson suffered a slight cut over his left eye in the fifth round. Jones tried to make it a larger one by jabs and by head-butting, but without success. It never bothered the champion again.

The fighters weighed 171½ pounds apiece. Johnson said afterward that he had hoped to be heavier and that the lighter weight weakened him a bit.

"I thought I could have knocked him out in that eleventh round when I had him between the ropes," said Johnson, "but I was too eager. I missed the best punches."

May 13, 1962.

LISTON KNOCKS PATTERSON OUT IN FIRST ROUND

END COMES AT 2:06

Favorite Wins World Heavyweight Title in Chicago Bout

By ROBERT L. TEAGUE
Special to The New York Times.

CHICAGO, Sept. 25—Nobody got his money's worth at Comiskey Park tonight except Sonny Liston. He knocked out Floyd Patterson in 2 minutes 6 seconds of the first round of their heavyweight title fight and took the first big step toward becoming a millionaire.

Liston's massive right fist exploded on a vulnerable target only once. It jarred Patterson loose from his senses and brought a startling finish to what had been billed as perhaps the fight of the decade.

Actually, this scheduled 15-rounder scarcely could be called a fight. Not more than half a dozen solid blows were struck before it was over.

Liston's first notable connection was a left hook to the head. Patterson sagged against the ropes. His glazed eyes probably did not see the favored challenger launch a chopping right to his head seconds later.

Patterson Tries to Rise

Patterson was still on the canvas struggling to regain his feet when Referee Frank Sikora counted him out.

Only two other championship bouts in the history of the heavyweight class had been settled with more speed and decisiveness.

Ironically, Patterson clearly was the faster man in the ring. But this was his only apparent advantage over his 214-pound opponent. Floyd weighed 189.

A decidedly startled gathering of 26.000 witnessed Patterson's dethronement. However, only 18.894 paid their way into the ball park. This, too, was a surprise. So were the gross receipts of $665,420 and the net of $556,119.96.

All those figures were well below the generous estimates yesterday by spokesmen for Championship Sports, Inc., the promoter. Receipts from the closed-circuit television at 263 locations across the nation were not immediately available.

$5,000,000 Gross Unlikely

It seemed likely, though, that the expectation of an over-all gross in excess of $5,000,000 would not be realized.

Liston, who lives in Philadelphia, eventually will collect 12½ per cent of the total revenue. Patterson, from Scarsdale, N. Y., will get 55 per cent of the gate receipts and 45 per cent of the proceeds from ancillary (television, radio and motion picture) rights.

This probably will mean more than a million dollars for Floyd and perhaps between $300,000 and $400,000 for the new champion.

Almost nothing worth repeating occurred until Liston started the knockout sequence. He did so with a left hook to the body near Floyd's corner.

From a safe distance, it did not seem to be an especially hard punch. But Patterson doubled over, perhaps because he was hurt or perhaps to avoid being socked in the same place.

As Liston towered over his crouching fee, he released the spring on his left hook again. This time, it crashed into Patterson's head. Floyd's hands fell limply but only a short distance, leaving him with an uncertain defense.

This blow was short and did not appear to carry knockout power. But Referee Sikora later described it as "terrific . . . the one that set him up."

In fact, the 27-year-old Patterson apparently would have gone down slowly from the aftereffects of that punch alone. Liston took no chances, though.

As Floyd leaned toward Sonny's left—as if headed for the canvas — Liston helped him along the way to oblivion with a chopping right to the head. Patterson crumpled, landing on all fours.

This deceptive three-punch sequence required no more than five or six seconds. It was executed with so little dramatics that hardly anyone expected Floyd to remain on the floor. Liston was the exception, or so he later said. But as he waited in a neutral corner for Sikora to complete the count, his normally impassive or glowering countenance did bear a trace of surprise.

When the count reached 3, Patterson made a tremendous effort to rise. He shook his bewildered head from side to side. The fuzziness in his mind refused to disappear. His expression was one of confusion and desperation, rather than that of a man seriously hurt.

Floyd's corner men yelled for all they were worth, begging him to get back into the fight. His brave attempt carried him as far as one knee. Both gloves remained on the floor.

Mighty Effort Fails

As the kneeling referee waved his hand and tolled the count, Floyd strained with all his remaining strength to lift his gloves from the canvas. They were hopelessly mired there, however—or so it must have seemed in his dazed mind.

Finally, at 9, he succeeded in putting a few inches of space between one hand and his shoes. It was too late, though. A second later, Referee Sikora yelled "10."

It was all over. Sikora assisted the deposed champion into an upright position and brushed away his mild pleas to let him go on with the fight.

As Liston's mighty hand was raised in triumph, the usual pandemonium broke loose. Dozens of well-wishers, ushers and special policemen swarmed into the ring, along with the fighters' handlers. Most of the traffic was aimed at the winner, of course.

By now the startled crowd had recovered sufficiently to express what must have been an odd mixture of cheers for Liston, wonderment over the power of his 14-inch fists and astonishment over the show of incompetence by the beaten sentimental choice. The roar was mightier than one would have expected from a such a modest-sized gathering.

Nearly everybody had come to Comiskey Park expecting to see a knockout. Professional odds makers had installed the 28-year-old Liston as the man more likely to accomplish the feat. The ringside odds were 7-5.

Patterson seemed to have a chance as the round began. He fairly charged from his corner and immediately launched a leaping left hook toward the head of the slowly advancing Liston. The punch missed.

Liston pawed ineffectively with his left. It bore little resemblance to the snappy weapon he had displayed while training in recent weeks. Then he threw a rather ponderous right that also missed the mark. A clinch ensued. Each man slapped the other about the ribs.

When they broke, Floyd lunged again and grazed Liston's midsection with a left. He scored with another light left to the body before Sonny hit him with a hard left in the side. During all these insignificant exercises, Liston barely took what could be called a backward step.

Liston kept stalking his obviously swifter target. Finally, he maneuvered Patterson into Floyd's corner. Then came the left hook to the body that doubled Patterson. The left hook and chopping right to the head soon followed.

24th Knockout for Liston

The knockout was the 24th of Liston's nine-year career as a professional fist fighter. All told, he has won 34 of 35 starts and never has been knocked off his feet.

Liston's only defeat came eight years ago. He lost an eight-round decision to Marty Marshall in Detroit. He since has beaten Marshall twice.

Patterson's defeat was only the third of a brilliant career that began ten years ago. He thus lost the title for the second time.

Patterson originally captured the crown on Nov. 30, 1956. He then was 21 years old. Ingemar Johansson of Sweden wrested it from him in 1959, but Floyd won it back a year later.

In all, Patterson has defended the crown seven times. Within a year from now, he will have an opportunity to try winning the most valuable prize in sports a third time, under a rematch clause in his contract with Liston for tonight's abbreviated bout.

The record book points up just how abbreviated it was. The only faster knockouts in heavyweight title bouts were scored by Tommy Burns over Jem Roche in 1:28 (March 17, 1908, at Dublin) and Joe Louis over Max Schmeling in 2:04 (June 22, 1938, at New York).

September 26, 1962

Associated Press Wirephoto

DEFEAT: Floyd Patterson lies stunned after being floored by Sonny Liston's attack

LISTON'S CRITICS REMAIN AT LARGE

Insist Police Record Makes Him an Unfit Champion

Wherever Charles Sonny Liston goes, suspicion and controversy always are close at hand. They are not likely to depart now that he has reached the pinnacle of the boxing world by wresting the heavyweight title from Floyd Patterson.

For more than a year, Liston was virtually the only logical contender for the big prize. His chance was delayed because he is one of the most controversial boxing figures since Jack Johnson, who had trouble staying out of jail while ruling the heavyweights half a century ago.

Some states, including New York and California, have refused to license Liston.

Liston's critics feel that his prison record and alleged association with underworld characters make him unfit to wear a hero's mantle and thus be admired by youngsters. His admirers say he has rehabilitated himself. And besides, many boxing fans had been waiting a long time to see a real slugger—with or without a halo—win the championship.

Strength Brings Deference

Few of Liston's detractors are bold enough to make their charges to his face, however. He is a hulking brute of a man with massive shoulders, enormous hands and a glowering countenance. The fact that he has served time in prison for armed robbery and has beaten up at least one policeman further inspires deference to him.

Although noted for his sense of humor, the 28-year-old Liston inadvertently bolsters his image as an adult delinquent with his quick changes of mood. He ranges from friendliness to black anger for little apparent reason, much like a Hollywood gangster.

Liston has been fighting his environment, circumstances or men for almost as long as he can remember. He says he never has been afraid of anything or anybody, and he looks the part.

His fighting mood always seems close to the surface. At weigh-ins, his face becomes a mask of hostility as he glares at his intended victim. Antagonism seems to seep from the pores of his muscular body. His large brown eyes appear flecked with evil and anger as he fixes the other fighter with a hypnotic stare.

Westphal Was Puzzled

One of his victim-to-be, Albert Westphal of Germany, said to Sonny, "You can talk to me. I'm your friend. Why do you look so angry?"

"You'll find out tonight," Liston replied curtly. He knocked out Westphal in the first round.

It all started with an unfortunate childhood. Sonny was one of 25 children in a poverty-stricken family in Pine Bluff, Ark. He already was hard and tough as a rock when the family moved to St. Louis. Sonny was 12 at the time. He admits to have been the meanest member of the St. Louis gang he joined.

At 18, Liston was arrested for robbing a service station. He was sentenced to concurrent five-year terms on three robbery counts and two counts of larceny.

Learned to Box in Jail

He learned to box in the state penitentiary at Jefferson City, Mo. By 1952, his reputation as a prison fighter was so awesome that no one would face him. With the help of the prison chaplain, Father Alois Stevens, Sonny gained a parole after 29 months behind bars.

He turned pro in 1953 and

compiled an amazing record, winning 33 of his first 34 bouts. He lost only to Marty Marshall, but whipped Marshall twice in rematches.

His deportment in the ring was superb, but his behavior as a private citizen landed him in trouble again and again. He was arrested by Philadelphia police for loitering and for disorderly conduct while impersonating a policeman.

Adding to his difficulties were persistent rumors that he was controlled by gangsters. During a Senate subcommittee investigation of boxing in 1960, a St. Louis police lieutenant, Joseph Kudna, testified that Frankie Carbo, the underworld czar, owned 52 per cent of Liston's contract, and that another known gambler, Blinky Palermo, owned 12 per cent.

Liston has denied those allegations. In an effort to remove the cloud, he purchased his contract from his manager of record, Joseph (Pep) Barone, who allegedly was a front man for Palermo.

Liston also sought to improve his public image by spending several weeks with the Rev. Edward F. Murphy in Denver last summer. Father Murphy taught him to read and write and gave him instructions in the proper way for a responsible citizen to behave.

Only time will tell whether Sonny Liston learned those lessons well.

He lives with his wife Geraldine in West Philadelphia. He is fond of listening to jazz records and does the twist with verve and style.

September 26, 1962

JAPANESE CAPTURES FLYWEIGHT CROWN

TOKYO, Oct. 10 (UPI)—Masahika (Fighting) Harada of Japan, considered by the World Boxing Association as an "unworthy" challenger, knocked out Pone Kingpetch of Thailand in the 11th round tonight to win the world flyweight championship.

With a shattering series of left and right punches, the 19-year-old Harada won at 2:59 of the eleventh.

Harada began his attack in the first round of the scheduled 15-rounder at Kuramae Sumo. He pressed his offense relentlessly as long as the fight lasted.

Kingpetch received a cut over his left eye in the fifth round. By the time he was counted out by the referee, Vongse Hiranyalekha of Thailand, he was bleeding profusely from the eye and nose.

Harada, who weighed 111 pounds to Kingpetch's 111¾, led on all three official scorecards. The judges were Nat Fleischer, American editor of Ring Magazine, and Koichi Takada of Japan.

October 11, 1962

Dick Tiger Wins Middleweight Title From Fullmer on Unanimous Decision

NIGERIAN SLASHES OPPONENT'S EYES

SAN FRANCISCO, Oct. 23 (AP)—Dick Tiger of Nigeria cut both of Gene Fullmer's eyes tonight in pounding out a unanimous 15-round decision for the World Boxing Association middleweight championship.

In a bruising battle the 159-pound Tiger used sharper punching to lift the title that his 160-pound foe from West Jordan, Utah, had held since 1959.

Blood gushed from a slash over Fullmer's left eye in the ninth round, and Tiger opened a cut over Fullmer's right eye in the 10th.

Though Fullmer's corner kept the cuts fairly well controlled and Gene battled back gamely, the Nigerian found the range consistently and kept Fullmer in trouble.

Referee Frankie Carter scored the bout 10—1 for Tiger, Judge Jack Downey 9—5 and Judge Vern Bybee 7—5.

A crowd of some 12,500 in Candlestick Park roared approval of the slugging brawl between the 31-year-old Fullmer and the 33-year-old Tiger. The bout was televised to 48 cities across the country on a closed circuit.

When the decision was announced, a group of Nigerians in colorful native robes lifted Tiger to their shoulders and did an impromptu dance in the ring.

Fullmer had not lost in his last 17 fights and had defended the crown seven times. He won it by beating Carmen Basilio here on Aug. 28, 1959. But Tiger, whose real name is Ihetu, had too much ammunition for him.

Tiger built an early lead while beating Fullmer to the punch. Fullmer alternately boxed and blasted to the body to stay in contention until Tiger's big ninth.

As the two battled on the ropes, Fullmer came away from a vicious exchange with a 1½-inch cut over his left eye. By the end of the next round, he was bleeding from both eyes, the nose and mouth.

Fullmer in Trouble

Tiger used a stunning left hook to the head and a right to the body to drive Fullmer into the ropes in the third round. In the fourth, Fullmer appeared to be in distress from a combination of rights and lefts to the head. In the eighth, Tiger took a hard right to the head, probably Fullmer's most telling shot of the night.

Fullmer's big smashes were largely to the body and the well-conditioned Tiger did not give much ground.

Fullmer drew a warning from Carter in the fourth to keep his punches up and in the eighth to "watch your head."

There were no knockdowns, though Fullmer twice slipped to the canvas. In the 14th, he was wrestled down.

During the late rounds, Fullmer went more to a boxing style to protect his eyes, and both finished with far more caution than they had shown at the start.

Tiger, who holds the British Empire 160-pound title, now owns a share of the world championship. Massachusetts, New York and Europe, including the British Boxing Board of Control, recognize Paul Pender of Massachusetts.

The triumph was the eighth straight for Tiger. His record is now 46—12—2. It was only the fifth loss for Fullmer, who has posted 55 victories. Since winning the crown, Fullmer had been held to draws by Joey Giardello and Ray Robinson.

It was Sugar Ray who had handed Fullmer his last previous defeat, a fifth-round knockout, that enabled him to regain sole possession of the world 160-pound title on May 1, 1957.

Tiger's quickness and constant stalking provided his edge over Fullmer. Now he must meet Fullmer in a contracted rematch. Then he hopes to fight Pender.

He became the second Nigerian ever to win a world title. The first, Hogan (Kid) Bassey, ex-featherweight king, was at ringside cheering on his countryman.

In the cool of the night, the fighters' breaths often were visible as they hammered each other. Tiger looked strong in the third, fourth and fifth rounds, with combinations of lefts to the body and head and a crossing right to the jaw.

Fullmer's Eye Examined

Following the vicious ninth, the California Athletic Commission's physician, Don Lastretto, was called into the ring to examine the cut over Fullmer's left eye. He allowed the fight to continue. Fullmer said later that an unintentional butt opened a big gash over his eye in the ninth.

Under California rules, the 5-point scoring system prevailed, with the winner of each round getting from 1 to 5 points and the loser nothing. On even rounds, no points were awarded.

October 24, 1962

Demands for Boxing Ban Grow As Davey Moore Dies of Injury

By GLADWIN HILL
Special to The New York Times

LOS ANGELES, March 25—Calls for the abolition of boxing grew today after the death here early this morning of Davey Moore.

The 29-year-old dethroned featherweight champion died at 2:20 A.M. at the White Memorial hospital of a brain injury received in his title bout with Sugar Ramos of Miami and Cuba here some 78 hours before.

[Moore's death touched off calls from all over the world urging that boxing be outlawed. However, some persons did not view it as cause for banning boxing.]

The injury, a panel of doctors had just decided from movies of the fight, was caused not by a punch, but by a blow to the back of his skull by a snapping ring-rope he fell against in the last 30 seconds of a bout that went to a tenth-round knockout at the Dodger Stadium Thursday night.

The injury was described as similar to that which might have been inflicted by the heel of the hand in karate, a form of judo. The boxer collapsed in his dressing room after the fight and had been in a coma ever since.

An autopsy confirmed that the rope-blow caused the fatal injury. But blows to the face could not be ruled out as a

Davey Moore

Associated Press

Sugar Ramos

contributory factor, reported the coroner, Dr. Theodore J. Curphey.

Dr. Curphey formally described the cause of death as "brain damage as a result of the application of blunt force to the head"—the blunt force being the impact of the rope. He added that hemorrhages around the temples probably caused by blows to the jaw could have aggravated Moore's condition.

The fighter's funeral was tentatively planned for later in the week at Columbus. His body will be on view here beginning at noon today at the Angeles Funeral Home, 1030 East Jefferson Boulevard and will be flown to Columbus Wednesday.

The Columbus, Ohio, Negro's wife Geraldine, mother of five children, was in a nearby hospital room when he succumbed. Commenting that she had never liked the idea of his fighting, she called the death an "act of God" for which she blamed no one. Later in the morning she went to a hotel to await the

completion of a county coroner's autopsy.

On March 24 last year, Benny (Kid) Paret, Cuban welterweight, was fatally injured in a New York fight with Emile Griffith—who was also on last Thursday night's program.

Last Sept. 21, Alejandro Lavorante, Argentine heavyweight, was hit so hard by Johnny Riggins in a fight here that he has been in a coma ever since at the California Lutheran Hospital and is not expected to recover.

There were 14 deaths in professional fighting last year, and there have been 216 since 1945, according to standard ring records.

This was the second opponent fatality for 21-year-old Sugar Ramos. Jose (Tiger) Blanco, a Cuban lightweight, died after a fight with him in Havana in November, 1958.

Ramos, who had remained in a hotel here since Thursday's fight, wept when told his opponent had succumbed. He responded noncommittally to a

leading question as to whether he might give up fighting.

Ramos visited the hospital yesterday and talked with Mrs. Moore in a reception room.

"I've been so anxious," he said tearfully, "I wanted to see him, or you. I'm very sorry."

Mrs. Moore replied: "I want you to understand I'm not blaming you for anything. Both of you went into the fight for the championship. One of you had to be the winner.

"I realize it's hard for you to know you aren't the one to blame. But I'm closest to Davey and I'm asking you not to take it that way. Just please pray for him."

Moore gained prominence as national Amateur Athletic Union 118-pound champion in 1952, and went on that year to represent the United States at the Olympic Games in Helsinki, Finland. He was eliminated in the third round of bantamweight competition.

He had fought 65 professional bouts, winning 28 by knockouts and 27 by decisions and one on a foul. He was disqualified in one, fought to a draw in one, lost five on decisions, and lost two by knockouts.

He had won the featherweight title from Hogan (Kid) Bassey of London March 18, 1959, by a knockout in a fight here.

His payment for the Thursday bout was $40,000.

Moore was born in Lexington, Ky., Nov. 1, 1933, the son of a minister. He lived for several years in Springfield, Ohio, moving three years ago to Columbus.

His lifetime ring earnings are estimated at about $500,000.

Mrs. Moore, married to him 11 years, said the family was not faced with any economic pinch—that the fighter had invested wisely. He had been planning to give up fighting to

be a real estate and insurance broker.

"I never wanted him to fight," his widow said today. "He knew this, and he respected my feeling about it. I never saw one of his fights. He didn't want me there and I didn't care to be there."

She said she "certainly will discourage" their two sons from going into pugilism.

Of Moore's injury, Dr. Cyril B. Courville, a neurologist, said after scrutinizing the fight films:

"It was highly unusual. I've never seen anything like it. The films answered what we suspected—that Moore suffered his injury not from punches but from a fall against the ropes."

A videotape of the contest was projected at the KTTV studios yesterday for Dr. Courville and two associates on the case. He is a professor of neurology at the Loma Linda University School of Medicine, like the hospital a Seventh Day Adventist institution. The associates were Drs. Philip J. Vogel and Kenneth H. Abbott.

Three punches to the chin late in the tenth round sent Moore falling backward. He landed sitting down near the edge of the ring. The highly elasticized lower rope, either struck as he fell or vibrating from some other cause, snapped against the nape of his neck like a whiplash, the films disclosed.

Moore regained his feet, took a mandatory eight-count, and got his hands up to defend himself, but staggered and flopped over the upper rope as the bell ended the round and the fight.

The rope-blow caused a bruise swelling against a critical area of the brain, rather than the more usual hemorrhage which might have been relieved by an operation, the doctors said.

March 26, 1963

Murder in the Ring

Davey Moore lies dead in Los Angeles, another sacrifice to the brutal pastime that goes by the name of the manly art of prizefighting.

How long will this go on, this wretched business which Pope John has rightly described as barbaric? How many more Davey Moores do we need before we call

a halt? How many more Kid Parets? How many more Alejandro Lavorantes?

Where is the political leadership clearsighted enough and courageous enough to say that we are fed up with the nauseating hypocrisy that permits this sordid business to be called a "sport" and that we intend henceforth to brand it as the crime it is in fact?

March 27, 1963

State Orders 8-Ounce Gloves and 3-Knockdown Rule for All Title Fights

By HOWARD M. TUCKNER

The New York State Athletic Commission banned the use of six-ounce gloves yesterday and ordered pilot programs for two other safety measures to reduce the hazards of professional boxing.

In reacting to a recent report by the New York State Joint Legislative Committee on Boxing, the Commission said two other safety measure were under discussion. with a decision expected soon. The Joint Legisla-

tive Committee recommended last Sunday that boxing be continued in New York, but under more stringent regulations.

The deaths of two world champions following savage beatings in the ring led the commission to order gloves of "not less than eight ounces" for all bouts. The bigger gloves already had been in use here for non-title fights. Now they become mandatory for title bouts as well.

The commission also ordered the mandatory eight-count, three-knockdown rule enforced in championship fights. It had been customary to waive these rules in such bouts.

The 8-count rule provides that a fighter knocked down cannot resume until the referee has counted at least 8. Under the three-knockdown rule, a fighter floored three times in one round automatically loses on a technical knockout.

Some Shorter Rounds

As an experiment, the Commission will institute two-minute rounds instead of the usual three for four-round preliminary fights. Boxing rings with four strands of rope instead of the customary three also will be tested in a pilot program.

Melvin Krulewitch, the chairman of the commission, said two other safety aspects considered by the Joint Legislative Committee were being studied by the commission.

One was a committee recommendation that a boxer knocked down at the end of a round should not be "saved by the bell." If this is adopted, the referee will continue his count after the bell. If the fighter fails to arise at the count of 10, the bout will be stopped.

The other matter was that of taping a boxer's hands. The commission hopes to determine whether less tape or no tape at all would increase saftey in the ring.

Krulewitch said a committee that included Floyd Patterson, the former heavyweight champion, as well as trainers and physicians would meet this week to talk about taping.

The commissioner said:

"We'll have to tread lightly on other recommendations by the committee until we see what legislation actually is passed. But the changes we have ordered are urgent ones."

In its report, the Joint Legislative Committee strongly recommended that 10-ounce gloves be instituted in all bouts. The committee also asked that authorized persons outside the ring be allowed to halt a one-sided bout. The committee suggested that this could be done through visual and audible signals.

Under current regulations, a commission doctor may stop a fight only by entering the ring.

"Before we decide about the 10-ounce glove." Krulewitch said, "we will await the Legislature's action. This is an important change, a vital element in professional boxing. We're not prepared at this point to go beyond insisting on gloves of eight ounces and eliminating the six-ounce gloves for all fights."

Opposition to 10 Ounces

Many boxing experts are against the use of 10-ounce gloves. They argue

that bigger gloves can stun an opponent, but cannot knock him out. According to their theory, this leaves the fighter open to continued punishment.

The Joint Legislative Committee was formed last May after the death of Benny (Kid) Paret. On April 24, 1962, Paret suffered brain injuries in a welterweight title fight at Madison Square Garden. He died 10 days later.

Last March 21, Davey Moore suffered brain damage in a featherweight title bout at Los Angeles. He died four days after the fight.

April 3, 1963

Pastrano Upsets Johnson On 15-Round Split Verdict

By United Press International

LAS VEGAS, Nev., June 1—Willie Pastrano, a second substitute and a 5—1 underdog, wrested the world light heavyweight championship from Harold Johnson tonight on a split 15-round decision.

Pastrano's victory before a crowd of only 2,500 broke the 34-year-old Johnson's winning string at 19.

The decision in the Las Vegas Convention Center was greeted with mingled cheers and boos because the fight was close and well-fought.

Pastrano, 27 years old, of North Miami Beach, Fla., weighed 174 pounds. Johnson scaled 173½.

There were no knockdowns.

Pastrano was the underdog because his recent record could not compare with that of the muscular Johnson.

Moreover, Pastrano was a third choice as a challenger. He got the title shot only after two others suffered training injuries and had to withdraw. They were Mauro Mina of Peru and Henry Hank of Detroit.

Pastrano was given the title chance because of his victory in this same ring May 4 over Wayne Thornton of Fresno, Calif.

Referee Jimmy Olivos of Reno voted for Pastrano on a 5-point-in front, must basis, 69—68. Judge John Romero of Las Vegas had Johnson, 69—68. Judge Harry Krause of Las Vegas made Pastrano the new champion—he scored him ahead, 69—67.

United Press International voted for Johnson, 69—68. A U.P.I. poll of writers at ringside favored Johnson, 9 to 5.

Johnson finished the fight with his left eye nearly closed because of a big mouse that kept pushing up from the cheek.

Both of Pastrano's cheeks were badly bruised.

It was Johnson's first defeat since his knockout, by Julio Mederos in the second round May 6, 1955—the night that someone gave Harold a doctored orange in the dressing room at Philadelphia.

Pastrano got his first shot at a title in his 11-year career, most of which was spent fighting out of New Orleans, before he moved to Miami Beach. He fought many high-ranking light heavyweights and heavyweights.

Jabs Fast, Effective

Tonight, his speedy jabs and whistling rights, thrown while he danced from side to side, were effective, particularly in the first, sixth, 10th, 12th, 14th and 15th rounds. He managed to fight on even terms in the fourth and eighth.

However, in the ninth it seemed that Willie might go down for the first time in his career. Johnson staggered him with a left-right combination to the head and then drove him around the ring. But Pastrano was fighting back at the close of that round.

Although the new champion had never been counted out, he was stopped in the fifth round by Brian London of England because of face cuts on Sept. 30, 1958.

In the fifth round here, Johnson hurt Pastrano with a punch that accidentally landed below the belt and then stunned him with a left hook to the head. Willie reeled as he walked to his corner at the bell. Referee Olivos did not penalize Johnson for the low blow although he did warn him to keep his punches up.

Johnson suffered his ninth defeat in 79 professional bouts.

It was Pastrano's 59th victory in 78 fights, in which he has scored only 13 knockouts.

Pat Oliveri, Johnson's manager, was so displeased with the decision against his fighter that he said:

"I think we were robbed and I want a return bout."

There was no return-bout clause in the contract for Johnson in case of a defeat.

From the gate estimated at only $32,000 and the television money of $60,000, Johnson was guaranteed $37,500 and Pastrano $22,500.

Pastrano said:

"I am going to rest for a while now and will decide about a return bout later. I'll say this for Harold—he was the best fighter I ever fought."

Johnson advanced persistently against his dancing opponent — but he apparently lost because he failed to do the leading. He insisted upon feinting Pastrano into leads so that he could counter. However, he was effective with his counters to the body and head at times.

Pastrano not only finished the stronger, but he also baffled

Johnson in the late rounds with his swift hitting tactics that included right-jabbing with his right foot forward.

Johnson said:

"I thought I won the fight, certainly because of my aggressivness. But I don't suppose he'll give me a return bout."

Johnson tried to win the light-heavyweight crown from Archie Moore in 1954 but was knocked out in the 14th round. However, in 1961 he won the World Boxing Association version of the vacant title on a ninth-round knockout over Jesse Bowdry. He defended that portion of the crown successfully against Von Clay and Eddie Cotton.

Next, he won sole possession of the world title by outpointing Doug Jones on May 12, 1962, and he defended successfully against Gustav Scholz in Berlin, June 23, 1962.

One of the remarkable facts about Pastrano's victory was that he had never gone 15 rounds before. His longest previous distance was 12 rounds.

June 2, 1963

GRIFFITH REGAINS TITLE

VERDICT IS BOOED

Griffith Regains Title From Rodriguez on a Split Decision

By DEANE McGOWEN

Emile Griffith last night became the first boxer to capture the welterweight title three times. But it was an achievement not universally applauded.

A chorus of boos at Madison Square Garden greeted his conquest of the champion, Luis Rodriguez, by a split decision in the 15-round bout.

Cries of "Robbery!" and "What must you do to win a fight?" rang out as Griffith was having his picture taken in the ring after the fight. And when Emile left the ring, whistles and boos echoed after him as he made his way to his dressing room.

Judge Tony Rossi scored it in favor of Griffith, eight rounds to seven. The referee, Jimmy Devlin, who was working his first title fight, also favored Griffith—by 9 to 6.

Rodriguez Gets 10-5 Vote

Judge Joe Armstrong gave 10 rounds to Rodriguez and five to Griffith. The New York Times score card favored Rodriguez, eight rounds to six with one even. In a ringside poll conducted by United Press International, 17 writers voted for Rodriguez and six for Griffith. One called it a draw.

Each fighter weighed 146½, half a pound under the division limit. As late as Friday Griffith had been the 13-to-10 favorite, but by weigh-in at noon yesterday the odds had narrowed to 6 to 5 and pick 'em. The officials did not see it that close, and the fans did not see what the officials saw.

It was Griffith's eighth title bout. He first won the crown from the late Benny (Kid) Paret on a 13th-round knockout in Miami in April, 1961. Paret regained the title at the Garden in September of that year, then Griffith took it back from Paret on March 24, 1962. Paret, knocked out in the 12th round, never regained consciousness and died 10 days later.

Griffith defended the title successfully against Gaspar Ortega, Ralph Dupas and Jorge Fernandez, then lost it to Rodriguez last March 21 in Los Angeles. That was a unanimous but a disputed decision. Most ringside reporters felt Griffith won that one.

Rodriguez Looked Better

Judging by reaction of the 8,081 fans who paid $35,148 to see last night's bout, and the 24 boxing writers who covered the fight, Rodriguez was clearly the victor.

Griffith's punching was heavier, but Rodriguez was the better boxer, faster of foot and faster of hand. But punchers usually sway officials, so Griffith's harder blows apparently swung things his way.

Seldom did either man gain a pronounced advantage, but Rodriguez did land the greater number of punches. He scored repeatedly with straight left jabs and long rights to the chin.

Griffith countered with crisp jabs and piled up points with a number of solid hooks to the body and head. As he had predicted, he tied up Rodriguez in the clinches and smothered the Cuban's flurries in close.

The 26-year-old Rodriguez was certainly the cleaner and sharper hitter. The Cuban native, who now makes his home in Miami, had his best round in the seventh when he forced the action all the way.

He put Griffith on the defensive at the start by nailing him with a short right to the chin as Emile was moving forward. The 24-year-old Griffith spent the rest of the round dodging, bobbing and weaving as Rodriguez landed hooks to the body and rights to the head.

Griffith's best round was the 10th when he staggered Rodriguez with a hard right to jaw. He pursued Luis and landed a succession of blows to the head and body, but just before the end of the round Rodriguez replied with a blazing offensive.

Last Rounds Decisive

Griffith grew stronger after this round, and this probably helped swing the decision in his favor. Referee Devlin gave Griffith the last three rounds and Armstrong awarded the last five to Rodriguez.

After 14 rounds, Rossi had the bout scored 7—7. When he gave Griffith the last round he gave Emile the title.

There were no knockdowns or cuts even though both men, in superb condition, fought hard the full three minutes of every round, as they vowed they would.

Griffith drew a warning from Devlin in the 12th. He pinned Rodriguez against the ropes, then ran the laces of his gloves up the left side of Rodriguez's face. That was the only unsportsmanlike action of the bout, brought on, perhaps, by Griffith's frustration by Rodriguez's superior boxing.

It was Griffith's third triumph over Rodriguez. Their first bout was a 10-rounder here before Griffith first won the title.

The defeat was Rodriguez's third in an eight-year professional career. He has won 50 and has had one no-contest bout. He has scored 21 knockouts.

For New Yorker Griffith, born in the Virgin Islands, it was his 36th victory against four defeats in six years. He has 12 knockouts.

Rodriguez had been guaranteed $40,000 from the gate and the $70,000 television fee. Griffith had been guaranteed $37,500.

With the television fee, the total receipts were $105,148.

There was no talk of a rematch. Teddy Brenner, the Garden matchmaker said it was "too soon to think about that."

One thing seems certain—if they meet again, the result should produce more controversy.

June 9, 1963

CHAPTER 3

ALI TO THE RESCUE

Float like a butterfly, sting like a bee—and keep talking. Muhammad Ali breathed life into a sport that was being strangled by seediness and fan indifference.

'Man, It's Great To Be Great'

By HOWARD M. TUCKNER

*Everyone knew when I
      stepped in town
I was the greatest fighter
      around.
A lot of people called me a
      clown
But I am the one who
      called the round.
The people came to see a
      great fight
But all I did was put out the
      light.
Never put your money
      against Cassius Clay,
For you will never have a
      lucky day.*
—CASSIUS MARCELLUS CLAY.

CASSIUS MARCELLUS CLAY, boxing's Cicero in resin, is a fresh breeze in an otherwise becalmed sport. But the world of the squared circle is not quite sure whether Cassius is a wonder boy or just another windbag putting his mouth where his gloves should be.

"I'm not the greatest," the 20-year-old heavyweight contender says modestly, "I'm the double greatest. Not only do I knock 'em out, I pick the round and then Cassius Clay of Louisville, Kentucky, does what he says he'll do. Cassius Clay is the double greatest 'cause Cassius Clay always keeps his promise."

Cassius Clay, it is true, usually does what Cassius Clay says he will do. In 16 fights since he became a pro-

FIGHTER-TALKER —Cassius Marcellus Clay, who proclaims himself the coming world's heavyweight champion. "It is true Cassius Clay usually does what Cassius Clay says he will do."

fessional loudmouth two years ago ("I've always been a loudmouth," the undefeated heavyweight says, "but it's so much sweeter getting paid for it"), Cassius has picked the moment of countdown 10 times right on the nose. In his most recent fight, known variously as the Great Debate and the Battle of the Mouths, Clay knocked out Archie Moore, boxing's consummate con man, in the fourth round.

"Moore will fall in four," Cassius had proclaimed. The 45- to 50-year-old Moore, the Sage of Punchville, said he would counter . with a new punch, "The Lip Buttoner." Clay retaliated with his "Pension Punch," and, as it turned out, it's poetic justice that a pop-off like Clay should succeed a pop-off like Moore.

Now Sonny Liston, the heavyweight champion who has been accused of everything except fraternizing with poets, has become a target for Clay's couplets. After watching Sonny make an ex-champion of Floyd Patterson in 126 seconds, Cassius wrote:

*When people left the park
      you could hear them say
Liston will stay the King
      until he meets Cassius
      Clay.*

"I'm the boldest, the prettiest, the most superior, most scientific, most skillfullest fighter in the ring today."

WINNER—"It's poetic justice that a pop-off like Clay succeeded a pop-off like Moore." Above, the moment of victory, Nov. 15.

Clay says at the drop of a breath. "I'm the onliest fighter who goes from corner to corner and club to club debating with fans. In my experience I received more publicity than any fighter in history. I talk to reporters till their fingers are sore, man— till they can't bend them.

"I'm just the heavyweight champion that the world needs," he goes on. "We need a man with personality, color, patience, charm, who'll talk to all reporters—give 'em just what they want. A man who's willing to cooperate in every way. A man who's not the greatest but the double greatest. Man, it's great to be great."

Liston reputedly is the strongest and most reticent heavyweight since King Kong, but the Louisville Lip got even him talking.

"Right after I annihilated Mr. Moore," Cassius said, "I shuffles over to Sonny's seat and say, 'Liston, you are next and you must fall in eight.' He looks at me, he thinks he scares me with those eyes of his, and he says, 'You don't go as long as Patterson. You go eight seconds, big mouth, I give you the fight.' Do I run back to my dressing room and cry? Do my knees knock? Nah, man. I look right at him and say, 'You keep popping off like that and I'll cut it to six rounds.' He wanted to say something else but my public

was waiting in the dressing room and Cassius Clay never keeps his public waiting."

IT may be a year before Clay risks lip and limb against Liston ("At 6-2 and 195 pounds I'm a Greek god now," he admits, "but in a year I'll be bigger and heavier"), but this man with the soul of a poet, the heart of a lion and the mouth of a river already knows how he will beat Liston in eight or six rounds.

"The man is nothin'," Cassius says. "The man will be in there with the fastest, the smartest, the boldest heavyweight in the world. I'll press him for the first five rounds and when he tries to punch me I'll call upon my natural talents and dazzle him with my blazing feet and hands. By the eighth round he'll be ready to drop from pain and fatigue, but he'll fall in limb in the sixth if he keeps popping off. Soon the world'll know the whole story. Right now, at this very moment, I am working on a poem about the fight. I'll recite it to the world when I'm ready. It will be my masterpiece."

CLAY was born and raised in Louisville, which also was the home of the abolitionist Cassius Marcellus Clay, who became President Lincoln's Ambassador to Russia. The fighting Clay, after winning the Olympic light-heavyweight championship at the age of 18, turned professional under the guidance of a group of wealthy Louisville businessmen. Except for Moore, who became his 13th knockout victim, his hand-picked opponents have included such anonymities as Tommy Hunsaker, Herb Siler and Duke Sabedong, as well as the much better-known LaMar Clark, Alonzo Johnson and Sonny Banks.

Some Eighth Avenue smart-money boys do not share Clay's opinion of his ability. They admire his size (he has a 32-inch waist and a 46-inch chest), his speed (as a child he never rode but raced the bus to school to make himself fast), his quick hands ("They're like blurred lightning, man") but they wonder if his opponents have tested anything more than Clay's ability to talk a good fight.

Other boxing savants, although not quite sure if Cassius can take a good punch, are unwilling to make book that the chesty chatterbox will **not become the youngest heavyweight champion in boxing history.** Marv Jenson, the manager of Gene Fullmer, says, "He has the fastest hands of any heavyweight I've ever seen, including Floyd Patterson." Lou Bailey, a sparring partner who has worked with Clay and Liston, swears, "Liston would not lay a glove on Cassius. What's his best punch? All of them."

Even Rudolph Arnett Clay, an 18-year-old amateur heavyweight who, under the influence of his bashful brother, has changed his name to Rudolph Valentino Clay, is convinced of Cassius's destiny. "He's the best what ever was," Rudolph says. "When we were kids he kept asking me to throw rocks at him. He dodged 'em all. I throw rocks faster than Liston throws punches."

So while the world keeps wondering if Cassius is for real, he keeps acting as if the original Cassius had something after all when he said, "The fault, dear Brutus, is not in our stars, but in ourselves, that we are underlings."

His even white teeth keep flashing out of an unmarked, walnut-colored face ("Girls tell me to quit fighting before I get hurt. I say, 'Don't worry, honey, nothin' gonna hurt Cassius,'"); he keeps taunting his rivals with good crosses and mediocre couplets ("I got through high school with a D-minus average and I never writ much poetry. The poetry comes to me from God, the poetry and the hands"). He keeps predicting the fatal round for his opponents apparently aware that the world may despise, but never

ignores, a braggart ("The people come to my fights 'cause they hate me. They come to see Cassius fall. But Cassius Clay won't fall 'cause boxing needs him. The country needs him. Archie Moore and Ray Robinson are finished. Floyd Patterson's got nothin' to say and Sonny Liston can't say anything").

AND because of his love of boxing and country, Cassius

Clay probably will continue to wear $100 suits, drive a pink Cadillac, wear a white "satiny" robe, white trunks and white shoes "with three coats of white polish," spread Vaseline on his arms before a fight "to make me look real musclely" and, during his travels, carry an overstuffed scrapbook labeled "Cassius Marcellus Clay."

"It's a beautiful name," he says. "Don't you think it's a

beautiful name? Makes you think of the Coliseum and those Roman gladiators. Cassius Marcellus Clay. Say it to yourself. Cassius Marcellus Clay. Feel the way it rolls out of your mouth. Say it out loud. Cassius Marcellus Clay. It's beautiful. It's a beautiful name. Cassius Marcellus Clay, Cassius Marcellus Clay, Cassius Marcellus Clay. . . ."

December 9, 1962

Clay Wins Title in Seventh-Round Upset As Liston Is Halted by Shoulder Injury

Associated Press Wirephoto
Cassius Clay lands left to the head of Sonny Liston during first round of the title bout.

Clay Is Exultant

By ROBERT LIPSYTE
Special to The New York Times

MIAMI BEACH, Feb. 25—Incredibly, the loud-mouthed bragging, insulting youngster had been telling the truth all along. Cassius Clay won the world heavyweight title tonight when a bleeding Sonny Liston, his left shoulder injured, was unable to answer the bell for the seventh round.

Immediately after he had been announced as the new heavyweight champion of the world, Clay yelled to the newsmen covering the fight: "Eat your words." Only three of 46 sports writers covering the fight had picked him to win.

A crowd of 8,297, on its feet through the early rounds at

Convention Hall, sat stunned during the one-minute rest period between the sixth and seventh rounds. Only Clay seemed to know what had happened; he threw up his hands and danced a little jig in the center of the ring.

The victory was scored as a technical knockout in the seventh round, one round less than Clay had predicted. Liston seemingly had injured the shoulder in the first round while swinging and missing with jabs and hooks at the elusive 22-year-old.

The fight was Clay's from the start. The tall, swift youngster, his hands carelessly low, backed away from Liston's jabs, circled around Liston's dangerous left hook and opened a nasty gash under Liston's left eye.

He never let Liston tie him up for short, brutal body punches, and although he faltered several times, he refused to allow himself to be cornered. His long left jab kept bouncing off Liston's face. From the beginning, it was hard to believe.

The men had moved briskly into combat. Liston stalking, moving flat-footedly forward. He fell short with two jabs, brushed Clay back with a grazing right to the stomach and landed a solid right to the stomach. The crowd leaned forward for the imminent destruction of the young poet.

Hands Still Low

But the kid hadn't lied. All those interminable refrains of "float like a butterfly, sting like a bee," had been more than foolish songs. The kid was floating. He leaned back from Liston's jabs and hooks, backed into the ropes, then spun out and away. He moved clockwise around Liston, taunting that terrible left hook, his hands still low.

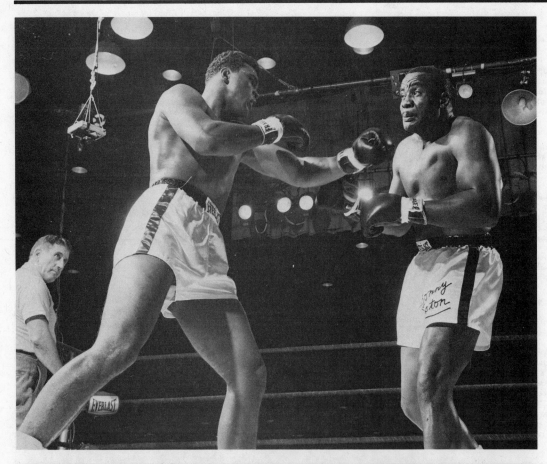

Champion Sonny Liston grimaces as Cassius Clay shakes him up with a left in the 6th round of their title bout in February 1964. Clay went on to beat Liston in a 7th round TKO.

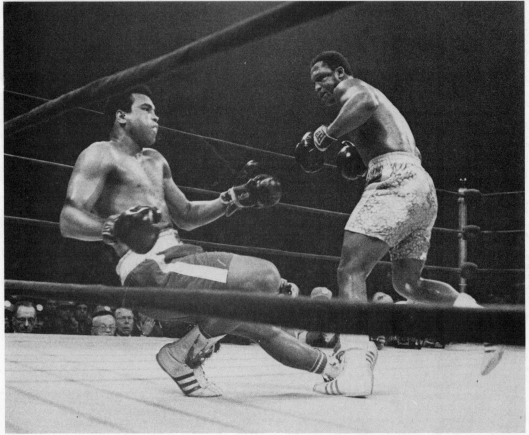

Joe Frazier sends Muhammad Ali to the canvas in their 1971 bout, the only one of the three they fought that Frazier won. When he fought Frazier in Manila in 1975, Ali said it was like facing death.

Then he stung, late in the first round, sticking his left in Liston's face and following with a quick barrage to Liston's head. They continued for long seconds after the bell, unable to hear the inadequate ring above the roar of the crowd.

It must have been somewhere in that round that Liston's shoulder was hurt.

[Jack Nilon, Liston's manager, said at the hospital that the former champion had hurt the shoulder during training. The Associated Press reported. He said Liston did not spar Feb. 3, 4, 5 and 14 because of the injury. Asked why he hadn't postponed the fight, Nilon said, "We thought we could get away with it."]

He strained forward with over-eager hooks that struck only air. For a moment, in the second round, Liston pummeled Clay against the ropes, but again, Cassius spun out and away.

Then the young man began to rumble as he had promised. His quick left jabs penetrated Liston's defenses, and he followed with right hands. He leaned forward as he fired rights and lefts at Liston's expressionless face. Liston began to bleed from a crescent-shaped cut high on the left cheekbone.

Liston Plunges Ahead

Like a bull hurt and maddened by the picadors' lances, Liston charged forward. The heavy muscles worked under his smooth, broad back as he virtually hurled his 218 pounds at the dodging, bobbing, dancing Clay.

His heavy arms swiped forward and he threw illegal backhand punches in his bear-like lunges. Once, Clay leaned the wrong way and Liston tagged him with a long left.

Cassius was staggered, but Liston was hurt and tired. He could not move in to press his advantage.

And now, a strange murmur began to ripple through the half-empty arena and people on blue metal chairs began to look at one another. Something like human electricity danced and flowed as the spectators suddenly realized that even if Cassius lost, he was no fraud. His style was unorthodox, but . . .

There was little action in the fourth, as Cassius continued to circle. Once he opened his eyes wide as a Liston jab fell short, and it seemed as if he were mocking the heavy-footed hunter. As it turned out, Cassius could barely see.

He began complaining to Angelo Dundee, his trainer, at the end of the round. Something had gotten into his eyes, from Liston's glove, from the sponge, somewhere. But he went out for the fifth anyway, and all Dundee could do was shout, "Stay way from him, stay away."

Clay tried to stay away. Sensing something, Liston bulled forward, slamming Cassius with a left hook in the nose and lefts and rights to the body. Blinking furiously, Clay kept circling away. He never hit back.

Both fighters were sluggish in the fifth round, breathing heavily. Liston's face was still impassive, but the grooves along his forehead seemed deeper, and the snorting breaths through his nose harsher.

He seemed even more tired in the sixth as Clay's eyes cleared and the younger man bore in, then leaped away, jabbing and hooking and landing a solid right to Liston's jaw. Clay's jabs were slipping through at will now, bouncing off that rock-like face, opening the cut under the left eye.

Liston walked heavily back to his corner at the end of the sixth. He did not sit down immediately. Then as Liston did sit down, Clay came dancing out to the center of the ring, waving his arms, all alone. It seemed like a long time before Drew (Bundini) Brown, his assistant trainer, was hugging him and Dundee was dancing up and down, and Jack Nilon, Liston's adviser, was wrapping yards of tape around the former champion's left shoulder.

"I just can't go back," a Liston aide reported Sonny to have said.

And then the crowd was cheering and booing, which is something like laughing and crying because it was the wildest thing they had ever seen. It didn't make sense. For weeks, Clay had played the fool and been tagged at will by unworthy sparring partners. This morning, at the weigh-in, he had acted bizarre and disturbed.

And tonight, he had been cool and fast and without fear.

Until the knockout, the officials had had the fight a draw. Referee Barney Felix had scored the six rounds 57—57 on the 10-point-must system. Judge Bill Lovitt scored it 58—56 for Liston, and Judge Gus Jacobsen 58—56 for Clay.

But points didn't really matter after all. Poetry and youth and joy had triumphed over the 8-1 odds. And until it had happened (and perhaps until they can look it up) people laughed at the thought that a night like this could happen.

The crowd had cheered lustily at 9:59 P.M., when Cassius came jogging down the aisle toward the ring, his face impassive, wearing a hip-length terry-cloth white robe on which was emblazoned The Lip. Nobody even snickered, for everyone knew Clay to be a braggart, not to be taken seriously.

He leaped through the ropes in a sudden motion, then waited in the ring for six minutes before Liston started down the aisle, shadow-boxing in a corner of the ring. He did not talk or shout. Liston, in a long, white robe, glared out from a white hood and climbed heavily through the ropes.

"Wipe my face off, hey, wipe my face off," said Clay to Dundee. The trainer was staring at the implacable Liston, and didn't hear Clay until he had repeated himself.

Both men stood in their corners, serenely as the inevitable

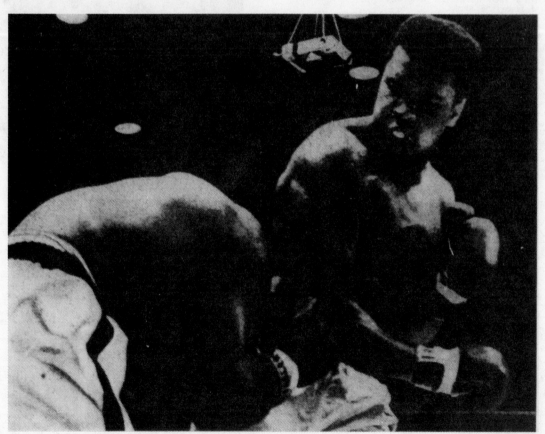

Associated Press Wirephoto

POWER: Cassius Clay lashes at Sonny Liston during the opening moments of their championship bout held in Miami

The Champion Speaks, but Softly

parade of notables—Rocky Marciano, Sugar Ray Robinson, et al—shook their gloved hands. Sonny, in white trunks with a black stripe and his name across a thigh, seemed malevolent and invincible. Clay, in white trunks with red piping, seemed only big.

Earlier, rumors had swept Convention Hall that Cassius was not going to show, that the thin line of hysteria he had trod during the morning weigh-in had become full-scale fear.

But even as the rumor mounted (that he was in a plane, en route to Mexico), Cassius was standing quietly in a far corner of the arena. He was waiting for his brother, Rudolph Valentino Clay, to make his professional debut.

Few people noticed him. He was dressed in a tight-fitting black tropical suit and wore a black bow tie on his ruffled, white dress shirt.

Clay was surrounded by aides—Brown; Archie Robinson, his personal secretary, and Dundee. Dundee was carrying a blue suitcase and Bundini kept a hand on Clay's back, as if he might have to restrain him at any moment.

But Clay hardly moved. Despite his height (6 feet 3 inches) e often had to stand on tiptoe to watch the action in the far-off ring. Once, when Rudy floored his opponent, Chip Johnson of Naples, Fla., in the second round, Clay shouted some encouragement. Otherwise he was silent.

Even during the one-minute rest periods between rounds, Cassius stared at the ring. His face seemed tense and alert, but his body was unmoving. At the end of the four-round bout, when it was announced that Rudy had won, Cassius turned abruptly, without saying a word, and followed a phalanx of Miami policemen with flashy gunbutts out of the arena and into his dressing room.

Once there, at about 9:15 P.M., he was re-examined by Dr. Robbins.

At the weigh-in, Dr. Robbins had said that Clay's pulse rate was around 120, more than double his norm of 54. Forty-five minutes before the fight, Clay's pulse was 64, the same as Liston's. Sonny had arrived at the hall a few minutes after 8 P.M. and gone to his dressing room to rest.

February 26, 1964

Clay Discusses His Future, Liston and Black Muslims

By ROBERT LIPSYTE
Special to The New York Times

MIAMI BEACH, Feb. 26—"I don't have to be what you want me to be," said Cassius Clay, the new heavyweight champion. "I'm free to be who I want."

Calm, poised, genial, but rarely smiling, the 22-year-old who beat Sonny Liston for the title last night faced a battery of cameras and newsmen today. Speaking softly (for the first time in recent memory) he talked of the fight, of his unresolved immediate plans, and of the tenets of the Black Muslim movement.

At first, he pleased his predominantly white audience with amiable and measured statements about his victory. They smiled at one another when Cassius said: "I'm through talking. All I have to do is be a nice, clean gentleman."

But they began to shift a little nervously when he put them down with such gentle truths as: "I'm sorry for Liston. You people put too much load on him. You built him up too big and now he has such a long way to fall."

The Nonsporting Side

And finally, there was a trace of antagonism when he refused to play the mild and socially uninvolved sports-hero stereotype, and began to use the news conference as a platform for socio-political theory.

"I go to a Black Muslim meeting and what do I see? I see that there's no smoking and no drinking and their women wear dresses down to the floor. And then I come out on the street and you tell me I shouldn't go in there. Well, there must be something in there if you don't want me to go in there."

Clay said that he wanted to be nice to everyone. But he warned that no one would make him into something he was not.

"I know where I'm going and I know the truth and I don't have to be what you want me to be. I'm free to be what I want," he said.

Someone asked: "Are you a card-carrying member of the Black Muslims?" Clay replied: "Card-carrying, what does that mean?" Then he spoke with revivalistic fervor about the group's separatist doctrine.

Separate With Equals

"In the jungle, lions are with lions and tigers with tigers, and redbirds stay with redbirds and bluebirds with bluebirds. That's human nature, too, to be with your own kind. I don't want to go where I'm not wanted."

Clay put down the civil rights movement ("I'm a citizen already"); defended Malcolm X, the Black Muslim leader ("If he's bad why don't they put him in jail?") and questioned those who attacked his leanings ("I catch so much hell, why? Why me when I don't try to bust into schools or march around or throw bricks?")

The conference had begun in a far different vein. A few minutes after the scheduled 11 A.M. starting time (there had been rumors, as usual, that Clay had left town), Cassius walked quietly into a large room in Convention Hall, wearing a gray tweed sport jacket, blue pants, a gray-and-red striped shirt open at the neck and buff-colored shoes.

Cassius was subdued. His voice was so soft that people had to strain to catch his words. After scoring his seven-round technical knockout over Liston last night, he said, he had gone to a private party with some friends at a local hotel. He had said last night that he "wanted to be with his people."

Associated Press Wirephoto

Sonny Liston, dark glasses covering injuries around his eyes and left arm in sling, at news conference yesterday.

He said he had known after the first round that he had the title. It was in that round that Liston separated some muscles in his left shoulder in swinging at and missing his elusive target.

Hands held carelessly low, leaning and backing away from punches rather than using more orthodox bob-and-weave technique, Clay never let Liston get close enough to hurt him.

While a crowd of 8,297 watched in some amazement, the 8-1 underdog proved he was no bragging fraud. Weighing 210½ pounds to Liston's 218, he danced and backpedaled away from Liston's vaunted hook, then leaped in to deliver quick barrages to Liston's head.

Clay opened a nasty gash under Liston's left eye in the third round. Later, six stitches were required to close the wound.

In the fifth, Clay had troubles of his own. He came out for the round blinking. Angelo Bundee, his trainer, has said that he had to shove Clay out to fight, that before the fifth began Clay had asked him to cut his gloves off and "leave me out of here."

Clay said today that he thought some caustic solution from Liston's glove or head had got into his eyes. He hinted that heavy bettors might have tried some "trick" and that he was "worried" and "watching out for something."

In that fifth round, Clay, claiming near-blindness for most of it, merely avoided Liston, never throwing punches. Several times he stretched his left glove to touch Liston's nose and keep the champion at arm's length. In his own news conference, Liston said he could have broken that outstretched arm but his own injury made him unable to lift his arm.

Liston also said that he considered Floyd Patterson, whom he beat twice in one-round knockouts, a better fighter than Clay.

His arm in a sling, and accompanied by a personal physician, Dr. Robert C. Bennett of Detroit, Liston quietly said that his big mistake was to throw everything in the first round.

He said he would have beaten Clay except for his arm injury, which Dr. Bennett said was a torn left biceps muscle.

Clay said that he would give Liston a rematch if "he wants one." Liston says he'll fight Clay again "if he gives me one."

None of the Clay ebullience was evident today, though some of the words were there. Directing his remarks at a press he feels sold him short, Clay said:

"I'm a wise man, a dignified man. You'd be surprised if you knew how wise I am. I talked up the greatest gate in history and you overlooked that I had the ability to back it up."

He also said that "for the right price I'd fight anyone in the world," later musing that he might retire. "I don't like to fight, don't like to hurt anybody. I just want to make a living and enjoy the good things in life."

He did not bad-mouth Liston, although he said Sonny never had hurt him and was constantly off-balance. He said that now that the fight was over there was no need to insult Liston, that that had been part of the whole act.

He led into his Black Muslim comments by stating his name was "magic" among the youth of the world and now people would listen to what he had to say.

Plans Not Firm

The new champion, who won the title in his 20th professional fight, seems to have no immediate plans. He may stay here for a few days, or he may drive in his bus to his home in Louisville, Ky.

Bill Faversham, head of the 11-man syndicate that owns Clay's contract, said that he had sold the promotional rights to Clay's next fight to Intercontinental Sports, Inc., a group in which Liston holds a 47½ per cent interest.

Clay's plans may very well be guided by the Muslims at this time. It was learned that his private victory party was held at Hampton House, a Miami motel, and one of the guests was Malcolm X.

February 27, 1964

GHANA REVERSES BOXING DECISION

Decrees Accra Fighter Won World Title Bout

By United Press International

ACCRA, Ghana, May 10—A Government agency today reversed the decision of last night's world featherweight championship bout here and gave the verdict to a Ghanaian.

Sugar Ramos of Cuba, the defending champion, originally had been awarded a split decision over Floyd Robertson at the Sports Arena in the first championship bout ever held at Accra. The decision was booed for several minutes by most of the crowd of 30,000.

The ruling of the Ghana Boxing Authority was the first reversal of a title bout decision in modern ring history. Immediately after the fight, the boxing authority ruled the bout "no contest."

Title Change Urged

Today it went a step further. It asked the World Boxing Association to recognize Robertson as the champion.

[In New York, Nat Fleischer of Ring Magazine, considered a leading American authority on boxing, said that "Ramos will still be considered champion." He said he would list him as such in his influential Ring Record Book.]

The Government of President Kwame Nkrumah had put up a guarantee of $150,000 to bring the bout to Ghana's capital. Ramos was assured of $50,000 and Robertson $10,000. No decision has been made on when

they will receive the money.

Ramos won the votes of the judges, but the referee gave the verdict to Robertson. Ed Lassman, of Miami Beach, the president of the World Boxing Association, and Ramon Valesquez of the Mexico Boxing Commission served as judges. The referee was Jack Hart of London.

The 24-year-old Ramos, who lives in Mexico City, was a 5-2 favorite. The 27-year-old Robertson knocked down the champion in the 13th round.

Jack Solomons of London promoted the fight. He called the original decision "incredible."

"This is robbery," he said. "Robertson won."

Special to The New York Times

ACCRA, Ghana, May 10 — Ohene Djan, Ghana's sports director, said before the reversal was announced today that the boxing authority would take into consideration "the total and absolute neutrality" of the British referee, Jack Hart, as against "the dramatic and irregular decision of the two American-based nominee judges of Sugar Ramos."

He said the authority would consider whether "the decision of the neutral referee should not outweigh that of the non-neutral judges."

Original Board a Failure

By GERALD ESKENAZI

The members of the original Ghana Boxing Authority were dismissed three months ago because they had failed to bring a title fight to Accra. Immediately afterward, a new six-man commission was formed.

In Washington, a spokesman for the Ghanian Government said on Sunday that the original commission—formed in 1960—had proved ineffective.

Sports in Ghana are controlled by the Central Organization of Sports. The C.O.S. is a Government agency whose members, according to the spokesman, are "fans." The boxing authority is an arm of the C.O.S.

Members of the authority do not work for the Government, but it is believed they generally accede to the Government's policy.

Boxing is becoming an increasingly popular sport in Ghana, although the quality of the fighters is generally poor. Like the other major sports in Ghana—soccer and cricket — boxing is subsidized by the Government.

Spokesman Is Doubtful

The spokesman, who did not wish his name to be used, said he didn't believe the reversal of the decision by his Government would be upheld.

"It seems to me it would be up to the World Boxing Association to make the final ruling. I find it hard to believe a local decision could outweigh the W.B.A.," he said.

It appears unlikely the W.B.A. will recognize Robertson. Abe Greene, the commissioner, said Sunday that "We would have to go with the ancient principle that officials are placed at a fight because they are competent."

Greene said any W.B.A. decision adverse to Robertson would not be an indication of unfriendly feeling to Ghana.

"We would take the same action if a member state here made the unilateral decision to change a verdict," he said.

For Ed Lassman, one of the judges, it marked the second time in three months one of his decisions had resulted in an international controversy.

It was Lassman who called upon the W.B.A. to strip Cassius Clay of recognition as the world heavyweight champion. His proposal brought antagonistic responses, especially from civil rights groups. One of Lassman's major reasons for wanting to deny recognition to Clay was Clay's membership in the so-called Black Muslims.

"It took a lot of guts for my dad to go to Africa after that." Lassman's son Everett said from Miami Beach on Sunday.

Lassman, because of his dual role of W.B.A. president and judge at the bout, will be placed in the position of reviewing his own decision.

There have been nine reversals of decisions in major bouts since 1897. Perhaps the most famous one involved Joey Giardello and Billy Graham in 1952.

Giardello won a split decision over Graham on Dec. 19, 1952, at Madison Square Garden. The decision was over-ruled by the New York Athletic Commission chairman, Robert K. Christenberry. Giardello brought the case before the State Supreme Court and the reversal was held invalid.

May 11, 1964

Philadelphian, 3 Russians and 3 Poles Gain Boxing Crowns

By JAMES ROACH

Special to The New York Times

TOKYO, Saturday, Oct. 24—Last night was fight night at the Olympics. The ten boxing titles were decided in a 5,000-seat skating and hockey rink called the Korakuen Ice Palace.

The winners included three Russians, three Poles, a Japanese who was thrown into the air several times by jubilant friends at ringside, and a Philadelphian who won the heavyweight title by a margin as thin as the sliced raw fish they serve as appetizers in Tokyo's Sushi Restaurant.

The heavyweight was the only finalist representing the United States—Joseph Frazier, whose nickname is Billy. He's a butcher boy by trade. He's 20 years old. He's a 6-footer. He weighs 195 pounds.

He beat a 30-year-old bus driver from Regensburg in Germany who is three inches taller, 10 pounds heavier and much less pugnacious.

The bus driver, Hans Huber, is a reformed wrestler. When he failed to get on the German Olympic wrestling team, he tried out for the boxing team and made it.

Huber retreated throughout the three-round bout. He backed and backed and backed. Frazier kept after him, forgot he had a right hand, and threw lefts repeatedly. Many missed.

Knockdown Hardly Counts

Olympic bouts are decided by five judges. The referee doesn't get a vote. The rules call for 20 points in each round to go to the more skillful boxer and proportionately fewer points to go to the opponent. The Olympic program says "amateur boxing places high value on technique and speed and does not attach importance to a strong blow or aggression." A knockdown counts no more than a good jab.

Huber's "to-the-rear, march" plan of campaign pleased two of the pacifists among the judges. They voted for him, 60—59 and 60—58. The three others voted for Frazier, 60—58.

Frazier got the chance to try for the gold medal here when America's No. 1 Olympic heavyweight, 293 - pound Buster Mathis, broke a knuckle.

Avery Brundage, the International Olympic Committee president, made a late arrival and presented the medals to the heavyweights in this next-to-last competitive program of the Tokyo games. Grand prix equestrian competition is the final event.

Four of Tokyo's prettiest girls, wearing four of Tokyo's prettiest kimonos, went into the ring carrying the medals on lacquer trays. In boxing, bronze medals go to both men beaten in the semi-finals by the gold medalist and the silver medalist.

7 Russians in Finals

The Soviet Union had seven finalists. Its winners were Stanislav Stepashkin of Moscow, a featherweight (125¾-pound maximum), Boris Lagutin of Moscow, a light middleweight (156 maximum), and Valery Popenchenko of Leningrad, a middleweight (165½).

Stepashkin officially beat Anthony N. Villanueva of the Philippines in a slashing bout that would have elicited cheers at any of New York's old fight pits. The Russian's nose bled. The Filipino's right cheekbone was cut and there was another cut over his right eye. The judges — from Italy, United

Arab Republic, Germany, Lebanon and Tunisia — picked Stepashkin, 3—2, and many in the crowd booed.

Villanueva cried. At trophy-presenting time, he got much more applause than Stepashkin.

Lagutin, in one of the best bouts, beat Joseph Gonzales of France. Popenchenko quickly finished Emil Schulz of Germany. Two right-hand punches floored Schulz, and the referee stepped in at 2:05 of the first round.

Schulz gladly sniffed smelling salts before walking over to get the silver medal.

The winning Poles who beat Soviet representatives in successive bouts were Jozef Grudzien, Jerzy Kulej and Marian

— that's right, Marian — Kasprzyk. In Olympic competition in previous years, Poland had a total of two gold medals.

Japanese Winner Soars

The Japanese winner, this nation's first in the history of Olympic boxing, was Takao Sakurai, a highly competent operator who had Shin Cho Chung of Korea so troubled in the second round that the referee called a halt. Friends of Sakurai grabbed him and his trainer in a corner of the ring after the medal presentation and joyously threw them into the air several times. Each time they caught them, too.

An Italian from Novara in the north of Italy beat a resident of Moscow in the light-heavy-

weight (178-pound maximum) final. The winner was Cosimo Pinto. The loser was Aleksei Kiseliov. These were two big, willing, clumsy, game hitters.

Italy had one other finalist, one other winner. He was the flyweight (112½ pounds) Fernando Atzori. He'd be right at home in the Aqueduct jockey room. He made four bows to the crowd when he was introduced, embraced his second when he won, then sobbed.

There were nine southpaws among the 20 finalists. Only three won—in bouts with other left-handers. These were in the bantam, feather and welter divisions. Two of the defeated leftists represented the Soviet Union.

October 24, 1964

Too Many Hands Often Spoil Boxing Pot of Gold

Even Bigger Purses Aren't So Big After the 'Cuts'

By ROBERT LIPSYTE

Traditionally, there is a pot of gold within punching range of every professional prizefighter. Actually, with the increasing revenues from such secondary rights as closed-circuit television, the gold is in greater abundance than ever. But, as always, the pot is dipped into by many hands.

From Cassius Clay, whose accountants have accountants, to the substitute preliminary boy in a borrowed robe, the fighter has legal right to more than half of the publicized purse. Personal contracts and secret deals may add to or subtract from the cash with which he goes home. For most, however, even the big pies turn out to be small potatoes.

Last week, after Madison Square Garden's first championship double-header, $190,000 in guarantees was distributed to four boxers. Willie Pastrano, who lost his light-heavyweight championship within 27 minutes of actual battle, got $100,000; José Torres, who should now command sizable purses as the new champion, got $10,000; Emile Griffith, who defended his welterweight title poorly but successfully, got $70,000, and José Stable, the night's biggest loser, got $10,000.

Stable, a 24-year-old Cuban immigrant who speaks no English, is, in many ways, typical of the middle-range fighter—a worthy, sometimes formidable, opponent with no particular drawing power. He earned $12,000 in purses for three main-

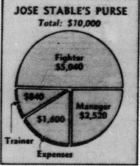

JOSE STABLE'S PURSE
Total: $10,000

Fighter $5,040
Manager $2,520
$840
$1,600
Trainer
Expenses

The New York Times   April 4, 1965

event fights last year (he won them all by knockouts). He lives in the Bronx, and his wife is expecting a second child. The $10,000 check—made out by the Garden to Stable and to his manager, Manny Gonzalez—represented his biggest payday.

José Stable will not get fat on that check. Before he even sees it, about $1,600 will be siphoned off to pay his training expenses. The largest item is for $720, paid to four sparring partners who allowed themselves to be punched for food, room and between $30 and $50 a day. The figure might have been much higher, but Stable has a reputation for punching hard, and sparring partners were difficult to get—so difficult, in fact, that Gonzalez, often allowed sparring rounds to go four minutes instead of the usual three.

Stable and Gonzalez got a break on food and lodging because it was the offseason and Kutsher's Country Club, an expensive hostelry, was looking for publicity. Gonzalez reports that the only expense there was $240 for tips and incidentals. Tickets

for the fight for family and friends cost $270.

Rubbing oils and vitamin pills cost $20, the services of a personal physician and a masseur $100. Such pieces of equipment as sweaters, a mouthpiece, two light punching bags and white sweaters for the men in Stable's corner came to $157.04, according to Gonzalez. Then there were tips for Garden attendants, a commission license and meals and a room in a New York hotel the night before the fight.

Similar expenses for a champion or a leading contender would be much higher. A champion has more tickets to buy and has to spend more money on sparring partners. He may also have two brothers-in-law (one a third assistant trainer, the other his gin rummy partner) on the payroll, an enormous telephone bill and a large entertainment bill.

The $8,400 Stable had after his expenses was decreased by 10 per cent—pay for Victor Valle, his chief trainer (who paid HIS assistant from that). According to the rules of the New York State Athletic Commission, the remaining $7,560 was then split between the fighter (two-thirds or $5,040) and the manager ($2,520).

As he does with most of his fighters, Gonzalez controls Stable's bank account. He had promised Stable $1,000 in cash for a victory. Because Stable lost, Gonzalez gave him $540 from Stable's percentage. The remaining $4,500 will be doled out to Stable at a rate of $70 a week. When the new baby is born, Gonzalez will increase the allowance to $85 or $90.

While every fighter and manager has a different private arrangement—depending upon who is more essential to the relationship—the breakdown on expenses and income is more or less standard. The manager of a preliminary boy

José Stable, whose purse from recent fight with Emile Griffith was cut just about in half by expenses.

who gets between $150 and $500 for a fight may let the fighter keep the entire purse until he is making enough to "cut."

A top fighter's manager is sometimes a front for a business syndicate, perhaps for a man whose underworld reputation prevents him from getting a license, or for the fighter himself. In this case, there might be kickback arrangements so complex as to leave somebody with nothing but an impressive Internal Revenue Service bill.

Closed-circuit television has in recent years added a new dimension, both for honest income and possible chicanery, to the dispersal of boxer's gold. The control of a championship promotion can be worth millions. When Inter-Continental Sports paid $50,000 for the right to promote Cassius Clay's first post-Sonny Liston fight, the group was not so much assuring Liston a rematch if he lost as it was assuring itself a continued hold on the heavyweight title, whatever the outcome.

Allegedly, José Torres was caught in the same kind of squeeze as Clay. Before Torres got a shot at Pastrano's title, his financial backers had to guarantee a Miami Beach promoter the right to Torres's first title defense, if he won. The promoter, Chris Dundee, is the brother of Pastrano's manager, Angelo Dundee.

Some managers earn their cut by booking their fighters shrewdly, others hold them in thrall through tight contracts made early in their careers. More and more often these days, fighters' affairs are being handled by non-fight men.

"Lawyers," says Joey Giardello, the middleweight champion who is handled by one, "are the best thing that ever

happened to boxers."

Frankie Narvaez, a fair lightweight, is managed by a young Wall Street broker; Ernie Terrell, the World Boxing Association's heavyweight champion, by the president of a small New York union; George Chuvalo by the Toronto businessman who once employed his mother, and Rubin (Hurricane) Carter by a deputy prison warden.

Many so-called "advisers," however, are neither benevolent Bernard Baruchs nor substitute fathers. Floyd Patterson's adviser, Al Bolan, is his personal promoter; men seen in the inner circles of other past and present champions have been reported to

be everything from neighborhood buddies to liaison officers from the Mafia.

While there are many fighters—Rocky Marciano, Rocky Graziano, Jack Dempsey, Gene Tunney, Ingemar Johansson, to name a few—who got out of the business with their wits and their wallets, there are many, many fighters who walk out of boxing on their heels.

Why?

First of all, as Tommy (Hurricane) Jackson, a leading heavyweight contender who has been shining shoes, pointed out, there is no pension fund or other provision for a boxer's post-bellum future.

Secondly, boxers are usually content to leave financial matters to managers who may be honest, but no more astute than they are. If the manager is dishonest, forget it.

But perhaps most important of all is the nature of the game itself, with its get-rich, bust-out structure. On the day the check comes through—whether it is for $10,000 or $100,000—it is easy for the boxer, the manager, the brother-in-law and the fan to take it at face value, and live up to it.

April 4, 1965

Laguna Wins Lightweight Title, Outpointing Ortiz in 15 Rounds

By The Associated Press

PANAMA CITY, Panama, April 10—Ismael Laguna, relatively unknown outside his native Panama, upset Carlos Ortiz and became the lightweight champion of the world tonight, scoring a 15-round decision in their title bout.

Ortiz, a Puerto Rican-born New Yorker, weighed 134¾ pounds for his fifth defense of the title he won from Joe Brown three years ago. Laguna came in at 132, three pounds under the class limit.

Jersey Joe Walcott, the former heavyweight champion who was the referee, voted for Laguna, as did a Panamanian judge. The other judge, Ben

Greene of New York, called it a draw.

Laguna, a 21-year-old from Colon, opened a cut over Ortiz's eye in the sixth, survived Ortiz's furious rally in the ninth and mixed it freely with the champion in the last two rounds.

The defeat ended Ortiz's 12-bout winning streak that began before he won the title from Brown in Las Vegas in 1962. He had defended the title four times successfully since then. In his last previous defense, a year ago in San Juan, P. R., he had defeated Kenny Lane of Muskegon, Mich.

Many of Laguna's followers jumped into the ring as soon as the fight had ended, certain that he had won. The announcement of the decision was delayed several minutes until the ring was cleared.

Laguna has a record of 38 victories in 40 bouts, but most of his previous 39 bouts were against little-known Panamanian opponents.

He had always fought as a featherweight and this bout was his first in the lightweight class. His speed helped him win the title from the 28-year-old Ortiz, whose record is 44-5 with one no-decision.

A crowd of 18,000 saw the bout at the Olympic Stadium.

The fight originally was scheduled for Feb. 15, but was postponed the day before when Ortiz suffered a stomach ailment.

April 11, 1965

Clay Knocks Out Liston in One Minute; Bout, Like First, Ends in Controversy

BY ROBERT LIPSYTE
Special to The New York Times

LEWISTON, Me., May 25—Cassius Clay retained the heavyweight championship tonight when he knocked out Sonny Liston in the first round of their rematch in the schoolboy hockey arena here.

Radio and television observers timed the knockout at 1 minute 42 seconds, but Maine boxing officials said it came at one minute. However, the bout, which slipped from the control of Jersey Joe Walcott, the referee, was not declared over until 2 minutes 17 seconds had elapsed. Clay and Liston actually squared off to fight again after it was over.

It will be listed as the fastest knockout on record in a heavyweight title bout, but some of the 4,280 spectators yelled "Fake, fake, fake!" Many were as angered by the controversial ending as were those who witnessed the confusing finish of their first bout 15 months ago.

The punch—a short right hand—that sent the 215¼-pound Liston to the canvas for the first time in his career did not seem to have knockout power.

It all happened something like this:

Clay, weighing 204 pounds, leaped out at the opening bell, skipping forward in his high white shoes, his 8-ounce red

gloves far in front of him.

He connected immediately with a right to Liston's head, then a left, Liston seemed to shake off the blows, as the crowd, for once, cheered for him.

For what seemed longer than the official 48 fighting seconds, Clay danced around Liston, counter-clockwise, jabbing him lightly, once more connecting with a solid right. Then he fired the short right and missed with a left hook as Liston sagged to his knees.

Liston collapsed slowly, like a falling building, piece by piece, rolling onto his back, then flat on his stomach, his face pressed against the canvas. Clay danced around him, waving at him, taunting him.

ing at him, taunting him.

Walcott, once the heavyweight champion, tried to wave Clay to a neutral corner. In doing so, he apparently lost the knock-down count being made by Francis McDonough across the ring.

As Walcott turned and leaned toward McDonough, Liston began to climb heavily to his feet.

Count Goes On

McDonough, a retired Portland printer, continued to count as Liston got back up to his knees, then went down again. McDonough reached the count of 12 before he and Walcott made contact.

By then, Liston was up again, squaring off with Clay and ready to fight. Walcott, confused, rushed across the ring and grabbed Clay. He held up Clay's arm, and Clay's entourage poured into the ring.

Liston merely dropped his hands to his sides and stood impassively.

Few in the sparse crowd in the cement-block Central Maine Youth Center realized what had happened.

The immediate confusion was much like that of the night in Miami Beach when Clay won the title. For six rounds that night Clay outboxed Liston bob-

bing out of range of long left hooks.

He opened a cut under Liston's left eye, but did not seem to do too much real damage to the so-called "ugly bear," who had twice scored one-round knockouts over Floyd Patterson.

Liston Stayed in Corner

But Liston never answered the bell for the seventh, remaining on his stool as the Miami crowd leaped, screaming, to its feet. Later, Liston said he had injured his left arm in the first round and was unable to use it.

Tonight there was the same kind of consternation. As the crowd surged forward against a cordon of state and city policemen — some yelling "Fix! Fix!"—Clay stood against the blue velvet ropes, telling the fans to "shaddup," telling them that his victory was a triumph of the "righteous life."

He said the winning blow was the "anchor punch," the secret weapon of the late Jack Johnson, taught to Clay by Stepin Fetchit, the 73-year-old comedian and old-time movie actor now in Clay's entourage.

The punch, said Clay, is part karate, part corkscrew.

Liston said the punch did not hurt him as much as other punches had in his life, but it caught him high on the right

cheekbone. Walcott, swamped by his first major refereeing assignment, said the winning punch was a left to the jaw and that it was followed by a right to the body.

"It was the easiest payday I ever had," Clay yelled from the ring. "I told you I had a surprise."

He had, indeed, said through the final days of training that he had a surprise. But he had refused to make a prediction because, he said, people might have thought the fight was fixed when his prediction came true.

Relaxed Through Week

He had been supremely relaxed, even through a week of rumors that Black Muslim defectors were en route from New York to kill him in revenge for the murder of Malcom X. The rumor grew stronger when two New York City homicide detectives arrived here and said that several of the defectors were "missing from their usual haunts."

Clay, guarded by several Black Muslims, maintained that the rumors had no effect on him, but were scaring Liston. Clay seemed always to be thinking past tonight's bout toward his next—with Floyd Patterson, "that Rabbit, with a habit of getting knocked out."

More Muslims, from Boston and New York, joined city, county, state and Federal officers scanning the crowd as it came in tonight. The Muslims also took pictures of the policemen, who were searching women's handbags and all packages and suitcases.

Clay, a member of the Black Muslim sect, went into the ring wearing a robe bearing his Muslim name: Muhammad Ali. He was introduced from the ring by that name.

Under Maine rules, Walcott would have had no vote had the bout gone to a decision. Three judges arrive at the verdict. The judges, all from Maine, were Joe Bovin, Russ Leonard and Coley Welch.

In one preliminary bout, Mike Bruce, 192½, of Westfield, Mass., outpointed Freddie Brown, 206½, New York, in six rounds.

Rudy Clay, the champion's brother who goes by the name of Ramanthan Ali, knocked out Buster Reed, 174½, of Louisville, Ky., in 58 seconds of the second round of a scheduled six-rounder. Clay weighed 186.

Joe Turnbow, 203, of Paterson, N.J., outpointed Cody Jones, 209, of Detroit, in six rounds.

Jim Ellis, 176, of Louisville, Ky., won by a technical knockout in 1:04 of the first round over Joe

THE END: Clay sneers at the abject challenger after knocking him down with a short right to the jaw

Blackwood, New York, in a scheduled six-rounder.

The weight-in was taped by SportsVision for inclusion in closed-circuit telecasts of the fight. More than 500 persons, the majority local residents on their lunch hours, watched from the permanent hockey seats around the rectangular arena. Few of them expected to attend the fight.

Liston Makes Appearance

It was a Liston crowd. At 12:31, an announcement that this would be the first title fight to be shown behind the Iron Curtain was drowned in a roar for the shuffling, sullen-faced former champion enwrapped in a white and gold silk robe. Liston was accompanied to the ring by two Androscoggin County officers, his trainers—Willy Reddish and Teddy King—and Ash Resnick, a well-known Las Vegas figure.

The crowd began to boo as Clay walked in, wearing a white terrycloth robe with Muhammad Ali written in red across the back. His entourage included Angelo Dundee, his manager, and Drew (Budini) Brown, his trainer.

Liston waited quietly in the ring while the Maine Boxing Commission tried to clear it. Supposedly, each fighter was to be accompanied only by two seconds and one commission doctor. Clay shadow-boxed as he waited. The fans on one side of the arena, under a huge sign proclaiming this an Inter-Continental Promotion, Inc. spectacular, began to yell at Clay, led by half a dozen roughly dressed young men.

"You'd better bring your pillow, Clay."

"Who is the greatest?. . .Sonny Liston."

Clay snorted as he jabbed and hooked and sent an occasional short right to the air, dancing about on black leather slippers. The three commissioners bumped into the two doctors, who pushed their way among clutches of hangers-on, mostly Liston's. Sam Margolis, the Philadelphia vending-machine operator and friend of under-world figures, sweated profusely under the glaring television lights. The Lewiston residents yelled. Liston was without expression. Clay pummeled the air.

"Hey, Muhammad, your camel's double-parked," yelled a youth.

Liston's weight was first announced as 219½ and Clay pinched his own lean flanks, pointed at Liston, and said: "Fat." Eventually, a plywood board was brought to balance the wobbly floor under the scale and Liston came off more than four pounds lighter. Clay leaned over Liston as he got off the scale and Liston shoved him away with a bent right wrist to the chest.

Clay was then weighed. The crowd booed when the champion flexed his considerable muscles at them. Then he turned to Liston, yelling, "you're in trouble."

THE AFTERMATH: Joe Walcott, the referee, raises Clay's left hand amid pandemonium

Associated Press Wirephotos

According to Margolis, Liston replied: "You shut that big mouth, I'll take care of you tonight."

And Teddy King yelled to Clay. "You won't be as lucky as you were in Miami."

Clay said to King: "I'll take care of him in six."

"Don't bull me," said Liston.

The dozens in the ring swirled back and forth and all around. When George Russo, the commission chairman, called the champion over, the young heavy-weight snarled, "don't call me no Clay."

A moment later, Clay was posing with Liston, the older man's right cocked for a haymaker, the younger's left and right flicking in and out.

"Hit him, Liston" yelled the crowd, and Sonny smiled for the first time.

The weigh-in was drab in comparison with the famous mad scene Clay staged 15 months ago in Miami beach. That afternoon, a commission doctor said that Clay was "scared to death." Clay went on to score a technical knockout and win the championship when Liston did not respond to the bell starting the seventh round.

Today, both doctors had only nice things to say. Dr. Leo Lemieux said that Clay was "normal" and his pulse was 72; Dr. Ralph Turgeon said Liston was in "fine shape," his pulse 60. After the weigh-in, the arena was cleared except for authorized personnel, and, according to Robert Nilon the Inter-Continental president, "searched from top to bottom."

May 26, 1965

Clay Knocks Out Patterson in the 12th And Keeps Heavyweight Championship

By ROBERT LIPSYTE
Special to The New York Times

LAS VEGAS, Nev., Nov. 22— Like a little boy pulling off the wings of a butterfly piecemeal, Cassius Clay mocked and humiliated and punished Floyd Patterson for almost 12 rounds tonight until the referee halted their heavyweight championship bout because the challenger was "outclassed."

After 2 minutes 18 seconds of the 12th round at the Convention Center, Harry Krauss, a local blackjack dealer, threw his body in front of Patterson's and the 30-year-old New York-er's attempt at a third world championship was—blissfully— over. It will go into the record books, of course, as a knockout.

It was bravura showmanship, a tour de force, but a sad and hopeless fight. From the moment the 23-year-old Clay stepped into the ring, cheered

only· by his Black Muslim cohorts who call him Muhammad Ali, he dominated the stage with contemptuous waves at Patterson, with jabs just hard enough to rock Patterson's head back, with rights just hard enough to hasten the swelling of Patterson's bewildered face.

Later, they would say that Patterson's back went out in the fourth round, and it is true that Patterson crouched after that. They said that Clay injured his right hand in the eighth from hitting Patterson so often, and it is true that he used his left more often in the later rounds. But from the beginning, Patterson had no chance against his bigger, younger, faster, stronger opponent. He could only hang on, wobbly but game, to take the slow punishment.

He had to stand there, weak and shaky, as Clay screamed, "No contest, get me a contender." And he had to keep trying with his only chance, a leaping left hook, although Clay easily danced away from it every time.

In the days before this fight, Clay and Angelo Dundee, his manager, had talked about buying Patterson a new hat because his head would be "so lumped up after the fight." Dundee had talked of his anger at Patterson for playing the Great Crusader, who was going to snatch the heavyweight title from the unworthy head of this loud-mouthed Muslim after Patterson had dodged rightful contenders through the years of his own championship. And Clay

had talked of this fool who was trying to create a religious war between Islam and Catholicism.

It seemed as if all Clay wanted to do tonight, before 7,402 paying spectators including several movie stars, was destroy Patterson forever as a boxer and as a dignified human being. Patterson's blind courage preserved some of his dignity, but it will be hard to ever think of him as a fighter again.

He was so small in that ring, extra-brightly-lit for some 500,-000 closed-circuit television viewers. Clay is 6 feet 3 inches tall, 3 inches taller than Patterson, and, at 210 pounds, 13¼ pounds heavier. He loomed above the man he mocked from the first round, standing tall, his hands low, his dancing feet moving from side to side, back and forth, as though loosening up for a training session.

The odds were 3-1 that Clay would win, but the sentimentalists, who wanted Patterson, outnumbered the gamblers.

Clay Shakes His Head

They screamed joyfully in that first round as Patterson rode in low to vainly pummel Clay's belly. And Clay looked out at the crowd, and shook his head.

"Watch it," he yelled at Patterson as he fired in his jabs, flicking them out until, in the second round, Patterson slipped to a knee.

"Boop, boop, boop," he called through his mouthpiece as the jab flicked out, just a little pain at a time. By the third round, Patterson was flat-footed, tired and missing open and haughty invitations at Clay's curling lip. Patterson was just pushing his hands in front of him like a sick man trying to wipe a foggy bathroom mirror. In the fourth, Clay shouted something about "knockdown"

to Patterson, and the referee yelled, "Shut up."

By the fifth, boop, boop, boop, the jab was shooting in at will, and Clay landed 19 jabs before Patterson reached and gently swatted his chest. Patterson had not landed a decent punch through the first five rounds.

In the sixth, it finally seemed as if this cruel dance was over. Clay opened up, slamming in left jabs at will, following with hooks and crosses until Patterson's head was snapping back and forth, until his mouth hung slack. Clay kept him wobbly, off-balance, until Patterson sank slowly to one knee like a nail slipping into melting butter. The mandatory 8 count was interrupted at 5 because Clay had not moved to a neutral corner fast enough.

Gloves Caress Face

Later, Clay was to say that Patterson was a good fighter, that he fought well. He would deny that he had carried Patterson through those 12 brutal rounds. But in that sixth round, it seemed as though Clay purposefully took his time going to a corner, afraid that he had jerked the butterfly's wings too hard.

Patterson got up, groggy, walking on his heels. And Clay treated him more gently now, red gloves caressing the swelling face in a gentle tempo. Through the next rounds, Clay let up. Dancing backward as the challenger stumbled after him, cocking his head away as Patterson missed with long and weary hooks.

Thus Patterson couldn't see and couldn't jump, as he staggered after Clay, and once in a great while he landed a long right, at the tailend of its force. And Clay would shake

his head, and punish Patterson for such presumption with a couple of flicking jabs, a few quick hooks.

They had to lower Patterson to his stool after the later rounds, and his handlers blocked his view so he couldn't see Clay's contemptuous waves. Clay relaxed in the eight and ninth and 10th, and toyed with Patterson, and poked him and stuck him and mocked him with his dancing legs.

And the crowd screamed for Clay to put him away, to knock him out, to stop torturing this man whose last few years have been filled with shame. They screamed as Patterson, a man who has run away from defeat in a mustache and beard, staggered after Clay, hardly seeing him as his eyes closed. Now bow-legged, now knock-kneed, Patterson staggered on as his legs no longer were strong enough—his body crouched and suddenly soft and vulnerable.

In the 12th, near the end, Clay was shaking his head at Patterson's futile efforts. The champion was throwing right jabs and left jabs and changing the pattern and the tempo and glaring down at the buckling Patterson, who slowly, painfully was punching at a phantom that wasn't there, as if he were in another fight.

"Put him away, Clay," yelled the white customers. "Knock him out, Ali," screamed the Muslims.

The Dealer Calls Bout

It was Krauss, the blackjack dealer, who stopped it. "He was taking too much punishment," said Krauss. But by the 12th round it was really too late. The crowd booed, a little sickened, and the shaven-headed Muslims screamed and clapped and charged the ring. The helmeted policemen got there at the same time, and there was a brief scuffle, a Muslim was hurled bodily out of the ring, down the steps and into a crowd of his brothers.

Some of the crowd cheered at that.

Krauss, who was escorted from the arena by policemen, had scored the fight 54-44 for 11 rounds, under the state of Nevada 5-point must system by which the winner of a round gets 5 points, the loser proportionately less. He had awarded the 11th round to Patterson. The terrible slaughter of the sixth round was 5-3, Clay, on Krauss's scorecard.

Judge Bill Stremmel of Reno scored the fight, 54-45, giving Patterson only the first round. He scored the sixth round, 5-3, the fourth even and all the rest 5-4. Judge Harold Buck of Las Vegas scored it 54-44. Buck also gave Patterson the first round. It was 5-3 Clay in the sixth on his scorecard, 5-4 for the other rounds.

Not in Friendly Sweden

This fight, Patterson's 49th as a professional in 13 years, was supposed to be a new and glorious chapter in his life. He had lost only four times before —once to Joey Maxim in 1954, once to Ingemar Johansson in 1959, and twice, by one-round knockouts, to Sonny Liston, in 1963 and 1964.

He had avenged the Johansson defeat by beating the Swede twice, and becoming the first heavyweight to regain his title. This fight was to be his redemption for the Liston defeats, and he prepared by beating four nonentities (three of them in friendly Sweden), and George Chuvalo, in New York.

Patterson said, after the fight, that Clay had never really hurt him, that he never felt in danger. He said that he would not use his back injury—a muscle spasm in the lumbar region of his lower back—as an excuse.

Clay, who has won all of his 22 professional fights, berated the press at his post-fight news conference. He praised Patterson, but challenged the press to come up with an excuse for his victory, an alibi to downgrade both him and his opponent. He said he would fight every three months, and said that he didn't care who.

The live gate was $300,011.

A chill rain swept Las Vegas through the day, and by fight time the airport was closed and cars were moving warily through the broad streets. The airport shutdown kept many scheduled last-minute arrivals from making the fight, including Elizabeth Taylor and Richard Burton.

On hand early were at least a hundred members of the Nation of Islam, Clay's adopted sect, better known as Black Muslims. Members of the so-called Fruit of Islam, with shaven skulls and red ties, moved around the arena as a kind of unofficial perimeter guard. More than 100 official law enforcement men were on hand, too.

Tickets were still available, for $100 and $50 seats, an hour before the fight. Although a sell-out has been predicted all week, there were many empty seats when Amos (Big Train) Lincoln and Thad (Babe) Spencer opened the night's fighting with a scheduled 10-round heavyweight semi-final.

The Lincoln-Spencer bout was booked to assure closed-circuit television viewers of at least two rounds of boxing. Three of the previous four heavyweight title fights' had ended in the first round.

Lincoln, a former sparring partner of Sonny Liston, and Spencer are both in the top 10 of most boxing rating lists. Both are heavyweights, and both are being groomed as possible title challengers.

Spencer opened a cut over Lincoln's left eye in the first round, but a few rounds later Big Train, encouraged by Spencer's slip to the canvas, pounded the smaller heavyweight with enthusiastic but awkward combinations.

By the later rounds, neither Spencer nor Lincoln, despite some pretty good punching ability, mounted any kind of sustained attack.

By the seventh round, the early arrivals had resumed looking around for more peaceful entertainers— big, blond showgirls with hard and varnished faces; light-stepping, tightly-trousered strip dancers, and an interchangeable procession of portly, baldish men striding down the aisles accompanied by cigar-smoke clouds and women who could eat apples off their heads.

There was also heavy betting would Eddie Fisher sing the national anthem as well as Robert Goulet did in Lewiston, Me., last May?

Goulet, in town for the fight, has been picked on every time he has entered a hotel lounge with an insulting comedian on stage.

Not only did Goulet read from a hand-card last May, but he blew the words. Fisher broke up his Riviera Hotel audience the other night by announcing that he had been prepping for his big moment with Goulet's help. The speculation subsided again in the last two rounds as Lincoln picked up the pace of the draggy fight, and managed to put two punches consecutively into Spencer's face.

Now and then even Frank Sinatra, sitting behind Billy Conn in the second row of the $100 ringside seats, stopped cracking up Dean Martin and Joey Bishop long enough to look up.

Lincoln was awarded the decision, 138-136, probably on the basis of those rounds.

November 23, 1965

Clay: A Ring Mystery

His Mockery of Sport, and Black Muslim Role Make Future of Boxing Uncertain

By ROBERT LIPSYTE
Special to The New York Times

SAN FRANCISCO, Nov. 27—Cassius Clay or Muhammad Ali, this bright, vain, talented, opportunistic 23-year-old will probably remain heavyweight champion of the world for some time to come, if it pleases him. What does boxing have, how did it come about, and where does it go from here?

First of all, the industry itself is not completely sure that Clay is the best thing that ever happened to it. Many of the sport's businessmen were hoping that Floyd Patterson would win in Las Vegas last week, returning the championship to predictable, money-hungry hands.

Secondly, many of the sport's commentators, fans and peripheral devotees were horrified at what they called the "mockery" Clay has made of what they say they believe is a fine and noble pursuit.

And, third, many people—white, black, fans and non-fans—believe that Clay's affiliation with the so-called Black Muslim movement has given a basically antisocial element a sporting pulpit from which to disseminate dogma and gather recruits.

Views of Champion

These three views of Clay add up to one half-truthful picture of the heavyweight champion. Obviously, he does not have Patterson's greed for money and material possessions. He never toned down his Muslim affiliation, although it cost him millions in endorsements, appearances and television and recording contracts.

And yet the publicity he has received—wider in scope than any other modern fighter—has created a greater public awareness of boxing than ever before, and hypoed the closed-circuit revenues of the last three title fights, each of which should logically have been a turkey.

Obviously, his sometimes bizarre performances have contrasted sharply with the public humility and professional savagery invested in other great fighters. One former champion, Rocky Marciano, has contended that Clay has created a climate in which young people don't treat the Rock with the same deference that their elders do.

And yet few still maintain —after the brilliant, well-conceived display of pure skill last week—that Clay is not the most gifted fighter of his time. There are many now, like Cus D'Amato, who say that Clay might have beaten Marciano and Dempsey and Louis in their primes. Clay says he could have beaten them all.

Muslim Role Hurts

His Muslim membership is unfortunate. Patterson has equated it with membership in the Ku Klux Klan, and many people feel it is a disservice to the revolution in civil rights. And yet others, some of whom don't like it any better than Patterson does, feel it makes perfect sense in the context of this unusual champion.

After all, they say, here is a boxer who turned professional after a thorough grounding in his trade, more than 100 amateur fights capped by an Olympic Gold Medal. He got himself a syndicate of liquor and advertising barons to sponsor him, and one of the most successful and best-connected managers in the business, Angelo Dundee, to train him.

From the beginning, he manipulated the press by charming them in private and boasting extravagantly in public. Sinister or saintly, Cassius Clay was good and easy copy.

Then, say his sympathizers, he looked around. Joe Louis, who always gets the big hand, was no model for a young Negro fighter—Louis has no real money of his own and is always available to dress up somebody else's promotion for walking around money. Patterson was hung up on what Clay calls "white man's religion," and was a slave to his neuroses and possessions. He was an emotional fugitive. Sugar Ray Robinson was fighting for peanuts at this time, Sonny Liston was an illiterate ex-convict and you had to search to find Jersey Joe Walcott, Ezzard Charles and the others.

The Muslims offered Clay a different kind of religion, a status within a community, a bastion from which to sortie into a world he felt was hostile toward him. Although the Muslims did not publicly claim him until he became champion, Clay was receiving instruction for years before he beat Liston.

With this emotional backing, and a realization that he had to use boxing harder than it used him, he opened the greatest personal publicity campaign in the history of sports. He says now that he wanted people to hate him, so they would come to his fights to see him knocked out. More likely, he was somewhat confused and hurt when his pitch for attention was not accepted in the same joyful spirit it was conceived. This, probably, drove him irrevocably into the Muslim fold.

The showmanship was taken badly because the public— through the press—was not ready to receive the antithesis of Louis and Patterson. Once before it had been presented with a nonconforming Negro champion, and society rejected, harassed and eventually persecuted Jack Johnson.

Trapped by Own Plan

So Clay was caught in his own plan. His showmanship got him the first Liston fight, and the basic hypocrisy of boxing—in this case a return-bout clause — got him the second fight. Patterson was dredged up for the third fight, and the promotion abetted the Holy War undertones of the match because it was all good box office. Boxing men would like to have "mixed matches," but if they can't have white against black, they will gladly settle for Eastern versus Western religions.

As long as there is money in it for someone, Clay will

be matched again. There has been a great deal of snide comment about Ernie Terrell, the 6-foot, 6-inch World Boxing Association champion, a man with little heart they say, gangster connections, and an inept right hand. But let there be a chance for a Terrell-Clay bout, and the favorable comparison of his left jab to Louis's left jab will fill the land.

So far, everything Clay has done professionally has turned out right for himself. He has won all his prizefights and he is up there with the Beatles as a world attraction. He has not always been a winner emotionally—Clay is seeking an annulment from his wife, and his early teacher, Malcolm X, was murdered.

But, Madison Square Garden, its boxing department on shaky ground, wants to do business with him, and the Louisville Sponsoring Group is wondering what it's going to do when its last option on Clay runs out next October. As long as he can keep his fists flying and his mouth running, Cassius Clay can defect to Mars and turn Trotzkyite and the boxing world, palms up, will play any game that pleases him.

November 28, 1965

Griffith Outpoints Tiger in Garden 15-Rounder and Wins Middleweight Title

NIGERIAN SUFFERS FIRST KNOCKDOWN

Griffith Floors Him in Ninth on Way to Gaining Close, Unanimous Decision

By DEANE McGOWEN

Emile Griffith, the 27-year-old welterweight boxing champion, turned a sports axiom around last night at Madison Square Garden by winning the middleweight title from Dick Tiger in a close 15-round bout.

Griffith, who spotted the 160-pound Tiger 9½ pounds, showed that a good little man could beat a good big man.

The decision was unanimous. Thus Griffith, who was born in St. Thomas, V.I., and has been a professional boxer nine years, became the third 147-pound king to succeed to the heavier title. Sugar Ray Robinson and Carmen Basilio also did it. Mickey Walker, Henry Armstrong, Kid Gavilan and the late Benny Paret failed.

The referee, Arthur Mercante, voted for Griffith, nine rounds to five, with one even. Judge Frank Forbes scored seven rounds for Griffith, six for Tiger and called two even. Tony Castellano, the other judge, voted for Griffith by the margin of a single point. He gave each seven rounds and called one even, but favored Griffith, 8 to 7, under the supplementary point system used in such cases.

Griffith, who had predicted he would catch up with Tiger in the later rounds, almost did so. After jabbing and moving away from Tiger's powerful left hook and solid right hand in the early rounds, Griffith changed his tactics with the start of the eighth, becoming more aggressive.

Hard Smash to Chin

The switch almost caught Tiger, the 2-1 favorite, for keeps. In the ninth Griffith dropped him with a hard right to the chin.

Tiger bounced up almost immediately. The knockdown time-

Emile Griffith connects with a right to Dick Tiger's chin to floor him for the first time

keeper, Johnny LoBianco, who is also a referee, said he had counted to 3, at which point Mercante picked up the count. It was the first time Tiger had ever been knocked down.

Tiger, standing, shook his head to clear the cobwebs while taking the mandatory 8-count that had been declared in effect. Then the fighters closed again. Tiger caught another right to the chin and lurched forward, almost off balance.

But the stocky Nigerian managed to keep his feet. That was by far the best action round of the fight and certainly the best for Griffith.

Except for the eighth and ninth rounds, Griffith had waged a cautious battle all the way. It was his plan to make the older man follow him, using up his strength. And it worked.

The challenger was content to box and run. When he moved into close range, he invariably was outgunned by Tiger in the exchanges, forced to yield ground or clinch.

The decision was received with cheers, mingled with boos, from the partisans in the crowd of 14,934.

Tiger's fans thought his superior punching power and relentless stalking should have counted more in his favor.

His First Defense

A ringside poll of sportswriters gave Tiger a big margin. Seventeen thought the Nigerian had won, while five saw Griffith as the victor.

Thus the Tiger, in his first defense of the title he regained from Joey Giardello here last October, gave up his crown again.

But his financial remuneration might have eased his pain. He had

166

been guaranteed $75,000 or 40 per cent of the net receipts. Griffith, to get the title shot, had to settle for a flat 20 per cent. The gate receipts alone totaled $147,536. In addition, there was revenue from a television hook-up in some 60 cities, with New York blacked out.

By winning, Griffith ran his record to 50 victories against seven defeats and one no-contest fight. Tiger, a professional for 14 years, lost his 15th fight. He has won 54 and fought three draws. He has a wife and six children back home in Aba.

Before the fight Griffith had said that, should he win, he would seek legal action to restrain the State Athletic Commission from forcing him to vacate the welterweight crown. Under Commission regulations, a fighter cannot hold two titles at one time.

Griffith and his managers, Gil Clancy and Howard Albert, contend he can properly defend at both weights within the six-month time limit imposed by the regulations. They also say it is "unreasonable to strip a champion of a title he did not lose in the ring."

In a four-round preliminary bout, Clyde Taylor, 161, of the Bronx defeated Rocky Halliday, 159½, of Wilkes-Barre, Pa.

In an eight-rounder, Candy McFarland, 157, of Philadelphia, outpointed Teddy Pagan, 161, of the Bronx.

In another eight-rounder Victor Melendez, 135, of Puerto Rico defeated Jose Colon, 130¾, of Puerto Rico.

April 26, 1966

The New York Times (by Larry Morris)

Griffith, after winning title, is lifted by Johnny Addie, left, announcer, and his handlers

Sports of The Times

By ARTHUR DALEY

Delayed Action Bombs

BILLY CONN, the referee, could never be described as one of those nice Nellies who flinch at the sight of blood. Before he won the light-heavyweight championship, the saucy and bellicose Billy the Kid had been something of a rowdy brawler as a youth and compassion was not one of his more notable qualities. Yet he acted with complete propriety and correctness in Mexico City Saturday after Carlos Ortiz, a Puerto Rican living in new York, had opened a wicked gash over the left eye of Sugar Ramos, a Cuban living in Mexico.

Conn stopped the fight in the fifth round, awarding the bout on a technical knockout to Ortiz, the lightweight champion of the blooming universe, because he said "Ramos was in danger of suffering permanent injury." That should have ended the matter. Unfortunately it didn't. Repercussions have been reverberating ever since.

The emotionally charged gathering of 35,000 persons in the El Torea bullring reacted violently to what they considered a gross miscarriage of justice for their idol, Ramos. They rioted. They hurled coins, bottles and rocks into the ring. They climbed through the ropes and carried on in disgraceful fashion as Ortiz, escorted by a flying wedge of policemen, escaped to his dressing room.

United Press International

Carlos Ortiz leaving the ring after the bout in Mexico City was stopped.

The Second Trigger

Half an hour later, Ramon Velazquez, secretary of the World Boxing Council—whatever that is—appeased the mob by announcing that he had overruled the referee. Because Ortiz had flatly refused to return to the ring for a resumption of the bout, Velazquez had awarded the championship to Ramos.

This triggered another riot on Sunday as about 2,000 protesting Puerto Ricans stormed a Bronx

theater where Mexican entertainers were performing. Explosive Latin-American temperaments, it would appear, should never be trifled with.

The first note of sanity emerged from Louisville, where Robert Evans, the president of the not always reliable World Boxing Association, resides. A clearer thinking man than most W.B.A. presidents have been, Evans stated that his organization would ignore Velazquez's expedient pronouncement and would continue to recognize Ortiz as champion. Eddie Dooley, chairman of the New York Athletic Commission, agreed.

"In the prize ring," Dooley said, "the referee's decision is final and irrevocable." The situation could not have been better expressed.

These statements were received with feelings of vast relief by Harry Markson, boxing director at Madison Square Garden, because he already is plotting an Ortiz title defense against Flash Elorde of the Philippines in late November, about a fortnight after his middleweight championship match between Emile Griffith and Joey Archer on Nov. 10.

As far as the oldest inhabitant can recall, there is nothing in boxing history analagous to the Ortiz-Ramos denouement. The closest to it, perhaps, came in 1952 when Billy Graham, who is one of nature's noblemen, dropped a split decision in the Garden to Joey Giardello, who is not. This outraged the sensibilities of Bob Christenberry, the boxing chairman and his fellow commissioner, Clion Powell.

After the decision had been rendered, they

studied the cards of the three ring officials and changed the scoring of Joe Agnello, one of their better judges. This arithmetical juggle gave the split decision to Graham, and an indignant Giardello sued in court to regain his victory.

Legal Ruling

State Supreme Court Justice Botein cracked the score-card changers across the knuckles. He ruled that the ring officials were the representatives of the commission and that their competence was attested to by the fact that the commission appointed them. That being the case, he tossed out Christen-

berry's arbitrary action and returned the decision to Giardello. In effect, this is what all thinking boxing people are doing in supporting Conn's verdict that Ortiz retained his title by a technical knockout.

There once was a referee who kept reversing himself, but the circumstances were rather unusual. In 1923, Mike McTigue, the light-heavyweight champion, rashly went to Columbus, Ga., to defend his title against Young Stribling, a Georgia boy. That was when the Ku Klux Klan was at the height of its power and neither McTigue nor his manager, Joe Jacobs, would have been eligible for Klan membership.

The referee was Harry Ertle, the same top-flight official who had handled the Jack Dempsey-Georges Carpentier fight. The McTigue-Stribling affair was a dreary dance with so little action that Ertle called it a draw. Into the ring surged steel-eyed Klansmen, who suggested to the referee that he might have been hasty. Ertle saw the light. He announced that Stribling had won. But as soon as he was safely back home, he returned to his original ruling, a draw.

At any rate, Ortiz is still the lightweight champion, Mexican Hayride to the contrary.

October 25, 1966

Ali's New Gimmick

Champion's Shuffle Confuses Foe, Amuses Fans, Sets Up Another Bout

By ROBERT LIPSYTE

The so-called Ali Shuffle, as seen through poor focus and distortion on the screen of the Warner Theater on Broadway off 47th Street, was clearly the cause of Cassius Clay's victory over Cleveland Williams last night. For starters, it kept the champion from getting bored.

Each of Clay's seven previous title fights has had a gimmick, built into the match (Would Sonny Liston kill him?) or the small-talk (I'm going to bring the title back to America," said Floyd Patterson) or the techniques (Can he take George Chuvalo's body punches?). But this one had nothing except an old heavyweight named Williams, never really that

good, now with a bullet in his body.

Thus, the Ali Shuffle, which looks like a Mexican Hat Dance done with great speed on a waterwheel. The Ali Shuffle, this fight's gimmick, had four major purposes.

The primary purpose was to spice Clay's training. This was his fifth title defense in 1966, and the constant training to a peak, and the travel, have tired him—sometimes left him irritable. Through these five fights, he has taken many days off, to gain weight, and rest.

Neither Clay, nor his advisers, thought the public could be sold on a fight with Williams. Since the shooting of Williams, Clay has considered the Houston heavy-

weight professionally dead. He needed something new, a challenge, the anticipation of some complicated and dangerous ring movement to carry him through the weeks of physical preparation for this fight.

The second purpose was the humiliation of Williams, the kind of affable, accommodating Negro that Clay and the Muslims hold in contempt. Clay's Muslim "commercial" on closed-circuit television after the fight—an obviously prepared speech giving his religion credit for his victory —was piped, without charge, into half-a-dozen Negro colleges, where the message of Clay superiority would reach the presumably most open minds in the black community. Williams, stiff-legged and clumsy, looked even more foolish as Clay strutted and postured and whipped his legs.

Purpose No. 3 was pure showmanship. This was Clay's first fight in the United States this year, and his first on closed-circuit television since he met Chuvalo last March. The Chuvalo fight

was a financial loser, and the last three fights were on home television from Europe.

Knowing he was tired and that he would probably put Williams away quickly, Clay devised the Ali Shuffle to give the television fans, some of whom paid as much as $10 for a seat, something to talk about on the way out, something to laugh about. Last night, in the Warner Theater, they were smiling and laughing over the shuffle, re-run after re-run.

Purpose No. 4, really a corollary of 3, was to set up the next fight. Clay is always thinking at least one fight ahead. If the memory of the Ali Shuffle would bring fans back again to see what he would do next, wouldn't it also create the thought, "He couldn't pull that stuff on Ernie Terrell, no sir, not with Ernie's reach and great left jab."

So Clay won again, but left the public laughing for a change, laughing while he shuffled to the bank.

November 15, 1966

Clay Fails to Get Ring's Annual Award

By ROBERT LIPSYTE

Ring Magazine, for the first time since 1933, has refused to designate a fighter of the year. It pointed out that "most emphatically is Cassius Clay of Louisville, Ky., not to be held up as an example to the youngsters of the United States."

The sport's leading periodical said, in its March issue, that "strictly on the basis of achievement with his fists, Cassius Clay-Muhammad Ali, heavyweight champion, merits the outstanding citation for the past year."

But the magazine goes on to cite Clay's affiliation with the Black Muslims, his appeal for draft exemption and "utterances which have not redounded to the credit of boxing" as disqualifications for the award.

Since the award was instituted in 1928, the magazine has failed to designate a top fighter only once be-

fore. In 1933, it refused to honor Primo Carnera, then heavyweight champion, because of the Italian boxer's business associates.

Clay Has Last Word

In Houston, where he is preparing for his sixth title defense within 12 months, Clay expressed some surprise that the magazine made such a point of refusing him the award instead of merely giving it to someone else. Then, counting his achievements as a boxer, drawing card, religious leader and controversial figure, he added:

"The whole world knows I'm not only fighter of the year, but fighter of the century."

Clay also expressed a feeling that Nat Fleischer, the 79-year-old editor, publisher and founder of Ring and its annual record book, was "overpowered by other pressures" into refusing to give

him an award that would have been "forgotten in two days" after delivery.

Fleischer was in Mexico City yesterday for a prize-fight, and no one was available at Ring's offices here for comment.

But Ernie Terrell, who will challenge for Clay's title in the Astrodome on Feb. 6, called Ring's reasoning "illegitimate."

Terrell Is Critical

"This is out of the realm of Ring to do this, and it's acting just like Clay. He brought all this political and religious business into boxing, and instead of ignoring it, Ring is keeping it in.

"They shouldn't judge Clay as a Muslim. Just because you disagree with someone, you shouldn't persecute him. It reminds me of the Julian Bond case."

Bond, a Negro who ex-

pressed strong anti-Vietnam War opinions, was barred from his elected seat in the Georgia Legislature until a recent Supreme Court ruling.

Terrell continued: "This will all be used as a stepping stone for the Muslims to say they achieved something. If Clay did something illegal, put him in jail. But he didn't. I dislike what Clay stands for, using boxing to further an extremist cause. But it's not against the law to be a clown."

Ring Magazine is a 46-year-old monthly, with a wide distribution in Europe and the Orient, that calls itself "the bible of boxing." In 1963, the year Clay won the title from Sonny Liston, Ring named him fighter of the year.

But Fleischer has always tended to discount the champion's boxing abilities in comparison to Jack Johnson, Jack Dempsey, Joe Louis and others.

The only other major fighter of the year award is given by the Boxing Writers' Association of New York, which honored Clay for 1965.

This year, the writers' award for 1966 went to Dick Tiger, the new light-heavyweight champion, with Clay among the top four candidates.

"You can't be loved by everybody," said Clay. "But I'm surprised this could happen in this country, a country with freedom of religion and belief where we go and fight in other countries for other people's freedom."

January 28, 1967

Clay Batters Terrell Severely and Retains Crown on Unanimous Decision

CHICAGOAN'S EYES CUT AND SWOLLEN

Clay Calls the 'Humiliation' Worse Than Patterson's —Record 37,321 at Bout

By ROBERT LIPSYTE
Special to The New York Times

HOUSTON, Feb. 6 In his own cruel time, Cassius Clay battered and dimmed the eyes of Ernie Terrell tonight and added the awkward giant's heavyweight title to his own.

A crowd of 37,321 at the Astrodome, an indoor record for a fight, watched Clay score a unanimous 15-round decision. The referee, Harry Kessler, scored the fight 148 points to 137; one judge, Jimmy Webb, had it 148-133, and the other, Ernie Taylor, made it 148-137. Under the Texas scoring system, each of the officials awarded Clay 13 rounds.

The victory, Clay's 28th in 28 professional fights, gave the 25-year-old fighter undisputed possession of the heavyweight throne. Terrell, a 27-year-old Chicagoan, had claimed the title under the aegis of the lightly regarded World Boxing Association.

It was not a good fight, although it re-established two important points lost in this match's recent buildup: Terrell is awkward, slow afoot and has nothing more than a left jab, and Clay is in a heavyweight class of his own.

Terrell Staggers On

Blinded and staggering in the later rounds, blood streaming from his eyes, Terrell hung on grimly through the "Floyd Patterson humiliation" Clay had promised him earlier in the week.

Clay, who recently announced he would move to Houston and assume Muslim ministerial and recruiting duties in the Southwest, had kept warning Terrell to call him Muhammad Ali, his name in the black racist sect.

When Terrell would respond, "I met you as Cassius Clay, I'll leave you as Cassius Clay," the

Clay's Professional Record

1960			
Date	Opponent Site	Outcome	
Oct. 29	Tunney Hunsaker, Louisville	W	6
Dec. 27	Herb Siler, Miami Beach	KO	4
1961			
Jan. 17	Tony Esperti, Miami Beach	KO	3
Feb. 7	Jim Robinson, Miami Beach	KO	1
Feb. 21	Don Fleeman, Miami Beach	KO	7
Aprl 19	Lamar Clark, Louisville	KO	2
June 26	Duke Sabesong, Las Vegas	W	10
July 22	Alonzo Johnson, Louisville	W	10
Oct. 7	Alex Miteff, Louisville	KO	6
Nov. 29	Willi Besmanoff, Louisville	KO	7
1962			
Feb. 10	Sonny Banks, New York	KO	4
Feb. 28	Don Warner, Miami Beach	KO	4
April 23	George Logan, Los Angeles	KO	4
May 19	Billy Daniels, New York	KO	7
July 20	Alex Lavorante, Los Angeles	KO	5
Nov. 15	Archie Moore, Los Angeles	KO	4
1963			
Jan. 24	Charlie Powell, Pittsburgh	KO	3
March 13	Doug Jones, New York	W	10
June 18	Henry Cooper, London	KO	5
1964			
Feb. 25	Sonny Liston, Miami Beach	KO	7
(Won World Heavyweight Title)			
1965			
May 25	Sonny Liston, Lewiston, Me.	KO	1
Nov. 22	Floyd Patterson, Las Vegas	KO	12
1966			
March 29	George Chuvalo, Toronto	W	15
May 21	Henry Cooper, London	KO	6
Aug. 6	Brian London, London	KO	3
Sept. 10	K. Mildenberger, Frankfurt	KO	12
Nov. 14	Cleveland Williams, Houston	KO	2
1967			
Feb. 6	Ernie Terrell, Houston	W	15

champion promised him the same kind of slow punishment he had administered to Patterson over a year ago.

It did not seem likely in the very early rounds. Clay weighed 212¼ pounds, only a quarter of a pound less than Terrell, but Terrell was 6 feet 6 inches tall, 3 inches taller than Clay.

Terrell's long, sharp left jab kept shooting out, doing little damage, but keeping the circling, dancing champion at a respectable distance.

Terrell Shuffles On

They clinched often in the early rounds, and Kessler, the portly, 60-year-old referee, had difficulty separating them. Terrell pounded at Clay's flanks in the clinches, but Clay merely held. When they broke, Terrell followed him on flat feet.

In the third round, Clay's jab began to slip through Terrell's guard. When Terrell covered up more carefully, Clay pounded at his gloves, driving Terrell's own thumbs into his eyes. The left eye began to swell early and was a puffy slit by the middle rounds. By the seventh, Terrell's right eye was often streaming blood.

Clay's gradual domination of the pace and pattern of the fight became absolute in the eighth round, when he began yelling, "What's my name?" After each

unanswered question, he rattled a combination off Terrell's head.

Clay's great speed, the asset he has exhibited most brilliantly in his career, never flagged as he danced around and into the taller man with less and less caution as Terrell's eyes closed. In the later rounds, Terrell was swinging wildly, lunging, lurching after Clay, falling into the ropes as Clay drew him in, then spinning off.

At times, Terrell connected, but always on an opponent moving away. Toward the end, Terrell was a blinded giant, gallantly staggering forward and swinging in the wild vain hope that a lucky one might do it.

Clay's only mark was a trickle of blood from his nose in the final round. Terrell was nearly helpless at the end. But the ringside physician had examined his eyes and allowed him to continue after the 13th. By that time, Terrell was feeling his way with his left, and could only return punches effectively in clinches.

Afterward, Clay said he had administered a worse "humiliation" to Terrell than to Patterson. That fight in November, 1965, was stopped in the 12th, with Patterson claiming a back

injury. At that time, Patterson had derided Clay's Muslim affiliation.

The crowd numbered 2,861 more persons than the previous indoor records of 35,460, set here in November when Clay knocked out Cleveland Williams. Tonight's fight might also turn out to be the most widely seen of all time.

It was televised live to Britain via Early Bird satellite and to Japan via Lani Bird, as well as to most of the major cities of Canada and the United States over closed-circuit television. Clay is to receive 50 per cent of all proceeds, a share that is expected to exceed $700,000. Terrell is to get 20 per cent of the gate receipts and 17½ per cent of the television proceeds.

The crowd paid $400,145, far from a record, and some fans seemed a bit disappointed at the outcome. There had been a sentimental feeling that Terrell, in his 44th prizefight, would become the conventional, kind, thoughtful, highly intelligent and articulate champion that many wanted in place of the controversial Clay.

But Terrell merely registered his fifth defeat and lost the corner of the throne he claimed

Benvenuti Outpoints Griffith at Garden and Captures Middleweight Title

ITALIAN RECOVERS FROM KNOCKDOWN

Benvenuti, Groggy in 4th, Jabs and Hooks His Way to a Unanimous Verdict

By ROBERT LIPSYTE

Nino Benvenuti, the coolly handsome Italian intellectual, rose slowly and glassy-eyed from a fourth-round knockdown and went on to win the middleweight championship of the world last night with a brilliantly fought decision over Emile Griffith.

A partisan crowd of 14,251 chanted "Nino! Nino!" as the lean Italian snapped quick jabs into Griffith's face and slammed solid hooks at his charging head. When the unanimous decision was announced, the crowd surged forward and into the ring through a lax cordon of Madison Square Garden police.

The referee, Mark Conn, and one judge, Leo Birnbaum, scored the fight 10 rounds to five for Benvenuti, as did The New York Times. The other judge, Al Berl, scored it 9-6.

The fight was Benvenuti's first in this country, and only his third, of 73, outside Italy. He stepped into the ring, his lean, bony face smiling, as a 13-5 underdog, considered by smart money as the Continental version of the Philadelphia fighter.

Nino Takes Command

But somebody hadn't been spying. Up on his toes, leaping nimbly away from Griffith's long looping body blows, Benvenuti took immediate control. In the first two rounds he set up the smaller man with brisk jabs, then belted him aside as Griffith charged. He scored with rattling head combinations, and, in the second, dumped Griffith on his backside with a quick flurry and a hard push to the chest.

The 29-year-old Griffith, whose pay supports 15 members of his family brought here from the Virgin Islands, rose with an anguished expression and attacked, low and hard, butting open a cut on the bridge of Benvenuti's Roman nose.

Through the next three rounds, the smart money rattled comfortably as Griffith drove in, slugging. In the fourth, a short inside hook shook up Benvenuti, an uppercut set him up and a

long right drove him across the ring.

On scattered-looking skinny legs, he staggered and fell into the four red velvet-covered ring ropes. His eyes bugged, glassy, as his chin caught on the third rope, and he seemed to be deciding whether the trip had been necessary.

Later on, in the tumult of his dressing room, Benvenuti would say, "I'm only sorry that he hit me with that one shot and I went down."

Griffith Loses Command

He should have been through then: he was bleary and out on his feet. But the 28-year-old from Trieste hung through that round and the next, clutching his opponent. Griffith, miffed, once slapped Benvenuti on the face at the break. Griffith never pressed his weakened opponent, and in the sixth round Nino had recovered and was coming on strong.

At 5 feet 11 inches and 159 pounds, Benvenuti was 3½ inches taller and 5½ pounds heavier than Griffith. He used the height and weight well, keeping the broad-shouldered, wasp-waisted Griffith out of

that danger zone in front of him, where a long punch can be lethal.

In close, he seemed to give as good as he got, trading sharp head and flank punches as the referee, Conn, seemed to have difficulty controlling the bout.

In the eighth, ninth and 10th, Griffith came back again, but his old weakness, a seeming inability to mount and sustain an attack, always gave Nino, now tired, breathing room.

This weakness may be understandable: As a welterweight, Griffith won one of his 147-pound championships in a fight in which Benny (Kid) Paret suffered the last of a career of hard punches that drove him into a coma and eventual death.

Frantic and confused, his left eye closing. Griffith swung vainly and clutched desperately through the later rounds as the final minutes of his middleweight reign—begun a year and two days ago here with a victory over Dick Tiger—flicked away on the bluish-white Garden clocks.

Italian flags waved in the balcony and from ringside through those final minutes, and the chants of "Nino! Nino!" grew louder as the Italian— a reader of books and a sipper of wine—eluded Griffith's pawing counters to his own quick head shots.

Benvenuti did everything right, and as is the tradition in boxing, will probably have to honor an agreement to meet Griffith in a return bout. But last night there was only today's champion, fast and superb, and the crowd hurled themselves over the ropes to touch him.

Griffith was guaranteed $80,-000 against 45 per cent of the gate of $141,251 and revenue from the sale of home television rights. Benvenuti received 15 per cent of the gate and television revenue.

Benvenuti and Griffith Take Turns on the Canvas

Emile Griffith sends Nino Benvenuti into ropes in fourth round. Referee is Mark Conn.

April 18, 1967

Clay Refuses Army Oath; Stripped of Boxing Crown

By ROBERT LIPSYTE
Special to The New York Times

HOUSTON, April 28—Cassius Clay refused today, as expected, to take the one step forward that would have constituted induction into the armed forces. There was no immediate Government action.

Although Government authorities here foresaw several months of preliminary moves before Clay would be arrested and charged with a felony, boxing organizations instantly stripped the 25-year-old fighter of his world heavyweight championship.

"It will take at least 30 days for Clay to be indicted and it probably will be another year and a half before he could be sent to prison since there undoubtedly will be appeals through the courts," United States Attorney Morton Susman said.

Statement Is Issued

Clay, in a statement distributed a few minutes after the announcement of his refusal, said:

"I have searched my conscience and I find I cannot be true to my belief in my religion by accepting such a call." He has maintained throughout recent unsuccessful civil litigation that he is entitled to draft exemption as an appointed minister of the Lost-Found Nation of Islam, the so-called Black Muslim sect.

Clay, who prefers his Muslim name of Muhammad Ali, anticipated the moves against his title in his statement, calling them a "continuation of the same artifically induced prejudice and discrimination" that had led to the defeat of his various suits and appeals in Federal courts, including the Supreme Court.

Hayden C. Covington of New York, Clay's lawyer, said that further civil action to stay criminal proceedings would be initiated. If convicted of refusal to submit to induction, Clay is subject to a maximum sentence of five years imprisonment and a $10,000 fine.

Mr. Covington, who has defended many Jehovah's Witnesses in similar cases, has repeatedly told Clay during the last few days, "You'll be unhappy in the fiery furnace of criminal proceedings but you'll come out unsinged."

As a plaintiff in civil action, the Negro fighter has touched on such politically and socially explosive areas as alleged racial imbalance on local Texas draft boards, alleged discriminatory action by the Government in response to public pressure, and the rights of a minority religion to appoint clergymen.

Full-Time Occupation

As a prospective defendant in criminal proceedings, Clay is expected to attempt to establish that "preaching and teaching" the tenets of the Muslims is a full-time occupation and that boxing is the "avocation" that financially supports his unpaid ministerial duties.

Today, Clay reported to the Armed Forces Examining and Entrance Station on the third floor of the Federally drab United States Custom House a few minutes before 8 A.M., the ordered time. San Jacinto Street, in downtown Houston, was already crowded with television crews and newsmen when Clay stepped out of a taxi cab with Covington, Quinnan Hodges, the local associate counsel, and Chauncey Eskridge of Chicago, a lawyer for the Rev. Martin Luther King, as well as for Clay and others.

Half a dozen Negro men, apparently en route to work, applauded Clay and shouted: "He gets more publicity than Johnson." Clay was quickly taken upstairs and disappeared into the maw of the induction procedure for more than five hours.

Two information officers supplied a stream of printed and oral releases throughout the procedure, including a detailed schedule of examinations and records processing, as well as instant confirmation of Clay's acceptable blood test and the fact that he had obeyed Muslim dietary strictures by passing up the ham sandwich included in the inductees' box lunches.

Such information, however, did not forestall the instigation, by television crews, of a small demonstration outside the Custom House. During the morning, five white youngsters from the Friends World Institute, a nonaccredited school in Westbury, L. I., who had driven all night from a study project in Oklahoma, and half a dozen local Negro youths, several wearing Black Power buttons, had appeared on the street.

Groups Use Signs

Continuous and sometimes insulting interviewers eventually provoked both groups, separately, to appear with signs. The white group merely asked for the end of the Vietnam war and greater efforts for civil rights.

The Negroes eventually swelled into a group of about two dozen circling pickets carrying hastily scrawled, "Burn, Baby, Burn" signs and singing, "Nothing kills a nigger like too much love." A few of the pickets wore discarded bedsheets and table linen wound into African-type garments, but most were young women dragged into the little demonstration on their lunch hours.

There was a touch of sadness and gross exaggeration throughout the most widely observed noninduction in history. At breakfast this morning in the Hotel America, Clay had stared out a window into a dingy, cold morning and said: "Every time I fight it gets cold and rainy. Then dingy and cool, no sun in sight nowhere."

He had shrugged when Mr. Hodges had showed him an anonymously sent newspaper clipping in which a photograph of the local associate counsel had been marked "Houston's great nigger lawyer."

Sadly, too, 22-year-old John McCullough, a graduate of Sam Houston State College, said: "It's his prerogative if he's sincere in his religion, but it's his duty as a citizen to go in. I'm a coward, too."

46 Called to Report

Then Mr. McCullough, who is white, went up the steps to be inducted. He was one of the 46 young men, including Clay, who were called to report on this day.

For Clay, the day ended at 1:10 P. M. Houston time, when Lieut. Col. J. Edwin McKee, commander of the station, announced that "Mr. Muhammed Ali has just refused to be inducted."

In a prepared statement, Colonel McKee said that notification of the refusal would be forwarded to the United States Attorney General's office, and the national and local Selective Service boards. This is the first administrative step toward possible arrest, and an injunction to stop it had been denied to Clay yesterday in the United States District Court here.

Clay was initially registered for the draft in Louisville, where he was born. He obtained a transfer to a Houston board because his ministerial duties had made this city his new official residence. He had spent most of his time until last summer in Chicago, where the Muslim headquarters are situated, in Miami, where he trained, or in the cities in which he was fighting.

After Colonel McKee's brief statement, Clay was brought into a pressroom and led into range of 13 television cameras and several dozen microphones. He refused to speak as he handed out Xeroxed copies of his statement to selected newsmen, including representatives of the major networks, wire services and The New York Times.

Associated Press Wirephoto

AT INDUCTION CENTER IN HOUSTON: Cassius Clay, having declined to be inducted into military service, is escorted out by Lieut. Col. J. Edwin McKee, commander.

The statement thanked those instrumental in his boxing career as well as those who have offered support and guidance, including Elijah Muhammad, the leader of the Muslims; Mohammed Oweida, Secretary General of the High Council for Islamic Affairs, and Floyd McKissick, president of the Congress of Racial Equality.

The statement, in part, declared:

"It is in the light of my consciousness as a Muslim minister and my own personal convictions that I take my stand in rejecting the call to be inducted in the armed services. I do so with the full realization of its implications and possible consequences. I have searched my conscience and I find I cannot be true to my belief in my religion by accepting such a call.

"My decision is a private and individual one and I realize that this is a most crucial decision. In taking it I am dependent solely upon Allah as the final judge of these actions brought about by my own conscience.

"I strongly object to the fact that so many newspapers have given the American public and the world the impression that I have only two alternatives in taking this stand: either I go to jail or go to the Army. There is another alternative and that alternative is justice. If justice prevails, if my Constitutional rights are upheld, I will be forced to go neither to the Army nor jail. In the end I am confident that justice will come my way for the truth must eventually prevail . . .

"I am looking forward to immediately continuing my profession.

"As to the threat voiced by certain elements to 'strip' me of my title, this is merely a continuation of the same artificially induced prejudice and discrimination.

"Regardless of the difference in my outlook, I insist upon my right to pursue my livelihood in accordance with the same rights granted to other men and women who have disagreed with the policies of whatever Administration was in power at the time.

"I have the world heavyweight title not because it was 'given' to me, not because of my race or religion, but because I won it in the ring through my own boxing ability.

"Those who want to 'take' it and hold a series of auction-type bouts not only do me a disservice, but actually disgrace themselves. I am certain that the sports fans and fair-minded people throughout America would never accept such a 'title-holder.' "

Clay returned to his hotel and went to sleep after the day's activities. He is expected to leave the city, possibly for Washington, in the morning.

April 29, 1967

Foster Knocks Out Tiger in 4th Round and Wins Light-Heavyweight Crown

LEFT HOOK SENDS LOSER TO CANVAS

Right Uppercut Precedes Decisive Punch—11,547 Attend Garden Bout

By DAVE ANDERSON

With a chopping left hook that made all his years of frustration worth while, Bob Foster knocked out Dick Tiger in the fourth round last night at Madison Square Garden and emerged as the new world light-heavyweight champion.

After a right uppercut had stunned the 39-year-old Biafran in the middle of the ring, Foster's left hook to the chin bounced Tiger onto the seat of his baby-blue satin trunks. He sprawled backwards, the back of his head resting momentarily on the white canvas.

As the referee, Mark Conn, began the count, Tiger lay still. After a few moments, he raised his head, but his eyes were bleary and he was unable to control his legs.

Tiger was still sitting down, unable to master the squat body that had earned him the world middleweight title prior to his light-heavyweight reign that began on Dec. 16, 1966, when he dethroned José Torres.

"I heard the next to last number," Tiger said, meaning nine, "but nothing before that."

A Long Wait Is Rewarded

When his victory was signaled by Conn after 2 minutes 5 seconds of the round, Foster leaped with joy. Deprived of an opportunity to win the title when Torres and Willie Pastrano were the champions, he quit in despair in 1965 and went to work on a bomb assembly line in York, Pa.

In the late months of 1966, Foster returned under the management of Morris (Mushky) Salow, a West Hartford, Conn., restaurateur who was denied a license in New York because of his history as a gambler.

Salow, however, guided his gladiator to the title bout and Foster justified the confidence,

The New York Times (by William E. Sauro)

Foster showing how it feels to be light-heavyweight champion. It was his 30th victory.

although his benefactor, Vince McMahon, a boxing and wrestling promoter in the Washington area, appears to have lost about $20,000. McMahon had pledged a $100,000 guarantee to Tiger for the bout.

With an assembly of 11,547 spectators representing a live gate of $113,728, and a television fee of about $25,000, the total income was about $30,000 short of Foster's break-even point. The new champion will collect 60 per cent of the net receipts.

Desperate to win the title that eventually should provide big money for his wife and four children, Foster used a slapping left jab to thwart Tiger's straight-ahead style. Through the first three rounds, Foster won every round but one, according to the cards of the three officials.

Conn and one of the judges, Tony Castellano, scored all three rounds for Foster. The other judge, Artie Aidala, had Foster ahead, 2-1, awarding Tiger the first round.

172

Foster Taller, Heavier

At a rope-muscled 6 feet 3 inches, Foster, who scaled 173¼ pounds to Tiger's 168 at the noontime weigh-in, towered over his 5-8 opponent. With an 8-inch advantage in reach, Foster was able to prevent Tiger from swarming towards the midsection, his favorite target.

"I was expecting him to press me more," the 29-year-old Foster said later. "But he didn't."

Tiger commented that "usually, I start after five, six rounds. I wasn't ready, this was a surprise to me." But the aging Biafran, after regaining his equilibrium, maintained his manner following the embarrassment of being knocked out for the first time.

"I didn't know what it was to be knocked out," Tiger said. "All the people I've knocked out, now I know how they feel."

Odds Prove Right

Foster had entered the ring as a 12-to-5 favorite, somewhat of a surprise. But the odds reportedly had been established by large amounts of money bet on him by people described as "connected with him," presumably in the hope of recouping their losses on Tiger's guarantee.

In two other light-heavyweight bouts, Johnny Persol of Brooklyn outpointed Angelo Oquendo of Puerto Rico and Frankie DePaula of Jersey City registered a fifth-round knockout over Freddie Williams of Brooklyn. For the quick-moving Persol, it might lead to a shot at Foster's title.

May 25, 1968

2 BOXING GOLD MEDALS

Foreman and Harris Gain Triumphs in Olympic Ring

By United Press International

MEXICO CITY, Oct. 26—George Foreman of Houston won the Olympic heavyweight boxing gold medal tonight by scoring a second-round technical knockout over Ionas Chepulis of the Soviet Union.

In two earlier bouts, Ronie Harris of Canton, Ohio, won the 132-pound gold medal by upsetting the defending lightweight champion, Jozef Grudzien of Poland, and Albert Robinson of Phoenix, Ariz., was disqualified for butting in his fetherweight championship match with Antonio Roldan of Mexico.

The 19-year-old, 6-foot 3½-inch Foreman battered the almost-helpless Soviet boxer around the ring from early in the opening round until Godfrey Amarteifo of Ghana, the referee, halted the uneven contest to save the baldish 29-year-old Chepulis from needless punishment.

The victory was the 22d against three losses for the 220-pound Ob Corps instructor and it was his 14th knockout triumph.

Foreman, the national Amateur Athletic Union champion, bloodied the nose of his opponent in the bout's opening moments and then staggered him repeatedly with jarring left hooks and powerful rights to the head and body.

Russian Stays on Feet

But the game loser, who was a last-minute substitute on the Soviet team, refused to go down and was on his feet at the end.

Foreman said after his victory that he was happy that he fought a good bout. He said his only immediate plans were to spend some time with his mother and he would have an announcement sometime next week about whether he intended to turn professional in the near future.

Foreman carried a small American flag around the ring before he was presented with his gold medal.

The 20-year-old Harris, a sophomore at Kent State (Ohio) Collége, boxed brilliantly during the contest, piling up points with sharp jabs to the head and occasional solid lefts to the face and body. The decision of the five judges was unanimous, with Harris receiving margins of from 1 to 3 points.

The 29-year-old Grudzien, the current European champion and gold medal winner in the 1964 Games at Tokyo, was unable to cope with Harris's superior speed and reach. His only good punch in the fight was a hard overhand right to the head in the second round.

Harris was penalized a point for butting early in the final round. But he rallied to win the roundn by staggering Grudzien with a right hook and then again with a straight left to the head.

Avery Brundage, president of the International Olympic Committee, presented the medal to Harris and shook his hand enthusiastically. The victory was the 61st in 65 amateur fights for Harris. For Grudzien, it was his 27th loss against 210 victories and eight draws.

Ironically, Grudzien gained the final in Tokyo by beating another American named Ronnie Harris. That Harris, from Detroit, is now a professional fighter.

Because of the disqualification, Robinson was not given the silver medal for second place, and it was left on the tray when medals were distributed in the class.

Roldan's cheek was streaming blood when the fight was stopped. Robinson slumped over the ropes in disgust but later shook hands with the Mexican.

Robinson, a Navy man, appeared to be leading by a comfortable margin while the fight lasted. The taller American, circling and jabbing, kept the Mexican at a safe distance during the first round. He jolted him with a hard right to the jaw and another to the body.

In the second round, Robinson landed several shots to the head. He was warned once for hitting with the inner side of his glove, but he resumed the attack and apparently clouted Roldan on the eye with a right-hand punch before the referee intervened after 2 minutes of the round had elapsed.

Robinson, almost in tears, was consoled by Pappy Gault, the American coach.

October 27, 1968

Frazier Flattens Ellis and Wins Undisputed Heavyweight Title

By DAVE ANDERSON

Actually smiling throughout a savage assault that typified his unstylish but undefeated career, Joe Frazier succeeded Cassius Clay last night as the undisputed world heavyweight champion by recording a fifth-round knockout over Jimmy Ellis at Madison Square Garden.

The bout ended when Ellis, who had been dropped twice in the fourth round, was kept on his stool by his manager, Angelo Dundee, as the bell rang for the fifth round. But moments afterward, the specter of Clay, who prefers to be called Muhammad Ali, penetrated the atmosphere in absentia.

Despite his 25 victories and 22 knockouts, Frazier announced his retirement unless a showdown could be arranged with Clay, the deposed champion.

"I'm retiring from boxing to sing rock 'n' roll," said Frazier, who has cut four records. "I'm not going to fight again unless Clay returns."

Clay's refusal to be drafted into the United States Army nearly three years ago created the confusion that Frazier cleared by demolishing Ellis with his brutal left hook. The 26-year-old Philadelphia slugger maintained his reign over six states, including New York, and conquered the World Boxing Association territory that Ellis had ruled.

But now, with Frazier claiming to be retired, new confusion appeared, so typical of boxing's affection for chaos.

Untypical of many boxing handlers, however, Dundee prompted almost as many cheers from the shouting, near-sellout crowd of 18,000 for his merciful decision to halt the bout as Frazier's brutal triumph evoked from among those who had wagered on him as a 4-1 betting favorite.

"I love my fighter," Dundee explained moments later in the ring.

All boxing managers like to profess their love for their gladiators, but in a moment of crisis, few prove it. Dundee

FINAL BLOW: Joe Frazier landing a right on Jimmy Ellis' jaw in the fourth round of the title fight last night.

did. He sculptured Ellis into a champion after he was Clay's sparring partner five years ago, but Frazier's left hook destroyed the manager's masterpiece.

Throughout the fourth round, Dundee saw Ellis battered to the canvas twice by Frazier's brutal left hooks.

Only once before in his 10-year career had Ellis been floored, and that was a momentary knockdown by Rubin (Hurricane) Carter in a middleweight match at the old Garden six years ago. But when Frazier leveled Ellis, it was not momentary. Each time the W.B.A. titleholder barely escaped a knockout.

Pummelled on Ropes

Frazier had stunned Ellis twice with left hooks to the jaw in the third round. Midway in the fourth, he was pummelling the 29-year-old former cement worker from Louisville, Ky., along the ropes when his left hook dropped him to the canvas on his face, his eyes closed.

As the referee, Tony Perez, counted four, Ellis blinked his eyes. At the count of eight, he wobbled to his feet.

Few boxers possess the "kil-ler instinct," as it is known, as joyously as Frazier, and he displayed it now. After the third round, he had returned to his corner with a wide smile beaming through his mouthpiece and now, as he assaulted Ellis, he was smiling in enjoyment.

Ellis, of course, was desperate. He was hoping to avoid Frazier's attack, finish the round and perhaps regain his strength and smartness during the one-minute intermission.

But as Ellis attempted to retreat, Frazier flung a left hook that resembled a hook shot by Dick Barnett of the Knicks more than it did a punch. Landing squarely on Ellis's jaw, it spun him backward on the canvas. Ellis lay supine, his maroon gloves above his face.

Moments Before Bell

The, gloves made it appear that Ellis may have been unconsciously beseeching Frazier not to hit him again, but he probably was trying to shield his unfocused eyes from the blinding, hot glare of the powerful lights that had been located above the ring for closed-circuit TV purposes.

But unknown to most of the shouting, stomping audience, the knockdown had occurred moments before the bell.

Suddenly, as Perez tolled five, the bell rang, but under New York State Athletic Commission rules, the count continues after the bell and the fighter can still be counted out. Apparently without realizing it, Ellis somehow struggled to his feet, as Perez shouted "nine," and stumbled onto the stool in his nearby corner.

Ellis in Control Briefly

During the intermission, Dundee attempted to revive Ellis by sponging his forehead and talking to him. When the bell rang, Ellis instinctively rose, but Dundee pushed him back.

Seeing that, Frazier leaped with joy. Moments later, Ellis staggered toward Frazier and acknowledged his defeat by draping his arms around his conqueror. Ellis had not been disgraced. He merely had been victimized by the left hook that had demolished virtually all of Frazier's foes.

Frazier, at 205 pounds, had been uncharacteristically cautious in the first round. Ellis, surprisingly heavy at 201 pounds, controlled the tempo with his left jab and a few long right hands, but after that the former Philadelphia slaughterhouse worker was in command.

Perez and the two judges, Tony Castellano and Jack Gordon, all awarded the first round to Ellis, the next three to Frazier.

For the disappointed Ellis, it was his first defeat as a heavyweight after 12 triumphs, although his career won-lost record is 27-6, including his four years as a middleweight. He will be consoled with 30 per cent of the $600,000 gate, plus the same percentage of the ancillary income.

Frazier's money will equal Ellis's, but now that he is abdicating his undisputed championship, he will have to make several hit records before he equals that amount as a singer. Strangely, when he sings, he has a sad expression. He doesn't seem to smile as he does when he's destroying somebody.

February 17, 1970

STATE WILL GRANT CLAY RING LICENSE

Surendering to a court order, the State Athlete Commission indicated yesterday that it would grant Muhammad Ali a boxer's license when he submitted an application. But relicensing will not automatically reinstate recognition of him as the world heavyweight champion.

Following a meeting of the three-man commission, Edwin B. Dooley, the chairman, issued the following statement:

"In the light of Federal Judge Walter R. Mansfield's decision rendered on Sept. 14, 1970, in the matter of Muhammade Ali, the New York State Athletic Commission has decided to consider his application for a boxer's license when he files. The commission also decided not to appeal the decision."

The commission has stripped Ali, also known as Cassius Clay, of his title on April 28, 1967, after he had refused military induction. Ali later was convicted of draft refusal but he has been free on bail pending appeal.

In his decision, Judge Mansfield called the commission's suspension of Ali an "arbitrary and unreasonable departure from the commission's established practice of granting licenses to applicants convicted of crimes or military offenses." He also described the action as apparent "discrimination."

A New Start

Dooley was unavailable for additional comment, but a commission spokesman explained why Ali would not be automatically reinstated as champion.

"One, he said earlier this year that he had retired; we can't give him back something that he gave up," the spokesman said. "Two, we have said in the past that if the courts were to reverse our ruling, that he would then be rated as the No. 1 contender."

Joe Frazier succeeded Ali as the world champion recognized by the commission. Jimmy Ellis earned recognition by the World Boxing Association in Ali's absence, but Frazier's knockout of Ellis earlier this year established Frazier's recognition worldwide as champion.

One of Ali's attorneys, Chauncey Eskridge, had requested the commission to update Ali's former license.

"But we can't do that," the commission spokesman said, "because it's against commission policy. He will have to go through the normal procedure of filling out an application to show his intention of wanting a license, submitting to a physical exam and having his application approved."

Training for Quarry Bout

Ali currently is in Miami, where he is training for his Oct. 26 bout with Jerry Quarry in Atlanta.

"Once his application is processed," the commission spokesman said, "it can be ruled on at the next meeting. We've been having meetings every week or 10 days."

Raymond J. Lee of Lockport, N. Y., and Albert Berkowitz of Granville, N. Y., are the other commission members.

But until Ali actually is licensed, the Garden promoters will not be able to arrange a bout for him. Harry Markson, the director of Garden boxing, hopes to stage a showdown between Ali and Frazier next winter.

"Our position," Markson said, "has been not to negotiate with a boxer who is persona non grata with the commission, but once they give him a license, we would reconsider our position. Once he gets it, we'd be happy to negotiate a bout for him."

Ali's licensing also would enable the Garden to become a site for the closed-circuit telecast of his Quarry bout.

September 18, 1970

Ali Scores Third-Round Knockout Over Quarry in Successful Return to Ring

SCORING WITH A RIGHT TO THE HEAD: Muhammad Ali connecting against Jerry Quarry in the second round

CUT EYE CAUSES REFEREE TO ACT

Bout Halted Before Fourth Round as Quarry's Trainer Signals for the End

By DAVE ANDERSON
Special to The New York Times

ATLANTA, Oct. 26—Dancing on the sands of time that had accumulated during his exile of three and one half years, Muhammad Ali returned to boxing tonight with a spectacular third-round knockout of Jerry Quarry.

With the speed and agility that always has been his trademark, Ali pounded the square-jawed Californian with his left jab and left-right combinations. Late in the third round, he opened a long cut over Quarry's left eye. Realizing his opportunity, Ali pounded for the kill with hammering right hands.

At the bell, Quarry returned to his corner, but moments later, his trainer, Teddy Bentham, beseeched Tony Perez, the referee, to stop the scheduled 15-round bout.

When the referee waved his arms, signaling the finish, Quarry leaped off his stool in protest. For a moment, he appeared to want to continue on his own as he ran toward Ali, but the returning champion's assistant trainer, Drew Brown, had his arms wrapped around Ali and Quarry realized his hopeless cause.

Referee Steps In

Perez intervened as Brown held Ali aloft and Quarry sulked in despair, to the delight of the Ali-oriented audience of 5,100 at the Municipal Auditorium.

"Bentham asked me to stop the fight," Perez acknowledged later, "and when I looked at the cut, I knew I had to. It was deep and the length of the eyebrow. When I stopped it, Quarry got mad and ran around, but when I explained it to him in the center of the ring, he calmed down. He knew."

Quarry required 11 stitches to close the wound.

Ali had dominated the nine minutes of action, winning all three rounds on the scorecards of the three officials—Perez and the two judges, Billy Graham and Lew Eskin.

"I'm just glad to be back, to clear up all this mess," Ali said in the ring, referring to Joe Frazier, the recognized heavyweight titleholder. "I'm sorry it ended that way, three rounds wasn't enough work for me. My combinations opened the cut. And my right hand did the rest of the damage."

Ali, acknowledged that a Quarry left hook to the body "hurt me one time" in the second round, but other than that the 28-year-old virtuoso was virtually untouched.

In successfully defending his invisible world championship and extending his unbeaten record to 30 victories with 24 knockouts, Ali stripped Frazier of the title in the eyes of the boxing public. Their showdown, assuming Frazier gets by Bob Foster on Nov. 18 in Detroit, should be an epic.

Madison Square Garden and the Houston Astrodome are believed to be under consideration for the Ali-Frazier match. It likely will occur in February, pending a United States Supreme Court ruling on Ali's appealed draft-refusal conviction.

Judging by his performance against Quarry, the 28-year-old Ali, now a resident of Philadelphia, developed no rust during his exile. For the first time in his career, Ali faced a younger foe, but with his lightning hands and dancing defense, he quickly turned the 25-year-old Californian into an old man.

The only unanswered question concerned Ali's stamina. The bout didn't last long enough to test that.

"But at the slow pace I was going," Ali said later, winking, "I could easily have gone 15 rounds."

At the opening bell, Quarry raced across the ring, as if in a Western-movie brawl, but stopped short as Ali circled. As it developed it was perhaps Quarry's best move because Ali, as if he had never been away, floated like a butterfly and stung like a bee in justifying his role as a 17-to-5 favorite.

Despite a 16-pound weight advantage, Ali, at 213½ pounds to Quarry's 197½, moved continually, circling to his left, away from Quarry's left hook.

Late in the opening round, he shook Quarry with a double left hook and jabbed at his nose at will.

In the second round, Ali, also known as Cassius Clay, maintained his pace. Below his corner, Brown exhorted him with shouts of "Stick, stick—at a distance," meaning to jab but stay away from Quarry's reputed punching power. And suddenly, in the third round, blood began trickling down from Quarry's sliced eyebrow.

In his desperation, Quarry moved Ali against the ropes, but he was unable to pin the returning champion there. Moments later, the round ended. Shortly after that, so did the bout.

For the disappointed Quarry, it was his fifth defeat against 37 victories (23 knockouts) and four draws. He lost title bouts to Frazier for the New York version in 1969, to Jimmy Ellis in the World Boxing Association tournament final in 1968 and now to Ali for the invisible throne.

But the estimated $250,000 live gate will help to console Quarry, who has now earned more than $1-million during his boxing career. He has been guaranteed $150,000 against 22½ per cent of the net income, including the lucrative ancillary rights generated by about 200 closed-circuit TV locations.

Ali's share, of course, will be 42½ per cent. His purse has been estimated as high as $1-million for his nine minutes of work, depending on the audit of the ancillary income.

But in destroying Quarry so quickly, Ali bettered Frazier's time. The recognized champion was awarded a seventh-round knockout when Quarry's right eye was virtually shut by a similar cut in New York 16 months ago. But now that Ali has returned to style, he has regained recognition by the public.

October 27, 1970

BENVENUTI LOSES

MONZON SCORES KNOCKOUT IN 12TH

Middleweight Title Won by Argentine in Rome Upset Before Crowd of 18,000

By The Associated Press

ROME, Nov. 7—Carlos Monzon of Argentina knocked out Nino Benvenuti of Italy with a right in the 12th round tonight to win the world middleweight championship in a stunning upset.

The end came two minutes into the round. The punch caught the 32-year-old champion flush on the chin.

Benvenuti was still on his back when the referee, Rudolf Durst of West Germany, finished counting him out.

Spectators jumped into the ring as Benvenuti hit the canvas and tried to attack the referee, but the police shoved them back.

Challenger in Command

Monzon was in command through most of the rounds and had the champion tiring. The 28-year-old Argentine's speed and longer reach gave him an edge over the more experienced champion. Both barely made the 160-pound limit at 159¾. The fight had been scheduled for 15 rounds.

It was only the second time in Benvenuti's career that he had been knocked out. The first was by Tom Bethea of New York in a nontitle fight in Melbourne, Australia, last March. Nino stopped Bethea in a title rematch at Umag, Yugoslavia, in eight rounds in May.

Benvenuti, making his fifth title defense, had held the crown since he defeated Emile Griffith of New York in 1968.

Monzon did not give Benvenuti a chance to get in the first blow. He snapped the champion's head back with a straight left at the opening bell. Hitting in flurries that moved Benvenuti around the ring, Monzon put on pressure and several times stung Nino with jabs and hooks.

Both were warned several times for infractions such as butting, hitting in the clinch and holding.

An overhand right dropped Benvenuti to his hands and knees in his corner. The capacity crowd of 18,000, which paid a record Italian indoor gate of $176,000, gasped as Nino, unbeaten in 31 previous appearances in Rome, was counted out.

Monzon had staggered Nino at least three times before the knockout.

Benvenuti bloodied the challenger's mouth in the 10th. It was the only effective shot thrown all night by the champion, who showed only flashes of his former brilliance.

The knockout was the 23d for Monzon, who was making his first ring appearance outside South America, and it ran his professional record to 69 victories, three losses and nine draws.

For Benvenuti it was his fifth defeat against 82 victories and a draw.

November 8, 1970

Frazier Floors Ali in 15th and Keeps Title on Unanimous Decision

Champion Floors His Rival With Left Hook in the 15th

By DAVE ANDERSON

In a classic 15-round battle Joe Frazier broke the wings of the butterfly and smashed the stinger of the bee last night in winning a unanimous 15-round decision over Muhammad Ali at Madison Square Garden.

Defying an anonymous "lose or else" death threat, Frazier settled the controversy over the world heavyweight championship by handing Ali his first defeat with a savage attack that culminated in a thudding knockdown of the deposed titleholder from a hammerlike left hook in the final round.

During the classic brawl, one man in the sellout throng of 20,455 died of a heart attack.

When the verdict was announced, Ali, also known as Cassius Clay, accepted it stoically:

Hurried to his dressing room rather than the postfight interview area, Ali remained there for about half an hour. Suddenly, he departed for Flower-Fifth Avenue Hospital for X-rays of the severely swollen jaw. He was released from the hospital after 40 minutes and left unbandaged.

But even before Ali's jaw began to bloat, the unbeaten Frazier had dulled the vaunted weapons of his rival in recording his 27th victory, although he failed in his quest for his 24th knockout. Ali's defeat ended his winning streak after 31 triumphs, with 25 knockouts.

"I always knew who the champion was," Frazier, his brow swollen above each eye, said later with a smile.

The officials agreed with the Philadelphia slugger. Judge Bill Recht awarded him 11 rounds to four for Ali, while the other judge, Artie Aidala, had Frazier ahead by 9-6. Referee Arthur

Mercante had it the closest, 8-6 for Frazier with one round even. During his uncharacteristic postfight silence, Ali sent this word to newsmen through Drew (Bundini) Brown, his assistant trainer: "Don't worry, we'll be back, we ain't through yet." But regarding a possible return bout, Frazier said, "I don't think Clay will want one."

Ali had predicted Frazier would fall "in six rounds" and he had maintained that there was "no way" the recognized champion could outpoint him. But the swarming Philadelphia brawler, battering his Cherry Hill, N. J., neighbor, ended the 29-year-old Ali's credibility as a prophet.

At the age of 27, Frazier justified his reign for all the world to see on a television network with an audience estimated at 300 million. Each fighter will receive $2.5-million from a posible $25-million in total worldwide receipts. The $1,352,951 gate at the Garden was a record for an indoor bout.

Ali remained unscratched, except for a slightly bloodied nose, but his jaw began to swell on both sides in the late rounds from Frazier's persistent hammering.

In the final round, Frazier landed a wild left hook that send Ali sprawling onto his back in a corner. But the 6-to-5 betting underdog was up almost instantly and took the mandatory eight-count on unsteady feet. Moments later, Frazier jolted his 215-pound rival with another left hook. But time was running out on the 205½-pound champion.

With a minute remaining, Ali desperately tried for a knockout, but his punches had virtually no effect. With the crowd roaring in the final seconds, the bell rang and Frazier playfully cuffed Ali across his head, bowed in apparent defeat.

Ali's strategy obviously had been to let Frazier grow armweary while pummeling him. But the chunky champion, despite a 6½-inch disadvantage in reach, defied Ali's tiring jab and moved in under it to convince the Garden audience he deserved the decision.

When the decision was announced, a patter of boos erupted, but the cheers soon thundered above them.

Except for the first round, when the red tassels on Ali's high white shoes flopped in rhythm to his ballerina moves, the deposed titleholder primarily used a flat-footed stance, a radical departure from his floating, stinging style prior to his 3½-year exile that ended last year.

Claiming exemption as a Muslim minister, Ali refused induction in the armed forces on April 28, 1967. He promptly was stripped of his title and license to box by the New York State Athletic Commission and the World Boxing Association, which governs boxing in most of the other states.

Not long after that, Ali was convicted of draft evasion. His sentence was five years in prison, plus a $10,000 fine, but an appeal currently is before the Supreme Court.

While his exile matured Ali's physique, it sabotaged his speed. But in red velvet trunks, he was as arrogant as ever even before the midring instructions. Twice he shouldered Frazier, in green-and-gold brocade trunks, as he whirled around the ring. And twice Frazier glared in contempt.

During the early rounds, Frazier pounded his left hook into Ali's midsection, but several times the deposed champion shook his head in the clinch as if to reassure his idolators.

At the end of the second round, Ali waved his right glove in derision at Frazier as they walked to their corners. And during that intermission, he showed his disdain by refusing to rest on his stool and moving threateningly to the center of the ring before the bell rang for the third.

Moments later, Ali's voice could be heard through the microphone hanging over the ring. Mercante warned Ali that "no talking" would be tolerated.

Soon, Ali wasn't talking anymore. Near the end of the fourth, Frazier's left hook bloodied Ali's nose. And in the fifth, Frazier strayed from his taciturn character. Holding his hands low, he permitted Ali to punch him at will in a demonstration of the blow's apparent Frazier literally was laughing in Ali's face now and he was in command. When the bell ended the fifth round, Frazier cuffed Ali across the top of the head.

In the tremendous tempo, Frazier was fulfilling his strategy to "kill the body and the head will die." But somehow, Ali's head remained alive through the middle rounds as his sixth-round prediction was unfulfilled. But before the eighth round, a chant of "Ali, Ali, Ali" began.

Momentarily inspired, Ali waved to the crowd and pointed to them as if to show Frazier it was his audience. But after the round, a roar of "Joe, Joe, Joe" disputed Ali's confidence.

More willing to trade punches, Ali slowed Frazier's pace. The champion's legs were weaving instead of churning. Sensing a knockout opportunity, Ali pounced but Frazier, in his typical fury, fought him off. In the 10th, Ali glanced at the ringside and shouted, "He's out," in a reference to Frazier's weariness.

Possum or a Fox?

In the 11th, Ali slipped to the canvas momentarily. Near the end of the round, he was made wobbly by a left hook. Frazier's savage flurry sent him stumbling into the ropes. He flopped around the ring on rubber legs, but appeared to be playing possum, perhaps to frustrate Frazier further.

But in the 12th, Frazier, strengthened by the surging of joy he receives from punishing an opponent, resumed his frantic pace—but soon it slowed. Each boxer was moving securely, but slowly, until Frazier uncoiled the left hook that dropped Ali in the final round.

It was only the third time Ali had been knocked down in his decade of competition.

Sonny Banks floored him in 1962 during his 11th bout and Henry Cooper flattened him in 1963 during his 19th bout.

But the knockdown by Frazier was the final embarrassment for the deposed champion, the sixth ex-heavyweight champion to fail in an attempt to regain his title. The others were Joe Louis, Jack Dempsey, Jim Jeffries, Bob Fitzsimmons and James J. Corbett. Only Floyd Patterson has succeeded in regaining it.

In his failure, Ali not only lost, but more embarrassing, he was silenced.

.March 9, 1971

Sports of The Times
Epic Worth the Price

By ARTHUR DALEY

The multimillion dollar fight in Madison Square Garden last night was worth every glorious, heartbreaking penny. Rarely does anything so expensive live up to advance billing or exceed expectations. But the wildly exciting exhibition of primitive savagery that Joe Frazier and Muhammad Ali put on over 15 exhausting rounds was an epic that fit the price tag.

Frazier won a decision because he punched himself out so completely that he just didn't have that extra little zing to put into the one wallop that would have finished it by a knockout earlier. And Ali was still vertical at the end because he was just too proud a man, too magnificent an athlete and too gutsy a warrior to let himself stay down.

He had been toppled in the 15th round by one of those uncountable Frazier left hooks that disarranged and puffed up the right side of the Ali face until it looked as though the former Cassius Clay had been stricken by a bad case of the mumps. But Frazier was no bargain at the final bell. His right eye was almost closed and his profile was a mass of welts.

The margin of superiority was reasonably clear-cut with Frazier ahead on the cards of all three ring officials. Nor did the crowd react in angry disapproval as is normally the case when the spectators let wishful thinking misdirect their emotions. Everyone sensed that Ali had failed.

Bee Is Stung Often

He failed gloriously, though, in a strange sort of bout where he neither floated like a butterfly nor stung like a bee, supposedly his normal method of operations. His dancing speed fled early. He was hit more often by Frazier in 15 rounds than he had been hit by all his other opponents together in a hitherto unbeaten career.

In the 11th round, the relentless Frazier—he attacks with the ceaseless whirr of a buzzsaw—began to take Ali cruelly apart with those ferocious left hooks. He exploded one and Ali went wobbling all over the ring, staggering woozily at the end of the round as Frazier's flailing left kept missing the finisher.

He was still missing it through the 12th and 13th when he had an inviting target in front of him, an Ali whose defenses were feeble and whose own punching fires were hardly embers. But in the 14th, Ali unexpectedly came back from the dead, pounded the startled Frazier and detoured his trip to oblivion. He almost went out again in the last round, but survived in some miraculous fashion.

Wait a minute. It wasn't a miracle. Frazier was just too tired to complete a job that had begun to look easy. As the hands of the clock advanced toward the finish of the fight, Frazier pinned Ali in a corner and leaned against him, his face a mask of weariness and his grin a bloody smirk.

If everything about this fight was not in accordance with the original ideas that had been plotted for it by the experts, it took on a new and appealing character of its own. There were times when Ali looked absolutely helpless. He flicked feeble little teasers at the never-stop foe. The man who had danced out of harm's way for all his fistic life stopped stepping even though there were two at hand to tango.

'Sticks and Stones'

He let Frazier corner him and pin him against the ropes.

At times he even stood there snarling, sneering and offering taunts. Frazier merely thought an old boyhood thought: "Sticks and stones can break my bones, but names will never hurt me." Maybe it was a quirk in the Ali defense mechanism, brought on by the unexpectedness of something that never had happened to him before.

How much his entire mental attitude was warped by the way his jaw was flailed by the Frazier hooks is beyond conjecture. This also was a new experience and a trip to the hospital afterwards for X-rays and diagnosis was proof positive that it was a physical handicap of unquestionable severity.

It was a thriller all the way, jam-packed with suspense and tingling from start to finish with the special brand of drama inherent in all heavyweight championship bouts. Not until the last third of the fight—if it is proper to partition it that way—did Frazier's thumping hooks carry him definitely into the lead.

So breathless was the pace that awed ringsiders sometimes were wondering near the end how either of them could still reach deeply within for a galvanic outburst that provided another electric shock of excitement. Thanks to the last-round knockdown, it was to stay exciting to the end.

Frazier left the ring with undisputed possession of the heavyweight championship of the world, a claim that always had rested in the shadow of his unfrocked predecessor, Muhammad Ali. The cash customers undoubtedly had to feel that they got their money's worth in a magnificent bout that was prize fighting at its best.

March 9, 1971

Ali Wins in Draft Case Appeal

Calling Up of Boxer Ruled Improper

By DAVID E. ROSENBAUM
Special to The New York Times

WASHINGTON, June 28 — Muhammad Ali was cleared by the Supreme Court today of the charge of refusing induction into the Army.

Four years after he was convicted by a jury in Houston, sentenced to five years in prison and then stripped of his heavyweight championship by boxing commissions, the Court declared that Ali was improperly drafted in the first place. The vote was 8-0, with Justice Thurgood Marshall abstaining.

In an unsigned opinion, the Court said that the Justice Department had misled Selective Service authorities by advising them that Ali's claim as a conscientious objector was neither sincere nor based on religious tenets.

Ali, who is now 29 years old and used to be called Cassius Clay, remained free on $5,000 bail after his 1967 conviction. It was not until last October, however, that he was permitted to fight professionally again.

Justice Marshall, the only black member of the court, abstained after sending an unusual note to the press room

United Press International
Muhammad Ali after he heard of Court's ruling.

saying that he could not take part in the case because he had been Solicitor General—the government's chief prosecutor—during the time Ali was being prosecuted.

The opinion overturning Ali's conviction was unsigned because no precedent was being set. Justices John Marshall Harlan and William O. Douglas filed concurring opinions.

In 1964, Ali was exempted from the military by his draft board in Louisville, Ky., because he failed the mental examination. Two years later, however, the Army lowered its qualifications, and Ali was reclassified 1-A, or draft eligible.

Ali appealed his classification to the Selective Service Appeal Board on the ground that he should have been declared a conscientious objector because of his Black Muslim religion.

The Justice Department wrote a letter to the Appeal Board asserting that Ali's claim should be denied because he did not satisfy any of the three requisites of conscientious objectors. The Department said that the boxer was not opposed to all wars, that his objection to military service was not based on religious training and belief and that his objection was not sincere. The Appeal Board then denied Ali's claim without giving any reason for doing so.

On April 28, 1967, Ali refused to step forward for induction, and on June 20 he was convicted in Federal Court.

In its opinion today, the Supreme Court declared that the sincerity of Ali's beliefs and their foundation in religious training were beyond doubt. It noted that the Government had conceded that Ali met these two criteria.

Whether Ali was opposed to all wars, the court said, was immaterial, since the Appeal Board could have made its decision on unlawful advice from the Justice Department.

"Since the Appeal Board gave no reasons for its denial of the petitioner's claim," the Court said, "there is absolute-

ly no way of knowing upon which of the three grounds offered in the Department's letter it relied."

The Court continued that "the department was simply wrong as a matter of law in advising that the petitioner's beliefs were not religiously based and were not sincerely held."

Selective Service officials said after the decision was announced that Ali would not now be liable for either the draft or alternative civilian service as a conscientious objector because he was over the age of 26.

In his separate concurring opinion, Justice Douglas suggested that Ali was opposed to all wars except "a religious war as sanctioned by the Koran."

Because of this belief, Justice Douglas said, Ali was "in a class honored by the First Amendment, even though those schooled in a different conception of 'just' wars may find it quite irrational."

Licenses to Fight Withheld

After Ali refused induction, and before he was even convicted, the New York State Athletic Commission took away his heavyweight title. He was also refused a license to fight in other states and was denied permission to fight outside the country.

After a 3½-year layoff, Ali began his comeback by knocking out Jerry Quarry last October and Oscar Bonavena in December.

On March 8, however, he was outpointed in a 15-round title bout by Joe Frazier, the current champion.

June 29, 1971

The State Athletic Commission reversed its long-standing policy yesterday and decided to permit "properly accredited" women journalists into dressing rooms at boxing and wrestling matches.

Commission Chairman Edwin B. Dooley said women would be allowed to enter the locker room once a commission official had de-termined "the male contestants are properly attired."

Women also will be allowed for the first time in the ringside press rows. A commission spokesman said impetus for the ruling came from the heavyweight title fight in Madison Square Garden last March between Muhammad Ali and Joe Frazier, when many foreign women journalists were astonished that the dressing rooms were closed to them.

March 3, 1972

Duran Gains Lightweight Title in 13th

Buchanan Is Floored by Disputed Punch After the Bell

By DAVE ANDERSON

In a chaotic finish created by a blow to the abdominal area with a punch and/or a knee, Roberto Duran of Panama dethroned Ken Buchanan of Scotland last night as the world lightweight champion.

After the bell ended the 13th round, they kept punching, as they had after several other rounds in the bitter bout. Suddenly, the 26-year-old Scot was on his back, holding his groin in agony. About 20 seconds later, he wobbled to his corner, still in obvious pain, but willing to continue.

Moments later, Referee John LoBianco awarded Duran the victory. It was recorded as a 13th-round knockout.

"They fought after the bell," LoBianco explained, "but the punch that put Buchanan down was in the abdomen, not any lower. It was impossible for him to continue. He was groaning in terrible pain. But it wasn't that punch alone, it was a culmination. Buchanan was unable to continue.

Duran had dominated the tempo throughout with a flailing assault that virtually erased the Scot's artistic left jab, to the delight of the Panamanian's loyalists among the 18,821 spectators at Madison Square Garden. The gate of $223,901 was an indoor record for the $135-pound division.

All the officials had Duran far ahead on points. Judge Jack Gordon scored nine rounds for Duran to three for Buchanan, with one even. LoBianco and Judge Bill Recht each forgot to mark their opinion of the 13th round, but after 12 rounds LoBianco had Duran ahead, 8-3-1, and Recht had him in front, 9-2-1.

But a controversy quickly developed as to the blow that leveled Buchanan after the bell.

"It was a right-hand punch, right here," Duran said, pointing to the waistline of his trunks.

"I don't know what it was," Buchanan said. "I was looking ahead. It could've been anything."

"It was definitely a knee," said Buchanan's trainer, Gil Clancy. "It lifted his cup up."

Like all boxers, Buchanan wore a protective cup under his trunks. It's also possible that the Scot crumpled because of both a punch and a knee. But whatever the reason, it didn't alter his failure to thwart the perpetual punches of the 21-year-old Panamanian, the second youngest lightweight champion.

Al Singer was 20 when he won the 135-pound title in 1930 with a first-round knockout of Sammy Mandell at Yankee Stadium.

Duran, who weighed 132¼ pounds, lived up to his reputations as a sneering streetfighter. At the weigh-in he had insulted Buchanan, 133½, with Spanish obscenities. And when the fight began, he insulted the Scot's reputation as perhaps the most artistic boxer today.

Shortly after the opening bell, Duran registered an official knockdown. Buchanan later said he had slipped while off-balance from a punch on the arm, but LoBianco ordered the mandatory 8-count. From then on Duran was in command, roughing up Buchanan constantly, nullifying the Scot's skills.

"He's what is known as a hustler," Buchanan said. "He bulls his way through and he got away with it."

Duran's manager, Carlos Eleta, a millionaire Panamanian, acknowledging that "I wasn't very much satisfied with the way the fight ended," mentioned November as a possible date for a Garden rematch. But in his annoyance at LoBianco, Buchanan demanded a "referee who'll protect me" in a rematch.

Buchanan, the 8-5 favorite, absorbed his second defeat against 43 victories. For the unbeaten Duran, it was his 25th knockout in 29 triumphs.

And no longer could Buchanan minimize Duran's credentials on the ground that the Panamanian had never defeated a world-ranking lightweight. Duran defeated Buchanan decisively.

June 27, 1972

Cuban Stops Bobick in the 3d, Ending Heavyweight's Streak

MUNICH, West Germany, Sept. 5 (AP)—Duane Bobick, the American heavyweight, was stopped in the third round today by Teofilo Stevenson of Cuba in a stunning Olympic upset. Stevenson knocked Bobick down twice in the third round.

They fought before the Games were brought to a halt after Arab commandos attacked the Israeli Olympic team quarters, killed the first man to resist and took hostages.

Bobick of Bowlus, Minn., became the first United States heavyweight eliminated in Olympic competition since Percy Price Jr. was beaten in a preliminary during the 1960 Olympics.

Joe Frazier, in 1964, and George Foreman, in 1968, won the Olympic heavyweight gold medals.

Before this year's Games someone was preparing a book on Bobick, and another man had him signed for the first-person account of his Olympic gold medal. That's all finished now. The career he wanted as a bigtime boxer may be over, too, along with his 62-fight winning streak.

"I'm gonna take me a few months off and I'll decide after that," Bobick said.

His eyes were covered by sunglasses that didn't fit and he wiped his nose with a gauze pad as he talked to reporters, slowly, a young man both hurt and embarrassed.

"I ran into some walls before and I've gotten up and started again," he said.

Bobick, who had beaten Stevenson last year in the Pan-American Games, tried to explain what happened this time.

"I had a bad day," he said. "Stevenson was in a lot better condition. He was a better fighter. Last time I faced him, all he had was a jab.

"I felt a little tense and a little slow. I just wasn't getting off real well. It just wasn't one of my best days. I wasn't at the top of my form. I wish I'd have given him a better fight."

Bobick has less than two months to serve in the Navy and expects to take the time to think over whether he has what a pro figher needs.

Stevenson, with an advantage in reach over Bobick, opened the fight with a series of left jabs. He pounded the sailor with a left-right combination and then finished the round jabbing so effectively that Bobick's left eye was almost fully closed.

The United States coach, Bobby Lewis, placed an ice pack over Bobick's eye between rounds. In the second round the Cuban switched to a right-handed attack, attempting to knock out Bobick.

Stevenson scored with combinations and seemed fully in control when Bobick pinned him in his corner for the last minute of the round. With Bobick on the outside, they traded slow punches until the bell ended the second.

Bobick looked slow and plod-

179

Roberto Duran (right) is shown here on his way to taking the middleweight title from Ken Buchanan in 1972. It has been said that Duran has been "pound for pound, the greatest fighter" of his time.

A prone Ken Norton seems to be saluting his conquerer as he is counted out in the second round of his 1974 fight with George Foreman. Foreman, although a fighter whose skills were never fully developed, was one of the most feared punchers to ever fight in the heavyweight division.

ding as the third round began and could not muster an effective defense.

Bobick had said he feared the Cuban the most. He had told reporters after he won on Sunday that Stevenson "is very, very tough, and has a very good left jab."

Bobick discounted Stevenson's threat with his right hand, however. "He couldn't have improved that much in a year," Bobick said Sunday. Bobick weighed in at 206

pounds. There was some mystery over the Cuban's weight because the official program listed him as 178 pounds; he appeared fully 25 pounds heavier.

Bobick's mother watched distraught at ringside and was shaking badly after the fight. Between sobs, she could only blurt out, "His face was hurt; his face was hurt."

September 6, 1972

United Press International

Foreman turning from Frazier as the referee, Arthur Mercante, signaled an end to the bout in Kingston.

Foreman Stops Frazier In 2d Round, Wins Title

By RED SMITH
Special to The New York Times

KINGSTON, Jamaica, Jan. 22 —Under Caribbean skies that had never witnessed anything remotely like it, big George Foreman smashed Joe Frazier to the floor six times tonight and won the heavyweight championship of the world in 4 minutes 35 seconds.

Arthur Mercante, the referee from New York, stopped the uneven match with Frazier on his feet but hardly in the contest.

A crowd of 36,000 paying $412,000, substantially more than had been expected, saw one of the most startling upsets in two and a half centuries of heavyweight title matches. Frazier, in his 10th defense of the title New York State conferred on him in 1968 and his third since he whipped the former champion, Muhammad Ali, in 1971, had been favored at 1 to 3 in the betting shops here.

Foreman, unbeaten in 37 fights and author of 34 knockouts since he won the Olympic heavyweight title in 1968, had been recognized as Joe's most formidable opponent since Ali but most boxing men doubted that he could stand up under the ceaseless pressure of a characteristic Frazier attack.

They'll never know now whether they were right or wrong, for Joe never got a chance to apply pressure. Looking rather thick in the middle at 214 pounds, the champion tried to "come out smoking" but Foreman used his greater size and longer reach to smother the fire. At 6 feet 3 inches, the challenger had three and a half inches in height and a five-inch advantage in reach.

Reaching out with both hands, he fended off Frazier's early rushes, turning the challenge aside. Then he sank a hook deep into Joe's body, and the crowd had the first hint of what was in store. In a moment Foreman was moving forward, using both hands with authority. Even so, there was an instant of shocked silence when an uppercut sent Joe sprawling.

The champion got to his feet immediately and resumed his jigging style, both hands high, as soon as Mercante completed the mandatory eight-count. By now there was bedlam in National Stadium, a tidy outdoor arena built for track and field. Sure of his power, Foreman forced Frazier into the champion's corner, brought up another uppercut to the chin, and Joe sank slowly to his knees.

He rolled over, pushed himself up and took two or three staggering steps while Mercante continued the count. This time George was on him hungrily. The challenger pumped both hands to the head, and just as the bell ended the first round, a straight right put Frazier flat on his back.

Under the rules, here a fighter cannot be saved by the bell. The count continues after the round ends and he must get up inside 10 seconds. Joe was dragging himself to his feet at 5, and Mercante stopped counting at 6.

Frazier's seconds could have saved themselves their frantic ministrations between rounds. The second was barely under way when a short right sent Frazier on a little wobbly walk. He shuffled unsteadily to his right, hands down, and as he passed, Foreman nailed him on the left ear. Down went the champion for the fourth time.

Again he beat the count. He wobbled into the ropes where Foreman slugged to the head again and again. When Joe crumbled for the fifth time, it was a left that dropped him. A moment earlier, Mercante had pushed Foreman off and

warned him for shoving Frazier. "But I was determined to keep chasing him," George said later, "no matter what."

Frazier Blames His Pride

He chased him. He caught him. He nailed him with one last right, and Mercante had had enough at 1:35 of the round.

Talking a trifle thickly because of a cut about an inch and a half long under his lower lip, Frazier blamed his pride. He said he hadn't realized how strong Foreman was, should have tried to bob and move away, but "my pride wouldn't let me." After the second knockdown, Joe said, the challenger simply overpowered him.

Beaten for the first time in 30 professional fights, Frazier said he would take a couple of

months off. "I'll be back," he promised.

Chances are he was thinking of the millions of dollars his manager, Yank Durham, had talked about whenever anybody mentioned a second bout with Ali, who split a $5-million purse with Joe the first time. Now the demand for a rematch will fade, and the long face on Angelo Dundee showed that Muhammad's little trainer realized it.

There was no rematch clause in the Foreman-Frazier contract. The new champion, who weighed 217½ pounds, was guaranteed $375,000 against 20 per cent of all receipts and Frazier was assured $850,000 against 42½ per cent.

January 23, 1973

Norton, a 5-1 Underdog, Breaks Ali's Jaw, Wins Split Decision

Ex-Champion Is Hurt Early in Second Loss

By WILLIAM N. WALLACE
Special to The New York Times

SAN DIEGO, March 31—The long slide downhill for one of the most famous athletes of our time, Muhammad Ali, began dramatically today when the 31-year-old former heavyweight champion suffered a broken jaw early in his fight with a 28-year-old unknown, Ken Norton, and lost a split decision.

Angelo Dundee, Ali's trainer, claimed his man suffered the broken jaw in the first round of the 12-round bout at the Sports Arena. Ali was able to hide his pain throughout the fight, remaining impassive and quiet, serious and hard-working, as his tank of energy ran down.

Ali, suffering only his second loss, was beaten by a man who had never before fought an opponent of world class. Norton beat him on speed, although for every punch the winner landed, at least 11 missed.

There were no knockdowns in the slow, sluggish fight, which was seen over nationwide television.

Ali bled briefly from the mouth, then slowly ran out of steam. In the final round, he was slow and dragging and Norton, who is not much of a puncher, got in some of his best blows. There were not many.

[Dr. William Lundeen said Ali's jaw was broken on the lower left side. He called it "a clean break, all the way through," The Associated Press reported.

[Ali, said little, taken to Clairemont General Hospital where he underwent 90 minutes of surgery, according to the doctor. "He was in considerable pain. If he broke it in the first round, as his manager says, I can't fathom how he could go the whole fight like that. That's real guts."

[The surgeon said Ali could be released from the hospital late Sunday or Monday. "I see no reason why he can't fight again after it heals."]

The referee, Frank Rustich, voted for Norton as did one of the judges, Hal Rickard. Rustich's card was 7-5, Rickard's 5-4. The dissenting judge, Fred Hayes, had it 6-5 for Ali. In California, the winner of a round receives from 1 to 5 points and the loser from 0 to 4. There are no points for an even round. Norton's purse was $50,000 while Ali earned $200,000. Ali seldom threw a right even though Norton kept his left low and never took command. This might have been his last big payday.

Ali seemed to be biding his time. Eventually Norton, a San Diego resident who began to fight professionally only six years ago, would make a mistake. But the courageous, trim athlete never did. Exceedingly quick, he never got caught by the circling Ali and never left space open.

After 10 rounds it was obvious to Dundee that the old champ had better do something in the final six minutes of action. Ali knew it too.

But when Muhammad reached for the extra, there was nothing at hand. His basic boxing skills were always evident—block, move, jab and move some more. But there was no way for him to trap the 210-pound Norton to deliver the big blow that would have ended the fight as expected. And everyone, including Norton's most loyal local supporters, expected Ali, who weighed 221, to take out the former sparring partner of Joe Frazier.

Frazier, the only other man to have defeated Ali, watched from near Norton's corner. He was delighted.

For Ali this was his second defeat in 43 fights since 1960. Norton's record, achieved for the most part against far lesser skills, is now 31 victories, 24 by knockout, against one defeat in 1970.

His is a new presence in the heavyweight picture, dominated by the new champion, George Foreman. For Ali, there now seems little demand for a fight against Foreman or a return against Frazier.

For the supporters of the man whose dressing robe proclaims him as the "People's Choice," it was all very sad—the beginning of the end of the line.

April 1, 1973

Ali Beats Norton on 12th-Round Rally

By DAVE ANDERSON
By The Associated Press

INGLEWOOD, Calif., Sept. 10—In the most dramatic fight of his career, with the victory and his future depending on the final three minutes, Muhammad Ali dazzled Ken Norton throughout the last round for a 12-round split-decision triumph tonight at The Forum.

Weary and weakened by a damaged right hand that later required X-rays, Ali realized the final round would be decisive.

"In the corner, they told me I needed the 12th round," Ali said later, flopped on a couch in his dressing room. "I knew if I closed the show, I'd stand a better chance of winning. I knew I had to move in for the attack. Jab, jab, move, move, then in again."

Hand Hurt in 6th Round

Confronted with the crisis, the 31-year-old Ali suddenly responded to the music that had deserted him after the sixth round. On his toes again, his white shoes circling nimbly, he moved as he did when he was the heavyweight champion from 1964 to 1967.

Norton, weary, too, was unable to catch Ali, as he

Winner Tires After 6th in Close Bout

had in the late rounds, and as he had in their March 31 bout in which the 28-year-old California heavyweight was awarded a 12-round split decision.

The round made the difference in the decision. By winning it Ali finished ahead, 6-5, on the scorecard of judge John Thomas and 7-5 according to Dick Young, the referee. The other judge, George Latka, gave the final round to Ali, but his scorecard had Norton ahead, 6-5, in the California system that awards 1 to 5 points for the winner of a round, 0 to 4 for the loser. No points are awarded in an even round.

Norton had dominated the scorecards, beginning in the seventh round, just as Ali had dominated the early rounds.

"I hurt my hand in the sixth round when I hit him with a right cross," Ali said later. "I couldn't do much after."

Norton disputed the decision, claiming that his punches were "more decisive,

they had more force." Norton called for a third match with Ali, but that was unlikely.

Ali is committed to a tour of the Orient, with a bout against Rudy Lubbers of the Netherlands in Jakarta, Indonesia. He also spoke of negotiating for a bout with Joe Frazier in New York.

George Foreman, the heavyweight champion, was at ringside. But he was there to inspect Jerry Quarry, who stopped Tony Doyle in the fourth round of the semifinal bout. Foreman is understood to be committed to a title bout with Quarry in about two months.

Ali, meanwhile, appears in no hurry to challenge Foreman, a wise philosophy. Despite his 42d triumph against only two losses (to Frazier and Norton), the 12-to-5 betting favorite who proclaims himself to be "The Greatest" was hardly that, to the disappointment of the estimated crowd of 12,100 that produced an estimated gate of $548,000.

Norton's Eye Cut

At a trim 212 pounds, to Norton's 205, Ali couldn't be honed much better. But his legs lasted through only six rounds. After that he was flat-footed much of the time,

Ali Beats Frazier On Decision Here

By DAVE ANDERSON

After 12 busy rounds that were virtually an extension of their 1971 classic, Muhammad Ali was awarded a unanimous decision over Joe Frazier at Madison Square Garden last night before a glamorous gathering of 20,748, who created a record gate of $1,053,688 for a nontitle, indoor bout.

Ali thereby evened his series with Frazier, the winner by a unanimous 15-round decision at the Garden nearly three years ago in their heavyweight title showdown.

Both former champions immediately looked ahead to a third bout, with Ali saying, "I'm not going to duck Joe, I'm going to give Joe all the chances he wants." Moments earlier, Frazier had said, "I want him again. One more time." Judging by the crowd's enthusiasm a third match is likely.

Ali's ability to land more punches, even though Frazier appeared to connect more solidly, apparently impressed the officials. Jack Gordon, one of the judges, had Ali ahead, 8 rounds to 4, on his scorecard. Judge Tony Castellano had it 7-4 with one even. Referee Tony Perez had Ali ahead, 6-5-1.

Ali justified his role as a 7-to-5 betting favorite with a flurry of jabs and occasional right hands that prevented Frazier from dominating the tempo.

Ali's right hand has a painful bursitis condition in the middle knuckle but it was the hand that registered perhaps his best punch—a straight right to Frazier's jaw late in the second round. Wobbling slightly, Frazier retreated to the ropes but the

referee leaped between them.

"Somebody called 'bell,'" Perez explained later, "so I stopped them both. Then the gong table yelled, 'Tony, the round isn't over.' Usually I hear the bell, but the bell was defective before the fight. They had to call the electrician to fix it. It was only five to eight seconds."

Afforded a moment's rest, Frazier easily finished the round, which ended perhaps 10 seconds later.

Unlike his attitude in the 1971 bout, Ali did not clown or attempt to minimize the strength of Frazier's punches. In recording his 44th victory against two losses, the 32-year-old Ali maintained his concentration. He also held Frazier in the clinches, angering his 30-year-old rival.

Except for the momentary clinches, Ali and Frazier maintained the brutal pace that marked their famous first fight, which attracted a record $20-million in gross income, including the ancillary revenue. The expected gross for last night's bout was in the $18-million area.

But throughout the bout, Frazier complained to Perez that Ali was holding in the clinches.

"The only violation," Perez said, "is if you held and hit at the same time. Ali was holding but he wasn't hitting."

Frazier's manager, Eddie Futch, occasionally complained to Perez between rounds.

Frazier, dethroned as champion by George Foreman in a second-round knockout a year ago, absorbed his second defeat against 30 victories. He will be consoled with 32½ per cent of the net income, which, like Ali's share, might equal the flat fee of $2.5-million each received in 1971.

At the opening bell, the pattern was established—Frazier, at 209 pounds, moving aggressively at his 212-pound

a relatively easy target for Norton's heavy punches. But in the final round, Ali's resumption of the dance resulted in Norton's second loss against 30 victories.

Throughout the bout, Ali displayed no theatrics. He didn't even use the Ali shuffle, as promised.

In the beginning, Ali took command, more with his speed than his punches. Circling mostly to the left, but occasionally moving to the right to confuse Norton, he flicked his red gloves into the muscular ex-Marine's face. Jab by jab, Ali produced the cut that eventually opened under Norton's eye late in the 10th round.

By the fourth, Norton was more aggressive, but still somewhat cautious. Between rounds, Ali had preferred to stand in his corner rather than sit on the wooden stool but after the fourth, he accepted the stool for the first time.

In the sixth, Ali jolted Norton with two hard right hands that quickened the tempo. In retrospect, he might have suffered his damaged hand with one of those punches. But with Ali content to punch instead of dance, Norton appeared more comfortable. Soon he began to bore

through Ali's defenses with hard right hands.

Suddenly, Ali was weary, still circling but not quite in flight as he was earlier. His punches no longer had any sting.

When the eighth round began, a chant of "Ali, Ali, Ali" erupted, presumably in hopes of inspiring their idol. But through the next four rounds, Norton landed the more damaging punches as Ali, flatfooted now, blinked in accepting them. But in the 10th, Norton's legs appeared questionable. Moments later, blood seeped from his cut cheek.

After the 11th round, Ali knew what he had to do. So did his trainer, Angelo Dundee.

"Take it to him," Dundee implored Ali in the corner. "You've got to win this round to win."

Quickly, reacting to the drama as he has throughout his magnetic career, Ali somehow regained his speed. His punches weren't any stronger, but his legs were. For three minutes they did what he asked them to do and, as the split-decision verdict would prove, his legs saved him. Some day they won't save him. But tonight they did.

September 11, 1973

How the Officials Scored Fight

REFEREE TONY PEREZ

1	2	3	4	5	6	7	8	9	10	11	12
A	A	F	E	A	A	F	F	A	F	A	F

Ali, 6 rounds to 5 and 1 even.

JUDGE TONY CASTELLANO

1	2	3	4	5	6	7	8	9	10	11	12
A	A	A	E	F	A	F	F	A	F	A	.A

Ali, 7 rounds to 4 and 1 even.

JUDGE JACK GORDON

1	2	3	4	5	6	7	8	9	10	11	12
A	A	F	A	F	A	A	A	F	F	A	A	A	F

Ali, 8 rounds to 4.

rival, willing to accept a fusillade of jabs in order to get under Ali's arms and land the left hook that had floored Ali in the 15th round of their Garden epic three years ago.

Through all 12 rounds, they maintained that pattern. In the ninth round, Ali began to bleed from the left nostril. In the next round, a tiny slice appeared on his right cheek, the target of Frazier's left hook, but there was hardly any flow of blood from the cut at his cheekbone.

As in the first fight, Frazier's face puffed in the late rounds, notably around the eyebrows.

Each wore white trunks, but it's doubtful if any spectator, either at the Garden or at any of the closed-circuit TV locations, had any trouble identifying them. Ali's trunks were his usual white

satin model, while Frazier appeared in white crushed velvet with a criss-cross stripe.

During the instructions from Perez in midring, Ali looked away from Frazier, who glared up at him. But near the end of the referee's lecture, Ali winked twice at the ringside spectators.

Ali had promised that he would dance for 12 rounds, but he seldom did. He was willing to trade three or four jabs or cuffing right hands in an effort to impress the officials, while Frazier was content to accept Ali's sometimes weak and wild punches in return for the opportunity to hook.

Occasionally, the gladiators talked to each other, as they had done three years ago.

"They kept talking to each other," Perez reported. "Frazier kept saying, 'I'll kill you, and Ali kept saying, 'I'll whip you bad.'"

But unlike most fights, there was no obvious turning point except for Frazier's attitude.

In the early rounds, Frazier appeared to control his assault. But, beginning in the seventh round, he obviously was trying to register a knockout. Time and time again, he rushed Ali, almost desperately, but Ali smoothly escaped, either with a flurry of punches or in a clever clinch.

Only once, in the sixth round, did Ali really dance as only he can, rapidly circling to his left, away from Frazier's hook.

Perhaps Frazier's best

punch was a hard right in the eighth to Ali's jaw. But again, Ali retreated successfully before his thickset rival could follow it up.

In the final rounds, Frazier lunged desperately, missing with his left hook. And by then, the officials had been impressed. Only a knockout by Frazier could have averted the verdict. Ali, typically, had impressed the crowd with a quick Ali shuffle after the bell ended the second round.

Other than that, Ali didn't try to be funny. He knew there was too much at stake —another multimillion-dollar extravaganza with Frazier, for example, as well as a heavyweight title bout with Foreman.

January 29, 1974

Valdez Knocks Out Briscoe, Wins Title

By MICHAEL KATZ
Special to The New York Times

MONACO, May 25 — Rodrigo Valdez, who used to fish the Caribbean with dynamite, landed one version of the world middleweight championship tonight with a left hook.

The 27-year-old Colombian, who gave up his illegal fishing habits for boxing when a local promoter offered anyone in the stands 10 pesos (about 40 cents) to fight, caught a charging Bennie Briscoe with the hook. He quickly followed it with some dynamite of his own. The knockout came at 1:45 of the seventh round.

A short right and another

left hook knocked Briscoe to the mat. The 31-year-old Philadelphian managed to get up at the count of 8, but the referee Harry Gibbs of England wisely stopped the bout.

Valdez, at 157½ pounds a quarter-pound heavier than his opponent, earned $50,000 —the same as Briscoe—and

the World Boxing Council title. The W.B.C. took away the crown from Carlos Monzon, taking the Argentine at his word that he is retired. The rival World Boxing Association, however, still recognizes Monzon, a big-money match with Valdez could easily bring the Argentine out of retirement.

Valdez, who was taken to the United States in 1969 by Gil Clancey, had won a close decision against Briscoe last September to become Monzon's No. 1 challenger.

Briscoe, after knocking out Tony Mundine of Australia in February, was rated No. 2. And for a while in that seventh round at the Stade Louis II, No. 2 was trying harder. Despite absorbing punishment from the first round, Briscoe had Valdez against the ropes.

The Colombian seemed tired, legs that had run circles around Briscoe now seemed weary.

In the corner Clancey led a chorus imploring Valdez to move. Instead, out flashed the left hook, sending Briscoe backward. Valdez moved in for the kill: a boxer who had thrown four, five and six-punch combinations earlier in the fight, was tired. But, the two-punch combinations were enough. After several, Briscoe was through.

Ironically, Briscoe had appeared to have changed the tempo of the fight early in the round. In the early rounds of the scheduled outdoors 15-rounder, Valdez had gained a large advantage with masterful counterpunching. In the first round leaning against the ropes he staggered Briscoe with a short right.

Combinations combined with combinations, yet Briscoe still charged. He seemed

Rodrigo Valdez knocks Bennie Briscoe to the canvas in the seventh round in Monaco

United Press International

to gain strength the more he was hit. In the end, he got hit too often.

Briscoe emerged quietly. "I just made a mistake," he said. "I thought I was getting to him, but I never saw that punch. It was a left hook, huh?"

For Valdez, it was his 50th victory against four losses and two draws in a professional career that began with that 40-cent fight

as a 16-year-old. Briscoe, knocked out for the first time, suffered his 13th loss against 49 victories and one draw.

In a rather classy semi-final, Emile Griffith, a former middleweight and welterweight champion of the entire world, W.B.C. and W.B.A., outpointed a 22-year-old Chilean named Renato Garcia.

May 26, 1974

Ali Regains Title, Flooring Foreman

By DAVE ANDERSON
Special to The New York Times

KINSHASA, Zaire, Wednesday, Oct. 30—Muhammad Ali became today the second man in boxing history to regain the world heavyweight championship, with an eighth-round knockout of George Foreman.

Under an African moon a few hours before dawn, the 32-year-old Ali sent his 25-year old rival crashing to the floor with a left and a chopping right. It was a bee harassing a bear, stinging incessantly until his arm-weary adversary succumbed to sheer persistence.

Inspired by the chant of "Ali, bomaye,' meaning "Ali, kill him" from the cheering assembly of nearly 60,000 in the Stade du 20 Mai, boxing's most controversial champion created the most bizarre chapter in his bizarre career in a bizarre bout in which each fighter earned $5-million in Africa's first heavyweight title bout.

Despite a violent siege, Ali, disdaining his usual butterfly tactics, took Foreman's most powerful punches without flinching and without wobbling except for a brief moment in the second round. Suddenly, with Forman stumbling on weary legs near the end of the eighth, Ali exploded a left-right combination.

Spinning backward, Foreman flopped onto the canvas. Ali had predicted that "after the 10th round, Foreman will fall on his face from exhaustion." As it developed, in the eighth Foreman toppled onto his rump from exhaustion. Groping to his feet, he was counted out by Zack Clayton, the referee, at 2 minutes 58 seconds of the round.

"Foreman was humiliated," Ali said later.

"I did it. I told you he was nothing but did you listen? I told you I was going to jab him in the corners, I told you I was going to take all his shots. I told you he had no skill. I told you he didn't like to be punched."

Ali's reaction was similar to his attitude in 1964 after he won the heavyweight title when Sonny Liston declined to come out for the seventh round of their Miami Beach bout. Ali, then known as Cassius Clay, was a 7-1 betting underdog that time. He was a 4-1 underdog to Foreman, unbeaten in 40 previous bouts.

"I lost the fight," Foreman commented, "but I was not beaten. He's now the champion. He has to be respected."

Ali had mentioned that this would be his "last fight" but he dodged questions pertaining to his retirement.

"Foreman was scared," Ali said, "and who would want a rematch. I got to get $10-million before I think about fighting."

At ringside, Joe Frazier, who outpointed Ali in a 15-round decision in 1971 but lost a 12-round decision to him early this year, hoped to arrange a title bout with Ali next year.

"I'm ready for him," said Frazier, also a former champion. "I know how to fight him now."

Ali joined Floyd Patterson as the only heavyweight champion to recapture the title. Patterson was dethroned by Ingemar Johansson in 1959 but knocked out the Swedish boxer the following year. Patterson also knocked out Johansson in a 1961 bout.

Ali has now won 45 of 47 bouts, wtih 32 knockouts. His only losses were to Frazier and to Ken Norton, the California heavyweight who broke Ali's jaw in winning a 12-round decision early last year. At that time Ali's career appeared to be waning rapidly.

Ali then outpointed Norton in a rematch and then outpointed Frazier to qualify as Foreman's foremost challenger.

In his three title bouts, Foreman had needed only 11 minutes 35 seconds in dethroning Frazier and successfully defending his crown against Joe (King) Roman and Norton, but in the ring under a canopy in the Zaire capital's soccer stadium, he was unable to pound Ali into submission with the same punches that had demolished the other three.

Ali took command of the spectacle even before Foreman entered the ring. Ali, who weighed 216½ pounds to Foreman's 220 at Saturday's weigh-in, arived in a white satin robe trimmed with what appeared to be an African blanket. He danced and shuffled for nearly 10

minutes before Foreman appeared in a red velvet robe with a blue sash.

During the playing of the national anthems, the Star-Spangled Banner and Le Zarois, while two American and two Zaire flags were in the ring, Ali mocked Foreman, who seemed not to see him. Later, while Foreman sat on his stool having his gloves tied on, Ali swooped near him and taunted him with a mock look, to the delight of the crowd.

At the bell, Foreman moved clumsily but quickly. He appeared to slow Ali with a long left hook to the body near the end of the first round. He also pinned Ali to the ropes and slammed punches with both hands to the rib cage. Ali covered up effectively. When the round ended, Ali sat on his stool and winked across the ring.

In the wait for the second round, the "Ali, bomaye," chant began. When the round started, Foreman again chased Ali, pinning him against the ropes. But suddenly Ali retaliated with a flurry of jabs. Midway in the round, Ali appeared to wobble and he grabbed Foreman's shoulder momentarily. But quickly he swung a right cross and threw several jabs.

During the third, Ali was content to lay on the top rope and permit Foreman to pummel him almost at will. But every so often, the old bee would sting the young bear with jabs that snapped back Foreman's head. Instead of sitting on his stool after the third, Ali strolled over to make a face into the closed-circuit TV cameras at ringside.

In the fourth, Ali opened with a quick flurry of jabs that jarred Foreman's head. But still Ali was content to lay on the ropes again. Foreman's legs appeared weary as he walked after Ali and

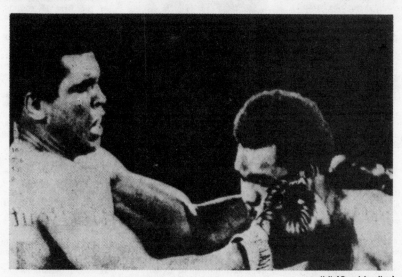

Muhammad Ali connecting with a right to George Foreman's head in an early round

often lunged ineffectively.

When the fifth began, Ali maintained his strange tactics. Other boxers had been toppled quickly by Foreman's sledge-hammer punches but Ali obviously had prepared himself well for this task. Surely his body will be sore tomorrow, but somehow, despite the punches to his face, there was no obvious sign of the punishment.

During the intermission before the sixth, Ali's trainer, Angelo Dundee, hurried across the ring apron to where a Zairian boxing official was trying to tighten the turnbuckle to control the top rope that Ali had been laying against. But instead of tightening it, the Zairian official was loosening it. The rope sagged.

Perhaps on Dundee's orders, Ali avoided those ropes during the sixth. Had he not, he might have toppled backward out of the ring. And in avoiding the ropes, he moved more than he had been before in jabbing Foreman effectively and often.

Stumbling along, Foreman chased Ali throughout the seventh, but his face had puffed, especially around the right eye that had been cut in training, causing a six-week postponement. Foreman was hoping to measure Ali for the big punch that had finished 24 consecutive opponents but his arms were powerless.

Suddenly, with the left-right combination, Ali produced the knockout. Moments later, perhaps overcome with emotion, he sat down in the ring for several moments as his idolators swarmed onto the canvas to surround him. The Zairian police and paratroopers needed several minutes to clear up the chaotic situation.

Not long after that the dawn broke here. But soon a heavy rainstorm crashed over the stadium. It was raining on an old and a new hevyweight champion.

October 30, 1974

Ali Retains Title as Fight Is Stopped After 14th

Battered Frazier's Pilot Ends Brutal Manila Bout

By DAVE ANDERSON
Special to The New York Times

MANILA, Wednesday, Oct. 1—In the most brutal confrontation of their five-year rivalry, Muhammad Ali retained the world heavyweight boxing championship today when Joe Frazier's manager, Eddie Futch, surrendered from the corner moments before the bell was to ring for the 15th round.

Frazier, dominating the middle rounds with the fury of his youth, had been battered by the champion throughout the three rounds prior to Futch's merciful decision.

"I stopped it," Futch explained, "because Joe was starting to get hit with too many clean shots. He couldn't see out of his right eye. He couldn't see the left hands coming."

Ali was far ahead on the scoreboards of the three officials. Using the 5-point must scoring system, referee Carlos Padilla Jr. had the champion ahead, 66-60. Judge Alfredo Quiazon had it 67-62 and Judge Larry Nadayag had it 66-62. On a rounds basis, Quiazon had Ali ahead 8-3, with three even. The others each had it 8-4-2.

Ali's victory was recorded as a knockout in the 14th round since the bell had not rung for the final round.

"My guy sucked it up," said Ali's trainer, Angelo Dundee. "When he looked completely out of gas, he put on another gas tank. I thought we were in front. My guy was hitting him better shots."

Futch believed that Frazier was ahead, which only added

Associated Press
Joe Frazier after being defeated in Manila contest by Muhammad Ali. At right, Frazier taking a punch to the head before fight was stopped.

to the humanity of his decision to surrender.

"Joe had two bad rounds in a row," Futch said. "Even with three minutes to go, he was going downhill. And that opened up the possibility in that situation that he could've been seriously hurt."

Wearing dark glasses to hide his puffed eyes, especially his right eye, Frazier agreed with Futch.

"I didn't want to be stopped, I wanted to go on," Frazier said, "but I'd never go against Eddie."

Frazier dismissed questions about retirement, saying, "I'm not thinking that way now." But the weary champion indicated that the "trilla in Manila" might have been his last fight.

"You may have seen the last of Ali," the champion said. "I want to get out of it. I'm tired and on top. What you saw tonight was next to death. He's the toughest man in the world."

Ali attempted to register the early knockout he had predicted while dominating the early rounds. But then Frazier, in his relentless attack, smashed and slowed the 33-year-old champion. They resembled two old bull moose who had to stand and slam each other because they couldn't get away from each other.

Through the middle rounds, Frazier took command. On the two scorecards of the New York Times, the 31-year-old challenger won eight of the first 11 rounds. But then Ali searched for the knockout punch that would assure the retention of the title.

Moving on weary legs, Ali began to measure Frazier in the 12th with a flurry of punches to Frazier's face, which resembled a squashed chocolate marshmallow. In the 13th, the champion quickly knocked out Frazier's mouthpiece with a long left hook, then landed a left-right combination.

Frazier was shaken now, wobblign on his stumpy legs, but his heart kept him going. But then Ali's straight right hand sent Frazier stumbling backward to the center of the ring but somehow the former champion kept his feet. His mouthpiece gone, Frazier kept spitting blood as he resumed his assault moments before the bell.

In the 14th round Frazier

hopped out quickly but Ali shook him with a hard right, then jolted him with several left-right combinations before the bell and Frazier stumbled to his corner.

Moments later, Futch waved his surrender to the referee. On the stool in his corner, Frazier appeared exhausted. He didn't protest.

Unlike their first two fights, Ali-Frazier III maintained a level of boxing violence seldom seen. During their 1971 classic, Frazier earned a 15-round unanimous decision and undisputed possession of the title with a relentless assault as Ali often clowned. In their 12-round nontitle bout early last year, Ali's holding tactics detracted from his unanimous decision.

But from the opening bell in the Philippine Coliseum, the estimated crowd of 25,-000, including President Ferdinand Marcos and his wife, realized that Ali had not come to dance. Moving out flat-footed, he shook Frazier with several right hands in the early rounds but Frazier kept attacking.

At the bell, Ali came out, hands high in a semipeek-aboo. He stood flat-footed rather than dancing, as if looking for the early knockout he had predicted. Frazier, in contrast, moved in aggressively, trying to unload his left hook but the champion tied him up effectively in two clinches.

Ali landed a left-right combination, then jarred Frazier with a left hook that sent him against the ropes. Ali also landed a hard right hand before the bell.

In the second round, Ali remained flat-footed, using his pawing jab to keep Frazier at bay. When he cupped his left glove around Frazier's head, the referee warned the champion. Ali then landed a hard right to the head that shook Frazier, then landed two more as Frazier kept coming in.

Ali covered up against the ropes, then easily pushed Frazier away, displaying complete control of the tempo.

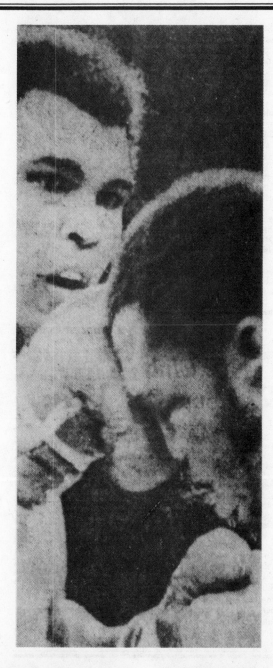

who broke Ali's jaw in winning a 12-round decision that Ali later reversed. Frazier's record is now 32-3, losing to Ali twice and being dethroned as champion by George Foreman in 1973.

In the decades to come, Ali and Frazier will be remembered as two of boxing's classic rivals through 42 rounds. As memorable as their first two fights were in Madison Square Garden, their masterpiece developed halfway around the world from where their rivalry began.

October 1, 1975

Joe Was Still Coming In

MANILA, Wednesday, Oct. 1—When time has cooled the violent passions of the sweltering day and the definitive history is written of the five-year war between Muhammad Ali and Joe Frazier, the objective historian will remember that Joe was still coming in at the finish. For more than 40 minutes, the former heavyweight champion of the world, who was now the challenger, attacked the two-time champion with abandoned, almost joyous, ferocity. For seven rounds in a row he bludgeoned his man with hooks, hounding him into corners, nailing him to the ropes. And then, when Ali seemed hopelessly beaten, he came on like the good champion he is. In the 12th round, the 13th and all through the cruel 14th, Ali punched the shapeless, grinning mask that pursued him until Eddie Futch could take no more.

Sports of The Times

After 14 rounds of one of the roughest matches ever fought for the heavyweight championship, Frazier's trainer, Futch, gave up. At his signal, the referee stopped the fight with Ali still champion.

All three Filipino officials had Ali leading on points at the end, but in The New York Times book, Futch snatched defeat from the jaws of victory. On the The Times' two scorecards, Frazier had won eight of the first 13 rounds when he walked into the blows that beat him stupid. He lost while winning, yet little Eddie was right to negotiate the surrender. Frazier's $2-million guarantee wasn't enough to compensate him for another round like the last.

So now the saga ended. It began on March 8, 1971, when Ali and Frazier met for the first time, both undefeated as professionals, both with valid claims to the championship, both in the glory and strength of youth.

But suddenly, Frazier landed a hard left hook to Ali's jaw before the bell.

Before the third round, Ali bowed and blew kisses to President Marcos and his wife. Ali then taunted Frazier with his pawing jab, using his six-inch advantage in reach to keep Frazier away. Ali landed a series of hard punches to the head, but Frazier burrowed through them to land a left.

Ali covered up against the ropes, and when Frazier stepped back, Ali waved his right glove at Frazier, as if inviting him to return. Ali was talking to Frazier now, then burst out of his cocoon with a flurry of lefts and rights in a toe-to-toe ex-change that had the spectators in a frenzy.

But in the fourth round Ali's tempo slowed as Frazier's increased. By the fifth round, a chant of "Frazier, Frazier" filled the round arena. As the struggle continued, the crowd sounded as if it favored Frazier, one of the few times that Ali hasn't converted the live audience into cheering for him.

Ali, at 224½ pounds at last Saturday's weigh-in, had been the 9-to-5 betting favorite in the United States but he was a 6-to-5 choice here. Frazier had weighed 214½ at the ceremonial weigh-in.

Ali's won-lost record is now 49-2 with 34 knockouts. He has lost only to Frazier in 1971 and to Ken Norton,

Associated Press
Frazier being caught with a right by Ali in the second

That time Frazier won it all. They fought again on Jan. 28, 1974, when both were ex-champions and Ali got a debatable decision. Today's might have been debatable, too, if a decision had been needed.

Many-Digit Inflation

It has been a series both men can remember with pride—and pride has been the spur for both. All three meetings were happenings, memorable chapters in the annals of the ring, and in many respects this was the best of the three. It will be some time before anybody knows whether the gross revenue from the live gate, closed-circuit and home television around the world will equal the $20-million drawn for their first encounter, but this day's business in the Philippine Coliseum may have broken all records for an indoor fight. Attendance was estimated at 25,000, with a gate of something like $1.5-million at $333 tops.

If a price can be put on the suffering of brave men, this returned a dollar in pain for every dollar involved. Curiously, the winner's suffering was the greater. Not many men could have stood up under the punishment Ali took from the fifth round through the 11th.

Yet Ali not only endured when he had taken all that Frazier could deliver, but he also had enough to win. Say what one will about this noisy extrovert, this swaggering, preening, play-acting slice of theatrical ham: the man is a gladiator. He was a callow braggart of 22 when Sonny Liston surrendered the title to him 11 years ago. At the ripe age of 33, he is a champion of genuine quality.

He has been saying he would have one more fight, probably with George Foreman, and then retire as the greatest of all time. It is not wise to accept his promises or faith, but he must take his leave some day. When he does, he will be remembered as one of the good ones.

Loser, and Still Champion

Whatever can be said to Ali's credit must be said with equal emphasis about Joe Frazier. This man was a good champion in his own right. He is the best man Ali ever fought, an opponent who searched Ali's inner depths and brought out qualities Ali never had to reveal to any other man.

It was Joe, rather than Muhammad, who made this a great fight. In the early round, Ali made half-hearted attempts to strut and posture the way he has done against men like Joe Bugner and Chuck Wepner, but Frazier's persistent advance brooked no such nonsense. Ali's faster hands and circling retreat held Joe off for a while. Joe was remorseless, though, and single-minded.

He brushed pawing gloves aside, rolled in under punches, bore straight ahead and slugged, and by the fifth round he was getting the message across. It was hook, hook, hook—into the belly to draw Ali's hands down, then up to the head against the ropes.

He beat the everlasting whey out of Ali. His attack would have reduced another man to putty. The guy in the white trunks was not another man. He was the champion, and this time he proved it.

October 1, 1975

Stracey Dethrones Napoles

MEXICO CITY, Dec. 6 (AP) — John Stracey of Britain halted the six-year reign of Jose Napoles in the welterweight division tonight stopping the 31-year-old champion in the sixth round of a World Boxing Council title fight.

Stracey, who was knocked down in the first round, opened up a cut above Napoles's right eye in the second round, continued to work on it with left jabs and then finished off the Cuban-born champion with a flurry of lefts and rights with 30 seconds to go in the sixth.

The 26-year-old British fighter had been given little chance to beat Napoles, who now lives in Mexico. Napoles had held the title twice over the last six years for all but a period of about six months.

Stracey came back from his knockdown, but took heavy punishment through the second round. In the third, Napoles began to ease his attack and Stracey moved in steadily with left jabs to Napoles's right eye. Napoles appeared to slip and fall in the round, but the Mexican referee, Octavio Mayran, ruled it a knockdown.

By the sixth round, the Mexican's eye was completely closed.

The end came with Napoles unable to protect himself or counterattack. Stracey backed him against the ropes and smacked his face with lefts and rights at will until the Mexican referee stopped the fight.

Angel Espada of Puerto Rico holds the World Boxing Association's welterweight championship, but most fans regarded Napoles as the true champion.

In a World Boxing Association bout on tonight's card, Alfonso Zamora of Mexico knocked out Socrates Batoto of The Philippines in the second round and retained his bantamweight crown.

Stracey, who fought his way out of London's End, has 44 victories, three losses and one tie. He has won 34 of his fights by knockouts.

Napoles, making his 15th title defense, now has a record of 76-7. He won the title the first time in 1969 from Curtis Cokes of the United States. He lost the title—stopped by a cut—in 1970 to Billy Backus of the United States, and regained it six months later.

Zamora, who has won all his fights by knockouts, put his challenger away with a left hook and a right cross with only five seconds left in the second round.

Stracey, who suffered a cut eyebrow and a bloody nose, said afterward that Napoles was a great champion.

December 7, 1975

Ali Struggles but Keeps Title on Unanimous Decision Over Young

By DAVE ANDERSON
Special to The New York Times

LANDOVER, Md., April 30 —Overweight and overconfident, Muhammad Ali retained the world heavyweight boxing championship tonight with a unanimous 15-round decision over Jimmy Young that was loudly booed by most of the 12,472 spectators attending the home-televised bout at the Capitol Centre.

Unable to register a knockdown even though he desperately tried for a late-round knockout, Ali was awarded 70 points to 68 for the 27-year-old Philadelphia challenger on the scorecard of Larry Barrett, a judge. Referee Tom Kelly had it 72-65 and the other judge, Terry Moore, had it 71-64.

On the scorecard of The New York Times, Young was ahead, 68-67, as the winner of eight rounds, including the 15th when some ringside observers thought the bout was at stake.

"I figured I'd win by a split decision," Young said later. "And when I heard the numbers announced, at first, I really thought it would be a split decision. I was never hurt. I was dazed once, somewhere between the third and the sixth. I didn't daze him, but I thought I shocked him a few times."

Ali and Don King, the promoter, agreed that Young deserved a rematch eventually but the champion didn't acknowledge the thinking that he had lost.

Ali 'Took Him Lightly'

"I thought I won," Ali said in the interview area, "but I

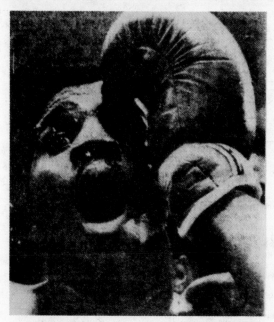

United Press International
Jimmy Young reacting as the referee announces the decision, in favor of Muhammad Ali, in Landover, Md.

would like to say that I underestimated Jimmy Young, that I didn't know Jimmy Young was so awkward, that he was as hard to hit, that he was as fast. I didn't worry about him. I took him lightly."

At yesterday's weigh-in, Ali had weighed 230, the heaviest of his career. He had predicted that he would be 233 in the ring.

"I didn't train hard and get down to 218," the 34-year-old champion said. "He hits hard. My people told me he didn't hit hard. I thought it would be an easy payday. But age does play some things on you. Age does move in on you."

Asked if he had been awarded the decision on his reputation or his performance, Ali replied:

"My performance. But also being the champion and the aggressor. Being the aggressor was important. I don't feel bad because I know what I done. My body's 34 years old. It won't let me train hard for all the guys, but I'll be ready for Norton."

In a scheduled 12-round bout that opened the TV show, Ken Norton, the top-ranked challenger, stopped Ron Stander, an unranked contender, in the fifth round. Ali has blueprinted Norton as his foe in a multimillion-dollar September bout.

"I'm fighting too much," Ali said,, "but I truly, after Norton, want to retire."

Young, at a nimble 209 pounds, joined Joe Bugner, Ernie Terrell and George Chuvalo as the only losers to survive the 15-round distance with Ali in a title fight. Joe

Frazier outpointed Ali over 15 rounds in their first championship bout five years ago.

"But he was much better," Ali said, "than the 15-to-1 underdog he was supposed to be. Look at him, not a mark on him."

In the beginning, Ali displayed the disdain he often does for an opponent. Except for a lunging left hook that missed shortly after the opening bell, the champion did not throw a punch during the first round. Instead he covered his face with his red gloves, as if daring the No. 3 contender to pierce that defense.

But as early as the second round, Ali discovered that Young was not an easy foe. By the third, Ali was missing more punches than usual, especially straight right hands that Young ducked under, frustrating the champion.

Young Doesn't Follow

In the third, Ali also leaned back against the loose ropes, hoping that Young would follow him there. But the challenger wisely remained in the middle of the ring and Ali, apparently thinking that he could register a knockout when he opened up, moved out to maintain the tempo as the aggressor.

Through the next several rounds, Ali appeared to be stalking his foe for a knockout but Young cleverly clinched whenever muscled against the ropes. As the aggressor, Ali was dominating the tempo but Young was foiling his punches.

In the seventh, Young

landed a left-right combination that jarred Ali, but the champion retaliated with a similar barrage. In the eighth, many of the spectators began chanting, "Ali, Ali," as if imploring the champion to display the ability that had earned him a $1.6 million fee for the bout.

But again Young, who collected $75,000 and another $10,000 for expenses, frustrated the champion's assault. By the ninth, Ali woke the crowd with a brief ballet, but his punches didn't have their usual power or precision.

Before the 13th round, Ali sat on a stool for the first time during the intermissions. Moments before the bell, Young was on his feet first, waving to the audience, which by now had become captivated with his stubborn defensive tactics that often included sticking his head through the ropes.

During one of Young's retreats through the ropes, the referee appeared to begin a standing count. But it was not recorded as a knockdown. In the final three rounds, Ali desperately tried to register a knockout that would assure the triumph and avoid embarrassment. But he flailed wildly.

At the final bell, Young had the look of a winner, jumping and waving to the crowd, as Ali retreated to his corner. But the scorecards were unanimous in Ali's favor, even though the voices of the spectators weren't. Ali's won-lost

record is now 51-2. Young has a 17-5 record with two draws.

Norton's triumph was never in doubt. From the opening bell, the 30-year-old part-time motion picture actor pummelled Stander as if the Council Bluffs, Iowa heavyweight was a punching bag. He cut Stander alongside the left eye in the opening round. In the third another cut opened above his right eye.

After the fourth round, Jack Cohen, the secretary of the Maryland Athletic Commission, told Dr. Steve Manekin, the ringside physician, "Tell him to stop it," meaning the referee, but Cecchini ignored Cohen's advice relayed by the doctor.

"He told me to get out of the ring," Manekin said as the fifth round was about to start. "The point is, Stander's taking a beating, it's not the cut. That's how you get brain damage."

But when Norton, 224, whose won-lost record is now 36-3 with 29 knockouts, resumed his relentless assault, the referee stepped between the fighters. For the unranked Stander, blubbery at 229, it was the ninth loss against 28 triumphs. He has 20 knockouts, but he never shook Norton with any of his few punches.

"Norton didn't look good," Ali said later, "but I'll be ready for Norton. I'll train for Norton, I'll kill myself for Norton."

May 1, 1976

What's Best Way of Scoring a Bout?

By LEONARD KOPPETT

When Muhammad Ali was declared the winner in his fight with Jimmy Young recently, two of the oldest controversies in sports were revived: what's the right way to determine the winner of a fight, and why shouldn't everybody know who's ahead while the fight is still on?

While distinct enough on one level, the two questions are closely related to another. One method of scoring used to judge a fight might lend itself much better to round-by-round announcement than some other method. Since there is no worldwide accepted standard for judging a fight in the first place, and since there is no truly effective centralized ruling body to impose any standards or procedures, the

arguments for and against "posting the score" vary with the nature of the judgment being made.

In any particular locality, regulations are set by state or national commissions, but the true power in boxing lies in the hands of those promoters and managers who control a champion or a top challenger. In other sports, either the promoters (teams organized into leagues) or the players (as in the Professional Golfers' Association) submit to a central authority. Boxing doesn't have that, and the method of choosing a winner is, in practice, one of the things taken into consideration in the negotiations to arrange a particular match.

Theoretically, however, the issues remain separate. No matter how a winner is chosen, why shouldn't the spectators and participants know how things stand during the fight as they do in every other sort of contest?

The Background

A knockout, or any other outcome where one fighter can't continue, is an objective event. But picking the winner of a fight that both men finish in reasonably sound physical condition is entirely a subjective judgment.

In some places (like in New Jersey), this judgment is left to one man: the referee, who is in the ring with the fighters. In other places, two ringside judges and the referee form a three-man panel. Elsewhere, three judges at ringside produce the verdict without the referee.

How do they exercise that judgment? One simplistic way would be to look at both fighters when the fight ends and decide which fared better. Or one could simply rely on an overall impression throughout the fight. Very early in boxing history, however, it was found best to consider each round as an entity, and award it to one fighter or call it even.

Simply adding up the number of rounds won, however, wouldn't take into consideration the degree of dominance within the round; it would be like deciding a baseball game by the number of "innings won," so that a six-run inning wouldn't be worth any more than a one-run inning, if the other team failed to score.

So point-scoring within rounds was devised. There is no single universally adopted system for this either, but most work on the following principle: the winner of the round is given 10 points, the loser 9 or less, an even round is 10-10; but it takes a decided margin, perhaps a knockdown, to make a score 10-8, and anything below 10-7 is very rare.

This means a fighter could win eight rounds by 10-9 margins, but lose seven, three of them by 10-8. Strictly on rounds, he would be the winner; but on points, he would wind up behind, 142-140. In such a case, there is no hard-and-fast rule which way the judgments go, but nowadays it would be likely to be by the points.

In any case, every judge looks at every round through his own preconceptions. Some give more weight to "aggressiveness" than others. Some pay more attention to the number of blows struck, some emphasize the damage done by effective blows. Some consider defense — the warding off of punches with arms and elbows, or dodging — more seriously than others. The de-

cision concerning a round is not made any less subjective by being expressed in numbers.

Against Posting

The idea of giving the score after each round seems so natural that the real question is why there hasn't been more pressure to adopt it long ago. Those in the boxing establishment who accept the present system (of a final announcement only) usually cite four factors.

1. Effect on the crowd—professional prize fights openly appeal to partisanship in the audience, and all the traditional publicity stimulates strong emotion among spectators. The very reaction that raises the controversy—the crowd's vocal dissatisfaction with the final verdict—might arise after every controversial round and quickly multiply the crowd's unrest beyond control. It is true that in other subjective scoring sports, like figure skating or diving, judges announce their scores after each segment; but the composition of the crowd at such events is distinctly different from that at most fights.

2. Effect on judges—it is acknowledged that in all sports, referees and umpires may be influenced to some degree by crowd reaction. In such objective decisions as safe or out, in bounds or not, the effect is easily resisted by a good official, and the majority of judgments made in most sports deal with objective measurement of space or time. Since the boxing judge is being almost entirely subjective, however, the crowd's response to his decision on Round Two may affect his judgment on Round Three. By the same token, knowing how other judges voted on Round Two could affect his judgment of Round Three.

3. Effect on fighters—past a certain point, the fighter who is trailing on points can win only by a knockout. But

many fighters are not punchers who can expect to get a knockout, and knowing conclusively (instead of merely suspecting or wondering) that a decision on points is no longer possible may discourage the fighter for the remainder of the fight. In the same circumstance suspense and "the quality of the show" can be ruined for the spectator if it is clearly established that one fighter has fallen too far behind to win.

For Posting

The arguments for a continuing scoreboard rest more on logic and ideal conditions than on practical experience.

1. The fighter deserves to know whether he's ahead or behind, so that he can alter his tactics accordingly, as competitors in all other sports can.

2. The spectator deserves to know how the bout is progressing, and what the judges are ruling at the time they make their judgments, while the action is still fresh in the spectator's mind.

3. Any possibility that a particular judge might be indulging in some sort of prejudice for one fighter or the other, for whatever reason, would be minimized if his decision on each round were publicly posted while the fight was still on. That is, his early round decisions would be subject to more scrutiny than under the present system.

4. "Suspense" based on the fact that both fighters and all spectators are ignorant of the true score is spurious, unworthy of any honest athletic contest, and unnecessary.

5. The requirement that scores be posted round by round might, in itself, promote the development of better and more objective methods of scoring a fight.

The Outlook

A few experiments have been made in the past with the announcement of decisions round by round, but they were abandoned. Until

and unless some truly powerful centralized system for regulating all boxing is developed, no general change is likely to be carried out. But if any existing power group—like a television network, or a closed-circuit promoter, or a champion's entourage, or a governor of a large state and his commission—wanted to push hard for such a scoring system, he could probably get it.

May 24, 1976

Monzon Defeats Valdes

By BERNARD KIRSCH
Special to The New York Times

MONTE CARLO, June 26—Carlos Monzon, who has always been certain of his invincibility in the ring, convinced almost everyone else tonight as he easily won a 15-round decision from Rodrigo Valdes and captured the middleweight title of the whole boxing world.

The 33-year-old Argentine was destructive against the 29-year-old Colombian as he raised his unbeaten streak to 61 fights, dating to 1964. Monzon added the World Boxing Council title to his World Boxing Association crown in the 160-pound division. The defeat was only the fourth for Valdes in 63 fights and his first in six years.

The French referee gave the fight to Monzon by 4 points and each French judge gave Monzon a two-point edge under a 10-point-must scoring system.

Monzon taunted Valdes with whispers when they were close and bombarded him with long rights when they were apart, the good big man slowly wearing out the good little man. When Valdes finally picked up speed—around the eighth round — Monzon never flinched. The Argentine was stunned with a right in the eighth, one of the few rounds he lost, but rebounded even more strongly, never tiring as he sent Valdes to the canvas for a mandatory 8 count with a straight right midway in the 14th.

Valdes, a beaten man, had one flurry left and vainly tried to knock out Monzon in the final round. But Monzon had not been down since

---

How Ali-Young Was Scored

REFEREE TOM KELLY

ALI	555,	555,	555,	545,	445—72 points
YOUNG	544,	444,	444,	454,	555—65

JUDGE TERRY MOORE

ALI	455,	555,	555,	545,	544—71
YOUNG	544,	444,	444,	454,	455—64

JUDGE LARRY BARRETT

ALI	545,	555,	555,	545,	444—70
YOUNG	555,	444,	444,	554,	555—68

The New York Times/May 24, 1976

United Press International

Perspiration flies from Carlos Monzon, rear, and Rodrigo Valdes during the fourth round in Monte Carlo.

1964, and he kept that mark intact. He was so confident about his indestructibility that he bet on himself in this city of gambling with any takers.

Besides his winning bets, Monzon received $250,000 for his victory. Valdes got $225,000.

It was a tense situation for Valdes, who earlier this week had his nerves somewhat shattered when he learned that a brother had been shot dead in Colombia. In addition, he was fighting for his pride against a fellow South American who had insulted his masculinity by calling him, "chico," a little boy.

Valdes's nerves and anxiety showed as he was overwhelmed by the early attack of Monzon, who was calm as always before the bout. Monzon's assortment of tricks had Valdes hurting and Valdes's trainer, Gil Clancy, complaining.

Clancy screamed from his corner during the early rounds, until the referee warned Monzon for thumbing in the 10th round. By then Valdes's left eye was bloodshot and almost closed.

Clancy also complained about Monzon's "rope-a-doping" at the Louis II Soccer Stadium, saying the ropes

had been loosened for Monzon's convenience and that Monzon was able to lean over the top strand when he wanted to move away from the ever-attacking Colombian.

Valdes had been told before the fight to push the action, to tire out Monzon. But nothing has ever worked against the Argentine, holder of an 88-3-9 won-lost-drawn record. Unless he is enticed by another huge purse, Monzon said he would become an actor and quit the ring. He'll be filming in Italy after the summer, his face after 13 years in the ring as unmarked as Muhammad Ali's.

Valdes' who is 57-4-2, is still the second best middleweight in boxing. He may be No. 1 if Monzon goes through with his retirement.

In another middleweight fight on tonight's card, Emile Griffith of New York and Benny Briscoe of Philadelphia fought 10 rounds to a draw.

Gratien Tonna of France failed to show up for his bout with Johnny Pinney of the United States, even missing the weigh-in. Tonna reportedly told a friend, "I don't feel like fighting today."

June 27, 1976

5 Boxers For U.S. Hit Gold

By STEVE CADY
Special to The New York Times

MONTREAL, July 31— Digging and blasting like prospectors who know exactly what they're doing, American boxers shook loose an avalanche of gold tonight in the Olympic finals at the Forum.

When the last stick of dynamite had been detonated by Leon Spinks in the light-heavyweight class, the young team many experts thought would be outslugged by East Europeans and Cubans had walked off with five gold medals. They could have used a pack-mule to lug the gold, because no other United States boxing team has ever won any more of it than they did tonight before an appreciative standing-room crowd of 20,000.

"This is the greatest night in the history of amateur boxing for America," said Rollie Schwartz, manager of the team.

The United States won five golds once before in the 1952 Olympics, but it got no silvers or bronzes that year. This time, a silver and a bronze increased the medal total to seven.

In order, the American winners on the 11-bout program were Leo Randolph, an 18-year-old bantamweight from Tacoma, Wash.; Howard Davis of Glen Cove, L.I., in the lightweight class; Sugar Ray Leonard, a light-welterweight from Palmer Park, Md.; Mike Spinks of St. Louis, Leon's younger brother, in the middleweights, and Leon, whose overhand right stretched Sixto Soria of Cuba flat on his face in the third round of their slugfest.

The Spinks-Soria bout was the most explosive of the night, almost completely upstaging Teofilo Stevenson's anticipated victory against Mircea Simon of Rumania in the heavyweight final.

Counting Stevenson's success, only three of six Cubans finalists won, compared to five of six finalists for the United States. In head-to-head confrontations, Ameri-

cans won all three of their bouts with Cubans.

Spinks, a 23-year-old Marine Corps corporal from St. Louis, mixed it with Soria right from the beginning, knocking him down with a vicious right five seconds from the end of the opening round.

Soria had been taking target practice with first-round knockouts in earlier bouts during this two-week-long tournament. But Schwartz had said, "Wait till the Cubans get hit."

Tonight, Soria was the target. In the third round, Spinks charged off the ropes and dropped him with a long right to the side of the jaw. Soria managed to struggle to his feet, but the Soviet referee stepped in and called off the war.

Leon's 20-year-old brother, Mike, also was a walking hand-grenade in his bout with Rufat Riskiev of the Soviet Union. The younger half of American boxing's first Olympic brother team decked his opponent with a long right in the second round, staggered him for a mandatory standing 8-count in the third and then doubled him up with a shot to the stomach. Riskiev complained that the blow was below the belt, but the Cuban referee disallowed the protest and stopped the bout with 1 minute 6 seconds to go.

"I was worried they might try to take it away from me," Mike said later. "I said a little prayer they wouldn't. He had to make up an excuse so his coaches wouldn't get mad."

While the Spinks brothers were climbing the podium to get their medals and listen to their national anthem again, they threw kisses to their mother, Mrs. Kay Spinks, who was flown here for the finals from her home in a public housing project by an anonymous St. Louis benefactor.

"She doesn't want us to fight," said Mike. "But all men have to grow up. We got to live our own lives. It's what we want to do." While the granite-jawed Spinks brothers provided the heaviest hitting of a star-spangled night, it was by no means the only dynamite set off by the American team. Davis and Leonard both put on dazzling displays of boxing and punching, Davis in a 5-0 decision over tank-like Simion Cutov of Rumania and Leonard against hard-punching Andres Aldama of Cuba.

Randolph had to rally for a 3-2 decision over Ramon Duvalon of Cuba, and Chuck Mooney, an Army sergeant from Fayetteville, N.C. dropped a 3-2 victory to Yong Jo Gu of North Korea.

Mooney, weakened by a severe cold, led the applause for the winner in a gracious display that did himself and his country credit. Like the other losing finalists, Mooney up a silver medal.

In the 1972 Olympics at Munich, the Americans collected only one gold and three bronzes. This time, Schwartz and the two coaches, Pat Nappi and Tom Johnson, built a powerhouse that relied on speed, science and uppercuts to penetrate the hands-high defenses of the favored East Europeans and Cubans.

Tonight, as they had in earlier bouts, American boxers nullified the punching power of more mature, stronger rivals by moving in close and digging to the body or catching them off guard with swiftly thrown punches.

But even in the toe-to-toe exchanges, the Americans showed class and courage and power. Leonard, for example, discarded his usual fancy tactics and hammered Aldama with left hooks and long rights. In the second and third rounds, he staggered the Cuban for two mandatory standing 8-counts and then sent him reeling into the ropes in the closing seconds.

"This is my last fight," Leonard said later. "My journey has ended. My dream is fulfilled."

The 20-year-old collegian, whose sore hands had to be iced before the bout, plans to major in business administration at the University of Maryland.

Because Aldama was a very aggressive, very unorthodox southpaw, Leonard's strategy was to work in close.

"He's tough," Sugar Ray said, "and I didn't want him connecting with any of those roundhouse lefts."

For pure ring mastery, the performance turned in by Davis against Cutov probably was the most polished of the night. It had skill, footwork, self defense and, when he elected to strike, awesome power for a lightweight. Cutov had been given a five-minute ovation the other day for a "war" with a Russian fighter, but Davis tagged him with a straight right in the first round to set the pattern. Another right in the second round dazed the Rumanian so badly he had to take a mandatory standing 8 count.

"He was real open to rights," said Davis. "But he's so tough, man, I hit him with Sunday punches and he kept coming back."

The 20-year-old Long Islander, who has been offered a pro spot on the Muhammad Ali-Ken Norton title card in September, said he wasn't sure about accepting that one. But he said he would definitely turn pro eventually.

"This is a big weight off my back," he said.

"This is what I came for—my mother, my father, my country."

Davis said he intended to take his gold medal with him when he visits the grave of his mother, whose recent funeral he didn't attend "because she would have wanted me to win the gold medal."

August 1, 1976

Ali Outpoints Norton and Retains His Heavyweight Crown

Champion Awarded 8 of 15 Rounds— No Knockdowns

By DAVE ANDERSON

With more votes than cheers, Muhammad Ali retained the world heavyweigth championship last night with a controversial but unanimous 15-round victory over Ken Norton at Yankee Stadium before 30,298 spectators, who created a gate of about $2.4 million.

Unable to register a knockout "inside five rounds" as he had predicted, the 34-year-old champion moved and manipulated enough in the 54-degree chill to earn eight rounds on the scorecards of the referee, Arthur Mercante, and the two judges, Barney Smith and Harold Lederman.

Mercante had Ali ahead by 8-6 with one round even. The judges each had Ali ahead, 8-7. On the scorecard of The New York Times, Ali also earned eight rounds, Norton seven.

Verdict Stuns Challenger

Many disagreed with the official verdict. At the announcement of the scorecards, Ali's triumph was not greeted with the usual cheers. But there weren't thunderous boos either. The muttering of surprise seemed to be the dominant reaction. But in his corner, Norton was crying in disbelief.

"I thought I won it," the 31-year-old Californian said later. "Ali knew I won it. The people knew I won it."

Ali's triumph created as much controversey as did his 15-round triumph over Jimmy Young in Landover, Md., on April 30. But as in his second fight with Norton in 1973, a 12-round split decision for Ali, the difference was Ali winning the final round on each of the official scorecards.

"I knew I was ahead," Ali said. "I didn't think I needed to win the last round to win. My corner was keeping tabs."

Ali's rally began in the ninth round. At the time, he trailed by 6-2 on Lederman's card and by 5-3 on the Mercante and Smith cards. But over the final six rounds, Ali obviously impressed with the officials. Lederman gave the champion six of the final seven rounds, Smith gave him five, Mercante gave him five, with one even.

Ali Stings Better

"Norton was the aggressor," Mercante explained later, "but Ali was scoring. You can chase a guy, but if you're getting hit, the other guy is winning points. Norton landed a lot of body punches, but Ali also blocked a lot of body punches. And at the end, Ali's punches seemed to have more Sting than Norton's did."

To those who agreed with the officials, Norton, like Jimmy Young, did not do enough to deserve dethroning the champion.

When in doubt, boxing officials have a history of voting for the champion. Not since James J. Braddock was awarded a 15-round decision over Max Baer at the Long Island City Bowl in 1935, a span of 41 years, has a heavyweight champion been dethroned on judgment.

Only two other heavyweight champions were dethroned on a decision—Max Schmeling by Jack Sharkey over 15 rounds in 1932 and Jack Dempsey by Gene Tunney over 10 rounds in 1926. In a 1949 elimination bout following Joe Louis's retirement, Ezzard Charles was awarded the title on a 15-round decision over Jersey Joe Walcott.

No Night for Knockdown

And so Ali, in his 20th title bout, remained the champion in the eighth defense of his second reign. Ali regained the title from George Foreman with an eighth-round knockout in Zaire almost two years ago.

That dramatic upset of Foreman and his epic of brutality with Joe Frazier in Manila a year ago had Ali thinking that he became a knockout puncher. But he couldn't knock out Norton; he couldn't knock down Norton; he couldn't even wobble him. But then Norton was unable to wobble Ali in their tedious tempo.

Perhaps the chilly breeze prevented both fighters from producing their best. The disappointing crown also prevented the Madison Square Garden promoters from establishing a record live gate, as they had anticipated. The record of $2.6 million was established at the second Dempsey-Tunney fight in Chicago in 1927.

Ali, as usual, had the spectators on his side. When he arrived in the ring, after keeping Norton waiting there for about five minutes, he prompted an "Ali, Ali" chant. Then the champion got the crowd chanting, "Norton must fall"

How the Officials Scored 15-Round Bout

Mercante	ANN	ANN	ANA	AAE	ANA—8-6-1
Lederman	ANN	NNN	ANA	AAN	AAA—8-7-0
Smith	ANA	NNN	ANA	NAN	AAA—8-7-0

in the moments before Mercante's instructions in midring.

Opens With a Windmill

At the bell, Ali was waving his right arms in a windmill notion, as he had done during his fifth-round knockout of Richard Dunn in Munich four months ago. And he moved out quickly in a flat-footed stance, obviously hoping to justify his prediction of a knockout within five rounds.

Norton was in a crouch, he would be throughout, and moving forward. Ali occasionallq held Norton's head with his left glove, prompting a warning by the referee.

In the fourth round, Ali could be heard saying, "I'm going to destroy you," before he backed the ex-Marine against the ropes, but Norton was controlling the pace. Ali, however, was controlling the theatrics. After the fifth, he wandered over toward Norton's corner to shout at him. Norton laughed.

In the fifth, Ali used the "rope-a-dope," backing against the ropes and covering up in the belief that Norton, like Foreman in Zaire, would punch himself weary. But the challenger, at a solid 217½ pounds to Ali's slightly beefy 221, had trained resolutely in order to avoid the pitfall that trapped Foreman.

Ali continued to use the rope-a-dope in the sixth, apparently willing to concede the round in order to save

his strength. But in the seventh Ali appeared to be taking command as Norton was content to block punches. Norton's best punch occurred in the eighth —a left hook to the hips as Ali winced.

Never the end of the 12th, Ali thumbed Norton in the left eye "ac-

cidentally," according to Mercante."

"When he got back to his corner," the referee said, "they put some ice on it and he was all right immediately."

Ending on a High Note

During the 13th and 14th, the champion flurried more, and at the bell for the final round, Ali danced quickly to his left. Norton was yelling, "C'mon, c'mon," and the champion opened up, obviously making sure that he would not lose the final round, while Norton punched desparately and ineffectively.

For the third time in three bouts, Ali and Norton had produced a close decision. In their first fight in San Diego in 1973, when Norton had fractured Ali's jaw in winning a 12-round split decision, Norton had earned 17 points to Ali's 14. In the rematch at Los Angeles, Ali was ahead, 18-16, in points.

But last night the title was at stake. Ali responded and Norton did not, at least in the judgment of the three officials.

The champion was guaranteed $6 million with Norton, the 2-to-1 betting underdog, assured $1.1 million of the gross income that the Garden promoters hoped would total $12 million including the TV income. But in the memorable career of Muhammad Ali, it was one of the few times that he was not worth his money.

September 29, 1976

King-ABC Fights Are Suspended Pending an Inquiry

MIAMI BEACH, April 16. (UPI)—The United States Boxing Championships, promoted by Don King and funded by ABC Television, have been suspended pending an investigation into boxers' rankings by Ring Magazine, which was also involved in the project.

ABC released a statement this afternoon saying it was suspending the so-called championship bouts following the investigation of the boxers' rankings and the possible falsifications of career records.

A grand jury investigation already is under way in Maryland, where Scott LeDoux, a heavyweight, charged the tournament with being rigged in favor of boxers handled by associates of King following his loss to Johnny Boudreaux at the Naval Academy in Annapolis. LeDoux also contended there were kickback payments made by boxers in order to get into the tournament.

Two Bouts Called Off

A semifinal bout scheduled for this afternoon between two unbeaten heavyweights—Larry Holmes (24-0), ranked fourth, and eighth-ranked Stan Ward (8-0-2), was suspended pending the investigation. A semifinal contest between Francisco Villegas of Puerto Rico and Frankie Baltazar of California, junior lightweights, also was suspended.

King was not immediately available for comment, but Irving Rudd, a spokesman, confirmed the suspension. Rudd said King concurred with the investigation and the suspension and promised

to aid the investigation.

The ABC statement said in part: "Since the early stages of the tournament, ABC has been investigating various allegations of improprieties and has subsequently turned over to the United States Attorney in Maryland evidence that it has uncovered such proprieties.

Records Termed Inaccurate

"On Friday, April 8, one aspect of this investigation resulted in ABC's obtaining and turning over to the United States Attorney an affidavit from a fighter stating that he had been contacted by a would-be manager who told him he could get him rated in Ring Magazine's top 10 United States rankings, although he had not fought in a year and had never been ranked before. He further stated that two fights, which became the basis for his being listed third in Ring's United States boxing rankings, never took place.

"On Tuesday, April 12, after further investigation and the publication of Ring Magazine's 1977 record book, ABC announced that it had further evidence indicating that several fighters in the tournament appeared to have inaccurate records, which had been compiled by Ring Magazine and used to determine the rankings of fighters entered in the tournament.

"ABC has now determined that the records of numerous fighters in the tournament as listed in the 1977 Ring Book are, in fact, inaccurate and con-

tain many fights which apparently never took place."

In New York, Ring Magazine denied any wrongdoing concerning the ranking of American fighters. "As always, Ring has immediately investigated and will continue to investigate inaccuracies in information that have been brought to its attention," the publication said in a statement.

"As it was recently reported by Ring, it has learned that there were errors in the records of some fighters in the tournament, which have been submitted by fight managers. Ring had commenced steps to determine the facts and act accordingly. As a result of its inquiry, Ring had advised the tournament committee, Don King and ABC that one fighter should be removed from the tournament, and has fully cooperated with all concerned parties to resolve this issue."

Two three-round exhibitions by Muhammad Ali, the world heavyweight champion, along with a three-round exhibition by the World Boxing Council lightweight champion, Esteban de Jesus, were all that were left of today's program.

ABC also said it was beginning its investigation of the tournament. According to the network's release, King concurred with the decision to suspend the tournament.

April 17, 1977

Boxing Inquiry Finds Deception in Tourney

A four-month investigation into the so-called United States Boxing Championships found evidence of "a good deal of unethical behavior by individuals involved with the administration and organization of the tournament."

The results of the investigation—commissioned by ABC television, which had telecast the tournament—were made public by ABC yesterday. The investigators said they uncovered no conduct in connection with the bouts that would warrant criminal prosecution. They also said there was no evidence that any of the fights was fixed.

The investigation was made at ABC's request by Michael Armstrong, former chief counsel to the Knapp Commission, who was retained by ABC's "outside counsel"—Hawkins, Delafield and Wood. The investigation began after allegations that some of the boxers' records had been altered and that some had been forced to pay kickbacks in order to enter the tournament.

The matches were promoted by Don King Productions with the aid of The Ring magazine, which supplied the records used as a basis for rankings in the tournament.

"It is plain from our investigation," the report said, "that at this time Ring lacks the credibility necessary for it to carry out its assigned role in the tournament."

As for King's involvement, the report said:

"On the subject of active wrongdoing, we were unable to find any evidence that King himself was involved in kickbacks, false ratings or other similar irregularities. The most disturbing action by King for which we were able to acquire direct evidence of personal involvement was his clearly improper payment of $5,000 to John Ort [associate editor of The Ring magazine] which seriously compromised the integrity of the selection process."

Nat Loubet, editor and publisher of The Ring, said:

"John was being paid for public relations work, which I allowed him to do. The only problem we had was several managers sent us phony records, and we accepted them."

The commission also exonerated ABC and James A. Farley Jr., then chairman of the New York State Athletic Commission, who served as chairman of the committee that oversaw parts of the tournament.

September 4, 1977

Duran Settles Title On Knockout in 12th

By United Press International

LAS VEGAS, Nev., Jan. 21—Roberto Duran knocked out Esteban DeJesus at 2 minutes 32 seconds of the 12th round today to gain the undisputed lightweight boxing championship.

Duran ended the fight with lightning quickness as he caught DeJesus with a right cross to the jaw midway through the 12th and sent him sprawling to the canvas.

DeJesus was on his feet at the count of three but was groggy. The fight continued, but Duran pummeled DeJesus in the corner with lefts and rights. DeJesus sagged into the ropes and the fight was stopped.

31 Straight for Duran

"I knew I had him, it was just a matter of time," said Duran, who won his 61st fight and made DeJesus his 51st knockout victim. Duran's only defeat was to DeJesus, and since then he has won 31 straight, including a previous rematch with DeJesus.

Duran was immediately surrounded in the ring by dozens of his followers from Panama. They cheered loudly as he strapped on the world championship belt with a large gold buckle.

"I was born for this, I was born to be champion," Duran said.

Duran led on all three officials' cards when the fight ended. He had bloodied DeJesus's nose in the 10th round and drawn blood from his opponent's mouth in the fifth.

The fight started slowly, Duran and DeJesus both showing caution and respect for one another after years of angry words. Both were champions when they entered the ring, Duran recognized by the World Boxing Association and DeJesus by the World Boxing Council.

For the first time in their three fights, Duran was not on the canvas in the opening round, and throughout the fight he remained unhurt.

A left uppercut to DeJesus's jaw early in the fifth snapped his head back and the Puerto Rican spit blood when the round ended. Duran, growing bolder, ripped a left to DeJesus's jaw in the sixth, then chased him across the ring to land a hard right to the temple.

Duran controlled the pace throughout with jabs and combinations. He caught DeJesus coming forward in the eighth round and tagged him with a straight right. He unleashed a two-fisted body attack at the start of the 10th and drew a trickle of blood from DeJesus nose with a left uppercut.

Duran's victory made him one of only three champions no longer disputed by the rival W.B.A. and W.B.C. The others are Muhammad Ali in the heavyweight division and Rodrigo Valdez in the middleweight division.

Duran, regarded as one of the hardest hitting small fighters in history, won the W.B.A. lightweight crown six years ago when he knocked out Ken Buchanan of Scotland in the 13th round. The 26-year-old Panamanian has successfully defended his title a record 12 times since then.

DeJesus, also 26, knocked down Duran in the first minute of a nontitle fight in 1972 and scored a unanimous 10-round decision in New York. DeJesus claimed he was tricked into taking their next fight, in 1974 in Panama, and blamed poor conditioning for his loss. Duran was also down in the first minute of that second bout but recovered to stop DeJesus in the 11th round.

De Jesus's loss today was only his fourth in 54 fights. He had claimed the W.B.C. title in 1976 and waited for three years for this rubber match.

Tempers were at the boiling point seven hours before the fight when the two weighed in. In top shape, both made the 135-pound limit easily, DeJesus at 134 and Duran at 134¼.

"You're too weak," De Jesus taunted Duran in Spanish at the weigh-in.

Duran snapped his fist near De Jesus's face and De Jesus swung at Duran's arm. Duran swung back but both were pulled away. A flare-up then followed among several of the 100 spectators. One lifted a chair and threatened to hit De Jesus's trainer and another grabbed De Jesus around the neck. Several small fights were broken up quickly.

In the preliminary bout, the W.B.C. junior middleweight champion, Rocky Mattioli of Milan, Italy, survived two cuts to win a unanimous nontitle decision from Jose Rodriguez of New York.

January 22, 1978

Spinks Captures Heavyweight Crown From Ali

A jubilant Leon Spinks after winning the heavyweight championship from Muhammad Ali last night in Las Vegas

Split Decision Gives Championship to Challenger, 24

By JAMES TUITE

Special to The New York Times

LAS VEGAS, Nev., Feb. 15—The second reign of Muhammad Ali as heavyweight champion of the world ended tonight. After a furious 15-round psychodrama of age against youth, brash defiance against jaded experience, the mantle passed to a real-life Rocky, Leon Spinks, only a year out of the amateur ranks.

Against incredible odds—the legal bookmakers in this gambling town wouldn't touch the fight—the 24-year-old Spinks destroyed the legend that was Muhammad Ali. The decision of the judges was divided but there were few viewers who could fault the determination of Spinks to fight back against every play in Ali's repertoire.

Of the three ring officials, Lou Tabat and Harold Buck voted for Spinks. Tabat voted, 145-140 and Buck 144-141. The third official, Art Lurie, voted for Ali, 143-142. Under Nevada rules the referee has no vote.

Olympic Champion in 1976

Ali, honed to his earlier sharpness to offset the flagging skills of his 36 years, did all of the things he had said he wouldn't do. He tried his rope-a-dope, his peek-a-boo stance, and Spinks penetrated it. He danced, but not well enough. He goaded Spinks, but the former Marine corporal snickered back.

Spinks, who rose from abject poverty in St. Louis to become the Olympic light-heavyweight champion at Montreal in 1976, got his biggest payday—a $320,000 windfall that he can now promote into millions.

For Ali, who has already taken in nearly $60 million in almost two decades of fighting, the fight was worth $3.5 million. He has not closed out his account, however.

"I want to be the first man to win the heavyweight championship for the third time," Ali proclaimed in a postfight interview. He won it for the second time when he knocked out George Foreman under a Kinshasa moon in 1974.

Would Spinks, the new king of the hill, grant a rematch?

"Definitely," said Leon, which for him is a long sentence.

There were tears in Ali's eyes as he stepped from the Hilton Pavilion ring after the judges' verdict was announced. Harold Buck (144 to 141) and Lou Tabat (145 to 140) voted for Spinks. The dissent was provided by Art Lurie, who picked Ali, 144 to 142.

"If I had to lose the title, I'm glad that I lost to a real man," said Ali in his dressing room as Dr. Charles Williams of Chicago examined him.

There is no return-bout clause in their contract but another fight seems inevitable. "Something tells you to take one more chance," said Ali in a jovial postfight mood. "I may not win it, but I'll try."

"I'm proud of myself," Spinks said. "I trained hard and I wanted to win. For the next few months, I want to relax."

Spinks had raised his hands in a victory sign as the two boxers entered the interview area together long after the bout.

"I wasn't getting tired," Spinks replied to a question about his stamina in the 10th round. "I tried to win all of the rounds, not just the last three. I never ever thought I had him. I feel very good. I turned on for the fight and I was really ready for it. I trained hard to be a great man. .

"This was my second goal—the first was winning the Olympic gold medal."

Until tonight, Ali had talked of retiring if he could get his price ($12 million) for a fight with Ken Norton. All that is blowing in the wind now, for the heavyweight picture was muddled by tonight's upset.

Spinks was the aggressor most of the way. He forced Ali time and again into the corners and pounded away with left jabs. At first, the peek-a-boo defense fended off the jabs, but as the fight wore on, more and more wedged through.

Ali danced and jabbed, danced and jabbed, and took Spinks's shots in an apparent effort to let the St. Louisian, who at 197¼ pounds was outweighed by 17 pounds, expend his energy. After all, how could a one-year professional with only seven money fights (six victories, one draw) endure against the mighty Ali?

Wasn't this the same Ali who had dominated boxing since his emergence as Olympic champion almost 18 years ago? Who had destroyed everyone in the heavyweight ranks and, after he lost the title to Joe Frazier in 1971, had won it back?

The answer is no, it was not the same Ali. It was an aging gladiator whose skills had flagged but who was still considered better than an up-and-coming youngster.

Ali did not even seem concerned in the fifth round, when Spinks drew blood from his mouth. He fought back, jarring the cagey challanger in some frantic exchange. In fact, by the 10th round Spinks seemed a bit drained, leaning across the ropes as Ali measured him with jabs and right crosses.

Even when Ali's jabs found their mark, even when his two-fisted flurry in the 11th round jarred Spinks, they could not stop his onrushing attack.

All the while Ali was light afoot, circling, moving, not with the old verve but enough to tire a less conditioned athlete than Spinks. Yet, the former Marine was noted for his casual training habits, just as he was known for his casual attendance record in the service.

The tempo picked up in the last two rounds, for the combatnats knew their fight was fairly even and a knockout would assure the victory. The 15th was a donnybrook that had most of the spectators on their feet.

With every vestige of animal desperation driving them on, they strove for that knockout punch. Then the bell sounded, tolling, perhaps the end of the career for sport's most celebrated personality.

For Spinks, a frail child with low blood pressure who took boxing lessons in self defense, the bell sounded the start of the reign of the new heavyweight champion, and a new era in boxing.

The raspy shouts of mother Spinks was heard above the din of the 5,298

spectators jammed into the Hilton Pavilion as son Mike got the evening off to a successful start for the family.

Although a World Boxing Council featherweight bout was next on the program, the crowd found more excitement in the eight-round slugfest won by Mike over chunky Tom Bethea of New York. The decision was unanimous.

In the featherweight title fight, Danny Lopez put away David Kotei for the second time. The 126-pound West Coast boxer sent David Kotei of Ghana to his knees in the sixth round and a few seconds later the referee stopped the scheduled 15-rounder at 1:18 of the round.

With Leon watching from ringside in a hooded robe, his younger brother (22) had a hard time fending off his more experienced rival. Bethea tried to offset Mike's longer reach by punching time and again to the body.

But this tactic took its toll and Mike met Bethea's onslaught with left hooks to the side of the head. In one round, the fifth, Mike landed 16 consecutive left hooks but they lacked any steam.

Kay Spinks, who raised her sons to be fighters on a diet of corn bread and peanut butter sandwiches that had to be shared with five siblings in St. Louis, beseeched Mike to defuse Tom The Bomb but he lacked a knockout punch.

A cut over Mike's left eye spattered Bethea's one white shoe with blood (his other shoe was black, in counterpoint not prove troublesome.

Bethea who at 172 held a two-pound advantage over Mike Spinks, like Leon a 1976 Olympic winner at Montreal, tried to force the issue with his infighting against the ropes, but Mike whittled away with left hooks and occasional combinations.

February 16, 1978

Spinks Stripped of Crown; W.B.C. Recognizes Norton

MEXICO CITY, March 18 (AP)—The World Boxing Council today withdrew its title recognition from Leon Spinks, who won the title a month ago from Muhammad Ali, and bestowed the crown on Ken Norton.

The action was taken by the W.B.C. president, Jose Sulaiman, and means the world now has two heavyweight champions. Spinks is still recognized as champion by the World Boxing Association.

Sulaiman said the action was taken because Spinks dealt in bad faith with the W.B.C. in connection with negotiations for a title defense against Norton. Spinks has said that he wanted his first title defense to be against Ali.

Suit Seems Likely

Bob Arum of Top Rank Inc., which has strong promotional ties with Spinks, said Top Rank and Spinks would sue the W.B.C. and termed Norton "a paper champion."

Sulaiman said that Norton was being

recognized as champion because he defeated Jimmy Young on Nov. 5, 1977, in a 15-round title-elimination fight.

Before Ali and Spinks fought, they agreed with a W.B.C. edict that the winner of their fight first defend the crown against Norton. The edict said that the champion had until March 17 to sign with a promoter of his choice to fight Norton by July 7, and that if he didn't, the fight would go to purse bidding, with the highest sealed bid to be opened April 7.

Sulaiman said that Spinks's letter of agreement was given to the W.B.C. in bad faith, and said that the W.B.C. executive committee voted 15-2, with one abstention, to strip Spinks of the title.

Sulaiman said the fact that CBS-TV has the rights to Spinks's first defense prevents negotiations from going to purse bidding, which is a violation of the second stage of the W.B.C. edict.

March 19, 1978

Ken Norton raises hands after sending Duane Bobick to the canvas, May 1977. Moments later, Petey Della, the referee, stopped the fight, giving Norton a TKO.

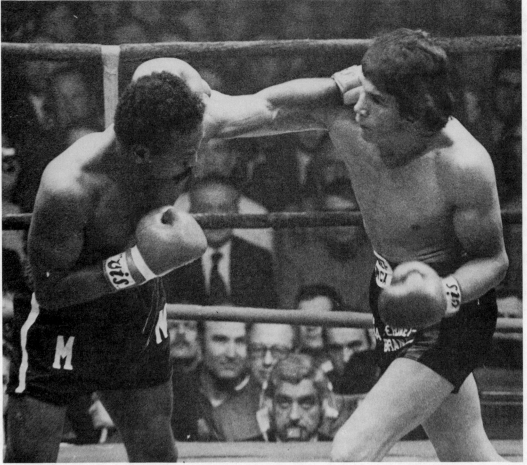

Carlos Monzon (right), shown here retaining his middleweight championship against Jose Napoles in 1974, held the title for six years and had an unbeaten streak spanning 61 fights from 1964 to 1976.

Holmes Takes Title From Norton on a Split Decision

Challenger's Jabs Take Toll —Jimmy Young Defeated

By MICHAEL KATZ
Special to The New York Times

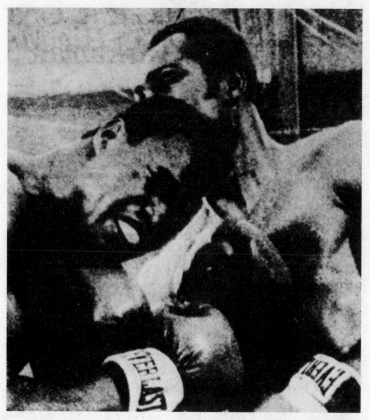

United Press International
Ken Norton landing a right to the chin of Larry Holmes in sixth round

LAS VEGAS, Nev., June 9—The title they fought for was controversial and so was Larry Holmes's decision over Ken Norton tonight that made the undefeated Holmes the new heavyweight champion, according to the World Boxing Council.

But there was no question that the two best heavyweights in the world—a controversial but majority opinion among boxing people—staged one of he great fights in recent history before a Caesars Palace Sports Pavilion audience and perhaps 40 million television viewers.

Holmes, the 28-year-old boxer from Easton, Pa., who has patterned his style on that of a former sparring partner, Muhammad Ali, took an early lead and, because he managed to remain on his feet during a furious 15th-round assault, won by the narrowest of margins.

Judges Harold Bock and Joe Swessel scored the fight, 143-142, for Holmes on the 10-points-to-the-round-winner system. Judge Lou Tabot had it 143-142 for Norton—the equivalent of an 8-7 score by rounds. In Nevada the referee does not score fights. The New York Times, and the majority of ringside reporters, had Norton ahead, 143-142. On all three official cards, the fight was even going into the final round.

"I thought I won the fight," said Norton, who dropped a similar split decision to Ali in September 1976, when the title belonged to one boxer and not two. "But you can't buck the judges."

Holmes had no immediate comment after the fight and disappeared from his dressing room after almost passing out in front of the television cameras. He later appeared in the interview room after a dip in the hotel pool.

Holmes had reason to be exhausted. He had just gone 15 gruelling rounds with one of the hardest punchers in the division. The fight was so exciting that Jose Sulaiman, the W.B.C. president so instrumental in withdrawing recognition from Leon Spinks for giving Ali an "illegal" rematch, said he would "definitely" recommend that the rematch restriction be waived.

"I would take a vote of the council," said Sulaiman, "if promoters request that. This was one of the best heavyweight fights in a long, long time."

Spinks, who dethroned Ali last Feb. 15, lost W.B.C. recognition for giving Ali a rematch instead of giving Norton, then the No. 1 contender, a title shot. The Ali-Spinks bout is scheduled for Sept. 15 at New Orleans.

Holmes vs. Evangelista?

Don King, the promoter of tonight's fight, said he would not try immediately for a rematch "because of the negative atmosphere," meaning he already had a title fight lined up for Holmes, probably against Alfredo Evangelista of Spain in Madrid later this year.

But Evangelista, the European champion, was unimpressive in gaining a 10-round split decision tonight over Jodie Ballard, a Holmes sparring partner. Jimmy Young, who had been the No. 1 contender, was upset by a young undefeated Puerto Rican, Osvaldo Ocasio, in 10 rounds. Norton is the only logical contender for the W.B.C. title.

Controversy was everywhere. Referee Mills Lane seized the water bottle from Holmes's corner after the 10th round and sent it to a laboratory for an examination that officials said would take a week to conclude. W.B.C. rules allow only water, and Fred Brown, Holmes's trainer, admitted the bottle contained a mixture of water and orange juice.

"There was no extra sugar, no medication in there," said Brown, "just orange juice and water."

Johnny Mag, a Nevada commissioner, smelled the bottle and thought he detected the odor of honey. But Mag did not think the decision would be reversed unless some very strong stimulant was found. A fine, cutting into Holmes's $500,000 share of the purse, seemed more likely.

Big Money, Little Solace

Norton, whose career has been marked by controversial split decisions (another loss to Ali and a victory over Young here last Nov. 5 in the bout that the W.B.C. decided last March was for the title), earned $2.3 million. But the 34-year-old former Marine is already a millionaire. What he wanted most was the universal title. He no longer has even the W.B.C. share because he started fighting tonight too late.

For the first five rounds, the 13-10 favorite stalked Holmes ineffectively. Holmes, who now has won all 28 of his professional fights, but has only this year begun to meet top competition, has perhaps the finest left jab in the heavyweight division.

He kept that left in Norton's confused face in the early rounds, occasionally setting himself and throwing a right in combination with the jab. In the second round Holmes had opened a small cut near Norton's right eye.

But a more important part of Holmes's game plan was to keep away from the harder-hitting Norton, who at 220 pounds outweighed his challenger by 11 pounds. Holmes moved gracefully sideways and backward, but it is difficult to throw punches with authority on the move.

Before long, Norton was moving in, willing to accept several punches for the opportunity to send one of his own. In the fifth round, Norton landed a solid looping right, the punch that so often connected against Ali, and the tempo began to accelerate.

Holmes Rocks, Doesn't Rattle

Norton landed another heavy right in the sixth and took mostly weak jabs in return. By the seventh, Norton had cut Holmes's mouth and in the eighth, he really opened up, rocking Holmes several times.

Holmes had proved in his March 25 fight here against Earnie Shavers that he could take a punch without getting rattled. He continued to jab, jab, jab.

Norton has a jab, too. "His may be faster than mine," Norton said before the fight, "but min eis more powerful." In the 10th, Norton, ever moving forward, used his jab to set up some more powerful right hands.

Holmes made Norton's defense easier by not going for the body. The 34-year-old Norton (he is two years older than his listed age), a good body puncher himself, was thus able to concentrate most of his defense on his head, several times allowing his midsection to go unprotected and unattacked.

In the 11th round, Norton finally achieved what he wanted—getting Holmes against the ropes. The younger fighter had said that he did not think Norton could corner him, and for most of the fight he was right. In the 11th, however, Norton had Holmes in trouble.

Holmes had never fought more than 12 rounds—he had gone that far only against Shavers—but in the 13th he suddenly surged and saved his victory. Holmes had been sneaking in some right hands occasionally, but now they came in series of three and four. Norton seemed unhurt by the first few, but he appeared frozen. Again and again Holmes hit him. There were no knockdowns in the fight, but Norton came close to falling in the 13th.

Norton Still No. 1?

Holmes started the 14th round with more quick right hands, but Norton pressed on. This was Norton's 45th professional fight—his fifth defeat against 40 victories—and he will not be remembered as one of the best heavyweights in history. But he is perhaps still the best heavyweight in the world. And by the end of the 14th round, he had found some reserve strength and had Holmes cornered again.

Norton opened the 15th with another powerful overhand right. Holmes countered with some combinations. They moved together, toe to toe, exchanging punches. A murderous left hook by Norton rocked Holmes. A right uppercut, one of the best punches in Norton's arsenal, landed. But Holmes would not go down. Instead, he fought back, throwing punches in flurries, and staggered Norton.

Now Norton would not go down. With a half-minute to go in the fight he landed another powerful left hook. Holmes was staggered. Instead of falling, he staggered Norton.

These two men genuinely do not like each other. "Just chemistry," said Norton. But after tonight, they must respect each other.

Before the fight, Teddy Brenner the president of Madison Square Garden boxing, had said, "no matter who wins here tonight, Leon Spinks will still be heavyweight champion of the world."

Perhaps, but Holmes and Norton showed that Spinks was not necessarily the best heavyweight in the world.

There was another split-title championship bout on tonight's card, but one which King and ABC were afraid to put on prime-time television because of "discrepancies" in the record of the challenger, Emillio Hernandez.

Zarate Gets 51st Knockout

Actually, Hernandez proved to be as worthy a challenger as Carlos Zarate has had. No one has come close to beating the W.B.C. bantamweight champion who knocked out Hernandez with a classic left-right combination at 2:10 of the fourth round.

Zarate, who weighed 118 pounds, the division limit, now has a 52-0 record as a professional—with 51 of the victories by knockout. No champion in boxing history has a better record than the 27-year-old Mexican, who has only Jorge Lujan of Panama, the W.B.A. champion, left among bantamweight contenders before moving up to the super-bantamweight and eventually the featherweight class.

Hernandez's record is another thing. The 116-pound Dominican-born fighter who now lives in Venezuela was listed with a 19-5-2 won-lost-drawn record In a statement issued before the fight was taped for possible showing, King said both he and ABC were "concerned" that the "credibility of Hernandez as an opponent for the world champion is in question."

"Latin fighter-records are extremely difficult to confirm," the statement added, after reports that Hernandez had many other unaccounted losses.

A Fast Learner

Only last weekend, King and ABC were embarrassed with the junior lightweight championship mismatch in which Alexis Arguello knocked out Diego Alcala in the first round. Hernandez was just as outclassed as Alcala was, but at least he put on a braver show. He won the first round when Zarate chose not to throw any punches, instead "scouting" his opponent.

Zarate quickly learned he could get

in left hooks when Hernandez attempted looping right-hand punches and floored the challenger in the second round, beat him in the third and ended the fight in the fourth by sending Hernandez into the ropes for a 10-count.

Young, fatter than ever, had trouble getting through the ropes for his bout with Ocasio. The No.1 contender, a position he had to maintain to be guaranteed a W.B.C. title shot within a year, risked his reputation and ranking against an unknown and undefeated fighter, for one reason.

"Money," said Young, who received $150,000 for his slow-fisted work tonight.

The 29-year-old Philadelphian weighed in yesterday at 220 pounds, the highest of his career, with rolls of surplus weight around his waist.

He tried counterpunching early, but was continuously beaten to the punch by Ocasio. Later, Young went more on the offensive and won some rounds with effective body-punching.

One of the three voting judges, Dave Moretti, gave Young the nod by a surprising 47-43 count. But Judge Bill Kipp scored the fight, 46-45, for Ocasio and Judge Ron Tabot concurred by 46-44.

Bill Daley, Ocasio's manager, said before the fight that he took the match because he wanted to see how his man would react to a loss. Previously, Ocasio had beaten 111 opponents, but the 205-pound Puerto Rican had never met anyone of Young's calibre.

Young, who said "if I had to do it again I'd have come in at 213," the weight at which he fought Norton, felt he had beaten Ocasio.

"We got robbed in Las Vegas again," said Ray Kelly, Young's co-manager.

"Me and the guy will fight again," said Young.

"Not in Las Vegas," added Kelly.

Young's record fell to 22-7-2.

June 10, 1978

BOXING, bok'sing, is the sport of fighting with the fists. It is engaged in by two participants who face each other in a roped-in square. Their only weapons are their gloved fists, and their only defenses are those they can effect by blocking with the gloves and arms and by evasive maneuvers.

Known also as *pugilism* and as *prizefighting,* boxing is one of the oldest and most universal of athletic endeavors. The word "pugilism" derives from the Greek *pugmè* (a fist or a fight with fists) and the Latin *pugnus* (fist) and *pugil* (boxer). The term "prizefighting" denotes that the contestants fight for a prize. The origins of the term "boxing," however, are in dispute. Some historians believe that it derives from the fact that the hand, when formed into a fist, resembles a box. Others maintain that it stems from an Italian cleric, later canonized as St. Bernardino, who in 1201, alarmed by the injuries and deaths that resulted from dueling with knives, encouraged his parishioners to fight with their fists and taught them how to employ tactics to "box up" an opponent.

Although often banned when its brutal aspects aroused public opposition, boxing has survived through the centuries because of its appeal to the basic instincts of aggression and self-defense. Its adherents contend that it is the most fundamental and fulfilling form of athletic competition.

The critics of boxing argue that the objective of a boxer is to inflict physical hurt, which may result in permanent injury and even death. Out of this controversy, as old as the sport, have evolved the refinements that have resulted in boxing as it is known today.

WEIGHT DIVISIONS, EQUIPMENT, AND REGULATIONS

From the earliest days of boxing until the middle of the 18th century contests, for the most part, were fought only between heavier and stronger men. In 1746 in England, the grouping of boxers into weight divisions, or classes, was introduced with the establishment of a "lightweight" category.

Weight Divisions. There are eight weight divisions in professional boxing today, each with its own champion. Occasionally, a boxer from one division will fight an opponent in a heavier division. Some boxers have won championships in more than one division.

In amateur boxing, international rules prescribe 10 divisions. These divisions are in effect during the Olympic Games and are recognized in the United States by the Amateur Athletic Union. The Golden Gloves Competition, although sanctioned by the AAU and conducted according to its rules, adheres to the professional classes.

WEIGHT DIVISIONS	PROFESSIONAL MAXIMUM WEIGHT		AMATEUR MAXIMUM WEIGHT	
Division	Pounds	Kilograms	Pounds	Kilograms
Flyweight	112	50.8	112	50.8
Bantamweight	118	53.5	119	54.0
Featherweight	126	57.2	125	56.7
Lightweight	135	61.2	132	60.0
Light-welterweight	. . .	. . .	139	63.0
Welterweight	147	66.7	147	66.7
Light-middleweight	. . .	. . .	156	70.8
Middleweight	160	72.6	165	74.8
Light-heavyweight	175	79.4	178	80.7
Heavyweight	Unlimited		Unlimited	

The Ring and Equipment. The square, raised platform on which a boxing match takes place is called a "ring," possibly because in Roman days a contestant declared his challenge by throwing his cestus, a leather hand-wrapping—sometimes metal-studded and often caked with gore from previous contests—into a circular arena. The ring floor is padded and covered with canvas, and three 1-inch ropes, supported by posts at each corner, form the boundaries. The area inside the ropes may be from 18 to 24 feet square, with the ring floor extending 2 or 3 feet beyond the ropes.

Boxers, stripped to the waist, wear trunks and high, leather soft-soled shoes. Under their trunks they wear a protective cup, and their hands and wrists are protected by wrappings of gauze and adhesive tape, called "bandages." Their gloves, mittenlike with padded back and thumb, are made of leather. Each weighs 8 ounces for professional bouts and from 8 to 12 ounces for amateur contests. A fitted rubber mouthpiece protects the teeth and mouth.

Rules and Regulations. Before entering the ring, boxers are assigned diagonally opposite corners, where they may rest on stools during the 1-minute periods between rounds. The beginning and end of each round are signaled by the sounding of a bell. In professional boxing a round lasts three minutes; in amateur boxing, two minutes. Professional contests are scheduled for 4, 6, 8, 10, 12, or 15 rounds, the last usually reserved for championship bouts. Amateur bouts are scheduled for three rounds.

A boxer is permitted three handlers, or seconds, who may assist him between rounds. During a round the only person permitted in the ring with the boxers is the referee, whose duty it is to enforce the rules and who usually also acts as a judge. In some countries and in some states of the United States the referee is the sole judge, but in most places bouts are judged by the referee and two judges, the latter seated outside the ropes at opposite sides of the ring. One or two timekeepers time the rounds and the count for knockdowns.

A boxer is considered "down" when any part of his body except his feet is touching the floor. Should the count, enunciated by the referee at 1-second intervals, reach 10 before he arises, then the boxer is declared a loser by a knockout (KO). A boxer is also "down" if he is helpless against the ropes or is outside the ring. When one man is down his opponent must go to a neutral corner and remain there until signaled by the referee.

A technical knockout (TKO) is scored when a bout has been halted by the referee because a boxer, in the official's judgment, is unfit to continue, or is so far outclassed that he has no chance to win. No count is necessary, and if one has been started it is discontinued.

When a fight lasts the scheduled number of rounds a decision is awarded to the boxer who, in the judgment of the majority of the officials, has won the most rounds or has acquired the most points. Each official keeps his own scorecard, awarding points on the basis of clean, effective punching and skillful defense. Points and entire rounds may be deducted for fouls. Fouls include hitting below the belt, hitting an opponent who is down or rising, butting, kneeing, elbowing, backhanding, thumbing, heeling with the glove, hitting with the open glove, hitting over the kidneys from a clinch, and hitting on the back of the neck. Deliberate and continued fouling can cause disqualification.

Governing Bodies. Professional boxing in the United States today is regulated by various state and local boxing commissions, which sanction matches, provide medical supervision, weigh the boxers before a bout, assign officials, and enforce rules. With several exceptions these commissions belong to the World Boxing Association (WBA), which has affiliates in a dozen other countries. Professional boxing in Europe is governed by the European Boxing Union, made up of the agencies regulating the sport in 17 countries.

Amateur boxing is included in the sports programs of many schools, colleges, clubs, boys' camps, and military organizations. The major controlling body is the Amateur Athletic Union. The most popular national tournament is the annual Golden Gloves competition, begun in 1927. Internationally, the best boxers from many countries meet every four years in the Olympic Games.

TRAINING AND TECHNIQUES

Before engaging in a contest, boxers go through a period of intensive training. When boxers are preparing for important matches and championship bouts, the training sessions may extend for a month or more. In such cases, the conditioning is usually carried out at a training camp located in a rural or semirural area where the boxer may enjoy privacy and where his living and training habits may be supervised.

Training Routine. The conditioning program is directed by a trainer, who may also be the boxer's manager. A daily schedule usually includes roadwork—running and walking to improve wind and endurance—and gymnasium work. The latter consists of calisthenics, work with pulley weights, rope skipping, punching light inflated and heavy filled bags, shadowboxing against an imaginary opponent, and boxing three rounds or more with sparring partners while wearing protective headgear and 12- or 14-ounce gloves. The sparring partners are hired to imitate the boxing style of the boxer's opponent. They aid the boxer in perfecting his skills and give him a physically taxing workout.

Offense and Defense. A boxer's style derives from his own adaptation of the basic offensive and defensive maneuvers that constitute the science of boxing. These maneuvers evolved in 18th century England from those employed in fencing and swordplay.

In the basic diagonal stance, or "on guard" position, the boxer faces his opponent turned slightly to the right, his left foot forward, his left arm partially extended, and his right arm bent and held near his upper body. (The rare left-handed, or southpaw, boxer reverses this stance.) From this position a boxer is able to launch punches and to block or avoid those directed at him. He can also advance, sidestep, or retreat as the situation demands.

The most common punches are those delivered with the straight arm, such as the left jab and the straight right, and the bent-arm blows, such as the left hook, the right cross, and the uppercuts, which are brought up from the waist or below. The boxer pushes off his right foot for jabs and right-hand blows, and off his left foot for hooks. Effective punching results when he links into a chain of power the muscles of his legs, upper body, and arms, and when the fists, turned at the last instant so that the palms are down, reach a vulnerable area at the peak of power. The vulnerable areas are the forehead, temples, chin, and the body between the waist and the rib cage. Openings to these areas may be made by feinting—the art of disguising intention and misleading an opponent by movement of eyes, head, hands, or feet, or by a combination of these.

Defensive maneuvers consist of blocking or catching a blow with the glove; parrying, or deflecting a blow from its target; and stopping a blow by applying restraint to the arm as the blow is launched. In addition, boxers avoid blows by ducking, turning, moving to the side, or moving inside or outside the arc of a punch.

Blocking. Warding off an opponent's blows with the gloves, arms, elbows, or shoulders.

Break. To come out of a clinch, voluntarily or on order of the referee.

Catch. To block a punch with an open glove.

Clinch. To hold or hug an opponent; also, the act of holding.

Counter Punch. A blow delivered directly following an opponent's punch and designed to land while the opponent is vulnerable.

Cross. A counter-blow crossing over the opponent's lead. For example, a straight right to the jaw crossed over the opponent's left lead (extended left arm), as the lead is slipped over either of the counterer's shoulders.

Decision. The official verdict that determines the winner. It may be based on a disqualification or on points awarded by the official or officials.

Ducking. Dropping under blows aimed at the head.

Feint. A simulated motion to deceive the opponent, forcing him to protect the area not actually hit.

Glass Jaw. The jaw of a boxer who is easily knocked down by a blow on the chin.

Handlers.. A boxer's seconds, or attendants.

Heeling. Pushing the inside of an open glove against an opponent's face.

Hook. A bent-arm blow delivered from the side and in close.

Infighting. Fighting at close range.

Jab. A light, straight punch by the leading arm to either head or body. Since most boxers are right-handed and lead with the left arm, the *left jab* is the one most often used.

Knockout. The end of a bout, when one fighter is either knocked unconscious or floored for 10 seconds.

Leading. Taking the initiative.

Mouse. A swelling under an eye.

One-two Punch. A left jab and a right-hand punch delivered in rapid succession.

Parrying. Turning an oncoming blow aside with a quick movement of the hand.

Rabbit Punch. An illegal blow delivered to the back of the neck at the base of the skull.

Reach. The measurement between the tips of the middle fingers of each hand when the arms are fully extended horizontally from the sides.

Ring. The roped-in area in which a bout is staged.

Round. The period in which the match is legally in process during a bout. Its duration is 3 minutes for professionals.

The beginnings and ends of rounds are usually signaled by a bell.

Roundhouse. A wide swing or hook to the head.

Seconds. See *Handlers*.

Slip a Punch. To avoid a blow by moving the head or body to either side.

Solar Plexus Punch. A blow that lands on the nerve center in the upper middle part of the abdomen.

Southpaw. A left-handed boxer who fights with the right foot forward and leads with the right hand.

Spar. To make offensive or defensive gestures without touching the opponent.

Stance. The posture or position a boxer assumes as a starting point for his maneuvers.

Swing. A blow delivered with a circular motion.

Technical Knockout. A verdict declared by the referee when he decides that a boxer is no longer able to defend himself.

Thumbing. Striking an opponent, usually in an eye, with the thumb of the glove; it is an illegal tactic.

Uppercut. A bent-arm blow delivered upward.

Weigh-in. The official weighing of boxers before their fight.

Bibliography

Amateur Athletic Union, *Official AAU Boxing Guide* (New York, annually).

Fleischer, Nat, *50 Years at Ringside* (New York 1958).

Fleischer, Nat, *The Heavyweight Champion* (New York 1949).

Fleischer, Nat, *The Ring Record Book and Boxing Encyclopedia* (New York, annually).

Fleischer, Nat, and Andre, Sam, *A Pictorial History of Boxing* (New York 1959).

Grombach, John V., *The Saga of Sock* (New York 1949).

Heinz, W.C., ed., *The Fireside Book of Boxing* (New York 1961).

Liebling, A.J., *The Sweet Science* (New York 1956).

BOXING CHAMPIONS

Heavyweights

Champion

John L. Sullivan	1889–92
James J. Corbett	1892–97
Bob Fitzsimmons	1897–99
James J. Jeffries	1899–1905
Tommy Burns	1906–08
Jack Johnson	1908–15
Jess Willard	1915–19
Jack Dempsey	1919–26
Gene Tunney	1926–28
Max Schmeling	1930–32
Jack Sharkey	1932–33
Primo Carnera	1933–34
Max Baer	1934–35
Jim Braddock	1935–37
Joe Louis	1937–49
Ezzard Charles	1949–51
Jersey Joe Walcott	1951–52
Rocky Marciano	1952–56
Floyd Patterson	1956–59
Ingemar Johannson	1959–60
Floyd Patterson	1960–62
Sonny Liston	1962–64
Cassius Clay	1964–67
Jimmy Ellis	1968–70
Joe Frazier	1970–73
George Foreman	1973–74
Muhammad Ali	1974–76
Leon Spinks Jr.	1978
Muhammad Ali	1978–

Light-Heavyweights

Champion

Jack Root	1903
George Gardner	1903
Bob Fitzsimmons	1903–05
"Philadelphia"	
Jack O'Brien	1905–12
Jack Dillon	1912–16
Battling Levinsky	1916–20
Georges Carpentier	1920–22
Battling Siki	1922–23
Mike McTigue	1923–25
Paul Berlenbach	1925–26
Jack Delaney	1926–27
Mike McTigue	1927
Tommy Loughran	1927–29
Maxie Rosenbloom	1930–34
Bob Olin	1934–35
John Henry Lewis	1935–38
Melio Bettina	1939
Billy Conn	1939–40
Anton Christoforidis	1941
Gus Lesnevich	1941–48
Freddie Mills	1948–50
Joey Maxim	1950–52
Archie Moore	1952–61
Harold Johnson	1961–63
Willie Pastrano	1963–65
Jose Torres	1965–66

Dick Tiger	1966–68
Bob Foster	1968–70
Vincente Paul Rondon	1971–72
Bob Foster	1972–74
Victor Galindez	1974–78
Mike Rossman	1978–79
Victor Balindez	1979–

Middleweights

Champion

Jack Dempsey ("The Nonpareil")	1884–91
Bob Fitzsimmons	1891–97
Tommy Ryan	1897–1907
Stanley Ketchel	1908
Billy Papke	1908
Stanley Ketchel	1908–10
Frank Klaus	1913
George Chip	1913–14
Al McCoy	1914–17
Mike O'Dowd	1917–20
Johnny Wilson	1920–23
Harry Greb	1923–26
Tiger Flowers	1926
Mickey Walker	1926–31
Tony Zale	1941–47
Rocky Graziano	1947–48
Tony Zale	1948
Marcel Cerdan	1948–49
Jake LaMotta	1949–51
Sugar Ray Robinson	1951
Randy Turpin	1951
Sugar Ray Robinson	1951–52
Bobo Olson	1953–55
Sugar Ray Robinson	1955–57
Gene Fullmer	1957
Sugar Ray Robinson	1957
Carmen Basilio	1957–58
Sugar Ray Robinson	1958–60
Gene Fullmer	1959–62
Paul Pender	1960–62
Dick Tiger	1962–63
Joey Giardello	1963–65
Dick Tiger	1965–66
Emile Griffith	1966–67
Nino Benvenuti	1967
Emile Griffith	1967–68
Nino Benvenuti	1968–70
Carlos Monzon	1970–77
Rodrigo Valdes	1977–78
Hugo Corro	1978–

Welterweights

Champion

Mysterious Billy Smith	1892–94
Tommy Ryan	1894–96
Kid McCoy	1896

Mysterious Billy Smith	1896–1900
Matty Matthews	1900–01
Rube Ferns	1901
Joe Walcott	1901–04
Dixie Kid	1904
Joe Walcott	1904–06
Honey Mellody	1906–07
Mike (Twin) Sullivan	1907–10
Ted Lewis	1915–19
Jack Britton	1919–22
Mickey Walker	1922–26
Peter Latzo	1926–27
Joe Dundee	1927–29
Jackie Fields	1929–30
Young Jack Thompson	1930
Tommy Freeman	1930–31
Young Jack Thompson	1931
Lou Brouillard	1931–32
Jackie Fields	1932–33
Young Corbett 3d	1933
Jimmy McLarnin	1933–34
Barney Ross	1934
Jimmy McLarnin	1934–35
Barney Ross	1935–38
Henry Armstrong	1938–40
Pritzie Zivic	1940–41
Freddie Cochrane	1941–46
Marty Servo	1946
Sugar Ray Robinson	1946–51
Johnny Bratton	1951
Kid Gavilan	1951–54
Johnny Saxton	1954–55
Tony DeMarco	1955
Carmen Basilio	1955–56
Johnny Saxton	1956
Carmen Basilio	1956–57
Virgil Akins	1958
Don Jordan	1958–60
Benny (Kid) Paret	1960–61
Emile Griffith	1961
Benny (Kid) Paret	1961–62
Emile Griffith	1962–63
Luis Rodriguez	1963
Emile Griffith	1963–65
Curtis Cokes	1966–69
Jose Napoles	1969–70
Billy Backus	1970–71
Jose Napoles	1971–75
Angel Espada	1975–76
Jose Cuevas	1976–

Lightweights

Champion

Joe Gans	1901–08
Battling Nelson	1908–10
Ad Wolgast	1910–12
Willie Ritchie	1912–14
Freddie Welsh	1914–17
Benny Leonard	1917–24

Jimmy Goodrich	1925
Rocky Kansas	1925–26
Sammy Mandell	1926–30
Al Singer	1930
Tony Canzoneri	1930–33
Barney Ross	1933–35
Tony Canzoneri	1935–36
Lou Ambers	1936–38
Henry Armstrong	1938–39
Lou Ambers	1939–40
Lew Jenkins	1940–41
Sammy Angott	1941–42
Ike Williams	1947–51
Jimmy Carter	1951–52
Lauro Salas	1952
Jimmy Carter	1952–54
Paddy DeMarco	1954
Jimmy Carter	1954–55
Wallace (Bud) Smith	1955–56
Joe Brown	1956–62
Carlos Ortiz	1962–65
Ismael Laguna	1965
Carlos Ortiz	1965–68
Teo Cruz	1968–69
Mando Ramos	1969–70
Ismael Laguna	1970
Ken Buchanan	1970–72
Roberto Duran	1972–

Featherweights

Champion

Abe Attell	1904
Tommy Sullivan	1904–08
Abe Atell	1908–12
Johnny Kilbane	1912–23
Eugene Cruqui	1923
Johnny Dundee	1923–25
Louis (Kid) Kaplan	1926–27
Benny Bass	1927–28
Tony Canzoneri	1928
Andre Routis	1928–29
Battling Battalino	1929–32
Tommy Paul	1932
Freddie Miller	1933–36
Petey Sarron	1936–37
Henry Armstrong	1937–38
Joey Archibald	1938–40
Harry Jeffra	1940–41
Joey Archibald	1941

Chalky Wright	1941–42
Willie Pep	1942–48
Sandy Saddler	1948–49
Willie Pep	1949–50
Sandy Saddler	1950–57
Kid Bassey	1957–59
Davey Moore	1959–63
Sugar Ramos	1963–64
Vicente Saldivar	1964–67
Raul Rojas	1968
Sho Saijo	1968–71
Alfredo Marcano	1971–72
Ernesto Marcel	1972–74
Ruben Olivares	1974
Alexis Arguello	1974–77
Cecilio Lastra	1977–78
Ruselio Pedroza	1978–

Bantamweights

Champion

George Dixon	1890–92
Vacant	1893
Jimmy Barry	1894–99
Terry McGovern	1899–1900
Harry Harris	1901–02
Harry Forbes	1902–03
Frankie Neil	1903–04
Joe Bowker	1904
Jimmy Walsh	1905–07
Vacant	1908–09
Johnny Coulon	1910–14
Kid Williams	1914–17
Pete Herman	1917–20
Joe Lynch	1920–21
Pete Herman	1921
Johnny Buff	1921–22
Joe Lynch	1922–24
Abe Goldstein	1924
Eddie Martin	1924–25
Charley Rosenberg	1925–27
Bud Taylor	1927–28
Al Brown	1929–35
Baltazar Sangchili	1935–36
Tony Marino	1936
Sixto Escobar	1936–37
Harry Jeffra	1937–38
Sixto Escobar	1938–40
Georgie Pace	1940
Lou Salica	1940–42
Manuel Ortiz	1942–47
Harold Dade	1947
Manuel Ortiz	1947–50

Vic Toweel	1950–52
Jimmy Carruthers	1952–54
Robert Cohen	1954–56
Mario D'Agata	1956–57
Alphonse Halimi	1957–59
Jose Becerra	1959–60
Eder Jofre	1961–65
Masahiko Harada	1965–68
Lionel Rose	1968–69
Ruben Olivares	1969–70
Jesus Castillo	1970–71
Ruben Olivares	1971–72
Rafael Herrera	1972
Enrique Pinder	1972–73
Romero Anaya	1973
Arnold Taylor	1973–74
Soo Hwan Hong	1974–75
Alfonso Zamora	1975–77
Jorge Lujan	1977–

Flyweights

Champion

Jimmy Wilde	1916–23
Pancho Villa	1923–25
Fidel La Barba	1925–27
Frankie Genaro	1928–31
Victor Perez	1931–32
Jackie Brown	1932–35
Benny Lynch	1935–38
Peter Kane	1938–41
Vacant	1941–42
Jackie Paterson	1943–47
Rinty Monaghan	1948–50
Dado Marino	1950–52
Yoshio Shirai	1952–54
Pascual Perez	1954–60
Pone Kingpetch	1960–62
Masahiko Harado	1962–63
Pone Kingpetch	1963
Hiroyuki Ebihara	1963–64
Pone Kingpetch	1964–65
Salvatore Burruni	1965–66
Horacio Accavallo	1966–68
Hiroyuki Ebihara	1969
Bernabe Villacampo	1969–70
Berkrerk Chartvachai	1970
Masao Ohba	1970–73
Charchai Chionoi	1973–74
Erbito Salavarria	1975
Alfonso Lopez	1976
Guty Espades	1976–78
Bertalio Gonzalez	1978–